The Definitive Guide to Power Query (M)

Mastering complex data transformation with Power Query

Gregory Deckler
Rick de Groot
Melissa de Korte

The Definitive Guide to Power Query (M)

Senior Publishing Product Manager: Gebin George

Acquisition Editor – Peer Reviews: Tejas Mhasvekar

Project Editor: Rianna Rodrigues

Content Development Editors: Shruti Menon and Shazeen Iqbal

Copy Editor: SafisE diting

Technical Editors: Aneri Patel and Kushal Sharma

Proofreader: SafisE diting

Indexer: Tejal Daruwale Soni

Presentation Designer: Pranit Padwal

Developer Relations Marketing Executive: Vignesh Raju

First published: March 2024

Production reference: 1260324

Published by Packt Publishing Ltd.
Grosvenor House
11 St Paul's Square
Birmingham
B3 1RB, UK.

ISBN 978-1-83702-525-1

www.packt.com

Foreword

Occasionally, the stars align in just the right way, and the result is something that is unexpectedly great. That's the story behind the book you're holding now. But I'm getting ahead of myself. Let's turn the clock back to the start of 2022, which is where the story of this book begins.

At that point, I had been a data professional and Excel user for over 30 years and was doing a lot of Power BI development while conducting online training as well. I had long used Power Query to clean and transform my data prior to performing analysis and building reports. But almost all of that prep was done through the Power Query user interface. As well designed as the Power Query UI is, it's also quite limiting, providing access to only a fraction of the 700+ available M functions. So, at the start of 2022, I decided that I was going to stop dabbling in M and make learning it thoroughly my top-priority training goal for the year. This was not easy in 2022, since while there were fantastic books on Power Query, they each had only a small percentage of their content dedicated to M. There were many great M resources online, but they offered deep insights into a grab bag of very specialized topics and applications, which also did not make for an ideal learning experience.

Despite these hurdles, by the end of 2022, I found that my deep dive into M had been transformative. My Power BI reports ran much faster, the DAX used in them was dramatically simpler, I was able to clean data faster than ever, and I now could easily build reusable custom functions to automate repetitive data tasks. I also found that learning how to visualize and manipulate complex data structures in M substantially improved my coding ability in other languages. However, I also realized that my experience was entirely unreplicable due to the fact that three of my friends (not coincidentally the authors of this book) happened to be among the most knowledgeable Power Query/M experts in the world, and I relied heavily on their expertise during my learning. I actually used to joke with both Melissa and Rick online about each of them being the "Chosen One" destined to write the M counterpart to *The Definitive Guide to DAX*, but I think that seemed too much of a monumental task to both of them.

During this time, I was the primary tester on a suite of apps that Gregory Deckler was developing. We would regularly talk about Power Query and M when we would discuss the potential future capabilities of those apps. One day, Greg mentioned to me that he was working on a book proposal outline for that same comprehensive guide to M that I had been joking about (but also genuinely wishing existed). He asked me who I would recommend as co-authors for that book, and I am beyond thrilled to say that my response can be found on the cover of this book.

Mastering M is neither a quick nor easy task. However, I am completely confident that whether you are a data analyst, Power BI developer, data scientist, business analyst, or even an Excel end user looking to level up your skills, having the same three clear, patient, and brilliant instructors I did will make learning M an enjoyable and game-changing experience for you too.

Brian Julius

Power BI Expert and Instructor

Contributors

About the authors

Gregory Deckler is a seven-time Microsoft MVP for Data Platform and an active blogger and Power BI community member, having authored over 6,000 solutions to community questions. Greg has authored numerous books on Power BI, including the first and second editions of *Learn Power BI*, the second editions of *Power BI Cookbook and Mastering Power BI*, and *DAX Cookbook*. Greg has also created several external tools for Power BI and regularly posts video content to his YouTube channels – *Microsoft Hates Greg* and *DAX For Humans*.

> *I would like to acknowledge my wonderful co-authors for this book; I learned so much from all of them. I'm also grateful to my son Rocket for supporting all of my endeavors. A special thanks to Brian Julius who inspired this book and without whom this book would not exist*

Rick de Groot is a Power BI consultant, blogger, YouTuber, and author who hails from the Netherlands. With a background in finance, he has devoted 14+ years to building his expertise in data analysis, particularly in the Power Query M language. He is an independent consultant who also provides training on Power BI, Power Query, and DAX. He regularly publishes articles on his blogs, *Power Query How* and *BI Gorilla*, which have emerged as important sources for M articles and tutorials. He contributes extensively to his YouTube channel *BI Gorilla* as well. Rick's commitment to sharing his expertise has earned him the Microsoft Data Platform MVP award for two consecutive years.

> *My deepest appreciation goes to Brian Julius . His belief in me nudged me to share more about Power Query and helped me grow as a writer for the M language. Without his support, I don't think my name would have been on the cover of this book. He also played an important part in our discussions and helped shape the contents of this book. I am profoundly thankful for your support, Brian.*
>
> *To my family – your patience and support while writing this book have meant the world to me.*
>
> *Also, a huge shout-out to all of you out there. All the discussions we've had have been incredibly valuable.*

Melissa de Korte is a passionate problem-solver known for simplifying complex problems with Power Query. With an impressive track record as an enterprise DNA expert and super user, she has become an asset to the community, actively engaging, supporting, and inspiring others. Behind her professional persona lies a genuine dedication to empowering others through sharing knowledge. Her portfolio includes blogs, tutorials, courses, and webinars to make Power Query and M more accessible.

To Marcel and Sam for filling every moment we share(d) with joy.

My gratitude goes to my co-authors, as well as Brian Julius, for their roles in this book's creation. To my family for their endless patience and support. And to all who generously share their knowledge, spark curiosity and promote a supportive and inclusive community. Your contributions are invaluable!

About the reviewers

Erin Ostrowsky is a digital nomad who endeavors to build healthy, happy relationships wherever she goes. She's passionate about STEAM – don't forget the Arts, folks! – and hopes to inspire others to join in the fun problem-solving this world needs. Erin loves learning, creating, making friends, traveling, and writing about life's many curiosities. Her current focus is running Fit 4 Duty Data, a data and reporting consultancy and training firm that supports the global mining and energy sectors.

I'd like to thank my Creator, my friends, and my family – you all make life beautiful, especially during the hard times.

Vahid Doustimajd is a recognized Microsoft MVP and certified trainer with over 15 years of experience. He is a technophile who is passionate about project management and data analytics. Currently, he works in Australia as a Project Controls and Analytics Manager. He is an active participant in the Microsoft Fabric and Power BI communities, enjoys sharing his expertise through blogs and videos, and organizes events for the Persian Power BI User Group.

I would like to extend my heartfelt gratitude to my wife for her endless support and patience. Her encouragement has been my guiding light.

Ahmed Oyelowo, a Managing Partner, lead trainer, and consultant at Foresight BI & Analytics Global Solutions, is a Microsoft Certified Power BI Data Analyst Associate and Azure Enterprise Data Analyst. He is also a Microsoft Certified Trainer, with a best-selling Power BI course on Udemy that has been taken by 90,000+ students. A four-time Microsoft MVP in the Data Platform category, he has developed cutting-edge solutions for various corporate clients.

My sincere appreciation to my Creator for the gift of all required to complete this review. I must also extend my gratitude to my dearest wife, Kafayat, and my lovely children, Yusraa and Yaasir, for their support and understanding while I was spending some time away from them to complete this task. Finally, I'd like to thank the authors of this book for this wonderful resource!

Learn more on Discord

Join our community's Discord space for discussions with the author and other readers:

`https://discord.gg/vCSG5GBbyS`

Table of Contents

Chapter 3: Accessing and Combining Data 49

Chapter 12: Handling Errors and Debugging 489

Preface

Over the last decade, the popularity of the Power Query's M language has continuously grown, such that it has become nearly ubiquitous within the Microsoft ecosystem, including Power BI, Excel, Power Platform, Dynamics 365, SQL Server, and Data Factory. Today, M and Power Query are indispensable tools for modern data professionals, such as business analysts, data scientists, and data enthusiasts.

This book seeks to make you a master of the M language. While M can be written using the Power Query Editor's **graphical user interface** (GUI), this approach severely limits you to only a small fraction of the 700+ core M functions. We estimate that the GUI for authoring M queries allows you to solve only about 50% of challenges related to data transformation. However, mastery of M allows you to bring that figure close to 100%. Starting with simple concepts and code, this book progressively moves you along a path of increasing complexity. Complex concepts are explained in clear and concise language with practical examples that demonstrate the concepts in action. By the end of this book, there will be few, if any, data transformation challenges that you won't be able to tackle head-on.

Get ready for an exciting and rewarding journey toward your mastery of the M language!

Who this book is for

If you're new to Power Query, then this book might not be the best choice for you. There are books out there that introduce the basics through the user interface and simple button-based actions, offering a straightforward way to get started.

On the other hand, if you are serious about fully understanding the M language, then this book is for you. If this is your first experience with M, you may find certain concepts challenging. Reading through the pages the first time will provide you with lots of information, but some topics may be too complex. As you become more familiar with M, reading the book again will likely make these complex topics easier to understand.

Overall, our goal was to write a book that blends theoretical knowledge with practical examples. The first few chapters are more theoretical and provide the M language fundamentals. As the book progresses and your understanding deepens, we include projects and exercise files for you to work along with.

The Power Query M language is useful for a variety of users. Power BI users may use M to prepare their data model, Excel users may transform data and output it on their spreadsheets, while data factory users could use M to query an API and transfer the result into a database. In this book, we aim to cater to all these different audiences.

Although some subjects, such as creating custom connectors or optimizing performance, may appeal more to those with advanced knowledge due to their technical nature, we believe it's beneficial for all users to understand the different ways the M language can be used.

Starting with the M language can be daunting, and mastering it took us several years. It's a challenging journey that requires focus and a lot of experimentation. However, if you persevere, our book offers unprecedented depth of all aspects of M, allowing you to become a true M expert.

What this book covers

Chapter 1, Introducing M, introduces M language basics such as the let expression and also covers the history of M and the formal and informal characteristics of M. It also discusses who should learn M, why you should learn M, and where and how to use M.

Chapter 2, Working with Power Query/M, introduces the Power Query Editor, the main application for coding M. In addition, it allows you to transition from only using the Power Query Editor's GUI to create M code to writing the code yourself via custom columns and the Advanced Editor.

Chapter 3, Accessing and Combining Data, explores the multitude of different data connectors available for M, including file and folder connectors, database and cube connectors, working with binary data, and finally, how to combine and merge data between queries.

Chapter 4, Values and Expressions in M, introduces the various kinds of values in the M language, as well as expressions, operators, control structures, and enumerations.

Chapter 5, Understanding Data Types, explores the importance of data types in the M language. It teaches you about their structure and their application in real-world scenarios. The chapter offers techniques to automatically detect data types and discusses why type conversion is important. Additionally, it presents the concept of facets and type ascription, which often lead to errors in your queries.

Chapter 6, Structured Values, covers some of the most important values in the M language,such as lists, records and tables. These values can store multiple values within them. You will learn the techniques for creating them, their typical uses, and the operators that work with structured values. Furthermore, the chapter explains how to access the individual values they contain.

Chapter 7, Conceptualizing M, explores some of the more abstract concepts of M that are critical to truly understanding how the M language works. The topics covered include the global environment, creating your own global environment, sections, closure, query folding, and metadata.

Chapter 8, Working with Nested Structures, presents several techniques to transform and manipulate structured values, such as lists, records, and tables, helping you move past the limitations of the GUI.

Chapter 9, Parameters and Custom Functions, begins by discussing the role of parameters in making queries flexible and dynamic. It then delves into how to create custom functions, covering their syntax, the importance of data types, and debugging techniques. Finally, you learn that the each expression is syntax sugar for a function.

Chapter 10, *Dealing with Dates, Times, and Durations*, explains how temporal analysis is key to unlocking many data insights and why you must be proficient in dealing with dates, times, and durations to perform such analyses. This chapter explores these subjects and more with numerous practical examples.

Chapter 11, *Comparers, Replacers, Combiners, and Splitters*, explores techniques for manipulating data. It demonstrates how to customize the way values are compared, ordered, replaced, combined, or split. These methods are essential for a wide range of common data transformation tasks.

Chapter 12, *Handling Errors and Debugging*, focuses on what errors are and provides guidance on how to handle them in the M language and debug your code successfully, enabling you to build more robust queries. In addition, it offers techniques to report errors.

Chapter 13, *Iteration and Recursion*, explains recursion through the use of the @ operator. The chapter then shifts focus to iteration techniques, using `List.Transform`, `List.Accumulate`, and `List.Generate`. You'll learn about memory considerations and what aspects to consider for the best performance.

Chapter 14, *Troublesome Data Patterns*, illustrates the versatility of the M language, covering various common text extraction techniques as well as providing a comprehensive approach to building a manageable custom solution for dealing with files in bulk.

Chapter 15, *Optimizing Performance*, examines factors that influence query performance. It introduces mashup containers and the importance of memory management. We'll delve into query folding, explore the formula firewall's mechanics, and present various methods to improve query performance.

Chapter 16, *Enabling Extensions*, demonstrates how to extend the M language by creating your own, reusable library of M functions, including a detailed example of creating a custom data connector.

To get the most out of this book

We expect you to have a basic knowledge of Power Query and some experience with analyzing data. If you have experience with the M language, that is helpful to understand concepts more quickly. However, knowing M is not a requirement.

Throughout the book, there are references to SQL and **Data Analysis Expressions (DAX)** code. However, you don't need to know these languages because the comparisons are simply meant to reflect on the different approaches between the languages. There's no need to worry if you don't understand a particular code snippet; that means the comparison is not as applicable to you.

In the more advanced sections of the book, we cover query folding, custom connectors, and memory usage. Some of you may not be familiar with these topics and that's okay. However, this information is an important element of what the M language is used for and we think it's good for everyone to read.

Download the example code files

The code bundle for the book is hosted on GitHub at `https://github.com/PacktPublishing/The-Definitive-Guide-to-Power-Query-M-/`. We also have other code bundles from our rich catalog of books and videos available at `https://github.com/PacktPublishing/`. Check them out!

Download the color images

We also provide a PDF file that has color images of the screenshots/diagrams used in this book. You can download it here: https://packt.link/gbp/9781835089729.

Conventions used

There are a number of text conventions used throughout this book.

CodeInText: Indicates code words in text, database table names, folder names, filenames, file extensions, pathnames, dummy URLs, user input, and Twitter handles. For example: "Navigate to the /ClientApp/src/app/cities folder."

A block of code is set as follows:

```
#date(
    year as number,
    month as number,
    day as number,
) as date
```

When we wish to draw your attention to a particular part of a code block, the relevant lines or items are highlighted:

```
#date(
    year as number,
    month as number,
    day as number,
) as date
```

Bold: Indicates a new term, an important word, or words that you see on the screen. For instance, words in menus or dialog boxes appear in the text like this. For example: "Navigate to the **Home** tab of the ribbon, click on the dropdown below the **Transform data** button, and select **Edit parameters**."

> Warnings or important notes appear like this.

> Tips and tricks appear like this.

Get in touch

Feedback from our readers is always welcome.

General feedback: Email feedback@packtpub.com and mention the book's title in the subject of your message. If you have questions about any aspect of this book, please email us at questions@packtpub.com.

Errata: Although we have taken every care to ensure the accuracy of our content, mistakes do happen. If you have found a mistake in this book, we would be grateful if you reported this to us. Please visit http://www.packtpub.com/submit-errata, click **Submit Errata**, and fill in the form.

Piracy: If you come across any illegal copies of our works in any form on the internet, we would be grateful if you would provide us with the location address or website name. Please contact us at copyright@packtpub.com with a link to the material.

If you are interested in becoming an author: If there is a topic that you have expertise in and you are interested in either writing or contributing to a book, please visit http://authors.packtpub.com.

Share your thoughts

Once you've read *The Definitive Guide to Power Query (M)*, we'd love to hear your thoughts! Scan the QR code below to go straight to the Amazon review page for this book and share your feedback.

https://packt.link/r/1835089720

Your review is important to us and the tech community and will help us make sure we're delivering excellent quality content.

Download a free PDF copy of this book

Thanks for purchasing this book!

Do you like to read on the go but are unable to carry your print books everywhere?

Is your eBook purchase not compatible with the device of your choice?

Don't worry, now with every Packt book you get a DRM-free PDF version of that book at no cost.

Read anywhere, any place, on any device. Search, copy, and paste code from your favorite technical books directly into your application.

The perks don't stop there, you can get exclusive access to discounts, newsletters, and great free content in your inbox daily

Follow these simple steps to get the benefits:

1. Scan the QR code or visit the link below

https://packt.link/free-ebook/9781835089729

2. Submit your proof of purchase
3. That's it! We'll send your free PDF and other benefits to your email directly

1

Introducing M

M is a powerful and versatile formula language specifically designed for data manipulation and transformation. The term M is an informal designation. M's official name is the **Power Query Formula Language**. For an explanation of this designation, see the *History of M* section later in this chapter. M is the language at the heart of Power Query, which is used in numerous applications like Microsoft Excel, Power BI, Power Platform, and Microsoft Fabric for data transformation and preparation.

The popularity of the M language has continuously grown over the last decade, and the language has been integrated into an impressive array of Microsoft tools and platforms. Today, M and Power Query are indispensable tools for modern data professionals such as business analysts, data scientists, and data enthusiasts.

This chapter is the beginning of your exciting journey that culminates in the mastery of the M language. We start with a brief history of M and then cover the basics of who, where, why, and how. Next, we introduce the absolute basics of the M language and finish with the formal and informal characteristics of M (in effect, what is M?). Overall, this chapter provides a firm foundation for the more in-depth exploration of the M language found throughout the rest of this book. Specifically, this chapter covers the following topics:

- The history of M
- Who should learn M?
- Where and how Is M used?
- Why learn M?
- M language basics
- The characteristics of M

The history of M

The process of extracting, transforming, and loading data is a challenge as old as information technology itself. Both business users and IT professionals have historically struggled with the challenge, and numerous software tools have been developed over the years to help deal with the challenge such as SQL **Server Integration Services (SSIS)** and **Alteryx**.

However, many of these tools were complex and not easily portable. The M language and Power Query were created to help solve these issues.

While there might be some more speculative history regarding the origins of M, we can at least definitively trace M back to a project originally code-named **Data Explorer**. Data Explorer was an Azure SQL Labs project circa 2011 that aimed to simplify the process of accessing, cleaning, and preparing data from various sources. The query language was thought of as a mashup language (hence the M for mashup).

In 2013, Microsoft released Power Query as an add-in for Excel. Power Query introduced a user-friendly interface, allowing business users to perform data transformations via a visual editor. Behind the scenes, Power Query utilized the M language as the underlying formula language to drive the data transformations, and as such, these data transformations became repeatable. Instead of, for example, business users continually performing the same manual data transformations on source data received as comma-delimited files, that process could now be effectively automated.

Following the success of Power Query in Excel, Microsoft included Power Query as part of its new product, Power BI Designer, which eventually became Power BI Desktop. As Power Query gained popularity, there was a need to standardize the underlying formula language. In 2016, Microsoft submitted the Power Query Formula Language specification to the **European Computer Manufacturers Association (ECMA)**, an international standards organization. This effort established a formal specification for the language, ensuring compatibility and interoperability between different implementations.

While the language was formally referred to as the Power Query Formula Language, it became commonly known as **M** among the user community. The informal name **M** gained widespread acceptance and is now widely used to refer to the language.

Microsoft continues to enhance and refine the M language as part of its ongoing investment in data integration and transformation technologies. New functions, features, and improvements are periodically introduced to provide users with more powerful and efficient ways to manipulate and prepare their data. In addition, Microsoft continues to introduce M within additional software tools and platforms, such as data integration within Microsoft Power Platform and dataflows within Power BI and Fabric.

Today, the M language is a key component of Microsoft's data transformation and integration toolset. The proliferation of M, as well as its versatility and extensibility, make it an invaluable language for today's modern data professionals.

Let's now turn our attention to who should learn M.

Who should learn M?

M is a powerful tool for data professionals and individuals who work with data on a regular basis. The versatility and capabilities of M make it a valuable language to learn for various roles, including the following:

- **Data analysts:** Data analysts who deal with data extraction, transformation, and preparation tasks can greatly benefit from learning M. It provides a comprehensive set of functions and operators that enable data analysts to efficiently shape and manipulate data from diverse sources. By mastering M, data analysts can automate repetitive tasks, handle complex data transformations, and ensure data quality, leading to more accurate and reliable data analysis.

- **Business intelligence professionals:** Professionals in the **business intelligence (BI)** space can greatly enhance their skills by learning M. It is a core component of Power BI. By understanding M, BI professionals gain the ability to connect to various data sources, perform complex data transformations, and create reusable data preparation workflows, enabling them to provide actionable insights and drive informed decision-making.

- **Data engineers:** Data engineers involved in the design and implementation of data pipelines and data integration processes can really benefit from learning M. It allows data engineers to efficiently **extract, transform,** and **load (ETL)** data from different sources into data warehouses or data lakes, specifically within Power BI and Microsoft Fabric. M also provides the flexibility and power to handle complex data formats, define custom transformations, and create efficient data processing workflows. By mastering M, data engineers can streamline data integration processes and ensure data consistency and quality.

- **Data scientists:** Data scientists who perform exploratory data analysis, model development, and advanced analytics can leverage the capabilities of M to efficiently prepare their data. M provides a robust set of functions for cleaning, shaping, and aggregating data, allowing data scientists to focus on the analytical aspects of their work. By incorporating M into their data preparation workflows, data scientists can streamline the pipeline of turning raw data into insights, spending less time on data cleansing and preparation and more time on data modeling and analysis.

- **Power users:** Power users in Excel and Microsoft's Power Platform who work extensively with data and perform complex data manipulations can benefit from learning M. It is integrated into Excel through Power Query, empowering users to perform advanced data transformations within the familiar Excel interface. In addition, M is integrated into the Microsoft Power Platform via data integration, allowing data to be transformed and mapped between systems. By mastering M, Power users can expand their data manipulation capabilities, automate repetitive tasks, and enhance the accuracy and reliability of their analyses.

- **Individuals in data-driven roles:** Beyond the specific roles mentioned above, individuals in various data-driven roles, such as project managers, consultants, researchers, and domain experts, can benefit from learning M. Mastery of M provides the ability for individuals in these roles to independently handle data-related tasks, extract meaningful insights, and make informed decisions based on reliable data.

M is a valuable language for a wide range of data professionals and other individuals who work with data. Whether you are a data analyst, BI professional, data engineer, data scientist, power user, or someone in a data-driven role, learning M empowers you to efficiently ingest, transform, and prepare data for analysis.

Now that we understand what types of individuals would want to learn M, let's next explore where those individuals can leverage their mastery of M.

Where and how is M used?

M is a versatile language included in various tools and platforms where data transformation and manipulation are essential. Its integration within the Power Query ecosystem enables users to leverage M's capabilities in different environments. In this section, we explore some key areas where M is widely used.

Experiences

Before discussing specific products where M is used, it is important to understand the different experiences available for authoring M. There are two experiences available for authoring M, one intended for on-premises use and the other for cloud-based applications. These experiences are the following:

- **Power Query Desktop:** Power Query Desktop is the experience for Power Query found in desktop applications such as Power BI Desktop and Microsoft Excel. While the experiences are similar, there are differences. For example, the **artificial intelligence (AI)** and **machine learning (ML)** integrations as well as the integrations with R and Python present in Power BI Desktop are not present in Microsoft Excel. Conversely, the **Structured Column** options available in Excel are not available in Power BI Desktop.

- **Power Query Online:** Power Query Online, a cloud-based service, allows users to create and manage data transformations within a web browser. M is used extensively in Power Query Online to define data transformations, connect to data sources, and perform complex data manipulations. Users can access and edit M queries directly within the browser interface, making it convenient to collaborate and work on data transformation tasks from anywhere with an internet connection. Power Query Online is integrated into a variety of Microsoft products, including the Power BI service, Power Apps, Power Automate, etc.

It is important to note that while two different experiences for authoring M exist, both provide nearly the exact same user experience. Even better, both provide the ability to edit the underlying M code, which is the primary focus of this book. Thus, the skills learned here apply equally to either experience used within any product or service.

Products and services

M is ubiquitous within the Microsoft ecosystem, including the following software and services:

- **Dataflows:** Dataflows are product-agnostic, cloud-based M queries that can be reused across multiple different products. Dataflows enable users to build and manage reusable data preparation and transformation processes. Dataflows leverage the Power Query Online experience.

- **Power BI Desktop:** M is a fundamental component of Power BI Desktop, a leading BI tool. M allows users to connect to different data sources, perform data transformations, and create interactive visualizations and reports.

  M enables users to extract, clean, and shape data from diverse sources, such as databases, Excel files, web services, and more. With M, users can define data transformation steps and create reusable queries that refresh and update data automatically when the underlying source changes.

  Within Power BI Desktop, M is used within the Power Query editor, a sub-program launched from within Power BI Desktop. The Power Query editor provides a powerful **graphical user interface (GUI)** for working with the M formula language, as shown in the following screenshot:

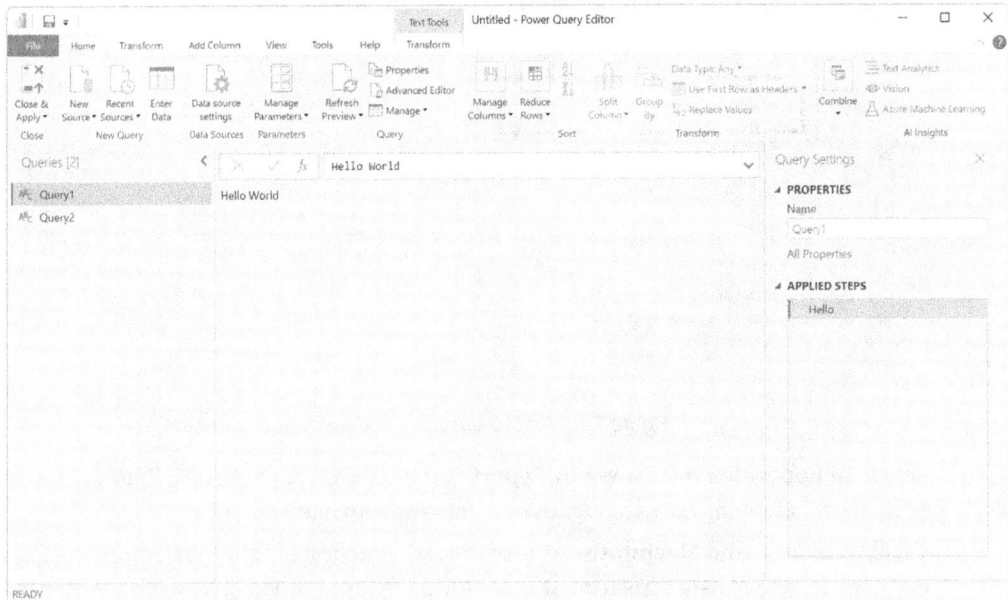

Figure 1.1: Power Query editor in Power BI Desktop

  The Power Query editor is covered in greater detail in *Chapter 2, Working With Power Query/M*.

  Power BI Desktop also supports the use of dataflows.

- **Power BI/Fabric service:** The Power BI/Fabric service (powerbi.com) is the cloud-based component of Power BI that enables you to share reports, dashboards, and other content. The service supports the use of M code via the creation of dataflows, using the Power Query Online experience.

To create a dataflow in the Power BI service, navigate to any workspace other than **My Work-space** and choose **New** and then **Dataflow**, as shown in *Figure 1.2*:

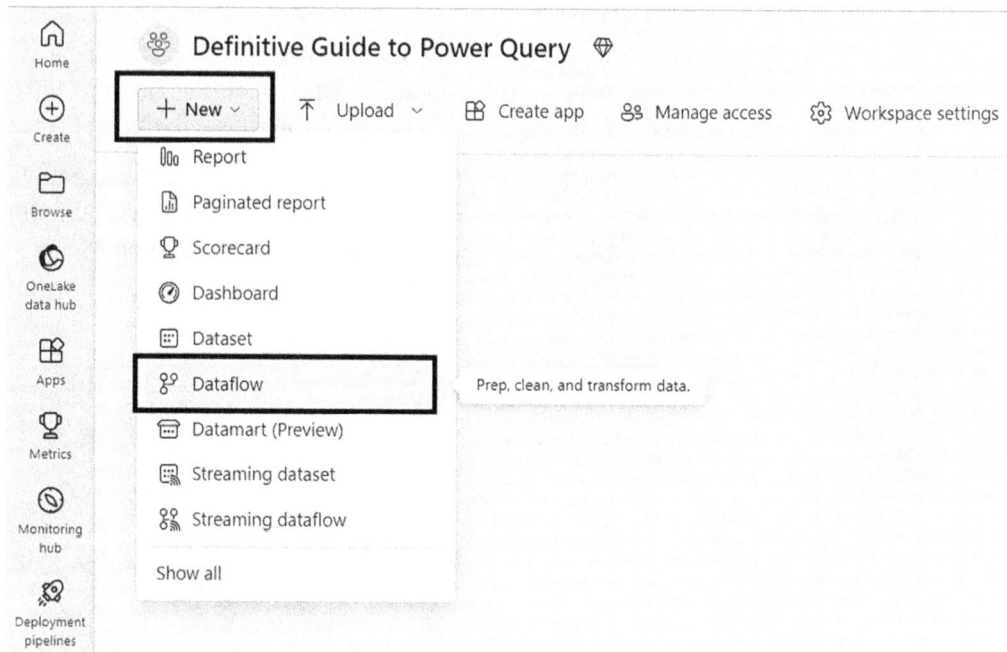

Figure 1.2: Create a dataflow in the Power BI service

- **Power BI Report Server: Power BI Report Server (PBRS)** supports the Power Query Desktop experience, allowing users to create rich data transformations via M.
- **Excel (Windows and Macintosh):** M is seamlessly integrated into Excel, empowering users to perform advanced data transformations within the familiar Excel interface. Power Query, the engine behind Excel's data transformation capabilities, is powered by M. Users can access the Power Query editor in Excel to apply M transformations, filter and sort data, remove duplicates, merge and append tables, and perform other data preparation tasks. M allows users to clean, reshape, and enrich data in Excel, enhancing the accuracy and reliability of their analyses.

In Excel, the Power Query editor interface can be accessed by using the **Data** tab of the ribbon and choosing **Get Data:**

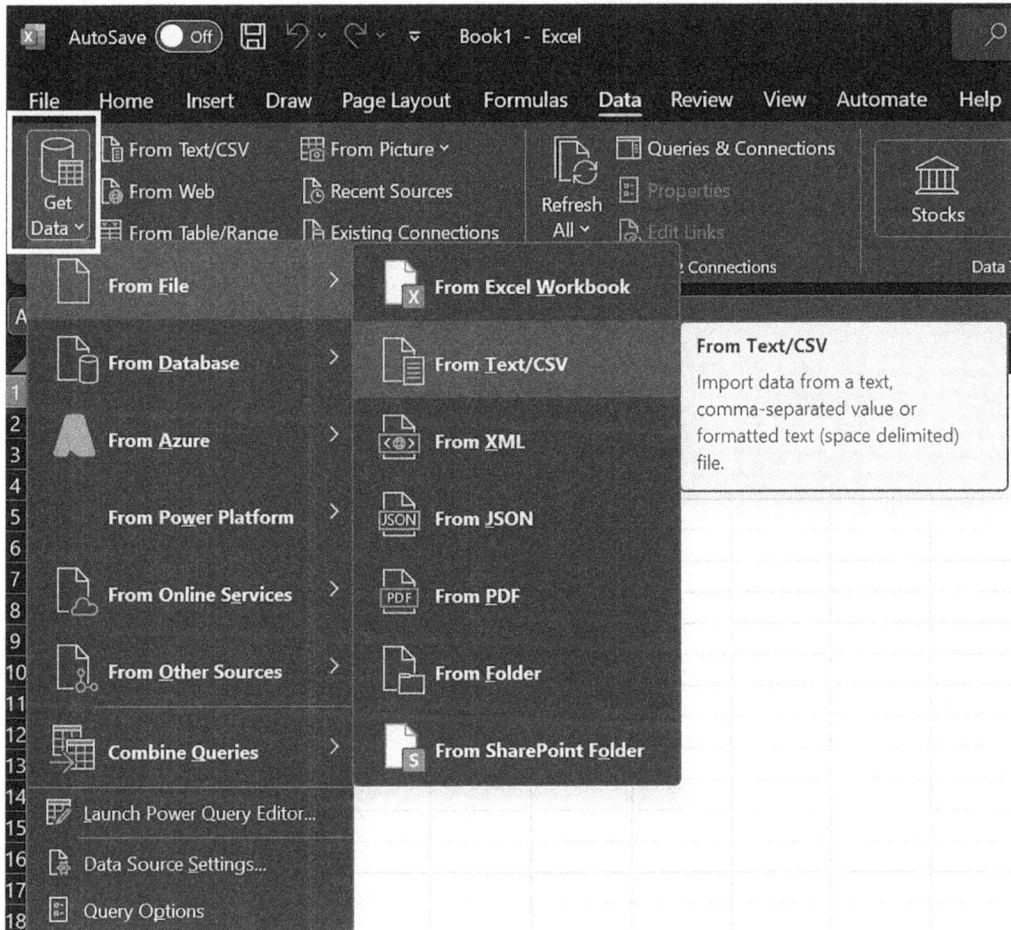

Figure 1.3: Get Data in Microsoft Excel

Once the data source is chosen, the Power Query Editor interface can be accessed by choosing the **Transform Data** button:

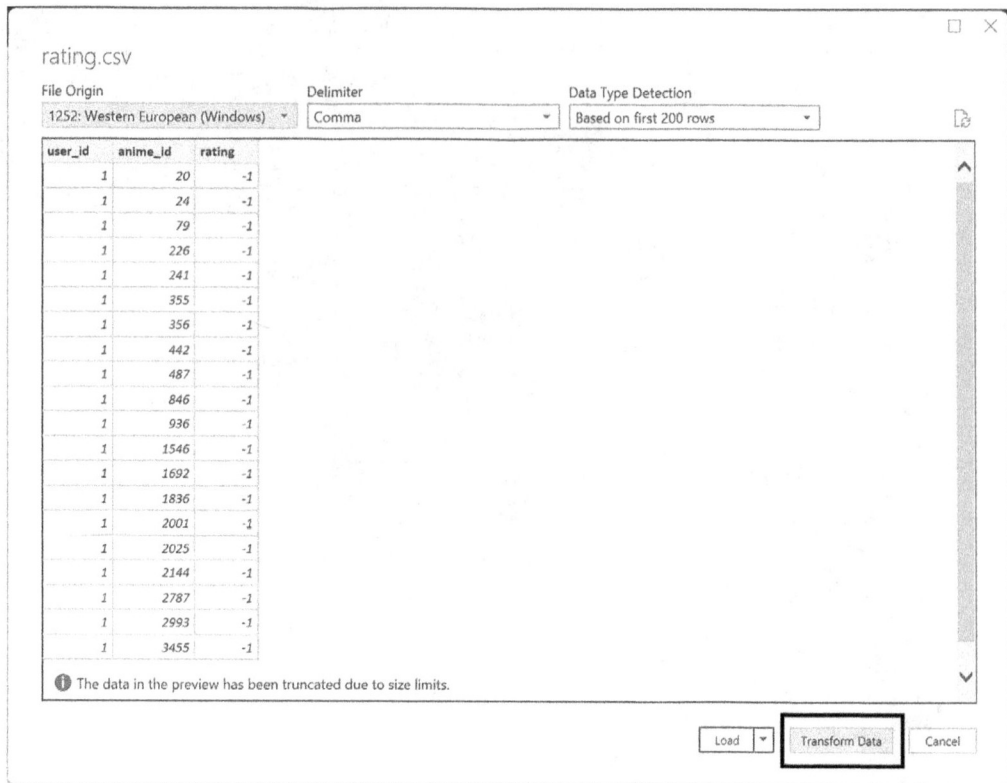

Figure 1.4: Transform Data option in Microsoft Excel

Both the Windows and Macintosh versions of Excel also support accessing and using dataflows.

- **Power Apps:** Power Apps is Microsoft's low-code platform for creating applications. Both the Power Query Online experience as well as the use of dataflows are supported. A common use case is to leverage M either via the Power Query Online experience or dataflows, allowing users to seamlessly bring their data into the Dataverse (formally Common Data Service).

- **Power Automate:** Power Automate is Microsoft's low code platform for automating workflows. Power Automate allows users to automate repetitive workflows and processes that may involve data manipulation and integration tasks. M can be employed within Power Automate to perform data transformations and handle complex data scenarios as part of the automated workflows, via the Power Query Online experience. By incorporating M into Power Automate, users can build sophisticated data integration and automation solutions that streamline their business processes. In addition, dataflows can be leveraged in Power Automate via Power Query Dataflows connector. This allows actions to occur once a dataflow completes and also provides the ability for a dataflow to be initiated as an action within a Power Automate flow.

- **Data Factory:** Data Factory is a managed cloud service specifically built for complex **extract-transform-load (ETL)** and **extract-load-transform (ELT)** integration projects. Data Factory allows the creation and orchestration of data-driven workflows, data movement, and transformation at scale. Both Azure Data Factory and Data Factory in Microsoft Fabric support M code, via both the Power Query Online experience as well as dataflows.

- **SQL Server:** SSIS supports the core M engine while **SQL Server Analysis Services (SSAS)** supports the Power Query Desktop experience.

- **Dynamics 365 Customer Insights:** Customer Insights within Dynamics 365 is Microsoft's **customer data platform (CDP)** that provides a holistic view of customers, enabling personalized customer experiences. Customer Insights supports both dataflows as well as the Power Query Online experience.

- **Visual Studio:** Visual Studio allows M to be integrated as a language. This is done via the Power Query Language Service for Visual Studio Code and is available in the Visual Studio Code Marketplace. This language service provides fuzzy autocomplete, hover, function hints, and other functionality for writing M code within Visual Studio.

  There is also the Visual Studio Power Query **Software Development Kit (SDK)**. This SDK consists of a set of tools designed to help create custom Power Query data source connectors. The Visual Studio Power Query SDK is covered in greater detail in *Chapter 16, Enabling Extensions*.

- **Other data integration scenarios:** M is not limited to the aforementioned software and services. M can also be leveraged in custom applications and programming environments that utilize Power Query libraries.

As you can see, M is widely used in different tools and platforms within the Microsoft ecosystem, such as Power BI Desktop, Excel, the Power BI and Fabric service, Power Platform, SQL Server, and Dynamics. M enables users to connect to various data sources, perform advanced data transformations, and automate data integration workflows. The skills learned in this book deal with the M language itself and, thus, transcend both the experience as well as the specific product or service. Thus, by mastering M, users gain the ability to create reusable data transformation processes and enhance their data manipulation capabilities across a wide range of data-related scenarios, as well as across any experience, product, or service that uses M as its underlying data transformation layer.

Let's now turn our attention to why data professionals and other individuals might want to add M to their repertoire of language.

Why learn M?

In today's data-driven world, efficiently and effectively transforming and analyzing data is a valuable skill. Power Query, a powerful data transformation and preparation tool, gained immense popularity due to its seamless integration with many popular software systems as well as its ease of use. At the heart of Power Query lies M, the Power Query Formula Language. But you may be asking yourself, why should you invest the time in order to learn M?

Here are seven reasons why we believe data professionals and other individuals should learn M:

- **Tapping into the full power of Power Query:** In Gil Raviv's book, *Collect, Combine, and Transform Data Using Power Query in Excel and Power BI*, Mr. Raviv estimates that the GUI for authoring M queries (see *Where and how Is M used?* in this chapter) allows you to solve only 40% of challenges related to data transformation, but mastery of M allows you to bring that figure closer to 99.99%. Later chapters demonstrate specific examples of solving data transformation challenges that cannot be done in the GUI. Since M serves as the backbone of Power Query's data transformation capabilities, by mastering M, you gain full control over the data transformation process, allowing you to extract, clean, transform, and reshape data from diverse sources.

- **Automation of repetitive tasks:** One of the primary reasons you should learn M is to automate repetitive data transformation tasks. Business and IT professionals are often tasked with receiving data on a recurring basis and then generating reports based on this data. Instead of manually transforming this data each time (often in Excel) to prepare it for reporting purposes, leveraging M for this data transformation allows the data transformation logic to be implemented once and then automatically run each time new data is received.

- **Flexibility and customization:** While Power Query provides a user-friendly interface for data transformation tasks, it does have its limitations. By learning M, you can extend the capabilities of Power Query and overcome these limitations. M allows you to write custom functions, perform advanced transformations, and apply complex logic that goes beyond the built-in capabilities of the Power Query interface. This flexibility empowers you to tailor your data transformations precisely to meet the unique requirements of your data sources and analysis.

- **Efficiency and performance optimization:** M is a highly efficient and optimized language for data transformations. The Power Query engine intelligently processes M expressions, optimizing performance by reducing unnecessary data loads and transformations. When working with large datasets or complex transformations, knowing M enables you to write efficient code that significantly speeds up your data processing, as demonstrated in *Chapter 15*, *Optimizing Performance*. By understanding the underlying principles of M and its performance considerations, you can optimize your data workflows and save valuable time. Finally, leveraging M can greatly reduce and simplify the formula and **Data Analysis Expressions (DAX)** code in downstream applications like Excel and Power BI Desktop.

- **Advanced data cleaning and transformation:** M provides a comprehensive set of data cleaning and transformation functions that go far beyond the basic operations available in traditional spreadsheet applications. With M, you can easily handle data quality issues, such as removing duplicates, handling missing values, splitting columns, merging sets of data, and performing advanced calculations. Learning M enables you to tackle complex data cleaning and transformation tasks efficiently, leading to accurate and reliable data analysis.

- **Integration with other programming languages:** M is not only a standalone language but also integrates well with other programming languages such as SQL, R, and Python. This integration allows you to leverage the capabilities of these languages within your Power Query workflows. You can combine M code with native SQL queries, call R or Python scripts, and seamlessly incorporate external libraries and functions into your data transformation process. By expanding your knowledge to include M, you unlock the potential to leverage the best features of various programming languages for data manipulation.

- **Career advancement**: Proficiency in M and Power Query has become a sought-after skill in the data industry. As organizations increasingly rely on data for decision-making, individuals who possess the ability to efficiently transform, clean, and analyze data are in high demand. By investing time and effort in learning M, you position yourself as a valuable asset to organizations that rely on data-driven insights. The knowledge of M can open up new career opportunities, enhance your job prospects, and enable you to take on challenging data-related projects.

In summary, learning M enables you to efficiently ingest, transform, and analyze data from diverse sources. It provides flexibility, customization, and performance optimization capabilities that extend the functionality of Power Query itself. By mastering M, you gain a competitive edge in the data industry and open doors to new career possibilities.

We hope that you are now excited about learning M! Let's turn our attention to the basics of the M language.

M language basics

As previously noted, M is a powerful language designed for data ingest and transformation within a variety of Microsoft software and services. Understanding the basics of the M language is essential for effectively leveraging its capabilities.

Here are some important fundamentals regarding the M language:

- **Expressions and functions**: In M, expressions form the building blocks of data transformations. An expression represents a computation or operation that evaluates to a value. M provides a wide range of built-in functions that can be used to perform operations on data. Functions in M are called using a syntax where the function name is followed by arguments within parentheses. For example, the function `Text.Start("Hello, World!", 5)` returns the substring `Hello` from the input text. More about expressions and functions are covered in *Chapter 4, Understanding Values and Expressions*, as well as *Chapter 9, Parameters and Custom Functions*.
- **Data types**: M supports various data types, including text, numbers, dates, times, lists, tables, and records. Understanding the data types in M is crucial for performing accurate transformations. M provides functions to convert between different data types and manipulate data, based on their inherent characteristics. For example, the `Text.From` function converts a value to text, while the `Date.Year` function extracts the year component from a date or datetime value. Data types are covered in *Chapter 5, Understanding Data Types*.
- **Variables and constants**: M allows you to define variables and constants to store and reuse values during data transformations. Variables are created within a let expression, followed by a comma-separated list of variable assignments. Constants, on the other hand, are fixed values that remain constant throughout the execution. Variables and constants help improve code readability, enable reuse, and make complex transformations more manageable. More about variables and constants can be found throughout this book.

- **Operators:** M supports a variety of operators to perform mathematical calculations, logical comparisons, and text manipulations. Arithmetic operators (+, -, *, /, and so on) are used for numeric calculations, while comparison operators (>, <, =, and so on) evaluate logical conditions. The combination operator '&' is used for concatenating text values, appending lists and tables, or merging records. Operators are covered in *Chapter 4, Understanding Values and Expressions*.

- **Step-by-step transformation process:** M follows a step-by-step transformation process where each step defines a data transformation operation. The Power Query editor provides a visual interface to define these steps and generates the corresponding M code. Steps can include operations such as filtering rows, removing duplicates, splitting columns, merging tables, and aggregating data. *Chapter 2, Working with Power Query/M*, covers this topic in more detail.

- **Query folding:** Query folding is an optimization technique in Power Query that pushes data transformations to the data source whenever possible. When using M, it is important to be aware of query folding to ensure efficient data processing. Query folding can improve performance by reducing data transfer between the data source and Power Query. However, not all transformations can be folded, so it is essential to understand which operations can be folded and which cannot. For example, when using Direct Query or Dual storage mode for tables, all M queries must fold, which can limit certain transformation operations. Query folding is discussed in *Chapter 7, Conceptualizing M*, and in *Chapter 15, Optimizing Performance*.

- **Error handling and debugging:** M provides error handling mechanisms to catch and handle exceptions during data transformations. By using functions like `try`, `otherwise`, and `error`, you can control the flow of execution and handle potential errors gracefully. Additionally, M supports debugging capabilities, such as the ability to step through the code to identify and resolve issues in complex transformations. Error handling and debugging are covered in *Chapter 12, Handling Errors and Debugging*.

- **Case sensitivity:** M is case-sensitive. This applies to all functions, expressions, variables, constants, and other aspects of the M language.

- **Commenting:** Comments in M follow the C language commenting style. Inline comments are proceeded by double slashes (//) while block comments use the slash-asterisk/asterisk-slash pattern (/* and */).

Now that we have a good understanding of the core components of the M language, let's next explore the most fundamental component of the M language, the `let` expression.

The let expression

At the core of the M language is the `let` expression, which must be paired with an `in` expression. In simple terms, the `let` expression contains the input and transformations, while the `in` expression contains the output. A simple `Hello World` for M looks like the following:

```
let
    Hello = "Hello World"
in
    Hello
```

This code would return the ubiquitous `Hello World` text.

It is important to note that every expression within a let statement must be followed by a comma (,) except the last expression prior to the in expression. Thus, if the let expression consists of multiple sub-expressions, then the code might look like the following:

```
let
    Hello = "Hello",
    World = "World",
    Return = Hello & " " & World
in
    Return
```

This code also returns Hello World as output.

Understanding the basics of M, including expressions, functions, data types, variables, operators, and the step-by-step transformation process, is vital for effectively manipulating and preparing data. By mastering these foundational concepts, you gain the ability to perform complex transformations, optimize data workflows, and unlock the full potential of the M language. The rest of this book is devoted to helping you master all of these foundational concepts and how to apply them to complex data transformations.

The characteristics of M

M is a programming language that serves as the backbone of Power Query, enabling users to extract, clean, and reshape data from various sources, such as databases, spreadsheets, web pages, and more. However, unlike general-purpose programming languages such as C, C#, Java, and Python, which are designed for a wide variety of applications, M is a domain-specific language, specifically designed for data ingest and manipulation. As such, M provides a rich set of functions, operators, and expressions that allow you to perform complex data transformations, calculations, and aggregations. Let's understand this better by taking a look at the characteristics of M from both formal and informal perspectives.

Formal classification

Programming languages are classified according to a number of properties, such as pure/impure, lower-order/higher order, statically/dynamically typed, strongly/weakly typed, eager/lazy evaluation, and imperative/functional.

Microsoft has described M as:

- **Mostly pure:** A programming language is said to be pure if it provides referential integrity. In other words, any expression can be replaced with that expression's value without changing the program's behavior or meaning.

  An impure programming language allows side effects, which are actions that cause changes outside the scope of a function's return value. In the case of M, it is commonly used for data transformation and retrieval tasks, which often involve interacting with external data sources, performing operations on data, and producing output. These actions constitute side effects because they affect the state of the data source or produce output beyond the function's return value.

While M provides functional programming constructs and supports immutability, allowing for the creation of pure functions, the language is not purely functional due to its impure nature. It embraces a combination of functional and imperative programming paradigms to facilitate efficient and practical data manipulation and retrieval.

- **Higher-order:** For lower-order languages, such as machine code or assembly language, each programming statement corresponds to a single instruction for the computer, while in higher-order languages, each statement corresponds to multiple instructions for the computer.

  Higher-order languages typically allow such things as functions, objects, and modules to be used as values within a program. Higher-order languages often treat functions as first-class citizens. Specifically, this means that functions can be assigned to variables, passed as arguments to other functions, and returned as values from functions.

  Power Query M supports higher-order programming by allowing you to define and manipulate functions as values. You can assign functions to variables, pass functions as arguments to other functions, and return functions as results. This enables you to create more modular and flexible code by abstracting and reusing function logic.

  With higher-order programming capabilities, M allows you to apply transformations and computations dynamically based on input parameters, control flow, and data characteristics. You can write functions that operate on other functions, enabling powerful data manipulation and transformation scenarios.

  For example, you can use higher-order functions in M to dynamically apply a series of transformations to a dataset, based on user-defined criteria, or to create reusable function pipelines for data processing.

  By providing higher-order programming features, M empowers developers to write expressive and modular code, making it easier to work with complex data transformations and customize the behavior of functions to suit specific requirements.

- **Dynamically typed:** Dynamically typed languages perform type checking at runtime instead of at compile time, as is the case with statically typed languages. Type checking is simply the process of ensuring that things such as parameters passed to a function are of the correct type, such as text, a number, or a date.

- **Weakly typed:** While closely related to the property of statically/dynamically typed, strongly typed and weakly typed refer to something quite different. Strongly typed languages are extremely sensitive to type compatibility and require explicit type definitions for variables before being used. Conversely, weakly typed languages like M do not require explicit type definitions, and some even perform automatic type conversion.

  M is not as weakly typed as programming languages such as Python, since variables are immutable once calculated. Thus, the weak type definition for M generally refers to the ability to use variables whose data types have not been explicitly specified.

Consider the following Python code:

```
a = 42
a = "Hello World"
print(a)
```

This code would not generate an error in Python, even though two different data types are assigned to the variable a. However, similar code is not possible in M, since variables, once calculated, are immutable (i.e., cannot be changed).

The flexibility in data typing allows Power Query M to handle a wide range of data sources and perform various data transformations effectively. It simplifies the process of working with heterogeneous datasets that may contain different data types and structures.

It is important to note that even though Power Query M is weakly typed, it still performs type checking during execution (runtime) to ensure the consistency of operations. If a particular operation is not compatible with the inferred type of a value, an error may occur at runtime.

Overall, the weakly typed nature of Power Query M strikes a balance between flexibility and data integrity, providing users with a versatile language for data transformation tasks.

- **Partially lazy:** In general, M follows an eager evaluation strategy, meaning that when you define transformations or computations, those transformations and computations are performed immediately as you apply them to the data. This eager evaluation approach ensures that data transformations occur promptly and that the results are readily available for further processing or analysis. Power Query M is designed to efficiently handle data manipulation and retrieval tasks, focusing on immediate evaluation to provide real-time feedback on transformations.

The term **partially lazy** refers to a specific feature within M called **lazy evaluation,** which is distinct from the overall evaluation strategy of the language. In M, lazy evaluation is applied to expressions within some specific constructs, specifically List, Record, and Table expressions as well as the let expression. These constructs allow you to define expressions that are evaluated only when needed, providing a form of on-demand or lazy evaluation within those contexts.

M also allows you to define optional arguments for functions. These optional arguments are evaluated lazily, meaning they are not computed unless explicitly used within the function body. Lazy evaluation of optional arguments helps optimize performance by avoiding unnecessary computations for optional values that are not actually used within the function. It ensures that the computations for optional arguments are deferred until their values are required within the function's execution.

M also supports conditional branching constructs like if-then-else statements. Only the branch that matches a condition is evaluated, while the other branch is not computed, resulting in lazy evaluation. This is in contrast to an eager evaluation strategy where both branches are evaluated regardless of the condition's outcome. This form of lazy evaluation within the if-then-else construct allows for efficient computation by avoiding unnecessary evaluations of expressions in the non-matching branch.

It is important to note that while M has these partially lazy features, the overall evaluation strategy of the language remains predominantly eager. Most expressions in Power Query M are eagerly evaluated, ensuring that data transformations occur promptly, and results are immediately available for further processing. Thus, M is primarily an eager programming language, but it incorporates partial lazy evaluation in specific constructs, such as for the List, Record, Table, and let expressions, as well as optional function arguments and conditional branching. These partially lazy evaluations offer flexibility and optimize performance within those contexts.

- **Functional:** M incorporates many functional programming concepts and features, making it a functional programming language. These functional concepts and features include immutability, higher-order functions, function composition, pure functions, and recursion.

  M encourages immutability, meaning that data values are not modified in place but transformed into new values. This promotes the functional programming principle of avoiding side effects.

  M supports higher-order functions, allowing functions to be treated as first-class values. You can pass functions as arguments to other functions, return functions from functions, and store functions in variables.

  M facilitates function composition, enabling you to combine multiple functions to create more complex transformations. This composability is a characteristic of functional programming.

  M promotes the use of pure functions, which have no side effects and produce the same output for the same input. Pure functions make code more predictable and easier to troubleshoot.

  M supports recursion. While recursion is not as extensively supported as in some other functional languages, M does offer limited support for recursive functions, allowing developers to solve problems through recursive techniques.

In terms of comparison with other languages, M is perhaps most similar to F#, a programming language developed and implemented by Don Syme of *Microsoft Research*, Cambridge, UK.

Now that we have covered the formal classification of the M language, let's next take a look at some more informal characteristics of M.

Informal characteristics of M

More informally, here are some key characteristics and features of M:

- **Functional language:** M is a functional language, meaning it is based on the concept of functions as the primary building blocks for data transformations. Functions in M can be combined, nested, and composed to perform intricate data manipulations. M provides over 700 built-in functions for common operations, as well as the ability to create custom functions tailored to your specific needs. Many of these functions, as well as custom functions, are covered in later chapters.

The extensive collection of built-in functions in M provides users with powerful tools to handle diverse data transformation scenarios. These functions are designed to simplify common data manipulation tasks and enable users to efficiently transform and shape their data.

- **Expressive and readable syntax:** The syntax of M is designed to be intuitive and easy to read, making it accessible to both beginners and experienced programmers. M expressions are written in a clear and concise manner, facilitating the creation of complex data transformations without sacrificing readability. The syntax follows a step-by-step approach, allowing you to define a series of sequential transformations to be applied to your data. Later chapters demonstrate the expressive and readable syntax of M with specific examples.

- **Data types and values:** M supports various data types, including primitive data types such as text, numbers, dates, and duration, as well as structured data types such as lists, tables, and records. It provides powerful functions to work with these data types, helping you to manipulate and transform data at a granular level. M also allows you to define and work with variables, constants, and parameters to store and reuse intermediate results during the data transformation process. Data types and values are covered in depth in *Chapter 4, Understanding Values and Expressions*, and *Chapter 5, Understanding Data Types*.

- **Integration with Power Query Editor:** M seamlessly integrates with the Power Query Editor, providing a user-friendly interface for interacting with and developing M code. The Power Query Editor allows you to visually build data transformation steps, preview the results, and generate M code automatically. It provides a robust development environment where you can write, debug, and refine your M expressions. See *Chapter 2, Working with Power Query/M*, for more on this subject.

- **Extensibility and customization:** One of the standout features of M is its extensibility. While M offers a wide range of built-in transformations, M also allows you to go beyond these capabilities and create custom transformations to suit your very own specific needs. You can define your own functions, write reusable code snippets, and create advanced data manipulation logic using M. This level of customization empowers you to handle complex data scenarios that are not covered by standard transformations accessible through the user interface. *Chapter 16, Enabling Extensions*, demonstrates M's flexibility and extensibility.

- **Performance optimization:** M is optimized for performance, enabling efficient data processing, even with large datasets. The Power Query engine intelligently evaluates and optimizes M expressions to minimize data loads and transformations, resulting in faster and more efficient data processing.

One specific performance optimization technique is called streaming semantically and is a property of `List` and `Table` expressions. Streaming semantically involves the repeated enumeration of table rows or list items. Instead of iterating through the table or list for each data transformation, streaming semantically each row of the table or item in the list is evaluated for all of the data transformations, and the results are collected as part of the output for the expression. Streaming semantically enable the transformation of datasets that do not fit within available memory.

Another performance optimization technique is called query folding. However, query folding is not a property of the M language itself. Instead, query folding is used within Power Query to *push* or *fold* data transformations back to source data systems. In essence, the transformation expressions within M are translated to equivalent transformation statements available within the source systems, such as SQL Server. This pushes the processing of transformations back to the source systems instead of the client system executing the M query. This can improve performance and efficiency by minimizing the data transfer and reducing the amount of data processed by Power Query.

By understanding the underlying principles of M and its performance considerations, you can write optimized code and improve the overall performance of your data workflows. *Chapter 15, Optimizing Performance,* provides more information on performance optimization, with specific examples.

In summary, M is a versatile and expressive language specifically designed for data transformation and manipulation within Power Query. Its functional nature, extensive set of functions, and integration with the Power Query editor make it a powerful tool for extracting, cleaning, and reshaping data from diverse sources.

Summary

The M language is the backbone of Microsoft Power Query's data transformation capabilities. M is widely used within the larger Microsoft ecosystem, including a variety of software applications and web-based services. Many different types of data professionals can benefit from learning M to efficiently and effectively ingest and transform data across a wide range of scenarios. By mastering M, you gain the ability to efficiently handle complex data transformations, customize your data workflows, and optimize performance, thereby tapping into the full potential that Power Query has to offer you for your data manipulation needs.

In this chapter, we have covered the essential questions of who, what, where, why, and how M is used, as well as provided a brief introduction to the fundamental aspects of the M language. In the next chapter, we introduce you to the primary interface in which you will be writing and working with M.

Learn more on Discord

Join our community's Discord space for discussions with the author and other readers:

`https://discord.gg/vCSG5GBbyS`

2

Working with Power Query/M

In *Chapter 1, Introducing M*, we introduced the fundamental aspects of the M language. In the section *Where is M used?*, we briefly introduced the concept of Power Query experiences, including Power Query Desktop and Power Query Online.

This chapter provides greater detail regarding working with M within the Power Query Desktop experience using Power BI Desktop. The knowledge covered here will allow you to start writing M code via an easy-to-use **graphical user interface (GUI)** provided by the Power Query Editor and is directly translatable to other desktop experiences, such as that found in Excel as well as the Power Query Online experience within websites such as powerbi.com. In effect, the Power Query Desktop experience allows you to create M code without actually writing the code yourself. Thus, you can immediately start using M to clean and transform your business data without knowing the language.

Since this book is primarily focused on the M language, this chapter does not provide comprehensive coverage of the Power Query experience. However, understanding the basics of where M code is written is important and thus this chapter covers the following topics:

- Touring the Power Query Desktop experience
- Tweaking experience-generated code
- Creating custom columns
- Using the Advanced Editor

Technical requirements

To complete the tasks in this chapter, you will require the following:

- Power BI Desktop
- The files for this chapter can be downloaded from the following GitHub repository: https://github.com/PacktPublishing/The-Definitive-Guide-to-Power-Query-M-

Power BI Desktop is where you will be introduced to the Power Query Editor experience in which you can start transforming and shaping your data.

Touring the Power Query Desktop experience

Power BI Desktop comes with a powerful sub-program called the Power Query editor. The Power Query Editor is a powerful tool for data preparation and transformation, enabling users to clean, shape, and combine millions or even billions of rows of data from different sources before using it in analytics, reporting, or visualization tools. Cleaning and transforming data plays a central role in creating a robust and well-structured semantic model for effective data analysis and reporting.

To access the Power Query Editor, you will first need to download and install Power BI Desktop. Power BI Desktop can be installed from the Microsoft Store. This is the recommended approach, although Power BI Desktop can also be installed from the following link: `https://www.microsoft.com/en-us/download/details.aspx?id=58494`.

To install Power BI Desktop from the Microsoft Store, perform the following steps:

1. Open the Microsoft Store app on your Windows PC and search for `Power BI Desktop`, as shown in *Figure 2.1*:

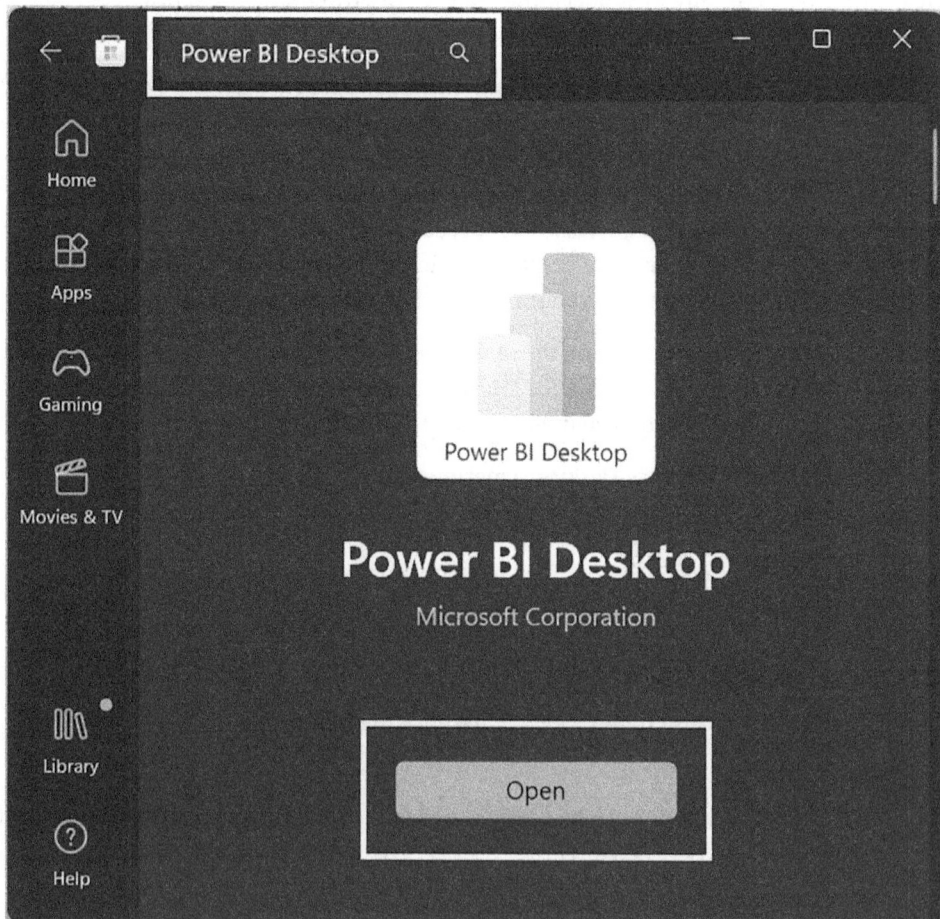

Figure 2.1: Power BI Desktop app in the Microsoft Store

2. Ensure that the name of the app is Power BI Desktop and not Power BI. These are two different apps.

3. If not already installed, the **Open** button in *Figure 2.1* will say **Install** instead. If the button already says **Open**, skip to step *5*.

4. Click the **Install** button and then once installed, the **Install** button will change to say **Open**.

5. Click the **Open** button to launch Power BI Desktop.

To access the Power Query Editor from Power BI Desktop, ensure that the **Home** tab is selected in the ribbon and then click the **Transform data** icon in the ribbon, as shown in *Figure 2.2*:

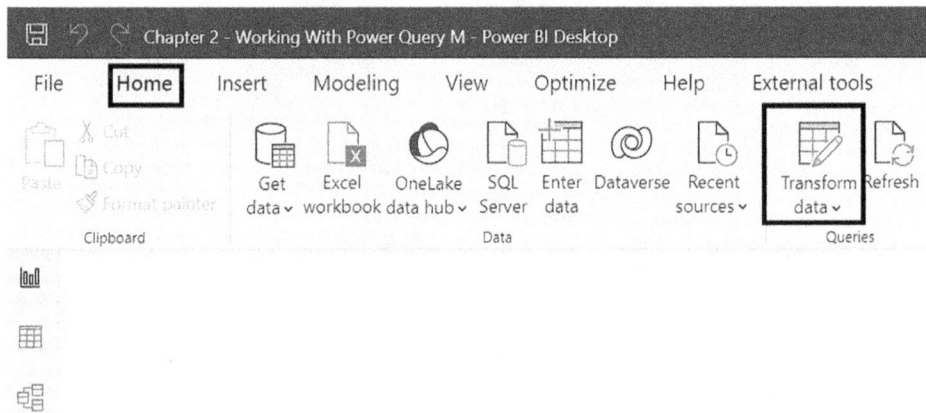

Figure 2.2: Transform data in Power BI Desktop

Now that you have Power BI Desktop installed and the Power Query editor launched, let's next take a brief tour of the Power Query Editor GUI and related settings.

A brief tour

The Power Query Editor interface has similar characteristics and shares common elements with Power BI Desktop. The Power Query Editor user interface comprises seven main areas. Refer to *Figure 2.3* while reading about these seven areas in the subsequent sections.

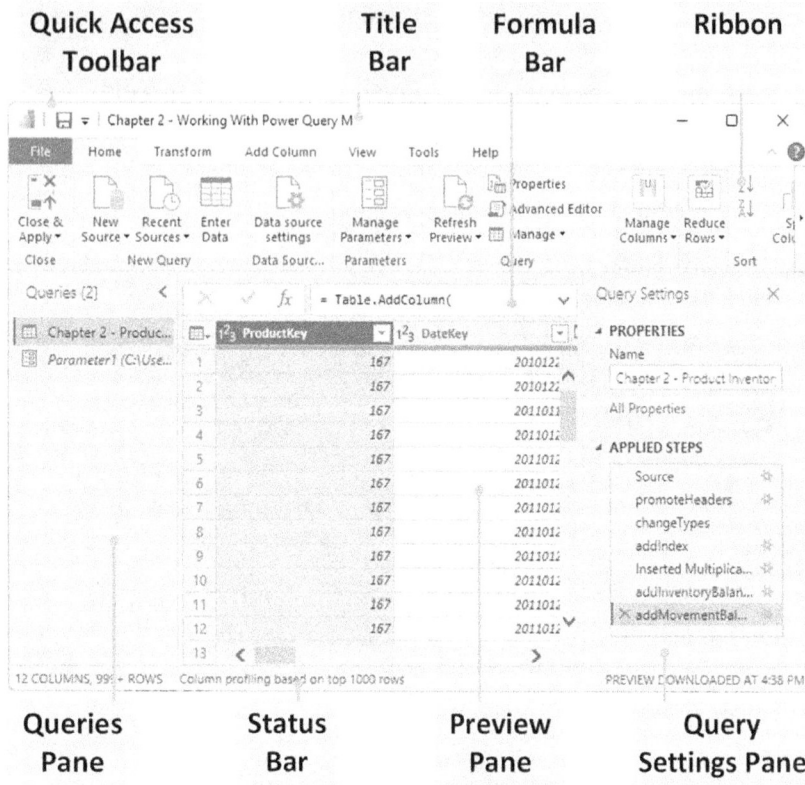

Figure 2.3: The Power Query Editor experience in Power BI Desktop

Let's briefly cover each of the main areas of the Power Query editor interface starting with the header area, which includes the Title Bar and Quick Access Toolbar.

Header

Nearly identical to Power BI Desktop, the header is the small strip at the top of the Power Query Editor window. This area is standard for Windows applications. Left-clicking the application icon in the left-hand corner provides the standard sizing and common exit commands, such as minimize, maximize, and close.

Next to this icon is the **Quick Access Toolbar**. This toolbar can be displayed above or below the ribbon, and commands within the ribbon can be added to this toolbar by right-clicking an icon in the ribbon and selecting **Add to Quick Access Toolbar**. By default, only the **Save** icon is displayed.

To the right of the **Quick Access Toolbar** is the name of the currently opened file. Finally, to the far right are the standard minimize, restore down/maximize, and close icons.

Formula bar

The Formula Bar allows you to view, enter, and modify the M code for a particular query step. As you may know from *Chapter 1*, *Introducing M*, M is a functional programming language comprised of functions, operators, and values that are used for connecting to and transforming data.

M is the language behind queries in Power BI Desktop. As you build a query in the Power Query Editor using the GUI, behind the scenes, this is really building an M script that executes to connect to, transform, and import your data. Each of the Applied Steps (see the **Query Settings** pane below) in a query is really a line of M language code. You do not need to worry about that just yet; we will explore this a little later in this chapter.

Ribbon

Below the Quick Access Toolbar and Title Bar in the header is the ribbon. If you are familiar with modern versions of Microsoft Office, you will recognize the function of this area, although the controls displayed are somewhat different. The ribbon consists of seven primary tabs plus one conditional tab:

1. **File:** The **File** tab displays a fly-out menu when clicked that allows Power BI Desktop files to be saved, as well as the Power Query Editor to be closed, and changes made within the Power Query Editor to be applied. In addition, the **File** menu provides access to **Options** and **Data Source Settings**.

2. **Home:** The **Home** tab provides a variety of the most common operations, such as connecting to sources, managing parameters, and common transformation functions such as removing rows and columns, splitting columns, and replacing values.

3. **Transform:** The **Transform** tab provides data manipulation functions that enable the transposing of rows and columns, the pivoting and unpivoting of columns, the merging of columns, adding R and Python scripts, and many scientific, statistics-related, trigonometry, date, and time calculations. It is important to understand that the functions on the **Transform** tab modify an existing column, in contrast with similar functions found on the **Add Column** tab, which instead add a new column with the specified data transformation.

4. **Add Column:** The **Add Column** tab provides operations that are focused on adding calculated, conditional, and index columns. In addition, many of the functions available on the **Transform** tab, such as scientific, statistics-related, trigonometry, date, and time calculations are also available on the **Add Column** tab; however, it is important to understand that the functions work much differently between the two ribbon tabs. On the **Transform** tab, these functions transform the currently selected column, while on the **Add Column** tab, these functions add an additional, calculated column to the data.

5. **View:** The **View** tab includes controls for controlling the layout of the Power Query interface, such as whether or not the **Query Settings** pane is displayed, and whether the **Formula Bar** is displayed.

6. **Tools:** The **Tools** tab provides access to diagnostic tools and options.

7. **Help:** The **Help** tab includes useful links for getting help with Power BI, including links to the Power BI Community site, documentation, guided learning, training videos, and much more.

8. **Tools | Transform:** The **Tools | Transform** tab is conditionally displayed when the query return type is not a table. This tab displays options for converting the value to a table, as well as contextual options depending on the data type returned. For example, an expression that returns text will have different options available than an expression that returns a number. In addition, the actual name of the tab changes based on the data type returned.

9. The **Tools | Transform** tab for a query returning a number is displayed in *Figure 2.4*:

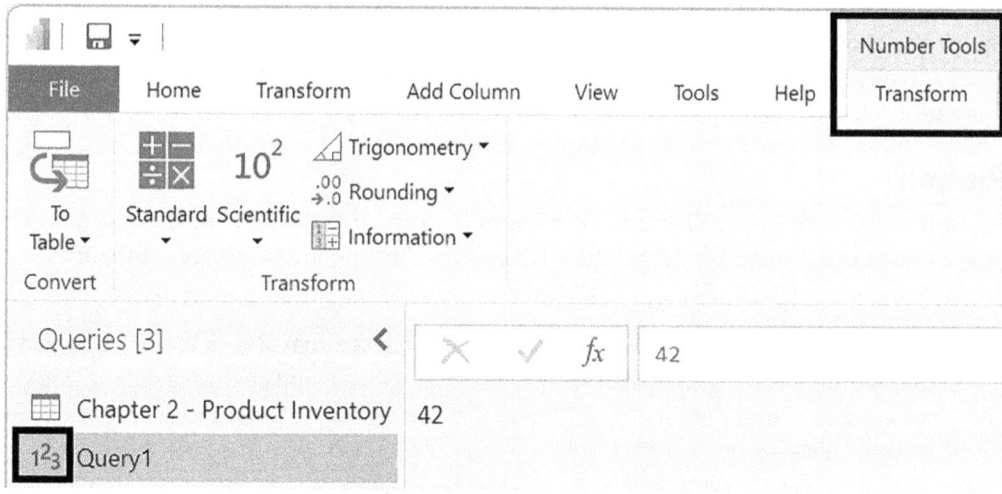

Figure 2.4: Contextual Tools, Transform tab

Now that we have reviewed the ribbon, let's move on to the **Queries** pane.

Queries pane

The **Queries** pane displays a list of the various queries associated with the current Power BI file. As queries are created, they are displayed here. In addition, if errors pop up during query execution, this area displays row sets of the errors generated by the query.

Right-clicking a query provides various options, such as deleting, copying, duplicating, referencing, and grouping the query. Some of these options require some additional explanation:

- **Copy**: This is the same as selecting the query and pressing *Ctrl* + *C* and then *Ctrl* + *V*. Copying a query creates a copy of the query as well as all referenced/associated queries and parameters. For example, if a query uses a parameter to define the data source, such as the name of a SQL server, database, or file path, and/or is a query that merges or appends multiple other queries, then copies of all of these associated queries and parameters are also created.
- **Duplicate**: Creating a duplicate of a query creates a copy of just the query itself. Essentially, all the M code for the query is copied and pasted into a new query. Associated queries and parameters are not duplicated, as with the **Copy** option.
- **Reference**: Choosing to create a reference creates a new query where the data source is the original query. References are often used on base queries that perform common data transformation operations required by multiple queries/tables.
- **Enable load**: Queries can be either enabled or disabled for loading within the ultimate client destination like Microsoft Excel or Power BI Desktop. Disabling loading maintains the query within the Power Query experience but that query no longer creates a table within the client application. Many times, referenced queries are disabled from loading because such queries perform intermediate data transformation steps.

Let's explore a practical application regarding how one might use these features. Imagine collecting activities from a **customer relationship management (CRM)** system, such as Dynamics 365. You might create a parameter that defines the source data system endpoint. This parameter would then be used in an Emails query that connects to the underlying Email table/entity to import data. You then select the User and Created On column and add a step to remove all other columns. Additionally, you add a custom Type column that simply returns Email for each row.

Now, if you wish to import appointments as well, a good choice here would be to duplicate your Email query and rename the duplicate query Appointments. You would not want to copy the query as this would create a duplicate of your parameter as well. You then simply edit the query to return Appointments for the type while all other data transformations remain the same.

Finally, you wish to end up with a final, single table called Emails and Appointments. This query simply appends the Emails and Appointments queries. These base queries are referenced by this new append query. You would then right-click the Emails and Appointments queries and disable loading as your final table contains all rows from both base queries.

Query Settings pane

The **Query Settings** pane provides access to properties for the query, such as the name of the query. By default, the name of the query becomes the name of the table within the semantic model.

More importantly, the **Query Settings** pane includes a list of **Applied Steps** for a query. A query is really just a series of applied steps, or transformations, of the data. As you transform the data imported by a query, a step is created for each transformation. Thus, executing a query to refresh data from a data source is just a matter of re-executing these steps or transformation operations.

Preview pane

The **Preview** pane provides a preview of the data being loaded and transformed. This area is contextual, displaying the data table for the currently selected step of a query. The column headers within the **Preview** pane area can be used to rename columns as well as access a wide variety of transformation and cleaning operations.

Status Bar

The **Status Bar** area is contextual based on what query is selected within the Power Query Editor. Helpful information, such as the number of rows and columns in a table and when the last preview of the data was loaded, is displayed here.

Now that we have completed a brief tour of the Power Query Editor, let's start writing some M code by creating our first query.

Your first query

To create your first query, you will need the *Chapter 2, Working with Power Query/M* file available with the supplemental content for this book. This file contains an export from the well-known and widely used sample database AdventureWorks DW and can be downloaded from the Packt GitHub repository for this book. See the *Technical Requirements* section at the beginning of this chapter.

To create the query, perform the following steps:

1. In the Power Query Editor, choose the **Home** tab and then click the **New Source** icon to display the **Get Data** window, as shown in *Figure 2.5*:

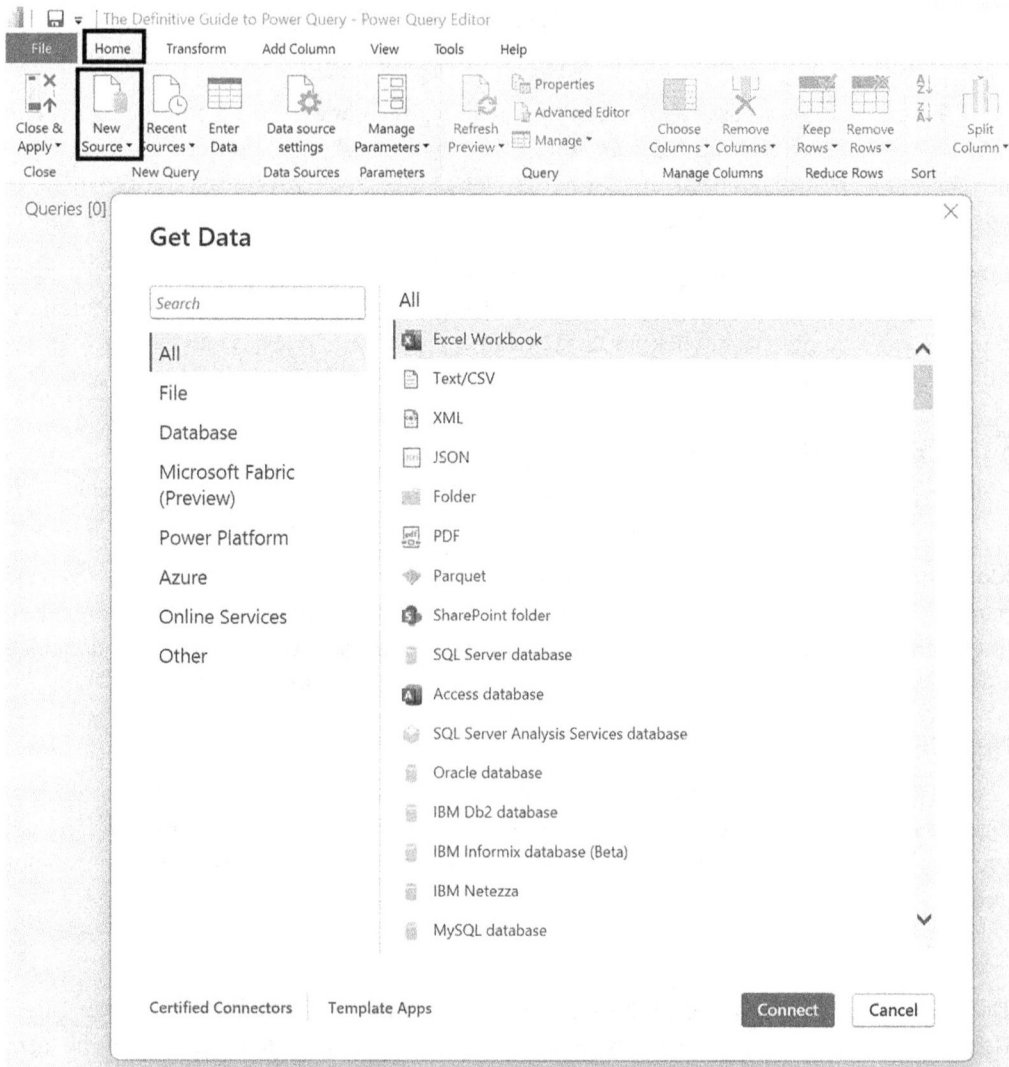

Figure 2.5: Get Data in Power Query Editor

2. Choose **Text/CSV** from the list of **All** data sources and then click the **Connect** button.

3. Navigate to the location of the *Chapter 2, Working with Power Query/M* file, select the file, and then click the **Open** button in order to display a preview of the data, as shown in *Figure 2.6*:

ProductKey	DateKey	MovementDate	UnitCost	UnitsIn	UnitsOut	UnitsBalance	EnglishProductName
167	20101228	12/28/2010	0.19	0	0	875	Metal Sheet 1
167	20101229	12/29/2010	0.19	0	0	875	Metal Sheet 1
167	20110119	1/19/2011	0.19	0	0	875	Metal Sheet 1
167	20110121	1/21/2011	0.19	0	0	875	Metal Sheet 1
167	20110122	1/22/2011	0.19	0	0	875	Metal Sheet 1
167	20110123	1/23/2011	0.19	0	0	875	Metal Sheet 1
167	20110124	1/24/2011	0.19	0	0	875	Metal Sheet 1
167	20110125	1/25/2011	0.19	0	0	875	Metal Sheet 1
167	20110126	1/26/2011	0.19	0	0	875	Metal Sheet 1
167	20110127	1/27/2011	0.19	0	0	875	Metal Sheet 1
167	20110128	1/28/2011	0.19	0	0	875	Metal Sheet 1
167	20110129	1/29/2011	0.19	0	0	875	Metal Sheet 1
167	20110130	1/30/2011	0.19	0	0	875	Metal Sheet 1
167	20110131	1/31/2011	0.19	0	0	875	Metal Sheet 1
167	20110201	2/1/2011	0.19	0	0	875	Metal Sheet 1
167	20110202	2/2/2011	0.19	0	0	875	Metal Sheet 1
167	20110203	2/3/2011	0.19	0	0	875	Metal Sheet 1
167	20110204	2/4/2011	0.19	0	0	875	Metal Sheet 1
167	20110205	2/5/2011	0.19	0	0	875	Metal Sheet 1
167	20110206	2/6/2011	0.19	0	0	875	Metal Sheet 1

Figure 2.6: Preview of data

> Depending on the data source selected, this interface changes and provides different options. For text/CSV files, one can choose the file origin (character set), the delimiter between columns, as well as whether or not to detect data types and whether that data type detection occurs on the entire semantic model or a subset of the semantic model. As noted via the information icon indicated by (i), the preview is generally truncated to only a subset of the rows within the semantic model.

4. Click the **OK** button to load a larger preview (up to 1,000 rows) into the Power Query Editor.

Now, the Power Query Editor window should look similar to *Figure 2.7*:

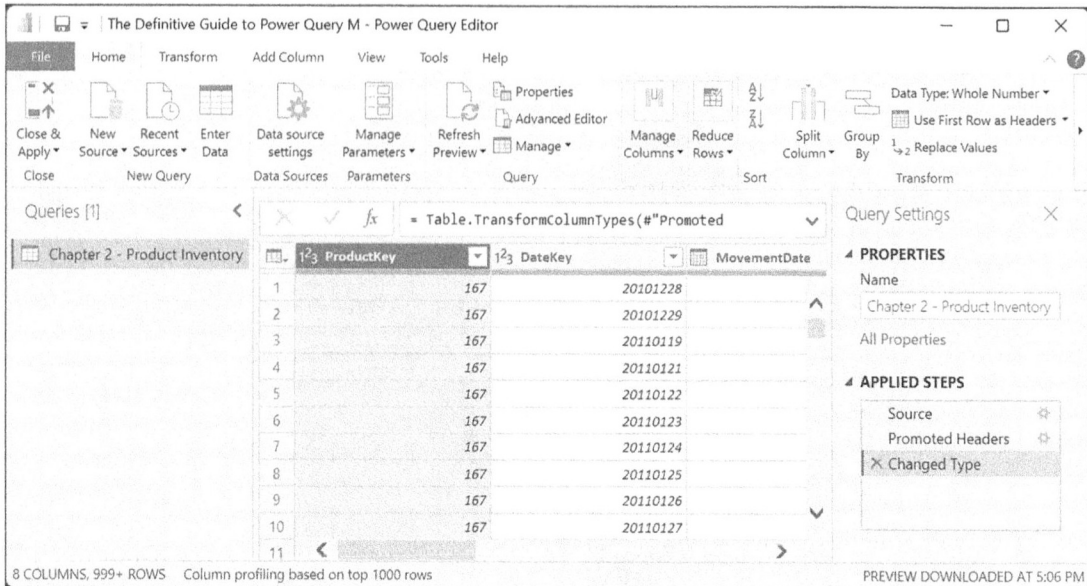

Figure 2.7: Power Query Editor with a preview of data

Note that the **Queries** pane displays the name of the query, which, in this case, is based on the name of the source file. The **Preview** pane displays the columns and data imported from the file. The **Query Settings** pane also displays the name of the query as well as three **Applied Steps**:

- **Source:** This is the step in the query that accesses the CSV file
- **Promoted Headers:** This step promoted the first row of values as the column names
- **Changed Type:** This step changed the data types for the columns using auto-detection based on the first 200 rows of data

The status bar indicates that there is a total of 8 columns and more than 999 rows of data and that column profiling (discussed later in this chapter) is based on the first 1,000 rows of data. Also, over on the right side of the status bar is information about when the preview was loaded.

Finally, the formula bar lists the actual M code behind the last query step, **Changed Type**. One can see that the M function used to change the data types of columns is the Table.TransformColumnTypes function. The data types chosen for each column are reflected in the column headers within the **Preview** pane, with whole numbers (Int64.Type) having a 123 icon, dates (type date) having a calendar icon, and currency (Currency.Type) having a $ icon.

And there you have it! You have written your first query as well as your first M code. Now that we have a query to work with in the Power Query Editor, let's next take a look at the various options available when working with queries as well as data source settings.

Options and data source settings

There are a number of options that can control the look and behavior of the Power Query Editor as well as how data is loaded into the system. In addition, creating a query that connects to a new data source also creates a data source on the local computer. This data source can be managed via the Power Query Editor.

Let's first take a look at **Options**.

Options

To access options that control the look and behavior of the Power Query Editor, click on **File** in the ribbon, then on **Options and settings**, and finally on **Options**, as shown in *Figure 2.8*:

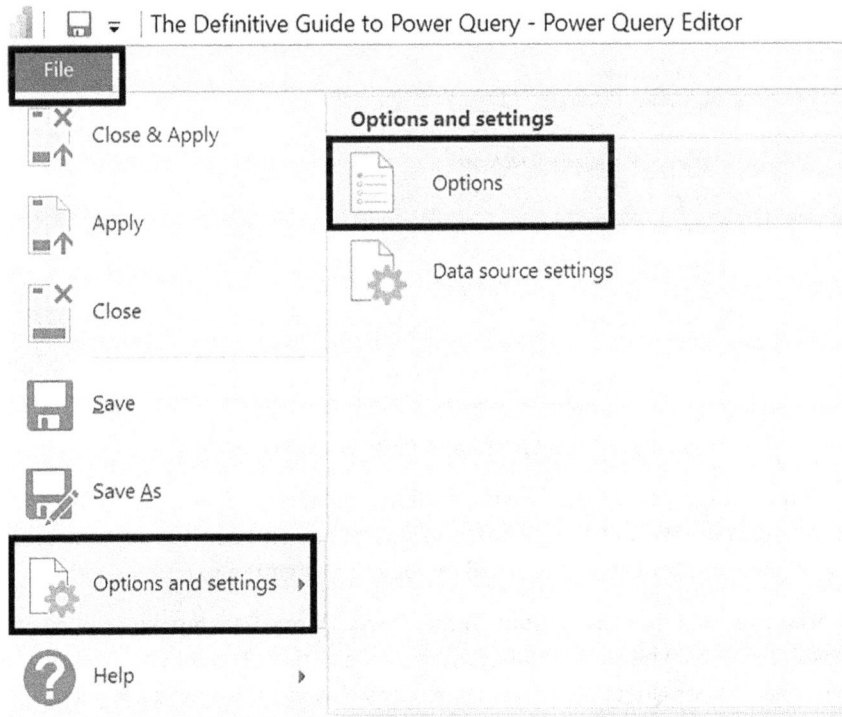

Figure 2.8: Accessing Options within the Power Query Editor

Performing this sequence of actions displays the **Options** window, as shown in *Figure 2.9*:

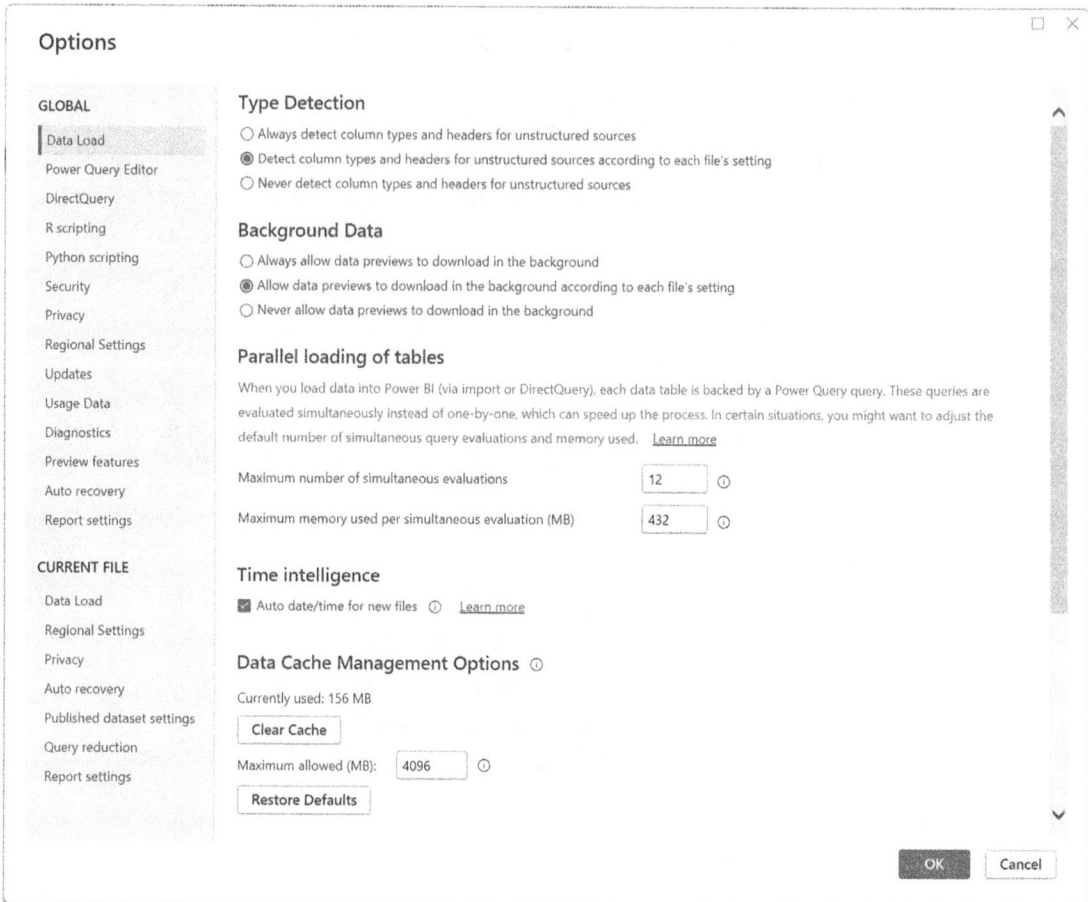

Figure 2.9: Options in Power BI Desktop/Power Query Editor

The **Options** window in *Figure 2.9* lists all of the options available for Power BI Desktop. Only a subset of these options impact the Power Query Editor and data transformation queries, specifically the **Data Load** and **Power Query Editor** categories listed on the left navigation pane.

It is also important to note that the options in the Power Query Desktop experience in other tools such as Microsoft Excel may be slightly different than the options listed here. However, overall, the options within other Power Query Desktop experiences closely mirror and are generally subsets of the options listed here. In addition, Power Query Online experiences do not generally offer the sorts of options covered in this section since Power Query Online experiences are provided as a service.

Figure 2.9 displays the **GLOBAL Data Load** options. The global options affect all files, although certain settings can be overridden at the report level (**CURRENT FILE**). These **GLOBAL** options include the following:

- **Type Detection:** This controls whether data types are automatically detected for unstructured data sources (such as text or Excel files). For structured data sources, the data types are inherited from the source. The default is to detect data types for columns (**Changed Type** step from *Figure 2.7*) as well as auto-detect headers (**Promoted Headers** step from *Figure 2.7*) in unstructured data sources according to the settings for each file. Recall from *Figure 2.6* how the **Data Type Detection** setting allowed us to control if and how data type detection occurred for your unstructured CSV file data source. Many data professionals recommend changing this setting to never auto-detect data types. However, there is certainly a convenience factor for the casual business user as Power Query's auto-type detection is quite good.

- **Background Data:** This setting controls whether data previews in the Power Query Editor and is downloaded in the background. Downloading previews in the background allows you to continue working within the Power Query Editor without being forced to wait for data previews to fully load. Typically, it is a good idea to leave this setting to the default of allowing background loading of data previews according to each file's settings.

- **Parallel loading of tables:** For files containing multiple queries, Power BI loads the queries in parallel to optimize performance. However, in certain situations, you may wish to adjust these parameters, including the **Maximum number of simultaneous evaluations,** and **Maximum memory used per simultaneous evaluation (MB).** For more information on these settings, refer to Microsoft's documentation: `https://learn.microsoft.com/en-us/power-bi/create-reports/desktop-evaluation-configuration` *Evaluation configuration settings for Desktop - Power BI | Microsoft Learn.*

- **Time intelligence:** By default, Power BI Desktop automatically creates a hidden date table for every date or date/time column. While this can be convenient for the casual user, most data professionals highly recommend turning this feature off. Having this feature activated can often lead to bloated semantic models that are much larger than necessary.

- **Data Cache Management:** The Power Query Editor caches preview results for queries in order to optimize performance for faster viewing. These settings show how much disk space is currently consumed by this cache, as well as allowing you to set the maximum amount of disk space used, and finally clear the cache if necessary.

As mentioned, the **GLOBAL** settings can be overridden on a per-file basis, using the **CURRENT FILE** settings for **Data Load** options. The **Data Load** options for **CURRENT FILE** are shown in *Figure 2.10*:

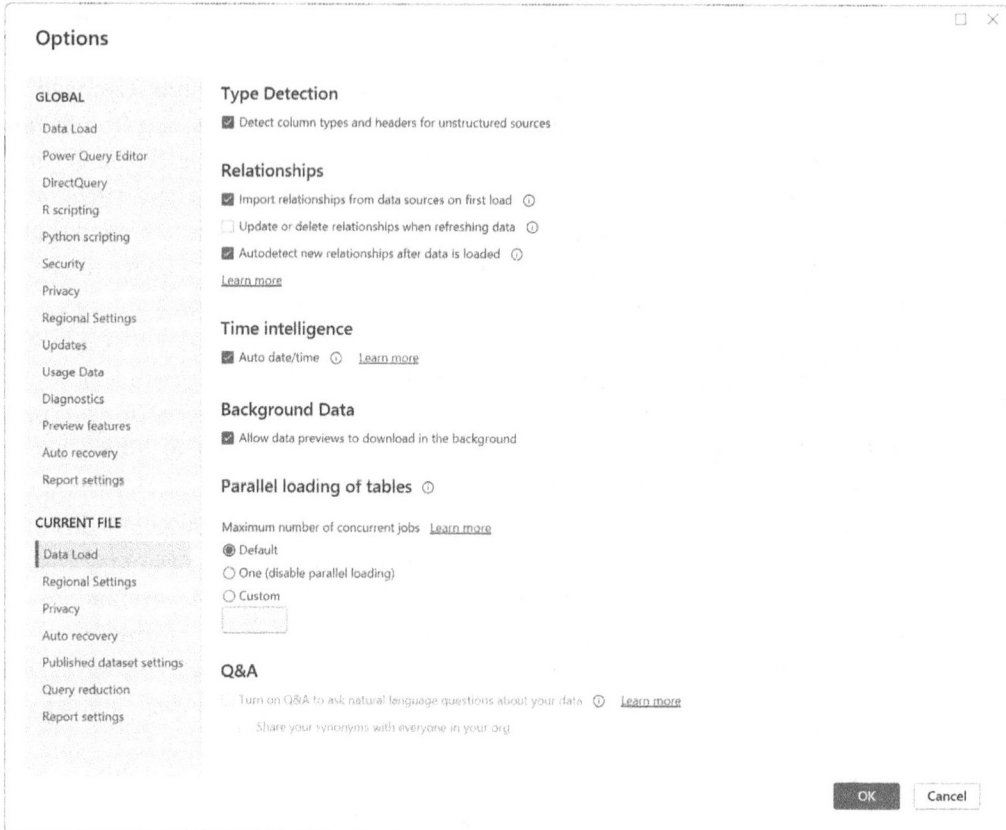

Figure 2.10: Data Load options for CURRENT FILE

The **Data Load** options for **CURRENT FILE** include the ability to override the **GLOBAL** settings for **Type Detection**, **Time intelligence**, **Background Data**, and **Parallel loading of tables**. In addition, there are two additional settings:

- **Relationships**: Controls the import and auto-detection of relationships between tables loaded via queries. The defaults for these settings are shown in *Figure 2.10*. Many data professionals recommend disabling the auto-detection of relationships. For more information about these settings, refer to *Create and manage relationships in Power BI Desktop - Power BI | Microsoft Learn* (https://learn.microsoft.com/en-us/power-bi/transform-model/desktop-create-and-manage-relationships#automatic-relationship-updates).

- **Q&A:** Enables or disables the natural language Q&A feature of Power BI. This setting is disabled in *Figure 2.10* because no queries have actually been loaded into the **semantic** model. For more information about these settings, refer to *Data sources for natural language Q&A* (`https://learn.microsoft.com/en-us/power-bi/natural-language/q-and-a-data-sources`).

In addition to the **Data Load** options for **GLOBAL** and **CURRENT FILE**, there are also options for controlling the look and behavior of the **Power Query Editor.** These options are shown in *Figure 2.11*:

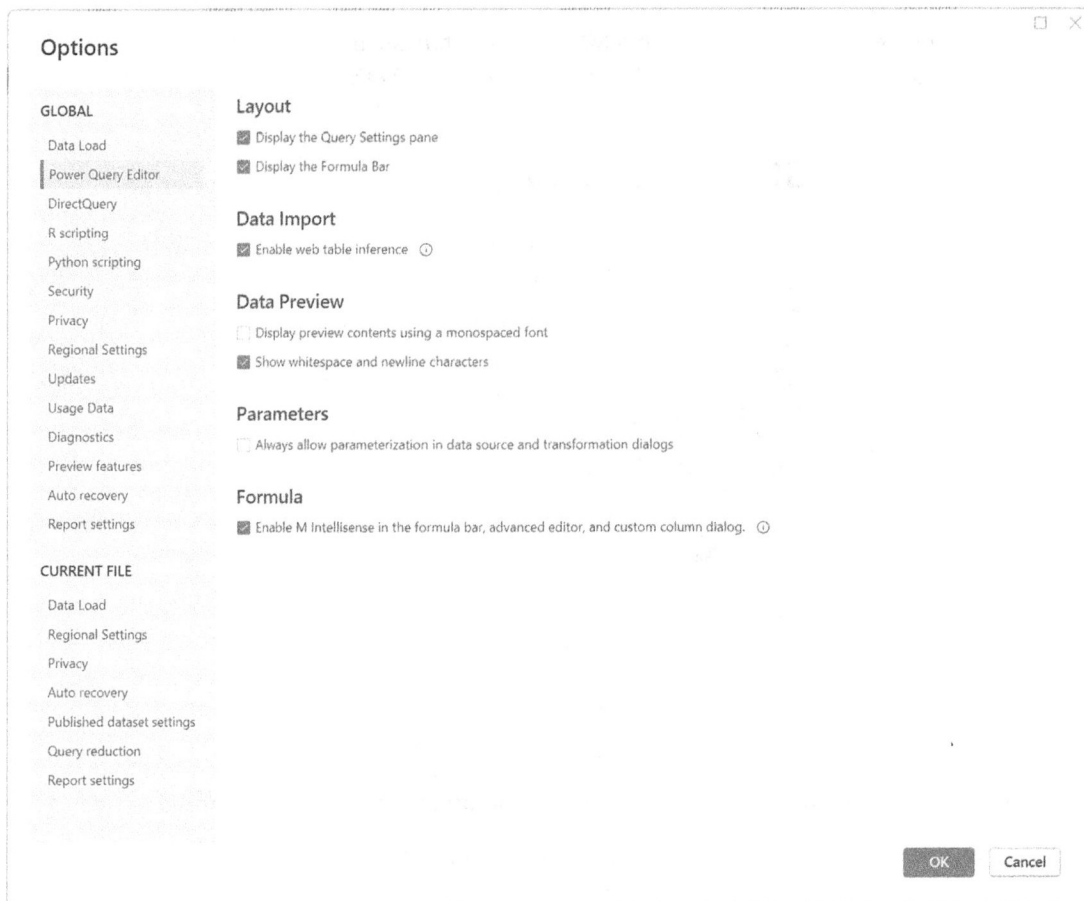

Figure 2.11: Power Query Editor Options in Power BI Desktop

The options listed in *Figure 2.11* include the following:

- **Layout:** Control whether or not the **Query Settings** pane and formula bar are displayed in the Power Query Editor.
- **Data Import:** Enabling this option leverages the Web.BrowserContents function when retrieving data from web pages. This function can detect repeating patterns within content that surpasses the simple detection of HTML tables.
- **Data Preview:** Controls the look and feel of preview content.

- **Parameters:** This setting can be quite useful in environments where reports move through development, test, and production phases. Without this setting enabled, developers are left with two choices. One, either edit the data source settings (see the *Data source settings* section in this chapter), or manually create query parameters (see *Chapter 9, Parameters and Custom Functions*) for things like server and database names, and then manually edit queries to use these parameters. With this setting enabled, parameter creation becomes built into the data source and transformation dialogs.

  For example, when connecting to a SQL Server database, having this feature activated provides a new dialog option to define a new parameter for both **Server** and **Database**, as shown in *Figure 2.12*:

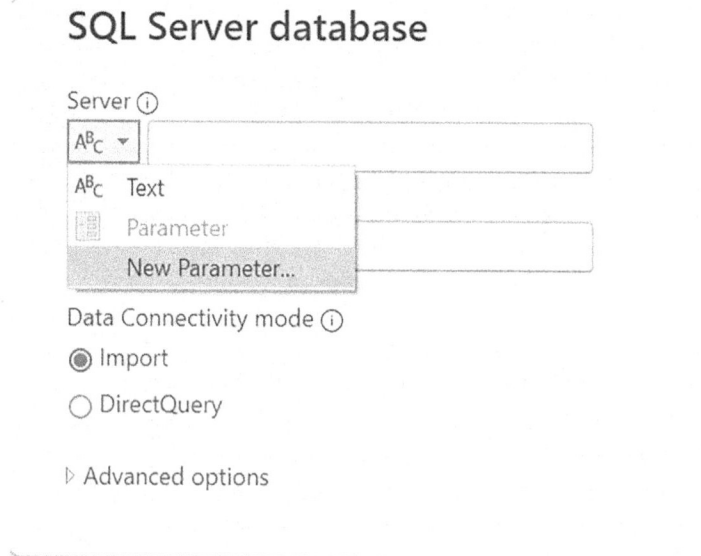

SQL Server database

Server ⓘ

| AᴮC ▾ | |

AᴮC   Text
▦   Parameter
New Parameter...

Data Connectivity mode ⓘ

◉ Import

◯ DirectQuery

▷ Advanced options

Figure 2.12: New Parameter… dialog option

- **Formula:** Enables or disables M IntelliSense (Microsoft's proprietary type-ahead technology).

Now that we have explored the options for controlling the look and behavior of the Power Query Editor, let's briefly discuss the **Data source settings** next.

Data source settings

Just as most tables within a data model are backed by M language queries, so too are most queries backed by a data source. These data source definitions are stored as part of the desktop file (either Power BI Desktop or Excel).

In addition, the credentials used to authenticate to these data sources are cached locally on the computer where the Power Query Desktop experience is running. Crucially, these data source credentials are not stored within the desktop file itself. This means that if opening the desktop file on another computer, the credentials used to authenticate to the data source must be re-entered.

Once one or more data sources are created, generally through the creation of a query, the settings for these data sources can be viewed and edited by clicking on **File** in the ribbon, then on **Options and settings**, and finally on **Data source settings**, as shown in *Figure 2.8*. Performing this sequence of actions displays the **Data source settings** window shown in *Figure 2.13*:

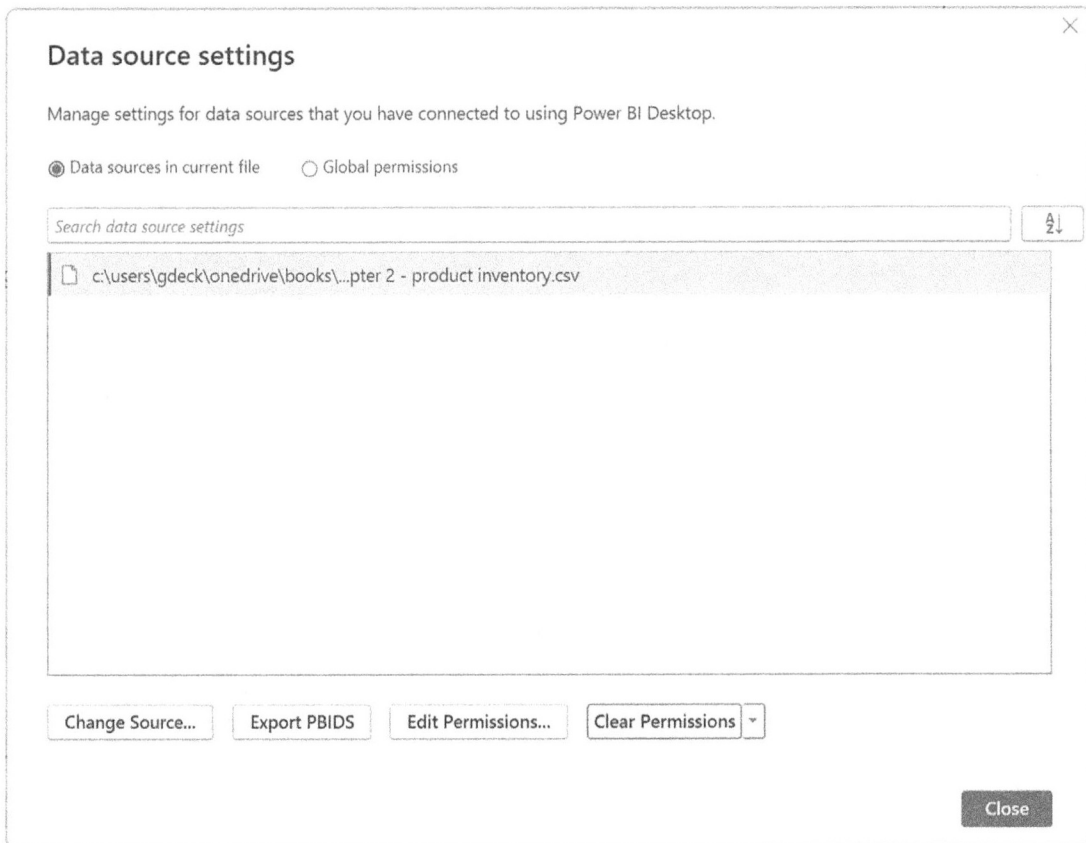

Figure 2.13: Data source settings window

The radio button **Data sources in current file** only displays the data sources contained in the current desktop file, while the **Global permissions** option displays data sources used across all your desktop files. The **Data sources in current file** option displays buttons for **Change Source...**, **Export PBIDS**, **Edit Permissions...**, and **Clear Permissions** while the **Global permissions** option only displays the latter three buttons.

Clicking the **Change Source...** button shown in *Figure 2.13* for the query created in this chapter allows you to view and change the configuration options for the data source as shown in *Figure 2.14*:

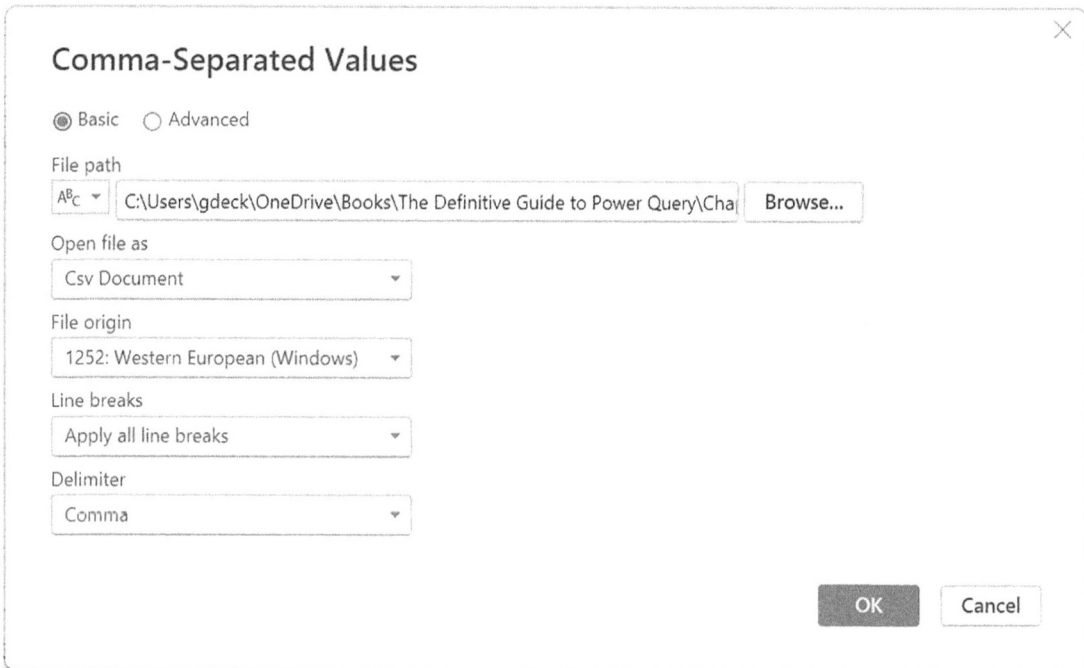

Figure 2.14: Comma-Separated Values data source settings window

The **Export PBIDS** button saves the data source as a JSON document. Note, if you are using the chapter PBIX file downloaded from GitHub, you will need to edit the Parameter1 parameter to point to a valid location for your system. For example, the data source created in this chapter in the *Your first query* section looks similar to the following when exported:

```
{
  "version": "0.1",
  "connections": [
    {
      "details": {
        "protocol": "file",
        "address": {
          "path": "c:\\temp\\Product inventory.csv"
        },
        "authentication": null,
        "query": null
      },
      "options": {},
      "mode": null
    }
```

```
    ]
 }
```

Depending on the type of data source, the **Edit Permissions...** button allows you to view and edit things such as the authentication credentials, privacy level, encryption, and any approved native database queries for data sources such as SQL Server.

This concludes our overview of the Power Query Desktop experience. Let's now move on to how to edit the M code generated by using the Power Query Editor.

Editing experience-generated code

As pointed out in this chapter's *Your first query* section, using the Power Query Desktop experience's **graphical user interface (GUI)** to connect to and transform data generates M language code. This code generated can be tweaked or edited using the formula bar.

For example, in the **Applied Steps** area of the **Query Settings** pane, by clicking on the **Source** step for the query and then clicking the down arrow to the far right in the formula bar, you can see the full M language code for the **Source** step, such as the following:

```
= Csv.Document(File.Contents("C:\Users\gdeck\OneDrive\Books\The
Definitive Guide to Power Query\Chapter 2\Chapter 2 - Product Inventory.
csv"),[Delimiter=",", Columns=8, Encoding=1252, QuoteStyle=QuoteStyle.None])
```

As you can see in this code, there are two nested functions being used to connect to the CSV file, Csv. Document and File.Contents.

- The File.Contents function has a single parameter passed to the function, the file path, and the name of the CSV file.
- The Csv.Document has two parameters passed to it, the first being the results of the File. Content function and the second being a record comprised of three key/value pairs. Records are discussed further in *Chapter 4, Understanding Values and Expressions*.

You can edit the M language code within the formula bar to make any necessary changes to the code. For example, a common change for CSV files is to completely remove the second key/value pair from the record, such as the following:

```
= Csv.Document(File.Contents("C:\Users\gdeck\OneDrive\Books\The
Definitive Guide to Power Query\Chapter 2\Chapter 2 - Product Inventory.
csv"),[Delimiter=",",Encoding=1252, QuoteStyle=QuoteStyle.None])
```

To effect this change, simply click inside of the formula bar, make the necessary changes and then click out of the formula bar or press the *Enter* key.

This edit is often done to help future-proof queries that access CSV files. For example, if a ninth column is added to the data source, the original version of the M code would ignore that additional column since only eight columns are specified. This is a common scenario with Excel spreadsheets where each month is added as a new column, for example.

Conversely, with the `Columns=8` key/value pair removed from the record that comprises the second parameter in the `Csv.Document` function, the additional column would automatically be recognized and included in the data when the query refreshes.

Another change that can be made involves the Changed Type function. Clicking on the **Changed Type** step within the **Applied Steps** section of the **Query Settings** pane displays the following M language code in the formula bar:

```
= Table.TransformColumnTypes(#"Promoted Headers",{{"ProductKey", Int64.Type},
{"DateKey", Int64.Type}, {"MovementDate", type date}, {"UnitCost", Currency.
Type}, {"UnitsIn", Int64.Type}, {"UnitsOut", Int64.Type}, {"UnitsBalance",
Int64.Type}, {"EnglishProductName", type text}})
```

You will learn more about this function and the syntax here in later chapters of this book, but simply put, this code is transforming each column into a particular data type (think numeric, text, logical, etc.).

The `MovementDate` column has a data type of `date`. However, you may wish to include a timestamp as well. You can do this by editing the code in the formula bar to the following:

```
= Table.TransformColumnTypes(#"Promoted Headers",{{"ProductKey", Int64.
Type}, {"DateKey", Int64.Type}, {"MovementDate", type datetime}, {"UnitCost",
Currency.Type}, {"UnitsIn", Int64.Type}, {"UnitsOut", Int64.Type},
{"UnitsBalance", Int64.Type}, {"EnglishProductName", type text}})
```

Performing this action adds a timestamp of 12:00:00 AM to all dates within the `MovementDate` column.

As you can see, the formula bar is the first, most obvious place where you can write your own custom M code. Next, we will explore another option for entering custom M code, adding custom columns.

Creating custom columns

Creating custom columns is a common data transformation activity when working with Power Query and the M language. While the number of scenarios for adding custom columns is effectively endless, a common example might be combining a unit price column and a quantity column into a single `total sales` column. In this section, we will explore several ways to create custom columns both using the GUI of the Power Query Editor as well as writing custom M code.

Adding an index column

A common column added to M queries is an index column, which numbers the rows in sequential order. Index columns are extremely beneficial in certain scenarios, such as **Mean Time Between Failure (MTBF)**, where it is necessary to compare the differences between two rows of data.

To add an index column to the existing query created in the *Your First Query* section of this chapter, do the following:

1. Click on the **Add Column** tab of the ribbon, then click the drop-down arrow to the right of the **Index Column** option, and finally choose an option, as shown in *Figure 2.15*:

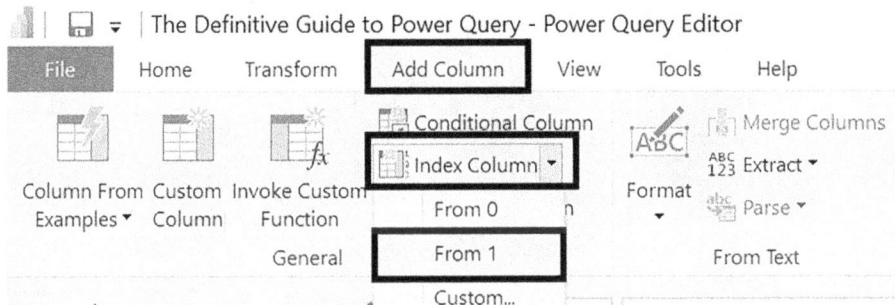

Figure 2.15: Adding an index column starting at 1

2. Performing this action adds an **Added Index** step in the **Applied Steps** area of the **Power Query Settings** pane. The formula bar displays the following M code with the **Added Index** step selected:

```
= Table.AddIndexColumn(#"Changed Type", "Index", 1, 1, Int64.Type)
```

In this case, the Table.AddIndexColumn function is being used to add a column called Index (second parameter) to the table returned by the #"Changed Type" step (first parameter). This Index column starts at 1 (third parameter), increments by 1 (fourth parameter), and has the whole number data type (Int64.Type).

Let's now take a look at adding columns using examples.

Adding columns with examples

Adding columns via examples applies advanced **machine learning** (ML) pattern matching to figure out the meaning behind example data entered into new rows by the user and automatically write the corresponding M code to effect the appropriate data transformation. A classic example is having a first name column and a last name column. Using add columns by example, one can enter the first and last name into a new column separated by a space and Power Query will automatically create the M code to concatenate the values in the two original columns.

We can test adding columns by example by following these steps:

1. Click on the **Add Column** tab of the ribbon, then click the **Column From Examples** function in the **General** area of the ribbon. This changes the **Preview** pane to look like *Figure 2.16*:

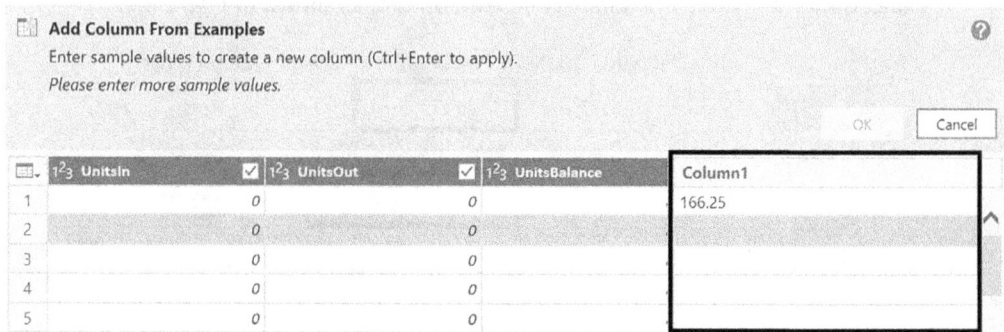

Figure 2.16: Add Column From Examples

2. As shown in *Figure 2.16*, type 166.25 in the first couple of rows. Power Query automatically determines that this number is the multiplication of the **UnitsCost** and **UnitsBalance** columns.
3. Click the **OK** button.

A new column is created called **Multiplication** with the following formula:

```
= Table.AddColumn(addIndex, "Multiplication", each [UnitCost] * [UnitsBalance],
type number)
```

Go ahead and remove this **Multiplication** column by either right-clicking the column header and choosing **Remove**, or simply clicking the X icon to the left of the **Inserted Multiplication** step that was added to the **Applied Steps** area of the **Query Settings** pane.

Let's now move on to creating/modifying columns using math operations.

Math operations

The data for the query created in the *Your first query* section in this chapter includes a UnitCost column and a UnitsBalance column. Instead of keeping both of these columns in the data, you may wish to consolidate these columns into a single column that contains the two columns multiplied together. In some scenarios, this can lead to smaller semantic model sizes. This can be done by following these steps:

1. On the **Preview** pane, click the column header for the **UnitCost** column.
2. While holding down the *Ctrl* key on the keyboard, next select the column header for the **Units-Balance** column.

3. Click on the **Add Column** tab of the ribbon, then click the **Standard** option within the **From Number** section of the ribbon, and finally, choose **Multiply**, as shown in *Figure 2.17*:

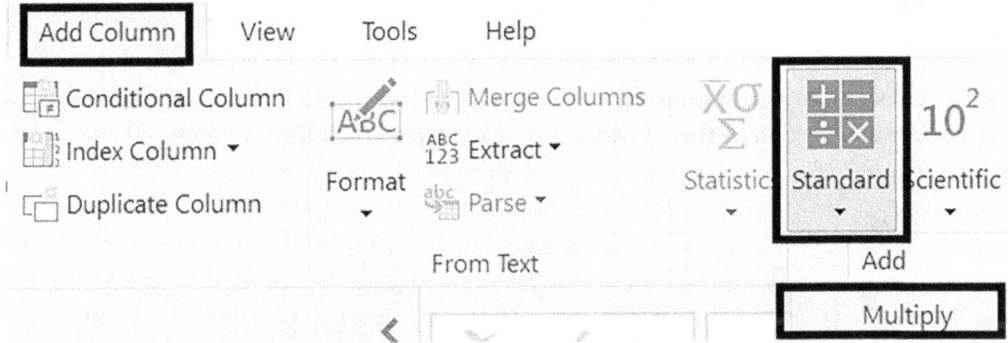

Figure 2.17: Multiplying two columns

Performing these actions adds an **Inserted Multiplication** step in the **Applied Steps** area of the **Power Query Settings** pane. The formula bar displays the following M code with the **Inserted Multiplication** step selected:

```
= Table.AddColumn(#"Added Index", "Multiplication", each [UnitCost] *
[UnitsBalance], Currency.Type)
```

Here, the `Table.AddColumn` function is used to add a column called **Multiplication** (second parameter) to the table returned by the #"Added Index" step (first parameter), where for each row, the **UnitCost** column is multiplied by the **UnitsBalance** column (third parameter) and the data type for the column is `Currency.Type` (fourth parameter).

Do not worry if some of the syntax, such as the use of the each keyword, does not completely make sense right now. This syntax has been well explained in the next chapters.

We have now explored two methods via which custom columns can be created using the GUI of the Power Query Editor. However, neither scenario required us to write any M code. In both cases, the M code was generated automatically for us. Therefore, let's now take a look at adding a custom column where we actually write at least a little M code ourselves.

Adding custom m code columns

In this next example, we will enter some simple M code ourselves. Here, again, we will still be leveraging the Power Query Editor to write most of the M code. To create a custom M code column, perform the following steps:

1. Click on the **Add Column** tab of the ribbon and then click the **Custom Column** option in the **General** section of the ribbon in order to display the **Custom Column** dialog, as shown in *Figure 2.18*:

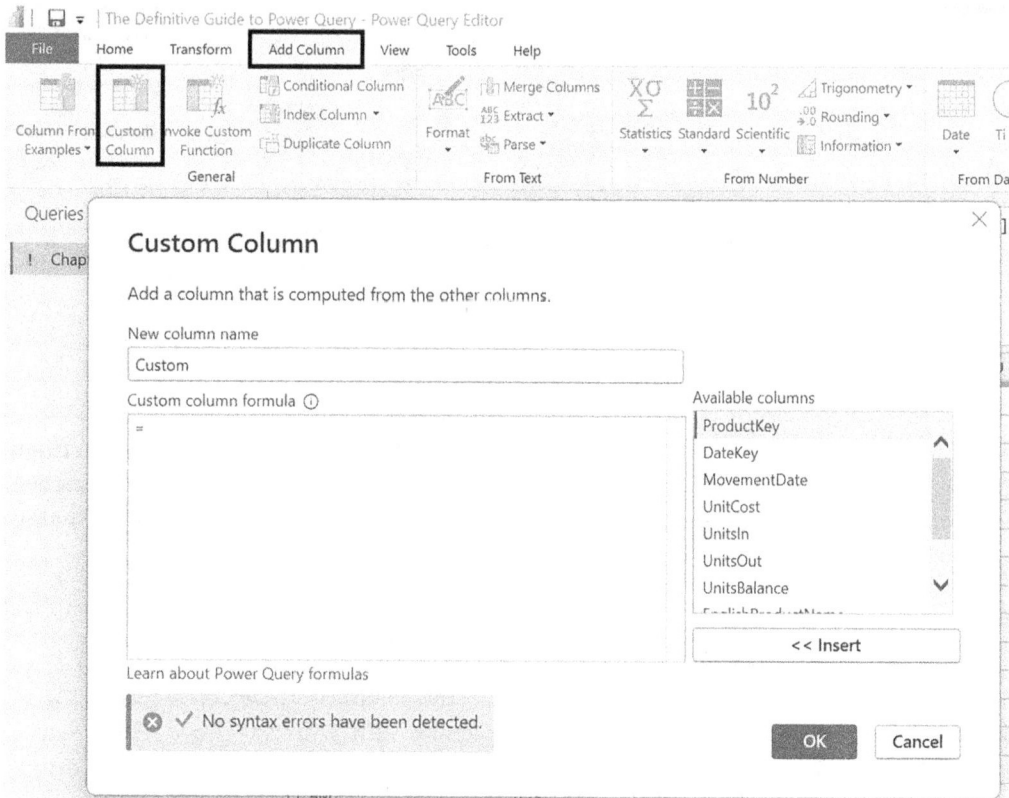

Figure 2.18: Custom Column dialog

2. Replace the word **Custom** under **New column name** with the text **MovementBalance**.

3. In the **Custom column formula** prompt, enter the following code:

```
( [UnitsIn] - [UnitsOut] ) * [UnitCost]
```

4. Click the **OK** button.

Like our previous **Multiplication** column, this column also performs some simple mathematical operations on multiple columns. In this case, for each row of data, the **UnitsOut** column is subtracted from the **UnitsIn** column and the result is then multiplied by the **UnitCost** column. The resulting column is named **MovementBalance** and contains the positive or negative cost of the difference in units moved in and out on each row.

Performing these actions adds an **Added Custom** step in the **Applied Steps** area of the **Power Query Settings** pane. The formula bar displays the following M code with the **Added Custom** step selected:

```
= Table.AddColumn(#"Inserted Multiplication", "MovementBalance", each (
[UnitsIn] - [UnitsOut] ) * [UnitCost])
```

This formula is extremely similar to our previous **Multiplication** column. A notable difference is the lack of a fourth parameter specifying the data type for the new column. Looking closely at the column header for our new column, we can see the data type icon at the left displays **ABC123**, indicating that this column has no specific data type. To rectify this situation, use the formula bar to modify the cost to the following:

```
= Table.AddColumn(#"Inserted Multiplication", "MovementBalance", each (
[UnitsIn] - [UnitsOut] ) * [UnitCost], Currency.Type)
```

We have now specified that the data type for our **MovementBalance** column is of the type Currency. Type and the data type icon for our column now displays a $.

Thus far, we have been slowly introducing how to write custom M code while still relying heavily on the Power Query Editor to write most of the code for us. Let's next explore how you can fully access the M code for queries using the Advanced Editor and make modifications without relying on the Power Query Editor to perform the heavy lifting.

Using the Advanced Editor

While most novices will rely heavily on the GUI and Power Query Editor to write all or the majority of their M code, advanced users will eventually migrate to wanting direct access to the M code, similar to how the source code is created and edited in most other programming languages. Luckily, the Power Query Editor provides such an interface, the **Advanced Editor**. By utilizing the Advanced Editor, the full power of the M language can be brought to bear during data transformation versus only a small fraction of the language that can be accessed using the GUI.

To access the **Advanced Editor**, click on the **Home** tab of the ribbon and then select **Advanced Editor** from the **Query** section, as shown in *Figure 2.19*:

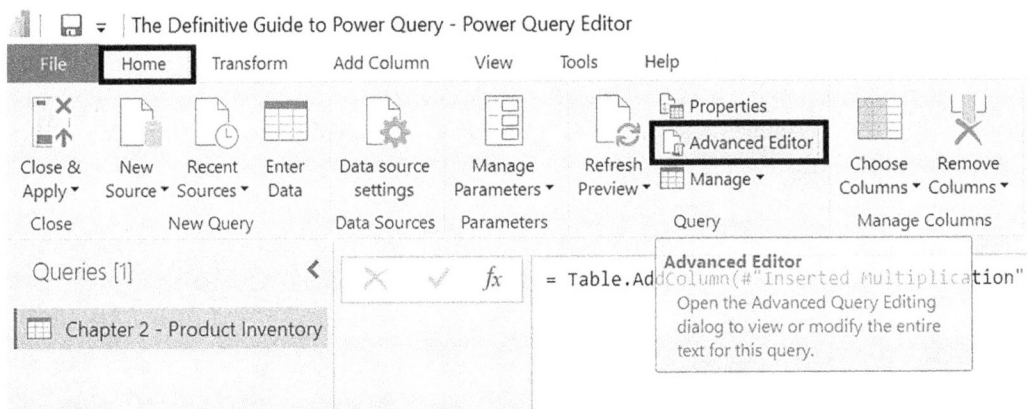

Figure 2.19: Accessing the Advanced Editor

This launches the **Advanced Editor** dialog, as shown in *Figure 2.20*:

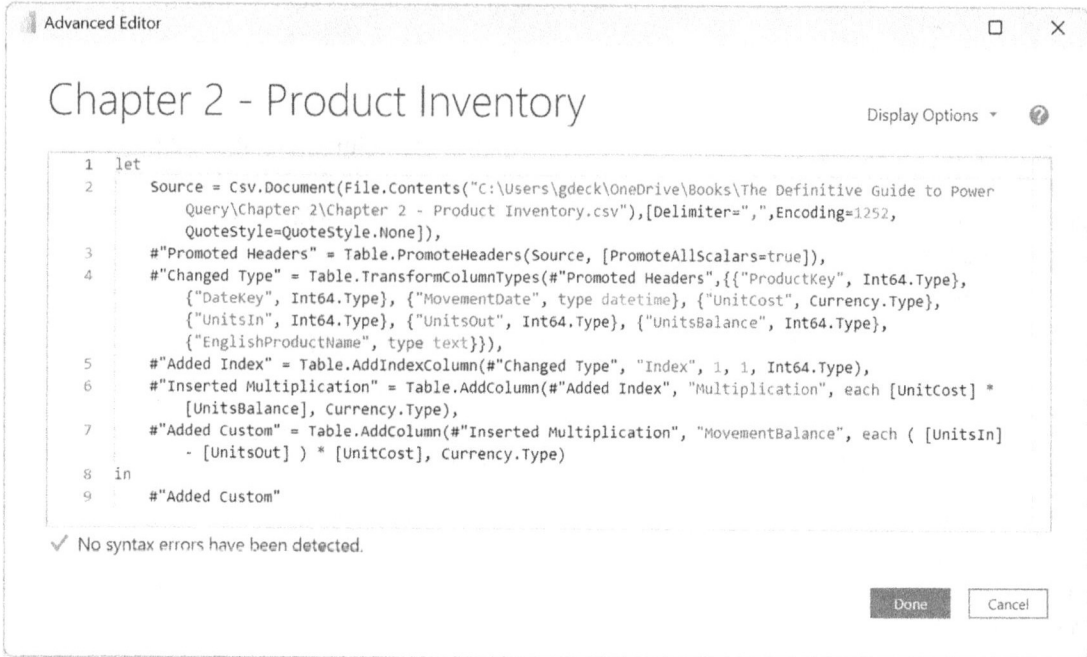

```
Advanced Editor                                                                         □   ✕

Chapter 2 - Product Inventory                              Display Options  ▾    ❓

1   let
2       Source = Csv.Document(File.Contents("C:\Users\gdeck\OneDrive\Books\The Definitive Guide to Power
            Query\Chapter 2\Chapter 2 - Product Inventory.csv"),[Delimiter=",",Encoding=1252,
            QuoteStyle=QuoteStyle.None]),
3       #"Promoted Headers" = Table.PromoteHeaders(Source, [PromoteAllScalars=true]),
4       #"Changed Type" = Table.TransformColumnTypes(#"Promoted Headers",{{"ProductKey", Int64.Type},
            {"DateKey", Int64.Type}, {"MovementDate", type datetime}, {"UnitCost", Currency.Type},
            {"UnitsIn", Int64.Type}, {"UnitsOut", Int64.Type}, {"UnitsBalance", Int64.Type},
            {"EnglishProductName", type text}}),
5       #"Added Index" = Table.AddIndexColumn(#"Changed Type", "Index", 1, 1, Int64.Type),
6       #"Inserted Multiplication" = Table.AddColumn(#"Added Index", "Multiplication", each [UnitCost] *
            [UnitsBalance], Currency.Type),
7       #"Added Custom" = Table.AddColumn(#"Inserted Multiplication", "MovementBalance", each ( [UnitsIn]
            - [UnitsOut] ) * [UnitCost], Currency.Type)
8   in
9       #"Added Custom"
```

✓ No syntax errors have been detected.

                                                                        Done   Cancel

Figure 2.20: The Advanced Editor

In *Figure 2.20*, the entire M code that comprises the *Chapter 2, Working with Power Query/M* query is displayed. All the steps of the query are contained within the let expression introduced in *Chapter 1, Introducing M*. In addition, the **Display Options** dropdown has been used to **Display line numbers** and **Enable word wrap**.

Clicking the question mark (?) icon opens a web browser to the Power Query M function reference web page. However, an excellent source that perhaps provides even more information is the powerquery. how website maintained by *Rick de Groot*. For example, powerquery.how contains an extensive list of M code enumerations (defined, fixed sets of possible values for a function argument), whereas such information is almost completely absent from Microsoft's official M language documentation.

In terms of useful websites external to Microsoft's official M language documentation, the website powerqueryformatter.com is a useful website for automatically formatting M code according to best practices. While the Advanced Editor includes type-ahead functionality and color formatting, it lacks any kind of automatic formatting features.

The following hot keys are available for zooming in and out:

- **Zoom in:** *Ctrl* + *Shift* + =
- **Zoom out:** *Ctrl* + *Shift* + -

Note that these hot keys for zooming also work within the Power Query Editor itself and not just the **Advanced Editor**.

Using the **Advanced Editor**, the entire contents of the query can be edited to allow proper indenting of the code for readability purposes, as well as cleaning up the step names, such as implementing camel case.

> As shown in *Figure 2.20*, step names with spaces in them must be prefixed by a hashtag character (#) and then the step name enclosed in double quotes.

For example, the entire contents of the **Advanced Editor** code can be replaced with the following code. Note that you will need to ensure that the file path corresponds to a file on your local system rather than the example file path provided:

```
let
    Source =
        Csv.Document(
            File.Contents("C:\temp\Product Inventory.csv"),
            [Delimiter=",",Encoding=1252, QuoteStyle=QuoteStyle.None]
        ),
    promoteHeaders = Table.PromoteHeaders(Source, [PromoteAllScalars=true]),
    changeTypes =
        Table.TransformColumnTypes(
            promoteHeaders,
            {
                {"ProductKey", Int64.Type},
                {"DateKey", Int64.Type},
                {"MovementDate", type datetime},
                {"UnitCost", Currency.Type},
```

```
                    {"UnitsIn", Int64.Type},
                    {"UnitsOut", Int64.Type},
                    {"UnitsBalance", Int64.Type},
                    {"EnglishProductName", type text}
                }
            ),
        addIndex = Table.AddIndexColumn(changeTypes, "Index", 1, 1, Int64.Type),
        addInventoryBalanceColumn =
            Table.AddColumn(
                addIndex,
                "InventoryBalance",
                each [UnitCost] * [UnitsBalance],
                Currency.Type
            ),
        addMovementBalanceColumn =
            Table.AddColumn(
                addInventoryBalanceColumn,
                "MovementBalance",
                each ( [UnitsIn] - [UnitsOut] ) * [UnitCost],
                Currency.Type
            )
    in
        addMovementBalanceColumn
```

With these changes, the code becomes much cleaner and easier to read, as shown in *Figure 2.21*:

Advanced Editor   ☐   ✕

Chapter 2 - Product Inventory   Display Options ▾   ❓

```
1    let
2        Source =
3            Csv.Document(
4                File.Contents(Parameter1),
5                [Delimiter=",",Encoding=1252, QuoteStyle=QuoteStyle.None]
6            ),
7        promoteHeaders = Table.PromoteHeaders(Source, [PromoteAllScalars=true]),
8        changeTypes =
9            Table.TransformColumnTypes(
10               promoteHeaders,
11               {
12                   {"ProductKey", Int64.Type},
13                   {"DateKey", Int64.Type},
14                   {"MovementDate", type datetime},
15                   {"UnitCost", Currency.Type},
16                   {"UnitsIn", Int64.Type},
17                   {"UnitsOut", Int64.Type},
18                   {"UnitsBalance", Int64.Type},
19                   {"EnglishProductName", type text}
20               }
21           ),
22       addIndex = Table.AddIndexColumn(changeTypes, "Index", 1, 1, Int64.Type),
23       #"Inserted Multiplication" = Table.AddColumn(addIndex, "Multiplication",
             each [UnitCost] * [UnitsBalance], type number),
24       addInventoryBalanceColumn =
25           Table.AddColumn(
26               #"Inserted Multiplication",
27               "InventoryBalance",
28               each [UnitCost] * [UnitsBalance],
29               Currency.Type
30           ),
31       addMovementBalanceColumn =
32           Table.AddColumn(
33               addInventoryBalanceColumn,
34               "MovementBalance",
35               each ( [UnitsIn] - [UnitsOut] ) * [UnitCost],
36               Currency.Type
37           )
38   in
39       addMovementBalanceColumn
```

✓ No syntax errors have been detected.

Done   Cancel

Figure 2.21: Advanced Editor with custom code changes

It is important to note that if you are using the **Advanced Editor** to rename step names, it is necessary to manually adjust any other expressions that reference those steps. For this reason, it may be preferable to use the **Applied Steps** area of the **Query Settings** pane to rename steps by right-clicking on the step name and choosing **Rename**.

Once you finish editing the M code within the Advanced Editor, you can apply the changes by clicking on the **Done** button. To actually load the data into the Power BI model or Excel, click the **Close & Apply** button on the far left of the **Home** tab of the ribbon, as shown in *Figure 2.19*.

This completes our exploration of the Advanced Editor in the Power Query Desktop experience.

Summary

The Power Query Desktop and Online experiences provide the primary interface for writing M code. These experiences largely shield you from having to directly write all or most of the M code that comprises queries. However, as your expertise with the M language grows, you will find yourself more frequently writing M code directly.

In this chapter, we toured Power Query using the Power Query Desktop experience in Power BI Desktop as our guide. This included an overview of the major components of the Power Query Editor interface as well as an exploration of options that control the look and behavior of this interface and how to view and modify data source settings. We also covered several ways of tweaking or writing M code, including using the formula bar as well as when adding custom columns. Finally, we explored the Advanced Editor for making mass edits and writing more advanced M code.

In the next and subsequent chapters, we delve into a more in-depth treatment of the M language, starting with an exploration of how to access and combine data within M.

Learn more on Discord

Join our community's Discord space for discussions with the author and other readers:

```
https://discord.gg/vCSG5GBbyS
```

3

Accessing and Combining Data

Given that M is a language used for retrieving and transforming data, it is natural that the M language has a large number of built-in functions devoted to retrieving data from various systems such as files, folders, databases, web pages, and standardized data structures and protocols such as **eXtensible Markup Language (XML)**, **JavaScript Object Notation (JSON)**, and the **Open Data Protocol (OData)**.

In fact, M includes over 100 standard data retrieval functions and provides the ability to write extensions to retrieve data from additional sources such as custom business systems like an in-house-developed **customer relationship management (CRM)** system or **warehouse management system (WMS)**. Creating such extensions is covered in *Chapter 16, Enabling Extensions*. With consideration of these extensions, there are over 350 data functions available for accessing data within the Power Query editor. Obviously, no book can cover that many individual functions. Thus, this chapter seeks to provide a broad treatment of many common data-accessing functions with specific examples that are applicable to most other such functions.

In addition to data retrieval, M also provides powerful capabilities when it comes to combining data from multiple sources, including the ability to combine (append) data together and join (merge) data. This merging capability even extends to fuzzy matching capabilities where the data values in the key columns being merged is similar but not necessarily identical.

Throughout this chapter, we will explore the M language's unique data-handling capabilities, uncovering the intricacies of working with hierarchical data structures, databases, and file systems. Additionally, we will delve into two of the most common techniques for data transformation; aggregation, and merging, enabling you to harness the full potential of M for data analysis and reporting. For additional information on performance optimization during data retrieval and transformation, see *Chapter 15, Optimizing Performance*.

As we progress, you will learn how to extract data from different sources and combine that data, all using the versatile capabilities of M. Specifically, this chapter covers the following:

- Accessing files and folders
- Retrieving web content

- Investigating binary functions
- Accessing databases and cubes
- Working with standard data protocols
- Addressing additional connectors
- Combining and joining data

Technical requirements

To complete the tasks in this chapter, you will require the following:

- Power BI Desktop
- The source files used in this chapter are included in the GitHub repository for this book (`https://github.com/PacktPublishing/The-Definitive-Guide-to-Power-Query-M-/tree/main/Chapter%2003`)

Accessing files and folders

Many users work with M by accessing files and folders on their local computer, network drive, or cloud storage. While most business users will likely retrieve data from Excel files or perhaps a folder of **comma-separated values (CSV)** files, there are numerous other file formats supported by M including those listed in *Table 7.1* along with their corresponding M data retrieval functions:

File Format	M Functions
Azure Storage	`AzureStorage.BlobContents, AzureStorage.Blobs, AzureStorage.DataLake, AzureStorage.DataLakeContents, AzureStorage.Tables`
Binary	`File.Contents`
Excel	`Excel.Workbook, Excel.CurrentWorkbook`
Folder	`Folder.Contents, Folder.Files`
HDFS	`Hdfs.Contents, `**`Hdfs.Files`**
HDInsight	`HdInsights.Containers, HdInsight.Contents, HdInsight.Files`
JSON	`Json.Document`
PDF	`Pdf.Tables`
RData	`RData.FromBinary`
Text/CSV	`Csv.Document`
XML	`Xml.Document, Xml.Tables`

Table 3.1: M Functions for different file formats

Data formats can be quite diverse and preferred formats have changed over time. In addition, there are specialized data formats used by particular segments of the technology world, such as **RData** files being used when using the R language for statistical analysis. The rise of *big data* introduced the **Hadoop Distributed File System (HDFS)**. Finally, the rise of data lakes and lakehouses has seen file formats such as Parquet become popular.

Let's take a closer look at these various file formats, only instead of working through them alphabetically as in the table, we will first look at what is arguably the core file-accessing function, File.Contents.

File.Contents

The File.Contents function is a foundational data-accessing function for files and folders. Seldom used on its own, the output from the File.Contents function generally serves as input for the first parameter of many other file-accessing functions such as Csv.Document, Excel.Workbook, Json.Document, Xml.Document, and Xml.Tables.

The File.Contents function takes two parameters, a required contents parameter as its first parameter and an optional options record as its second parameter. If you are familiar with other programming languages, the concept of parameters used with functions is exactly the same. If you are unfamiliar with functions and parameters, refer to *Chapter 9, Parameters and Custom Functions*. In addition, records are covered in *Chapter 6, Structured Values*.

The output of the function is the contents of the file specified in the contents parameter formatted as binary (non-text). The contents parameter specifies the location of the file, such as C:\accounting\invoices.csv. The second parameter is a record that contains options for processing the file.

The second options parameter is common to many data-accessing functions. However, the available options are notoriously not well documented within official M documentation available online, and the valid options vary depending on the particular data-accessing function being used. In the case of File.Contents there is a known valid option, PreserveLastAccessTimes, which can be either true or false.

There is a way to uncover these *hidden* options for data-accessing functions. Within the Power Query editor, simply construct a query such as the following:

```
let
    Source = File.Contents
in
    Source
```

As shown, simply specify the function as the source of data. Inside the Power Query editor, documentation is returned regarding the function:

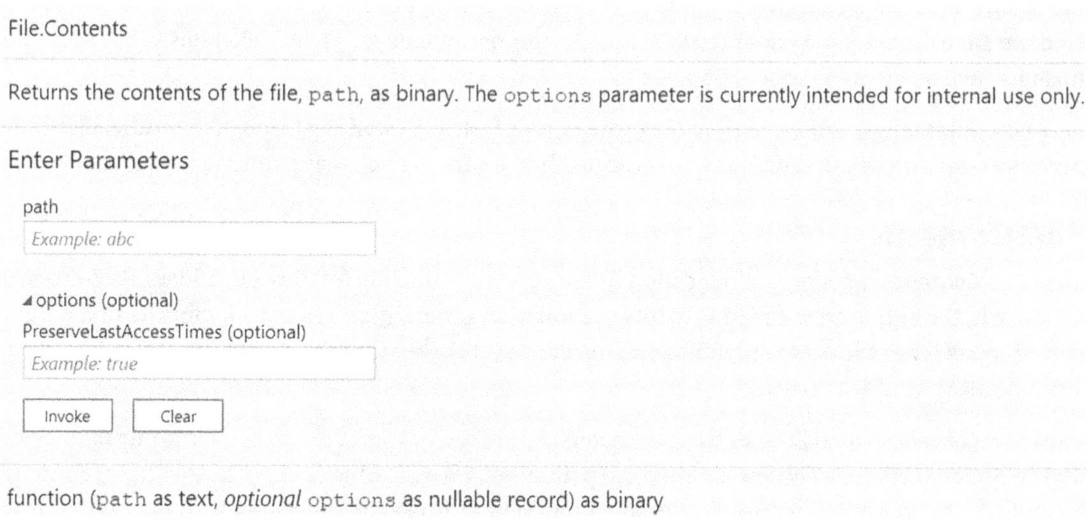

File.Contents

Returns the contents of the file, path, as binary. The options parameter is currently intended for internal use only.

Enter Parameters

path

> Example: abc

⊿ options (optional)
PreserveLastAccessTimes (optional)

> Example: true

[Invoke]   [Clear]

function (path as text, *optional* options as nullable record) as binary

Figure 3.1: File.Contents documentation

The mechanism behind how this documentation is provided is covered in *Chapter 7, Conceptualizing M*.

It must be noted that when using the Power Query interface for the functions covered in this section, *Accessing files and folders*, the interface assumes a local or network file is being accessed and thus utilizes File.Contents as the function to return the binary contents of the file. However, File.Contents is not required as the base function to return these binary contents. In fact, any function that returns the binary contents of a file can be used instead. For example, if the file exists on a website, the Web. Contents function can be used instead of File.Contents as Web.Contents returns the binary contents of a file from a URI. For more information on Web.Contents, see the *Retrieving Web Content* section in this chapter.

Let's now look at using File.Contents in a practical manner on **comma-separated values (CSV)** files.

Text/CSV

Text and CSV files are common file types used with data and have near-universal support as an export option within software systems that deal with data. Such files are often the output from exporting data from a data warehouse or other centralized data store.

As their name suggests, text files are simply text with fields or columns most often separated by tabs or commas. Tab-delimited and comma-delimited files are common data export options for many systems. To explore text/CSV files in greater detail, we will use the Avocado Prices.csv file. This file is included in the GitHub repository for this book. Download this file from the GitHub repository and save this file in a folder on your local computer.

The *Avocado Prices* data is a common public data source used for demonstrating variations in sale prices and volumes over time (time series analysis). The file contains the average price and total volume of avocados sold by city, state, and region over a period of approximately 3 years.

To create a CSV file query, perform the following steps:

1. In the Power Query editor, click the **New Source** button on the **Home** tab of the ribbon and choose **Text/CSV**:

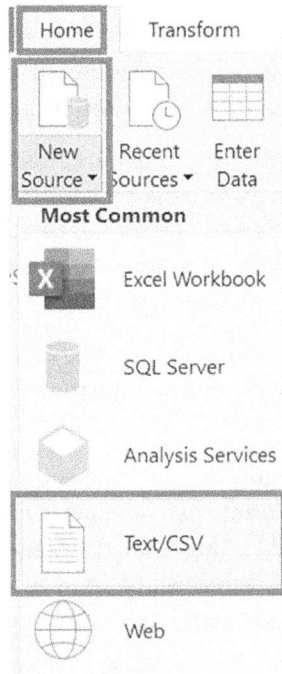

Figure 3.2: Creating a Text/CSV query

2. Use the File Explorer window to navigate and select the file and then press the Open button.
3. In the Avocado Prices.csv dialog, press the OK button.

After performing these steps, the Source step can be viewed in the **Advanced Editor** and looks like the following:

```
    Source = Csv.Document(File.Contents("C:\data\Avocado Prices.csv"),
[Delimiter=",", Columns=14, Encoding=1252, QuoteStyle=QuoteStyle.None]),
```

As can be seen in the code, the File.Contents function is used to retrieve the contents of the C:\data\Avocado Prices.csv file as binary data. Accessing and retrieving source data is an obvious and necessary step when it comes to data analysis. Regardless of the analysis to be performed, if one cannot ingest or access the necessary data, no analysis can proceed.

The output of the File.Contents function is used as the first parameter for the Csv.Document function. The second parameter for the Csv.Document function is an options record with options defined for the following:

- Delimiter: Specifies that columns in the data are separated by a comma (,).
- Columns: Specifies that there are 14 columns in the data.
- Encoding: Specifies the 1252 code page (Windows character encoding). A code page is simply a specification of how printable characters and non-printable characters (such as control characters like carriage return and line feed) are associated with unique numbers.
- QuoteStyle: Specifies that line breaks are treated as the end of the current row regardless of whether the line break occurs within a quoted value.

The second parameter of the Csv.Document function can actually be null, a table type, a list of column names, the number of columns, or, as with the code provided, an options record. The Csv.Document function determines how to treat the second parameter based on the value's type, such as a number, list, or record. We will look at the options record provided by this second parameter shortly, but first, let's enumerate the additional optional parameters available. There are three such additional parameters.

The third parameter is the delimiter parameter. The default is a comma (,) character. A delimiter value of an empty text string ("") indicates that the rows should be split into columns based on consecutive whitespace characters.

To use special characters, such as a tab character, you must use M escape sequences. Character escape sequences are formatted as #(<character>). Some characters have special names such as tab (tab character), cr (carriage return), and lf (line feed). For example, for tab-delimited files, specify #(tab) as the delimiter. However, any character can be used as a delimiter by specifying the character's four-digit Unicode hex code such as #(2605) for a black star character (U+2605).

The official documentation for this function claims that you can also provide a *list of characters*. However, specifying { ",", "|" } returns an error that a value of type List cannot be converted to type Text. Thus, what this means is that instead of a single-character delimiter such as a comma (,), several characters can be used as the delimiter, such as #(tab)#(2605) in the case of a tab and a black star character being used as a delimiter. This allows quite a bit of flexibility to support complex data formats.

The fourth parameter is the extraValues parameter. This parameter dictates how the Csv.Document function should handle additional, unexpected columns. This parameter accepts values according to the ExtraValues.Type enumeration. Specifically, the allowed values are as follows:

Friendly Name	Value	Comments
extraValues.List	0	Returns extra columns as a list
extraValues.Error	1	Raises an error
extraValues.Ignore	2	Ignores extra columns

Table 3.2: Allowed values for the extraValues parameter

The default is `ExtraValues.Ignore`. This means that if a fifteenth column was added to the `Avocado Prices.csv` file, because our options record includes specifying 14 for the **Columns** option, this additional fifteenth column would be ignored. This can help prevent errors during data ingest in the case of errors introduced while creating the data. Conversely, one may want to be alerted to any changes to the underlying data format and thus use `ExtraValues.Error` in order to ensure that any data format changes must be specifically addressed.

Alternatively, it may be advisable to omit the **Columns** option all together in order to help future-proof your query. By not specifying the number of columns, if a fifteenth column appeared in the data, the query would process the CSV file and include this fifteenth column.

The fifth and final parameter is the encoding parameter. This parameter specifies the file encoding type. Common text encoding types are provided by the `TextEncoding.Type` enumeration, including:

Friendly Name	Value	Comments
`TextEncoding.Utf16, TextEncoding.Unicode`	`1200`	Little endian binary form (UTF16)
`TextEncoding.Unicode`	`1200`	Little endian binary form (UTF16)
`TextEncoding.BigEndianUnicode`	`1201`	Big endian binary form (UTF16)
`TextEncoding.Windows`	`1252`	Windows binary form
`TextEncoding.Ascii`	`20127`	ASCII binary form
`TextEncoding.Utf8`	`65001`	UTF8 binary form

Table 3.3: Text encoding types

However, there are many additional encoding values that can be provided. In fact, the `Avocado Prices.csv` dialog provides a **File Origin** option as part of the dialog. Using the dropdown, one can see additional encoding values and a description for that encoding. For example, a value of `10017` is the encoding value for `Ukrainian Macintosh` computers.

Let's now circle back to the record used for our second parameter in our example. To use an options record as the second parameter, the third, fourth, and fifth parameters must be null or otherwise not included in the function call. When this is the case, the following options can be included in the record:

- `Delimiter`: Works exactly like the third `Delimiter` parameter for `Csv.Document`.
- `Columns`: Works exactly like the second `Columns` parameter for `Csv.Document` other than it cannot be a record.
- `Encoding`: Works exactly like the fifth parameter for `Csv.Document`.

- `CsvStyle`: Impacts whether quotes in a field are only significant immediately following the delimiter, or are always significant. Accepts `CsvStyle.Type` enumerations. `CsvStyle.Type` enumerations include the following:

Friendly Name	Value	Comments
`CsvStyle.QuoteAfterDelimiter`	0	Quotes are only significant if they are immediately preceded by a delimiter. This is the default.
`CsvStyle.QuoteAlways`	1	Quotes are always significant.

Table 3.4: CsvStyle enumerations

- `QuoteStyle`: Determines how quotes are treated within the string (whereas `CsvStyle` only impacts quotes that directly follow the delimiter). Accepts `QuoteStyle.Type` enumeration. `QuoteStyle.Type` enumerations include the following:

Friendly Name	Value	Comments
`QuoteStyle.None`	0	Quotes are ignored. This is the default.
`QuoteStyle.Csv`	1	Quotes are the start of a quoted string. Two quotes represent nested quotes.

Table 3.5: QuoteStyle enumerations

For a specific example, see the following link: `https://powerquery.how/quotestyle-none/`.

Considering everything that has been coved thus far, this means that instead of using an options record for the `Source` line in our `Avocado Prices.csv` file example, we could have alternatively used the following and achieved a similar result:

```
Source = Csv.Document(File.Contents("C:\data\Avocado Prices.csv"), 14, ",",
null, TextEncoding.Windows),
```

However, this alternative `Source` expression only works because there are no commas within our column values. If there were, then those rows would be parsed incorrectly. Thus, it is recommended to always use an options record for text/CSV files as the options.

Let's move on to Excel files.

Excel

The M language has two standard data-accessing functions for Excel, `Excel.Workbook` and `Excel.CurrentWorkbook`. These functions are essential for automating the extraction of financial data, sales metrics, or any other data from Excel files, which is one of the most popular file formats used by business users.

Let's first take a look at the Excel.Workbook function. To investigate this function, perform the following steps:

1. Open the Avocado Prices.csv file in Microsoft Excel and save the file as an .xlsx file, Avocado Prices.xlsx.

2. In the Power Query editor, click the **New Source** button on the **Home** tab of the ribbon and choose **Excel Workbook**.

3. Use the **File Explorer** window to navigate and select the file created in *step 1* and then press the **Open** button.

4. In the **Navigator** dialog, select the Avocado Prices sheet and then press the **OK** button:

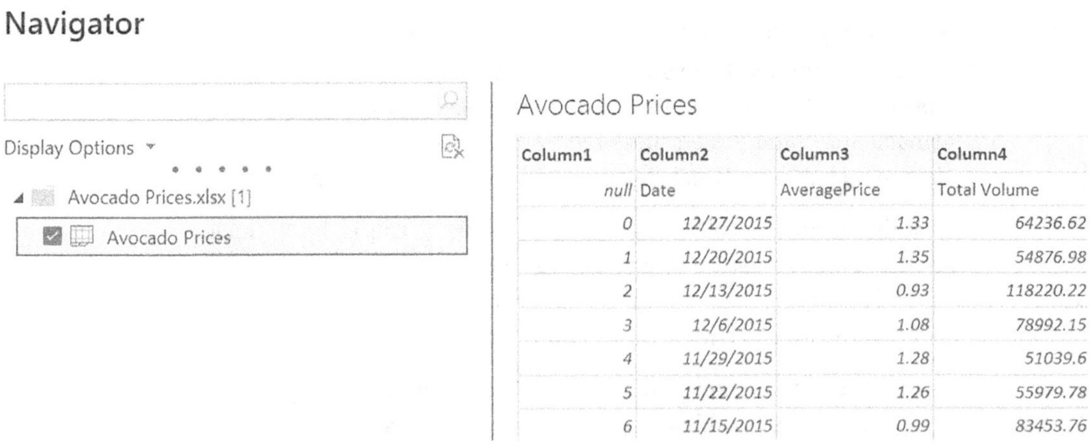

Navigator

Figure 3.3: Importing a sheet from an Excel file

After performing these steps, the following M code is generated for the first two expressions within the let statement, which can be viewed in the **Advanced Editor**:

```
Source = Excel.Workbook(File.Contents("C:\Users\gdeck\OneDrive\Books\The
Definitive Guide to Power Query\Chapter 7\Avocado Prices.xlsx"), null, true),
    #"Avocado Prices_Sheet" = Source{[Item="Avocado Prices",Kind="Sheet"]}
[Data],
```

Let's first look at the Source line. As shown, the Excel.Workbook function has three parameters. Similar to Csv.Document, the first parameter is the output of the File.Contents function, which accesses the Excel file and returns binary data.

The second parameter is the useHeaders parameter. This parameter can be null, true, or false and defaults to false. Alternatively, this parameter can also be an options record as long as the third parameter is null. Specifying true causes the Excel.Workbook function to use the first row of the table returned as column header names. In our example, Power Query did not automatically recognize that the first line of data was made up of column names (because of the null value in the first column of the first row). Thus, we could change this to true or we could simply promote the headers in a subsequent query step (Table.PromoteHeaders).

The third parameter is the `delayTypes` parameter. This parameter can also be `null`, `true`, or `false` and defaults to `false`. Specifying true causes the `Excel.Workbook` parameter to not assign types to columns. Many data analysts promote the best practice of assigning data types manually and not automatically. However, automatic assignment of data types can be a convenient time saver for business users.

As mentioned, the second parameter, `useHeaders`, can alternatively be an options record as long as the third parameter (`delayTypes`) is set to `null`. For a review of options records, see the *File.Contents* and *Text/CSV* sub-sections within this section. In this case, the options record supports the following options:

- `UseHeaders`: Operates exactly like the `useHeaders` parameter other than it cannot be an options record.
- `DelayTypes`: Operates exactly like the `delayTypes` parameter.
- `InferSheetDimensions`: This value can be `null`, `true`, or `false` and the default value is `false`. This option is only supported by the modern Open XML file format and not legacy Excel file formats. Specifying `true` causes the `Excel.Workbook` function to ignore the dimensions metadata included in the Excel file and infer the area of a worksheet by reading the worksheet.

Let's now look at the second line, `#"Avocado Prices_Sheet"`. This is the **Navigator** step in our query shown in *Figure 3.3*. This expression refers to the `Source` expression, accessing the table returned as a list of records and retrieving the record with an item of `Avocado Prices` and a kind of `Sheet`. Finally, the `Data` field of this record is retrieved as the table output.

As an experiment, change the expression after the `in` keyword in the generated query to `Source`. A single-row table is returned with column headers of `Name`, `Data`, `Item`, `Kind`, and `Hidden`. This is the actual table returned by the `Excel.Workbook` function. If multiple sheets, tables, named ranges, and/or dynamic arrays were included in the Excel file then multiple rows for each item would appear in this table. This information is used by the Power Query editor to build the **Navigator** window seen in *Figure 3.3* to demonstrate how this experimentation relates to what is going on within the Power Query editor, which is how you visually select your data.

Since our Excel file only includes a single sheet and no tables or named ranges, next try switching the expression after the `in` keyword to `Source{[]}`. Here the single row in the table is returned as a record. If multiple rows were present, this notation would return an error. For more information about this notation and selecting items in tables, see *Chapter 6, Structured Values*.

Let's next look at the `Excel.CurrentWorkbook` function. This function is used within Power Query for Excel and refers to the current open Excel file. As such, this function takes no parameters. Unlike the `Excel.Workbook` function, this function does not return sheets but rather only tables, named ranges, and dynamic arrays. In addition, for each item two columns are returned, `Content` and `Name`. Items are otherwise accessed in a similar manner to the `Excel.Workbook` function, such as:

```
Source = Excel.CurrentWorkbook(){[Name="Table2"]}[Content])
```

Having covered Excel files, let's next tackle importing multiple files from a folder, a situation that often comes up when data is regularly exported from a source system on a daily, weekly, or monthly basis.

Folder

In addition to accessing single files, two functions are included for dealing with file system folders containing any number of files, Folder.Contents and Folder.Files. Both functions are extremely similar, taking a text file path as their first parameter and the options record as their second parameter. Similar to File.Contents, the options record for both functions supports a single option, PreserveLastAccessTimes, which can be either true or false.

The two functions differ only in their output. The Folder.Contents function returns a table consisting of a row for every folder and file within the specified folder path while File.Contents only returns rows for each file. Thus, both would return exactly the same table of information if there were no sub-folders within the specified folder path.

To explore these functions in greater depth, we will use the Atlantic and Pacific Hurricanes 1851-2014.zip file included in the GitHub repository for this book. Follow these steps:

1. Download the Atlantic and Pacific Hurricanes 1851-2014.zip file and extract the four files included in the .zip file to a single folder on your local computer. There are two CSV files, atlantic.csv and pacific.csv, along with two PDF files, atlantic.pdf and pacific.pdf.

2. In the Power Query editor, click the **New Source** button on the **Home** tab of the ribbon and choose **More...**.

3. In the **Get Data** dialog, choose **File** in the left-hand pane, choose **Folder** in the right-hand list, and then press the **Connect** button.

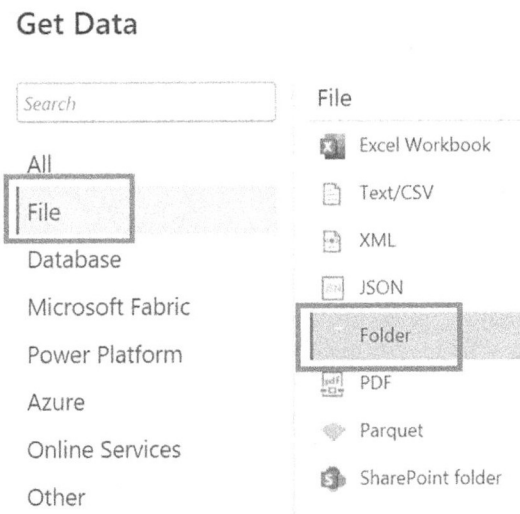

Figure 3.4: Get Data dialog

4. In the **Folder** dialog, click the **Browse...** button.

5. Using the **Browse For Folder** dialog, navigate and select the folder where you extracted the files in *step 1* and then press the **OK** button.

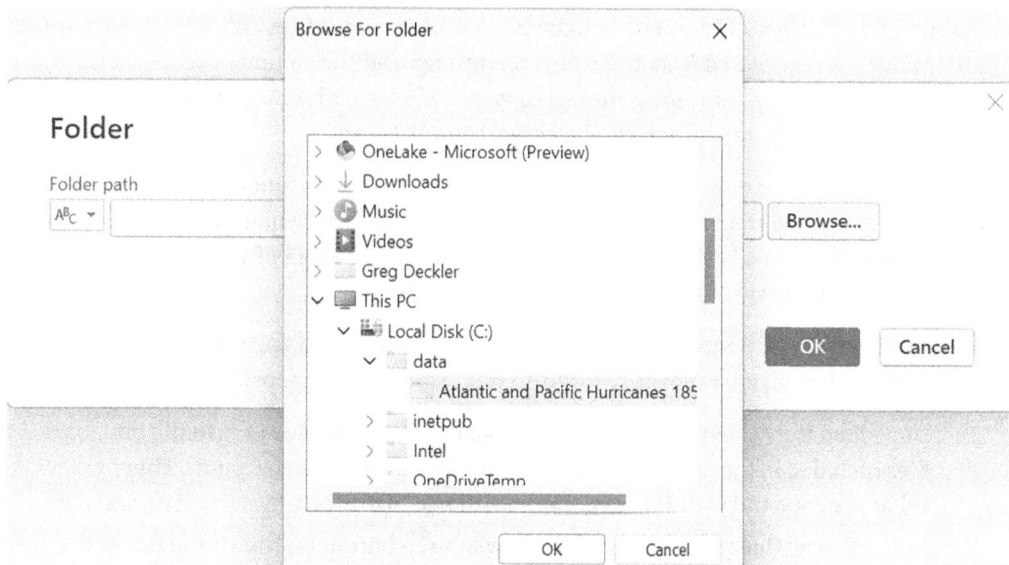

Figure 3.5: Browse for folder

6. Back in the **Folder** dialog, press the **OK** button.

7. In the next dialog, a preview of the four files is displayed. Click the **Transform Data** button.

C:\data\Atlantic and Pacific Hurricanes 1851-2014

Content	Name	Extension	Date accessed	Date modified	Date created	Attributes	Folder Path
Binary	atlantic.csv	.csv	3/3/2024 8:35:35 AM	7/24/2023 10:08:25 AM	3/3/2024 8:35:35 AM	Record	C:\data\Atlantic and Pacific Hurricane
Binary	atlantic.pdf	.pdf	3/3/2024 8:35:35 AM	7/24/2023 10:08:25 AM	3/3/2024 8:35:35 AM	Record	C:\data\Atlantic and Pacific Hurricane
Binary	pacific.csv	.csv	3/3/2024 8:35:35 AM	7/24/2023 10:08:25 AM	3/3/2024 8:35:35 AM	Record	C:\data\Atlantic and Pacific Hurricane
Binary	pacific.pdf	.pdf	3/3/2024 8:35:35 AM	7/24/2023 10:08:25 AM	3/3/2024 8:35:35 AM	Record	C:\data\Atlantic and Pacific Hurricane

Figure 3.6: Files preview

Performing these steps generates M code similar to the following that can be viewed in the **Advanced Editor**:

```
let
    Source = Folder.Files("C:\data\Atlantic and Pacific Hurricanes 1851-2014")
in
    Source
```

This code is quite straightforward and results in a table with the following columns: Content, Name, Extension, Date accessed, Date modified, Date created, Attributes, and Folder Path. The Content column holds the content of each file as binary data and the Attributes column holds a record. The rest of the columns are text except for the three Date columns, which are datetime values.

Now create a new folder in the folder where you extracted the four files and then refresh your data. Note that no additional rows are displayed. Next, edit the Source line of the query to use the Folder. Contents function instead of the Folder.Files function. Notice that an additional row is added to the table returned. This row is for the new folder created and has a Table value in the Content column and no value in the Extension column.

In the row for the atlantic.csv file, click the **Binary** link in the Content column. Many additional steps are added to the query and the result is a table imported from the CSV file. Looking closer at the two expressions immediately after the Source expression we observe code similar to the following in the **Advanced Editor** (some steps may have different names depending on the exact location of the folder on your computer):

```
    #"atlantic csv" = Source{[Name="atlantic.csv"]}[Content],
    #"Imported CSV" = Csv.Document(#"atlantic csv",[Delimiter=",", Columns=22,
  Encoding=1252, QuoteStyle=QuoteStyle.None]),
```

In the #"atlantic.csv" expression, we see that the desired data is accessed in a similar manner to how particular sheets of data are accessed from the output generated by the Excel.Workbook function (see the *Excel* section). The table is accessed as a list of records specifying the particular record using the Name field. From this selection, the Contents field is returned. The next expression, #"Imported CSV" uses the output from the #"atlantic.csv" record as the first parameter of the Csv.Document function (see the *Text/CSV* section).

As you can see, accessing the data of individual files using the Folder.Files or Folder.Contents functions is rather simple. However, a common scenario is to process and combine multiple files in a folder that all have the same format such as monthly or quarterly financial statements or a daily report on inventory status. To explore this option, create a new query performing the same steps as before, except this time, for *step 7 choose the* **Combine & Transform Data** button instead of the **Transform Data** button.

The Combine Files dialog is displayed. The **Sample File** dropdown defaults to the first file but using the dropdown a particular file can be specified. Also note the **Skip files with errors** checkbox. For now, however, simply press the **OK** button.

Performing these steps generates more than just a single query. In fact, in addition to the main query, a query group is created named after the source folder name. Within this query group is a query group called **Helper Queries** and a **Transform Sample File** query. Expanding the **Helper Queries** group, we see a parameter, **Parameter1**, another query, **Sample File**, and a function, **Transform File**:

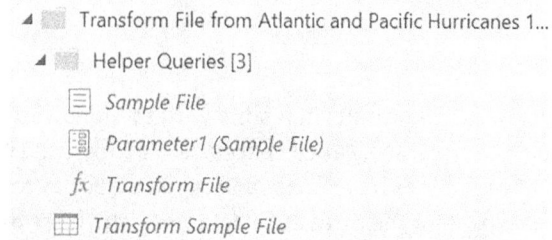

Figure 3.7: Queries, functions, and parameters created by Combine & Transform Data

Note that all of these queries and parameters are italicized within the Power Query editor. This means that none of these have been loaded into the data model. The dependencies between these various queries are as follows:

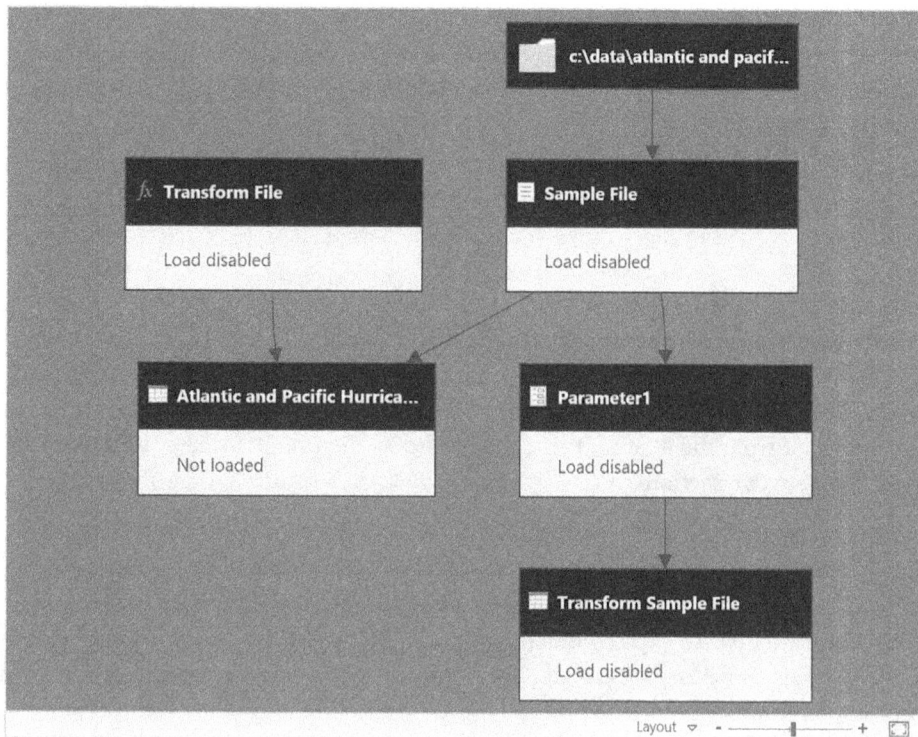

Figure 3.8: Query dependencies for the Folder query

Let's explore the queries created in further detail starting with the Sample File query. The Sample File query contains the following code:

```
let
    Source = Folder.Files("C:\data\Atlantic and Pacific Hurricanes 1851-2014"),
    Navigation1 = Source{0}[Content]
in
    Navigation1
```

As you can see, this query has code similar to what we have seen previously. The Source expression uses Folder.Files to return a table of files as rows. The Navigation1 expression accesses the content for one of these files, the first file in the table accessed as a list {0}. Changing the 0 to a 1 would access the second file and so on. Alternatively, if we had selected a particular file as part of the **Combine Files** dialog using the **Sample File** dropdown, the expression would look similar to the #"atlantic csv" expression in the earlier code example.

Let's next look at the Parameter1 (Sample File) parameter. This parameter is simply set to Sample File, a reference to the Sample File query.

The Transform File function is linked to the Transform Sample File query. This means that any changes to the Transform Sample File query are automatically reflected in the Transform File function. In fact, on opening the Transform File function in the **Advanced Editor**, you will receive a warning to this effect.

The Transform File function contains the following M code:

```
let
    Source = (Parameter1) => let
        Source = Csv.Document(Parameter1,[Delimiter=",", Columns=22,
Encoding=1252, QuoteStyle=QuoteStyle.None]),
        #"Promoted Headers" = Table.PromoteHeaders(Source,
[PromoteAllScalars=true])
    in
        #"Promoted Headers"
in
    Source
```

This function definition takes a single parameter, with the default being Parameter1. Parameter1 is a reference to the Parameter1 Power Query parameter, which is currently set to Sample File. By specifying a default value, this allows the function to operate and return a table of values for preview purposes but allows the function to also operate on data passed into the function via an argument.

The M code within the second `let` expression actually reflects the M code in the `Transform Sample File` query as you can see if you open the `Transform Sample File` query in the **Advanced Editor**:

```
let
    Source = Csv.Document(Parameter1,[Delimiter=",", Columns=22, Encoding=1252,
QuoteStyle=QuoteStyle.None]),
    #"Promoted Headers" = Table.PromoteHeaders(Source,
[PromoteAllScalars=true])
in
    #"Promoted Headers"
```

The `Source` line references `Parameter1`, which is currently set to reference the `Sample File` query and uses the `Csv.Document` function to retrieve the data. This is because the first file in the folder is a CSV file. Had we specified one of the PDF files, the data access function would be different. The query also contains a single transformation step using the `Table.PromoteHeaders` function. The net effect of this is that you can modify the `Transform Sample File` query to perform additional data transformations, such as removing and renaming columns. These data transformations are reflected in an updated `Transform File` function.

Let's now look at the main query created. In the **Advanced Editor**, this query includes the following three expressions immediately after the `let` statement:

```
    Source = Folder.Files("C:\data\Atlantic and Pacific Hurricanes 1851-2014"),
    #"Filtered Hidden Files1" = Table.SelectRows(Source, each
[Attributes]?[Hidden]? <> true),
    #"Invoke Custom Function1" = Table.AddColumn(#"Filtered Hidden Files1",
"Transform File", each #"Transform File"([Content])),
```

The expression `#"Invoke Custom Function1"` uses the `Table.AddColumn` function to add a column called `Transform File` whose contents are the output from calling the `Transform File` function with the `Content` column for each row. In effect, this returns the row with a column, `Transform File`, whose contents is the output from the `Transform File` function with the `Content` column for the row passed in as a parameter, meaning that ultimately, the transformations from the `Transform Sample File` query are applied to the contents of each file returned from the `Source` expression, which uses the `Folder.Files` function to enumerate the files within the folder.

The subsequent two expressions (not shown in the code sample) in the main query rename and remove columns such that only a `Source.Name` column and the `Transform File` columns remain. These expressions use the `Table.RenameColumns` and `Table.SelectColumns` respectively. The next expression then expands all rows in the `Transform File` column using the `Table.ExpandTableColumns` function.

We now have the contents of each file as transformed by the `Transform Files` function loaded into a single table along with a `Source.Name` column that contains the file names. The last step in the query simple changes the types for the columns using the `Table.TransformColumnTypes` function.

If you were to load this query into the data, model rows for the PDF files would be included. However, these rows would be blank or null for every column other than the Source.Name column. This is because the transformation steps do not correctly process the PDF files since the transformations are for CSV files. To correct this, click on the Source step in the **Applied Steps** area of the Power Query editor for the main query created.

Use the dropdown for the Extensions column to filter the rows to just the csv rows. The first two expressions in the main query now look like the following:

```
Source = Folder.Files("C:\data\Atlantic and Pacific Hurricanes 1851-2014"),
#"Filtered Rows" = Table.SelectRows(Source, each ([Extension] = ".csv")),
```

Here, the Table.SelectRows function filters the files returned by the Folder.Files function to just the files with a .csv extension.

This completes our exploration of the folder functions in M. Let's next look at processing PDF files.

PDF

Developed in 1992 and standardized as *ISO 32000*, **Portable Document Format** (PDF) files have long been a standard file format used to exchange formatted documents that include formatted text, tables, images, annotations, form-fields, rich media such as video content, layers, etc. Given their long, over-30-year history as a free and open standard for document exchange independent of hardware, operating system, and application software, there is a wealth of potentially useful data stored within PDF documents. For example, PDF documents are often used for monthly or quarterly financial statements. Thus, the ability to import such PDF files into a single semantic model provides the opportunity for tracking changes over time as well as trend analysis. Luckily, the M language includes a data-accessing function to extract data from PDF files, the PDF.Tables function.

To explore the PDF.Tables function in further detail, we will use the PDF files included in the Atlantic and Pacific Hurricanes 1851-2014.zip file included in the GitHub repository for this book. If you have not done so already, download the Atlantic and Pacific Hurricanes 1851-2014.zip file and extract the four files included in the ZIP file to a single folder on your local computer. There are two CSV files, atlantic.csv and pacific.csv,along with two PDF files, atlantic.pdf and pacific.pdf.

Once you have downloaded and extracted the PDF files, follow these steps:

1. In the Power Query editor, click the **New Source** button on the **Home** tab of the ribbon and choose **More...**.
2. In the **Get Data** dialog, choose **File** in the left navigation, choose **PDF** in the right-hand list, and then press the **Connect** button.
3. Use the **File Explorer** window to navigate to the folder where you extracted the files contained in Atlantic and Pacific Hurricanes 1851-2014.zip.
4. Select the atlantic.pdf file and press the **OK** button.

5. In the **Navigator** dialog, note that several **Table** and **Page** elements appear. The `Pdf.Tables` function attempts to automatically identify tables within the PDF document and includes these as potential data selections along with each page of the PDF file. Select the **Table001 (Page 1)** item and then press the **OK** button:

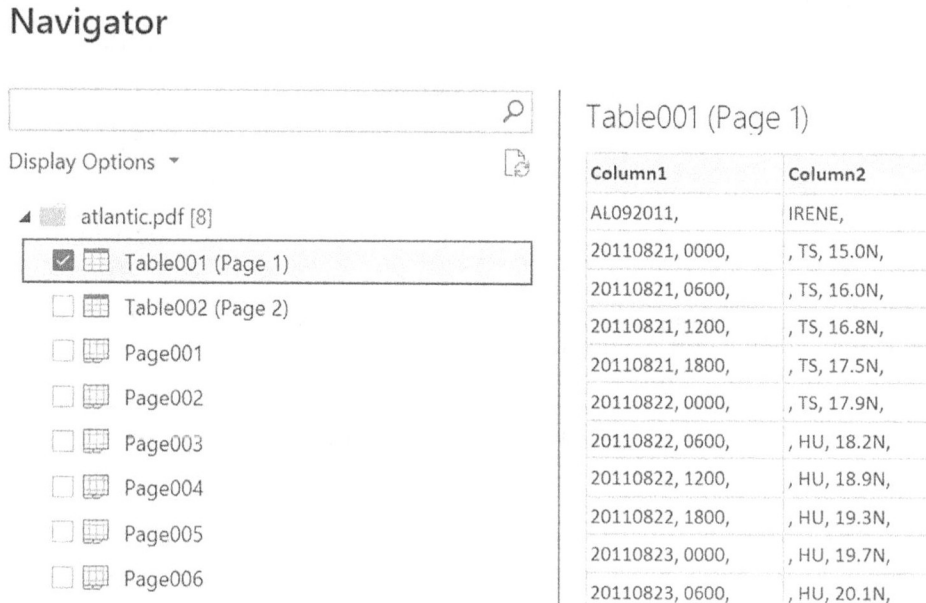

Navigator

	Column1	Column2
	AL092011,	IRENE,
	20110821, 0000,	, TS, 15.0N,
	20110821, 0600,	, TS, 16.0N,
	20110821, 1200,	, TS, 16.8N,
	20110821, 1800,	, TS, 17.5N,
	20110822, 0000,	, TS, 17.9N,
	20110822, 0600,	, HU, 18.2N,
	20110822, 1200,	, HU, 18.9N,
	20110822, 1800,	, HU, 19.3N,
	20110823, 0000,	, HU, 19.7N,
	20110823, 0600,	, HU, 20.1N,

Display Options ▾

▲ atlantic.pdf [8]

   ☑ Table001 (Page 1)

   ☐ Table002 (Page 2)

   ☐ Page001

   ☐ Page002

   ☐ Page003

   ☐ Page004

   ☐ Page005

   ☐ Page006

Table001 (Page 1)

Figure 3.9: Navigator for PDF file

After performing these steps the following M code is generated for the first two expressions within the `let` statement which can be viewed in the **Advanced Editor**:

```
Source = Pdf.Tables(File.Contents("C:\data\Atlantic and Pacific Hurricanes
1851-2014\atlantic.pdf"), [Implementation="1.3"]),
    Table001 = Source{[Id="Table001"]}[Data],
```

Let's first look at the `Source` line. As shown, the `Pdf.Tables` function has two parameters. As with the other file-accessing functions we have covered, the first parameter is the output of the `File.Contents` function, which accesses the PDF file and returns binary data.

The second parameter is an optional options record. This options record works identically to options records for the other file-accessing functions we have covered and includes the following options:

-   `Implementation`: Microsoft has implemented a number of different algorithms to identify tables in PDF files. This option determines which algorithm is used with valid values being `1.3`, `1.2`, and `1.1`. You should always use the latest value of the algorithm as the other values are provided solely for the purposes of backward compatibility.
-   `StartPage`: Defaults to 1 and specifies the first page to include in the data retrieval.
-   `EndPage`: Defaults to the last available page and specifies the last page to include in the data retrieval.

- **MultiPageTables**: Specifies whether to treat tables that span multiple pages as a single table or multiple tables. This value can be `true` or `false` and defaults to `true`. Note that the identification of tables spanning multiple pages is not always successful.
- **EnforceBorderLines**: Specifies whether table borderlines are enforced as the boundaries of cells within the table. This value can be `true` or `false` and defaults to `false`.

The next expression, `Table001`, operates exactly like the navigation step we explained in the *Excel* section of this chapter.

Let's now move on to XML files.

XML

XML, or eXtensible Markup Language, is a widely used file format for storing arbitrary data. Its flexibility and standardization make it well suited for exchanging data between organizations. For example, **Health Level 7 (HL7)** is a global, XML-based standard for exchanging health data between applications. Another example is OpenTravel Alliance, a consortium of travel and hospitality companies that uses standard XML files to exchange data between systems.

The XML family of functions includes `Xml.Tables` and `Xml.Document`. The first argument of both functions is required and specifies the contents of a file. The last argument of both functions is an optional encoding number (`TextEncoding.Type`). The `Xml.Tables` function also has an optional second parameter to specify options.

While both functions parse XML files their internal implementations are different. `Xml.Tables` parses the XML and returns the elements as column headers while `Xml.Document` returns a hierarchical table structure with the column headers `Name`, `Namespace`, `Value`, and `Attribute`.

To examine the differences in these two functions, we will use the `books.xml` file sample found here: `https://learn.microsoft.com/en-us/previous-versions/windows/desktop/ms762271(v=vs.85)`

This file is also included as part of the GitHub repository for this chapter. For ease of reference, here is a sample of the file contents:

```
<?xml version="1.0"?>
<catalog>
    <book id="bk101">
        <author>Gambardella, Matthew</author>
        <title>XML Developer's Guide</title>
        <genre>Computer</genre>
        <price>44.95</price>
        <publish_date>2000-10-01</publish_date>
        <description>An in-depth look at creating applications
        with XML.</description>
    </book>
    <book id="bk102">
        <author>Ralls, Kim</author>
```

```
        <title>Midnight Rain</title>
        <genre>Fantasy</genre>
        <price>5.95</price>
        <publish_date>2000-12-16</publish_date>
        <description>A former architect battles corporate zombies,
        an evil sorceress, and her own childhood to become queen
        of the world.</description>
    </book>
</catalog>
```

The file contains a root node called catalog. Within the catalog are multiple book nodes. Each book node contains numerous properties such as author, title, genre, price, etc.

Xml.Tables

Using the Power Query editor's GUI to connect to this file displays a table labeled book in the **Navigator**. Selecting this table for data retrieval generates the following query:

```
let
    Source = Xml.Tables(File.Contents("C:\data\Books.xml")),
    Table0 = Source{0}[Table],
    #"Changed Type" = Table.TransformColumnTypes(Table0,{{"author", type text},
    {"title", type text}, {"genre", type text}, {"price", type number}, {"publish_
    date", type date}, {"description", type text}, {"Attribute:id", type text}})
in
    #"Changed Type"
```

As one can see in the code, the Source step retrieves the file contents using File.Contents and then further processes the file contents using Xml.Tables. The elements under the root node are returned as a list. Thus, the Table0 step accesses the first item in the list {0} and then the [Table] portion uses field selection and returns the contents of a record field named Table. The #Changed Type step automatically attempts to identify the data types of the columns returned. Note that this attempt is not fully successful as the price column is identified as a decimal number instead of a fixed decimal number (currency).

The net effect of the code is that the XML document is returned with column headers of author, title, genre, price, publish_date, description, and Attribute.id. The data for each book is presented as a row in this table. Note that the Attribute.id column contains the ID attribute for each book node.

Before moving on to the second function, Xml.Document, let's first explore the second parameter of the Xml.Tables function, options. The options parameter of the Xml.Tables function is not well documented. Current research on the subject indicates that only a single record field is supported, NavigationTables, which defaults to true. The optional third parameter specifies an encoding type (TextEncoding.Type enumeration) such as TextEncoding.Windows, which is simply the number 1252.

As one can see, using `Xml.Tables` enables just a few lines of M code to generate a table of books with the properties of those books returned as columns. The same cannot be said about using `Xml.Document`.

Xml.Document

For the same file, using `Xml.Document` instead of `Xml.Tables` requires the following code to return the exact same data table:

```
let
    Source = Xml.Document(File.Contents("C:\data\Books.xml")),
    #"Removed Columns" = Table.RemoveColumns(Source,{"Namespace", "Attributes",
"Name"}),
    #"Expanded Value" = Table.ExpandTableColumn(#"Removed Columns", "Value",
{"Value", "Attributes"}, {"Value.1", "Attributes"}),
    #"Expanded Attributes" = Table.ExpandTableColumn(#"Expanded Value",
"Attributes", {"Value"}, {"Value"}),
    #"Expanded Value.1" = Table.ExpandTableColumn(#"Expanded Attributes",
"Value.1", {"Name", "Value"}, {"Name.1", "Value.2"}),
    PivotedColumn = Table.Pivot(#"Expanded Value.1", List.Distinct(#"Expanded
Value.1"[Name.1]), "Name.1", "Value.2"),
    #"Renamed Columns" = Table.RenameColumns(PivotedColumn,{{"Value",
"Attribute.id"}}),
    #"Changed Type" = Table.TransformColumnTypes(#"Renamed
Columns",{{"Attribute.id", type text}, {"author", type text}, {"title", type
text}, {"genre", type text}, {"description", type text}, {"price", type
number}, {"publish_date", type date}})
in
    #"Changed Type"
```

As you can see, the `Source` step is nearly identical other than the use of the `Xml.Document` function instead of the `Xml.Tables` function. This source step returns a single-row table as follows:

Name	Namespace	Value	Attributes
catalog		Table	Table

This row represents the root element of the XML document, `catalog`. In order to return the books elements, we first remove the `Name`, `Namespace`, and `Attributes` columns using the `Table.RemoveColumns` function. We then expand the `Value` column for both `Value` and `Attributes` using the `Table.ExpandTableColumn` function. This step returns a row for each book element with column headers of `Value.1` and `Attributes`. Both columns contain a table for each row.

In the next two steps, we again use `Table.ExpandTableColumn` to first expand the `Attributes` column, for just the `Value` column. This is the `#Expanded Attributes` step. We then expand the `Value.1` column for just the `Name` and `Value` columns. Note that the order of these two steps is irrelevant. The only difference is a slight variation in the names of the columns generated.

At this point, we have a table where the first few rows look like the following:

Name.1	Value.2	Value
author	Gambardella, Matthew	bk101
title	XML Developer's Guide	bk101
Genre	Computer	bk101

Table 3.6: The expanded table

We now need to pivot the table such that the first column, `Name.1`, becomes the column headers. Our table is now in the same basic format as that returned by the `Xml.Tables` function described earlier in this section. All that is needed is to rename the `Value` column to `Attribute.id` and change the column types.

As you can see, the `Xml.Tables` and `Xml.Document` functions behave quite differently. The `Xml.Tables` function returns child elements as tables while the `Xml.Document` function allows you to drill through the hierarchy of the XML document using the same four columns, `Name`, `Namespece`, `Value`, and `Attributes`. In our example, the `Xml.Document` function takes many more data transformations to return a suitable table with the desired information. However, the number of data transformations for each function will vary depending on the exact structure of the XML file.

Azure Storage

While a complete treatment of Azure Storage concepts is beyond the scope of this book, as a brief overview consider that Microsoft Azure provides several different mechanisms for storing files and information. At the core of this storage is what is known as an Azure Storage account. Azure Storage accounts can store different data objects such as blobs, files, queues, tables, and data lake storage. Each of these storage accounts has a unique namespace and is often accessed using an automatically generated account key.

The core M library contains several functions for accessing these storage objects including:

- `AzureStorage.Blobs`
- `AzureStorage.Tables`
- `AzureStorage.BlobContents`
- `AzureStorage.DataLake`
- `AzureStorage.DataLakeContents`

Let's look at the `AzureStorage.Blobs` function. A sample query for using this function might be:

```
let
    Source = AzureStorage.Blobs("mystorageaccountname")
in
    Source
```

Here, mystorageaccountname would be replaced with the name of your Azure Storage account. When authenticating, you can choose the **Account key** option. This account key can be retrieved using the **Access keys** option when viewing the properties of your Azure Storage account on portal.azure.com:

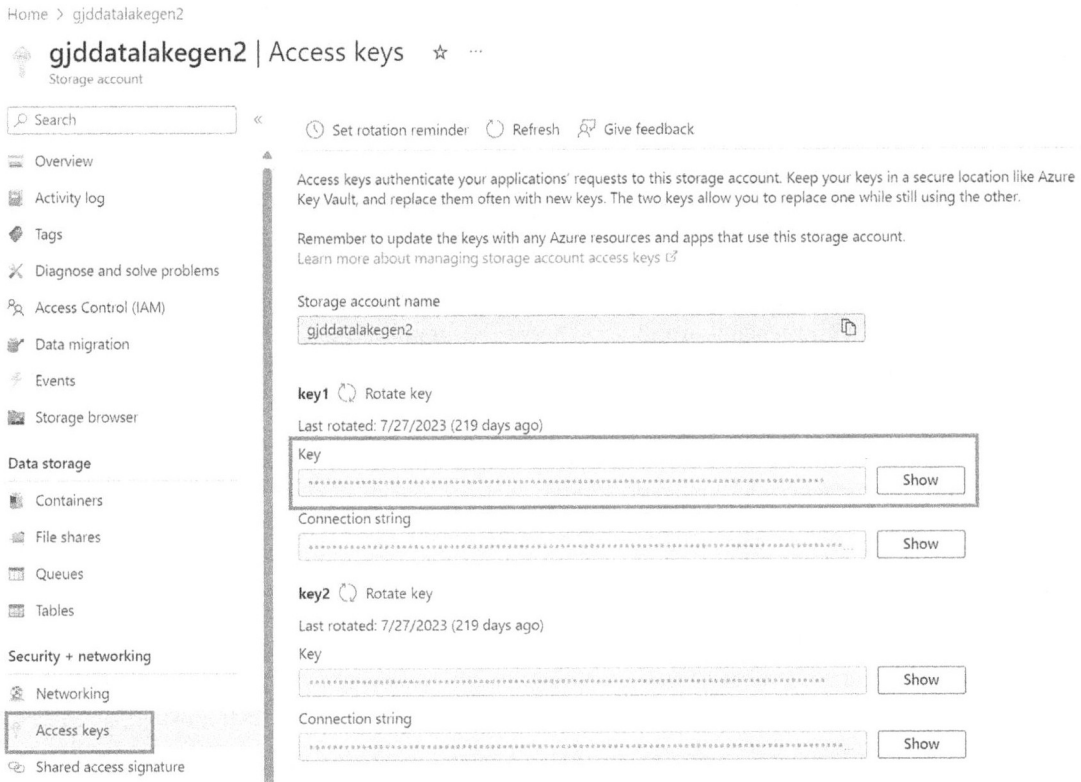

Figure 3.10: Storage account access keys on portal.azure.com

The function returns a two-column table consisting of any blob containers present within the storage account. This table consists of a Name column for the blob container name and a Data column that returns a Table object. You can navigate into this Table object to view the folders and files within the blob container. The experience is extremely similar to using the Folder.Contents or Folder.Files functions. In fact, once at the blob (file) level, the columns returned are identical.

The AzureStorage.Blobs function also supports a second, optional parameter. This parameter is an options record that can contain the options BlockSize, RequestSize, and ConcurrentRequests. The defaults for these options are 4MB, 4MB, and 16 respectively. These parameters can be adjusted to potentially speed up downloads at the expense of greater memory utilization. For example, the ConcurrentRequests parameter could be adjusted to 32, meaning that there would be 32 simultaneous requests for data, each requesting 4MB (if using the default RequestSize). Thus, the memory utilized would be 32 * 4MB or 128MB.

The `AzureStorage.Tables` function operates identically to the `AzureStorage.Blobs` function except that it returns tables instead of blob containers from the Azure Storage account. Another difference is that the function's second parameter, an options record, only supports the option `Timeout` specified as a duration value. The default value for this option is provided by the source.

The `AzureStorage.BlobContents` function takes a URI as its first parameter and an optional options record with the same options as the `AzureStorage.Blobs` function. The URI must be the full URI to a blob within the Azure Storage account.

The `Azure.DataLake` function takes the data lake endpoint for the Azure Storage account as its first parameter. This is a URI in the form of `https://mystorageaccountname.dfs.core.windows.net/`.

This function operates like the `Folder` family of functions, even providing the same **Combine & Transform Data** option within the Power Query editor. This function also takes an optional second parameter, an `options record` with the same `BlockSize`, `RequestSize`, and `ConcurrentRequests` options and default values as the `AzureStorage.Blobs` function as well as an option for `HierarchicalNavigation`. This last option can be `null`, `true`, or `false` and defaults to `false`.

As you might expect, the `Azure.DataLakeContents` returns the contents of an individual file stored within the data lake endpoint of the Azure Storage account. The first parameter is the full URI to the file. An options record can be provided as the second parameter and has the same options and default values as the `AzureStorage.Blobs` function.

Additional file formats

The standard M library contains additional functions for accessing files. These functions operate similarly to the functions covered in this section. These functions include the following:

- `Hdfs.Contents`: Retrieves a table of folders and files from a Hadoop file system. Takes a single parameter, `url`, as text. This is a URI for a Hadoop folder. Similar to `Folder.Contents`.
- `Hdfs.Files`: Retrieves a table of files from a Hadoop file system. Takes a single parameter, `url`, as text. This is a URI for a Hadoop folder. Similar to `Folder.Files`.
- `HdInsights.Containers`: Retrieves a table of containers from an Azure HDInsights storage vault. Azure HDInsights is a managed Azure service that provides the ability to use open-source frameworks such as Hadoop, LLAP, Apache Hive, Apache Spark, and Apache Kafka. Takes a single parameter, `account`, as text. This is the account URI for the Azure HDInsights storage vault. Each row returned links to the container blobs.
- `HdInsights.Contents`: Also retrieves a table of containers from an Azure HDInsights storage vault. Takes a single parameter, `account`, as text. This is the account URI for the Azure HDInsights storage vault. Each row returned links to the container blobs.
- `HdInsights.Files`: Retrieves a table of blob files from an Azure HDInsights storage vault. Takes a single parameter, `account`, as text. This is the account URI for the Azure HDInsights storage vault. Each row returned includes properties of the file and a link to the contents of the file.
- `Json.Document`: Returns the contents of a JSON document. Has two parameters, `jsonText` (often the output of `File.Contents` or `Web.Contents`) and encoding, which takes an `TextEncoding.Type` enumeration (see the *Text/CSV* section).

- `RData.FromBinary`: Used to return a record of the data frames from an `RData` file. Takes a single parameter, `stream`, as the binary contents of the file.
- `Parquet.Document`: Not part of the core M library but rather implemented as an extension (connector). For an overview of extensions and connectors, see *Chapter 16, Enabling Extensions*. Retrieves a table from the contents of a Parquet document. Has two parameters, `binary`, the binary contents of the file (often output of `File.Contents` or `Web.Contents`) and an optional options record. This options record can contain options or `MaxDepth`, `Compression`, `PreserveOrder`, `LegacyColumnNameEncoding`, and `TypeMapping`.

This completes our exploration of file and folder formats. Let's next turn our attention to databases and cubes.

Retrieving web content

In the last section, we covered accessing data within files stored on a local computer or network file system. However, another common source of data is the internet. The standard M library includes a number of functions for retrieving data from the internet, including:

- `Web.BrowserContents`
- `Html.Table`
- `Web.Page`
- `Web.Contents`
- `Web.Headers`
- `WebAction.Request`

To see these functions in action, first perform these steps:

1. Select **Get Data** from the **Home** tab of the Power Query editor and then choose **Web**.
2. In the **From Web** dialog, use the following for the URL, `https://subscription.packtpub.com/search`.
3. Press the **OK** button.
4. Select **Anonymous** authentication and press the **Connect** button.
5. In the **Navigator** dialog, choose **HTML Code** under the **Text** folder.

Following these steps generates the following M code as viewed in the **Advanced Editor**:

```
let
    #"HTML Code" = Web.BrowserContents("https://subscription.packtpub.com/
search")
in
    #"HTML Code"
```

The output of this query simply returns the raw **HyperText Markup Lanaguage (HTML)** for the web page. The `Web.BrowserContents` function simply returns the raw HTML for the URI specified as the first parameter. An options record can be provided as an optional second parameter.

This options record can contain the ApiKeyName and WaitFor fields. You can learn more about these option fields at the following URL: https://powerquery.how/web-browsercontents/.

Now, create the same query as before but this time select **Displayed Text** instead of **HTML Code** in *step 5*. This time, the following M code is generated:

```
let
    Source = Web.BrowserContents("https://subscription.packtpub.com/search"),
    #"Extracted Table From Html" = Html.Table(Source, {{"Column1", "BODY"}}),
    Column1 = #"Extracted Table From Html"[Column1]{0}
in
    Column1
```

In this query, Web.BrowserContents is still used to get the raw HTML for the web page. However, the Html.Table function is then used to select the BODY of the web page. It should be evident that the first parameter for the Html.Table function is HTML content as text.

The second parameter to the Html.Table function is actually a list of **Cascading Style Sheets** (CSS) selector pairs used to extract information from the provided HTML. A full discussion regarding CSS is beyond the scope of this book but note that all web pages have the following basic structure:

```
<html>
    <head>
    </head>
    <body>
    </body>
</html>
```

This HTML code, when viewed as a table at the root level (html), is thus a single-column table consisting of head and body. Thus, a selector of *BODY* makes sense as this selects the body portion of the web page. Note that Html.Table does not return the raw HTML but rather what is actually visible on the page as text.

A third parameter is also available, an options record. This options record supports a single field, RowSelector. This RowSelector uses a CSS selector to only return particular rows from an HTML table.

A final note about Html.Table is that the Html.Table function is used whenever you select an identified table or use the **Add Table Using Examples** feature in the **Navigator** dialog when using the **Web** connector. In these scenarios, the Power Query editor uses CSS selectors in the HTML document to extract the table data.

Let's next look at the Web.Page function. Create the following query:

```
let
    Source =
        Web.Page(
            Web.BrowserContents("https://subscription.packtpub.com/search")
```

```
        ),
    Data = Source{0}[Data],
    Children = Data{0}[Children]
in
    Children
```

The Web.Page function takes a single parameter, html. In our case, we used the output from the Web.BrowserContents function for this parameter since the Web.BrowserContents function returns the raw HTML as text.

The output from the Web.Page function is remarkably similar to the Xml.Document function discussed previously in this chapter, as is the user's interaction when navigating through the document.

The output of the query is a two-row, four-column table. The columns returned are Kind, Name, Children, and Text, and the rows have values of HEAD and BODY for the Name column. You can continue navigating the hierarchical tree structure returned by this query by clicking on any cell that contains a table. Refer back to the *XML* section of this chapter and specifically the section on Xml.Document for further explanation.

The last web-related data-accessing function we will discuss is the Web.Contents function. The Web.Contents function returns the contents of a web request as binary data, similar to how the File.Contents function returns the contents of a file as binary data. This means that anywhere we used File.Contents in the *Opening files and folders* section of this chapter, we could have instead used Web.Contents.

Like the File.Contents function, the Web.Contents function has two parameters. The first parameter is a text URI (URL). The second parameter is an options record. This options record can have the following fields:

- Query: Adds query string parameters to the URL programmatically.
- ApiKeyName: Used to specify the name of the key parameter used in the *URL*.
- Headers: Supplies additional HTTP headers used in a request.
- Timeout: A duration value specifying how long to wait for a response before timing out. The default timeout is 100 seconds.
- ExcludedFromCacheKey – A list of HTTP header keys to be excluded from the calculation for caching.
- IsRetry: Can be true or false. Specifying true ignores any existing response in the cache.
- ManualStatusHandling: A list of HTTP status codes. Responses with these codes will not be handled automatically by the Web.Contents function.
- RelativePath: Appends the specified value to the base URL when making a request.
- Content: A binary value. Changes the request from GET to POST with this value as the content.

To observe these options in use, create the following query:

```
let
    Source =
        Web.Contents(
            "https://subscription.packtpub.com",
            [
                RelativePath = "search",
                Query = [ query = "power+query",
                          products = "Book"
                        ],
                Timeout = #duration(0,0,0,30)
            ]
        )
in
    Source
```

This query specifies a 30-second timeout and returns the contents of the following URI as binary:
`https://subscription.packtpub.com/search?query=power+query&products=Book`

The value for `RelativePath` is appended to the base URL specified. The query string (the portion after the ?) is built automatically from the record value of the `Query` parameter.

This completes our exploration around retrieving web content. We will now move on to investigating binary functions.

Investigating binary functions

As we have discussed, `File.Contents` and `Web.Contents` serve as core data-accessing functions. One accepts a file path while the other accepts a URI but both return the accessed file or web page as binary data. It stands to reason then that there is an entire group of functions dedicated to processing and handling binary data built into the core M library. These are the functions that start with the word `Binary`.

In fact, there are over 40 functions in the Binary family. Many of these functions are somewhat esoteric. However, a common use for these functions can be observed in `Enter Data` queries.

To observe these binary functions in action, create an `Enter Data` query in the Power Query editor with the following data:

Column1	Column2
One	1
Two	2
Three	3

Table 3.7: Sample data

This generates the following M code after proper formatting:

```
let
    Source =
        Table.FromRows(
            Json.Document(
                Binary.Decompress(
                    Binary.FromText(
                        "i45W8s9LVdJRMlSK1YlWCinPB7KNIOyMolSQjLFSbCwA",
                        BinaryEncoding.Base64
                    ),
                    Compression.Deflate
                )
            ),
            let _t = ((type nullable text) meta [Serialized.Text = true]) in
type table [Column1 = _t, Column2 = _t]
        ),
    #"Changed Type" = Table.TransformColumnTypes(Source,{{"Column2", Int64.
Type}})
in
    #"Changed Type"
```

Here we can see that the data we entered was converted to compressed, binary-encoded text. This is the long string of text and numbers beginning with i45w8 and ending with FSbCWA. This string is converted to binary data using the Binary.FromText function.

Binary encoding and compression are complex subjects. However, the basic concept is easy enough to explain. Imagine that within a given set of data, the word the appears dozens or even hundreds of times. Instead of storing the word the for each instance, we can instead choose to represent the with the number 1. Thus, we would only need to store a single digit, 1, for each instance of the word the, along with a translation table that mapped the number 1 to the word the.

The Binary.FromText function has two parameters. The first parameter is the text to convert to binary data and the second parameter is the encoding for that text. This second parameter is a BinaryEncoding. Type enumeration and can be either BinaryEncoding.Base64 or BinaryEncoding.Hex.

Once converted to binary data, the binary data is decompressed using the Binary.Decompress function. The Binary.Decompress function has two parameters. The first parameter is the binary data to decompress. The second parameter is the compression type. This second parameter is a Compression. Type enumeration and can have the following values:

- Compression.None
- Compression.Gzip
- Compression.Deflate
- Compression.Snappy

- Compression.Brotli
- Compression.LZ4
- Compression.Zstandard

While an extensive treatment of these difference compression types is beyond the scope of this book, in short, the use of one compression format or another really comes down to whether one values compression ratio versus speed. For example, LZ4 and Snappy compression are much faster than Gzip but produce larger files. On the other hand, Brotli compression was designed for compressing video streams on the fly and actually performs better than Gzip and produces smaller files.

Once the text is decompressed, the `Json.Document` function and `Table.FromRows` functions are used to transform the data into a table of columns and rows.

One might be curious where the long string of numbers and letters comes from. To uncover this, we first need to know exactly what text was compressed and encoded. We can accomplish this using the `Text.FromBinary` function as follows:

```
let
    Source =
        Text.FromBinary(
            Binary.Decompress(
                Binary.FromText(
                    "i45W8s9LVdJRMlSK1YlWCinPB7KNIOyMolSQjLFSbCwA",
                    BinaryEncoding.Base64
                ),
                Compression.Deflate
            )
        )
in
    Source
```

In this code, instead of processing the decompressed binary data using the `Json.Document` and `Table.FromRows` functions, we instead use the `Text.FromBinary` function to return the following text:

```
[["One","1"],["Two","2"],["Three","3"]]
```

The `Text.FromBinary` function has two parameters. The first parameter is the binary data. The second parameter is a `TextEncoding.Type` enumeration. The `TextEncoding.Type` enumeration was covered in the *Text/CSV* section of this chapter.

As seen in the output, in this case, each row is surrounded by square brackets with the values of the columns in the row stored as strings surrounded by double quotes. The column values are separated by commas. Finally, the entire contents are encased in square brackets. We can use this output to recreate the compressed, encoded text seen in the original `Enter Data` query using the following code:

```
let
    Source =
        Binary.ToText(
            Binary.Compress(
                Text.ToBinary(
                    "[[""One"",""1""],[""Two"",""2""],[""Three"",""3""]]",
                    BinaryEncoding.Base64,
                    false
                ),
                Compression.Deflate
            )
        )
in
    Source
```

Note that because the double-quote character is present within a string, we must use two double-quote characters as an escape sequence. This code reverse-engineers how the original compressed and encoded string was created.

First, the Text.ToBinary function coverts the text string to binary. The Text.ToBinary function takes three parameters. The first parameter is the text to convert into binary data. The second parameter is TextEncoding.Type enumeration as covered in the *Text/CSV* section of this chapter. In the referenced code, an encoding type of BinaryEncoding.Base64 is used. The third parameter is the includeByteOrderMark parameter and can be true or false.

Once the text is converted to binary, the Binary.Compress function is used to compress the data. The Binary.Compress function has two parameters, the first of which is the binary data to compress. The second parameter is the Compression.Type enumeration covered earlier in this section.

We can now use the Binary.ToText function to return the compressed, binary-encoded text as text, which results in the following output:

```
i45W8s9LVdJRMlSK1YlWCinPB7KNIOyMolSQjLFSbCwA
```

Here we can see that this is the exact same text that appeared in our original Enter Data query. The Binary.ToText function has two parameters, the binary data and a BinaryEncoding.Type enumeration.

Let's now have a look at an additional class of functions and how they can be used to help us access and retrieve data.

Lines functions

In addition to the Binary family of functions, there are additional functions for dealing with binary data and the content of files such as the following:

- Lines.FromBinary
- Lines.FromText

- `Lines.ToBinary`
- `Lines.ToText`

The `Lines` family of functions convert lists of text to and from single text values or to and from binary data. By default, these functions use the carriage return and line-feed characters as separators.

To see how these functions can be used, consider a file containing multiple JSON documents with one per line, such as:

```
{"Column1": "One",   "Column2": "1"}
{"Column1": "Two",   "Column2": "2"}
{"Column1": "Three", "Column2": "3"}
```

While each line is a JSON document, attempting to parse this file using the `Json.Document` function will fail as the file as a whole is not valid JSON. Luckily, we can use the `Lines.FromBinary` function to help us successfully convert the data in this file into a single table using the following code:

```
let
    Source =
        Table.FromColumns(
            {
            Lines.FromBinary(
                File.Contents(
"C:\data\MultipleJSONDocs.json"), null, null
            )
            }
        ),
    #"Transformed Column" = Table.TransformColumns(Source, {"Column1", Json.
Document}),
    #"Expanded Column1" = Table.ExpandRecordColumn(#"Transformed Column",
"Column1", {"Column1", "Column2"}, {"Column1", "Column2"}),
    #"Changed Type" = Table.TransformColumnTypes(#"Expanded
Column1",{{"Column1", type text}, {"Column2", Int64.Type}})
in
    #"Changed Type"
```

In this code, the `Lines.FromBinary` function is used to read each line of the file and return these lines as a list:

	List
1	{"Column1": "One", "Column2": "1"}
2	{"Column1": "Two", "Column2": "2"}
3	{"Column1": "Three", "Column2": "3"}

Figure 3.11: Output of the Lines.FromBinary function

This list is converted to a single-column table via the `Table.FromColumns` function and then further transformed using the `Json.Document` function to process each row as a JSON document. This is done with the help of the `Table.TransformColumns` function. In this case, the `Json.Document` function returns a record for each row, which we can expand into columns using the `Table.ExpandRecordColumn` function.

This completes our exploration of Binary functions. Additional information on other Binary functions can be found here: `https://powerquery.how/binary-functions/`. Let's now move on to learning how to access databases and cubes.

Accessing databases and cubes

Just as the standard M function library supports many different standard file formats, there are also core functions for accessing a variety of different industry-standard database/cube formats. Here we use the term cube to refer to database systems classified as **Online Analytics Processing (OLAP)** systems. The term database refers to relational databases classified as **Online Transactional Processing (OLTP)** systems. OLAP systems are suited for the multi-dimensional analysis of data while OLTP systems are suited for transactional operations.

OLTP systems tend to use highly normalized data structures that value the efficiency of data storage and speed of write operations over other concerns. Think high-transaction scenarios such as inventory management within a warehouse or retail sales. Conversely, OLAP systems aggregate (de-normalize) historical information and value the speed of read operations and the efficiency of analysis and reporting.

The core M library includes functions for accessing the following types of databases and cubes:

System	Description	M Functions
Microsoft SQL Server	Microsoft's relational database system.	`Sql.Database` `Sql.Databases`
Microsoft Analysis Services	Refers to **SQL Server Analysis Services (SSAS)** and **Azure Analysis Services (AAS)**. Supports both tabular and multidimensional cubes. Tabular cubes use **Data Analysis Expressions (DAX)** for queries and calculations while Multidimensional cubes use **Multidimensional Expressions (MDX)** for the same.	`AnalysisServices.Database` `AnalysisServices.Databases`
Microsoft Access	The relational **Access Database Engine (ACE)**, formerly the Jet database engine.	`Access.Database`

Adobe Analytics cubes	Adobe Experience Cloud's cube analytics service, a leading system for web analytics. Adobe Experience Cloud was formerly known as Adobe Marketing Cloud. Adobe Systems acquired the analytics components of Adobe Experience Cloud from Omniture.	`AdobeAnalytics.Cubes`
IBM DB2	A relational database system developed by IBM.	`DB2.Database`
IBM Informix	A relational database system originally developed by Informix, which was acquired by IBM in 2001.	`Informix.Database`
Oracle Essbase	A multidimensional cube system originally developed by Arbor Software Corporation, which merged with Hyperion Software in 1998. Oracle later acquired Hyperion Solutions Corporation and originally marketed Essbase as DB2 OLAP Server.	`Essbase.Cubes`
Oracle MySQL	MySQL is a free and open-source relational database released under the GNU General Public License in 1995. Originally owned and sponsored by the company MySQL AB, which was acquired by Sun Microsystems, which was itself acquired by Oracle in 2010.	`MySQL.Database`
Oracle Database	Commonly referred to as simply Oracle, Oracle Database is a relational database that supports OLTP and data warehouse workloads.	`Oracle.Database`
PostgreSQL	Also simply known as Postgres, PostgresSQL is a free and open-source relational database originally released in 1996.	`PostgreSQL.Database`
SAP HANA	A column-oriented, in-memory, relational database system developed by SAP.	`SapHana.Database`
SAP Business Warehouse	Originally a relational database, SAP's Business Warehouse later evolved to leverage the SAP HANA in-memory database and provide advanced OLAP functionality.	`SapBusinessWarehouse.Cubes`
SAP Sybase	A relational database system originally created by Sybase and then later acquired by SAP.	`Sybase.Database`
Teradata	Teradata's relational database system.	`Teradata.Database`

Table 3.8: M functions for accessing databases and cubes

As you might expect, the functions ending with `.Database` are generally designed to work with relational databases (OLTP) while those ending with `.Cubes` are for accessing analytics systems (OLAP). The exception is the `AnalysisServices` family of functions.

While there are exceptions, most functions operate similarly and take either two or three parameters. The first parameter is the server parameter, which specifies the connection string for the connection to the database server. If there are three parameters for the function, the second parameter is the database parameter, which specifies the name of the database to access. The last parameter is an options record.

The options available for the options record vary depending on the function. However, common options include the following:

- Query: A SQL, MDX, DAX, or other native query supported by the source system.
- CommandTimeout: Specifies the duration for how long the query is allowed to run before being canceled. This is a duration value and the default is ten minutes.
- ConnectionTimeout: Specifies the duration for how long to attempt a connection before timing out. This is a duration value and the default is dependent on the driver used.
- CreateNavigationProperties: Specifies whether to create navigation properties. Can be either true or false and defaults to true.
- NavigationPropertyNameGenerator: Specifies a function used to create the names for navigation properties.
- HierarchicalNavigation: Specifies whether objects are grouped by their schema name. Can be either true or false and defaults to false.

As an experiment, create the following two queries:

```
let
    Source = Sql.Database("ServerName", "DatabaseName", [HierarchicalNavigation
= false])
in
    Source
```

and

```
let
    Source = Sql.Database("ServerName", "DatabaseName", [HierarchicalNavigation
= true])
in
    Source
```

Replace ServerName and DatabaseName in the code with the actual name of the SQL Server and SQL database. The first query returns a five-column table listing the tables, views, and functions within the database. The columns returned are Name, Data, Schema, Item, and Kind. The second query returns a two-column table listing the schemas within the database. The columns returned are Schema and Data.

In our next example, we utilize the options record to run a native SQL query to return only a few columns and the top 1,000 rows from a specific table:

```
let
    Source =
        Sql.Database(
            "localhost",
            "AdventureWorksDW2019",
            [Query="SELECT TOP (1000) [CustomerKey],[FirstName],[MiddleName]
FROM [AdventureWorksDW2019].[dbo].[DimCustomer]"])
in
    Source
```

Here, we retrieve data from the `dbo.DimCustomer` table of a database called `AdventureWorksDW2019` available on a local SQL Server instance (localhost). The `Query` field is used to run a `SQL SELECT` statement.

The AdventureWorks sample database can be downloaded here: `https://learn.microsoft.com/en-us/sql/samples/adventureworks-install-configure`.

Cube functions

Functions that access cubes have a special family of functions that can be used to transform the data. These functions start with Cube. There are 16 such functions as follows:

- `Cube.AddAndExpandDimensionColumn`
- `Cube.AddMeasureColumn`
- `Cube.ApplyParameter`
- `Cube.AttributeMemberId`
- `Cube.AttributeMemberProperty`
- `Cube.CollapseAndRemoveColumns`
- `Cube.Dimensions`
- `Cube.DisplayFolders`
- `Cube.MeasureProperties`
- `Cube.MeasureProperty`
- `Cube.Measures`
- `Cube.Parameters`
- `Cube.Properties`
- `Cube.PropertyKey`
- `Cube.ReplaceDimensions`
- `Cube.Transform`

When working with cubes in the Power Query editor, a special **Cube Tools | Manage** tab appears in the ribbon. This ribbon exposes an **Add Items** option and a **Collapse Columns** option. The **Add Items** option invokes the Cube.AddAndExpandDimensionColumn function while the **Collapse Columns** option invokes the Cube.CollapseAndRemoveColumns function.

If using the Power Query editor to access a Power BI dataset published in the cloud via Analysis Services, the M code generated looks something like this:

```
let
    Source =
        AnalysisServices.Databases(
            "powerbi://api.powerbi.com/v1.0/<tenant>/<workspace>",
            [TypedMeasureColumns=true, Implementation="2.0"]
        ),
    #"MyCube" = Source{[Name="MyCube"]}[Data],
    Model1 = #"MyCube"{[Id="Model"]}[Data],
    Model2 = Model1{[Id="Model"]}[Data],
    #"Added Items" = Cube.Transform(Model2,
        {
            {
                Cube.AddAndExpandDimensionColumn,
                "[FactInternetSales]",
                {
                    "[FactInternetSales].[CarrierTrackingNumber].
[CarrierTrackingNumber]",
                    "[FactInternetSales].[CurrencyKey].[CurrencyKey]"
                }
            }
        })
in
    #"Added Items"
```

As you can see in the Source line, the AnalysisServices.Database function is used to connect to the workspace. The connection string format for accessing the XMLA endpoint for a workspace takes the following format: power-bi://api.powerbi.com/v1.0/<tenant>/<workspace>

Here, <tenant> is the name of the Microsoft 365 tenant and <workspace> is the name of the Power BI workspace.

The options record for the AnalysisServices.Database function can include options for CommandTimeout and ConnectionTimeout covered previously but can also include the following options:

- TypeMeasureColumn: Specifies whether the types in the cube are used for the types of added measure columns. Can be true or false. The default is false and thus all measure columns added are of type number.

- Culture: Specifies the culture used for the data. This is analogous to the Local Identifier property available in Analysis Services connection strings.
- SubQueries: Controls the behavior of calculated members on subcubes or subselects. Can be 0, 1, or 2 and defaults to 2. This is analogous to the SubQueries property available in Analysis Services connection strings.
- Implementation: Specifies the implementation version.

The next three expressions after the Source expression simply navigate to the desired cube using standard data-accessing syntax described previously. Finally, the Cube.Transform function is used in conjunction with the Cube.AddAndExpandDimensionColumn function to return the desired information from the cube.

Similar to how File.Contents and Web.Contents are base data-accessing functions for files and websites respectively, the Cube.Transform function has a similar role with respect to accessing data from cubes. The Cube.Transform function takes two parameters, the cube to transform and a list of transformations to apply to the cube. In the example code, a single transformation is specified via the Cube.AddAndExpandDimensionColumn function. More information about the Cube family of functions can be found on powerquery.how.

This completes our investigation of data access for databases and cubes. We will next turn our attention to standard data protocols.

Working with standard data protocols

Over the years, a number of standards have been developed to facilitate efficient and seamless communication and data exchange between various platforms and systems. The standard M library provides functions for many of these data-accessing standards including:

Standard	Description	M Functions
ADO.NET	**ADO.NET (ActiveX Data Objects .NET)** is a data access technology in the Microsoft .NET framework that provides a set of libraries and classes for accessing and manipulating data from different data sources, such as databases, XML files, and more. ADO.NET is specifically designed for building data-driven applications and is a fundamental component in the .NET framework for working with relational databases.	AdoDotNet.DataSource AdoDotNet.Query
Delta Lake	Delta Lake is an open-source data storage layer that extends compute engines such as Apache Spark, PrestoDB, and Hive for building scalable, reliable, and performant data lakes. Originally developed by Databricks, Delta Lake provides several advanced features and optimizations to address common data lake challenges and improve data management.	DeltaLake.Table

ODdata	OData, short for Open Data Protocol, is an open standard for querying and updating data over the web. It is a RESTful protocol that allows clients to interact with data resources by using standard HTTP methods, such as `GET`, `POST`, `PUT`, `PATCH`, and `DELETE`. OData is designed to provide a standardized way to expose and access data from various sources, making it easier to create data-driven applications that can consume and interact with data across different platforms and services.	`OData.Feed`
ODBC	ODBC stands for Open Database Connectivity. It is an industry-standard **application programming interface** (**API**) that enables software applications to access and interact with databases using a common interface, regardless of the **database management system** (**DBMS**) being used. ODBC was developed by Microsoft in the early 1990s and has since become a widely adopted standard for database connectivity.	`Odbc.DataSource` `Odbc.InferOptions` `Odbc.Query`
OLE DB	**OLE DB** (short for **Object Linking and Embedding Database**) is a Microsoft technology that provides a data access interface for accessing and manipulating data from various data sources. It is a set of **Component Object Model** (**COM**) interfaces and protocols that enable applications to interact with diverse data sources, including relational databases, spreadsheets, text files, and more. OLE DB was introduced by Microsoft as an evolution of the earlier **ODBC** (**Open Database Connectivity**) technology and is considered a successor to ODBC.	`OleDb.DataSource` `OleDb.Query`
SODA	**Socrata Open Data API** (**SODA**) is an API provided by Socrata (now Tyler Technologies), a company that specializes in data management and open data solutions. The SODA API allows developers to access and interact with datasets published on Socrata's open data portals. These portals are used by various government agencies, non-profit organizations, and businesses to share and make their data publicly accessible.	`Soda.Feed`

Table 3.9: M functions for data-accessing standards

Every Windows computer comes with a number of ODBC drivers. Drivers are software components that act as intermediaries to different database and file formats. Windows comes with ODBC drivers for dBASE files, Excel files, Microsoft Access files, CSV files, SQL Server, and other database systems. Additional ODBC drivers are also available from a wide array of third parties.

There are 32-bit and 64-bit ODBC drivers. You must use the appropriate driver compatible with your application software (64-bit for Power BI Desktop).

To use ODBC, you must first install the appropriate driver on your system. You then create an ODBC **Data Source Name (DSN)** that defines the connection details and settings for a specific data source. This can be done by typing ODBC Data Sources in the Windows search bar. This DSN is then used in the connection string for the ODBC connection:

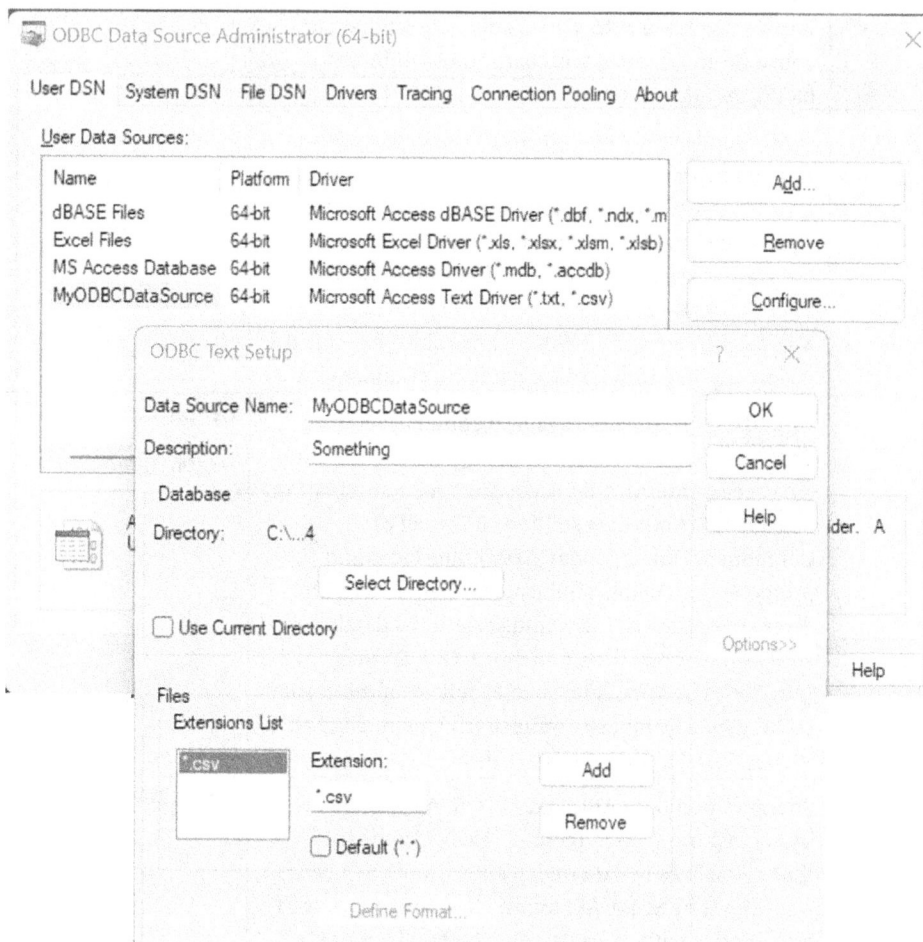

Figure 3.12: ODBC DSN

For example, after setting up a 64-bit DSN called MyODBCDataSource using the Microsoft Access Text Driver to point to the folder for our Atlantic and Pacific Hurricanes 1851-2014 dataset, we can use the following query to retrieve the contents of the atlantic.csv file using ODBC:

```
let
    Source = Odbc.DataSource("dsn=MyODBCDataSource",
[HierarchicalNavigation=true]),
```

```
    #"C:\DATA\ATLANTIC AND PACIFIC HURRICANES 1851-2014_
Database" = Source{[Name="C:\DATA\ATLANTIC AND PACIFIC HURRICANES
1851-2014",Kind="Database"]}[Data],
    atlantic.csv_Table = #"C:\DATA\ATLANTIC AND PACIFIC HURRICANES 1851-2014_
Database"{[Name="atlantic.csv",Kind="Table"]}[Data]
in
    atlantic.csv_Table
```

The data-accessing structures are similar to what we have seen in other examples within this chapter. The `Odbc.DataSource` function supports two parameters, the first being the connection string and the second being an options record. Available options record fields include many of the common database and cube data-accessing function options covered in the *Accessing Databases and Cubes* section of this chapter, including `CreateNavigationProperties`, `HierarchicalNavigation`, `ConnectionTimeout`, and `CommandTimeout`. In addition, there is a logical `true`/`false` field, `SqlCompatibleWindowsAuth`, that specifies if the connection string is compatible with Windows authentication. The default is `true`.

OData is another common and popular data protocol standard. We can retrieve data from an OData endpoint using the following query:

```
let
    Source = OData.Feed("https://services.odata.org/TripPinRESTierService/
People", null, [Implementation="2.0"])
in
    Source
```

Here, the `OData.Feed` function is used to retrieve data from a URI configured for OData. In our case, we are using one of the reference services provided by `odata.org`. The `Odata.Feed` function has three parameters. The first parameter is the connection URI. The second parameter is a headers record (usually `null`). The third parameter is an `options` record. This `options` record supports many of the same fields as the `Web.Contents` function. However, there are many options available that are particular to OData. You can find out more about these options here: https://learn.microsoft.com/en-us/powerquery-m/odata-feed

This completes our exploration of standard data protocols. Let's now take a look at any standard data-accessing functions we may have missed.

Addressing additional connectors

Thus far we have covered most, but not all, of the data-accessing functions available within the standard M library. Note that many more data-accessing functions are available within the global M environment in products such as Power BI Desktop. These additional data-accessing functions provide the ability to connect to a wide variety of specialized business systems such as **customer relationship management (CRM)** systems, **enterprise resource management (ERP)** systems, and others. These additional data-accessing functions come from external connectors included with Power BI Desktop.

External connectors are covered in *Chapter 16, Enabling Extensions*. A full list of data-accessing functions available in the global environment for Power BI Desktop can be found here: `https://powerquery.how/accessing-data-functions/`

Let's briefly address the remaining data access functions available in the standard M library. These generally fall into two categories, popular software systems and identity functions.\

Popular software systems

The standard M function library includes several functions for connecting to popular software systems such as the following:

System	Description	M Functions
Microsoft Active Directory	**Active Directory** (**AD**) is a directory service developed by Microsoft that is used primarily in Windows-based networks to manage and organize resources such as users, computers, printers, and other network objects. It provides a centralized database that stores information about network resources and allows administrators to control and manage access to these resources within a domain environment.	`ActiveDirectory.Domains`
Microsoft Exchange	Microsoft Exchange is a popular and widely used email server and calendaring software developed by Microsoft. It is part of the Microsoft Office family of products and is designed to provide email communication, calendar scheduling, and collaboration capabilities for businesses and organizations.	`Exchange.Contents`
Microsoft SharePoint	Microsoft SharePoint is a web-based collaborative platform and content management system developed by Microsoft. It is part of the Microsoft 365 (formerly known as Office 365) suite of productivity tools and is designed to facilitate teamwork, content sharing, and document management within organizations.	`SharePoint.Contents`, `SharePoint.Files`, `SharePoint.Tables`
Salesforce	Salesforce is a leading cloud-based CRM platform developed by Salesforce.com, Inc. It is designed to help businesses of all sizes manage their customer relationships, sales processes, marketing efforts, and customer service interactions more efficiently and effectively.	`Salesforce.Data`, `Salesforce.Reports`

Table 3.10: M functions fro connecting to software systems

The use of these data-accessing functions is generally fairly straightforward. For example, the following query will return all of the contacts for a mailbox from Exchange Online:

```
let
    Source = Exchange.Contents("user@company.com"),
    People1 = Source{[Name="People"]}[Data]
in
    People1
```

The SharePoint family of functions deserves some clarification. Consider the following query:

```
let
    Source = SharePoint.Files("https://<tenant>.sharepoint.com/<site>/",
[ApiVersion = 15])
in
    Source
```

This query uses the `SharePoint.Files` function and returns a table in the same format as the `Folder.Contents` functions. Every file within the specified site, regardless of document library, is included in the table.

Conversely, consider the following query:

```
let
    Source = SharePoint.Contents("https://<tenant>.sharepoint.com/<site>/",
[ApiVersion = 15])
in
    Source
```

This query uses the `SharePoint.Contents` function and also returns a table in the same format as the `Folder.Contents` function. However, individual document libraries are returned as rows. Thus, you can navigate to the folders and files contained within a specific document library by clicking on the `Table` link in the `Content` column. Both folders and files are returned as rows.

Finally, consider this query:

```
let
    Source = SharePoint.Tables("https://<tenant>.sharepoint.com/<site>/",
[ApiVersion = 15])
in
    Source
```

This query uses the `SharePoint.Tables` function. This function returns a table where each row is a list or document library within the specified SharePoint site. The table has three columns, `Id`, `Title`, and `Items`. The `Id` column is a unique identifier, the `Title` column contains the name of the list or document library, and the `Items` column contains a `Table` object that can be navigated into in order to list the individual items within the list or document library.

Identity functions

The standard M library includes a few functions related to handling identity. These functions are not generally used by users but rather classified as helper functions for internal implementation within the M engine. These functions include the following:

- `GoogleAnalytics.Accounts`: Returns Google Analytics accounts available with the current credential.
- `Identity.From`: Creates an identity given an identity provider as a function and a value.
- `Identity.IsMemberOf`: Returns `true` or `false` depending on whether a specified identity is a member of an identity collection specified as a record.
- `IdentityProvider.Default`: Returns the default identity provider for the current host.

Even advanced M users will seldom ever encounter a use case for these functions. More information about these functions can be found on `powerquery.how`.

We have now covered all of the data-accessing functions available in the standard M function library. We will now turn our attention to some basic data transformation functions that allow us to combine and merge data from multiple sources.

Combining and joining data

Thus far, we have been focused on accessing and retrieving data from individual data sources with minimal data transformation. However, in addition to accessing data, one of the strengths of the M language is the ability to transform and combine that data. This provides the ability to combine data from multiple sources together such as merging inventory data with sales data or combining customer data from multiple CRM systems. Therefore, we will briefly cover five basic functions that allow us to combine and merge our data together. These five functions are:

- `Table.Combine`
- `Table.NestedJoin`
- `Table.Join`
- `Table.FuzzyNestedJoin`
- `Table.FuzzyJoin`

As you read this section, it will be helpful to reference *Rick de Groot's Join Types Cheat Sheet*, which can be found here: `https://gorilla.bi/power-query/join-types/`. For ease of reference, the cheat sheet is included here:

Join Types - Cheat Sheet   BI GORILLA

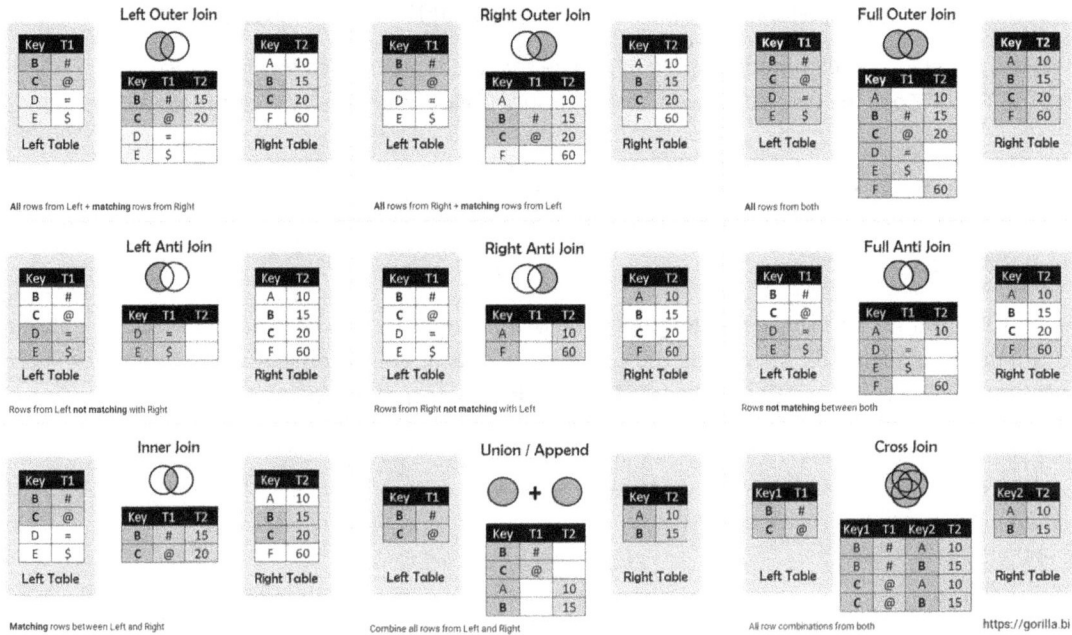

Figure 3.13: Output of Table.NestedJoin function

Let's start with the `Table.Combine` function.

Table.Combine

The `Table.Combine` function appends or unions two or more tables together. Explore the `Atlantic.pdf` file included in the `Atlantic and Pacific Hurricanes 1851-2014.zip` file included in the GitHub repository for this book. If you have not done so already, download the `Atlantic and Pacific Hurricanes 1851-2014.zip` file and extract the four files included in the `.zip` file to a single folder on your local computer. There are two CSV files, `atlantic.csv` and `pacific.csv`, along with two PDF files, `atlantic.pdf` and `pacific.pdf`.

Once you have downloaded and extracted the PDF files, follow these steps:

1. In the Power Query editor, click the **New Source** button on the **Home** tab of the ribbon and choose **More...**

2. In the **Get Data** dialog, choose **PDF** and press the **Connect** button.

3. Use the **File Explorer** window to navigate to the folder where you extracted the files contained in `Atlantic and Pacific Hurricanes 1851-2014.zip`.

4. Select the `atlantic.pdf` file and press the **OK** button.

5. In the **Navigator** dialog, select the **Table001 (Page 1)** and **Table002 (Page 2)** items and then press the **OK** button.

6. Rename these queries to `atlanticPDFTable1` and `atlanticPDFTable2` respectively.

Because the `PDF.Tables` function failed to realize that the table in question spans two pages, we can use the `Table.Combine` function to correct this issue. Create a new query with the following code:

```
let
    Source = Table.Combine( {atlanticPDFTable1, atlanticPDFTable2})
in
    Source
```

As shown, the `Table.Combine` function takes a list of tables as its first parameter. A second, optional parameter is available for specifying the columns to return. For example, this version of the query only returns one column, `Column1`, instead of 17 columns as in the original:

```
let
    Source = Table.Combine( {atlanticPDFTable1, atlanticPDFTable2},
{"Column1"})
in
    Source
```

Rename this query to `atlanticPDFTableCombined`.

Let's now look at merging tables.

Table.NestedJoin and Table.Join

The `Table.NestedJoin` and `Table.Join` functions merge or join tables together. These two functions are similar to one another but have certain nuances. Merging tables together can help aid in data analysis, such as enriching a customer table with geographic information from a geography table or enriching a sales table with customer demographic information.

Continuing with our last example, from the *Table.Combine* section, first rename `Column1` in the output of the `atlanticPDFTableCombined` query to `Column0`. Next, create the following two queries:

```
let
    Source = Table.NestedJoin(atlanticPDFTableCombined, {"Column0"},
atlanticPDFTable1, {"Column1"}, "atlanticPDFTable1", JoinKind.LeftOuter)
in
    Source
```

and

```
let
    Source = Table.Join(atlanticPDFTableCombined, {"Column0"},
atlanticPDFTable1, {"Column1"}, JoinKind.LeftOuter)
```

```
in

    Source
```

One can immediately see the major difference between these functions in the output of these two queries. The first query returns a two-column table with column headers of Column0 and atlanticPDFTable1 as shown in *Figure 3.14*:

$^{AB}_C$ Column0	atlanticPDFTable1
1	AL092011,	Table
2	20110821, 0000,	Table
3	20110821, 0600,	Table
4	20110821, 1200,	Table
5	20110821, 1800,	Table
6	20110822, 0000,	Table
7	20110822, 0600,	Table
8	20110822, 1200,	Table
9	20110822, 1800,	Table
10	20110823, 0000,	Table

Figure 3.14: Output of Table.NestedJoin function

The atlanticPDFTable1 column contains Table values. This column can be expanded to only the particular columns desired using the divergent arrows in the column header.

Conversely, the second query returns a table with Column0 from the atlanticPDFTableCombined query as well as all the columns from the atlanticPDFTable1 query as shown in *Figure 3.15*:

$^{AB}_C$ Column0	$^{AB}_C$ Column1	$^{AB}_C$ Column2	$^{AB}_C$ Column3	1^2_3 Column4	1^2_3 Co
1	AL092011,	AL092011,	IRENE,	39,	null	
2	20110821, 0000,	20110821, 0000,	, TS, 15.0N,	59.0W,	45	
3	20110821, 0600,	20110821, 0600,	, TS, 16.0N,	60.6W,	45	
4	20110821, 1200,	20110821, 1200,	, TS, 16.8N,	62.2W,	45	
5	20110821, 1800,	20110821, 1800,	, TS, 17.5N,	63.7W,	50	
6	20110822, 0000,	20110822, 0000,	, TS, 17.9N,	65.0W,	60	
7	20110822, 0600,	20110822, 0600,	, HU, 18.2N,	65.9W,	65	
8	20110822, 1200,	20110822, 1200,	, HU, 18.9N,	67.0W,	70	
9	20110822, 1800,	20110822, 1800,	, HU, 19.3N,	68.0W,	75	
10	20110823, 0000,	20110823, 0000,	, HU, 19.7N,	68.8W,	80	

Figure 3.15: Output of Table.Join function

Both functions perform what is known as a join where a key column from both tables is selected and these key columns are compared to find matching rows. The tables and key columns are the first four parameters to both the Table.NestedJoin and Table.Join functions. The first parameter is the "left" table and the third parameter is the "right" table. Note that the key columns (second and fourth parameters) are specified as a list.

This means that the merge can occur on multiple columns versus just a single column. Also, it is worth noting that the join columns should be the same data type such as text, numbers, or dates, for example.

The fifth parameter of the `Table.NestedJoin` function is the name of the column to store the `Table` values (matching rows from the join operation). The fifth parameter of the `Table.Join` function is the type of join to perform, `joinKind`. This is also the sixth parameter of the `Table.NestedJoin` function.

The `JoinKind` parameter uses the `JoinKind.Type` enumeration. This enumeration can have the following values:

Friendly Name	Value	Comments
JoinKind.Inner	0	Only matching rows returned.
JoinKind.LeftOuter	1	All rows from the left table, only matching rows from the right table. This is the default.
JoinKind.RightOuter	2	All rows from the right table, only matching rows from the left table.
JoinKind.FullOuter	3	All rows from both tables returned. Unmatched rows have null values for columns.
JoinKind.LeftAnti	4	All rows from the left table that do not match any rows in the right table.
JoinKind.RightAnti	5	All rows from the right table that do not match any rows in the left table.

Table 3.11: joinKind enumerations

Anyone familiar with SQL will be familiar with these types of joins.

The sixth parameter of the `Table.Join` function is the `JoinAlgorithm` parameter. This parameter allows you to specify the algorithm used during the join process. This parameter takes a `JoinAlgorithm.Type` enumeration that can have the following values:

Friendly Name	Value	Comments
JoinAlgorithm.Dynamic	0	Automatically determine the join algorithm to use. This is the default.
JoinAlgorithm.PairwiseHash	1	Recommended for small tables only. Buffers both tables until one of the tables is completely buffered. Depending on which table was buffered, it performs a `LeftHash` or `RightHash`.
JoinAlgorithm.SortMerge	2	Assumes both tables are sorted by their join key columns. Performs a streaming merge, which is extremely fast but returns incorrect results if the tables are not sorted as expected.

`JoinAlgorithm.LeftHash`	3	Buffers the left table rows. Performs a streaming merge for the right-table rows. Recommended when the left table is small and most right-table rows match.
		Consider this algorithm for merging fact tables and dimension tables when the dimension table is the left table.
`JoinAlgorithm.RightHash`	4	Buffers the right-table rows. Performs a streaming merge for the left-table rows. Recommended when the right table is small and most left-table rows match.
		Consider this algorithm for merging fact tables and dimension tables when the dimension table is the right table.
`JoinAlgorithm.LeftIndex`	5	Operates in batches using the keys from the left table to query the right table. Recommended when the right table is large with few expected matches.
`JoinAlgorithm.RightIndex`	6	Operates in batches using the keys from the right table to query the left table. Recommended when the left table is large with few expected matches.

Table 3.12: JoinKind enumerations

Using the `JoinAlgorithm.SortMerge` algorithm can dramatically speed up merge operations (by orders of magnitude). However, you must be careful that your tables are, in fact, sorted correctly or you will get incorrect results. In our case, we can use `SortMerge` with our example as follows:

```
let
    Source = Table.Join(atlanticPDFTableCombined, {"Column0"},
atlanticPDFTable1, {"Column1"}, JoinKind.LeftOuter, JoinAlgorithm.SortMerge)
in
    Source
```

Finally, both functions have a seventh parameter, `keyEqualityComparers`, that is intended only for internal use.

It is important to know that when performing the join or merge, both functions require that the key columns exactly match one another. However, M does provide join functions where that is not necessarily the case so let's look at those next.

Table.FuzzyNestedJoin and Table.FuzzyJoin

As indicated, the `Table.FuzzyNestedJoin` and `Table.FuzzyJoin` functions allow the merging or joining of tables even when the key values in both tables are not an exact match. This is known as fuzzy matching.

The parameters for both of these functions are analogous to their non-fuzzy counterparts, `Table.NestedJoin` and `Table.Join`, with the exception that `Table.FuzzyJoin` does not support the `joinAlgorithm` parameter.

The algorithm used by Power Query to measure the similarity between pairs is called the Jaccard similarity algorithm. The Jaccard similarity algorithm simply takes the number of items that occur in both pairs (the intersection or inner join) and divides this by the total number of items in both pairs (the union). This produces a number between 0 and 1 with 0 indicating no items in common (less similar) and 1 indicating that both pairs have the same items in common (more similar).

The last parameter for each function is the `joinOptions` parameter. The `joinOptions` parameter is an options record for controlling the fuzzy matching criteria used to join the tables. This record can contain the following fields:

- `ConcurrentRequests`: Defaults to 1. Specifies the number of parallel threads to use for fuzzy matching. Can be a number between 1 and 8.
- `Culture`: Defaults to `""`, which is invariant English culture. If specified, can match rows based on culture-specific rules. Cultures are specified via the ISO 639 standard such as `ja-JP`, `en-US`, `en-UK`.
- `IgnoreCase`: Can be `true` or `false` and defaults to `true`. Ignores the case of letters when matching, so grapes, "Grapes", "gRapes", "GrApEs", and "grapeS" would all match.
- `IgnoreSpace`: Can be `true` or `false` and defaults to `true`. Permits the combining of text parts to find matches. For example, "grapes", "gra pes", and "grape s" would all match.
- `NumberOfMatches`: Defaults to all matching rows. Specifies a whole number representing the maximum number of matching rows returned.
- `SimilarityColumnName`: Specifies a name for a column that returns the calculated similarity of the matched rows. The similarity of matched rows is calculated as a value between `0.00` and `1.00`. Defaults to `null`, meaning that no such column is returned. Rows with a similarity above the specified `Threshold` option are considered matching rows.
- `Threshold`: A decimal number between the values of `0.00` and `1.00`. Defaults to `0.80`. Specifies the threshold for matching rows based upon the fuzzy matching algorithm.
- `TransformationTable`: A table with a `From` column and `To` column. Allows matching rows to be determined based on this custom mapping table. For example, a transformation table that includes a row with grapes and raisins will match rows where key columns hold values of grapes and raisins or grapes are yummy and raisins are yummy.

This completes our exploration of data-accessing functions as well as combining and joining data.

Summary

The standard M function library contains a plethora of functions designed to facilitate data access and retrieval from a wide array of different systems and data storage formats. In addition, the M language also provides functions for combining and joining data together. Practical examples were included throughout this chapter to allow the reader to experiment with and visualize the output from these functions.

In this chapter, we explored data-accessing functions for a variety of file formats, folders, web content, databases, cubes, and standard data protocols such as OData and ODBC. We also covered a variety of binary functions, identity functions, and specialized functions for accessing popular software systems such as Microsoft Exchange and Microsoft SharePoint. Finally, we explored five functions for combining and joining data, including the ability to perform fuzzy matching when joining tables.

In the next chapter, we continue to explore the M language by seeking to understand values and expressions in greater detail.

Learn more on Discord

Join our community's Discord space for discussions with the author and other readers:

```
https://discord.gg/vCSG5GBbyS
```

4

Understanding Values and Expressions

Now that we have covered an overview of M, reviewed the elements of the Power Query **user interface (UI)**, and discussed how to access and combine our data, we are ready to dive into the specific components of the M language. Values comprise the first component, following naturally from our previous chapter since every time you ingest files into Power Query, each of the individual elements of data is a value.

If you think of Power Query and M as the lab where you go to clean and shape your data so that it's well-prepped for data modeling and reporting, then values are the atoms of M code – the smallest single units. These values are combined to form expressions, making them the molecules of our lab. One or more expressions can be integrated to form the extremely powerful compounds (i.e., queries) that allow you to transform your data in an infinite number of ways.

In this chapter, we closely examine these values, looking at all the different kinds you will encounter, and how the kind of value directly affects what you can (and can't) do with it. We also look at the basic structure of expressions and queries, as well as the bonds that tie values together within expressions – operators and control structures.

This chapter covers all of the different kinds of values, including key issues to watch out for when working with each kind of value. We also delve into how operators and control structures are used to combine values into expressions and queries, and, finally, how enumerators are used to define how certain function values operate.

This chapter covers the following topics:

- Introducing the types of values
- Expressions
- Operators
- Control structures
- Enumerators

Let's start by taking a closer look at values in M.

Introducing the types of values

The M language recognizes 15 different kinds of values, spread across the following categories:

- **Primitive values**: Individual data elements that M treats as a single unit for purposes of processing and operations. In the DAX context, these are referred to as scalar values.

- **Structured values**: These can hold multiple values with a specific structure, although it is possible that a given structured value only holds a single value or no values at all. The three kinds of structured values are lists, records, and tables, which will be covered in detail in *Chapter 6, Structured Values*. Structured values that hold other structured values (also referred to as nested structures) will be addressed in depth in *Chapter 8, Working with Nested Structures*.

- **Function values**: A function is a value that represents a mapping from a set of argument values to a single value. The M language includes over 700 defined functions, and users have the ability to develop custom functions of their own that can be reused and applied across multiple queries. The development of custom functions will be covered in *Chapter 9, Parameters and Custom Functions*.

- **Type values**: These can be thought of as meta values that provide information about the data type of another value. The classification of values into their appropriate data type is a process covered extensively in *Chapter 5, Understanding Data Types*.

The following table provides a brief summary of each of the 15 recognized values across these four groups. Additional information can be found throughout the rest of this chapter as well as in *Chapters 5, 6, 8,* and *9*. Note that the term **literal** refers to the textual representation of a value as it is written in a programming language.

Kind	Literal	Description
Primitive		
Date	`#date( 2023, 12, 29 )`	Date values are specified in the format: `#date(year, month, day)`.
Binary	`#binary( "QRST" )`	Binary data is represented as a sequence of byte values, which are most frequently used in ingesting web content, multimedia content, and for custom connectors.
DateTime	`#datetime( 2023, 11, 26, 24, 59, 01 )`	Date values are specified in the format: `#datetime( year, month, day, hours, minutes, seconds )`.
DateTimeZone	`#datetimezone( 2023, 11, 26, 24, 59, 1, 08, 00)`	Date values are specified in the format: `#datetime( year, month, day, hours, minutes, seconds, offset hours, offset minutes )`.

Duration	`#duration( 1, 5, 30, 0 )`	Duration values represent a specific period, defined as `#duration(days, hours, minutes, seconds)`.
Logical	`true false`	One of two truth values, `true` or `false`, typically used in comparisons and conditions.
Null	`null`	An unknown or missing value is denoted by `null`.
Number	`-1 0 1 1.5 2.3e-5`	Numerical values can be integers or decimals.
Text	`"Canada"`	Textual data is represented within double quotes.
Time	`#time( 23, 59, 15 )`	Time values are specified in the format: `#time( hours, minutes, seconds)`.
Structured values		
List	`{ 1, 2, 3 }`	A sequence of values defined in curly brackets.
Record	`[ A = 2023, B = "Argentina" ]`	A collection of named values bundled in square brackets.
Table	`#table( { "a", "b"}, {{1,2},{3,4}})`	A collection of rows, where each row is a record.
Function Values		
Function	`(x) => x * 2`	An expression that takes one or more input values and returns a value.
Type values		
Type	`type date, type table`	Types are used to classify values based on their kind.

Table 4.1: Kinds of values in M

Each of the 15 kinds of values is uniquely structured, has different uses, and works with different M code functions. In addition to addressing these characteristics for each kind of value, this section will also highlight the subtle issues related to each value kind that can derail you if you are not aware of them.

Now that you've been introduced to the kinds of values you will encounter in M, we're going to explore them each in more detail.

Binary values

Binary values are those that are stored as bytes (sequences of zeros and ones). These are typically specific program-readable files, such as images. Power Query processes binary data in three primary use cases:

- Ingestion of local data (via the `File.Contents` function)
- Ingestion of data from the web (via the `Web.Contents` function)
- Ingestion of data through custom connectors

In addition, when values are input by the user via the **Enter Data** button, they are converted to binary in the process of storing those values. For example, if we input the following data manually using the **Enter Data** option, the data is converted to binary and then encoded into text:

	A^B_C Author	A^B_C Country
1	Brian	USA
2	Greg	USA
3	Melissa	NED
4	Rick	NED

```
let
    Source = Table.FromRows(Json.Document(Binary.Decompress(Binary.FromText
        ("i45WcirKTMxT0lEKDXZUitWJVnIvSk1H4vqm5mQWFycCRfxcXcAiQZnJ2TBuLAA=", BinaryEncoding.Base64),
        Compression.Deflate)), let _t = ((type nullable text) meta [Serialized.Text = true]) in type table [Author
        = _t, Country = _t])
in
    Source
```

Figure 4.1: Creation of binary value via the Enter Data option

Additional details regarding this process are found in *Chapter 3, Accessing and Combining Data*.

Structure

The following code creates a binary value from a list of numbers or a Base64-encoded text value:

```
#binary( value as any ) as any
```

The two examples shown in the following screenshot will both produce the same binary value:

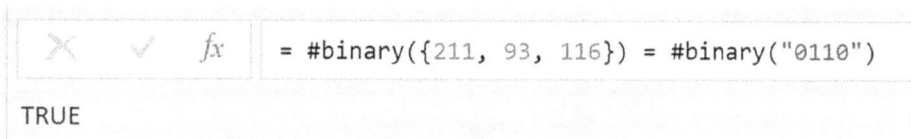

```
fx   = #binary({211, 93, 116}) = #binary("0110")
```

TRUE

Figure 4.2: Direct creation of a binary value from text and list of numbers

Related functions

There are 40 related binary functions, spanning the following seven categories:

- **Buffering and compression:** The functions buffer binary values into memory and compress and decompress binary values.
- **Byte ordering:** This function specifies the byte ordering of a binary value.
- **Creation and conversion:** These functions create and covert binary values to and from other kinds of values.
- **Informational:** These functions return information on the length and inferred content type of binary values.

- **Reading:** This category represents over half of the total related binary functions and specifies how different binary values should be read
- **Transforming:** These functions combine, split, and extract specified portions of binary values
- **Viewing:** These functions are used to create and manipulate views of binary data without modifying the underlying binary content

Special considerations

A special consideration when creating binary values is the unique data structure. Images, text, numerical data, and many other types of data can be handled as binary data within M. Understanding how each of these different kinds of values is structured, coded, and encoded is essential for working successfully with binary values.

The use of binary values in custom connectors is addressed in *Chapter 16, Enabling Extensions*, while the role of binary values and functions in the ingestion of local and web data is expanded upon in *Chapter 3, Accessing and Combining Data*.

The Date/Time family of values

Many of the data values you will come across are connected to specific moments in time. Whether you're analyzing patterns in product sales, improvements in the capabilities of AI models, changes in storm intensity, or Olympic 100-meter dash results, knowing when these events occur is highly relevant. Therefore, this group of values, which helps us understand when something happened, is one of the most significant and commonly encountered types of data in M.

Additionally, skilfully handling these values is an important skill for Power BI developers, since any analysis with a temporal element requires a `Date/Calendar` table within your Power BI data model. If you're not getting this table from a data warehouse or another source, creating it in Power Query using M is highly recommended. This approach is considered a best practice. For a deep dive into working with dates, times, and durations, including advanced topics such as temporal data analysis, be sure to check out *Chapter 10, Dealing with Dates, Times, and Durations*.

Because these functions all help characterize the temporal aspect of your data, we address the `Date`, `Time`, `DateTime`, `DateTimeZone`, and `Duration` values together in this section. However, the discussion of computations involving `Date`, `Time`, `DateTime`, `DateTimeZone`, and `Duration` values can be found in the subsequent section dealing with operations.

Date values

Dates are often the most detailed level at which data are gathered. Therefore, if you understand how Power Query handles dates and learn how to adjust them using M, you'll find it easier to handle the other types of values in this category. This is because many of the same general concepts and patterns carry over to the others.

Structure

Date values can be created using the following structure:

```
#date(
    year as number,
    month as number,
    day as number,
) as date
```

The inputs have the following additional restrictions or the expression will return an error:

```
1 ≤ year ≤ 9999
1 ≤ month ≤ 12
1 ≤ day ≤ 31
```

The #date literal expression is case-sensitive with no alternate specifications – thus, #Date and #DATE will return errors.

An example of this is #date(2023, 11, 1), which returns a value representing November 1, 2023.

Related functions

There are nearly 60 functions that aid in manipulating Date values. Broadly, these fall into the following categories:

- Date.Add functions (e.g., Date.AddMonths): These functions accept a Date, DateTime, or DateTimeZone value, and a number, and add the specified number of time periods to the original value. Note that the number can be negative, to move backward in time.

- Date.Component functions: These accept any kind of date value and return the specified component as a number (e.g., Date.Month) or a text value (e.g., Date.MonthName).

- Date.Start and Date.End functions (e.g., Date.EndOfMonth): These functions accept a Date, DateTime, or DateTimeZone value and return the same value kind for the date that fulfills the function. For example, using our previous example, Date.EndOfMonth(#date(2023, 11, 1)) returns November 30, 2024.

- Date.IsIn functions (e.g., Date.IsInPreviousYear): These functions accept a Date, DateTime, or DateTimeZone value and provide a true or false outcome. The relevant DateTime component, used to evaluate the logical value of the expression, is based on the system value at the date/time of evaluation. For example, consider evaluating the function Date.IsInPreviousYear(# date(2023, 11, 1)) on August 1, 2023. This function checks if the provided date, November 1, 2023, falls in the previous year, that is, 2022. Since the date is in 2023 and not 2022, the function returns false.

- Date.To and Date.From functions: These functions transform a Date value to another kind of value or extract a date value from a different value type. For instance, the function Date.ToText(#date(2023, 11, 1)) returns 11/1/2023 on my computer, reflecting the default local settings for the date format. The influence of local settings, including how the culture parameter affects such conversions, is thoroughly explored in *Chapter 5, Understanding Data Types*.

The Date.ToText function also includes an optional format parameter that allows you to specify the format of the output. So, while Date.ToText(# date(2023, 11, 1)) returned 11/1/2023, Date.ToText(# date(2023, 11, 1), [Format="dd MMM yyyy"]) returns 1 Nov 2023. Additional information on this function and other date functions can be found in *Chapter 10, Dealing with Dates, Times, and Durations*.

Special considerations

A special consideration when using Date values is the date system in Power Query. Though the #date(year, month, day) structure is the primary way to specify dates in Power Query, it is very helpful to know the underlying date system that Power Query (in both Excel and Power BI Desktop) uses. Dates are computed as whole numbers representing the total number of days elapsed from December 30, 1899.

This comes in handy for functions that won't accept dates as inputs but will accept numbers. For example, the list generation expression using the A..B form, which will be discussed in detail in *Chapter 6*, will return an error if you enter the inputs as dates directly. Yet, as shown in the following screenshot, if you first transform the date inputs to their underlying serial numbers, evaluate the expression using whole numbers, and then transform the resulting list back to dates, it works perfectly:

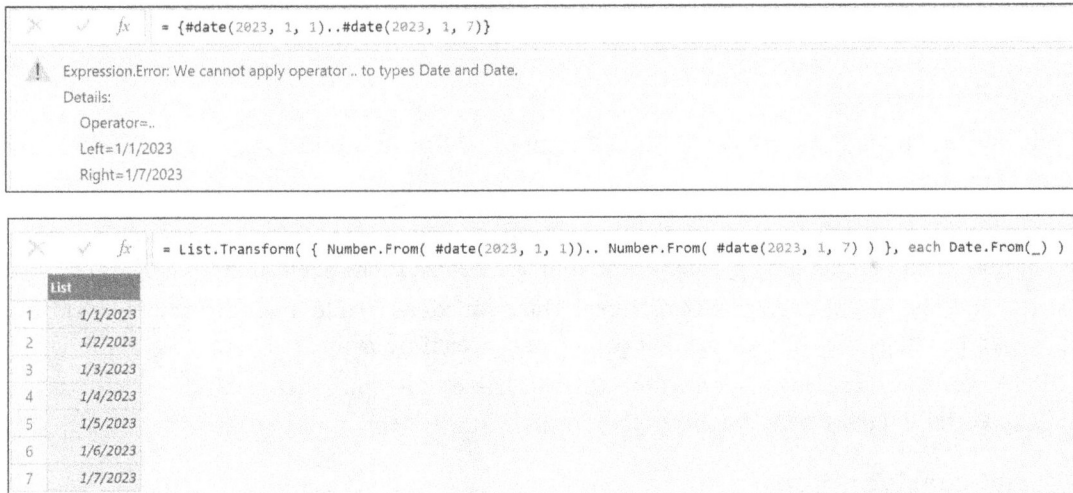

```
fx    = {#date(2023, 1, 1)..#date(2023, 1, 7)}
```
Expression.Error: We cannot apply operator .. to types Date and Date.
Details:
    Operator=..
    Left=1/1/2023
    Right=1/7/2023

```
fx    = List.Transform( { Number.From( #date(2023, 1, 1)).. Number.From( #date(2023, 1, 7) ) }, each Date.From(_) )
```

	List
1	1/1/2023
2	1/2/2023
3	1/3/2023
4	1/4/2023
5	1/5/2023
6	1/6/2023
7	1/7/2023

Figure 4.3: Transforming a date to its underlying serial number prior to generating a list

This concludes our overview of Date values, but advanced concepts and applications involving the Date/Time family of values will be covered in much greater detail in *Chapter 10, Dealing with Dates, Times, and Durations*.

Time values

Time values in M represent a particular point in a day, expressed using a 24-hour cycle. Here, we present some of the basics of time values. More information can be found in *Chapter 10, Dealing with Dates, Times, and Durations*.

Structure

Time values can be created using the following structure:

```
#time(
  hour as number,
  minute as number,
  second as number,
) as date
```

The inputs have the following restrictions or the expression will return an error:

- 0 ≤ hour ≤ 24
- 0 ≤ minute ≤ 59
- 0 ≤ second < 60

If the value of hour is 24, then the value of both minute and second must be 0. Also, as with the #date literal expression, the #time expression is case-sensitive. Some examples of this are as follows:

```
#time( 7, 23, 30)  // returns 7:23:30 AM
#time(23, 59, 59)  // returns 11:59:59 PM
#time(24, 0, 0)    // returns 12:00:00 AM
```

Related functions

While the date family has nearly 60 related functions, M has only 9 time functions, which fall into three categories:

- Time.To and Time.From functions: These functions allow you to convert a time value to a record or text value, and extract time values from other appropriate value kinds.
- Time.EndOfHour and TimeStartOfHour: These functions enable you to determine the starting and ending times of the hour component of a given time value.
- Time.Hour, Time.Minute, and Time.Second: These allow you to extract the hour, minute, and second components as number values from a time value.

Special considerations

The following are some special considerations when working with Time values:

- **Location awareness:** #time does not include any information about the time zone. If you need to express time relative to location, #datetimezone should be used instead, and, if necessary, the time component can be extracted from that value.
- **Precision:** Power Query supports tracking and computing time values down to the microsecond level (millionth of a second), but it is unlikely that users will ever need a level of precision greater than the millisecond level.

DateTime values

DateTime values represent the concatenation of Date and Time values. Basic information about DateTime values is presented here, with more information in *Chapter 10, Dealing with Dates, Times, and Durations*.

Structure

DateTime values can be created using the following structure:

```
#datetime(
    year as number,
    month as number,
    day as number,
    hour as number,
    minute as number,
    second as number
) as datetime
```

The inputs have the following additional restrictions or the expression will return an error:

- 1 ≤ year ≤ 9999
- 1 ≤ month ≤ 12
- 1 ≤ day ≤ 31
- 0 ≤ hour ≤ 23
- 0 ≤ minute ≤ 59
- 0 ≤ second < 60

Also, as with the #date literal expression, the #datetime expression is case-sensitive.

The following example returns a value of 11/1/23 7:15:00 AM:

```
#datetime( 2023, 11, 1, 7, 15, 0 )
```

Related functions

There are 25 functions related to DateTime, most of which mirror the Component, IsIn, and To/From categories of the #date functions. However, there are also three DateTime functions that have no analog in the #date-related functions.

- DateTime.LocalNow and DateTime.FixedLocalNow: Both functions return a datetime value set to the current date and time on the system. The difference is that the former can change over the course of the execution of an expression, while the latter remains constant.

  An important point to note is that these functions return the datetime value associated with the system on which the query is executed. This means if your dataset is refreshed in Australia but you're in Canada, the function will yield the time in Australia. If you want to return the time in Canada, you will need to add a time zone offset to adjust the time to account for the time zone difference.

- `DateTime.AddZone`: This function takes a valid #datetime value, an hour value, and a nullable minutes value as input and returns a #datetimezone value, in order to add a locational element to the #datetime value to adjust for local time and/or daylight savings time.

Special considerations

`DateTime` values should be used cautiously and only when absolutely necessary since they have two major disadvantages relative to `Date` and `Time` values:

- The use of `datetime` values can dramatically increase the cardinality of the columns containing them, which can blow up the file size needed to store all of those distinct values, as well as negatively impact performance and memory usage. In most cases, a better practice will be to split the `datetime` into separate `date` and `time` fields, with each joined in a one-to-many relationship with separate `Date` and `Time` tables in the Power BI (or Excel) data models.
- `DateTime` values do not contain information regarding time zones. This means that if you are comparing `datetime` values across locations, you will need to take the time zone difference into account.

DateTimeZone values

`DateTimeZone` values are very similar to `DateTime`, with the only difference being that they include a time zone offset value expressed in hours and optional minutes, which represents the difference between the local time and **Coordinated Universal Time (UTC)**.

UTC is the worldwide standard, based on atomic time and used for navigation and scientific time measurements. It replaced the prior standard, `Greenwich Mean Time`, and all time zones can be expressed as an offset from UTC. *Chapter 10, Dealing with Dates, Times, and Durations*, contains additional information on `DateTimeZone` values.

Structure

`DateTimeZone` values can be created using the following structure:

```
#datetimezone(
  year as number,
  month as number,
  day as number,
  hour as number,
  minute as number,
  second as number,
  offsetHours as number,
  offsetMinutes as nullable number,
) as datetimezone
```

The inputs have the following additional restrictions or the expression will return an error:

- $1 \leq year \leq 9999$
- $1 \leq month \leq 12$

- $1 \le day \le 31$
- $0 \le hour \le 23$
- $0 \le minute \le 59$
- $0 \le second < 60$
- $-14 \le$ offset-hours + offset-minutes $/ 60 \le 14$

Also, as with the #datetime literal expression, the #datetimezone expression is case-sensitive.

The following code returns the value of 11/1/2023 7:15:00 AM -05:00: #datetimezone(2023, 11, 1, 7, 15, 0, -5, 0)

Related functions

Power Query has 15 DateTimeZone functions, most of which mirror the component, LocalNow/ FixedLocalNow, and To/From categories of the #datetime functions. However, there are also four DateTimeZone functions that have no corresponding match in the DateTime-related functions:

- **DateTimeZone.UtcNow and DateTimeZone.FixedUtcNow**: Both functions return a DateTimeZone value set to the current date and time on the system. The difference is that the former can change over the course of the execution of an expression, while the latter remains constant.
- **DateTimeZone.RemoveZone and DateTimeZone.SwitchZone**: These functions allow manipulation of the time offset values, respectively enabling the user to remove the time zone component, thereby converting the value to a datetime value, or switching the time offset values to correspond to a different zone.

Special considerations

Here are the key considerations for working with DateTimeZone values:

- **Daylight saving time**: The time zone offset in a DateTimeZone value does not automatically adjust for daylight saving time, and different countries that observe daylight saving time may adjust seasonally on different dates. We will discuss a comprehensive approach to address this issue in *Chapter 10*.
- **Conversion**: When converting DateTimeZone values, it is important to consider how M handles the conversion of the offset. For example, when a DateTimeZone value is converted to a DateTime value, the time zone offset is discarded, which effectively presents the time as **UTC**.

Duration values

Duration values in M are used to represent lengths of time expressed in days, hours, minutes, and (fractional) seconds. The basics of Duration values are covered here with additional information available in *Chapter 10, Dealing with Dates, Times, and Durations*.

Structure

The following is the structure that can be used to create a #duration:

```
#duration(
  days as number,
```

```
  hours as number,
  minutes as number,
  seconds as number,
) as duration
```

Some examples are as follows:

```
#duration(0,1,2,3)        // returns 0.01:02:03
#duration(9,8,7,6.543210) // returns 9.08:07:06.5432100
#duration(3,32,74,82)     // returns 4.09:15:22
```

Related functions

There are 12 functions that belong to the duration category, which are spread evenly and quite predictably across three categories:

- **Component extraction:** These functions allow you to extract the day, hour, minute, or second value from a duration value.
- **Computation:** These functions compute the days, hours, minutes, or seconds in a given duration value.
- **Creation and conversion:** These functions provide a direct means for converting duration values to or from another value kind.

Special considerations

Some of the important considerations for Duration values are:

- **Negative values:** Durations can take on negative values, either directly when created or when a larger duration value is subtracted from a smaller one.
- **Arithmetic calculations:** Because durations represent lengths of time rather than specific points in time, they have a greater range of arithmetic operations that can be applied to them. This topic is addressed in detail in the following section on operators.

Logical values

Logical values are essential for performing logical operations on your data, and also for controlling the flow of data through expressions via control structures, as we will discuss at length later in this chapter.

Structure

Logical values are very simple, referring only to the values of true or false.

Related Functions

Logical values have three related functions, which all pertain to conversion:

- **Logical.From:** This converts any value that can be evaluated as true or false to the appropriate logical value
- **Logical.FromText:** This creates a logical value from the text values true and false

- Logical.ToText: Returns the text true or false given a logical value

Special considerations

The following are the special considerations to keep in mind:

- **Conversion:** Logical values have some unique conversion patterns that are important to know in order to make optimal use of this value kind:

  - false equates to 0, true to 1. This can be demonstrated by:

    ```
    Number.From( true )  // returns 1
    Number.From( false ) // returns 0
    ```

  - In converting numbers to logical values, 0 converts to false, and any other number will convert to true – this can be demonstrated by:

    ```
    Logical.From( 0 )     // returns false
    Logical.From( -2 )    // returns true
    Logical.From( "csv")  // returns expression.Error:
                          // We couldn't convert to Logical
    ```

- **Short-circuit evaluation:** Like many other languages, M uses this method of evaluating logical expressions, where the second argument is only executed or evaluated if the first argument is insufficient to determine the value of the expression. This means that in a logical expression using and, if the first condition is false, the second condition will not be evaluated. For an or expression, if the first condition is true, the structure will exit before evaluating the second condition.

  This can lead to problems where the second condition is specified in a way that will trigger an error if it is ever reached, but can remain undetected until that point. Let's look at a specific example (note that Number.PI is simply a constant that returns the number pi to 16 decimal places):

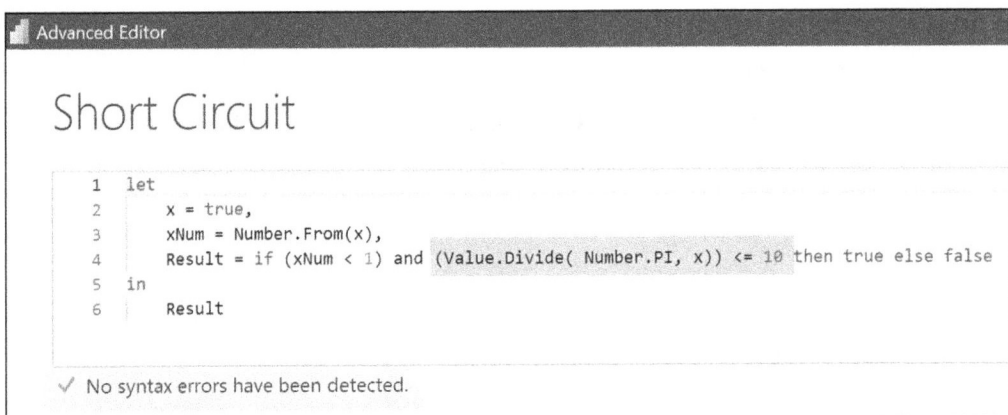

```
Advanced Editor

Short Circuit

1   let
2       x = true,
3       xNum = Number.From(x),
4       Result = if (xNum < 1) and (Value.Divide( Number.PI, x)) <= 10 then true else false
5   in
6       Result

✓ No syntax errors have been detected.
```

Figure 4.4: Potential pitfalls related to short-circuit evaluation

In this expression, we know from our discussion of conversion of logical expressions above that Number.From(true) will evaluate to 1, and thus the first condition of the Result expression will evaluate to false. Given that Result requires both conditions in the expression to be true in order to evaluate to true, the control structure exits immediately after evaluating the first condition and returns a value of false for the entire expression.

However, we can see that when x is of the logical value kind, this second expression will always return an error, since it is attempting the divide a number (pi) by a logical value (x), rather than by x's numeric equivalent (defined in this expression as xNum). However, M will let us try to do this since the expression takes the correct syntax, and if the values we evaluate for x are such that xNum will be >= 1 for all values, then we will not trigger the error and it could go undetected.

We will explore techniques in *Chapter 5* on data types that will help prevent this type of problem.

Null values

A null value is used to represent the absence of a value, or a value of indeterminate or unknown state (i.e., in the case of a missing value).

Structure

A null value is written using the literal null. It is critical to note that null is different from 0. The former is the absence of a value, while 0 is a specific numerical value, just like 1 or 732.

An example of where you could use this is:

```
if [Value] = null then "NA" else [Value]
```

Related functions

There are no functions that are directly related to null values, but the related functions for many other values take null values explicitly into account.

Special considerations

The key considerations include:

*   **Equality comparisons:** null has some unique properties concerning how expressions involving the quality operator are evaluated. For example, null is only strictly equal to itself:

```
null = null   // returns true
null = true   // returns false
null = false  // returns false
null <= null  // returns null
null >= null  // returns null
null <> null  // returns null
null < 0      // returns null
```

- **Concatenation with nulls:** Concatenating values with null will return a null. For example:

```
null & " orange "    //   returns null
```

- **Propagation of nulls:** This term in M refers to the fact that a null value plus a value that is compatible with the + operator will return the value null. For example:

```
null + number type   // returns null
null + datetime       // returns null
null + duration type // returns null
```

- **Nullability:** All data types in M can be made nullable; in other words, they are compatible with a value of null. We will explore this concept in greater depth in *Chapter 5* on data types.

- **Coalesce:** The M language includes a specific coalesce operator to make handling null easier, denoted by a double question mark (??). Coalesce allows you to return a different value instead of null. When the value on the left-hand side of the operator is null, it returns the value on the right side of the operator.

  For example, let's look at the following if statement in M:

```
if [FirstLetter] <> null then [FirstLetter] else
if [SecondLetter] <> null then [SecondLetter] else
  "ZZ"
```

  The Coalesce operator allows us to write this expression much more simply as:

```
[FirstLetter] ?? [SecondLetter] ?? "ZZ"
```

Chapter 12, Handling Errors and Debugging, delves much more deeply into how to properly handle null values.

Number values

Number values in M are used to express numeric amounts and for mathematical calculations. While the concept of "a number" is familiar to everyone, number values in M have the most varied literal forms of any value kind.

Structure and examples

All of the following expressions represent valid types of number values in M:

$^{AB}_C$ Expression	$^{AB}_C$ Description	1.2 Result
2.998	Fractional number	2.998
-3.2	Fractional number	-3.2
1.00e+3	Fractional number with exponent	1000
1.0e-3	Fractional number wiht exponent	0.001
36	Whole number	36
2e4	Whole number with exponent	20000
0x62	Whole number in hex	98

Figure 4.5: Number values in M

Related functions

Due to the wide range of mathematical operations that can be performed on number values, there are 52 different related number functions in M, spread across the following six categories:

- **Bitwise:** These functions directly manipulate the bits of a number. However, because M is a functional language and typically does not involve low-level binary transformations, bitwise operations are not well documented nor commonly used in M.

- **Creation and conversion:** These functions are used to create number values or convert them to or from compatible kinds of values.

- **Informational:** These functions determine whether a number value is even, odd, or **Not a Number** (NaN).

- **Mathematical:** These functions perform mathematical calculations on number values. Almost half of the mathematical functions relate to trigonometric calculations.

- **Random:** These functions are used to create random numbers within defined ranges.

- **Rounding:** These functions control the number of decimal places to which a number value will be expressed.

Special considerations

Here are some of the important considerations relevant to Number values:

- **Data types versus formats:** One of the most important concepts to understand regarding numbers in M is that while a number's data type is set within Power Query/M, its format is set in the visual layer of Power BI (or Excel), and not in Power Query. The primary implication of this difference is that the type controls the way a number is stored, which in turn can affect a number's level of precision and memory requirements. On the other hand, the format controls only how it appears when used in visuals. This issue will be addressed in detail in *Chapter 5* on data types.

- **Facets:** You can specify more detailed information on number types in M by using a range of subtypes called **type claims**. These belong to the **facets** category. Facets impact the different storage options, such as currency, decimal, and whole number, thus affecting the precision of a value. Values that fall outside of the defined range will return an error. The proper use and implication of number facets will be addressed in *Chapter 5* on data types.
- **Division by zero:** In M, dividing by zero will produce different results depending on the numerator:
  - Dividing a positive number by 0 will return positive infinity (∞)
  - Dividing a negative number by infinity will return negative infinity (-∞)
  - Dividing 0 by 0 returns NaN

  In many calculations in M, division by zero will cause a runtime error, so steps should be taken to guard against this scenario. Error handling will be addressed in detail in *Chapter 12*.
- **Constants:** There are six numeric constants defined in the M language:
  - `Number.E`: This returns e, or Euler's number, with an accuracy of 16 decimal places.
  - `Number.Epsilon`: This returns the smallest possible positive number for a floating point value.
  - `Number.NaN`: This returns a constant value that represents 0 divided by 0.
  - `Number.NegativeInfinity`: This returns a constant value that represents 1 divided by 0.
  - `Number.PI`: This returns the number pi to an accuracy of 16 decimal places.
  - `Number.PositiveInfinity`: This returns a constant value that represents 1 divided by 0.

Text values

In M, text values are sequences of characters, which are used to represent text data. More information about text values can be found in *Chapter 5, Understanding Data Types*.

Structure

Text values in M are indicated by " ".

The following are some examples:

```
" Basketball "
"23 "
"November 9, 1993"
```

Related functions

Because all non-abstract, non-structured value kinds except for null can be converted to and from text values, it's not surprising that there are 45 text-related functions, spread over the following categories:

- **Conversion and creation:** Functions that create text characters and values and convert them to other kinds of values
- **Extraction and position:** Functions that determine the position of characters within text values and extract different subsets from within text values

- **Formatting:** Functions that clean unwanted characters and control text case and other formatting characteristics
- **Information:** Functions that determine the length and contents of text values
- **Transformation:** Functions that combine, split, insert, or remove text or subsets of values

Special considerations

Here are the key features:

- **Concatenation:** You can concatenate text values in M using the ampersand (&) operator. For example:

```
Sentence = "M code is not that hard " & "if you know the basic
principles."
```

This M code returns:

```
"M code is not that hard if you know the basic principles."
```

- **Escape characters:** Certain characters and codes that are reserved for special purposes in the M code language, such as line feeds (lf) and carriage returns (cr), require an "escape character" sequence preceding them to instruct the program to read these as literal text characters. For example, they could be written as #(lf) and #(cr).
- **Evaluation of comparability operators:** Text values support all of the common comparison operators, which by default are case-sensitive. However, the case is not evaluated as one might think – lowercase letters receive a higher value than their uppercase equivalents:

```
"gza" < "rza"          // returns true
"rza" = "Rza"          // returns false
"rza" > "Rza"          // returns true
"RZA" < "Rza"          // returns true
```

When in doubt about the evaluation order of text values, you can use the `Character.ToNumber` function to return the numeric value (on which the evaluation is based) of any text character. To compare text values without considering the case, we can use the `Comparer.OrdinalIgnoreCase` option. For example, the following example returns `true`:

```
Comparer.Equals(Comparer.OrdinalIgnoreCase, "rza", "RZa ")
```

While text values may appear simple at first glance, they often present complex data cleaning challenges. These issues are explored in *Chapter 14, Troublesome Data Patterns*, and *Chapter 11, Comparers, Replacers, Combiners, and Splitters*. In addition, for Power BI Premium and Premium per user licensees, Power Query includes AI text analytics, which provides advanced capabilities including text processing and sentiment analysis.

List values

A list is a series of values. In M, a single column of values is a list, and lists can contain any type of primitive or structured value. Lists are covered in depth in *Chapter 6, Structured Values*.

Structure

Lists are initiated by curly brackets, { }. For example:

```
{ 1, 2, 3 }
{ "Cat", "Dog", "Monkey" }
{ { 1, 2, 3 }, { "Cat", "Dog", "Monkey" } }
```

Related functions

Lists are one of the most flexible and powerful value kinds in M, which explains why there's a wide range of functions associated with them. There are a total of 71 related functions, categorized into five distinct groups:

- **Generation**: Functions that create lists with different specified characteristics, e.g., lists of date, numbers, and random numbers, as well as more complex functions that let you create lists recursively
- **Informational**: Primarily functions that output a logical value depending on the contents of a given list
- **Selection**: Functions that select an item or group of items from a list based on specified criteria
- **Statistical**: Functions that return the results of computations on a given list (e.g., sum, median, max, etc.)
- **Transformational**: Functions that take a list as input and create a new list by modifying the structure of and/or the items in the original list

Special considerations

A critically important characteristic to be aware of regarding lists in M is that they work with a zero-based index. This means that the index that defines the position of items within a list starts with 0. Note that this is different from **Data Analysis Expressions** (**DAX**), which uses a one-based index, where the first item in a list is found at position 1.

For example, to find the third letter in the word Method, in M, you can use the following:

```
Text.At("Method", 2)
```

This returns t, the character at the third position (0, 1, 2) of the text string. Conversely, to achieve the same result in DAX, you can use:

```
MID("Method", 3, 1)
```

This returns 1 character, starting at the third position (1, 2, 3).

Lists will be addressed in detail in subsequent chapters, starting with *Chapter 6* on structured values.

Record values

A record is a named list of values. You also can think of a record as a single row in a table, where each field in the row has a column name and a value. Like lists, records can contain either primitive or structured values. Additional information about record values can be found in *Chapter 6, Structured Values*.

Structure

Records are initiated by square brackets, [ ]. Here is an example and the associated record created:

```
[Planet = "Earth",  MilesFromSun = 92960000, AdjacentPlanets = { "Venus",
"Mars" }]
```

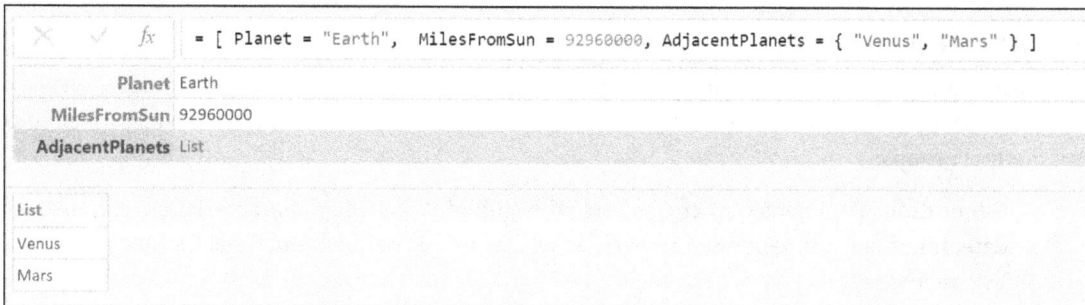

f_x	= [Planet = "Earth", MilesFromSun = 92960000, AdjacentPlanets = { "Venus", "Mars" }]
Planet	Earth
MilesFromSun	92960000
AdjacentPlanets	List

List
Venus
Mars

Figure 4.6: Creation of a record in M, also showing the values within a nested list

Related functions

The 23 functions related to records are spread across five categories that largely parallel the categorization of list functions. However, there are no statistical records functions and you'll find that a new category is added:

- **Conversion:** Functions that create a record from a list or table, or a table or list from a record
- **Geospatial:** Functions that handle geospatial data in point or **well-known text (WKT)** form
- **Informational:** Functions that output a value depending on the contents of a given list
- **Selection:** Functions that select the field or the value of a specified field from a record based on specified criteria
- **Transformational:** Functions that modify the structure or contents of a record

Special considerations

Similar to how { } allows access to an item in a list using a positional index, [ ] with a field name within it gives access to a specific field in a record.

Records are addressed in greater detail in *Chapter 6, Structured Values*.

Table values

A table is composed of three key elements:

- **Rows**, where each row represents an individual record
- **Columns**, where each column defines a field within a record and is assigned a specific data type
- **Headers**, which identify the names of each column

In M, tables can be constructed using various methods, including using the #table constructor, or by transforming values, lists, records, columns, or rows with the appropriate M function.

Additional information about table values can be found in *Chapter 6, Structured Values*, as well as numerous other chapters.

Structure

The following is the structure that can be used to create a table:

```
#table(
   columns as any,
   rows as any,
) as any
```

Let's look at an example:

```
let
   Source = #table(
      type table [ProductID = text, ProductQuantity = number,
               Column3 = date],
      {
         {"P001", 10, #date(2023, 8, 13)},
         {"P002", 25, #date(2023, 8, 14)},
         {"P003", 30, #date(2023, 8, 15)}
         }
      )
in
   Source


#table({}, {}) // empty table
```

There are many ways to construct tables using #table, as well as other functions that create tables from other kinds of primitive and structured values. These methods will be addressed in detail in *Chapter 6, Structured Values.*

Related functions

Given that tables are the most frequently used type of structured values, it is not surprising that they have the highest number of associated functions (116) among all the types of values. These functions are spread across five major categories that define their use:

- **Creation and conversion:** These functions create tables and transform them from and to other kinds of values.

- **Informational:** Tables are characterized by many different attributes, such as dimensions, schema, relationships, and contents. The functions can extract information about any of the specific attributes of a given table.

- **Column specific:** These functions allow the manipulation of the fields and headers of a table.

- **Row specific:** These functions enable the manipulation of individual or groups of records within a table.

- **Other functions:** These functions control buffering, query folding, and user-defined handlers for query operations. With the exception of `Table.Buffer`, they are rarely used.

Special considerations

The following are some of the key features to take note of when working with tables:

- **Selection and projection:** A critical aspect of working with tables is the ability to filter a table down to only the rows (selection) and columns (projection) needed in a given transformation. The ways in which you perform selection and projection have implications for the performance and readability of your M code. Particularly as you begin to use nested structures in M, selection and projection can become quite complex. This issue is addressed in depth in *Chapter 8, Working with Nested Structures*.

- **Performance:** As most steps within a query return a table value, much of the focus on optimizing performance within Power Query centers on optimizing the creation and transformation of tables. Performance optimization is covered in *Chapter 15, Optimizing Performance*.

Tables will be addressed in great detail in subsequent chapters, starting with *Chapter 6* on structured values.

Function values

Function values are those that when invoked with a set of input values (i.e., arguments) produce a new value.

Structure

In M, functions are specified by listing the input parameters of the function in parentheses, then the "goes to" operator (=>), and then the expression that defines the function. The following is an example:

```
Concatenator =
  (parameter1, parameter2) => (parameter1 & parameter2)
```

```
DifferentDistinct =
  (x) => List.Difference(x,List.Distinct(x))
```

Related functions

Function values have five related functions – two for creating functions, two for invoking custom functions, and one informational function to check if a specific function acts as a data source.

Special considerations

Here are some of the key considerations:

- **Flexibility and power:** Functions can be assigned to variables, passed as arguments, and returned from other functions, making them some of the most versatile and powerful kinds of values in M.
- **Importance of data types:** To avoid errors in M, it is important to assign appropriate data types to the function parameters. We will address the issue of enforcing proper data types in the next chapter, as well as in *Chapter 9*, which is specifically dedicated to custom functions.
- **Performance:** When calling complex functions, particularly recursive functions, and higher-order functions that take one or more functions as arguments and/or return a function, be mindful of the potential adverse impacts on performance that such functions can impose.

User-defined functions are one of the most powerful elements of M and are addressed in detail in *Chapter 9*.

Type values

Type values can be thought of as *meta* values that provide information about the data type of another value.

Structure

Because they classify value types, they can take on any of the descriptors of the values (i.e., Date, binary, DateTime, DateTimeZone, Duration, logical, null, number, text, time, list, record, table, function, or type).

In M, the Value.Type function returns a value that reflects the data type of the value input into the function:

```
Value.Type( 400 ) = number
Value.Type( "Book" ) = text
Value.Type( { 2, 3, 5, 7, 11, 13 } ) = list
```

Related functions

A total of 22 functions are associated with type values. Because type values convey information about other values instead of being structures on their own, these functions primarily provide further details about a value's type. For instance, Type.TableRow and Type.TableColumn return the type values for specified rows or columns, respectively, within a table.

Special considerations

The key aspects include the following:

- **Data integrity:** Type values are important for ensuring the integrity of the data inputs and outputs of functions. In addition, they are used to ascribe data types to unstructured data and for converting data types from one to another as transformations are performed.

- **Abstract type values:** There are a number of *abstract* types that do not uniquely classify any values. These include the data types any, anynonnull, and none, which respectively encompass all values, all non-null values, and no values. The first two values are used to support input values of multiple types, whereas type none does not classify any value and is generally not used.

- **Custom type values:** Any data types outside the union of primitive and abstract datatypes are considered custom data types, which are relevant mainly to describe structured values and for the creation of custom Power Query connectors. Custom data types and their associated custom type values will be discussed further in *Chapter 5*.

We have now looked at the different types of values available within M. Up next, we will explore operators – the "bonds" that tie values together within expressions.

Operators

Just as there are different types of bonds that join atoms, there are also different categories of operators in M that connect values. The following table lays out the distinct categories and the specific operators included within each category:

Operator Category	Operators Included	Description
Arithmetic	Addition (+)	Performs mathematical operations
	Subtraction (-)	
	Multiplication (*)	
	Division (/)	
Comparison (also known as common operators, since they are used by all primitive value operators)	Equal to (=)	Compares two values (returns a Boolean result)
	Not equal to (<>)	
	Less than (<)	
	Less than or equal to (<=)	
	Greater than (>)	
	Greater than or equal to (>=)	

Logical	and	Performs logical (Boolean) operations
	or	
	not	
Text	Concatenation (&)	Joins text strings
List	Equal to (=)	Used for creating, comparing, combining, and accessing lists
	Not equal to (<>)	
	Concatenation (&)	
	List indexer ({})	
Record	Equal to (=)	Used for creating, comparing, combining, and accessing records.
	Not equal to (<>)	
	Concatenation (&)	
	Record lookup ([])	
Table	Equal to (=)	Used for comparing and combining tables
	Not equal to (<>)	
	Concatenation (&)	
Function	Goes to (=>)	Used for mapping inputs to outputs in function definitions
Type compatibility and assertion	is	Used for data type checking and asserting the type of a value
	as	

Table 4.2: Categories of operators in M

Just as the kind of value determines what functions will and won't work with a given value, the type of value also determines the set of compatible operators. The following figure maps the value types discussed earlier in this chapter, with the operator categories and the specific operators applicable to them:

Value Type	=	<>	>	>=	<	<=	+	-	*	/	+x	-x	and	or	not	??	&	{}	[]	=>	Meta	is	as
Primitive Values																							
Null	●	●	●	●	●	●										●					●	○	○
Logical	●	●	●	●	●	●							●	●	●						●	○	○
Number	●	●	●	●	●	●	●	●	◐	◐	●	●									●	○	○
Time	●	●	●	●	●	●	○	◐									○				●	○	○
Date	●	●	●	●	●	●	○	◐									○				●	○	○
DateTime	●	●	●	●	●	●	○	◐													●	○	○
DateTimeZone	●	●	●	●	●	●	○	◐													●	○	○
Duration	●	●	●	●	●	●	◐		◐	◐	●	●									●	○	○
Text	●	●	●	●	●	●		◐									●				●	○	○
Binary	●	●	●	●	●	●															●	○	○
Structured Values																							
List	●	●															●	●			●	○	○
Record	●	●															●		●		●	○	○
Table	●	●															●		●		●	○	○
Function Values																							
Function	●	●																		●		○	○
Type Values																							
Type	●	●																			●	◐	◐

Column groups: Comparison (= <> > >= < <=), Arithmetic (+ - * / +x -x), Logical (and or not), Coal. (??), Conc. (&), List ({}), Rec. ([]), Func. (=>), Meta (Meta), Type (is as).

- ● **Self-Only** — Operates exclusively with its own value type.
- ◐ **Self+Other** — Operates with its own and some other value types.
- ○ **Other-Only** — Operates exclusively with other value types.

Figure 4.7: Mapping of kinds of values to operator categories and operators

Applying arithmetic and concatenation operators to Date, DateTime, DateTimeZone, Duration, and Time values presents numerous special cases, as summarized here:

Operand LHS => / RHS	Date	DateTime	DateTimeZone	Duration	Time	Number
Date	All comparison - = duration			+, - = Date	& = DateTime	
DateTime		All comparison - = duration		+, - = DateTime		
DateTimeZone			All comparison - = duration	+, - = DateTimeZone		
Duration	+, - = Date	+, - = DateTime	+, - = DateTimeZone	All comparison +, - = duration	- = Time	*, / = Duration
Time	& = DateTime			+, - = Time	All comparison - = duration	
Number				* = duration		All comparison +, -, *, / = Number

Figure 4.8: Listing of valid arithmetic and concatenation operations and resulting value types for Date, DateTime, DateTimeZone, Duration, and Time values

In general, the following rules hold for arithmetic operations involving `Date`, `Time`, `DateTime`, and `DateTimeZone` values:

- When you subtract two values of the same kind from each other, the result is a positive or negative `Duration`
- When you add or subtract a `Duration` from one of these kinds of values, the result is the same kind of value
- Adding or subtracting two `Durations` will produce a `Duration`
- Multiplying or dividing a `Duration` by a number value will produce a `Duration`
- Concatenating a `Date` value and a `Time` value will produce a `DateTime` value

One last special case to note pertains to arithmetic operations. Numeric operations in M follow the standard mathematical order of operations abbreviated as **PEMDAS** (**parentheses, exponents, multiplication, division, addition,** and **subtraction**). However, unlike many languages that use the caret (^) as the operator for exponentiation, M requires the use of the `Number.Power` function to raise a number value to a power. A full list of operator precedence can be found here: `https://learn.microsoft.com/en-us/powerquery-m/m-spec-operators`.

There are some additional, less common operators within the M language, including:

- **Coalesce** (`??`): Returns the result of the left operand if not `null`; otherwise, returns the result of the right operand. Example: `x ?? y`. This operator was covered in the *Null values* section in this chapter.
- **Metadata** (`meta`): Adds metadata to a value. Example: `x meta y`. This operator is explored in *Chapter 7*, *Conceptualizing M*, and *Chapter 16*, *Enabling Extensions*.
- **Unary Plus** (`+x`): The identity operator for number values. For example, + 12 returns 12.
- **Negation** (`-x`): The negation operator for number values. For example, -12 returns -12.

In the next section, we will look at how to combine operators and values (which we explored earlier in this chapter) into expressions.

Expressions

Expressions in M are like formulae – by using operators and values as inputs, they allow you to output a new value. These expressions are evaluated or computed to always return a single value as the outcome. Ultimately, every expression in M must produce either a value or an error. It's also through expressions that M transcends mere data representation and allows you to transform your data.

So, what is the distinction between values and expressions? While values represent data points in their simplest form, expressions are the formulas through which these values can be manipulated or generated. These expressions can be as simple as returning a single constant or as complex as a statement containing hundreds of intermediate expressions.

For instance, the following examples are single value expressions:

```
1                                      // returns a number value
"We love Power Query"                  // returns a text value
[ Fruit = "Apple", Fruit = "Plum"] // returns a record value
```

Yet, Power Query also allows you to combine multiple values or lets you create logic to return another value. For example, the following lines of code are also considered expressions:

```
1 + 5                    // the sum of two numbers
List.Count({1,2,3})      // an expression using a function
( x, y ) => x - y        // a function that subtracts y from x
let age = 2 in age * 2 // a let expression
```

In these examples, expressions are the input recipes for generating results, whereas values are the outcomes of such recipes.

The preceding examples are relatively straightforward. However, it's perfectly valid to create more complex expressions by combining multiple expressions. For instance:

```
Date.AddMonths( #date( 2024,1,1), 1 )
```

This example consists of 6 values. You can find the following:

- **Function values:** Both Date.AddMonths and #date are functions that perform an operation.
- **Number values:** You can find three number values used in Date.AddMonths and one number value is used in the #date function.

Working on values through expressions is an important element of performing transformations. Yet, things can get complex quickly once you get more comfortable with creating expressions. Imagine that you nest 20 different values together. In such a situation, you may consider storing your logic within a let statement. A let statement allows you to define a series of variables, make references to them, and output a result. But instead of looking at a sea of code, the variable names it includes help in splitting up the code in chunks that are easy to understand.

For instance, if we continue our previous date example, but now also format it in a particular way, we can use this code:

```
Date.ToText( Date.AddMonths( #date( 2024,1,1), 1 ), [Format = "yyyy-MM-dd"] )
```

This expression returns the date February 1, 2024. But the more values we include in our expression, the harder it reads. To improve this situation, we could format the code as follows:

```
Date.ToText(
  Date.AddMonths(
    #date( 2024,1,1 ),
    1 ),
  [Format = "yyyy-MM-dd"] )
```

The code is now easier to read but still requires some mental processing. To make things even easier, let's include variables by using a let statement:

```
let
  myDate = #date( 2024,1,1 ),
  addMonth = Date.AddMonths( myDate, 1 ),
  formatDate = Date.ToText( addMonth, [Format = "yyyy-M-d"] )
in
  formatDate
```

Here, the let keyword is followed by three variables, and the result is indicated by the variable name formatDate that comes after in. The outcome of this code is identical for all three snippets, but by providing clear variable names, the expression is much easier to understand.

You have now seen an easy example of using a let statement. The most common place where you will find such a statement is in the **Advanced Editor**. When performing operations, Power Query automatically creates a let statement in the **Advanced Editor**. While this specific let statement is auto-generated, you can manually include additional let statements within any of your applied steps. Let's explore what that looks like.

Nesting let expressions

Power Query uses a let expression to represent the applied steps in your query. To make your transformation logic for a step easier to digest, you can nest multiple let expressions.

In this section, we'll explore the *Palindromes* query, which uses a nested let expression. This query aims to analyze a column of words and determine which of those words are palindromes, that is, words that read the same both backward and forward. We will then return a table of these words, sorted in ascending alphabetical order.

Here is what the query looks like in the **Advanced Editor**:

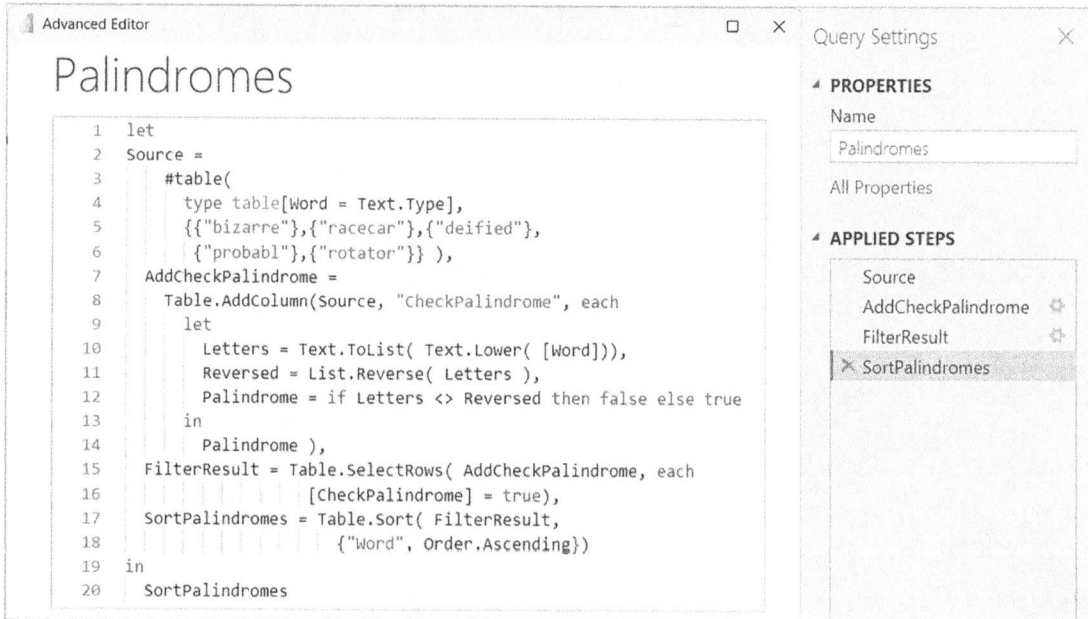

Figure 4.9: A more complex query containing expressions, values, operators, controls structures, and enumerations.

For ease of reference, here is the `Palindrome` query as text:

```
let
  Source =
    #table(
      type table[Word = Text.Type],
      {{"bizarre"},{"racecar"},{"deified"},
       {"probabl"},{"rotator"}} ),
  AddCheckPalindrome =
    Table.AddColumn(Source, "CheckPalindrome", each
      let
        Letters = Text.ToList( Text.Lower( [Word])),
        Reversed = List.Reverse( Letters ),
        Palindrome = if Letters <> Reversed then false else true
      in
        Palindrome ),
  FilterResult = Table.SelectRows( AddCheckPalindrome, each
                  [CheckPalindrome] = true),
  SortPalindromes = Table.Sort( FilterResult,
                  {"Word", Order.Ascending})
in
  SortPalindromes
```

The query uses a let statement with four variables and returns a table in a step called SortPalindromes. These represent the four applied steps in our query.

Nested within that let statement is a step called AddCheckPalindrome. This step contains another let statement composed of three expressions that produce a value for each word, indicating whether it is a palindrome (true) or whether it is not a palindrome (false). While this may sound confusing at first, don't worry. You'll get used to working with let-statements. They are simply a way to split your code into variables and return an outcome.

Let's break down what this query is doing by examining it step by step:

- Source: This expression provides the source data for the expression – a single column table identified as Source. As discussed in *Chapter 3*, we typically ingest data from an external structured or unstructured data source. However, for purposes of clarity, we are generating our source data within the let expression.
- AddCheckPalindrome: This step adds a new column named CheckPalindrome to the Source table using a nested let statement. This statement unfolds into three interim expressions:
    - The first, Letters, transforms each word to lowercase and splits the word into a list of the letters of which it is composed.
    - The next step reverses the Letters list in a step called Reversed.
    - The final expression, Palindrome, uses if then else logic to test whether the original list of letters is identical to the same list in reversed order. It populates the CheckPalindrome column with true/false values for each row.
- FilterResult: This step applies a filter to the CheckPalindrome column to retain only those rows that have a true value (that is, those that are considered a palindrome).
- SortResult: The final step sorts the remaining palindromes in the Words column in ascending order. Order.Ascending in this step also marks the first appearance of an enumeration – we will address these values at length later in this chapter.

> Note that in the **Applied Steps** panel to the right of the Advanced Editor code, each of our variable names in the outer let statement shows up listed as a separate step, but the intermediate expressions in our nested let statement do not.

Had we not nested the Letters, Reversed, and Palindrome expressions within that second let statement but instead added them as separate steps in the outer let statement, they would have shown up in **Applied Steps**. Because they were sub-steps of the process necessary to produce the CheckPalindrome results and not needed for any other purpose in the expression, we chose to nest them within that second let statement. This ensures our logic is represented by a single applied step instead of three separate ones.

Also, note that next to the AddCheckPalindrome and FilterResult steps appears a small gear icon. The presence of that gear icon indicates that you can click on it (or double-click on the step name) and then modify that step using the Power Query UI.

For example, if we click on the gear next to the `FilterResult` step, the following screen will pop up, and we can revise our filter conditions using the UI, and Power Query will write the changes back to our M code expression:

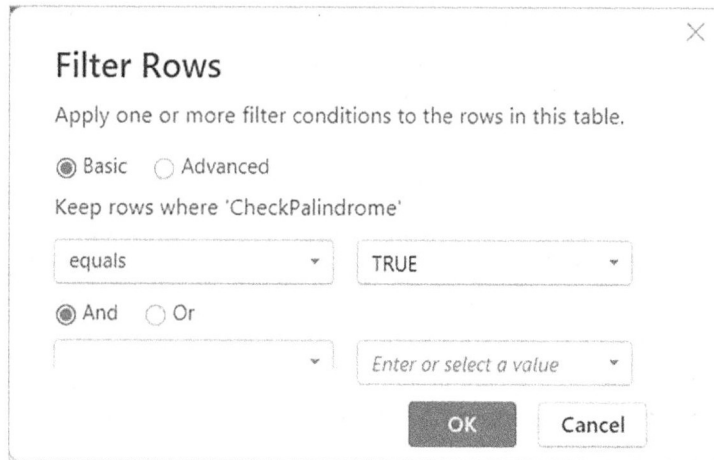

Figure 4.10: Example of options that appear when clicking the gear icon next to a specific step

Once you become comfortable writing M code directly in the **Advanced Editor**, you may find that making these types of changes can be quicker and easier to do via coding rather than using the UI. Still, the gear icons allow you to use the UI if you desire.

It's also important to note that we could have placed our final operation after the `in` keyword, as shown in the following screenshot:

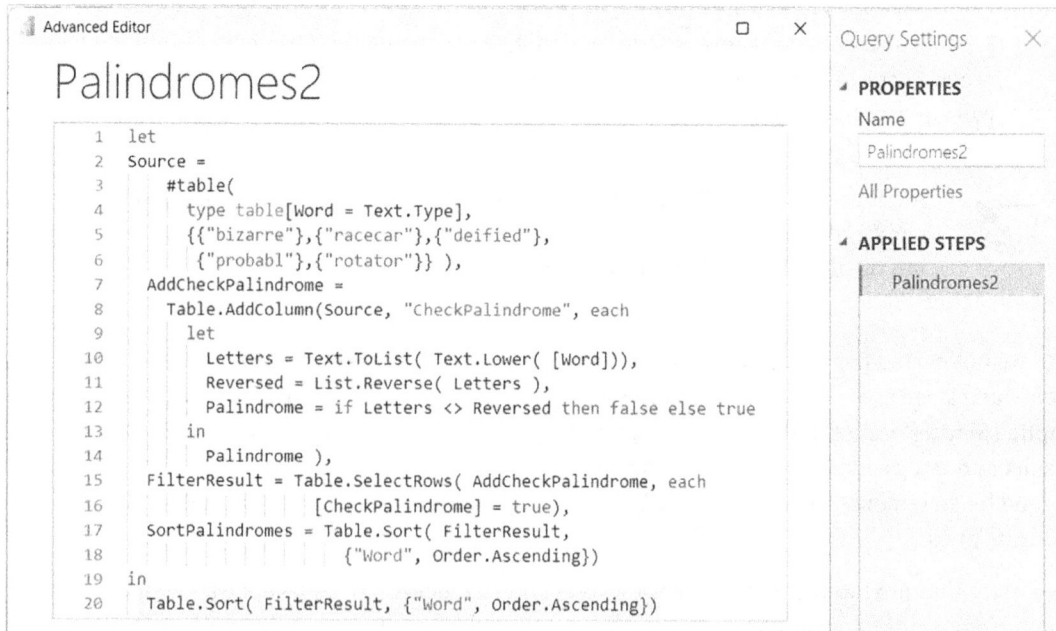

Figure 4.11: Shifting the final expression collapses the Applied Steps list

Rather than referencing a variable, the part after in now shows an expression. This change does lead to the desired outcome, yet observe how it affects the **Applied Steps** list. All operations are consolidated into a single step, labeled with the query's name, Palindromes2. A major strength of Power Query is the ability to navigate through each expression in the Applied Steps to inspect their outcomes. Therefore, structuring your queries to return a single variable name after the final in, and with that, showing each transformation step, is considered a best practice.

Coding best practices for expressions

In addition to writing your outermost let expression with a single identifier after the in operator to keep the **Applied Steps** list from collapsing, here are some other recommendations for writing expressions that we consider best practices:

- **Use descriptive identifiers**: It can be tempting to use single letters, acronyms, or abbreviations for the identifiers of your expressions. However, doing so will likely make your code more difficult for others to understand (or even yourself a month or two from now) to understand.

- **Avoid the use of spaces in your identifiers**: There are two distinct reasons to avoid spaces:

  - When your identifier includes spaces, you must reference it in subsequent expressions with hashtags and quotes (for example, #"Filter Result"). This signals Power Query that it is a single identifier rather than separate variables. These additional symbols can make your code look cluttered and difficult to read and are also just an unnecessary source of potential error.

  - Power Query has the ability to call Python and R scripts directly from within an M code expression. This capability gives M superpowers – the ability to do highly advanced statistical analyses, complex machine learning, and much more. However, both Python and R prefer identifiers without spaces. So, if you intend to leverage this feature, it is wise to use identifiers that avoid spaces.

- **Use a consistent case for identifiers**: If you choose to adhere to the preceding recommendation, it is best to pick a specific case for your identifiers and stick with it for consistency and readability. The particular case you choose to use (e.g., PascalCase, camelCase, snake_case, etc.) is largely a matter of personal preference.

- **Comments**: There are two ways to comment your M code at the individual expression level:

  - You can use // at the start of a line to comment out that line and use it to provide descriptive comments about the corresponding expression. Alternatively, /* and */ can be used to open and close a multi-line comment block.

- If you right-click on an expression within the **Applied Steps** list, you can select **Properties** and it will provide the following dialog box for you to enter comments regarding that expression:

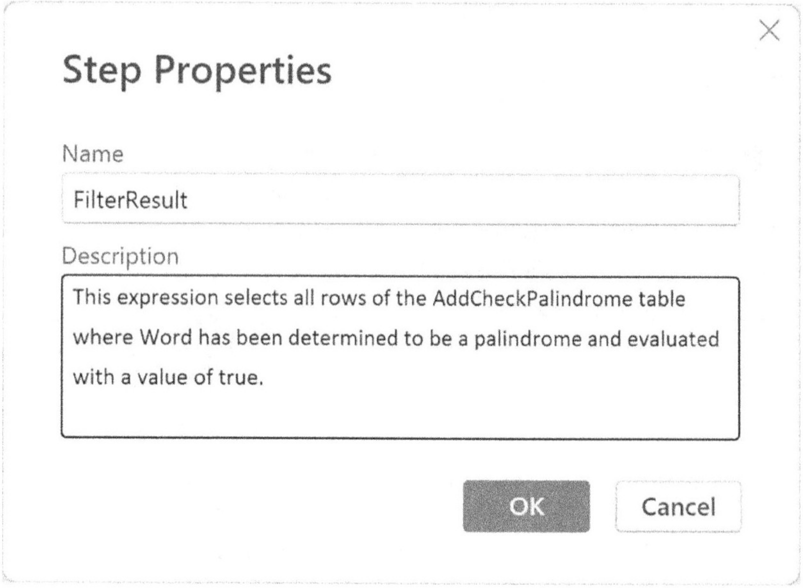

Figure 4.12: Using Step Properties to document expressions

In both cases, your comment will show up in green in the **Advanced Editor**, and a small, circled information icon will now appear on the right-hand side of the relevant step in the **Applied Steps** list.

Now that we've covered the basic structure of expressions, let's next turn our attention to control structures, which help you control the flow of program logic within your queries.

Control structures

As we continue to break down the components of queries and expressions that allow us to use values in different ways, we will briefly look at the role of control structures in M. Control structures are constructs that manipulate the flow of execution, allowing a program to branch in different directions and loop over sections of code based on the evaluation of conditions.

This section is brief, not because control structures are unimportant but because (as we covered in *Chapter 1*) M is a functional language and thus has far fewer control structures than a procedural language like C, object-oriented languages such as Python or C++, or event-driven languages like JavaScript.

In fact, M only has one formal control structure – the if-then-else statement, otherwise known as a conditional. This works exactly as it sounds. If a condition evaluates to true, then return the true expression (the then clause). If the condition evaluates to false, then return the false expression (the else clause). If the condition results in a non-logical value (neither true or false), then an error is returned.

For example, the following simple expression returns 1:

```
if true then 1 else 0
```

Similarly, this simple expression returns 0:

```
if false then 1 else 0
```

The following example returns an error since the condition is a text value, not a logical value:

```
if "12345" then 1 else 0
```

Finally, it is important to note that while logical true is often represented by 1 and logical false by 0, the following expression also returns an error:

```
if 1 then 1 else 0
```

This is because the number one is not a logical value but rather a number value.

You can nest if-then-else statements such that if the condition evaluates to true, then the true expression can be a second if-then-else statement, and so on. Unfortunately, M does not have a switch or case control structure like DAX or SQL that allows you to account for more than two outcomes for a given condition. Thus, those scenarios typically are addressed using multiple nested if-then-else statements.

The following example that demonstrates the use of nested if-then-else control structures is based on a classic programming challenge called **FizzBuzz**, which is commonly used to evaluate candidates for developer positions. The task is to create a list of integers from 1 to 100, and then for each number, if it is evenly divisible by 3, it gets a value of Fizz; if evenly divisible by 5, it gets a value of Buzz; and if it is evenly divisible by both numbers, it gets a value of FizzBuzz. Rows meeting none of those conditions just return the number in that row. To do that, we use the following code:

```
Advanced Editor                                                    □  ✕

Fizzbuzz

1   let
2       Source = Table.FromList({1..100}, Splitter.SplitByNothing(), {"Numbers"},
            ExtraValues.Error),
3       AddFizzBuzz = Table.AddColumn(Source, "FizzBuzz", each
4           if Number.Mod([Numbers], 3) = 0 and Number.Mod([Numbers], 5) = 0 then "FizzBuzz" else
5           if Number.Mod([Numbers], 3) = 0 then "Fizz" else
6           if Number.Mod([Numbers], 5) = 0 then "Buzz" else
7               [Numbers],
8           Any.Type)
9   in
10      AddFizzBuzz
```

Figure 4.13: Illustration of nested if-then-else statements in the FizzBuzz challenge

For convenience, here is the `FizzBuzz` query as text:

```
let
    Source = Table.FromList({1..100}, Splitter.SplitByNothing(), {"Numbers"},
ExtraValues.Error),
    AddFizzBuzz = Table.AddColumn(Source, "FizzBuzz", each
        if Number.Mod([Numbers], 3) = 0
            and Number.Mod([Numbers], 5) = 0 then "FizzBuzz" else
        if Number.Mod([Numbers], 3) = 0 then "Fizz" else
        if Number.Mod([Numbers], 5) = 0 then "Buzz" else
            [Numbers],
        Any.Type)
in
    AddFizzBuzz
```

The following screenshot shows the first 15 rows that the query returns:

	ABC 123 **Numbers**	ABC 123 FizzBuzz
1	1	1
2	2	2
3	3	Fizz
4	4	4
5	5	Buzz
6	6	Fizz
7	7	7
8	8	8
9	9	Fizz
10	10	Buzz
11	11	11
12	12	Fizz
13	13	13
14	14	14
15	15	FizzBuzz

Figure 4.14: Sample data from the FizzBuzz query

So what happened with this query? `Number.Mod` is a function that takes two number kind values, divides the first by the second, and returns the remainder. So, using that function within the nested control structures, this problem becomes quite straightforward:

- **Line 1:** This initiates our expression with `let`.
- **Line 2:** This creates our list of integers using the `list` operator and converts that list to a table.
- **Line 3:** This adds a column called `FizzBuzz` to the table to hold the results of our evaluation.
- **Line 4:** This is the start of our if-then-else control structure. First, we evaluate the strictest condition (`FizzBuzz`) so that the control structure doesn't exit prematurely when both conditions are `true`. If both conditions are `true`, the value of `FizzBuzz` is returned and the program exits the control structure. If it's not `true`, it proceeds to the next line.
- **Line 5:** When this line is executing, we know that both conditions did not evaluate to `true`, so we test each condition individually. First, we test `Number.Mod` with a divisor of 3. If that divides evenly into our value, we return a value of `Fizz`. Otherwise, continue to **Line 6**.
- **Line 6:** Here, we test `Number.Mod` with a divisor of 5. If that divides evenly into our value, we return a value of `Buzz`. Otherwise, continue to **Line 7**.
- **Line 7:** This is our *catch-all* if none of the preceding statements evaluate to `true`. If the control structure reaches this point, then we just return the original number value.
- **Line 8:** This sets the data type of our added `FizzBuzz` column to a text type because it contains a mix of text and number values. We will discuss this process, referred to as "data type ascription," at length in our next chapter.
- **Lines 9–10:** These just close out our initial let expression, and return the final value of our expression.

This problem represents an extremely common scenario with many real-world applications, which is why it has been such a frequently used test question. Note that the initial condition in our control structure can be something very simple such as `[color] = "red"`, or an extremely complex multiple nested let expression. All that is required is that the initial condition returns a logical value (`true` or `false`).

While M has only one formal control structure, that does not mean it is not a powerful language. It has other functions and capabilities that can replicate the actions of control structures in other languages:

- The `List.Accumulate` function can execute an expression multiple specified times, in the same manner as a typical `for` loop control structure
- The `List.Generate` function can execute an expression repeatedly an unspecified number of times as long as an evaluation condition remains `true` in the same manner as a typical `while` loop control structure
- M also reserves the @ symbol for use in creating custom recursive functions that can replicate `for` or `while` loop control behavior.

Finally, many programs, such as R, include a map function that acts as a type of control structure, applying a specified function to all rows of a column. M has multiple ways of doing this, including the `Table.TransformColumn` and `List.Transform` functions

These more complex looping and recursive structures will be the sole focus of *Chapter 13, Iteration and Recursion*, since they are very flexible and powerful, with a wide array of common, practical applications.

We now arrive at the last of our components related to values, known as enumerations.

Enumerations

Enumerations are a fundamental concept in programming. They are sets of named values that specify the behavior of functions. These names make it easier for us to pick options in our code, making our intentions clear. Users can specify an enumeration by using either the corresponding index number or its textual representation. The textual representation often makes code easier to understand.

Take the `Table.Sort` function as an example. This function sorts table data using an enumeration to specify the order. Recall that we discussed sorting palindrome words in ascending order. To do so, we created the following expression:

```
SortPalindromes =
    Table.Sort(FilterResult, {"Word", Order.Ascending})
```

Here, `Order.Ascending` tells how the `FilterResult` table should be sorted. There is another way to write this that achieves the same outcome, which is shown in the following screenshot:

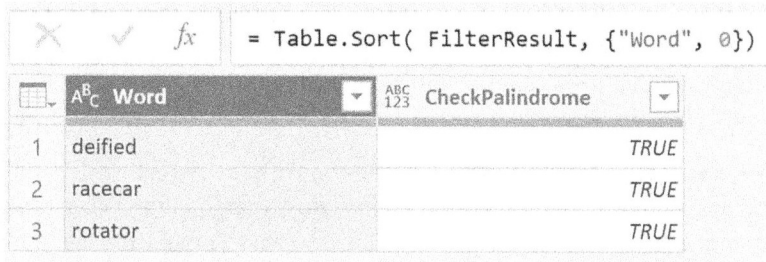

Figure 4.15: Alternate method for specifying enumeration value using numbers

This code works because, in M, every enumeration option has an integer equivalent that we can use in place of the corresponding text value of that enumeration. A quick glance at the Microsoft online documentation for this enumeration indicates you have the option to use 0 or `Order.Ascending` for ascending sort order, and 1 or `Order.Descending` for descending sort order.

Name	Value	Description
Order.Ascending	0	Sorts the values in ascending order.
Order.Descending	1	Sorts the values in descending order.

Figure 4.16: Allowed values for Order.Type enumeration

An interesting point about enumerations is they can be swapped based on their underlying index number. For example, Day.Sunday and Order.Ascending both have a corresponding number value of 0. So, if Day.Sunday is used in Table.Sort, it reads it as 0 and sorts in ascending order. This shows how numbers behind the names can lead to different uses, where the same index value can lead to contextually different behaviors across functions.

For instance, the following snippets return the same results:

```
List.Sort( { 4, 3, 2, 1 }, Order.Ascending )
List.Sort( { 4, 3, 2, 1 }, Day.Sunday )
List.Sort( { 4, 3, 2, 1 }, 0 )
```

This illustrates that enumerations are syntax sugar for an integer value. Functions that include an enumeration have been designed to behave in a particular way based on these integers.

Besides Order.Type, other commonly used enumerations are:

- RoundingMode.Type: This tells functions like Number.Round, Currency.From, and Int64.From how to round numbers. Whether you need to round up, down, or to the nearest number, this enumeration makes it clear.

- MissingField.Type: It's not uncommon to encounter missing fields in data. This enumeration lets you decide what action to take–ignore, return an error, and so on—when such a scenario arises. It's useful for functions like Record.RemoveFields, Table.SelectColumns, and Table.TransformColumns.

- GroupKind.Type: You may have different requirements when grouping data. This enumeration guides how the Table.Group function brings data into groups. Depending on the used enumeration, it respects the order of the data when grouping.

- JoinKind.Type: Deciding the nature of a join is crucial when combining data sets with Table.Join, Table.NestedJoin, or their fuzzy counterparts. This enumeration guides the type of join—inner, outer, left, right, and so on.

- Day.Type: For date-related calculations, deciding which day starts the week can affect our results. This enumeration allows us to set that starting day for functions like Date.StartOfWeek, Date.EndOfWeek and Date.WeekOfMonth.

At the time of writing, there are a total of 30 different enumerations in M, with many of these used in multiple functions. You can take a look at the following overview:

Enumeration	Description
BinaryOccurrence.Type	Specifies how many times the item is expected to appear in the group.
Occurrence.Type	Specifies the occurrence of an element in a sequence.
Order.Type	Specifies the direction of sorting.
PercentileMode.Type	Specifies the percentile mode type.
Precision.Type	Specifies the precision of comparison.
RankKind.Type	Specifies the type of ranking.
RoundingMode.Type	Specifies rounding direction when there is a tie between the possible numbers to round to.
AccessControlKind.Type	Specifies the kind of access control. This enumeration is not currently used in any function.
ODataOmitValues.Type	Specifies the kinds of values an OData service can omit.
SapBusinessWarehouseExe...	Valid options for SAP Business Warehouse execution mode option.
SapHanaDistribution.Type	Valid options for SAP HANA distribution option.
SapHanaRangeOperator.Type	A range operator for SAP HANA range input parameters.
BinaryEncoding.Type	Specifies the type of binary encoding.
Compression.Type	Specifies the type of compression.
ExtraValues.Type	Specifies the expected action for extra values in a row that contains columns more than expected.
MissingField.Type	Specifies the expected action for missing values in a row that contains columns less than expected.
BufferMode.Type	Describes the type of buffering to be performed.
ByteOrder.Type	Specifies the byte order.
CsvStyle.Type	Specifies the significance of quotes in Csv documents.
LimitClauseKind.Type	Describes the type of limit clause supported by the SQL dialect used by this data source.
QuoteStyle.Type	Specifies the quote style.
RelativePosition.Type	Indicates whether indexing should be done from the start or end of the input.
TextEncoding.Type	Specifies the text encoding type.
GroupKind.Type	Specifies the kind of grouping.
JoinAlgorithm.Type	Specifies the join algorithm to be used in the join operation.
JoinKind.Type	Specifies the kind of join operation.
JoinSide.Type	Specifies the left or right table of a join.
Day.Type	Specifies a day of week.
TraceLevel.Type	Specifies the trace level.
WebMethod.Type	Specifies an HTTP method.

Figure 4.17: Enumerations in M (source: https://learn.microsoft.com/en-us/powerquery-m/enumerations)

You can get more information about each of these enumerations, including which functions support them and how you can use them, at `https://powerquery.how/enumerations/`. Similarly, when reading the documentation on functions, you will find references to the enumeration documentation when applicable.

In summary, enumerations play an important role in making your code more expressive and easier to read. By allowing for both numerical and textual representations, users can either choose the concision of code or readability.

Summary

In this chapter, you have acquired a solid foundation of the basic values necessary to start creating your own M queries, enabling you to clean and transform your data. We have discussed what values and expressions are and why they are so important within M. We explored the four categories of values in M and the 15 different kinds of values within those categories. We acquired a detailed understanding of each kind of value, including their structure, the categories of related functions for each, and how many of them build upon each other. We also covered some of the special considerations that should be taken into account when using each kind of value to avoid subtle errors and potential inaccuracies. Finally, we discussed the "connective bonds" that are used to tie values together within expressions, including operators, control structures, and enumerators

In the upcoming chapters, we will gather the last two remaining elements, namely, data types (*Chapter 5*) and structured values (*Chapter 6*). Armed with this knowledge, we will be set for the advanced stages of our journey. There, we will learn how to assemble these basic components into increasingly complex structures that can help address nearly any data challenge we might encounter.

Learn more on Discord

Join our community's Discord space for discussions with the author and other readers:

```
https://discord.gg/vCSG5GBbyS
```

5

Understanding Data Types

In the previous chapter, we looked at the role of values in shaping expressions and queries within the M language. We learned how values interact with various operators and functions and their unique characteristics. Building upon this knowledge, let's continue this journey by turning our attention to data types.

Data types serve as a classification system for values, providing information about their structure and usage within M. Understanding data types is crucial for effectively using M and storing values efficiently. In this chapter, we provide a comprehensive overview of data types, their significance, and their application in practical scenarios.

We will start by examining why data types are important. You'll discover the various data types in M and the contexts in which they are used. We also explain how to identify and understand different data types, with a focus on type conversion. Additionally, this chapter introduces facets and explains how to assign data types to values.

Here's a quick overview of the chapter:

- Importance of data types
- Data types available in M
- Type detection
- Type conversion
- Facets
- Type ascription
- Type equivalence and compatibility

By the end of this chapter, you will have a thorough understanding of data types in M. This equips you with the knowledge to build effective queries without running into data type errors.

What are data types?

The M language has both values and data types. In the official documentation, data types are formally referred to as **types** because they don't just classify data but also classify functions and the data type itself. Throughout this book, we use both the terms **data types** and **types** so as not to get confused when comparing them with value types. So, what exactly are data types, and how do they compare to values?

The type system

The type system in Power Query helps classify values, offering information about the structure of your data. When creating custom functions, data types specify the required values. Additionally, they convey essential information to any system into which the data is loaded. Let's start by delving into an example.

Each kind of value in the M language has a data type. It's a special kind of value that characterizes the kind of value and carries additional metadata that is specific to the shape of the value. This may all sound complex at the moment, but hang in there; we will illustrate everything with clear examples.

A data type is a value, just like a number is a value. To illustrate this, let's look at a simple example. Suppose you need to add a new column to your table. You can do that with a statement like this:

```
Table.AddColumn(
  #"Changed Type",   // A table value
  "Addition",        // a text value
  each [Value] + 10, // a function value
  type number        // a type value
)
```

In this expression, each argument of the `Table.AddColumn` function received a value of a different type:

1. The first argument refers to a table in a step called `Changed Type`.
2. The second argument contains a text value with the name of the new column.
3. The third argument defines a function that generates the value to populate the new column.
4. The fourth argument defines a data type for the new column.

You can find a total of 15 kinds of values in the M language, and a type is also a value. By using the literal syntax (the notation) associated with each value, Power Query differentiates between different values. *Figure 5.1* shows an overview of all values and their literal syntax.

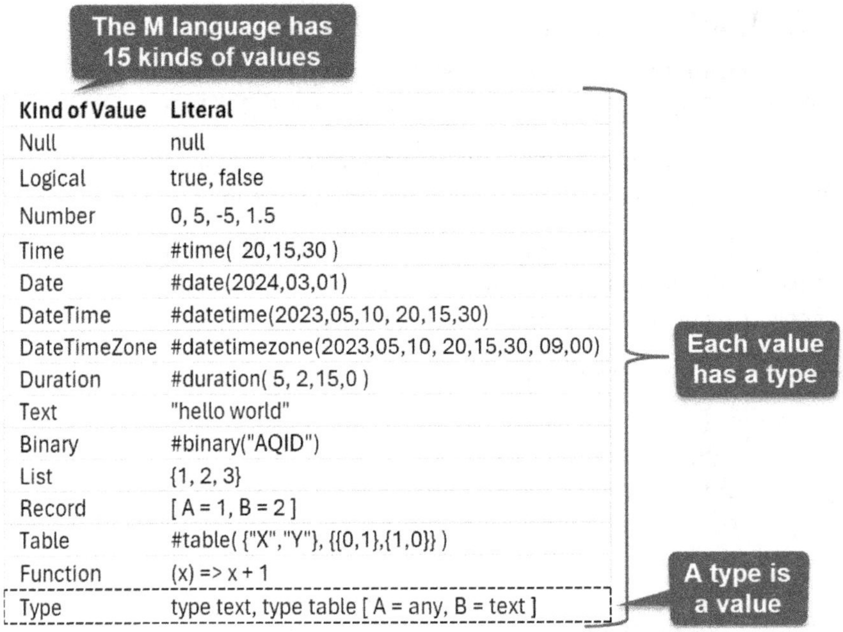

The M language has 15 kinds of values

Kind of Value	Literal
Null	null
Logical	true, false
Number	0, 5, -5, 1.5
Time	#time(20,15,30)
Date	#date(2024,03,01)
DateTime	#datetime(2023,05,10, 20,15,30)
DateTimeZone	#datetimezone(2023,05,10, 20,15,30, 09,00)
Duration	#duration(5, 2,15,0)
Text	"hello world"
Binary	#binary("AQID")
List	{1, 2, 3}
Record	[A = 1, B = 2]
Table	#table({"X","Y"}, {{0,1},{1,0}})
Function	(x) => x + 1
Type	type text, type table [A = any, B = text]

Each value has a type

A type is a value

Figure 5.1: Different kinds of values in the M language

As the table shows, there are many different types of values. Have a look at how the following expressions return four different values:

```
"MyText"        // Returns a text value
2024            // Returns a number value
{ 1, 2, 3 }     // Returns a list value
type list       // Returns a type value
```

Focus your attention on the last example that shows the type list. Just like any other value, the (data) type is also a value and there is a specific syntax to return a type. Examples of types are:

```
type number // returns a type value holding numbers
type binary // returns a type value holding binary values
type text   // returns a type value holding text values
```

This indicates there are different types available. So, if a value has a type associated with it, when does this nuance become relevant?

Columns with mixed types

When you're dealing with tables in Power Query M, the difference between data types and values becomes especially clear. Columns have a data type that describes the kind of values the column contains.

To follow along with the following example, you can open the accompanying exercise files that come with the book. We encourage you to try different transformations and test your knowledge.

Imagine a situation where a column's data type isn't straightforward. Your data comes from an unstructured source (like Excel), and you will find that it can contain different kinds of values. In this specific example, your column contains a variety of values, including text, numbers, logical values, and dates.

You can create such a column by writing:

```
Table.FromColumns(
    { { "abc", 123, true, #date(2024,1,1) } } ,
    {"Mixed Data"}
)
```

This code creates a column called **Mixed Data** with four unique values. Since we did not specify a data type, Power Query automatically assigned type any to this column, represented by **ABC123** in the column header:

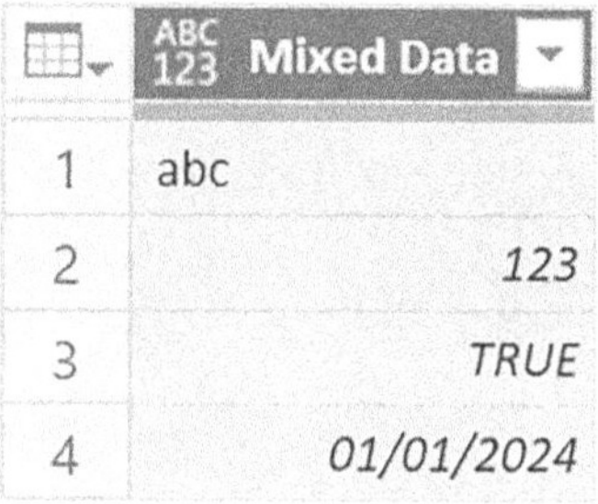

ABC123 Mixed Data
1	abc
2	123
3	TRUE
4	01/01/2024

Figure 5.2: A column with a mix of different values

Assigning a more specific data type to such a column can be hard since it contains different kinds of values. When we don't set a data type in our expression, Power Query, therefore, defaults to the any data type. The any type allows for a variety of value types within the same column. Yet, the choice of data type ultimately depends on your specific needs and the calculations or transformations you plan to apply.

For example, if you expect to work exclusively with date values, you might consider setting the column's data type to date. But the values in your column also need to support this. So, how would you set such a data type?

To specify a column's data type, click on the *data type* icon located on the left of the column header. The following example sets the data type of the **Mixed Data** column to the **Date** type:

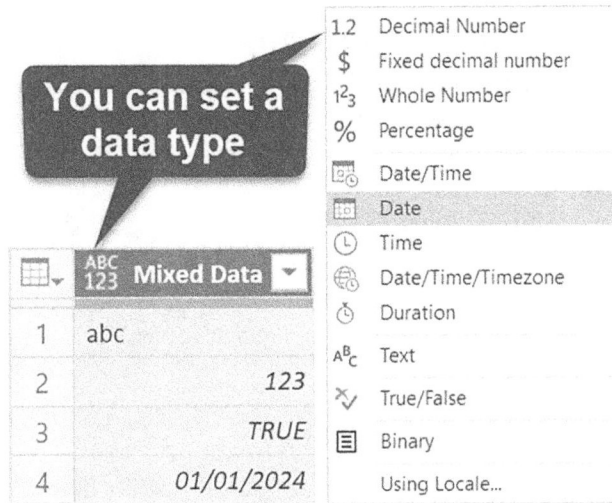

Figure 5.3: Set a data type for a column

Through this operation, Power Query will try to transform the column values to type **Date**, and it checks whether the underlying values conform to this data type. If, for some reason, the engine can't transform the value to the new data type, an error is shown. For example, converting the column's data type to **Date** gives the following results:

Figure 5.4: Converting a column containing various data types can lead to errors

In this example, the engine successfully converts the values 123 and the date 01/01/2024 to a date value but throws an error for the text and logical value. What this tells us is that M does not support transforming all values to type date and in this case of mixed values, the data type any is more suitable. This indicates that even though each value individually may be of a particular type, the column accepts a mix of values with the type any. Later this chapter, we provide an overview of which transformations between data types are supported in the M language.

The preceding example is meant to illustrate that a data type can be different depending on what values it describes. With a mix of values, type any may be most appropriate.

Now, let's move on to another example where we'll have a look at the subtle but important difference between a data type and a value type. The difference is important because a column of a particular type can contain values of another type. Let's learn what that means.

Column data type versus value type

A (data) type is different from the value it describes; after all, each value has a type. Consider a table that includes columns for **Invoice ID, Date,** and **Sales Amount.** You can follow along by opening the accompanying exercise files that come with the book. Suppose you wish to add a new column to show a 5% discount across all rows.

To insert this new column, you would:

- Navigate to **Add Columns** and choose **Custom Column.**
- Input the value 0.05 and assign the column name Discount.

This creates the table in the following figure:

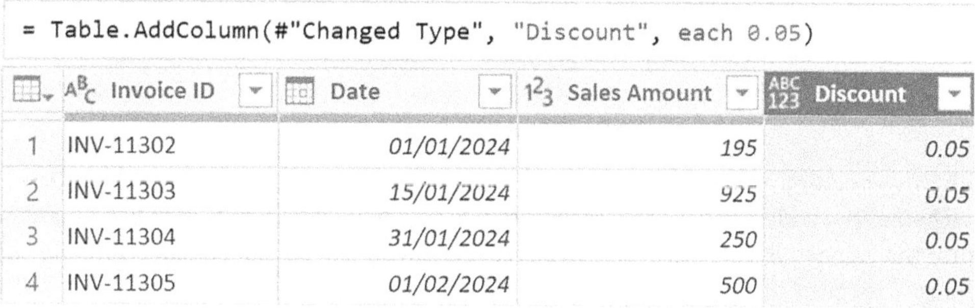

```
= Table.AddColumn(#"Changed Type", "Discount", each 0.05)
```

	ABC Invoice ID	Date	123 Sales Amount	ABC 123 Discount
1	INV-11302	01/01/2024	195	0.05
2	INV-11303	15/01/2024	925	0.05
3	INV-11304	31/01/2024	250	0.05
4	INV-11305	01/02/2024	500	0.05

Figure 5.5: Table with the Discount column of type any

When we add the **Discount** column, Power Query automatically gives it the any data type because we haven't defined a specific type for it. However, this is where it gets a little tricky: the **Discount** column is labeled as type any, yet the actual values in that column are number values. The column simply does not have a label announcing the values.

We can demonstrate this by using the Value.Type function on the **Discount** column's values. To do that, follow these steps:

1. Navigate to **Add Column** and select **Custom Column.**
2. This time, enter the formula: Value.Type([Discount]).
3. Press **Ok.**

You end up with the following table:

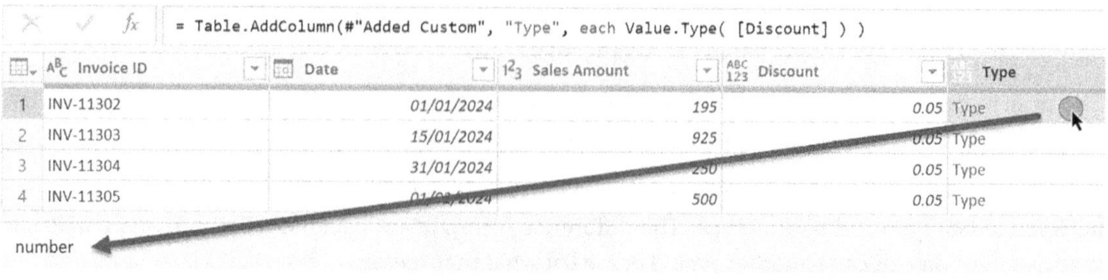

```
fx   = Table.AddColumn(#"Added Custom", "Type", each Value.Type( [Discount] ) )
```

	ABC Invoice ID	Date	123 Sales Amount	ABC 123 Discount	Type
1	INV-11302	01/01/2024	195	0.05	Type
2	INV-11303	15/01/2024	925	0.05	Type
3	INV-11304	31/01/2024	250	0.05	Type
4	INV-11305	01/02/2024	500	0.05	Type

number

Figure 5.6: Power Query can recognize the kind of value even without a data type assigned

By applying the `Value.Type` function on each value in the **Discount** column, we end up with a column that for each row shows what type of value it contains. To preview the type, you can click on the *whitespace* within the cell, where you can see that the value is of type `number`.

Now, this is interesting. So, even without a data type assigned to the column, the function still recognizes the kind of values we are working with. How does that work?

Remember how we entered the discount value earlier? We passed the value `0.05` to the `Table.AddColumn` function. Power Query recognizes the literal syntax (notation) used to input the discount value. This allows the engine to recognize what kind of value we are working with.

That goes to say that having a type, like any, in the column header, does not mean the underlying column values are of the same type. All it indicates is that the values conform to the data type of that column.

As we've seen so far, M can work with values of type any and recognizes what values we are working with. A reasonable question to ask at this point is: if M recognizes what kind of value we are working with anyway, why not just make things simple and use the Any data type for the entire dataset? That's what we'll cover in the next section.

Importance of types

The M language is a query language that is dynamically typed. What that means is that you don't have to declare variables and their (data) types before you can use them. And, as you just learned, Power Query can recognize what kind of data it receives, but not being explicit about your data types is risky in data. When your column is labeled as type any, it signals that it can contain any value. When you then perform an operation that only works on a particular type of value, your operation may result in an error.

In this section, we're going to explore why it's better to be clear about your data types. Think of data types like labeling boxes when you move; it requires some attention when storing, but saves a lot of confusion later on. So, why are data types important?

Clarity and consistency

Data types have an important role in improving clarity and ensuring consistency within datasets. They do this by clearly signaling the nature of values contained within a column. When you define a data type for a column, you are setting clear expectations and rules for the data it contains. Data that does not conform to the data type raises an error, flagging inconsistencies and helping maintain data integrity.

Imagine you're handling a set of invoices. Previously, your company used a simple numerical sequence for invoice numbers: `10000`, `10001`, `10002`, and so on. With the new year, the format was updated to include a prefix and a dash, like `INV-11000`, `INV-11001`, and `INV-11002`.

Without specifying a data type, a quick glance through the dataset might mislead you to believe you are dealing with numerical data. After all, it's only when you reach row 220 that you see the new data format:

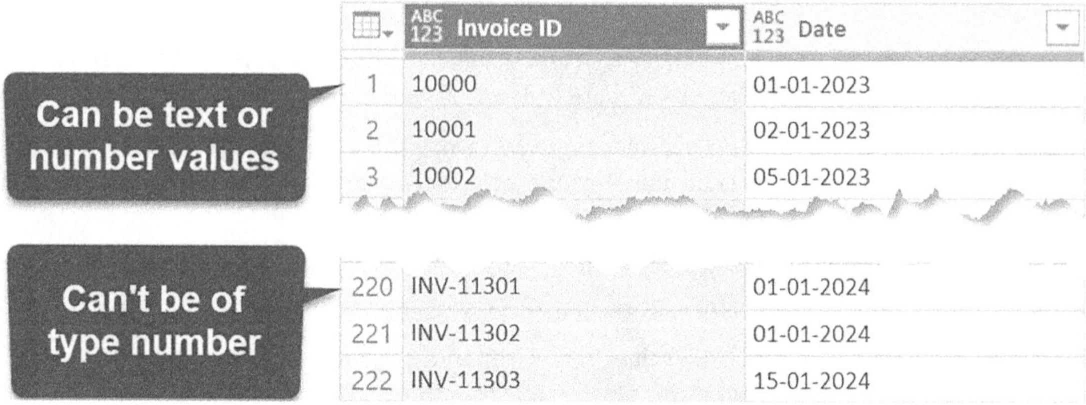

Figure 5.7: Dataset where a scan of the top 200 rows may lead to wrong data type assumptions

What this example shows is that the absence of a defined data type might lead to wrong assumptions about your data and possibly result in processing errors. If you then apply functions that are compatible with numbers only, you will run into errors. After all, the entire dataset is processed when loading your data into a destination like Power BI or Excel. Once the engine tries to process the text values, the number operations then fail.

Conversely, a clearly defined data type for the column prevents such issues by communicating the exact nature of the data, ensuring all values conform to the specified format. This clarity, together with the consistency it brings, allows you to work confidently with your data. But that's not the only reason for assigning data types. They're also useful for validating your data, as we will discuss in the next section.

Data validation

Data types play an important role in data validation and preventing errors. By setting data types, you can make sure that the data conforms to a specific type. This is important because many operations depend on receiving the correct type of data.

Take, for instance, the action of adding values together. It would not make sense to sum text values. Similarly, when you are merging tables, the Merge Columns operation requires that the columns used for merging have matching data types. Suppose your merge gives unexpected outcomes. In that scenario, pinpointing the problem can be challenging if you don't define your data types.

Perhaps the most obvious example of why data types are important is when creating custom functions, a topic we delve into in *Chapter 9, Parameters and Custom Functions*. Custom functions accept parameters, perform operations with them, and return a result. When you define a function, it is recommended to declare the expected data type for each parameter. For instance, the following function expects values of data type text as input and returns a value of type text as output:

```
( myText1 as text, myText2 as text ) as text => myText1 & myText2
```

What this function does is it takes two text values as input, combines them, and returns the combined value. Explicitly setting data types communicates to the engine that any value passed to the function should conform with the declared data type, it validates the input. In the scenario where the function receives an input value of a different type, let's say number, it throws an error and signals the user something is wrong. This immediate feedback helps to make sure the function is used as expected. Besides the two reasons we just covered, there are also other reasons for providing data types, which we discuss in the next section.

Other reasons

Besides providing clarity, consistency, and data validation, data types are important for the following reasons:

- **Performance:** Defining data types can make your queries run faster. When you set types for columns, Power Query optimizes how it stores and retrieves that data, cutting down on memory use. On the other hand, if you don't specify types, Power Query will try to infer (guess) them. Type inference consumes extra computational resources, slowing down your queries. To learn more about improving query performance, refer to *Chapter 15, Optimizing Performance*.

- **Error handling:** By specifying a data type, Power Query can better handle errors. If Power Query encounters a value that doesn't fit the assigned type, it either rejects it or converts it, depending on your expression. A variety of error-handling techniques are discussed in *Chapter 12, Handling Errors and Debugging*.

- **Compatibility:** Data types can be important when integrating with other systems or when exporting data. Certain systems require specific data types for their operations or interfaces. By using data types, Power Query ensures compatibility with these systems.

  For example, while you can call *R scripts* from within Power Query to perform advanced statistical analysis, if your data are expressed as currency (perfectly valid within M) they will be read into R as text, and the majority of the statical functions called in the script will not work.

As discussed previously, data types have more than a descriptive purpose; they play an important role in maintaining data consistency and integrity, improving performance, error handling, ensuring system compatibility, and improving overall clarity.

In the next section, we go deeper into the different kinds of data types available in the M language. We will introduce the available types, explain their properties, and show how to use them.

Data types available in M

The M language has a range of different (data) types. They provide a way to classify values and sometimes constrain the kind of data that is allowed in a custom function. You could say data types define a value's shape and indicate the operations that can be performed on it.

The *type system* in M can be seen as a hierarchy. At the base, all values conform with the any type. From here, we can get down to more specific types.

A layer down in the hierarchy, you can find more specific types. Think of primitive types, as well as more complex constructions like records, lists, and tables. The type system also allows for the definition of custom types, giving users the flexibility to specify custom data structures.

One can also distinguish between values that can and cannot hold null values through **nullable types**. This distinction is helpful when dealing with data sources where the absence of a value, represented by null, is a possibility and should be handled correctly. So, what are all these different types and how can you use them?

Primitive types

Primitive types are the fundamental data types from which all other data types are created. They can be used to classify primitive values but also as building blocks of the more complex data types like records, tables, or functions.

You can find a total of 18 primitive types in the M language. Six of these are *abstract types* that classify more than a single value and four can be used as *custom types*:

Primitive Types	Type Qualifiers	Value
binary		Binary
date		Date
datetime		DateTime
datetimezone		DateTimeZone
duration		Duration
list	Custom	List
logical		Logical
null		Null
number		Number
record	Abstract, Custom	Record
text		Text
time		Time
type		Type
function	Abstract, Custom	Function
table	Abstract, Custom	Table
any	Abstract	
anynonnull	Abstract	
none	Abstract	

Abstract: type is considered an abstract type

Custom: type can also be used as custom type

Figure 5.8: Overview of primitive types in M

In the preceding table, you can find the following information:

- The first column, **Primitive Types**, lists all the primitive types available in the M language, which includes the *abstract types*.

- The **Type Qualifiers** column identifies which primitive types are *abstract* and also indicates which *primitive types* can be used as custom types. We delve more into these terms later in this chapter.

- The **Value** column in the third position displays the specific values classified by each type. It reveals that certain types (such as any, anynonnull, and none) do not correspond to a single value, resulting in these cells being left blank.

> **Note:** The table does not include types such as Int64.Type (*whole number*), Currency.Type (*fixed decimal number*), and Number.Type (*decimal number*). The reason is that these are Type Claims, which belong to the facets category. Each of these has a base type that is included in the table provided earlier. For a more detailed exploration of these and other facets, refer to *the Facets* section of this chapter.

One reason to learn about data types is that different types of operations are supported by different values. Understanding and identifying the types of data you are working with therefore signals what you can do with them. Here are five example values and their syntax:

```
2024                    // Returns a value of type number
[ a = 10, b = 20 ]      // Returns a value of type record
#date( 2024, 12, 31 )   // Returns a value of type date
{ 1 }                   // Returns a value of type list
null                    // Returns a value of type null
```

Now, these examples show the different kinds of values. If instead, you want to return the (data) type you're dealing with, you can make use of the Value.Type function. This function accepts a value and returns its data type. For example:

```
Value.Type( 2024 )                  // Returns 'type number'
Value.Type( [ a = 10, b = 20 ] )    // Returns 'type record'
Value.Type( #date( 2024, 12, 31 ) ) // Returns 'type date'
Value.Type( { 1 } )                 // Returns 'type list'
Value.Type( null )                  // Returns 'type null'
```

What's interesting is that the Value.Type function can also return type type. For instance:

```
Value.Type( type function ) // Returns 'type type'
```

What this output indicates is that we are dealing with a type value, a special kind of value used to classify other values. In Power Query, that looks like the following:

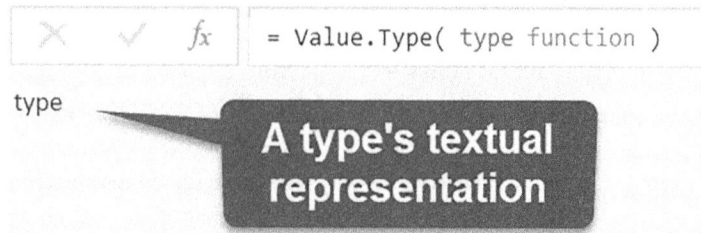

Figure 5.9: The Value.Type function returns the textual representation of a type

While the output of this expression looks like text, remember that this is just a textual representation of a type, not the actual value or its properties. To extract additional information about a type, Power Query provides a suite of functions prefixed with Type. These functions are designed to delve into the specifics and characteristics of types.

Now that you know about the general primitive types and how you can recognize them, let's have a closer look at abstract primitive types.

Abstract primitive types

In the M language, primitive types are divided into two categories: abstract and non-abstract types. There are 6 abstract and 12 non-abstract types and the primary distinction lies in how these types classify values. Non-abstract primitive types are specific; they uniquely identify a single, specific value. Abstract types, in contrast, are broader and less specific. They don't completely classify a single, unique value.

Take the type function as an example. While all functions in M conform to this type, the type function alone is insufficient to describe a function's details, such as its parameters and data types. For a complete and specific classification, a custom type would be necessary. Custom types are covered later in this chapter.

This concept extends to type table and type record as well. These types broadly classify tables and records, yet they fall short in describing specifics like column or field names, or the data types of the columns or fields. A custom type is required for such detailed classification.

Also, consider the types any and anynonnull. Every possible value in M conforms to type any, and every non-null value fits type anynonnull. However, neither of these types specifies a unique, individual value.

Finally, there's the none type, which is unique in that it is impossible to produce a value that conforms to it. An expression of type none must invariably result in an error (errors are not considered a value) or enter an endless loop. With this reasoning, type none does not classify a unique value since no value conforms with it. It's therefore not a type you will use when writing your code.

> The takeaway here is that whenever you describe a value with one of the abstract data types, it is never a precise classification of the value.

A classification using abstract types does not represent the underlying value accurately or the classification does not classify a type at all (as is the case with type none). Generally speaking, abstract types require more nuanced handling since they can describe a variety of values or no value.

For columns that expect multiple types of values, you could use broad types like any or anynonnull. But there's another useful concept that makes other data types support null values. You can do that by making them nullable, which we will cover next.

Nullable primitive types

Primitive types are not just limited to the basic forms we've covered previously. There's an important variation of these types which is the **nullable primitive type**. This type builds on the standard primitive types by incorporating an additional capability: the ability to represent the absence of a value with null.

Imagine **nullable primitive types** as a system capable of holding two kinds of values. The first kind is similar to their non-nullable counterparts, where they store specific values such as a number or text. The second kind is the ability to hold a null value. This null signifies the absence of a value. You can consider **nullable primitive types** as abstract values, as they can contain both the primitive value and the absence of a value, null.

The importance of **nullable types** becomes evident in scenarios where operations require a specific type of data, yet also need the flexibility to handle instances of missing values. To better understand this concept, let's explore an example.

Consider the Power Query functions: Number.IsOdd and Number.Sign. They have the following syntax:

```
Number.IsOdd( number as number ) as logical
Number.Sign( number as nullable number ) as nullable number
```

The Number.IsOdd function is straightforward. It takes a number and returns true if that number is odd, and false otherwise. It does not accept null values, but strictly requires a value of type number.

On the other hand, Number.Sign is more accommodating. It accepts a nullable number, meaning it accepts either a number or a null value. This is significant because it allows the function to be applied to a dataset where some values might be missing.

Let's consider a practical example: you have a dataset with an Amount column containing numerical values, but some entries are missing and represented as null. When applying the Number.IsOdd and Number.Sign functions to this column, different behaviors emerge, as shown in the following screenshot:

	1²₃ Amount ▼	ABC 123 Number.IsOdd ▼	ABC 123 Number.Sign ▼
1	-10	FALSE	-1
2	-5	TRUE	-1
3	null	Error	null
4	0	FALSE	0
5	null	Error	null
6	3	TRUE	1
7	8	FALSE	1

Figure 5.10: The behaviour of functions with and without nullable types

Figure 5.10 shows us that:

- With `Number.IsOdd`, the function processes only the entries with actual numeric values. Entries containing a null value will return an error, as `Number.IsOdd` does not accept `null` values.

- Conversely, the `Number.Sign` function can handle all rows. For numbers, it will return 1, 0, or -1, depending on whether the number is positive, 0, or negative. For `null` values, it will simply return `null`, acknowledging the absence of a value without causing an error.

The concept of **nullable types** is especially important when dealing with functions. For functions, you want to know if they accept null as an input or might give null as a result. Understanding how to use **nullable types** helps prevent errors. In *Chapter 9, Parameters and Custom Functions*, we'll delve deeper into this topic. You'll learn how to use nullable types for function parameters, making your custom functions more flexible and less prone to errors.

Applying the nullable keyword on types

Now that we've established the significance of **nullable types**, let's examine the impact of applying the `nullable` keyword to data types in M language. The rule of thumb is straightforward: prefixing any data type with the keyword `nullable` allows that type to accommodate both its **primitive value** and `null`. Here's what it looks like in action:

```
nullable text  // describes both text and null values
nullable table // describes both table and null values
```

In some cases, using `nullable` with a data type results in a type transformation. This is specifically true for the types anynonnull and none:

```
nullable anynonnull // Returns type any
nullable none       // Returns type null
```

However, there are exceptions to this transformation rule. When `nullable` is applied to a type that already accommodates null, the type remains unchanged. For instance, applying nullable to type text transforms it to `nullable text`, describing a value that can contain both text or null values. But applying `nullable` to type any, which already accepts any value including `null`, does not change the type. The following examples remain the same when applying the `nullable` keyword:

```
nullable any   // returns type any
nullable null  // returns type null
```

These examples show how the `nullable` keyword can modify a type value to support nulls. You can also achieve the reverse by using the function `Type.NonNullable`:

```
Type.NonNullable( type nullable number )
```

Having discussed all the primitive types, we are now ready to examine their practical application.

Setting data types for columns

The most common use case for types is setting data types for columns. Let's see how that can work. Imagine you have a dataset with columns like **Date**, **Product**, and **Sales**. These columns contain primitive values, but they currently have no data type set. In those cases, Power Query defaults to using the any type, represented by the **ABC123** icon in the column header:

	ABC 123 Date	ABC 123 Product	ABC 123 Sales
1	2024-01-05	Bread	2.50
2	2024-02-10	Milk	1.99
3	2024-03-15	Cereal	3.75
4	2024-04-20	Pasta	1.29

Figure 5.11: Table with columns of type any

Let's say we want to set the data types for these columns. For the columns **Date**, **Product**, and **Sales** you want to set the types to date, text, and number respectively. Before setting a data type, make sure to review your column values to confirm that they match the intended type to avoid transformation errors.

After inspecting your data, you can specify a data type by clicking the icon at the left side of each column header and selecting the desired type. Selecting the relevant types for each column results in the following code:

```
Table.TransformColumnTypes(
  Source,
  { {"Date",    type date},
    {"Product", type text},
    {"Sales",   type number} } )
```

This code uses the `Table.TransformColumnTypes` function, which does two things. It defines the data types for each column and when a value does not conform with the new type, it tries to transform the relevant value into the new type. This can, for example, happen when transforming a column with number values into `text`. Later in this chapter, we will further delve into what it means to convert data types in the *Data type conversion* section.

Using primitive types for data filtering

Before moving on, let's look at another scenario where you can benefit from knowing your primitive data types. Consider a scenario where you have a table with mixed values, including Booleans, dates, times, and numbers. You want to keep only the number values. Unfortunately, converting the entire column to number type won't work as it would transform other types, too, as shown in the following screenshot:

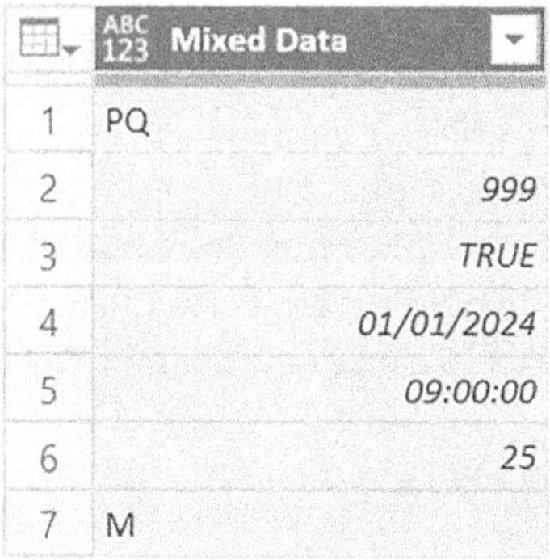

Figure 5.12: Table with different kinds of values

To tackle this challenge, the M language provides functions that can identify the type of each value, enabling you to filter the relevant types. The Value.Type function is particularly useful here. It accepts a value as input and outputs its data type. In a custom column, you might use an expression like the following:

```
Value.Type( [Mixed Date] )
```

This results in a new column populated with the data types of each value:

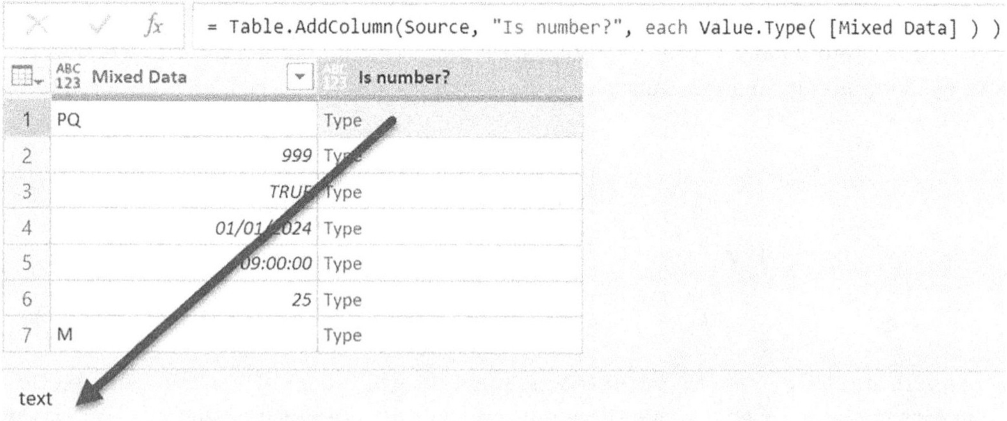

Figure 5.13: The Value.Type function returns the (data) type of a value

By clicking on the whitespace around the cells, you can bring up a preview that shows the data type for each cell. It's important to note that this returned data type is a descriptor of the value's type, not the value itself.

Next, we want to test whether we are dealing with number values. To do that, we can use another function named Type.Is. This function determines whether the value specified in the first argument conforms to the data type indicated in the second argument. Applying this to our scenario, you can check if the new type column matches type number by using the following expression:

```
Type.Is( Value.Type( [Mixed Data] ), type number )
```

Incorporating the expression into a custom column provides you with an easy method to filter exclusively for number values:

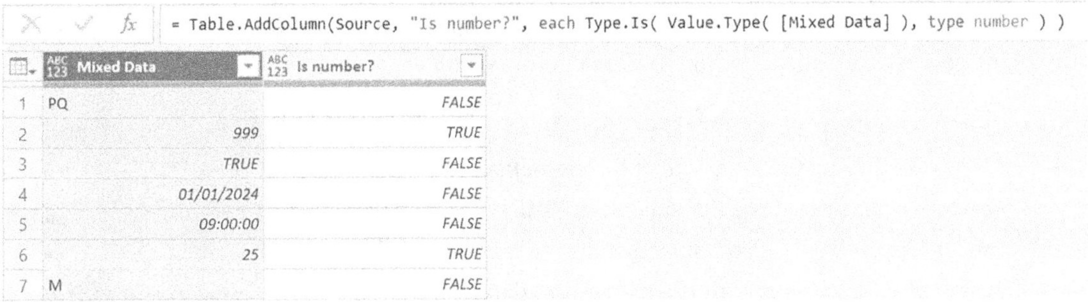

	Mixed Data	Is number?
1	PQ	FALSE
2	999	TRUE
3	TRUE	FALSE
4	01/01/2024	FALSE
5	09:00:00	FALSE
6	25	TRUE
7	M	FALSE

fx = Table.AddColumn(Source, "Is number?", each Type.Is(Value.Type([Mixed Data]), type number))

Figure 5.14: An expression that validates whether a value is of a particular type

The resulting column contains Boolean values that return true for number values. From here, you have two options for filtering. One is to directly apply a filter to the new custom column. The other, more succinct approach, is to use the expression within the Table.SelectRows function. The syntax for this would be:

```
Table.SelectRows(
    Source,
    each Type.Is( Value.Type( [Mixed Data] ), type number ) )
```

Applying that operation leaves us with a table containing only number values:

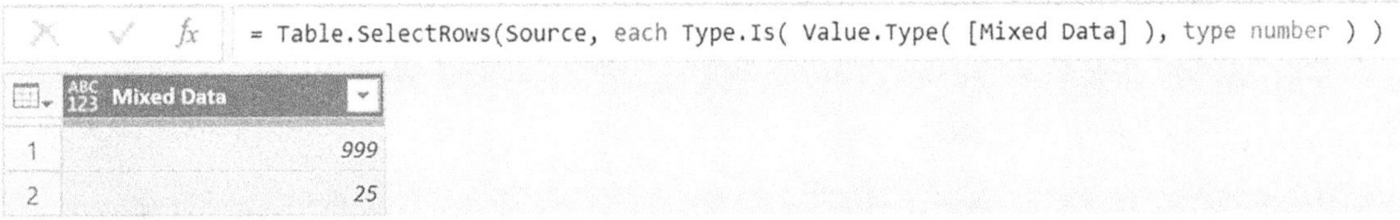

fx = Table.SelectRows(Source, each Type.Is(Value.Type([Mixed Data]), type number))

	Mixed Data
1	999
2	25

Figure 5.15. Expressions can filter values of a particular type

Alternatively, you could also use a simplified syntax using the is operator:

```
Table.SelectRows(
    Source,
    each [Mixed Data] is number )
```

This alternative not only reduces the amount of code but also improves readability. As this example shows, with the right functions, it's relatively easy to filter values of a particular type. We'll delve deeper into the use of this syntax and its implications when discussing type equivalence later in this chapter.

After covering primitive types in this section, we'll now have a look at **custom types**. These types are more complex but very useful to accurately describe your structured values and functions.

Custom types

Custom types are not part of the closed set of **primitive types**. While **primitive types** describe simple values like text or numbers, custom types describe more complex values. They are relevant for structured values and custom functions. To precisely describe what these values contain, we need a framework that incorporates one or more primitive types.

The M language knows four custom types: lists, records, tables, and functions. They can be constructed using type expressions that allow you to classify more complex structures.

For custom types, you can think of types for:

- Lists: Classifying the data type of the elements in the list.
- Records: Specifying both the names and data types for each field in a record.
- Tables: Specifying both the names and data types for each column in a table.
- Functions: Specifying both the names and data types of function parameters, as well as defining the data type of the function's return value.

These custom types are built upon the primitive and abstract types but add constraints to their structures. While primitive types are important, custom types are also widely used in Power Query. Just like primitive types classify primitive values, custom types add an additional classification layer for more complex values. To illustrate the application of custom types, we will use Table.AddColumn. This function allows you to ascribe data types to columns.

Ascribing a type is like declaring that a value conforms to a specific type without performing any checks. In that case, the M language does not verify whether the values in the column match the ascribed type. This means you might inadvertently ascribe a type that does not conform with the underlying values in the column. For now, it's enough to be aware of this behavior; we will delve into the concept of ascription later in this chapter when covering ascribing types.

Let's delve deeper into each custom type, starting with the type list.

List type

The custom list type can be used to classify list values. By using a custom list type, you can specify a value of type list but also include the data type of the values it contains. Let's see how that works.

List values are a collection of items that can be of any data type. You can create such a value using curly brackets, like {1, 2, 3}, a list containing only numbers. Creating a column and setting its data type to type list will not specify the types of values contained within it.

For instance, the following image shows you how to create a new column containing a list of numbers. The fourth argument of Table.AddColumn allows you to ascribe the data type of a column; in this case, we used the primitive type list.

Now, here's where things get interesting: when you expand the `mylist` column with the icon in the header and select **Expand to New Rows**, the new rows don't have a specific data type defined:

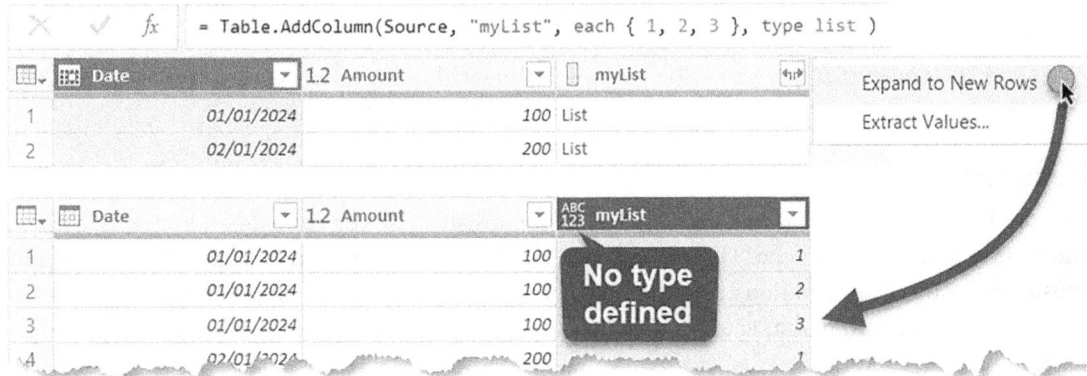

Figure 5.16: Types are lost when expanding a column with a primitive list type

This is because a type `list` is generic and does not specify the type of values it contains. However, you can classify a list with a more specific custom type to indicate that all its elements conform to a certain data type.

For instance, to classify different types, you can use:

```
type { text }        // Returns a list type containing text values
type { number }      // Returns a list type containing number values
```

To specify this custom type, you start with the word `type`, followed by the type within curly brackets. Applying this more complex type, which also classifies the values within the list, ensures Power Query can output a table with the relevant types:

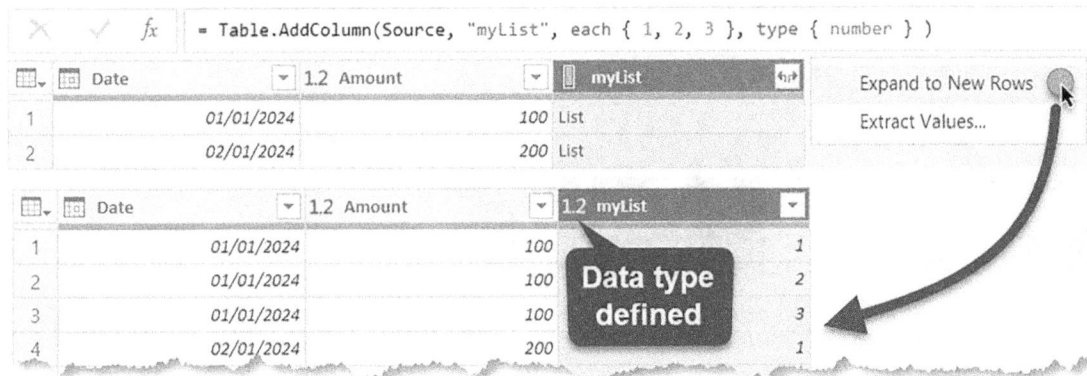

Figure 5.17: Types are retained when expanding a column with a custom list type

In this way, a custom type allows you to set your data types and keep them intact when expanding them. As the preceding examples show, the column header does not differentiate between a primitive-type list and a custom-type list; the list icon is identical.

If you're dealing with a custom list type and want to test what kind of values a list accepts, you can use the `Type.ListItem` function:

```
Type.ListItem( type { number } ) // Output: type number
```

This allows you to extract the type value you are dealing with. Like a `list` type, a `record` type is also a custom type that allows you to describe a record, which we will cover next.

Record type

A record in Power Query M is like a row in a table. It consists of one or more fields, each with a name and a corresponding data type. The `record` type, similar to `list` type, broadly classifies a value but doesn't provide any information about the types a value can have. To describe what type of values are expected for each field name, you can make use of a custom record type. The syntax for defining a record might look like:

```
type record            // primitive type
type [ Date = date ] // custom type
```

The custom type includes the field name and type within square brackets, whereas the primitive type provides no such details. So, how can we use them? Suppose you wish to create a `record` type with two fields: `Column1` with text values and `Column2` with numeric values. You can represent this as:

```
type [ Column1 = text, Column2 = number ]
```

When you add a new column with a record value and expand it, the data type is preserved only if it's explicitly set in the custom record type. Additionally, if you have fields in your record that are not specified in its type definition, the Expand Record operation does not suggest these missing fields, as shown in the following image:

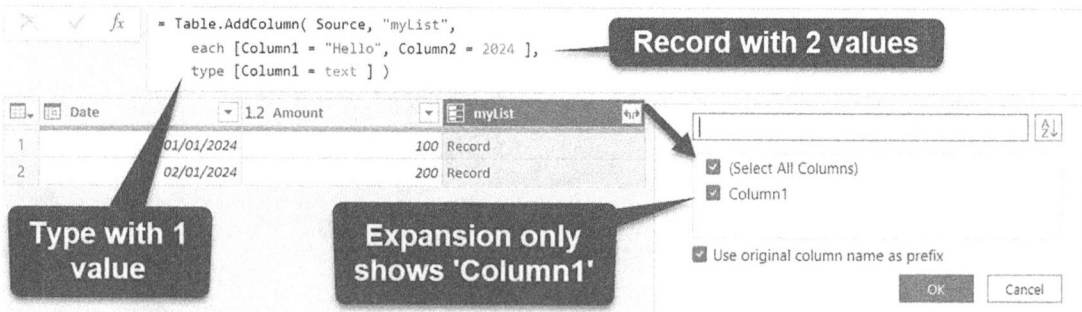

Figure 5.18: Fields missing in a custom record type do not show when expanding columns

Whenever you are missing fields when expanding a record column, make sure to check the type definition. It likely misses a few fields. Also, when creating a `custom record` type, it is not necessary to specify the type of each column. For instance, it's perfectly valid to define the same record and only provide `Column1` with a data type:

```
type [ Column1 = text, Column2 ]
```

Just keep in mind that when expanding a record column, any fields that do not have their types specified will receive type any.

Another interesting syntax you can use is that of an open record. The open-record marker, represented by three dots (…), allows you to define a record that allows for new (unknown) fields in the future. For instance, imagine you have a record with a range of field names. You only want to specify the types of Date and Amount; all others can be of type any. You can achieve that by using the open-record marker as follows:

```
type [ Date = type date, Amount = type number, ... ]
```

This custom record type sets an expectation that the record may or may not contain more values than the ones described. The primitive type record definition is equivalent to an open record. Hence, the following statement returns true:

```
type [...] = type record // returns true
```

This shows that type record is considered an open record. Having seen the **type list** and **type record**, let's move on to one of the most important custom types: **type table**. As most transformations in Power Query revolve around tables, you will commonly find this custom type. Let's see how it works in the next section.

Table type

Another common type you will find is the table type. You can consider a table as a list of records with a defined structure. Each column in a table has a specified data type, and all records (rows) in the table conform to this structure. The table type is the base type of all tables. It is specified as:

```
type table
```

This represents a row type with an empty open record, identical to:

```
type table []
```

This is also the only time where a table type is allowed to have an open row type. Custom table types should always have the form of a closed record.

The custom type table definition is similar to type record. A common scenario where you will find it used is when using the **Group By** feature. When performing that operation, the M engine automatically generates a custom table type to specify the relevant table column names and types. A basic example of a table type with text and number columns is:

```
type table [ Column1 = text, Column2 = number ]
```

This type indicates all rows in the table conform to these values, where Column1 always contains text data, and Column2 contains numeric data. If you wanted to, you could even use a custom record type and use it to provide the information for your table type:

```
let
    myRecordType = type [ Column1 = number, Column2 = text ],
```

```
    myTableType = type table myRecordType
  in
    myTableType
```

The code returns a table type, which, as a value by itself, is not often used. It's often found within a table function to specify the column and data type details of a table. This example illustrates that a table type can include a record type in its definition. However, there are subtle distinctions between a record type and a table type. To be valid, the record types used in defining a custom table type must be of a closed type. This means they cannot have optional fields; all fields in the record must be explicitly defined and required for the table type to be properly recognized. It would have been useful to be able to provide an open table type so that you could specify types of specific columns and indicate you're not sure about the type of the others. Unfortunately, this is not allowed.

In line with what was illustrated for both the list types and record types, when you add a custom table type to a column and don't include certain columns, they don't show up in the **Expand Columns** dialogue box. We will delve more into structured values in *Chapter 6*.

Something unique to table types is that they can include the definition of the table's keys. Power Query uses key information to improve functionality performance, such as joining operations. You can use the Type to set the key on a table's type.AddTableKey function. For instance, the following code sets Column1 as the primary key for the table type:

```
  let
    myType = type table [ Column1 = text, Column2 = number ],
    setKeys = Type.AddTableKey( myType, {"Column1"}, true )
  in
    setKeys
```

The output of this code is a table type with key information. Again, these types are used to classify a table, which can then be used for subsequent operations. Once a key is set, you can retrieve the existing ones using the Type.TableKeys function or replace them using Type.ReplaceTableKeys. We will delve more into custom table types in *Chapter 6*, *Structured Values*. Having covered most custom types, up next is the last one: **type function**.

Function Type

We can also define a custom function type. You could assign a function the primitive type function, and any expression will work. However, this does not impose any restrictions on the input parameter types or types a function can return. Defining a custom function type allows you to overcome this limitation.

A function type consists of a return type and a list of zero-or-more function parameters. A function type is compatible with another function type if the return types are compatible, and the parameter types are identical.

Defining a **custom function type** can be done with a syntax like the following:

```
  type function ( date as date, days as number) as date
```

What's interesting is that you can define a **function value**, without specifying a type:

```
( date, days ) => Date.AddDays( date, days )
```

In that case, the value automatically receives a **custom function type** of:

```
type function ( date as any, days as any ) as any
```

That shows that type assertions are optional when defining a function value. However, when specifying a custom function type, you are required to include type assertions. The following statement returns a syntax error:

```
type function ( date, days ) as date
```

When defining a data type for a parameter in a custom function, you can only use primitive types. Providing a custom type will result in an error. We will delve more into custom functions and their syntax in *Chapter 9, Parameters and Custom Functions*.

For cases where you need to apply a custom function type to a function, you can only achieve this using an ascribed type using the `Value.ReplaceType` function.

So far in this chapter, we have looked at the available data types and how we can specify them using primitive and custom types. That's often a tedious process requiring manual work. However, you don't always have to manually identify your data types. Power Query has different methods for doing so automatically, which we will cover next.

Type detection

Your first interaction with datatypes in Power Query is likely when you import data. Your data often comes in the form of a table, and the columns for the table can have a data type. When using the default settings, Power Query automatically recognizes the data types of any tables you import. Yet, how Power Query detects the data types of the values in your dataset will depend on the data source used and your Power Query settings. There are two available methods:

- Retrieving data types from data sources
- Automatically detecting types

The following sections look at how these two methods work.

Retrieving data types from a data source

When you import data from a structured data source (e.g., SQL, Oracle, Azure Data Lake, OData feed, etc.), Power Query automatically accesses the table schema from these sources. This table schema is only available in structured data sources and defines the structure of tables in a database. It contains information about the different data types found in each column.

If the source system contains information about the data types of the imported columns, Power Query sets the types in line with this definition. However, the engine can't rely on any schema if you are importing data from an unstructured data source. The reason is that those data sources don't come with a table schema. In those cases, the engine uses another approach, which we will discuss next.

Automatically detecting types

Power Query has a feature designed to automatically identify the data types of columns in your datasets. This is particularly useful when dealing with unstructured data sources such as Excel files, CSVs, or text files, where there is no predefined schema to guide the data types for different columns. The feature works by examining the first 200 rows of your dataset to determine the most suitable data type for each column.

Suppose you work with a table without any specified data types, as shown in the following figure:

	ABC 123 ISO2	ABC 123 Country	ABC 123 Neighbors
1	NL	Netherlands	2
2	PO	Poland	7
3	US	United States	2

Figure 5.19: Table without any type information

You can use the **Detect Data Type** operation to automatically assign data types to these columns. This involves the following steps:

1. Selecting all the columns in your table.
2. Navigating to the **Transform** tab.
3. Clicking on **Detect Data Type**.

Power Query then analyses your data and makes an educated guess about the appropriate data types, converting the columns accordingly. This process is visualized in the following image:

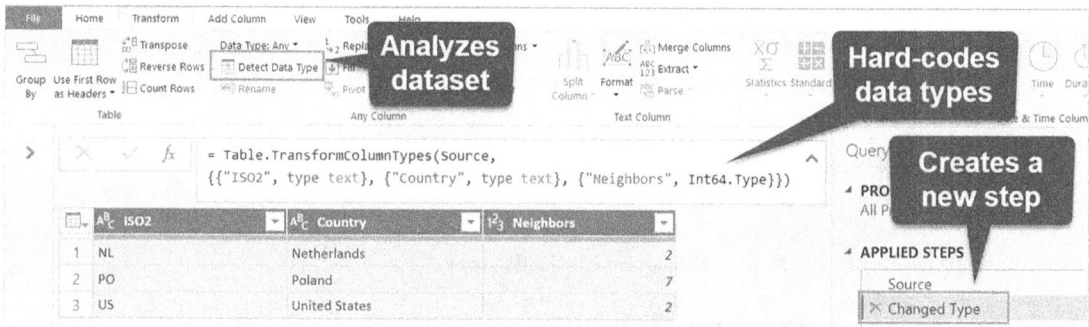

Figure 5.20: The Detect Data Type operation hardcodes data types in a new step

By default, Power Query performs the **Detect Data Type** operation when you connect to a data source without a structured schema. But you have the option to change this setting in your Power Query settings. This can be done by doing the following:

1. Going to the **File** menu.
2. Selecting **Options** and **settings**.
3. Clicking **Options**.

In the settings window, you can choose how your data is loaded in the **Data Load** section of the **Global** options. This selection process is illustrated in following image:

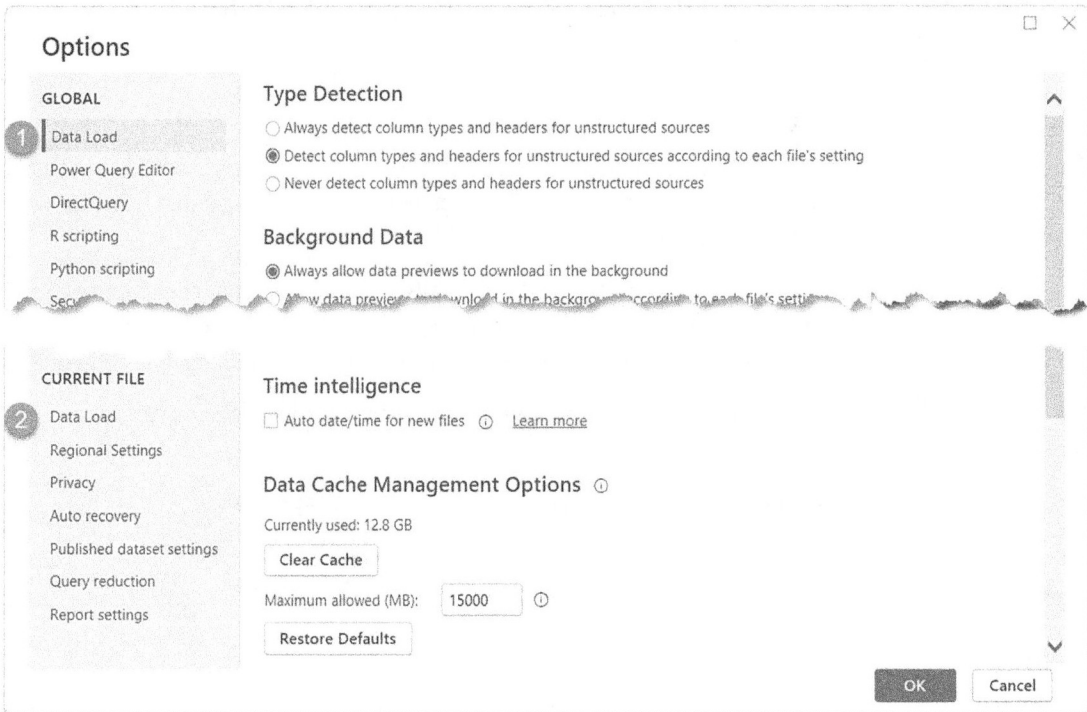

Figure 5.21: The Power Query Options menu allows you to set Type Detection preferences

In terms of settings for handling **Type Detection**, Power Query offers three options:

- **Always**: This examines the first 200 rows of each column in every file. Power Query then uses pattern recognition algorithms to deduce each column's most probable data type.
- **According to each file's setting**: The use of automatic type detection depends on the user's choice in the **Current File Data Load** settings.
- **Never:** This prevents Power Query from automatically inserting a changed type step to identify column types.

Even if auto-type detection is turned off, either in the global or individual report settings, users can still apply the **Detect Data Type** feature manually. This is done by selecting the desired columns, navigating to the **Transform** tab, and choosing **Detect Data Type** from the Power Query ribbon.

When deciding which settings to use in Power Query, consider your specific needs and circumstances. While the auto-detect feature is generally effective at predicting column types, it only bases its analysis on the first 200 rows. Therefore, whether you enable auto-detection at the global or report level, thoroughly reviewing each column type is always a good idea. Verifying or adjusting the detected data types using your understanding of the data is a best practice to ensure accuracy.

So far, we have looked at the different data types in the M language and why they are important as a concept. What we haven't seen yet is that different values support different operations. Because of that, you often need to convert a value into another type of value to be able to work with it. That's what we're looking at next.

Data type conversion

Whether you import or create data yourself, setting the correct data type is essential. Sometimes, you'll need to change a data type temporarily to make things work—like making sure a piece of data is accepted by a certain function, or when you're mixing different types of data.

Let's say you have a number that's been input as text. To do any math with it, you'll need to change it from text to a numeric format. Or, if you're trying to add a date to a text message, you'll need to switch the date to a text format first. This kind of switching is often needed when your data is stored in tables.

For these situations, the M language has two main ways to convert your values to another type. You could:

- Create a new column and use a conversion function within an expression
- Transform entire columns to another type

We will look at both approaches in the following sections.

Converting value types

First, let's look at a range of functions that allow you to convert a value from one type to another. They fall into two categories:

- **Type extraction functions**: These functions extract a specific type of value from a more general input, which can be any kind. The purpose is to identify a particular type from a potentially mixed or undefined data type. Common examples of these functions include `Date.From`, `Text.From`, and `Number.From`. They are available for various data types, such as `binary`, `date`, `duration`, `function`, `logical`, `number`, `time`, `datetime`, `datetimezone`, and `text`.
- **Type conversion functions**: This category contains functions that convert data between specific types. They are capable of handling conversions in both directions. For instance, `Date.ToText` and `Binary.ToText` transform date and binary data into a text format. On the other hand, `Date.FromText` and `Binary.FromText` reverse these conversions, turning text into date values and text into binary data.

The functions that convert or extract types are typically used during the evaluation of an expression. For example, the following expressions extract `date` and `number` values:

```
Date.From( "31 dec 2024" ) // Output: #date( 2024, 12, 31 )
Date.From( 45657 )          // Output: #date( 2024, 12, 31 )
Number.From( "550" )        // Output: 550
Number.From( true )         // Output: 1
```

As you can see, the extraction functions have a level of flexibility in what values they allow. On the other hand, conversion functions require a more specific type. For instance:

```
Number.ToText( 125 )                    // Output: "125"
Record.ToList( [A = 1, B = 2, C = 3] ) // Output: {1, 2, 3 }
```

When you work with tables, using the conversion functions in an expression has two benefits:

- **Preserving original columns:** The original structure of the table can remain unchanged, maintaining its original data types.
- **Preventing clutter:** There is no need for an additional step to transform data types, preventing your queries from clutter.

For the next exercise, we'll start with the following table:

	Date	AᴮC Product Name	$ Price
1	01/01/2024	Chef's Knife	45.00
2	02/01/2024	Cast Iron Skillet	30.50
3	03/01/2024	Cutting Board	15.75
4	04/01/2024	Digital Kitchen Scale	22.00
5	05/01/2024	Dutch Oven	55.99
6	06/01/2024	Silicone Spatula Set	10.25
7	07/01/2024	Stainless Steel Cookware Set	120.00
8	08/01/2024	Programmable Slow Cooker	75.00

Figure 5.22: Table containing dates, text, and number values

To follow along, you can download the exercise files on the book's GitHub page (`https://github.com/PacktPublishing/The-Definitive-Guide-to-Power-Query-M-`). The preceding dataset has three columns with different data types: `Date`, `Text`, and `Number`. Your goal is to merge the information from these columns into a single, coherent sentence. However, in the M language, you must first convert values into text before combining them into a sentence. This is where conversion functions come in.

Let's say you aim to construct a sentence like:

```
"On [Date] we sold [Price] worth of [Product Name]s."
```

To concatenate the different values, you must ensure that the `Date` and the `Price` values are turned into text. The `Text.From` function is perfect for this task. It converts the Date and Price values into text, providing the correct format for concatenation.

After converting the values you can use the concatenation operator (&) to piece together your custom sentence. The following code would achieve that:

```
"On "
  & Text.From( [Date] )
```

```
& " we sold "
& Text.From( [Price] )
& " worth of "
& [Product Name]
& "s"
```

If you add this to a **Custom** column, you end up with the following situation:

```
          fx    = Table.AddColumn(#"Changed Type", "Custom",
                    each "On " & Text.From( [Date] ) & " we sold " & Text.From( [Price] ) & " worth of "& [Product Name] & "s"  )
```

	Date	A^BC Product Name	$ Price	ABC 123 Custom
1	01/01/2024	Chef's Knife	45.00	On 01/01/2024 we sold 45 worth of Chef's Knifes
2	02/01/2024	Cast Iron Skillet	30.50	On 02/01/2024 we sold 30.5 worth of Cast Iron Skillets
3	03/01/2024	Cutting Board	15.75	On 03/01/2024 we sold 15.75 worth of Cutting Boards
4	04/01/2024	Digital Kitchen Scale	22.00	On 04/01/2024 we sold 22 worth of Digital Kitchen Scales
5	05/01/2024	Dutch Oven	55.99	On 05/01/2024 we sold 55.99 worth of Dutch Ovens
6	06/01/2024	Silicone Spatula Set	10.25	On 06/01/2024 we sold 10.25 worth of Silicone Spatula Sets
7	07/01/2024	Stainless Steel Cookware Set	120.00	On 07/01/2024 we sold 120 worth of Stainless Steel Cookware Sets
8	08/01/2024	Programmable Slow Cooker	75.00	On 08/01/2024 we sold 75 worth of Programmable Slow Cookers

Figure 5.23: Conversion functions allow you to transform values into text before concatenating them

This example illustrates how you can use a conversion function within a custom column to create a custom sentence. By using a conversion function, the table's column types remain intact for any future operations.

The preceding examples showed a successful conversion from various data types to text. However, the M language does not support converting data types into just any type. Some combinations result in an error. The following matrix shows which conversions are supported. The values on the left side show the current value and the icons indicate whether you can transform the value into the type indicated in the top row:

Data Types	1.2	$	1²3	%	📅🕐	📅	🕐	🌐	⏱	A^B_C	✗✓
1.2 Decimal number		⊖	⊖	✓	✓	⊖	⚠	⊕	✓	✓	✓
$ Currency	✓		⊖	✓	✓	⊖	⚠	⊕	✓	✓	✓
1²3 Whole number	✓	✓		✓	✓	✓	⚠	⊕	✓	✓	✓
% Percentage	✓	⊖	⊖		✓	✓	✓	⊕	✓	✓	✓
📅🕐 Date/Time	✓	⊖	⊖	✓		⊖	⊖	⊕	⚠	✓	⚠
📅 Date	✓	✓	✓	✓	✓		⚠	⊕	⚠	✓	⚠
🕐 Time	✓	✓	✓	✓	⊕	⚠		⊕	⚠	✓	⚠
🌐 Date/Time/Zone	✓	⊖	⊖	✓	⊖	⊖	⊖		⚠	✓	⚠
⏱ Duration	✓	⊖	⊖	✓	⚠	⚠	⚠	⚠		✓	⚠
A^B_C Text	✓	✓	✓	✓	✓	✓	✓	✓	✓		✓
✗✓ True/False	✓	✓	✓	✓	⚠	⚠	⚠	⚠	⚠	✓	

✓ Conversion possible

⚠ Conversion fails with error

⊕ Conversion possible, adds detail to the original value

⊖ Conversion possible, loses detail of the original value

Figure 5.24: Data type conversion matrix

Having explored how conversion functions let you change a value without changing the original column types, let's transition to another approach. The next section delves into transforming a column type, and with it, all column values.

Converting column types

Next, we delve into the process of converting entire column types. Unlike the individual value conversions we discussed previously, this method involves changing the data type of an entire column. This approach is particularly useful when you want to load the appropriate data type into a host like Power BI or when you need the outcome of this transformation for multiple other calculations. So, how does that work?

The following image presents a small dataset with the **Neighbours** column formatted as Whole Number:

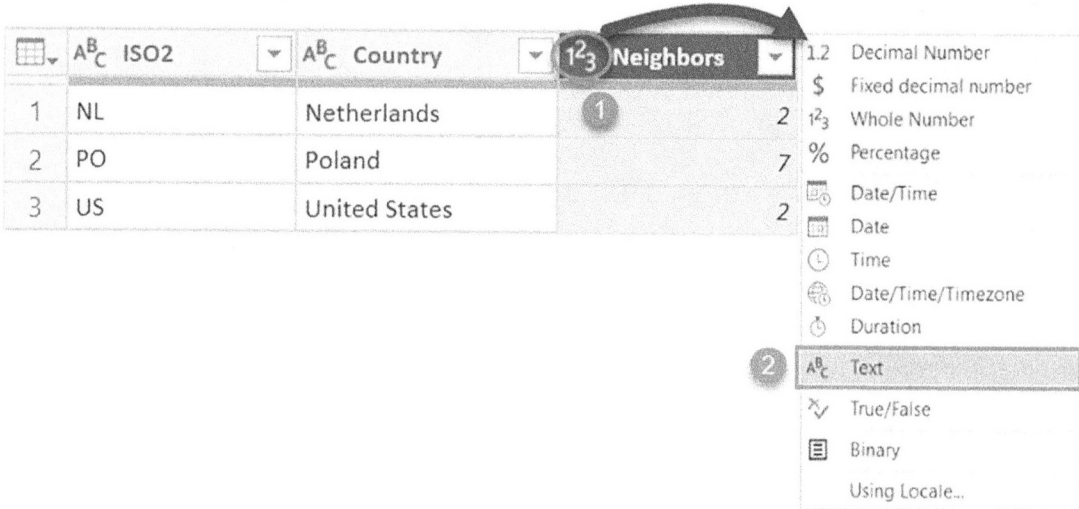

Figure 5.25: Transform a column to the desired type by selecting it in the column header

Suppose that in the **Neighbors** column, we want the values to be of type text instead of type number. A simple way to make this change is to click on the column icon next to the column name and select the type **Text**. This operation transforms your column from a whole number to type text by using the Table.TransformColumnTypes function. It uses the following expression:

```
Table.TransformColumnTypes(
    #"Changed Type",
    { {"Neighbors", type text} } )
```

So, how does this function work? Table.TransformColumnTypes requires two arguments. The first is the table that you want to modify, in this case, #"Changed Type". The second argument is a list where each element is a pair: a column name and a new data type. For example, { {"Neighbors", type text} } indicates that the Neighbors column's data type will be changed to text.

The function executes two key operations:

1. **Data type assignment:** The function assigns the new data type to the specified column, as directed. The table's column header will reflect this new data type.

2. **Value conversion:** The function attempts to convert the existing values in the column to the new data type.

Setting the data type of a column always works as the icon in the header will change. However, the value conversion isn't always successful. For instance, if we try to convert a column from a whole number to a time data type instead of text, it results in the following error:

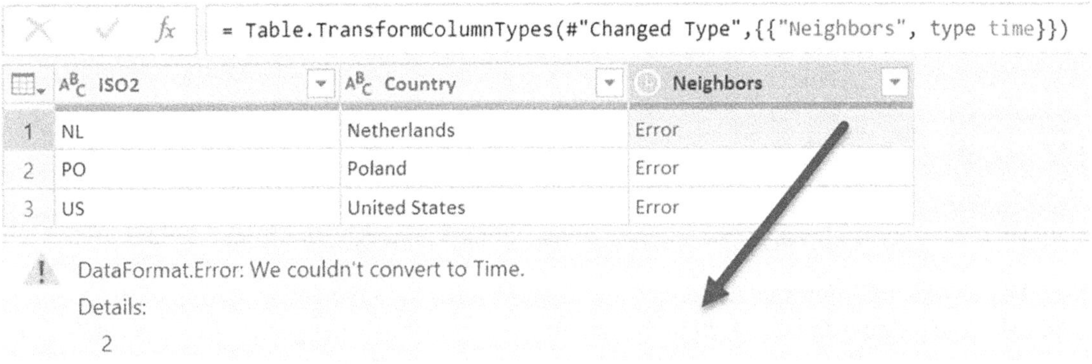

Figure 5.26: Converting a value to an unsupported value results in DataFormat.Error

The reason for this error is that a number can't be transformed into a time value. You can refer to *Figure 5.24* to check which conversions are supported in the M language.

As this section showed, you can convert column types, just like you can convert values. You learned which data type conversions are supported and when you can run into errors. There's one important topic to still add, though. Even if a conversion is successful, some conversions can lead to a loss of data. The next section delves into when this happens.

Avoiding data loss during conversion

When you change values from one data type to another, it's important to be cautious and fully grasp what that change means. During type conversion, Power Query will try to make the conversion if it can, but be aware that this might lead to losing or gaining data or precision in the process. This process impacts how data is stored and finally provided to a host application like Power BI.

Contrastingly, the practice of applying format strings within the visualization layer of Power BI Desktop operates differently. Unlike type conversion in Power Query, which directly influences data storage, format masks merely adjust the presentation of values without changing the underlying data storage. This distinction helps in understanding how data adjustments affect the backend (storage) versus the frontend (display) in Power BI. Let's see an example where data loss is an issue.

Consider a dataset of daily paid parking in *Seattle, Washington*. The data types were defined according to the dataset's accompanying data dictionary:

	AᴮC Transaction ID ▼	AᴮC Meter Code ▼	▦ Transaction Date ▼	AᴮC Payment Mean ▼	1.2 Amount Paid ▼
1	1250162207	12028002	7/11/2023	PHONE	0.26
2	1250162278	19232002	7/11/2023	PHONE	1.52
3	1250131414	19127010	7/11/2023	PHONE	9.67
4	1250134465	5073002	7/11/2023	CREDIT CARD	4
5	1250134860	19161010	7/11/2023	PHONE	6.73
6	1250134876	5019002	7/11/2023	PHONE	0.3
7	1250134941	19126010	7/11/2023	PHONE	8.77

Figure 5.27: Table with the Amount Paid column containing decimal numbers

Now, let's say we are interested in doing some analyses related to the dollar portion of the **Amount Paid** field (and for now don't care about the remaining cents). If we change that field to a whole number using the UI, it will work:

	AᴮC Transaction ID ▼	AᴮC Meter Code ▼	▦ Transaction Date ▼	AᴮC Payment Mean ▼	1²₃ Amount Paid ▼
1	1250162207	12028002	7/11/2023	PHONE	0
2	1250162278	19232002	7/11/2023	PHONE	2
3	1250131414	19127010	7/11/2023	PHONE	10
4	1250134465	5073002	7/11/2023	CREDIT CARD	4
5	1250134860	19161010	7/11/2023	PHONE	7
6	1250134876	5019002	7/11/2023	PHONE	0
7	1250134941	19126010	7/11/2023	PHONE	9

Figure 5.28: Table with the Amount Paid column converted to whole numbers

However, reverting `Amount Paid` to a decimal type to include cents will restore the field type but lose the original cent values. This highlights a key point: changing a field's data type impacts its storage and can reduce the data's granularity. On the other hand, modifying the format through the Power BI visualization layer only changes how data appears in visuals, not its storage format.

In some instances, changing data types can seem to increase data detail, but this can be misleading. For example, converting the **Transaction Date** column to a datetime type adds time values to the dates:

⊞▾	A^BC Transaction ID ▾	A^BC Meter Code ▾	🕘 **Transaction Date** ▾
1	1250162207	12028002	*7/11/2023 12:00:00 AM*
2	1250162278	19232002	*7/11/2023 12:00:00 AM*
3	1250131414	19127010	*7/11/2023 12:00:00 AM*
4	1250134465	5073002	*7/11/2023 12:00:00 AM*
5	1250134860	19161010	*7/11/2023 12:00:00 AM*
6	1250134876	5019002	*7/11/2023 12:00:00 AM*
7	1250134941	19126010	*7/11/2023 12:00:00 AM*

Figure 5.29: Converting a date to a datetime value adds a default time of 12 AM

However, the added time does not correspond to an actual Transaction Time field. Instead, it adds 12 AM by default, illustrating that while data may appear more detailed, it may not be accurate.

These examples show the importance of fully understanding the implications of a datatype conversion before you implement it. As shown previously, Power Query will not stop you from executing conversions that will result in data loss.

A datatype conversion can have one of four different outcomes:

- **Success:** The datatype change is implemented with no gain or loss of data.
- **Success with data lost:** The datatype change is implemented but with some level of data loss.
- **Success with data gained:** The datatype change is implemented with some level of data gained. The data gained may or may not be correct.
- **Failure:** The datatype change was not implemented due to incompatibility of input and output types.

It should be noted that while data loss due to datatype conversion is usually an outcome to be avoided, in some cases, it can be intentional. For example, converting a datetime value to a date removes the time component but has a positive impact on the compression when loading your data into Power BI.

So far, we have seen that converting a value from one type to another can lead to data loss. We have also seen that transformations are only supported between certain types. Another topic relevant to conversion is the effect of locale. Depending on local formatting conventions, one value may be interpreted differently. That what's we'll cover in the next section.

Effect of locale/culture

Different regions around the world follow varied data conventions. This includes choices like which separator to use in numbers (comma or period), the format for dates, and whether to use an AM/PM designator. These regional conventions have a big influence on how data types are transformed since the conversion process relies on recognizing the format of the underlying value. This section demonstrates how regional settings can affect the outcomes of your data transformations.

Imagine a situation where you have a column of text values that represent dates from January 1 to January 12, 2024. Depending on the conventions used, these dates might be interpreted in various ways. They could be seen as dates from January 1st to January 12th, 2024, or as the first day of each month throughout 2024. What the right approach is depends on the convention used when providing the data. Power Query addresses these ambiguities using Locale settings. By default, it matches the language and regional settings of your computer. So, if your computer is set to interpret dates in the MM/DD/YYYY format, Power Query will respect this format when converting text values to a date.

However, what if you need to convert these text values into date formats, and your settings are different from those of a colleague? How do you ensure consistent date recognition across different systems? The key is in using Locale settings to guide the transformation of the values. So, how does that work?

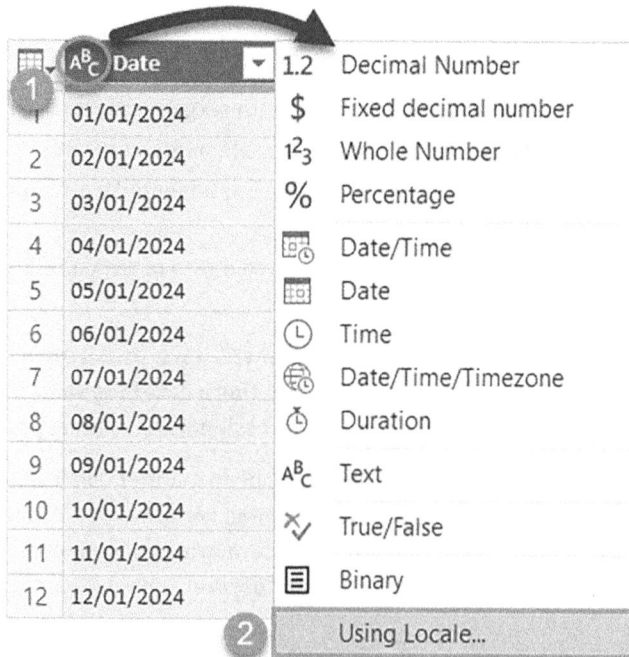

Figure 5.30: The UI allows you to change a data type using the Using Locale… option

When you click on the **data type** icon located in a column's header, a dropdown menu appears. This menu offers various options for data types. The last option in this dropdown enables you to modify the data type according to specific **Locale** settings, as illustrated in the image above. Choosing this option opens a dialogue box where you can select both the desired data type and the **Locale**. This feature is designed to accommodate local formatting conventions during the data type transformation process.

For example, when you choose **Date** as the data type in this dialogue box, a preview is displayed. This preview shows what input values Power Query expects using the chosen Locale. That means that the country you select represents the format of the source data and not the format you want the output to be in. The output will be in line with your current regional settings. This preview is particularly useful for verifying that the data matches the expected format for the selected **Locale**. You can see an example in the following image:

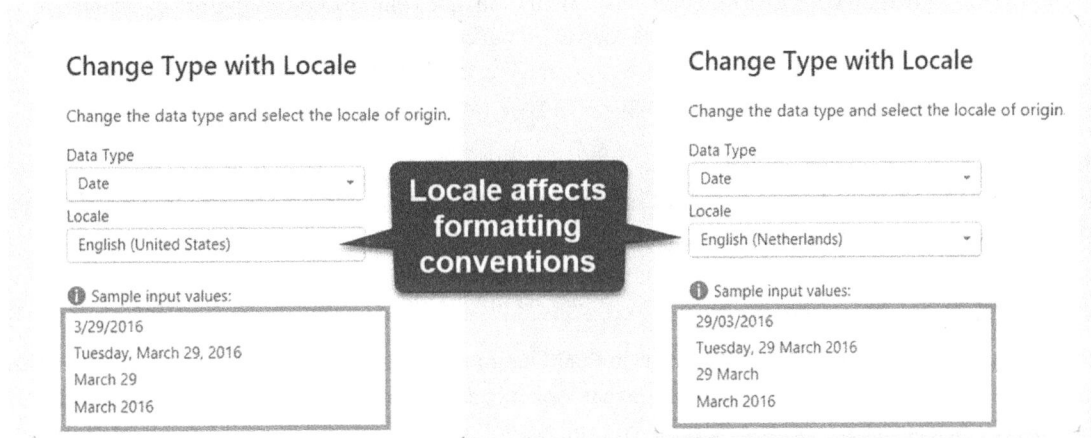

Figure 5.31: Changing the type using Locale shows a preview of the expected formatting conventions of the input

Confirming the transformation using the **English (Netherlands)** locale transforms the dates and makes use of the following formula:

```
Table.TransformColumnTypes( Source, {{"Date", type date}}, "en-NL")
```

In this function, the third argument is an optional culture code. The en-NL locale expects dates to be in the format of dd/mm/yyyy.

Should you need to use the English (United States) locale instead, expecting a format of m/d/yyyy, the culture code changes to en-US:

```
Table.TransformColumnTypes( Source, {{"Date", type date}}, "en-US")
```

This approach offers a user-friendly way to change column types through the interface. Moreover, Power Query includes several functions that accept a culture code to guide the conversion process. These functions are often used for extracting or converting data types, as well as formatting values as text.

For instance, the interpretation of dates varies with the culture code in the `Date.From` function:

```
Date.From( "01-12-2024", "nl-NL" )      // Output: #date(2023,12,1)
Date.From( "01-12-2024", "en-US" )      // Output: #date(2023,1,12)
```

Additionally, the `Text.Upper` function shows different behaviors with different locales. When using the Turkish Locale `tr-TR` compared to the English `en-US` locale, the capitalization outputs vary:

```
Text.Upper( "i am lucky", "tr-TR" )     // Output: "İ AM LUCKY"
Text.Upper( "i am lucky", "en-US" )     // Output: "I AM LUCKY"
```

That can mean a world of difference for your transformation needs.

> **Pro tip:** Whenever a function's documentation mentions an optional culture parameter, it indicates you can use a culture code to influence the output. When a culture parameter is available in a function, we recommend using it. That ensures your output is predictable regardless of the machine language of your users.

Having explored different data types, type detection, and value conversion in Power Query, we now turn to the next section. This section will introduce facets, a concept that allows you to provide additional details about your data types.

Facets

So far, we have looked at the base data types in the M language, both the primitive and the custom ones. However, you may have encountered values that look like data types, but with a different notation. For instance, when selecting a new data type, you see the following popup:

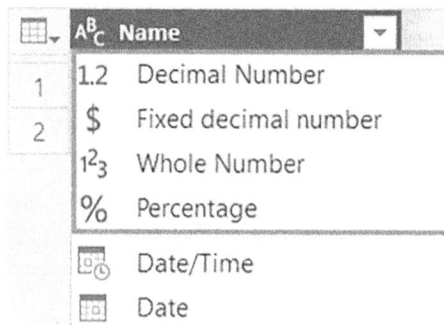

Figure 5.32: The drop-down menu for changing column types

Notice how the menu shows four different ways to label number values. Now, suppose we change a column to **Decimal Number** and a column to a **Fixed decimal number**. The UI produces the following code:

```
Table.TransformColumnTypes( Source ,
    { { "Name",  type number    },
      { "Value", Currency.Type } } )
```

The first type transformation references the familiar type number. However, what exactly is `Currency.Type`? The answer is this is one of the Type Facets, commonly referred to as facets.

Type Facets provide additional information about your data types. They become useful when Power Query needs to talk to other systems, such as Power BI or other applications to which Power Query provides data. Even though facets don't change how Power Query works with the data on its own, they provide valuable information to other systems.

For example, facets allow Power Query to tell a system exactly what kind of data to expect, like using the `Int64.Type` facet to say, *"These are all 64-bit integers."* An application that receives this data may use the type information to reserve the right amount of space and handle the data properly.

Facets can also give hints about the data, such as how long a text field can be or how exact a number is. While you can use the default library functions to work with facet information, you won't see facets at work much inside Power Query. It tends to only be used when receiving data from or transferring data to other systems. These other applications often possess more complex type systems compared to Power Query.

While many facets are not essential for everyday use, **Type Claims** are an exception. This specific facet is important, as it frequently appears, even in the UI, and is seen in many functions. For most users, a detailed understanding of all facets isn't necessary to become proficient in Power Query. However, since you will likely encounter **Type Claims** (a particular kind of facet), even when using the UI, we will briefly cover the topic in the next section.

Depending on how you import your data, your tables will or will not have facets information associated with them. If your SQL database contains facet information and you connect to a table, Power Query retrieves the type information for your table.

For instance, suppose you have a basic table type. By default, there won't be any facets associated with that value. You can add some custom information to your facets using the `Type.ReplaceFacets` function. Then to return the facets associated with your type, use the `Type.Facets` function:

```
let
  myType = type table,
  myFacets =
    [
      NumericPrecisionBase = 10,
      MaxLength            = 4,
      NativeTypeName       = "INTEGER"
    ],
  addFacets = Type.ReplaceFacets( myType, myFacets ),
  showFacets = Type.Facets( addFacets )
in
  showFacets
```

The preceding expression provides facet information for `NumericPrecisionBase`, `MaxLength`, and `NativeTypeName` and adds it to the table type. To inspect the facet information, we can use the `Type.Facets` function and reference the table type that includes the facet information, as shown in the following figure:

× ✓ *fx*	= Type.Facets(addFacets)

NumericPrecisionBase	10
NumericPrecision	null
NumericScale	null
DateTimePrecision	null
MaxLength	4
IsVariableLength	null
NativeTypeName	INTEGER
NativeDefaultExpression	null
NativeExpression	null

Figure 5.33: Simple facets associated with a table type

As you can see, there is a lot of additional information a (data) type can hold. The Type Facets shown in the preceding image are considered **Simple Facets**. You generally won't be adding these kinds of values yourself, but it's good to know that it's perfectly valid to use these in your expressions. Remember that external applications working with Power Query will often use this information to help improve storage and data handling.

The preceding example provided us with some information about the general table type, but you may want to retrieve this information for each column within your table. To do that instead, you can use the `Table.Schema` function. The following example creates a table value and then returns its facet information:

```
let
  myTable = #table(
    type table[ ProductKey = Int64.Type, Product = Text.Type ],
    {{ 1, "Apple" },{ 2, "Prume" }} ),
  tableFacets = Table.Schema( myTable)
in
  tableFacets
```

The result of this expression is a table providing schema information for each column, as shown in the following:

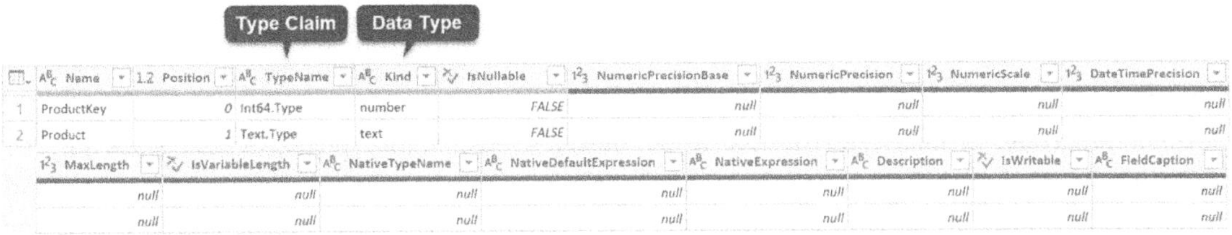

Figure 5.34: Type Facet information for columns returned by Table.Schema

You can find Type Claim and Data Type as the third and fourth columns respectively. Directly following these two columns, you can find other facet information.

An alternative way to display the same information is by retrieving it from the table type, instead of from the table itself. You can do that using the Type.TableSchema function as follows:

```
let
  myTableType =
    type table[ ProductKey = Int64.Type, Product = Text.Type ],
  typeFacets = Type.TableSchema( myTableType)
in
  typeFacets
```

The outcome using this code snippet is identical to the preceding image. The main difference is that Table.Schema is applied on a table, whereas Type.TableSchema can be used on table types.

As you've learned so far, facets are Power Query's way of storing additional type information received from an external system. Power Query can then pass this information on to the external system it provides data to. Now the Simple facets (returned by Type.Facets), are often system specific and don't allow an easy exchange between applications.

However, some of the facets are more generic and can be used to communicate type information between systems. These are the Type Claims. Type Claims are the facets you will most likely work with. For that reason, the next section focuses on these values.

Type Claims

Earlier in this chapter, we explored the range of primitive and custom data types available in the M language, such as type date for dates and type logical for Boolean values. While Power Query's mashup engine primarily uses these standard data types, external applications may work with more specific type classifications. This is where Type Claims come into play.

Type Claims belong to the category of facets within the M language. They provide a way to specify more detailed information about data types, beyond what is typically used within Power Query. For example, while Power Query might treat numbers uniformly, a database might distinguish between numeric, decimal, 8, 16, 32, or 64-bit integers, to mention a few. These detailed specifications are not important within Power Query itself, but they are valuable for external applications that process and store the data received from Power Query. Think of Type Claims as a universal language for conveying data type information from one system to another.

Let's now have a look at what type claims are available in the M language.

Available Type Claims

In the M language, various **Type Claims** correspond to specific data types. The table shown in the following figure lists these **Type Claims** and their base types. For example, Currency.Type and Decimal.Type both have type number as a base type, whereas Text.Type and Password.Type belong to type text.

So, which **Type Claims** are available?

Type Claim	Base Type	Description
Any.Type	type any	Represents all values
Binary.Type	type binary	Represents all binary values
Date.Type	type date	Represents all date values
DateTime.Type	type datetime	Represents all date and time values
DateTimeZone.Type	type datetimezone	Represents all date and time values relative to a timezone
Duration.Type	type duration	Represents all duration values
Function.Type	type function	Represents all functions
List.Type	type list	Represents all lists
Logical.Type	type logical	Represents all logical values
None.Type	type none	Represents no values
Null.Type	type null	Represents null
Byte.Type	type number	Represents all bytes
Currency.Type	type number	Represents currency value
Decimal.Type	type number	Represents fixed-point decimal number
Double.Type	type number	Represents double precision floating point number
Int16.Type	type number	Represents signed 16 bit integer
Int32.Type	type number	Represents signed 32 bit integer
Int64.Type	type number	Represents signed 64 bit integer
Int8.Type	type number	Represents signed 8 bit integer
Number.Type	type number	Represents all numbers
Percentage.Type	type number	Represents percentage value
Single.Type	type number	Represents single precision floating point number
Record.Type	type record	Represents all records
Table.Type	type table	Represents all tables
Character.Type	type text	Represents all characters
Guid.Type	type text	Represents a GUID value
Password.Type	type text	Represents a text password
Text.Type	type text	Represents all text values
Uri.Type	type text	Represents a text URI
Time.Type	type time	Represents all time values
Type.Type	type type	Represents all types

Figure 5.35: Overview of Type Claims and their corresponding base data types

It's important to note that Type Claims are not data types themselves. Rather, they function by assigning a base type to a value and supplementing it with additional facet information. Nonetheless, when dealing with a function that requires a data type as input, it's valid to provide either the base type or the Type Claim as the argument. Since you now know what type claims are available, let's have a look at how we can use these to convert values.

Converting values using type claims

Consider a scenario where you need to convert a column into a number type. You can use either a base type or a Type Claim:

```
Table.TransformColumnTypes( Source, {{"Sales", type number}} )
Table.TransformColumnTypes( Source, {{"Sales", Int64.Type}} )
```

Both expressions are valid, but using a base type or a Type Claim might result in slightly different behaviors with the following number types:

- **Currency type:** `Currency.Type` returns a number with up to 4 decimal places.
- **Integer types:** `Int8`, `Int16`, `Int32`, and `Int64` return whole numbers, trimming any decimal points.

Let's examine the impact of applying Type Claims for value conversion in Power Query. In the following figure, we use a table with four columns as an example, as shown in the following figure. Each of these columns contains an identical text value. Our objective is to observe and understand the changes that occur when these text values undergo conversion using different Type Claims in Power Query.

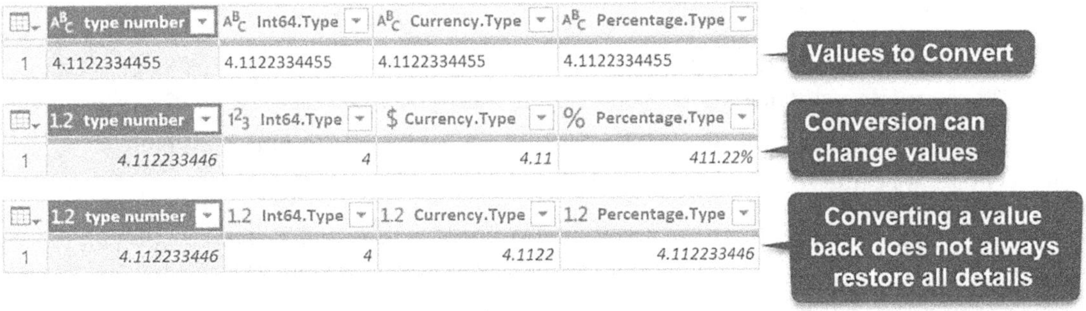

Figure 5.36: Type conversion can result in a loss of precision

The middle row of the table demonstrates what the different values look like after the conversion, based on the Type Claim specified in the respective column headers. An important aspect to note during this conversion process is the change in data precision. For instance, when text values are converted to `Int64.Type`, the process eliminates any decimals, resulting in whole numbers. Conversely, converting values to `Currency.Type` preserves precision up to four decimal places. This illustrates how different Type Claims affect the precision and format of the converted data.

Now, have a good look at the bottom row. When we convert the different data types back to a decimal type, which can hold a large number of decimals, we can see the loss of precision for the **Int64.Type** and `Currency.Type` column.

It's essential to understand that using a Type Claim for converting a value type can result in an irretrievable loss of precision of that value. Remember, once a value transforms, the only way to revert to the original precision is by undoing the conversion step. Earlier in this chapter, you saw how you can return the data type of a value. But how does that work for Type Claims?

Inspecting Type Claims

In the M language, Type Claims are primarily used within table types. Due to this specific use, the M language only allows us to inspect them using the table function `Table.Schema`. However, there may be situations where you might need to explore the facets associated with a specific value.

As of the current writing, the most straightforward method to investigate these facets is by embedding the value within a table. This approach allows you to use the **Table.Schema** function to reveal the underlying Type Claim details.

Consider the following example, where we create a table specifically to inspect a particular type – `Character.Type`:

```
let
    myType   = Character.Type,
    mySchema = Table.Schema( #table(type table [Col1 = myType], {} ) ),
    typeInfo = mySchema[[TypeName], [Kind]]
in
    typeInfo
```

In this code, we do the following:

- We define `myType` as `Character.Type`.
- We create an empty table with a single column, specifying `Character.Type` as the column type.
- We use the `Table.Schema` function to extract the schema information of this table.
- Finally, we extract both the `TypeName` and `Kind` columns.

The preceding expression returns a record displaying the type name and its kind:

```
[ TypeName = Character.Type, Kind = text ]
```

This output indicates that `Character.Type` belongs to the base type text.

In conclusion, you have now learned that facets provide additional information to data types. This additional information is particularly useful when communicating data to and from various external systems that Power Query interfaces with. The most common scenario where an analyst runs into facets, more specifically type claims, is when setting a data type. Make sure to pay attention to Type Claims that change the precision of a value as they may change your values without you noticing.

Moving forward, our focus will shift to the concept of ascribing types. Ascription can make use of both data types and Type Claims, and unlike simple value conversion, ascription adopts a more daring approach – one that requires caution due to its potential risks. Let's find out how that works.

Ascribing types

In this section, we'll delve into the purpose of ascription and how you can use it. You'll also learn the risks and what scenarios can cause errors.

What is ascription?

Ascribing a type is a process where you declare that a value conforms to a specific type. To some extent, this process instructs the engine to accept your assessment of the value's type. In contrast to data type conversion, where Power Query actively converts values to a designated type, ascribing a type labels the type of a value without changing the value itself. During ascription, a limited conformance check is conducted. This check verifies that the type you declare is compatible with the value's intrinsic primitive type.

However, this approach can lead to some complexities. For instance, if you ascribe type text to a column that contains whole numbers, Power Query will label the column type as text, but the values are stored numerically. Consequently, you won't be able to apply text-specific functions to these values, as they are still numbers.

This differs significantly from converting values. When you convert a column's data type, the system labels the values, checks compatibility, and transforms them into the new data type. If a value cannot be converted, Power Query flags an error. This ensures that the resulting values genuinely match the chosen data type or give an error. During the ascribing process, however, you don't receive this error.

Let's have a look at how you can ascribe a value. We continue our example with a table containing only a date column. When we select the column, then navigate to **Add Column** in the ribbon, select **Date**, and then **Day of year**, we end up with the following situation:

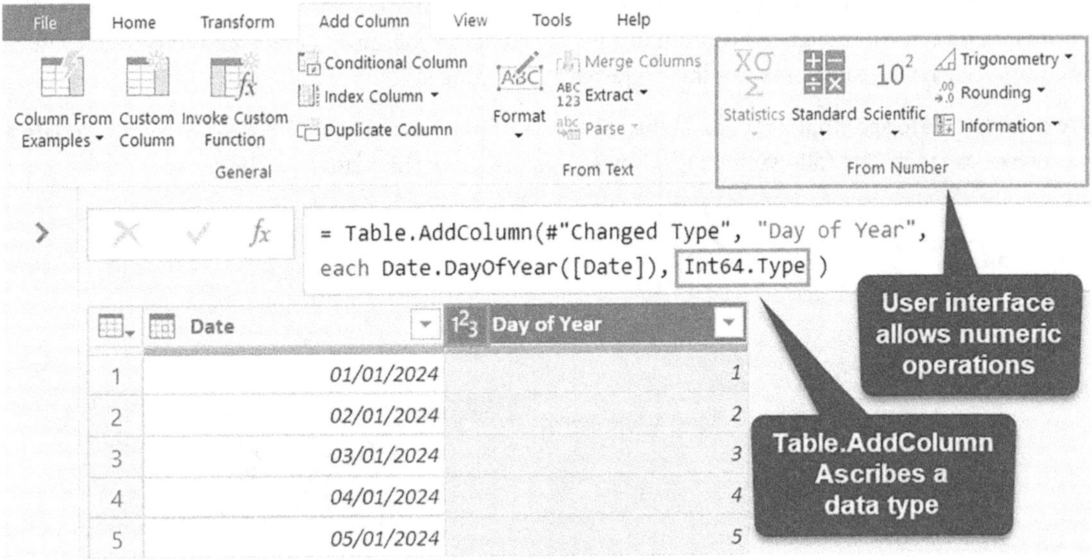

Figure 5.37: Table.AddColumn ascribes the Int64.Type to a column with number values

This operation created a new column called **Day of Year** and automatically received a whole number (`In64.Type`) as column type. The `Table.AddColumn` function received the data type in the fourth argument. Notice that this function does not transform a column type but ascribes one. That means no value conversion takes place. Now, let's adjust the formula and insert a type that's incompatible with number values, such as a text type:

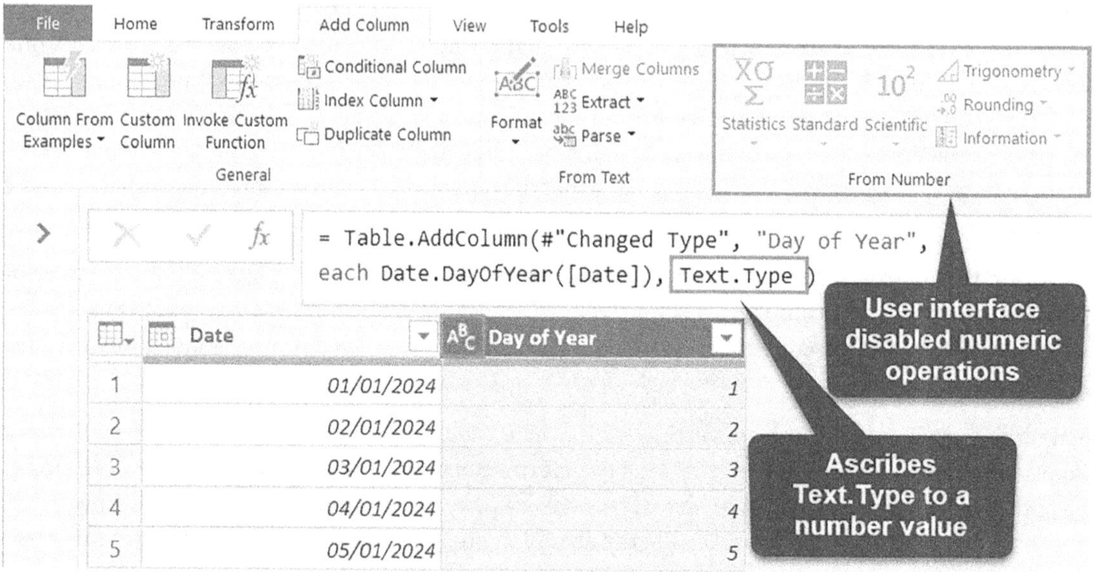

	Date	Day of Year
1	01/01/2024	1
2	02/01/2024	2
3	03/01/2024	3
4	04/01/2024	4
5	05/01/2024	5

Figure 5.38: Table.AddColumn ascribes the Text.Type to a column with number values

By adjusting the formula from `Int64.Type` to `Text.Type`, you can see the text type icon in the column header. Also, notice that the column no longer supports numeric operations. Now, here comes the confusing part. Even though the column header declares the column is of type text, the actual values are numeric. Trying an expression that requires a text value still throws an error.

We can test this to see what happens. If the value was of type text, we should be able to concatenate a value like `Day` to it. The following image, however, shows that this returns an error:

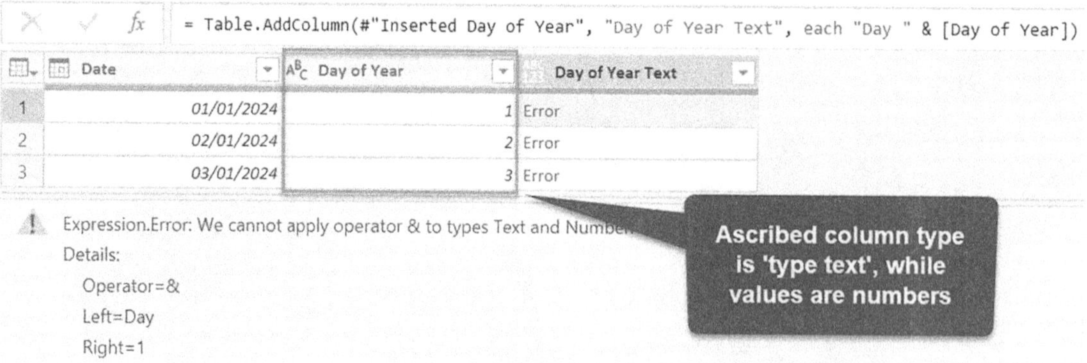

	Date	Day of Year	Day of Year Text
1	01/01/2024	1	Error
2	02/01/2024	2	Error
3	03/01/2024	3	Error

Figure 5.39: The ascribed column type is Type.Text but values are still of type number

That gives you an idea of what it means to ascribe data. This example labels a column as being of a particular type without performing additional checks. So, why is it beneficial to understand ascription?

It's helpful to understand ascription for several reasons:

- **Performance**: Ascribing a data type does not require the engine to scan all your data. By declaring a type, Power Query trusts its correctness, potentially enhancing performance as it bypasses extensive data type validation.

- **Risk management**: An essential aspect of ascription is the risk involved. If you ascribe a data type to a column that contains values incompatible with this type, errors can occur during data loading into applications like Power BI. This is because Power BI, during the loading process, expects data to conform to the ascribed types and may return errors if there are discrepancies.

- **Integration with host applications**: Ascribing types is particularly relevant when loading your data to a destination like Power BI or Excel. These applications may use the ascribed data type information for their processing and storage requirements. Incorrect ascription can lead to compatibility issues and errors when loading data into these applications.

Now that you know what ascription is for and why it's helpful to understand, you may wonder which functions can ascribe a data type to a value. Let's find out.

Functions that support ascribing types

This section is meant to deepen your understanding of ascription. It introduces you to functions that allow you to ascribe a type and should make you more familiar with their syntax.

Ascribing types when creating records

Records in Power Query can have multiple fields, each with a specific data type. To define these data types, functions like `Record.FromList` support a custom record type. The inclusion of a custom record type provides the function with both the custom field names and their corresponding types. Here's an example:

```
Record.FromList(
    { 2024, "M-Language", true },
    type [ Year = number, Topic = text, LearningM = logical ]
)
```

In this case, `Record.FromList` is used to create a record where `Year` is a number, `Topic` is text, and `LearningM` is a logical value.

Ascribing types when creating tables

Several functions allow for the creation of tables with custom data types. The most common ones are `#table`, `Table.FromRecords`, `Table.FromList`, `Table.FromColumns`, `Table.FromRows`, and `Table.FromValue`. These functions allow you to specify both column names and their data types.

For example, the following M code creates a table by specifying column names and values:

```
#table(
    { "BookID", "Title" },
    { { 1, "Animal Farm" }, { 2, "Brave New World" } }
)
```

In this example, we specify the column names BookID and Title in the first argument, and the table's columns are automatically assigned the any type. This shows that providing column types is not necessary.

However, in cases where you want to be more specific, you can provide the #table function with a custom table type to specify the column BookID as integer and Title as text. To ascribe the relevant column names and types, you can use the following code:

```
#table(
    type table[ BookID = Int64.Type, Title = text ],
    { { 1, "Animal Farm" }, { 2, "Brave New World" } }
)
```

The outcome of these two code snippets is shown in the following figure:

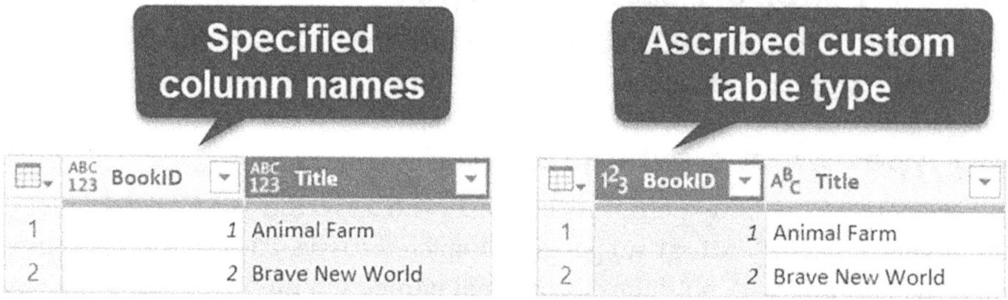

Figure 5.40: Two tables where one receives column names and the other also gets column types

This image demonstrates two scenarios: a table where only the column names are specified and another with defined column types. Despite differing syntax among various table-creating functions, the underlying concept of ascribing data types is uniform. Hence, this chapter will not detail every function, but instead focuses on the core principle of type ascription.

Ascribing types when modifying tables

In addition to creating tables, Power Query offers functions for modifying tables and assigning types to them. The most commonly used functions for this purpose are Table.TransformColumns, Table.AddColumn, and Table.Group.

Consider a table like the one provided previously, where the Title column contains text values. To modify this column using Table.TransformColumns, you can use the Power Query editor's UI. For example, by selecting the **Title** column, navigating to the **Transform** tab, choosing **Format**, and then selecting **UPPERCASE**, the following code is generated:

```
Table.TransformColumns(
    Source,
    {{"Title", Text.Upper, type text}} )
```

In this function, the first argument specifies the table to be transformed. The second argument is a list detailing the operation performed on the column, formatted as {"column name", transformation, new column type}. This format not only transforms the column but also allows you to assign a specific type to it.

Ascribing types to any value

The final example in this section is Value.ReplaceType, which is a function dedicated to replacing a data type of a given value. It requires two arguments: the value itself and the type you wish to ascribe. For example:

```
Value.ReplaceType( 5, type number )
```

The preceding statement ascribes type number to a value. However, the function is not just limited to ascribing primitive types. It can also handle the more complex custom types.

```
Value.ReplaceType( { "a", "b", "c" }, type { text } )
```

So far, that all seems predictable. Now, let's make some adjustments that could come as a surprise. Consider the following examples:

```
Value.ReplaceType( { "a", "b", "c" }, type { number } )
Value.ReplaceType( [ a = 1, b = true ], type [ a = date, b = text ] )
```

Notice that in the first line, a list of text items receives a data type describing a list of numbers. In the second line, a record is ascribed a custom record type, but again with mismatched data types. Interestingly, the Power Query UI does not return an error.

Having reviewed these previous examples, you might think it's possible to ascribe any chosen type to a value. However, this isn't always possible. There are scenarios where attempting to ascribe a type can lead to errors. In the next section, we'll delve into specific situations where type ascription might not work as intended and ultimately result in an error.

Errors when ascribing types

Ascribing is a common cause for errors in Power Query, but errors don't occur in all situations. So, why do we get errors in some cases and not in others? There are three situations where ascribing a type to a value can return an error.

Type ascription errors occur under these circumstances:

- The base type of the ascribed type is incompatible with the value it's assigned to.
- The base type is compatible, but the Type Claim itself does not conform with the value.
- The ascribed type is applied to a structured value that contains values that are incompatible with the type.

Let's look at each of these causes a little closer.

The base type is incompatible with the value

Whenever you ascribe a Type Claim to a value, the base type needs to be compatible with the value you are working with. In other words, the structure of your value and the type needs to be the same. If these two are incompatible, you receive an error. For an overview of the different Type Claims and their base types, please refer to the *Available Type Claims* section in this chapter, as well as *Figure 5.35*.

Here are some examples that throw an error due to an incompatible type:

```
Value.ReplaceType( "myString", type number )
Value.ReplaceType ( #date( 2024, 12, 31 ), type logical )
Value.ReplaceType( 123, type text )
```

The first code example returns the following error:

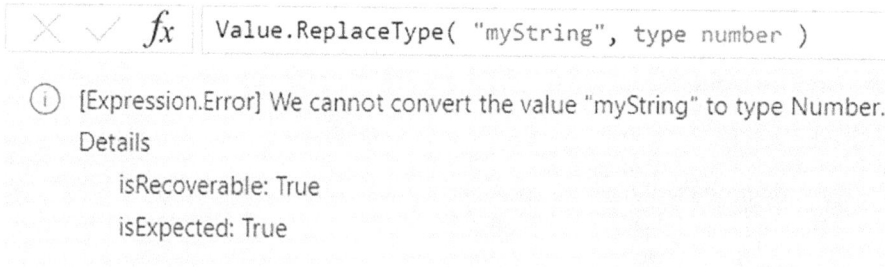

Figure 5.41: When ascribing a type, its base value must be compatible with the value

Changing the data type to one that is compatible with the value's structure would solve these errors.

The Type Claim does not conform with the value

Another scenario where you can run into errors is when you ascribe a type where the base type conforms with the value, but the Type Claim does not. For example, consider a scenario where you have a value with decimal points, such as 5.33353. Power Query allows you to ascribe this value with an Int64.Type representing whole numbers. You can do that with the following code:

```
Value.ReplaceType( 5.33353, Int64.Type )
```

This returns a number value:

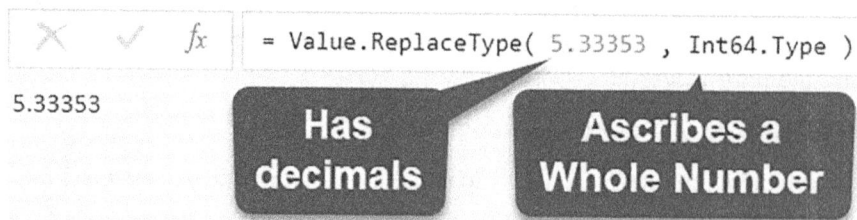

Figure 5.42: Incompatibility between the Type Claim and value

The underlying base value, being a type number, initially seems compatible; thus Power Query does not throw an error. It's important to note that Power Query only performs a basic check during ascription. This check only verifies whether the value's base type aligns with the ascribed type. However, complications arise when loading the query into a destination like Power BI. Here, Power BI examines the specified Type Claim information and attempts to process the values as integers, leading to the following error:

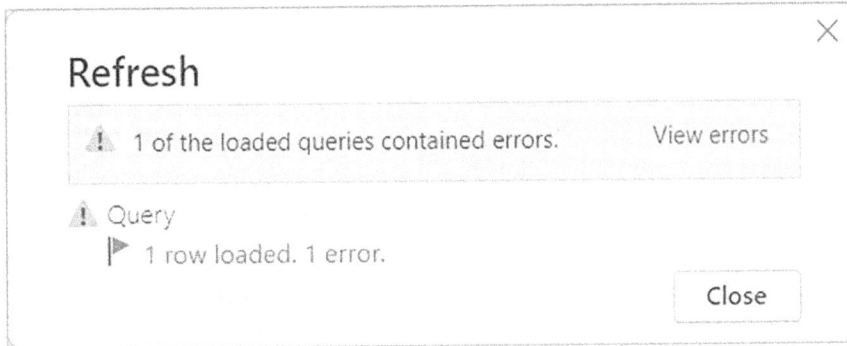

Figure 5.43: Ascribing a Type Claim that's incompatible with a value returns an error

Frustratingly, when you click on **View errors**, a window pops up saying: **Unable to get errors for your queries. Please refresh your queries and try again.**

This scenario can be confusing because Power BI flags an error that isn't visible in the Power Query editor. So, here's some advice: if you encounter an error and Power Query can't pinpoint it to a specific row, it's a good idea to review your queries carefully. You likely ascribed a wrong type to a column.

Ascribing incompatible types to structured values

Errors in Power Query can also arise from improperly assigning types to the elements within structured values. These errors appear only after loading your data into Power BI. Let's delve into what this means.

You can ascribe Type Claims to structured values like lists, records, tables, and functions. Power Query assesses whether the value conforms with the base type of the ascribed Type Claim. Therefore, if certain values don't conform to the base type of a Type Claim, they will result in an error, just like the following two examples show:

```
Value.ReplaceType( [A = 1, B = 2 ], Int64.Type )
Value.ReplaceType( {1, 2, 3}, type text )
```

In both expressions, the base types are incompatible with the underlying values. A record is not a whole number; neither is a list a text value. Adjusting the types as follows would make both expressions valid:

```
Value.ReplaceType( [A = 1, B = 2 ], type [ A = number, B = number ] )
Value.ReplaceType( {1, 2, 3} , type { number } )
```

In this case, we provided the correct list types and record types. However, it's important to understand that when you ascribe a type to a structured value, the values contained within the structured value are not validated for compatibility.

This means you can ascribe a complex list type to a value where you indicate that the values within the list are of a different type than they actually are. Also, this operation won't throw an error. For instance, look at the following expression:

```
Value.ReplaceType( { 1, 2, 3} , type { date } )
```

Even though the list contains only number values, you ascribe a list containing dates without receiving an error in the Power Query editor. That is, until you load your data into a host application like Power BI. When Power BI receives type information, it will use it to ingest and compress the data. When the type information then conflicts with the actual values, Power BI returns an error.

The same happens for records, tables, and function types. You can indicate within the type value that you expect a value of a particular type, but Power Query does not check whether that claim is correct. It's only when you load the data into Power BI that you may run into errors.

Knowing this, let's delve into the most common scenario where you will encounter this issue. Suppose you want to add a custom column to your table. To prevent an additional Change Type step, you can ascribe a type to the newly created column using `Table.AddColumn` fourth argument:

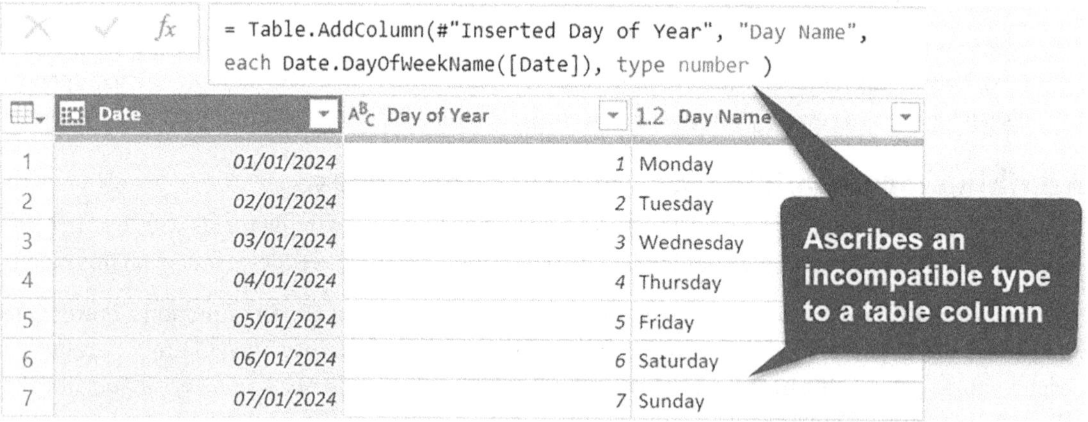

Figure 5.44: Table.AddColumn allows you to ascribe a type that's incompatible with a column's values

Ascribing the type in this expression is very convenient to prevent additional steps. Just remember that ascribing a column type to a structured value (like a table) skips the conformance check of the underlying values. It only checks whether the base type (type table) conforms with the value. When you load this query into Power BI, you will run into the following error:

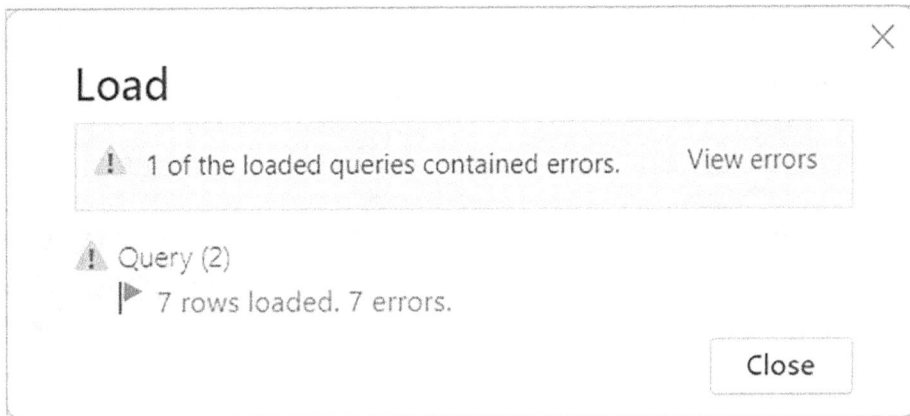

Figure 5.45: This error appears when loading a table with an incompatible type into Power BI

When you click **View errors**, a new query will open showing you the type errors. Only after you fix the wrongly ascribed column type will you be able to refresh the query successfully.

To provide you with another typical example that suffers from the same issue, let's look at the Table.Group function. Suppose you have the following table:

	Date	123 Week of Year	Start of Week
1	03/01/2024	1	01/01/2024
2	04/01/2024	1	01/01/2024
3	05/01/2024	1	01/01/2024
4	06/01/2024	1	01/01/2024
5	07/01/2024	1	01/01/2024
6	08/01/2024	2	08/01/2024
7	09/01/2024	2	08/01/2024

Figure 5.46: The dataset that we will use to summarize values

Now, if you want to summarize the table by Week of Year, you can do that by:

1. Selecting the **Week of Year** column.
2. Going to **Home** in the ribbon and selecting **Group By**.
3. Creating a **New column** named Details and selecting the **All Rows operation**.

You end up with the following situation:

```
= Table.Group(#"Inserted Start of Week", {"Week of Year"},
  {{"Details", each _,
  type table [Date=nullable date, Week of Year=number, Start of Week=date]}})
```

123 Week of Year	Details
1	1 Table
2	2 Table

Hardcoded table type

Figure 5.47: Grouping your data with the All Rows operation hardcodes the data type

The operation makes use of the `Table.Group` function and hardcodes the custom table type in its expression. Since the types fit with the existing values, there is no problem. Suppose you want to make a change earlier in your query. You change the `Start of Week` column values from a date to the day's name (text). The original expression was:

```
Table.AddColumn( Source, "Start of Week",
    each Date.StartOfWeek([Date]), type date )
```

To turn this into the day name of the respective dates, you use the following expression:

```
Table.AddColumn( Source, "Start of Week",
    each Date.DayOfWeekName( Date.StartOfWeek([Date]) ), type text)
```

This is where the trouble begins. The **Group By** operation referenced the `Start of Week` column but hardcoded the data type `Date`. We adjusted our column earlier in the query, which is now of type text. The effect of this is that when you expand the details column, it ascribes a data type to the column, which no longer conforms with its values. Loading this data into Power BI then results in an error.

To solve this situation, you have a few options. First of all, you can adjust the `Table.Group` function to reflect the correct data type. This is a manual task where there is a risk of forgetting to change the table type. Alternatively, you can dynamically retrieve the previous step's table type dynamically using the `Value.Type` function. The following expression picks up the table type of the prior step called `Inserted Start of Week`:

```
Table.Group(
    #"Inserted Start of Week",
    {"Week of Year"},
    {{"Details", each _, Value.Type( #"Inserted Start of Week" )}}
)
```

Any future changes that come up earlier in the query are automatically picked up, ensuring your table always has the correct data types associated with it.

In conclusion, understanding and correctly using type ascription is essential to ensure your queries remain error proof. Ascribing types correctly allows you to classify data efficiently, avoiding the need for Power Query to scan all your data. However, it is a task that requires accuracy and attention to detail, as mistakes can lead to errors that may not become visible until the data is loaded into an external application. Thus, while ascribing types helps classify values, it must be done with careful consideration to prevent errors.

Since you now know how to ascribe values, let's look at how we check whether types are equal or compatible.

Type equivalence, conformance, and assertion

Knowing whether a value is equal or compatible with another type is useful for some operations. This would allow you to set up conditional statements that handle different data types with appropriate operations. This section delves into the topic of type equivalence and compatibility. Knowing more about these topics should equip you with the knowledge to create logic on them.

Type equality

Let's say you want to check whether two data types are the same; consider the following comparison:

```
type text = type text // Output: true
```

This straightforward comparison appears to confirm equality; after all, it returns `true`. However, comparing more complex types may give a different outcome:

```
type [ a = text ] = type [ a = text ] // Output: false
```

The result is `false` in this case, although the contents compared seem identical. How can that be? The reason is that the outcomes of type comparisons in Power Query M are not guaranteed to be consistent or predictable. This is because type equivalence is not defined within the M language itself.

Consequently, different implementations of M might apply their own rules when comparing types. This variability means the same type comparison could yield different results depending on your specific environment, such as Excel or Power BI. Although current versions may agree that particular comparisons return true, the absence of a formal definition for type equivalence in the language means these behaviors could change in future updates or versions.

Rather than directly comparing type values, the M language offers a variety of library functions designed for handling type values. A notable example is the `Type.Is` function. This function checks whether the type provided as the first argument is compatible with the type given as the second argument. For instance:

```
Type.Is(type date, type nullable date)   // true
Type.Is(type nullable date, type date)   // false
Type.Is(type text, type number)          // false
```

The `Type.Is` function can accept any type, including custom types, as its first argument. However, the second argument must be a nullable primitive type. For example:

```
Type.Is(type [ A = number], type [ A = number] ) // Output false
Type.Is(type [ A = number], type record )         // Output true
```

The first example demonstrates that using a custom type as the second argument in the `Type.Is` function consistently results in `false`. In contrast, the second example shows the function's ability to test whether the first type value conforms with the second one. As custom record types inherently conform to the type record, this specific comparison returns `true`.

This indicates that it is feasible to check whether a custom type matches a certain base type using `Type.Is`. However, it's important to note that the M language currently lacks a built-in function specifically for assessing compatibility between a standard type and a custom type.

Despite this, the standard library in M includes functions that can identify specific characteristics of a custom type, enabling the creation of tailored compatibility tests. Examples of such functions include:

```
Type.IsNullable( type nullable text )   // Output: true
Type.NonNullable( type nullable text )  // Output: false
Type.ListItem( type { number } )        // Output: type number
```

These functions are just a glimpse of the available type functions in the M language. In total, there are 22 type functions, each allowing you to perform different operations with types. We encourage you to check out the options available and their syntax at https://powerquery.how/type-functions/.

Besides checking whether a type is equal to another, there are cases where checking whether a value conforms to another is useful. We will cover how to do that next.

Type conformance

Besides checking whether a type conforms with another, you can perform a similar kind of check for values. When you have a value and a data type and want to determine if that value is consistent with (i.e., "conforms to") that data type you can use the `Value.Is` function. It takes any kind of value as an input and any data type and returns either `true` or `false`, depending on whether the input value conforms to the input data type. This process helps in validating data, preventing errors, and maintaining consistency in your queries.

The syntax is as follows:

```
Value.Is(value as any, type as type) as logical
```

When you apply the function to different types of values, it returns you a `true` or `false` value that indicates whether the value is of a particular kind:

```
Value.Is(9, Number.Type)      // returns true because 9 is a number.
Value.Is("126", Number.Type)  // returns false: "126" is a text value
Value.Is(36, Value.Type(36))  // returns true: self-conformance.
```

Using `Value.Is`, you have an easy way to test whether your values conform to a particular type. It's also possible to perform this comparison in a simplified way by using the is operator. The following expressing tests whether 49 is of number type:

```
49  is number
```

It is essentially the same comparison but written in a simpler way. Just note that the simplified method shown previously only works with primitive values. You can't use Type Claims, like `Number.Type` or `Int64.Type` here. Thus, the following expressions both evaluate to `true`:

```
Value.Is( "Hello", Text.Type)
"Hello" is text
```

Knowing whether a value conforms to a particular type is useful. It even allows you to filter your data down to the rows that conform with a particular type. In other situations, if you want to enforce a data type, you can also make use of type assertion, a topic that we will cover next.

Type assertion

Type assertion in Power Query is implemented through the `Value.As` function. This function is used to explicitly enforce a specific data type on a given value. It acts as a checkpoint to verify whether a value conforms to a desired data type, providing you with another option to ensure data integrity in your queries.

The `Value.As` function accepts two parameters: a value of any type and a primitive data type to check against. Its primary role is to return the original value if it matches the specified type. However, if there's a mismatch between the value and the type, the function generates an error. This behavior is helpful for maintaining data consistency and preventing unexpected errors.

Here's the basic syntax of `Value.As`:

```
Value.As(value as any, type as type) as any
```

You can apply `Value.As` in several ways, for instance:

```
Value.As( 36, Number.Type ) // 36
Value.As( "36", Text.Type ) // 36
Value.As( 36, Text.Type )    // Expression.Error: We cannot convert the
                             // value 36 to type Text
```

An alternate expression of this concept is direct type casting, such as:

```
36 as number
```

This expression is `true` when `Value.Is(36, Number.Type)` is compared, validating that 36 is indeed a number. A helpful feature of `Value.As` is that it returns errors as values. This characteristic enables the development of intricate error-handling strategies, essential when values do not match the expected types. By using this function, you can create custom logic to manage errors. This could range from simple error logging to providing fallback values, ensuring that your data processing remains uninterrupted. The detailed exploration of these error-handling techniques will be the focus of *Chapter 12*.

In conclusion, `Value.As` is a useful function that ensures that values conform to specified types. Coupled with the broader concepts of type equivalence and conformance, you now have different options to ensure type integrity and create reliable queries.

Summary

As we conclude this chapter, let's reflect on what we've learned about data types in the M language. We began by introducing the fundamental concept of data types, an important concept for understanding and using the M language effectively.

We explored both primitive and custom data types. We learned how different functions in M handle these data types, noting the nuances between functions that accept nullable types and those that require more stringent type conformity. This distinction is important for crafting precise and functional queries.

We also delved into the potential pitfalls associated with data types. You saw how data types could lead to various errors. While some, like conversion errors, are immediately apparent, others are more subtle. Particularly, errors resulting from ascribing incompatible types can be challenging to identify and rectify.

Now, with this foundation in data types, you are well equipped to integrate them into your queries, functions, and expressions more effectively. While this chapter provided specific examples, it merely scratches the surface of what is possible with data types in M. In the upcoming chapters, we will expand on these concepts, offering you additional examples on how to incorporate them while working with structured values, when creating custom functions, and how they are useful when writing efficient code using `List.Generate`.

Learn more on Discord

Join our community's Discord space for discussions with the author and other readers:

```
https://discord.gg/vCSG5GBbyS
```

6

Structured Values

In this chapter, we focus on an important concept in the Power Query M language: **structured values**. Whereas we introduced both values and data types in *Chapters 4* and *5*, structured values are more complex and require additional attention. Unlike simple or primitive values, they can include multiple other values within them. This complexity allows them to hold a range of primitive values, or even other structured values, opening up a wide range of possibilities for data manipulation and analysis.

The importance of structured values within the M language is such that we're dedicating an entire chapter to them. The constructs you will learn not only contribute to more efficient and effective code, but also form the backbone of many operations within the M language.

This chapter covers the following topics:

- Introducing structured values
- Lists
- Records
- Tables

In each section, we will provide a clear explanation of the concepts, clarify them with appropriate examples, and highlight their use cases. This structured approach will make it easier for you to understand these concepts, see how they relate to each other, and apply them effectively in your work.

Introducing structured values

As we delve further into the M language, we arrive at one of the most important concepts: structured values. These values form the foundation of data shaping and manipulation in Power Query M. But what exactly do we mean when we say *structured values?* You can think of them as a container or package that can contain one or more values. These containers are organized in a way that allows us to perform transformations on them. As a developer, getting a thorough understanding of how to use these values allows you to perform challenging data transformations more easily.

Structured values allow us to deal with complexity by splitting data into manageable chunks. Each structured value – be it a list, record, table, or function – has its unique characteristics and applications, and understanding when to use each helps in writing effective code.

As we go through this chapter, you might find some concepts slightly more challenging than others. But by taking the time to understand these fundamental concepts, you'll lay a solid foundation that enables you to confidently handle more complex tasks in the future.

This chapter aims to clarify structured values and provide you with a comprehensive understanding of their role and application in Power Query M. We'll delve into the specifics of lists, records, tables, and functions, discussing what they are, how they work, and their importance in data transformation tasks.

Lists

Beginning our exploration of structured values, we first encounter lists. So, what is a list?

Introduction to lists

A list contains a sequence of comma-separated values of any type. That includes primitive values (like text, numbers, dates, or times) and structured values (lists, records, or tables).

So why should lists interest you to begin with? You will find that lists are used extensively throughout Power Query. For example, selecting a column returns its values in the form of a list. Similarly, when functions take multiple values as input (like `List.Count`) or return multiple values as output (like `Table.ColumnNames`), you will often find that these functions involve lists. Let's have a look at how you can create a list.

Creating a list is a straightforward process. You can define a list value by enclosing values in curly brackets { }, formally known as *list initialization*. Each value within the list is separated by a comma.

For instance, you can create a list of three number values as follows:

```
{1, 2, 3}
```

This list can then be viewed, as shown in the following screenshot:

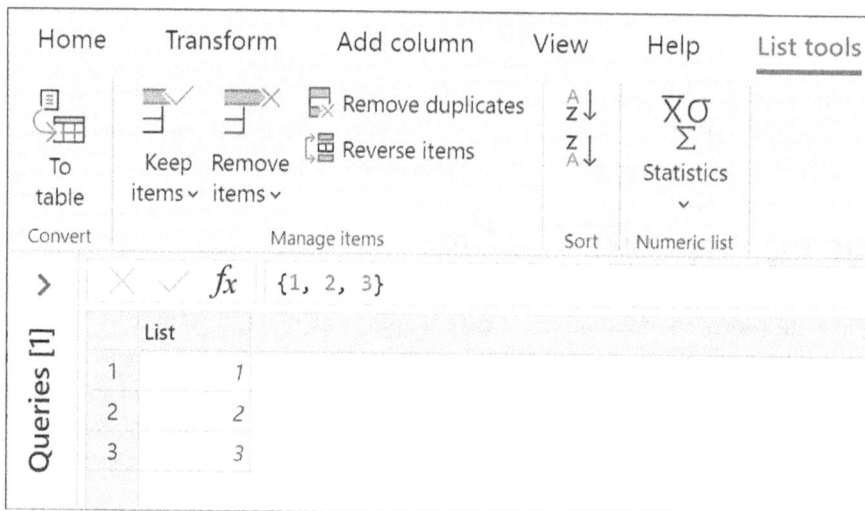

Figure 6.1: Initialize a list in Power Query using { }

A list can also contain a mix of values. The following statement creates a list containing a number, text, and a logical value:

```
{1, "Hello", true}
```

In the same way, you can enclose other structured values inside a list. The following expression returns a list that contains a text, list, record, and table value:

```
{
  "a",
  {4,5,6},
  [Column1 = 1, Column2 = "v"],
  #table( { "ID", "Product" }, {{ 1, "Apple" }} )
}
```

We will discuss records and tables later in this chapter.

When a list does not contain any items, it is considered an *empty list*. To return an empty list, you can write:

```
{} // Output: empty list
```

To check the number of items in a list, you can use a function like `List.Count`:

```
List.Count( {1, 2, 3} ) // Output: 3
List.Count( {} )        // Output: 0
```

To learn more about the available `List` functions and their expected input and output data types, we recommend taking a look at the `List` functions overview at `https://powerquery.how/list-functions/`.

List operators

As we deepen our understanding of lists, let's turn our attention to operators. We briefly introduced operators in *Chapter 4* and provided an overview of which values support which operators. This section delves into operators that work with lists.

Lists support the following operators:

Operator	Notation	Description
Equal	=	Checks if two lists are identical.
Not equal	<>	Checks if two lists are different.
Concatenation	&	Appends two lists.
Coalesce	??	Returns the first non-null value from two values.

Table 6.1: Operators supported by lists

Equal

The equal (=) operator inspects whether two lists are identical, both in terms of the order in which they appear and whether the values in the lists are equal.

When comparing the following lists, the operator returns true since both lists match perfectly:

```
{1, 2, 3} = {1, 2, 3}
```

However, reordering the items as shown below returns false:

```
{1, 2, 3} = {3, 2, 1}
```

This shows that the order of elements is important when comparing lists. The equal operator works, irrespective of whether the list contains primitive or structured values (like nested lists). For instance:

```
{ {1,"a","b"}, 2, 3} = { {1,"a","b"}, 2, 3} // Output: true
```

One way we could use this is when comparing column names in two tables. When appending tables using the Table.Combine function, columns with the same column names are combined. Suppose you want to verify whether the column names in the two tables are identical. To retrieve the column names in a table you can use:

```
Table.ColumnNames( YourTable )
```

As we have just seen, when testing if lists are equal, the order of values is important. We should therefore sort the lists before comparing them. You can do that with the following code:

```
let
  ColumnNamesTable1 =
    List.Sort( Table.ColumnNames( Table1 )),
  ColumnNamesTable2 =
    List.Sort( Table.ColumnNames( Table2 )),
  ColumnsAreEqual = ColumnNamesTable1 = ColumnNamesTable2
in
  ColumnsAreEqual
```

The output of this query is a Boolean value indicating whether the two lists are equal.

Not equal

The not equal operator does the exact opposite of the equal operator. It verifies if two lists differ. The following example is slightly different from the previous one:

```
{1, 2, 3} <> {3, 2, 1} // Output: true
```

Despite containing identical elements, the list order difference makes them *not equal*, hence the output true.

Concatenate

The concatenation operator is used to combine two lists, essentially appending one list to the end of another. For example, you can combine two lists as follows:

```
{1, 2} & {4, 5} // Output: {1, 2, 3, 4}
```

This is an excellent way to combine your lists. Instead of manually combining the lists, you can also make use of the `List.Combine` function. `List.Combine` requires you to provide the lists to combine into another list; that is, two inner lists within an outer list, like so:

```
List.Combine( { {1, 2}, {4, 5} } ) // Output: {1, 2, 3, 4}
```

The combining of lists is useful in a range of scenarios. For instance, you may want to select all numbers and letters from a string. Instead of doing that manually, you can generate a range of values and concatenate them.

Suppose you have the following string:

```
"inv-1006-!**!-(act)"
```

To extract only text and numbers, you can generate two lists of values as follows:

```
{ "a".."z" } // Generates a list of lowercase letters
{ "0".."9" } // Generates a list of numbers
```

These two statements use the AB-construct, which we will discuss in more depth later in this chapter. To combine the generated lists and extract values from the string, you can use the following code:

```
let
    LowercaseLetters = { "a".."z" }
    Numbers = { "0".."9" }
    CombinedCharacters = LowercaseLetters & Numbers
    SelectCharacters =
        Text.Select( "inv-1006-!**!-(act)", CombinedCharacters )
in
    SelectCharacters
```

The & operator is used to combine lists of lowercase letters and numbers. `Text.Select` then filters the desired characters from the given string, returning: `inv1006act`.

Coalesce

The coalesce operator is effective for handling null values in data. It is placed between two values: the primary value (on the left) and a fallback value (on the right). The operator evaluates the primary value first. If this value is not null, it is returned as the result. If the primary value is null, the operator returns the fallback value instead.

Consider this example, which returns {1, 2, 3}:

```
{ 1, 2, 3 } ?? null
```

In this case, since the first list is not null, the coalesce operator retains it. However, if the order is reversed as in the following:

```
null ?? {1, 2, 3}
```

The expression returns {1, 2, 3}. This behavior guarantees a non-null result, which is useful in scenarios with potential null values.

For a practical application, imagine a product catalog with a Features column listing product features. If some products lack a specified feature list, you can provide a default list using this code:

```
each [Features] ?? {"Feature 1", " Feature 2"}
```

In this way, encountering a null in the Features column results in a standard list of features being returned. This approach guarantees uniformity in product descriptions, providing default features where specific lists are missing.

Now we know how to create lists and what operators can work on them, let's have a look at how you can easily generate lists of values.

Methods to create a list

So far, you have seen the basics of a list in terms of how to use operators on them. Let's now review the different ways to create lists.

Creating lists using the list initializer

The first method to create a list is by using the list initializer, as shown earlier. The simplicity of creating a list manually is its biggest charm. Here's how you can combine diverse values to form a list:

```
{ 1, true, #date( 2023, 12, 31 ) }
```

Creating lists using functions

Another easy way to create a list of values is by using generator functions. The following functions generate a list from scratch:

- List.Dates
- List.DateTimeZones
- List.DateTimes
- List.Durations
- List.Numbers
- List.Times

These functions follow a similar pattern requiring three key ingredients:

- A starting value for the list.
- The number of values to create in the list.
- An increment that is added to every value for each step.

Creating a list of numbers is easy with the `List.Numbers` function. With 1 as the starting value, let's create 5 values, incrementing each one by 1:

```
List.Numbers( 1, 5, 1 ) // Returns { 1, 2, 3, 4, 5 }
```

With an increment of 2 and the same starting value and count, you get:

```
List.Numbers( 1, 5, 2 )  // Returns { 1, 3, 5, 7, 9 }
```

The magic of lists also extends to dates. The `List.Dates` function allows you to create a list of dates, such as five dates starting from `December 31, 2023`, incrementing each one by a day:

```
List.Dates( #date(2023,12,31), 5, #duration(1,0,0,0) )
```

If you want to create a list of random numbers, you can make use of `List.Random`. For example, the following expression creates a list with 3 random numbers:

```
List.Random( 3 )
```

When we ran this query, the output returned this list:

```
{0.42290808419832404,0.76420168008850964,0.75750946894172089}
```

Alternatively, there are many other predefined functions in the M language that return a list, for instance:

- **Field names:** You can find functions that return the field names found in tables (`Table.ColumnNames` or `Table.ColumnsOfType`) or in records (`Record.FieldNames`).
- **Reshape structured values:** Other functions transform a structured value into a list. You can reshape tables into a list with functions like `Table.ToColumns`, `Table.ToRecord`, `Table.ToRows`, or `Table.ToList` or reshape records with `Record.ToList`.
- **Split text:** When working with strings, the functions `Text.Split` and `Text.SplitAny` can split a string based upon a specified delimiter and return the result as a list.

Besides these common ones, two other powerful functions create a list with custom logic. These functions are `List.Accumulate` and `List.Generate`. We will cover both in *Chapter 13, Iteration and Recursion*.

Referencing a table column

Another elegant way to return a list is by referencing a table column. Imagine you have a Product table as shown in *Figure 6.2*, with **Product** as the first column:

▦	ABC Product ▾	ABC Size ▾	ABC Category ▾
1	Shoe	Medium	Clothes
2	Hat	Large	Clothes
3	Shirt	Medium	Clothes
4	Belt	Extra Small	Accessories

Figure 6.2: Dataset with three columns

If the Power Query step returning this table is called `Source`, you can return the values of the **Product** column in the form of a list by using the following expression:

```
Source[Product] // Output: {"Shoe", "Hat", "Shirt", "Belt"}
```

This process, known as **field-selection**, will be further explored in upcoming sections on records and tables.

Using the a..b form

A useful functionality for lists is the ability to generate a list of sequential items using the `a..b` form. This can be particularly useful when you want to create a list of consecutive numbers, letters, or special characters.

In its simplest form, the `a..b` syntax generates a series of values within a specified range of numbers. For instance, to create a list of numbers from 1 to 10, you can use:

```
{1..10} // Output: {1, 2, 3, 4, 5, 6, 7, 8, 9, 10}
```

This tells Power Query to generate a list of integers, starting at 1 and ending at 10. Such a list can be useful for tasks such as looping, iterating, data generation, or even creating calendars.

You can also use this construct to create a non-continuous series of values. Here are two examples:

```
{ 1..3, 11..13 }    // Output: { 1, 2, 3, 11, 12, 13}
{ -1..1, 5, 8..10 } // Output: { -1, 0, 1, 5, 8, 9, 10 }
```

However, it's important to note that this functionality is designed for incrementing lists. If you attempt to create a decrementing list with this syntax, Power Query will return an empty list:

```
{10..1} // Output: {}
```

To create a descending list from 10 to 1, two easy methods involve using the `List.Reverse` or `List.Numbers` functions:

```
List.Reverse( {1..10} )
List.Numbers( 10, 10, -1 )
```

Just as you generated a sequence of numbers, you can also produce a sequence of letters. For instance, to generate a list with the first 6 letters of the alphabet, you can use:

```
{"a".."f"} // Output: {"a", "b", "c", "d", "e", "f}
```

But remember, the M language is case-sensitive. Consequently, changing the case to {"A".."F"} yields a list of the first 6 capital letters of the alphabet:

```
{"A".."F"} // Output: {"A", "B", "C", "D", "E", "F}
```

You may be wondering if there's more to the a..b form. Indeed, there is. To grasp how this feature works, it's important to understand what's happening behind the scenes.

When Power Query generates these lists, it uses Unicode characters, whether you specified a number, letter, or capital letter.

Consider the following example. If you were to generate values starting from the letter "Y" up to "a", you would get:

```
{ "Y" .. "a"}
// Output: { "Y", "Z", "[", "\", "]", "^", "_", "`", "a" }
```

What's happening here? The letter "Y" corresponds to the Unicode decimal 89, while "a" equals 98. You can verify this by writing:

```
Character.ToNumber( "Y" ) // Output: 89
Character.ToNumber( "a" ) // Output: 97
```

When you only have the Unicode decimal, you achieve the reverse by using:

```
Character.FromNumber( 97 ) // Output: "a"
```

Thus, to fully understand the sequence in which characters are generated, it's helpful to refer to the Unicode Standard: https://en.wikipedia.org/wiki/List_of_Unicode_characters#Latin_script.

Accessing items in a list

Once you've grasped how to create lists, the next step is to learn how to access their values, a process that is known as **selection**.

The M language uses the same curly brackets used in defining a list to select an item, a fact that is often confusing. To extract an item from a list by its position, apply an index number inside curly brackets after the list. Bear the following in mind:

- Lists in Power Query's M language follow a *zero-based* indexing system, meaning the first item in your list has an index of 0.
- Attempting to select an item at a non-existent position will result in an error.

Let's illustrate both points with some examples.

Accessing list values by index

Suppose we have a list that increments in steps of 10, ranging from 10 to 50: {10, 20, 30, 40, 50}. Accessing a value is as simple as specifying its index. For instance, to get the first element, you would use myList{0}, yielding 10. Likewise, myList{4} will return 50, the list's last element.

Here's how you would use the item-access-expression in code:

```
{10, 20, 30, 40, 50}{0} // Output: 10
{10, 20, 30, 40, 50}{4} // Output: 50
```

The curly brackets serve a dual role here. The initial set constructs the list, while the second set identifies the index of the value we aim to extract. Keep in mind that the selection statement always represents a single numerical value – the index.

We can achieve the same outcome with the List.Range function. The following statement grabs the second value from a list:

```
List.Range( { 1, 2, 3}, 1, 1 ) // Output: 2
```

The concept of selection reaches even further. When you're working with nested lists (lists within lists), you can pick values from multiple layers. Consider a list that has a list as the first item. If you want to return the first item, which itself is a list, you would use the following code:

```
{{1,2,3}, "a", "b"}{0}    // Output: {1, 2, 3}
```

But what if we aim to extract the second value within that nested list? Well, nothing stops you from selecting that value by adding another set of curly brackets:

```
{{1,2,3}, "a", "b"}{0}{1} // Output: 2
```

The added {1} here signifies that we're selecting the second value from the first list in our parent list. Remember, we're using zero-based indexing.

Handling non-existent index positions

Now, let's explore what happens when we try to retrieve an item at an index position that doesn't exist in our list. Imagine we have some code attempting to access the sixth value in a five-element list:

```
{10, 20, 30, 40, 50}{5}
```

Power Query will return an expression error stating: There weren't enough elements in the enumeration to complete the operation.

To prevent this error, the M language offers an operator that instructs optional item selection. This can be achieved by appending a question mark at the end of an expression attempting to access a list. If the index position doesn't exist in the list, it will return a null value:

```
{10, 20, 30, 40, 50}{4}? // Output: 50
{10, 20, 30, 40, 50}{5} // Output: Expression error
{10, 20, 30, 40, 50}{5}? // Output: null
```

So, now you know how to create lists and access their values, when are lists useful?

Common operations with lists

Lists play an important role in a wide range of operations. To illustrate their use, let's walk through some tangible examples that show the applicability of lists in your data transformation tasks.

Suppose you are working with a table consisting of three columns.

You wish to pinpoint the maximum value across these columns. You can provide a list to the `List.Max` function to achieve this:

```
List.Max( { [Column1], [Column2], [Column3] } )
```

That returns:

```
Table.AddColumn(Source, "Max", each List.Max( { [Column1], [Column2], [Column3] } ))
```

	ᴬᴮC Column1	ᴬᴮC Column2	ᴬᴮC Column3	ABC 123 Max
1	5	20	12	5
2	26	8	10	8
3	14	20	90	90

Figure 6.3: You can use List.Max to return the maximum of multiple columns

In this code, the list surrounds the columns you are interested in, allowing you to extract the maximum value across all of them.

Now, what if you want to evaluate whether a value in the column **Color** matches one of three specific colors? The Power Query M language does not possess a traditional IN operator as seen in SQL or DAX. However, you can replicate it by providing a list to the `List.Contains` function:

```
List.Contains( { "Blue", "Green", "orange" }, [Color] )
```

The result looks as follows:

```
Table.AddColumn(Source, "IsMyColor", each List.Contains( { "Blue", "Green", "Orange" }, [Color] ))
```

	ᴬᴮC Product ID	ᴬᴮC Color	ABC 123 IsMyColor
1	1	Orange	TRUE
2	2	Pink	FALSE
3	3	Blue	TRUE
4	4	Green	TRUE
5	5	White	FALSE

Figure 6.4: List.Contains is a great alternative to mimic the IN operator

The above code tests whether the column [Color] contains at least one of the specified colors. It's a good example of how lists facilitate conditional logic.

Consider another scenario where you're dealing with the string: ISBN: 978-3-16-148410-0. You only wish to extract the numbers and hyphens. You can effectively handle this by using the a..b form to generate the required characters:

```
Text.Select( "ISBN: 978-3-16-148410-0", {"0".."9","-"} )
```

In this example, the list helps to specify the character set we want to keep, extracting only the desired text.

Another use case for lists is to provide values for creating a table. For instance, you can generate a table with a single column containing three values as follows:

```
Table.FromList( { "Apple", "Pear", "Banana" } )
```

Lastly, the Table.Group function is another instance where lists are used extensively. It uses lists to specify columns for grouping and for defining aggregations:

```
Table.Group(    Source,
    {"Column1", "Column2"},
    {{"Count", each Table.RowCount(_), Int64.Type}} )
```

In this code, the lists are used to both group the data (by Column1 and Column2) and to provide the details for creating an aggregation column with a row count. This produces the following:

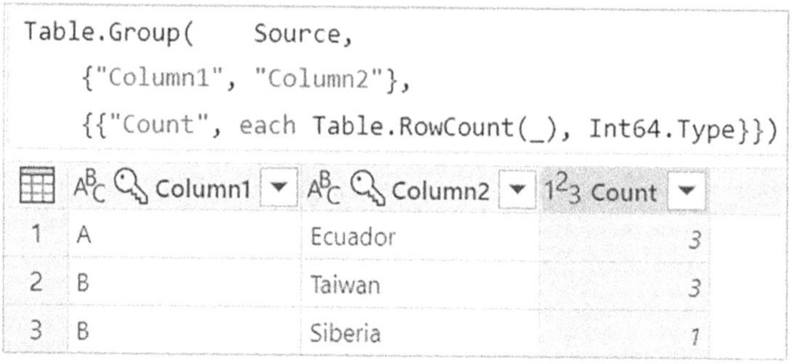

Figure 6.5: Functions like Table.Group require lists as input for their arguments

These examples show the multi-purpose role of lists in the M language. Understanding how to manipulate and use lists is an essential skill to becoming a better M coder.

As this chapter showed, lists can contain any value. Now what options do you have when specifying the data type for a list? That's what we'll discuss next.

Assigning data types to a list

As mentioned in *Chapter 5*, on data types, each value has a data type associated with it. That goes for primitive values, but also for lists and their contents. Let's build on the knowledge gained in this chapter so far and delve deeper into the data types belonging to lists.

When a list contains values belonging to a single data type, you can specify their data type when creating a column. As an example, let's recall the steps to create a list from earlier in this chapter. Once you have this list, you can incorporate it into a custom column using the Table.AddColumn function, as shown below:

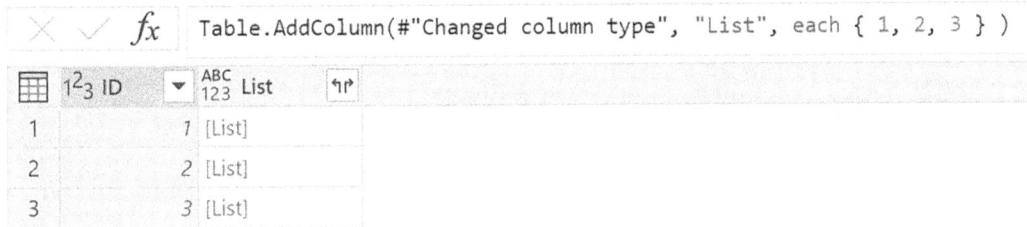

Figure 6.6: Adding list values into a column without assigning a data type

In the above code, the Table.AddColumns function didn't receive any specific data type instruction, so it created a **List** column of type any. As a consequence, when you expand the column values, they remain of type any, as the following screenshot shows:

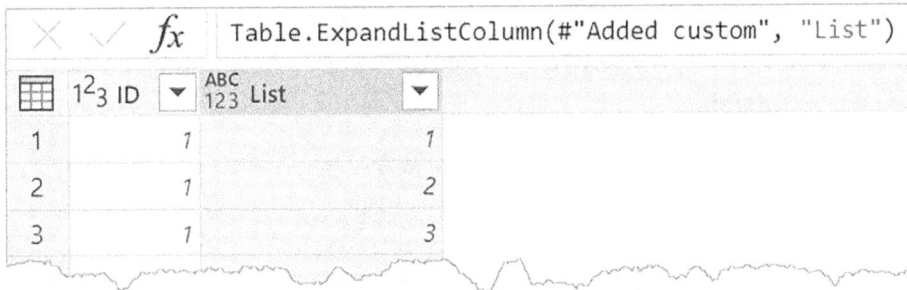

Figure 6.7: Columns remain of type "any" when expanded without a pre-assigned data type

The good news is that you can assign a data type to your list values. Achieving this involves filling in the optional columnType argument of the Table.AddColumn function. With lists, much like any other value, you can specify the type using any data type value that's available. The only difference for lists is that you should wrap the type in curly brackets. So, if you want to specify a list with whole numbers, you would write:

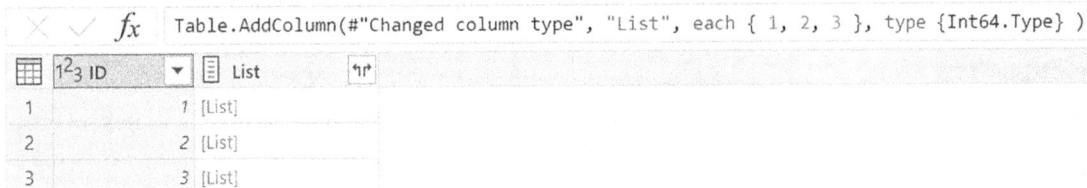

Figure 6.8: Adding list values into a column with an assigned data type

When you expand this newly created column, it appears as a column of the type Whole Number. Specifying the data type prevents you from having to dedicate a separate step to change the column's data type, as the following image shows:

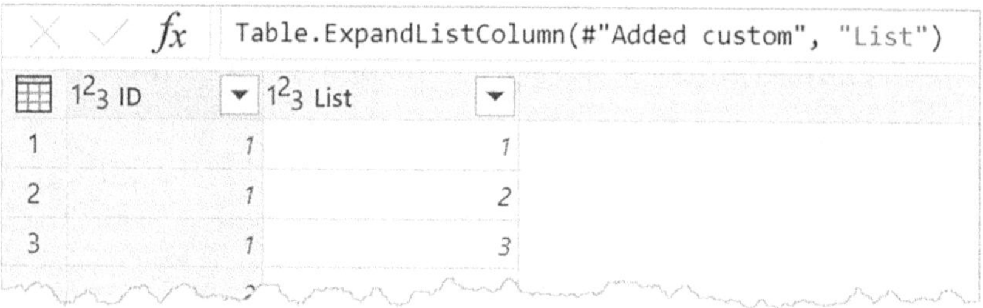

Figure 6.9: When expanded, the List column includes the assigned data type

The preceding screenshot is based on assigning a data type to a list during the Table.AddColumn operation. But what if you have tables already containing lists to which you want to assign a data type?

Suppose we have the same situation as before, but we did not define a data type for the **List** column. It's also possible to convert the type of a column with list values. For instance, to turn the existing column into a list of values of the Whole Number type, you can use the Table.TransformColumns function. The following code achieves this:

```
Table.TransformColumns(
    Source,
    {{"List", each _ ??_, type {Int64.Type}}} )
```

What's important to be aware of here is that the Table.TransformColumn function requires you to perform an operation on the underlying list. Failing to do so leads to Table.TransformColumns not assigning a data type. In the above example, we apply the coalesce operator to the underlying value. Because of that operation, the function also successfully assigns the data type.

To conclude, the benefit of assigning a type to a list is that when you expand the list to new rows, it will have a data type assigned to the column. That eliminates the need to add a separate change type step to define the data type.

Now that we have explored lists, let's next explore another structured data type, records.

Records

Next on our journey through structured values in Power Query's M language, we encounter records.

Introduction to records

A record is a named list of values. While lists are a simple, ordered collection of values, records associate a field name or key to each value. This leads to a more complex, yet organized data structure.

You can think of a record as a single row in a table, where each field in the row has a unique column name and a value. Just like lists, records can contain any type of value, be it primitive (such as text, numbers, or dates), or structured (like lists, records, or tables).

You can create a record with the record initialization operator. This involves specifying pairs of keys and values within square brackets [], also known as record initialization. What's important here is to remember that:

- Every record is surrounded by square brackets.
- A key (the field name) is followed by an equal sign (=). Records allow you to provide the field names without quotation marks.
- The field value follows the equal sign.
- Pairs of keys and values are separated by a comma.

Consider the example in the following figure. This code creates a record with a person's details:

```
[ Name = "John Doe", Age = 30, City = "Seattle" ]
```

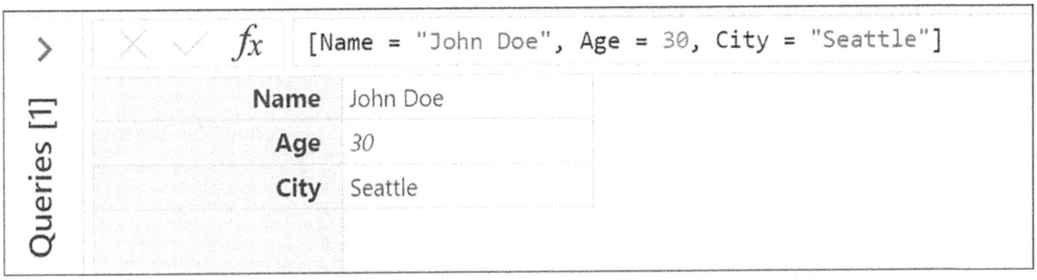

Figure 6.10: Initialize a record in Power Query by using []

In the preceding example, Name, Age, and City are the keys (field names) and John Doe, 30, and Seattle are the corresponding field values. Bear the following in mind when creating a record:

- Key and value combinations are separated by commas.
- Each field name specified should be unique based on a case-sensitive comparison.

An error is returned if the same field name is repeated, like in this faulty record:

```
[ Name = "John Doe", Age = 30, Age = 31 ]
```

The error message states The name 'Age' is defined more than once due to multiple definitions of the field Age. Always make sure to give your records unique field names.

A record can contain other primitive or structured values. Here's an example of a record with a nested list and record:

```
[ Full Name = "John Doe",
  Ages = { 20, 30, 49 },
  Name = [ Initials = "J", Last Name = "Doe" ]
]
```

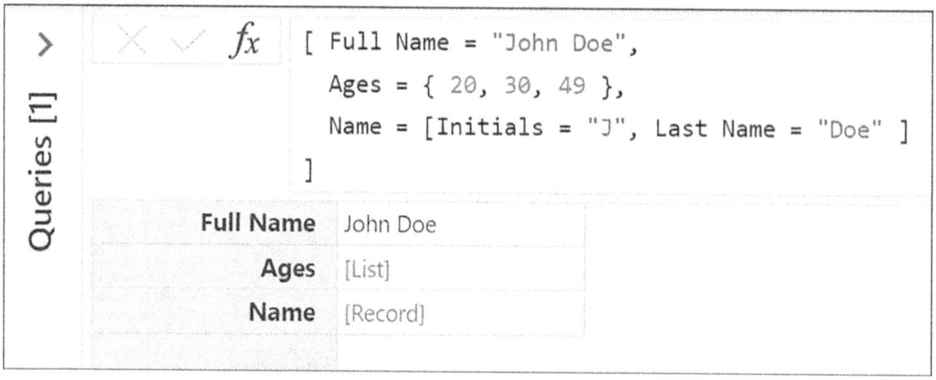

Figure 6.11: A record can contain primitive and structured values

You can return an empty record as follows:

```
[ ] // Output: empty record
```

To count the number of fields in a record, you can use the `Record.FieldCount` function:

```
Record.FieldCount( [ Name = "John Doe", Age = 30 ] ) // 2
Record.FieldCount( [] )                               // 0
```

Apart from using functions, you can also use operators to work with records, which we'll discuss next.

Record operators

Record operators provide the functionality for manipulating and comparing records, just as they do for lists. Let's explore some of these operators that are useful for working with records.

Operator	Notation	Description
Equal	=	Checks if two records are identical.
Not equal	<>	Checks if two records are different.
Concatenation	&	Appends two records.
Coalesce	??	Returns the first non-null value from two values.

Table 6.2: Operators that are used with records

Equal

The equal (=) operator is used to evaluate whether two records are identical. The M language considers records equal when:

- The total number of field names is identical.
- Each field name exists in both records.
- Corresponding field names have identical values considering both their field names and associated values.

For example, the following statement returns `true` as both records are identical:

```
[ Name = "John", Age = 32 ] = [ Name = "John", Age = 32 ]
```

You can freely move around field names in records. When testing for equality, the comparison returns true if the sets of field names and values are identical in each record, regardless of the order. The following statement returns `true`:

```
[ Name = "John", Age = 32 ] = [ Age = 32, Name = "John" ]
```

But if there's any difference in either the field names or the values, it will return `false`. For instance:

```
[ Name = "John", Age = 32 ] = [ Name = "Jane", Age = 32 ]
```

In this case, the `Name` fields of the two records are different, leading to `false` being returned. Remember, the comparison is order-agnostic and case-sensitive for both the field names and the values.

So how can you use this? Consider a situation where you need to determine if a list of records is identical, but the order of fields within these records varies. A common misconception might lead you to believe that aligning the fields in a uniform order is necessary. However, you just learned record equality does not depend on order, so this extra step is unnecessary.

Consider the following example:

```
let
    RecordsList =
        { [ID = 1, Product = "Widget"],
          [Product = "Widget", ID = 1],
          [ID = 1, Product = "Widget"]  },
        UniqueRecords = List.Distinct( RecordsList ),
        CountRecords = List.Count( UniqueRecords )
in
        CountRecords
```

In this script, we begin with a list of records (`RecordsList`) where the order of fields is not consistent across the records. By applying the `List.Distinct` function, we eliminate any duplicate records. The final step, `CountRecords`, calculates the total number of unique records remaining in the list. The result of this operation is 1, showing that the field order within records is irrelevant when determining record equality.

Not equal

The not equal (`<>`) operator serves as the logical opposite of the equal operator. It returns `true` if the records are not identical and `false` otherwise:

```
[ Name = "John", Age = 32 ] <> [ Name = "Jane", Age = 32 ]
```

In this case, the result is `true` as the Name field differs between the two records.

Concatenation

The concatenation operator is valuable for merging records. It allows you to combine two records into one. For example, the following code returns: [Name = "John", Age = 32, Gender = "Male"]

```
[Name = "John", Age = 32 ] & [ Gender = "Male"]
```

In case of overlap between fields, the concatenation operation uses the field from the record on the right to overwrite the field value in the record on the left. With that in mind, the following expression returns [Name = "John", Age = 45]:

```
[ Name = "John", Age = 32 ] & [ Age = 45 ]
```

You can achieve the same outcome with the `Record.Combine` function by providing the records to combine as a list:

```
Record.Combine(
  { [ Name = "John", Age = 32 ],
    [ Age = 45]
  } )
```

So, what is a practical use case for combining record values? Let's consider a scenario where you need to access data from an API. The process typically begins with an API call to retrieve an authorization token. For this request, certain header information is necessary, which must be provided as a record.

Here's an example showing only the header portion of the code required for the initial authorization request:

```
MyHeaders =
[ #"Content-Type" = "application/json",
  #"Api-Client-Identifier" = "ccurr",
  #"Api-Client-Token" = "11d8373-9y3f-9agw-piwr" ]
```

After receiving the authentication token, a subsequent API call is usually made. This call often requires the same header information. Since it's good practice not to repeat yourself, the code for the API call references the `MyHeaders` variable multiple times. For the second request, we just need to enrich the record with the newly received authorization token. That looks as follows:

```
Json.Document(
  Web.Contents("https://myAPI.product.com/api/v4/products/",
    [ Headers =  MyHeaders & [ Authorization = Token ] ]
  ) )
```

On line 3, the concatenation operator combines the MyHeaders record with a record containing the authorization token. This example illustrates how combining records can be useful when providing an options record to functions. Explaining the API call logic of this example is beyond the scope of this book. However, if you are interested, in *Chapter 13, Recursion and iteration,* we cover a more basic example of how you can call an API.

Coalesce

Just like with list values, the coalesce operator (??) works for records. Its usage involves placing the operator between two values: a primary value (on the left) and a fallback value (on the right). The operator first evaluates the primary value. If this value is not null, it is returned. Otherwise, the fallback value is chosen.

Consider this example:

```
null ?? [ Age = 13, Name = "Marc" ]
```

Here, the coalesce operator checks the primary value. Since it's null, the operator returns the fallback record [Age = 13, Name = "Marc"]. While you may not frequently see the coalesce operator used with records, its use becomes clearer when employing it within functions.

Imagine a function designed to count the number of fields in a record:

```
Record.FieldCount( [ Age = 13, Name = "Marc" ]  )
```

This function returns 2, indicating two fields in the record. Now, let's extend this example to a column containing both records and null values, aiming to count the fields in each row. For rows with null values (indicating no fields), you want to return 0. However, the below code does not meet that requirement:

```
Record.FieldCount( null )
```

The Record.FieldCount function does not accept null values. It instead returns the following error:

```
Expression.Error: We cannot convert the value null to type Record.
```

To solve this, the coalesce operator becomes useful. Assume the record and null values are in a column named myRecords. To handle null values without error, incorporate the coalesce operator as follows:

```
Record.FieldCount( [myRecords] ?? [ ] )
```

With this approach, when the function encounters a null value within the myRecords column, it defaults to an empty record. Record.FieldCount can then accurately count the fields in this empty record, correctly returning 0 for null values. That prevents future errors from occurring.

Methods to create a record

This section will provide you with the methods to create and retrieve records, each useful for specific scenarios.

Creating records using the record initializer

Creating a record manually is often the simplest route. In line with what we learned in the previous section, the record initialization operator allows us to create a record in no time. Consider this example:

```
[ Name = "John Doe", Age = 30, City = "Seattle" ]
```

Just like that, we have a record.

Creating records using functions

Next to manual creation, you can also form records using certain functions. Consider the Record.FromList function. This handy function enables us to create a record from given values and fields like so:

```
Record.FromList(
    {"John Doe", 30, "Seattle" },
    { "Name", "Age", "City"    } )
```

The Record.FromTable function offers another alternative to turn a table into a record:

```
Record.FromTable(
    #table( { "Name", "Value"    },
            { { "Name", "John Doe" },
              { "Age",  30         },
              { "City", "Seattle"  } }
        ))
```

The result of this operation is identical to the first code snippet. Yet, the syntax is slightly different.

Retrieving a record by referencing a table row

The third approach to acquire a record is by referring to a table row, formally known as **field selection**. For instance, if you have a table named Source, the first row of this table can be returned as a record with the expression:

```
Source{0}
```

Alternatively, when you're using the Table.AddColumn function, you can reference a table row by writing an underscore (_). Each cell in the new column then contains a record that contains the current row's values.

The following figure illustrates this:

	A^BC Name ▼	1²3 Age ▼	A^BC Gender ▼	A^BC City ▼	A^BC Occupation ▼	ABC 123 CurrentRow
1	John	32	Male	New York	Engineer	[Record]
2	Sarah	27	Female	Los Angeles	Teacher	[Record]
3	Michael	45	Male	Chicago	Doctor	[Record]

`Table.AddColumn(Source, "CurrentRow", each _)`

Table cell details

Name	Sarah
Age	27
Gender	Female
City	Los Angeles
Occupation	Teacher

Figure 6.12: The underscore references the current row in a table

The objective of this section is merely to introduce field selection as the third method. We will explore tables and their characteristics in more depth in the following sections.

Power Query has different methods and functions to accomplish the same task. The choice among these largely depends on the scenario at hand. Manual record creation, using square brackets, is typically the most straightforward route. Yet, in situations where you reference lists or column values, a function like `Record.FromList` can come in handy. Familiarity with these different methods will guide you to the most effective choice for creating your records.

With this new understanding of record creation, let's turn our attention to operators.

Accessing fields in a record

Records can hold one or more fields and values. Accessing these requires understanding two fundamental methods—field selection and record projection.

Operator	Notation	Description
Field selection	[A]	Selects a field from a record.
Record projection	[[A], [B]]	Selects multiple fields from a record.

Table 6.3: Operators used to access fields in a record

Field selection

To access a single field in a record, you can reference the key associated with that value. This is formally referred to as **field selection**. For instance, if you want to return the value from the Name field from a record, you would write:

```
[Name = "John Doe", Age = 30, City = "Seattle"][Name]
```

Notice the use of square brackets here? It's similar to how you access elements in a list, but instead of an index position within curly brackets {}, you're specifying a field name in square brackets.

You can achieve the same outcome by using the Record.Field as follows:

```
Record.Field(
    [Name = "John Doe", Age = 30, City = "Seattle"],
    "Name"
)
```

As your records get more complex, you may encounter records nested within other records. For instance, a second record within the Info field might include more information like Age or Gender. To retrieve the Gender data from such nested structures, you would write it as:

```
[Info = [Age = 20, Gender = "Male"]][Info][Gender]
```

The critical difference between creating and selecting fields within a record lies in the notation within the square brackets. Record definition includes a field name, an equal sign (=), and a value, while field selection only specifies the field name within the brackets. Spotting the difference may take some practice but you will get used to it.

However, be cautious while selecting fields. Attempting to select a field that does not exist in the record will result in an error, as illustrated in the following example:

```
[Name = "John", Age = 30][City] // error
```

The above code returns the Expression.Error: "The field 'Gender' of the record wasn't found.". To prevent this error message, you can use the optional field selection operator (?) to return a null value and bypass the error:

```
[Name = "John", Age = 30] [City]  // error
[Name = "John", Age = 30] [City]? // null
```

This is identical to using the Record.FieldOrDefault function:

```
Record.FieldOrDefault( [Name = "John", Age = 30], "City", null )
```

The examples so far return the value of a field. Records, however, also support returning part of the record so you can retrieve multiple values at once, which we will cover now.

Record projection

Record projection expands on the concept of field selection, allowing you to call upon more than one field simultaneously. In other words, it lets you perform field selection multiple times and *glue* them together. This creates a new record with the selected fields from the original record.

To achieve this, simply enlist the names of the fields you wish to retrieve, separated by commas within square brackets, like:

```
[Ab=1,Bo=2,Ed=3][[Ab],[Ed]] // Output [Ab=1,Ed=3]
[Ab=1,Bo=2,Ed=3][[Ab]]      // Output [Ab=1]
```

When you try to select a nonexistent field, Power Query will raise an error. To circumvent this, you can use the *optional record projection operator* (?) just like you did with field selection, and it will return a null value for the missing field:

```
[Ab=1,Bo=2,Ed=3][[Ab],[Z]]  // Output error
[Ab=1,Bo=2,Ed=3][[Ab],[Z]]? // Output [Ab=1, Z=null]
```

You can replicate this behavior by using `Record.SelectFields`:

```
Record.SelectFields([Ab=1,Bo=2,Ed=3], {"Ab", "Z"}, MissingField.UseNull )
```

In this section, we learned more about accessing elements in records, but when are records useful?

Common operations with records

Now that you're acquainted with creating records and accessing fields with selection and projection, you may wonder about their practical use. In this section, we will explore real-world applications and scenarios where record values are useful in data manipulation.

Structure for variables

A first use case for records is to use them as a structure for variables. In DAX, as you may know, a variable is prefixed by the word VAR and ends with the text RETURN. The advanced editor works with the let..in construct, which does the same thing. Now, what does this have to do with records? The let..in statement in the advanced editor is essentially a record, and you can use it to your advantage for variables.

So why would you want to use variables? For three reasons:

- When you re-use parts of your code, you have less repetition and possibly more efficient code when saving the result of an expression in a variable.
- By splitting up a complex statement your code becomes easier to read.
- Variables help with troubleshooting because you can return interim calculations as a result.

Let's look at an example. Imagine you have a table with a Date column containing the text value 31-12-2024. Your goal is to create the code to dynamically state what day of the week New Year's Eve is falls on.

The steps to do this are:

i.   Transform the text value into a date.

ii.   Retrieve the year and the day of the week name of this date.

iii. Create a string to combine this information.

You can manually do this by adding the following code to a custom column:

```
"New year "
    & Text.From( Date.Year( Date.From( [Date] )))
    & " is on a "
    & Date.DayOfWeekName( Date.From( [Date] ))
```

The output of this statement is: `New year 2023 is on a Sunday`. Notice how this statement converts the text value from the `Date` column to the data type date twice.

If instead you want to use a record structure and work with variables, you can write:

```
[
    _Date   = Date.From([Date]),
    _DoW    = Date.DayOfWeekName(_Date),
    _Year   = Text.From(Date.Year(_Date)),
    _Result = "New year " & _Year & " is on a " & _DoW
][_Result]
```

The output of this code looks as follows:

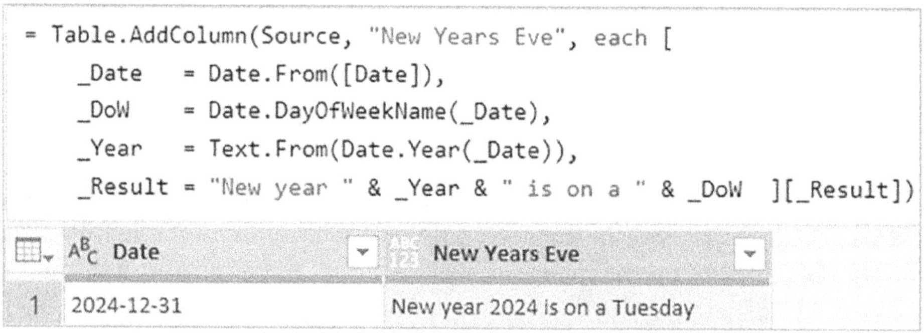

```
= Table.AddColumn(Source, "New Years Eve", each [
    _Date   = Date.From([Date]),
    _DoW    = Date.DayOfWeekName(_Date),
    _Year   = Text.From(Date.Year(_Date)),
    _Result = "New year " & _Year & " is on a " & _DoW ][_Result])
```

AᴮC Date	ABC 123 New Years Eve
1 2024-12-31	New year 2024 is on a Tuesday

Figure 6.13: Records are an effective way to store variables

The code ends by returning the field named `_Result`. Should an error arise, you can pinpoint the problematic step by swapping the final line for another field within the record.

You could even return the entire record, as shown in the following figure:

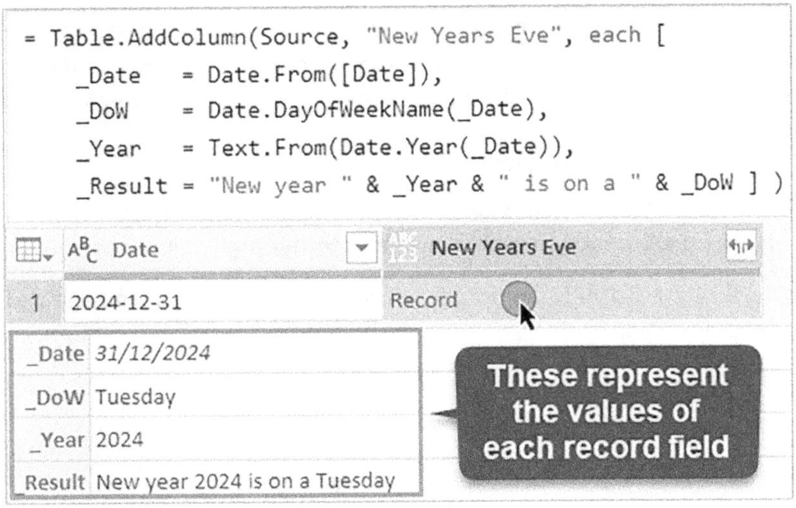
= Table.AddColumn(Source, "New Years Eve", each [
_Date = Date.From([Date]),
_DoW = Date.DayOfWeekName(_Date),
_Year = Text.From(Date.Year(_Date)),
_Result = "New year " & _Year & " is on a " & _DoW])
Date
New Years Eve
1
2024-12-31
Record
_Date 31/12/2024
_DoW Tuesday
_Year 2024
Result New year 2024 is on a Tuesday
These represent the values of each record field

Figure 6.14: By returning the entire record, you can inspect the values of each variable

That would allow you to see the result of each field in your record. The use of a record construct in this manner is particularly beneficial for troubleshooting, as it allows for a systematic review of the variable values at each stage. You can find the above example in the exercise files provided in the GitHub repo for this book.

Referencing the current row

Another scenario where records are useful is when making calculations on the current row values. The following figure depicts a table containing a column with store location names and all other columns containing the months of the year.

	Store	January	February	March	April
1	Denver	501	490	477	522
2	Seattle	780	869	840	700
3	New York	1100	1250	1219	1846

Figure 6.15: Dataset for retrieving the current row as a record

If you want to add a column with average sales without taking data from the store column, you could manually write:

```
List.Average( { [January], [February], [March], [April] } )
```

However, record structures make for a more dynamic way to reference values from a row. To get the same result without hardcoding the month columns, you can write:

```
List.Average(
 Record.ToList(
   Record.RemoveFields( _, "Store" ) ) )
```

This code first retrieves all values from the current row as a record using the underscore. The `Record.RemoveFields` function then removes the `Store` field from this record. Finally, `Record.ToList` transforms the record into a list so that `List.Average` can average all the remaining values.

Providing options for functions

Records are also commonly used to provide options in function parameters. Using a record as input for a function argument allows you to specify the input for multiple options in an easy way.

Take, for example, the `Date.ToText` function. To specify the output format and culture for the English language, you can use:

```
Date.ToText( #date( 2023, 12, 31 ),
  [Format = "dd MMM yyyy", Culture = "en-US" ] )
```

Doing something similar for the German language is as follows:

```
Date.ToText( #date( 2023, 12, 31 ),
  [Format = "dd MMM yyyy", Culture = "de-DE" ] )
```

The result of this operation can be found in the following figure:

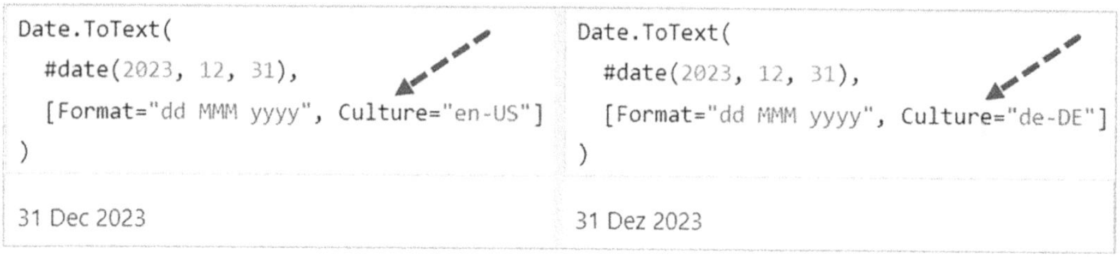

Figure 6.16: Records are used in function arguments

The difference between these two examples can be found in the `Culture` code. In this case, the abbreviated month name shows a different result depending on the culture code used.

In short, being able to provide options to a function is another good reason to learn about records. You will find a great number of functions that require a record to specify additional options.

Keeping track of intermediary results

Records also play an important role in saving intermediary results in complex functions. A function that can use records for more complex calculations is `List.Generate`.

This function generates a list of values based on a starting value, a condition that determines when to stop generating values, and a function that describes how to generate each subsequent value. Without the use of records, this function can, for example, generate a list of increasing values from 1 to 5:

```
List.Generate(
    () => 1,      // the starting value is 1
    each _ <= 5,  // until the value reaches 5
```

```
      each _ + 1     // increment the initial value by 1
  )
```

Here, the List.Generate function generates a list of values. However, this operation is still quite simple, and this is where records come in. Records play an important role when dealing with multi-variable iterations in List.Generate. A record can hold the current state of all variables involved in the iteration. By generating a list of records, you can store more than one of your required values. For instance, the following example creates a running total by increasing value x by one in each step, and then adding this new value to the previous value in the RT (for running total) variable:

```
List.Generate(
      () => [ x = 1, RT = 1 ],
      each [x] <= 5,
      each [ x = [x] + 1, RT = [RT] + [x] + 1 ],
      each [RT]  )
```

Note that this illustration is meant to show you where records are useful. List.Generate is a complex function that we will cover in more detail in *Chapter 13* as we delve into recursion and iteration. Up next is the topic of assigning data types to records.

Assigning a data type to records

A record is a structured value capable of holding one or more distinct values. When you generate these records, Power Query defaults to the any type if no specific data type is assigned, as illustrated in the following figure:

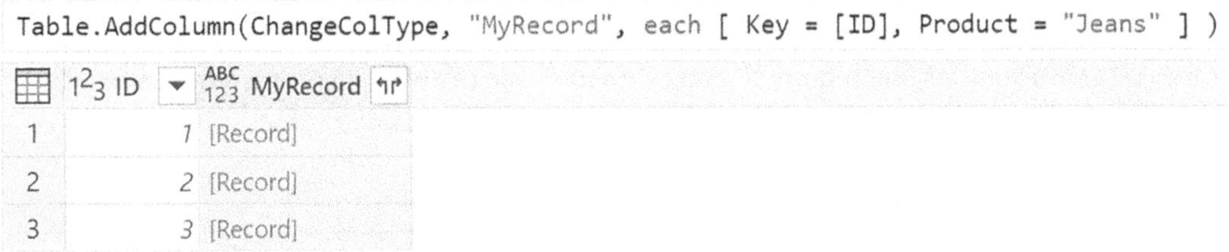

```
Table.AddColumn(ChangeColType, "MyRecord", each [ Key = [ID], Product = "Jeans" ] )
```

1²₃ ID	ABC 123 MyRecord
1	1 [Record]
2	2 [Record]
3	3 [Record]

Figure 6.17: Generating a Record column without assigning a specific data type

Expanding the **Record** column then adds the new columns and assigns the data type any as illustrated here:

```
Table.ExpandRecordColumn(Custom, "MyRecord", {"Key", "Product"}, {"Key", "Product"})
```

1²₃ ID	ABC 123 Key	ABC 123 Product
1	1	1 Jeans
2	2	2 Jeans
3	3	3 Jeans

Figure 6.18: Expanding a Record column that does not have a data type assigned

To allocate a data type to a record, you can input a record type that defines the data type for each record field. The syntax for this mirrors the record's creation, with the sole difference being that it specifies the data type rather than the field value, as shown below:

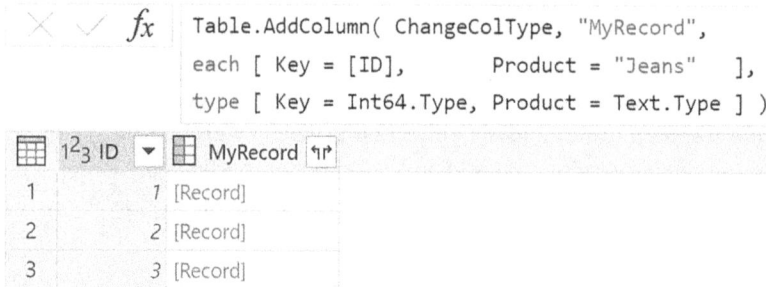

```
fx   Table.AddColumn( ChangeColType, "MyRecord",
        each [ Key = [ID],        Product = "Jeans"    ],
        type [ Key = Int64.Type, Product = Text.Type ] )
```

1²₃ ID	MyRecord
1	1 [Record]
2	2 [Record]
3	3 [Record]

Figure 6.19: Creating a Record column with assigned data types

In the next figure, we expand the **Record** column that has an assigned type. This creates new columns that reflect the provided data types.

```
Table.ExpandRecordColumn(AddRecord, "MyRecord", {"Key", "Product"}, {"Key", "Product"})
```

1²₃ ID	1²₃ Key	A_C Product
1	1	1 Jeans
2	2	2 Jeans
3	3	3 Jeans

Figure 6.20: Extending this Record column keeps the assigned data types

As this section showed, records provide a structured way to hold and manipulate data. Their utility becomes clear in scenarios that require dealing with multiple related data points simultaneously. With this in mind, we now arrive at the remaining structured value, the table value.

Tables

Now that we've taken a deep dive into lists and records, it's time to extend our understanding to table values. As with lists and records, tables hold an important place in the M language due to their role in structuring and organizing data. So, what is a table?

Introduction to tables

At its most basic, a table is a structured value that arranges data in rows and columns. You could also say that a table is a list of records where each record represents a row of the table. Because of its two-dimensional form, it is easy to preview your data in a table and you will find that most queries that are loaded into Power BI or Excel have a table value as output. So how do you create a table?

Creating a table in Power Query's M language is often done by calling an accessing data function as described in *Chapter 3*. For instance, when you import an Excel or CSV file, Power Query automatically creates a table for you.

However, to illustrate the characteristics of tables, this section makes use of the `#table` function that manually creates a table. This function takes two arguments:

- A list of column names.
- A list of lists, where each inner list forms a row.

Let's look at an example expression that uses `#table`:

```
#table(
    {"ID", "Name", "Country"},
    { {1, "John Doe", "USA"},
      {2, "Jane Doe", "USA"},
      {3, "Jane Doe", "Canada"}
    } )
```

The above code returns the table shown below:

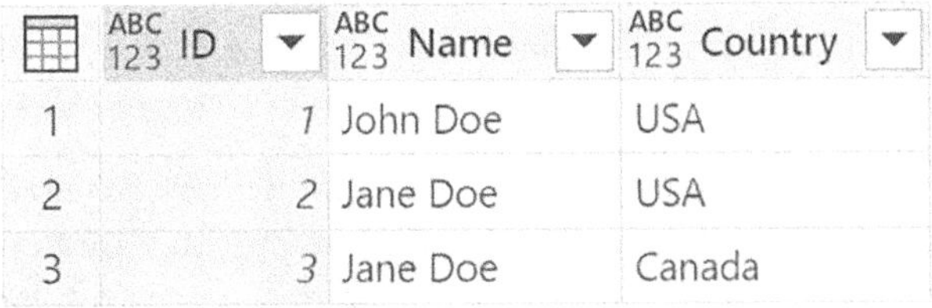

	ABC 123 ID	ABC 123 Name	ABC 123 Country
1	1	John Doe	USA
2	2	Jane Doe	USA
3	3	Jane Doe	Canada

Figure 6.21: A table created using the #table function

The created table has three columns (**ID, Name, Country**) and three rows of data. To specify data types, you can specify a custom table type as covered in *Chapter 5, Understanding Data Types*. We will delve into some aspects of this later in this chapter. Next, we will look at how different operators behave with tables.

Table operators

As we deepen our understanding of tables, let's turn our attention to operators. Tables support the following operators:

Operator	**Notation**	**Description**
Equal	=	Checks if two tables are identical.
Not equal	<>	Checks if two tables are different.
Concatenation	&	Appends two tables.
Coalesce	??	Returns the first non-null value from two options.

Table 6.4: Operators supported by tables

Equal

The equal (=) operator is used to determine whether two tables are the same, both in their structure and in the values they contain. For two tables to be considered equal, they must meet the following criteria:

- They have the same number of columns.
- Each column name is available in both tables.
- They contain an identical number of rows.
- Corresponding cells across these rows hold identical values.

Consider the following example where two tables have their column names ordered differently:

```
#table( {"ID", "Name", "Country"},
        {{1, "John Doe", "USA"}, {2, "Jane Doe", "USA"}} ) =
#table( {"Name", "Country", "ID"},
        {{"John Doe", "USA", 1}, {"Jane Doe", "USA", 2}} )
```

This expression returns `true`, showing that the order of column names does not impact the equality of the tables. The key factor is that the data aligns correctly in terms of values and structure.

A common use case for this type of comparison is in data validation. For example, suppose you have imported a budget table into Power Query. To ensure accuracy, you want to verify that the uploaded data matches the latest budget file you received. When comparing the two tables using the equal operator, a result of `true` confirms that the data in both tables is indeed identical. This ensures that no discrepancies exist between the old budget version and the latest file.

Not equal

The not equal operator does the exact opposite of the equal operator. It checks whether two tables differ in any way. Taking our previous example, we can change the country from USA to US:

```
#table( {"ID", "Name", "Country" },
      {{1, "John Doe", "USA"}, {2, "Jane Doe", "USA"}}) =
#table( {"ID", "Name", "Country" },
        {{1, "John Doe", "US"}, {2, "Jane Doe", "USA"}})
```

The above expression returns `false` because the country name in the third column of the first row differs. It's good to be aware that the not equal operator works, irrespective of whether the values compared are primitive or structured values.

Concatenation

You can use the concatenation operator, represented by &, to combine two tables. The operation appends one table to the end of another. For example, the following code combines two tables:

```
#table({"ID", "Name", "Country"}, {{1, "John Doe", "USA"}}) &
#table({"ID", "Name", "Country"}, {{2, "Jane Doe", "USA"}})
```

This expression returns the following table:

```
fx    #table( {"ID", "Name", "Country"}, {{1, "John Doe", "USA"}}) &
      #table( {"ID", "Name", "Country"}, {{2, "Jane Doe", "USA"}})
```

ABC 123 ID	ABC 123 Name	ABC 123 Country
1	1 John Doe	USA
2	2 Jane Doe	USA

Figure 6.22: Combining two tables with identical columns

Here, the two tables are successfully merged, aligning the rows from both tables into one continuous sequence. In cases where the tables have different columns, the merge operation intelligently fills in missing data with null values to ensure the integrity of the merged table. You can try this using the following code:

```
#table({"ID", "Name", "City"}, {{1, "John Doe", "Texas"}}) &
#table({"ID", "Name", "Country"}, {{2, "Jane Doe", "USA"}})
```

The output of this expression is as follows:

```
fx    #table( {"ID", "Name", "City"}, {{1, "John Doe", "Texas"}}) &
      #table( {"ID", "Name", "Country"}, {{2, "Jane Doe", "USA"}})
```

ABC 123 ID	ABC 123 Name	ABC 123 City	ABC 123 Country
1	1 John Doe	Texas	null
2	2 Jane Doe	null	USA

Figure 6.23: Merging tables with different columns adds null values

Another useful scenario for combining tables is when using the **Enter Data** functionality. This functionality allows you to manually provide data and import it into your query. Simply go to the **Home** tab and select **Enter Data** as shown below:

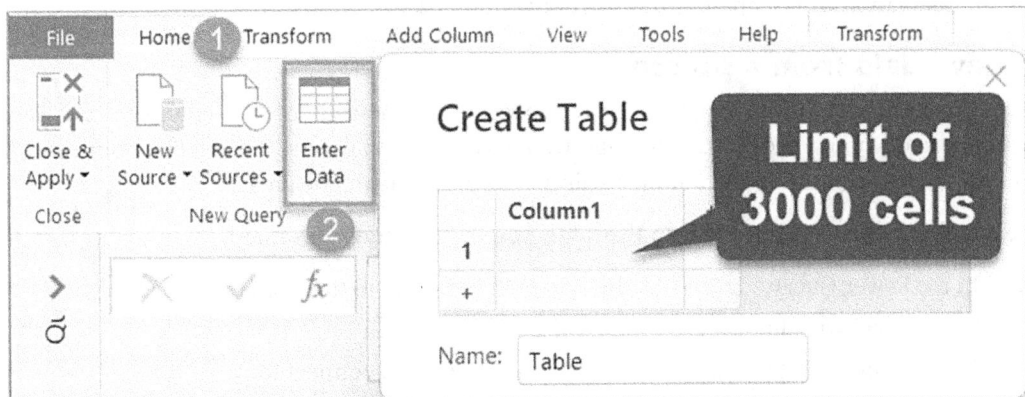

Figure 6.24: The Enter Data functionality is limited to 3,000 cells

You can then paste your values into the table. However, there is a limit of 3,000 cells that you can paste in. A workaround for this limit is to split up your table into multiple tables that are within that 3,000-cell limit. You can then use the concatenation operator to reference the different tables and combine them into a single table.

Alternatively, if you prefer a functional approach, `Table.Combine` offers a similar outcome. This function requires the tables to be combined within a list, as shown below:

```
Table.Combine( Table1, Table2 )
```

This method is just as effective and more explicit, especially when dealing with multiple tables.

Coalesce

The coalesce operator (`??`), which we showed for lists and records, is equally effective when applied to table values. It allows you to provide fallback values in cases where the primary table might be null. This ensures your queries remain robust and error-free.

An example of the coalesce operator in action on a table value is as follows:

```
null ?? #table( {"ID", "Name"}, {{1, "John Doe"}})
```

In this statement, if the first value is `null`, the operator defaults to returning the table specified after `??`. Consequently, the table value is returned.

You will generally find the coalesce operator used in combination with tables when creating custom functions. Here, it acts as a safeguard, preventing errors that could arise from null inputs. By providing an alternative table when the expected table is null, you ensure that your custom functions are resilient and reliable. You can find the details of how to create custom functions in *Chapter 9*.

Having explored the creation of tables and the application of operators, the next section focuses on accessing items in a table, a helpful skill when transforming your data.

Methods to create a table

Tables are a fundamental concept in the M language. This section will guide you through various methods of creating tables, opening a world of possibilities.

Retrieve data from a source

The most common way to create a table is to connect to a data source. You can connect to a variety of data sources, including Excel files, CSV files, web pages, and databases. Once you've connected to a data source, Power Query M will automatically create a table from the data.

For example, to create a table from an Excel file, you would follow these steps:

1. In the Power Query editor, click the **New Source** button in the ribbon.
2. Select **Excel Workbook**.
3. In the **Open** dialog box, select the Excel file you want to connect to.
4. Select the table or sheet you want to import.
5. Click the **OK** button.

Power Query M will automatically create a table from the Excel file using the Excel.Workbook function together with File.Contents.

Manually input data into functions

The second way to create table values is by manually building them using library functions. The functions that allow you to create tables manually are:

- #table
- Table.FromColumns
- Table.FromList
- Table.FromRecords
- Table.FromRows
- Table.FromValue
- Table.FromPartitions
- Record.ToTable

Each function brings its own set of capabilities to the table (pun intended). The most used function to manually create a table is the #table function. This function takes a list of column names as the first argument and a list of lists as the second argument to form the rows. Consider the following example:

```
#table( {"ProductKey", "Product"},
        {{1, "Apple"}, {2, "Prume"}} )
```

The preceding code uses lists as input and returns the following table:

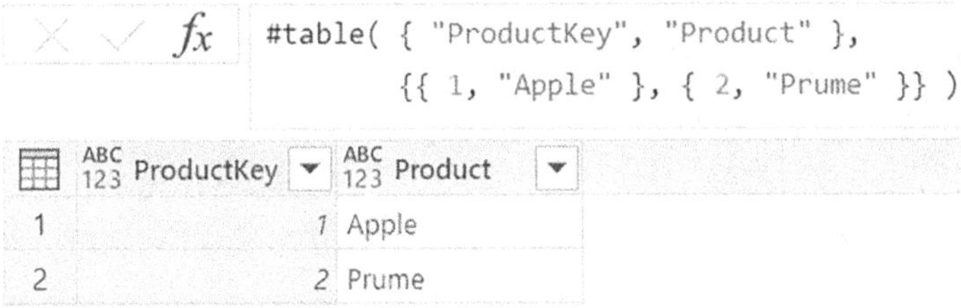

Figure 6.25: The #table function creating a table

The first argument takes a list of column names, whereas the second argument takes a list of lists for the rows in the table.

Another popular function, Table.FromRecords, accepts a list of records as input. These records house both the column names, portrayed by the record field names, and the row values, represented by the record field values. You can use it as follows:

```
Table.FromRecords( { [ ProductKey = 1, Product = "Apple"  ],
                     [ ProductKey = 2, Product = "Prume" ] })
```

This code returns an identical table, but instead uses records as input:

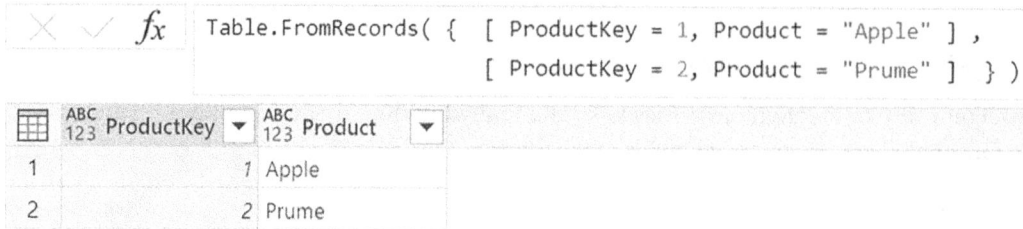

```
fx    Table.FromRecords( { [ ProductKey = 1, Product = "Apple" ] ,
                           [ ProductKey = 2, Product = "Prume" ] } )
```

ABC 123 ProductKey ▼	ABC 123 Product ▼
1	Apple
2	Prume

Figure 6.26: An illustration of creating a table using Table.FromRecords

The number of methods for creating tables in Power Query is vast, and covering every function here would be overwhelming. However, becoming an M language expert involves understanding the different methods of table creation.

Consider a scenario where you generate a list of running total values using the List.Generate function. The output of this function is a list value. To tie the values in this list to an existing table, you'll need to combine some of these functions.

In another instance, you might be tasked with creating a reconciliation table that performs various checks answering questions like: is the final table's row count the same as the initial count? Does the total revenue of Query1 align with that of Query2?

In these scenarios, knowing how to store the output values of these checks in a table proves helpful. And the good thing is that you have a great range of functions at your disposal to create a table that meets your specific needs.

Re-use existing tables/queries

Now you know the methods to create tables manually, it's time to explore two other important ways of adding tables in Power Query: referencing and duplicating queries.

Referencing tables/queries

Referencing tables is the process of pointing to the output of other tables or queries. This approach enables you to use existing tables or queries without modifying or affecting their original content. Think of referencing as creating a link. This process allows you to link to the output of an existing table or query and continue working on it without any disruptions or changes to the source. So how do you do it?

Referencing tables or queries is easy. For instance, let's assume we have a table called **Calendar**. You want to use the output of the **Calendar** table as the base of a new query. All you would need to do is *right-click* the **Calendar** query and click **Reference**, as shown below:

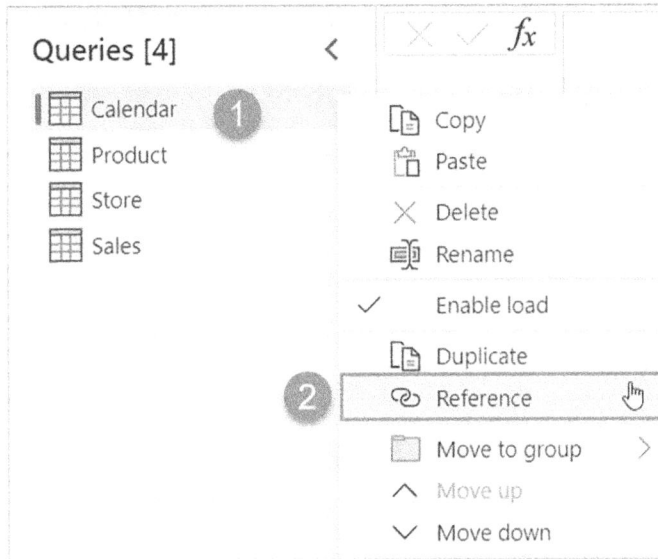

Figure 6.27: Illustration of the reference query operation

This creates the query, shown below, that references (or links to) the **Calendar** query.

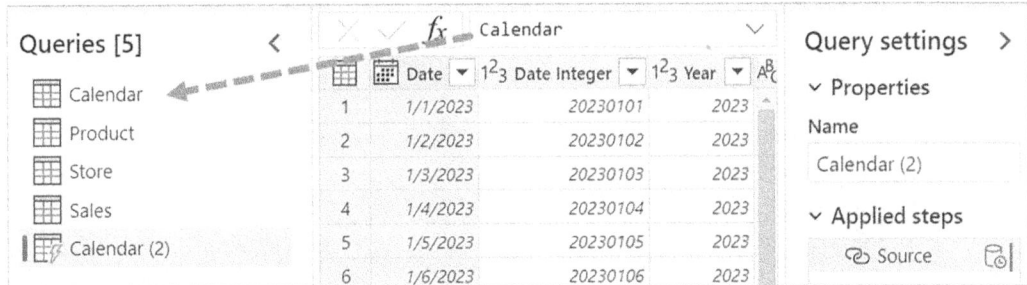

Figure 6.28: The reference query operation links to the original table

Any updates to the original calendar will flow into the referenced query. In that way, there is a chain of logic. Besides referencing, you can also duplicate tables.

Duplicating tables/queries

Duplicating tables in Power Query is the act of creating an exact copy of an existing query. The duplicated query has the same query steps and content as the original but functions as a separate entity.

To duplicate a query, you *right-click* an existing query and click **Duplicate** as shown in the following figure:

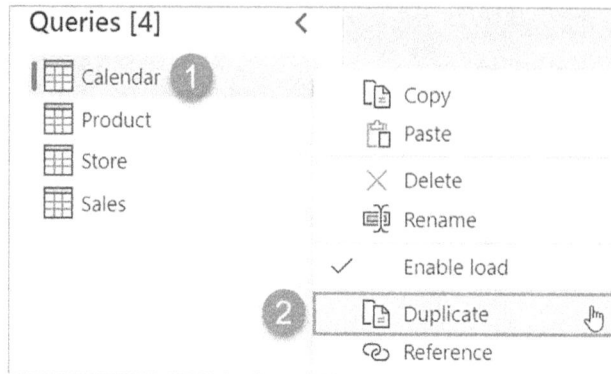

Figure 6.29: You can duplicate a query by right-clicking and selecting Duplicate

The process is different from referencing a query: while referencing creates a link to an existing query, duplication creates an entirely new query that merely resembles the original. This copy includes all query steps in the original query, as illustrated by the following figure.

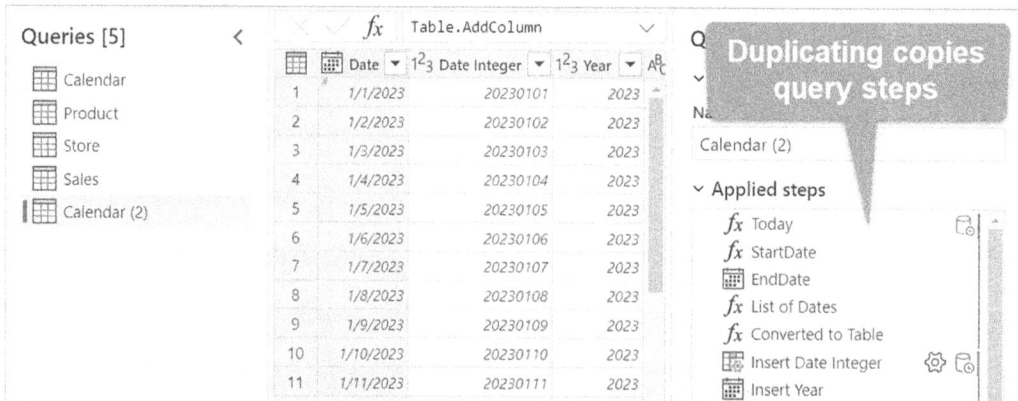

Figure 6.30: The Duplicate query operation also copies query steps

When trying out different approaches on your data, we recommend duplicating a query and using it as a backup. This way, you can always restore the original query in case your trials fail.

Using the Enter data functionality

This list wouldn't be complete without mentioning the **Enter data** functionality. The Power Query editor provides a user-friendly way to create tables manually by simply entering data on a screen.

To enter data manually, navigate to the **Home** tab in the ribbon. In the **New query** section, you'll find the **Enter data** button as shown in *Figure 6.31*. This is where you can manually create tables without writing any M code.

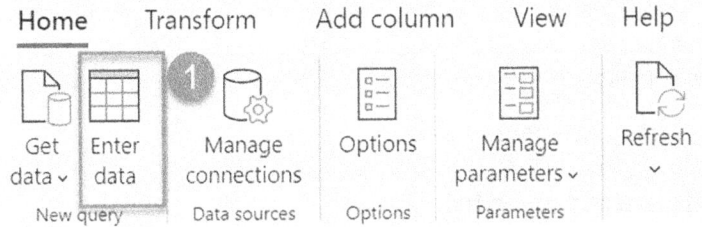

Figure 6.31: Enter data button in the Home tab

Once you click on **Enter data**, a window appears with an empty table, ready for you to populate. Both the column names and values are editable, and you can directly enter your data as shown in the following figure:

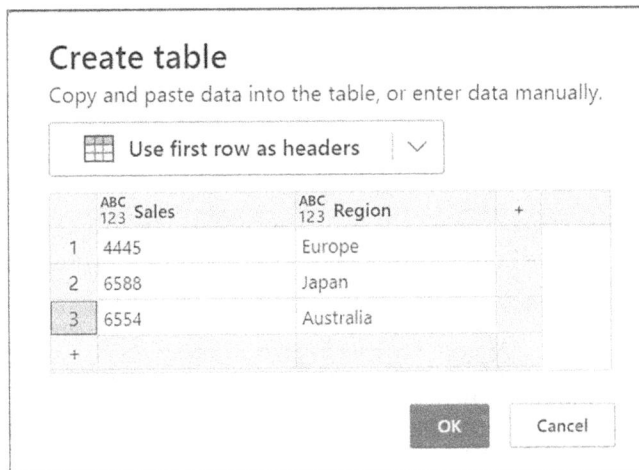

Figure 6.32: The Create table dialog screen

To add rows, you simply click the cells (highlighted in gray) at the end of the last row, and a new row will appear. Similarly, to add columns, you click the rightmost column header (also in gray), and a new column will be created.

After you have populated your table with data, click on **OK** in the bottom-right corner of the window. This action will close the window and load the data into Power Query as a new table.

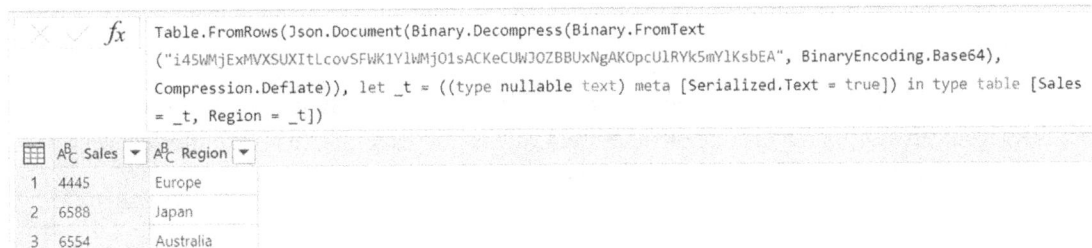

```
Table.FromRows(Json.Document(Binary.Decompress(Binary.FromText
("i45WMjExMVXSUXItLcovSFWK1YlWMjO1sACKeCUWJOZBBUxNgAKOpcUlRYk5mYlKsbEA", BinaryEncoding.Base64),
Compression.Deflate)), let _t = ((type nullable text) meta [Serialized.Text = true]) in type table [Sales
= _t, Region = _t])
```

Sales	Region
1	4445	Europe
2	6588	Japan
3	6554	Australia

Figure 6.33: Binary code generated with the Enter data functionality

As this image shows, the **Enter data** functionality compresses the data into binary code and uses the `Table.FromRows` function to create the table. Since this is such an easy way to create a table, we wanted to mention it separately. Be aware that this functionality supports up to 3,000 cells with values.

Next, we delve into accessing different elements in a table.

Accessing elements in a table

Much like lists and records, accessing elements in a table is a useful skill to have when working with Power Query. You might want to select a single column, multiple columns, a row, or even a single cell value. Let's have a look at how we can use the principles of selection and projection in the context of a table.

Item access

In the context of a table, the item access expression is used to return a row. Let's say the following table is created in a step called `Source`.

	ABC 123 ID	ABC 123 Name	ABC 123 Country
1	1	John Doe	USA
2	2	Jane Doe	USA
3	3	Jane Doe	Canada

Figure 6.34: Table for accessing items

Using the item-selection operator in the context of a table returns a row in the form of a record.

You can, for example, return the first row of the table by writing:

```
Source{0} // Output: [ID=1, Name="John Doe", Country="USA"]
```

This is identical to using the `Table.Range` function and specifying you want to return a single row:

```
Table.Range( Source, 0, 1 )
```

Just like with lists, trying to retrieve an item where the requested position does not exist in the table throws an error that you can prevent with the *optional item-selection operator*:

```
Source{3}  // Row 4 does not exist, returns an Error
Source{3}? // Returns null
```

Tables allow you to access rows in an additional way. Instead of providing an index number in curly brackets, you can also search for one or more field values. For example, to return the second row of our table, we can use any of the following expressions:

```
Source{1}        // Returns the second row
Source{[ID = 2 ]} // Returns the row where ID = 2
```

You can narrow down your search further by providing multiple search values. Simply extend your record with additional fields and return it within curly brackets, like so:

```
Source{[ID = 2, Name ="Jane Doe" ]}
```

It's important to remember that item selection by providing a record should return a unique row. The following expression matches two rows and throws an error, as shown in *Figure 6.35*:

```
Source{[Name ="Jane Doe"]}
```

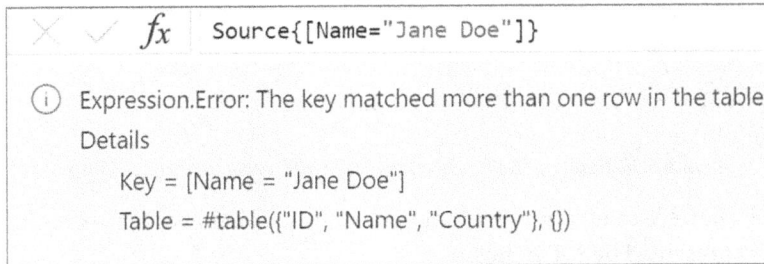

Figure 6.35: Error when item selection returns multiple rows

This behavior closely resembles the following expression, which expects a single row as a result:

```
Table.SingleRow(
    Table.SelectRows( Source, each [Name] = "Jane Doe" ) )
```

If you want to return multiple rows, you can resort to a function like:

```
Table.SelectRows( Source, each [Name] = "Jane Doe" )
```

Field access

Whereas item-selection returns a row, the *field-selection operator* allows you to return the values from a column as a list. To return the values from the Name column as a list, you can use the same syntax as you did for records:

```
Source[Name] // Output: { "John Doe", "Jane Doe", "Jane Doe" }
```

Alternatively, you can use the Table.Column function for a similar result:

```
Table.Column( Source, "Name" )
```

This behavior is useful when you want to reference all column values to perform an operation on them similar to when you use List.Sum. You can then use the result to state each value as a percentage of the total.

Now let's say you want to access multiple columns from your table, how would you achieve this? Field projection allows you to project a table to one with fewer columns.

```
Source[[Name],[Country]] // Returns two columns
```

It's like providing a list of column references, but instead of surrounding the column with curly brackets, you provide square brackets. This method works for both single and multiple columns. The benefit of this approach is that the output provides you with columns in table format instead of a list, as illustrated below:

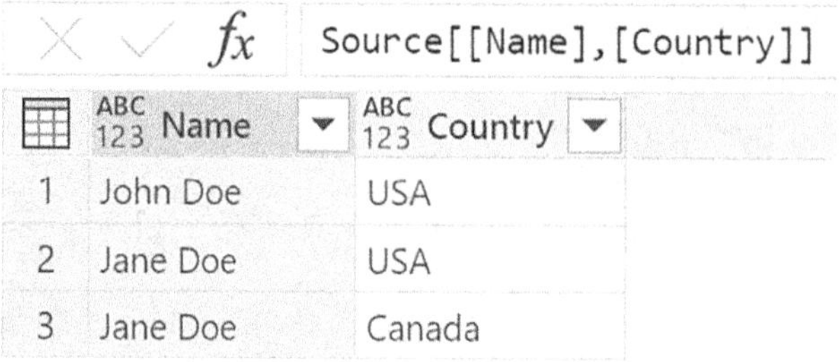

	ABC 123 Name	▼	ABC 123 Country	▼
1	John Doe		USA	
2	Jane Doe		USA	
3	Jane Doe		Canada	

fx Source[[Name],[Country]]

Figure 6.36: Required field projection projects a table to fewer columns

An error is raised when selecting a non-existent field, but you can prevent the error by using optional field projection, represented by ?. For instance:

```
Source[[Name],[Location]]  // Error
Source[[Name],[Location]]? // Returns null in Location column
```

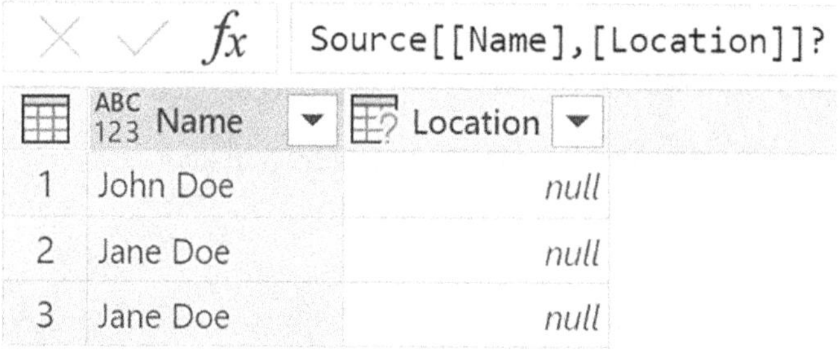

	ABC 123 Name	▼	Location	▼
1	John Doe		null	
2	Jane Doe		null	
3	Jane Doe		null	

fx Source[[Name],[Location]]?

Figure 6.37: Optional field projection returns null for missing columns

This behavior is identical to using the Table.SelectColumns function together with the MissingField. UseNull enumeration:

```
Table.SelectColumns(
    Source,
    {"Name", "Location"},
    MissingField.UseNull
)
```

So far, we have seen how to select a row as a record (item-selection) and we know how to return one or more columns from a table (field-selection and field-projection). To return a single value from a table, you can combine both concepts. Let's say you want to return a value from the third row in the Name column – you can use either of the following expressions:

```
Source[Name]{2}
Source{2}[Name]
```

This can be useful when you want to drill down into a single value in your table. Now that you know how to create tables and access items within them, let's look at some situations where tables are useful.

Common operations with tables

Generally, tables are what we are looking for when working with Power Query. It may be obvious, but here's a few areas where tables are often used:

- **Helper tables:** Tables are helpful when joining or appending data. This can be an import from another file or database, but you can also manually create helper tables to enrich your data or use them to merge or join.
- **Inspect data and debug:** Tables are often the most effective structure with which to inspect your data. With columns and rows, you can see many cells at the same time. And with each transformation you perform, you can easily see the effect on your table.
- **Integrate with Power BI and Excel:** After performing transformations on your data, you usually end up with one or more clean tables. You can then load them to your desired destination, like an Excel worksheet or a Power BI dataset. From there you can continue working with your data.

There are currently over 117 table functions and it is the largest function category in the M language. In subsequent chapters, you will learn techniques that incorporate the most important table functions.

You now know how to create, manipulate, and access values in a table. What's left is to learn about assigning data types to tables, which we will cover next.

Assigning a data type to tables

Table values are structured values with complex data types. After all, they can contain other primitive values or structured values. Yet, you can still define data types for each column in your table. So how should you approach data types for table values?

Imagine you're manually constructing a table value for each row in a table. You can do this by using the #table function together with the Table.AddColumn function, as shown in the following screenshot:

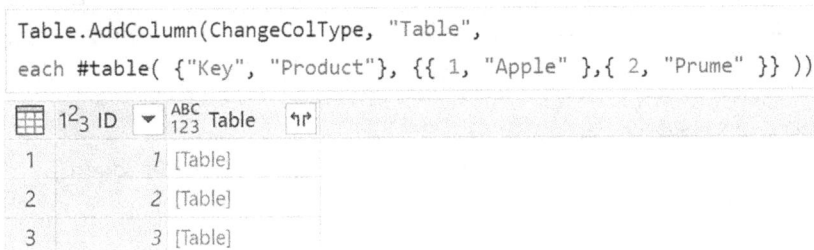

```
Table.AddColumn(ChangeColType, "Table",
each #table( {"Key", "Product"}, {{ 1, "Apple" },{ 2, "Prume" }} ))
```

1²3 ID	ABC 123 Table
1	1 [Table]
2	2 [Table]
3	3 [Table]

Figure 6.38: Creating a table value using the #table function

In line with our expectations, the newly formed column is automatically assigned the type any. When you expand the column, it yields additional columns, all set to the data type any. So, how do we assign a table type during the table creation process?

This is very similar to how we defined a record type, with the key difference being that this time, the word type is followed by the word table, as shown in the following figure.

```
fx   Table.AddColumn(ChangeColType, "Table",
         each #table( {"Key", "Product"},
                      {{ 1, "Apple" },{ 2, "Prume" }} ),
                      type table[ Key = Int64.Type, Product = Text.Type ] )
```

1²₃ ID	Table
1	1 [Table]
2	2 [Table]
3	3 [Table]

Figure 6.39: Creating a table column with data types assigned

Expanding the column then adds new columns with data types assigned, as shown below:

```
Table.ExpandTableColumn(#"Added Custom", "Table", {"Key", "Product"}, {"Key", "Product"})
```

1²₃ ID	1²₃ Key	Product
1	1	1 Apple
2	1	2 Prume
3	2	1 Apple

Figure 6.40: Expanding a table column retains the types provided through a custom table type

Note that you can also supply a table type within the #table function. When you construct a table solely using this function, without using Table.AddColumns, the table type provides the engine with the necessary data type information.

However, when using the Table.AddColumn function, adding the table type to the #table function does not influence the output data type. It is only the fourth argument that impacts the output type, as shown below:

```
fx   Table.AddColumn(ChangeColType, "Custom",
         each #table( type table[ Key = Int64.Type, Product = Text.Type ],
                      {{ 1, "Apple" },{ 2, "Prume" }} ))
```

1²₃ ID	ABC 123 Custom
1	1 [Table]
2	2 [Table]
3	3 [Table]

Figure 6.41: The Table.AddColumn function determines the output data type

In the above figure, the column type is not set for `Table.AddColumn` but it is included in the table expression. Therefore, the column type is not retained. In these situations, it is important to add the table type to the fourth argument of `Table.AddColumn`.

Summary

In this chapter, we explored lists, records, and tables, showing how important they are when you're using the M language.

We learned that structured values serve as containers holding one or more primitive or structured values. Learning about them is useful in many different areas. For instance, lists and records are often used to provide multiple items in function arguments and they help in simplifying your code by using them. Record structures are also great structures in which you can create variables.

We also investigated how to access items from the different structured values through selection and projection, enabling you to easily extract values. You will find that these skills help you understand code created by the user interface, but also help you create shorter code yourself.

We then looked at the creation of these values and how operators work on them. You also learned about complex data types, highlighting their importance and how to assign them.

Finally, this chapter provided tangible, real-world examples and scenarios. These served as practical demonstrations to show the power of structured values and how you can handle them with ease.

We will now continue to the next chapter, in which we focus on conceptualizing M and delve deeper into the fundamental principles of the M language.

Learn more on Discord

Join our community's Discord space for discussions with the author and other readers:

`https://discord.gg/vCSG5GBbyS`

7

Conceptualizing M

As with any programming language, it is important to understand both the abstract principles of the language as well as more practical topics, such as what functions are available and how to use them. This chapter aims to provide you with a solid conceptual understanding of key, perhaps more abstract aspects of Power Query M, such as scope, the global environment, closure, and metadata. These concepts are crucial to truly becoming a master of Power Query M.

We will begin by delving into the concept of scope in Power Query M. Understanding scope is essential for controlling the visibility and accessibility of variables and functions within your queries. We will explore the distinction between local and global scope, examining how variables and functions interact within different scopes to produce effective data transformations.

Any discussion of scope naturally leads to a discussion of the global environment for Power Query M and how we can create our own global environment through the use of the `Expression.Evaluate` function. We will explore different aspects of the global environment and how the `Expression.Evaluate` function can be used to create dynamic queries and programmatically modify query logic based on specific conditions or inputs.

Closures are an essential concept in Power Query M that amplify the capabilities of functions. We will explore how closures allow functions to encapsulate data and maintain references to variables from their lexical environment, enabling sophisticated data manipulations and iterative calculations.

Finally, understanding and utilizing metadata can be useful when working in Power Query M. We will explore how metadata can be harnessed to improve data governance, trace data sources, and ensure data quality.

Specifically, this chapter covers the following:

- Understanding scope
- Examining the global environment
- Understanding closures
- Managing metadata

Technical requirements

To follow along with this chapter, you will need to have Power BI Desktop installed.

Understanding scope

In Power Query M, **scope** determines where variables and functions can be accessed and used, and it plays a critical role in controlling the flow of data transformations and data manipulation operations:

- **Global scope:** Global scope refers to variables and functions that are defined at the query level, outside of any specific query step or function. Variables and functions with global scope can be accessed and utilized across all steps and functions within the entire query. They provide a way to store and share data or calculations between different parts of the query, ensuring consistency and reusability.

- **Local scope:** Local scope is the most common type of scope in Power Query M. It refers to variables and functions that are defined within a specific query step or a function definition. Variables and functions with local scope are only accessible within the step or function where they are defined. They cannot be referenced or used outside of their local context, making them ideal for temporary calculations or intermediate results within a specific transformation.

- **Using let expressions for scope management:** In Power Query M, the let expression is a powerful tool for managing scope. It allows you to define local variables within a specific query step while keeping the global scope clean and organized, making your code more **readable** and **maintainable** by segregating temporary calculations and intermediate results from the main data transformations.

- **Function scope and parameters:** Functions in Power Query M have their own scope. The parameters of a function are considered to be local variables within the function's scope. They are accessible and usable within the function's body but have no meaning outside of it. Function parameters allow you to pass data and values between different parts of the function, ensuring data flow and modularity.

- **Resolving scope conflicts:** When variables or functions share the same name in different scopes, Power Query M uses a process called **lexical scoping** (also known as **static scoping**) to resolve scope conflicts. Lexical scoping prioritizes local scope over global scope, meaning that if a variable or function with the same name exists both locally and globally, the local one will take precedence within its specific context.

Let's look at some specific examples of scope. Consider the following query:

```
let
    x = 10,
    y = 20,
    z = 30
in
    x * y * z
```

Ignoring the global environment (see *Examining the global environment* later in this chapter), the following table summarizes the scope for the query and each expression within the query:

Item	Global Scope	Local Scope
Query	x = 10, y = 20, z = 30	
X		y = 20, z = 30
Y		x = 10, z = 30
Z		x = 10, y = 20

Table 7.1: Summarizing the scope for a query and the expressions used

As can be seen in the table, at the query level, all three variables or expressions, (x, y, z) are in scope for the query. However, each variable has its own local scope. Within this scope, each expression can see the other global variables; however, their own expression is not in scope and generally cannot be referenced without causing an error. For example, the following is invalid code:

```
Let
    x = 10,
    y = 20,
    z = x * y * z
in
    z
```

This results in the following error:

```
Expression.Error: The name 'z' wasn't recognized.  Make sure it's spelled
correctly.
```

This type of error is generally the results of misunderstanding scope. To prevent such errors, verify that your variables and function definitions are defined within the proper scope and thus accessible where you intend to use them.

In this particular case, the error is caused by the expression z = x * y * z because z is not in scope for that line of code.

It is possible for an expression to self-reference using the @ symbol as a prefix. However, this too generally results in an error. For example, the following code is syntactically valid:

```
let
    x = 10,
    y = 20,
    z = x * y * @z
in
    z
```

However, this query results in the following error:

```
Expression.Error: A cyclic reference was encountered during evaluation.
```

This error is caused by the expression z = x * y * @z because the Power Query M engine has determined that there is no end condition where the self-reference will terminate. Self-referencing is generally only useful, and will not cause an error, in the context of a recursive function with some form of termination condition. See *Chapter 13, Iteration and Recursion,* for more about recursive functions.

Continuing with our example, let's explore a more complex query that demonstrates using the let expression to control scope and demonstrates lexical scoping where local scope is given precedence over global scope:

```
let
    x = 10,
    y =
        let
            x = 1,
            z = x
        in
            z
in
    y
```

The result of this query is 1. Let's explain how this occurs:

Item	Global Scope	Local Scope
Query	x = 10, y = ?	
x		y = ?
y		x = 10
x		x = 10, z = ?
z		x = 1

Table 7.2: Summarizing the scope for a query and its expressions

Here we have used ? to denote values that are resolved as part of the explanation given here in the following paragraphs. As covered earlier, the global scope for the query includes all of the variables or expressions defined in the query (x and y). Each of these variables has a local scope that includes every other global variable but not itself.

For the expression for the variable y, we use a let expression to control scope. Within this scope we define a variable x with a value of 1. The local scope for this variable cannot see itself but can see the global scope variable x whose value is 10.

It can also see the local variable z. The z variable cannot see itself but can see x. However, because of local precedence, the value for x that z sees is 1 and not 10. Thus, z returns 1 and thus y returns 1 and thus the query itself returns 1.

Now consider the following example:

```
let
    x = z,
    y = 20,
    z =
        let
            a = 30
        in
            a
in
    x
```

This query returns 30. This is because z is in the scope for x and obviously the order of the code does not matter. The fact that the definition of z comes after x is irrelevant as the M engine recognizes that the value for x is dependent on the value of z.

Consider this final example:

```
let
    x = a,
    y = 20,
    z =
        let
            a = 30
        in
            a
in
    x
```

This query results in an error, "The name 'a' wasn't recognized". This is because while x and y are within the scope of a, the same cannot be said with regards to a being in the scope of x or y. Variables (expressions) defined within nested let structures are not available to expressions defined higher in the nested hierarchy.

Understanding scope is essential for writing efficient and maintainable Power Query M code. Properly managing scope ensures that variables and functions are used in the right context and that calculations and data manipulations are performed accurately. By leveraging local and global scope strategically, you can create flexible, modular, and organized data transformation processes in Power Query M.

Let's continue our exploration of scope by addressing the top scope level, the global environment.

Examining the global environment

In Power Query M, the **global environment** refers to the top-level scope that encompasses the entire Power Query query. It represents the highest level of visibility and accessibility for variables and functions, making them available throughout the entire query's code. The global environment serves as a container for global variables, functions, and settings that can be accessed and used across all query steps and functions.

When creating queries within Power Query Editor in Power BI Desktop, the global environment comprises the following three components:

- **Standard library:** A programming language's **standard library** is a non-volatile collection of resources such as configuration data, documentation, classes, values, types, and pre-written code. M's standard library consists of the following elements:

  - Built-in functions
  - Built-in types
  - Built-in enumerations

- **Shared extension functions:** Functions in Power Query extensions are defined with the shared keyword. See *Chapter 16, Enabling Extensions,* for more information.
- **Current queries:** These are queries defined within the current session.

You can actually *see* this global environment by using the #shared keyword. In Power Query Editor, create a new blank query. Open the query in **Advanced Editor** and replace the entire contents with, simply, #shared. Note that #shared is one of about a dozen, predefined keywords/identifiers in the core M language that start with a hashtag (#). Most of these keywords/identifiers are constructors for specific datatypes, such as #binary, #date, #time, etc. Two additional keywords/identifiers are #infinity, which returns the symbol for infinity, and #nan, which returns NaN.

What is returned is a table with the columns Name and Value. Scrolling through the list, you will find any existing queries defined within your Power Query Editor session and all of the standard M functions, types, and enumerations, as well as functions for third-party connectors that come bundled with Power BI Desktop.

By leveraging the global environment effectively and complementing it with local scope management, you can create powerful, flexible, and cohesive data transformation processes in Power Query M, as you will see in the practical examples throughout this book. Before we move on, let's tackle two additional topics that involve the global environment, starting with sections.

Studying sections

Sections are covered more extensively in *Chapter 16, Enabling Extensions.* However, we will briefly cover this topic here to explain the overall concept without getting into detail. Sections in Power Query M are containers of *things*, such as queries, parameters, functions, expressions, and so on. These *things* are referred to as **members**. **Sections** cannot be created in Power Query editor but rather must be implemented as **extensions** to the global environment, which is the subject of *Chapter 16, Enabling Extensions.*

While sections cannot be created in Power Query Editor, we can see the sections available within the global environment by using the #sections keyword. Create a blank query and then use Advanced Editor to entirely replace the contents of the query with the keyword: #sections.

A record is returned with a single field called Section1 that contains a record. Section1 is the default section created automatically by Power Query. Now, modify your query such that the code is as follows:

```
#sections[Section1]
```

We now have a record with fields for each query currently in our Power Query Editor session. Suppose that one of these queries is Query1. We can access this query using the following syntax (in a different query than Query1):

```
#sections[Section1][Query1]
```

This code returns the results from Query1. However, a more preferred syntax to accomplish the same thing is simply:

```
Section1!Query1
```

Here we reference Section1 directly without the #sections keyword and use the exclamation mark (!) as shorthand to access Query1.

For every Power Query Editor session, the global environment contains a single section, Section1, which contains all of the queries within the Power Query Editor as members of Section1. This is what effectively allows us to reference a query from another query. This allows us to create intermediate queries that are not loaded into the semantic model, such as the intermediate queries, parameters, and functions created when combining files in a folder (see *Chapter 3, Accessing and Combining Data*).

Interestingly, if you were to execute the #sections expression from within a section and return the results, you would get very different results. Instead of a single section, Section1, the expression would return a section for every extension included with Power BI Desktop as well as any custom extensions.

Similarly, if one were to execute the #shared expression from within a section and return the results, you would also get different results than executing #shared within the default global environment. In this case, the record returned would only include the expressions tagged with the keyword shared within the section as well as all of the M standard library functions, types, and enumerations.

With a brief treatment of sections behind us, let's next take on how we can create our own global environment, allowing you to precisely control the variables and functions available within your expression.

Creating your own global environment

The global environment we just covered is the standard global environment in which queries operate in Power Query Editor. However, it is possible to create your own global environment for executing Power Query M code. This is done using the Expression.Evaluate function.

The Expression.Evaluate function has two parameters. The first parameter is the document parameter. This is the M expression to be evaluated. The second parameter is an optional environment parameter as a record. This is the environment in which to evaluate the M expression.

By default, this second parameter is null. Thus, the following query returns a null record:

```
Expression.Evaluate("#shared")
```

Since this is an empty **global environment**, there are no sections present either. We can confirm this by using this code:

```
Expression.Evaluate("#sections")
```

This also returns a null record.

However, if we add an environment record such as the following, it returns a record with fields of x, y, and z with values of 10, 20, and 30 respectively:

```
Expression.Evaluate("#shared", [x = 10, y = 20, z = 30])
```

You can even pass functions into the environment. For example, consider the following more complex example:

```
Expression.Evaluate(
    "let Source = List.Sum( {x, y, z} ) in Source",
    [x = 10, y = 20, z = 30, List.Sum = List.Sum]
)
```

This evaluates to 60 (10 + 20 + 30).

You can even use this to rename standard M functions within your own environment. The following code also returns 60:

```
Expression.Evaluate(
    "let Source = SumThatList( {x, y, z} ) in Source",
    [x = 10, y = 20, z = 30, SumThatList = List.Sum]
)
```

Running expressions within our own environment consisting of only the elements required for evaluation can be considered a security measure. Of course, if you are not concerned with such things, passing #shared into Expression.Evaluate as its second argument evaluates the expression in the same global environment as covered earlier. For example, the following is a valid expression and evaluates to 60 as well:

```
Expression.Evaluate(
    "let x = 10, y = 20, z = 30
    in List.Sum( { x, y, z } )",
    #shared
)
```

This concludes our exploration of the global environment. Let's next cover an important but rather abstract topic, closures. Understanding closure will help you create dynamic, reusable code within the M language.

Understanding closures

In programming languages, a **closure** is a powerful concept that allows a function to capture and retain references to variables from its lexical environment (the environment where the function is defined). This means that even after the outer function has finished executing or has gone out of scope, the inner function (the closure) still retains access to the variables from its enclosing scope.

Closures are created when an inner function references variables from its containing function or any other surrounding scope. The inner function *closes over* those variables, hence the term closure.

The ability of a closure to maintain access to variables from its lexical environment is particularly useful in scenarios where you need to create functions with behavior that depends on the values of certain variables at the time the function was defined.

Here's a simple example of a closure in Power Query M:

```
let
  x = 10,
  closureFunction = () => x * 2
in
  closureFunction()
```

This query results in a value of 20. In this example, the variable x is defined within the let block and has a value of 10 (global query scope). closureFunction is a closure because it captures the reference to the variable x from its lexical (current) environment. When closureFunction is invoked later in the query, it still has access to the value of x (10), and it will return the result of x * 2, which is 20.

Let's now consider a more complex example of closure in Power Query M. Consider the following query:

```
let
  x = 10,
  closureFunction = () => x * 2,
  Evaluation =
    Expression.Evaluate(
      "closureFunction()",
      [
        closureFunction = closureFunction,
        x = 20
      ]
    )
in
  Evaluation
```

Given our explanation of scope and local scope precedence, you might expect that this query returns 40 (20 * 2). However, this is not the case. This expression actually returns 20 (10 * 2). Did we just throw all of our scope discussion and local scope precedence out the window? Not at all, and the explanation is the closure.

Observe that `closureFunction` is originally defined in the scope where x equals 10. Just as in the original example, `closureFunction` still captures the reference to the variable x from its original lexical (current) environment. Thus, this closure of capturing the current values in the context of where the function is originally defined takes precedence over passing a different value for x (20) into the environment of our `Expression.Evaluate` expression, where we invoke `closureFunction`. In other words, the value for x from the scope of where the function was originally defined is "closed off" and cannot be changed.

Let's take this concept of original (defining) context one step further. Consider the following query:

```
let
    multiplyFunction = ( x ) as function =>
        ( multiplier ) => x * multiplier,
    closureFunction = multiplyFunction( 10 )
in
    closureFunction( 2 )
```

This query also returns 20, but how does it actually work? At first glance, it might seem like the code would generate an error since there is seemingly never a time where the expressions x and `multiplier` are in the same scope. The secret lies in the creation of a function that returns a function and the application of closure.

The function, `multiplyFunction`, accepts a single parameter, x, and returns a function that accepts a single parameter, `multiplier`. We define `closureFunction` as the function that is returned from invoking `multiplyFunction` with a value of 10.

The closure comes into play here because `closureFunction` remembers its original defining context where x is set to 10 via invoking `multiplyFunction` with an argument of 10. Thus, the definition of the function returned by `multiplyFunction` is *closed off* and defined as a function where x equals 10. Therefore, when we later invoke `closureFunction` with a value of 2, the parameter passed in is the `multiplier` parameter of the function returned from invoking `multiplyFunction` with a value of 10, and hence 10 * 2 = 20.

Closures are beneficial for creating reusable functions with dynamic behavior. They allow you to define functions that are dependent on values outside of the function's body, giving you more flexibility and adaptability in your Power Query M code. Closures are often used in advanced scenarios where you need to build functions with specialized behavior based on specific context or conditions.

In terms of practical use, closures are particularly handy to understand when dealing with transformation functions, see *Chapter 6, Structured Values*. In addition, closures are fundamentally required for implementing query folding.

Query folding

Query folding is a feature of Power Query as a whole and requires specific implementation logic within data connectors via the `Table.View` function. Query folding occurs when M code is rewritten into a native data source query.

In general, query folding improves the performance of Power Query since server-side resources and native queries are used to perform data transformation. We will cover query folding in depth in *Chapter 15, Optimizing Performance*, but it is worth mentioning here that closures come into play when implementing query folding.

First, it is important to understand that the M language itself knows nothing about query folding. That is to say that query folding is not part of the core M engine or its standard library.

Essentially, when M code is executed within Power Query Editor/Power BI Desktop, the process is intercepted and the query is rewritten using the defined event handlers within the data source connector, if such event handlers exist. In other words, instead of the M engine performing the query transformations, the code is rewritten as native source queries and executed by the source system, not Power Query. Event handlers are triggered when a specific event happens, such as querying a SQL Server database table. The event triggers the event handler, which then performs the task. In the case of query folding, the event handler is responsible for rewriting the M query as a query that is native to the source system. Since query folding is not part of the core M language, we will only briefly cover the concept here from a technical perspective.

For query folding to work, a data source connector must implement a function that returns a `Table.View` type. This `Table.View` definition must include specific event handlers passed as a record. There are two types of event handlers, `Get` and `On`. The `On` class of event handlers handles capturing when a particular event is requested, such as `OnSort`, `OnTake`, `OnSkip`, or `OnSelectColumns`, while the `Get` class of event handlers returns data or information about data such as `GetType`, `GetRows`, and `GetRowCount`.

Consider the following M query, which retrieves the `DimCurrency` table from a SQL Server database and sorts the table by the `CurrencyAlternateKey` column:

```
let
    Source = Sql.Database("localhost", "AdventureWorksDW2022"),
    dbo_DimCurrency = Source{[Schema="dbo",Item="DimCurrency"]}[Data],
    #"Sorted Rows" = Table.Sort(dbo_DimCurrency,{{"CurrencyAlternateKey",
Order.Ascending}})
in
    #"Sorted Rows"
```

Because the connector for SQL Server supports query folding and also supports the `GetRows` and `OnSort` event handlers, this query is rewritten as the following SQL query:

```
select [_].[CurrencyKey],
    [_].[CurrencyAlternateKey],
    [_].[CurrencyName]
from [dbo].[DimCurrency] as [_]
order by [_].[CurrencyAlternateKey]
```

This native query can be seen within Power Query Editor by *right-clicking* the last step in the **APPLIED STEPS** area for the query and choosing **View Native Query**.

While it is obvious what the Get class of event handlers returns, what does the On class of event handlers return? Simple: the On class of event handlers performs closures to capture the information pertaining to the folding request and return a Table.View object that remembers this information. Thus, when a Get class event handler accesses the Table.View returned from an On class of event handler, the Table.View has encoded the details of the folding request.

The mechanism for how this works is essentially the same mechanism as our last example, where closureFunction effectively *remembers* that the value of x is 10. You can find out more about implementing query folding here: https://learn.microsoft.com/en-us/power-query/samples/trippin/10-tableview1/readme#using-tableview.

With a basic understanding of closures, query folding, and how closure are used to facilitate query folding, let's next move on to the concept of metadata.

Managing metadata

Simply put, metadata is *data about data*. In Power Query M, metadata can be associated with any value using the meta keyword to define a metadata record. Metadata in and of itself does not *do* anything, nor does it change the behavior of a value in any way.

Consider the following query:

```
let
    x = 10 meta [Type = "Whole number", OoM = 1],
    y = 20 meta [Type = "Whole number", OoM = 1],
    z = 30 meta [Type = "Whole number", OoM = 1]
in
    x * y * z
```

This query still returns 6000, just as before. However, the metadata associated with each value can be accessed and returned by using the Value.Metadata function, as follows:

```
let
    x = 10 meta [Type = "Whole Number", OoM = 1],
    y = 20 meta [Type = "Whole Number", OoM = 1],
    z = 30 meta [Type = "Whole Number", OoM = 1]
in
    Value.Metadata(x)[Type]
```

This query returns Whole Number.

Two additional metadata functions exist, Value.RemoveMetadata and Value.ReplaceMetadata. Value.RemoveMetadata removes all metadata from a value. For example, the following code returns a null record:

```
let
    x = 10 meta [Type = "Whole Number", OrderOfMagnitude = 1],
```

```
        x1 = Value.RemoveMetadata(x)
    in
        Value.Metadata(x1)
```

The function Value.ReplaceMetadata replaces all metadata with a new metadata record. For example:

```
    let
        x = 10 meta [Type = "Whole Number", OrderOfMagnitude = 1],
        x1 = Value.ReplaceMetadata(x, [Divisors = 4])
    in
        Value.Metadata(x1)
```

This query returns a record with a single field, Divisors, with a value of 4. Conversely, the following code appends additional metadata to the original metadata:

```
    let
        x = 10 meta [Type = "Whole Number", OrderOfMagnitude = 1],
        x1 = Value.ReplaceMetadata(x, Value.Metadata(x) & [Divisors = 4])
    in
        Value.Metadata(x1)
```

This query returns a record with three fields, Type, OoM, and Divisors with values of Whole Number, 1, and 4 respectively.

Finally, consider this example:

```
    let
        x = 10 meta [Type = "Whole Number", OrderOfMagnitude = 1],
        x1 = Value.ReplaceMetadata(x, Value.Metadata(x) & [Divisors = 4]),
        multiply = x * x1
    in
        Value.Metadata(multiply)
```

Is the output the metadata for x, the metadata for x1, or both? The answer is none of those, as the output is actually a null record. This is because metadata is not carried forward during operations.

As stated, metadata by itself does nothing and there are no special metadata values recognized by the M engine. However, software applications such as Power Query Editor do make use of metadata to change their behavior.

One example of this can be seen when using Get Data and specifically the Navigator dialog. Metadata controls the display of the Navigator, such as the icons displayed for navigation items as well as whether the item is a folder or leaf node that returns preview data. More about this topic can be found in *Chapter 16, Enabling Extensions*.

Another example is if you create a query that uses the function `Value.Metadata` against another query. This returns a record with a `QueryFolding` field that has a record as a value. Expanding this record returns fields and values for the following:

- `IsFolded`
- `HasNativeQuery`
- `Kind`
- `Path`

A more practical application of metadata within Power Query Editor is function documentation. Create a blank query and use the Advanced Editor to replace the entire contents of the query with `Value.Metadata`. The following information is displayed:

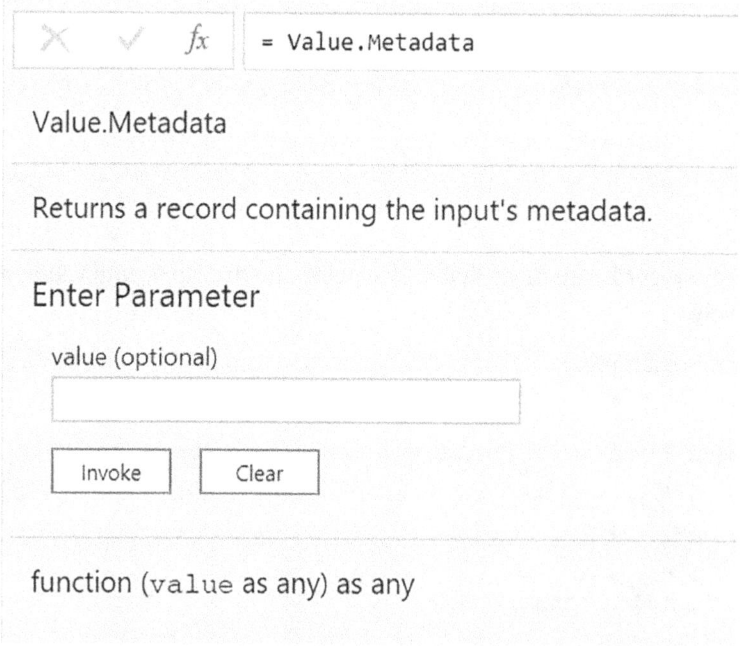

Figure 7.1: Internal documentation for the function Value.Metadata.

Compare this to the output returned from a custom function, such as a query named `multiplyFunction`, with the following definition:

```
let
    Source = ( multiplier as number ) as number =>
    let
        x = 10
    in
        x * multiplier
in
    Source
```

In this case, much less information is displayed by a query that simply references `multiplyFunction`:

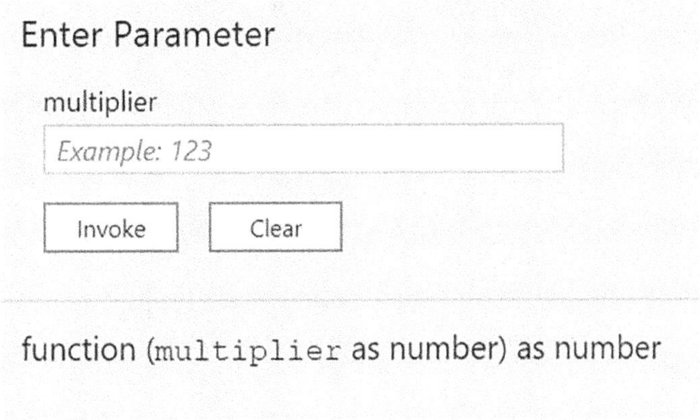

Figure 7.2: Default custom function documentation

However, we can use metadata to spruce up our function documentation as follows:

```
let
    Source = ( multiplier as number ) as number =>
    let
        x = 10
    in
        x * multiplier,
    Type = type function (value as number) as number
        meta[
            Documentation.Name = "multiplyFunction",
            Documentation.LongDescription = "Multiplies the number 10 by the
multiplier.",
            Documentation.Examples =
            {
                [Description = "Multiply by 1", Code = "multiplyFunction(1)",
Result = "10"],
                [Description = "Multiply by 2", Code = "multiplyFunction(2)",
Result = "20"],
                [Description = "Multiply by 3", Code = "multiplyFunction(3)",
Result = "30"]
            }
        ]
in
    Value.ReplaceType(Source, Type)
```

This produces the following output:

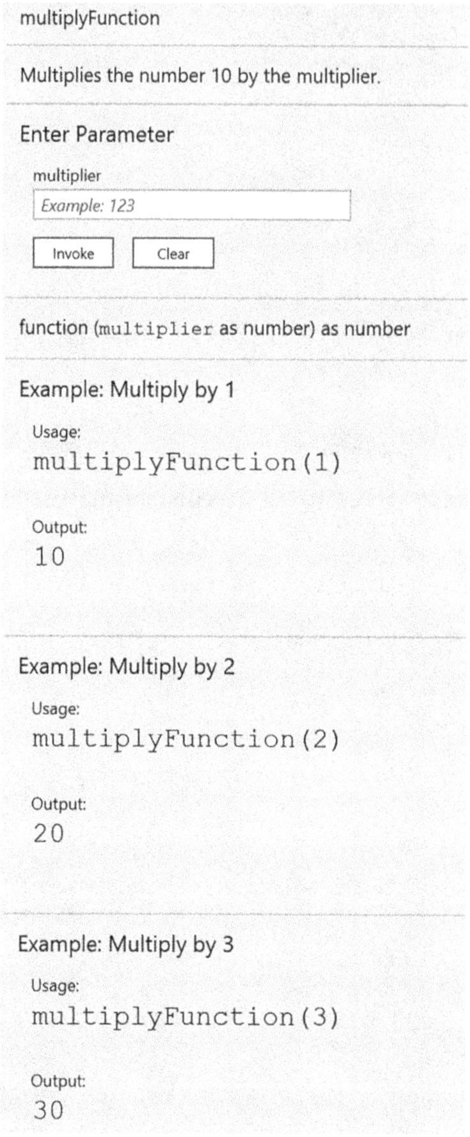

multiplyFunction
Multiplies the number 10 by the multiplier.

Enter Parameter

multiplier

Example: 123

Invoke	Clear

function (multiplier as number) as number

Example: Multiply by 1

Usage:
```
multiplyFunction(1)
```

Output:
```
10
```

Example: Multiply by 2

Usage:
```
multiplyFunction(2)
```

Output:
```
20
```

Example: Multiply by 3

Usage:
```
multiplyFunction(3)
```

Output:
```
30
```

Figure 7.3: Enhanced custom function documentation

The metadata record fields used in this last example are special fields recognized by Power Query Editor. These special metadata record fields must be attached to a function's type, not to the function itself. This is why it was necessary to create a new function type with the desired metadata record and then associate that type with our function via the Value.ReplaceType function.

Other metadata record fields exist other than those used thus far. Documentation.Description also changes the description of the function. This metadata record is overridden by Documentation. LongDescription if both exist. Documentation.Syntax and Documentation.Result both have no effect on the Power Query user interface.

There are also special metadata record fields that can be used for the parameters of functions. Here is an example of using a metadata record for our `multiplier` parameter:

```
let
    Source = ( multiplier as number ) as number =>
    let
        x = 10
    in
        x * multiplier,
    Type =
        type function
        (
            multiplier as
            (
                type number
                    meta
                    [
                        Documentation.FieldCaption = "Multiplier - The
multiplier of 10",
                        Documentation.AllowedValues = { 1, 2, 3, 4, 5, 6, 7, 8,
9, 10}
                    ]
            )
        ) as number
        meta
        [
            Documentation.Name = "multiplyFunction",
            Documentation.LongDescription = "Multiplies the number 10 by the
multiplier.",
            Documentation.Examples =
            {
                [Description = "Multiply by 1", Code = "multiplyFunction(1)",
Result = "10"],
                [Description = "Multiply by 2", Code = "multiplyFunction(2)",
Result = "20"],
                [Description = "Multiply by 3", Code = "multiplyFunction(3)",
Result = "30"]
            }
        ]
in
    Value.ReplaceType(Source, Type)
```

Here we associate a metadata record within the type definition for the multiplier parameter. `Documentation.FieldCaption` replaces the default parameter caption while the `Documentation.AllowedValues` changes the input field to a dropdown list of the specified values. This does not actually change the values that can be passed into the function, only the interface within the Power Query Editor is affected. This metadata has the following effect on the user interface:

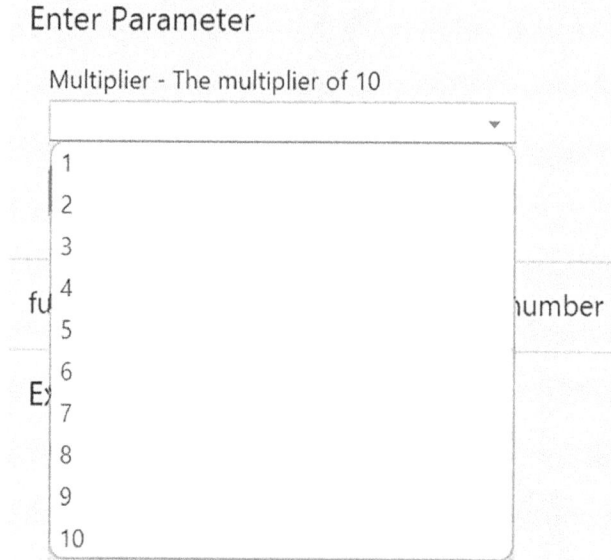

Figure 7.4: Enhanced custom function parameter documentation

Other documentation-related metadata record fields are available for parameters such as `Documentation.FieldDescription`, `Documentation.IsMultiLine`, and `Documentation.IsCode`. However, these do not seem to affect the Power Query Editor interface. Another field, `Documentation.SampleValues`, takes a list as a value, but only the first value in the list shows up as an example. Additional information regarding documenting functions can be found here: `https://learn.microsoft.com/en-us/power-query/handling-documentation`.

The practical uses for metadata are effectively endless; however, metadata is rarely used by the majority of M language users. This is unfortunate as metadata is a huge area of untapped potential that can allow you to do things in M code that would otherwise be impossible. For example, consider the following `PreviousSteps` query:

```
let
    Step1 = 10,
    Step2 = Step1 * 2,
    Step2a = Step2 meta [PreviousStep = Step1],
    Step3 = Step2 * 2,
    Step3a = Step3 meta [PreviousStep = Step2a]
in
    Step3a
```

This query returns 40. If we create another query that references this query, then this also returns 40. Normally, only the output from the last step of a query is accessible to other queries. However, because we have added metadata, we can actually access the values of previous steps within the query. For example, the following query returns 20, the value from Step2:

```
let
    Source = Value.Metadata(PreviousSteps)[PreviousStep]
in
    Source
```

In contrast, the following query returns 10, the value from Step1:

```
let
    Source =
        Value.Metadata(
            Value.Metadata(PreviousSteps)[PreviousStep]
        )[PreviousStep]
in
    Source
```

This completes our exploration of metadata within the Power Query M language. As mentioned, metadata is perhaps the greatest source of untapped potential in the whole of the M language, so keep metadata in mind as you continue to expand your practical knowledge of M.

Summary

In this chapter, we covered some important but perhaps rather more obscure and abstract aspects of the M language, including scope, global environments, closures, and metadata. We also briefly explored sections as well as creating our own global environments using the Expression.Evaluate function. Sections are covered in depth in *Chapter 16, Enabling Extensions*.

While the information covered in this chapter might appear to be less practical than that of other chapters, the concepts conveyed within this chapter are critical to truly understanding the M language and fully leveraging its potential.

In the next chapter, we start to put the abstract concepts from this chapter to practical use by working with nested structures, where the concept of scope is vitally important.

Learn more on Discord

Join our community's Discord space for discussions with the author and other readers:

`https://discord.gg/vCSG5GBbyS`

8

Working with Nested Structures

Nested structures are very common and refer to the hierarchical organization of data, where a table, record, or list is contained within another. This provides an efficient way to organize relationships and hierarchies and store arrays of values. Common data sources supporting nested structures include relational databases, JSON, and XML. In addition, there is a wide range of M functions that yield structured values. Getting a good grasp on how to handle these structures is crucial; it unlocks a wealth of possibilities.

This chapter covers common functions for working with nested structures in the Power Query M language. These functions allow you to extract specific elements from nested tables, lists, and records, filter and transform nested data, and create new structures based on existing ones. It aims to equip you with the necessary knowledge to apply these transformations in your own workflows. The main topics covered in this chapter are:

- Transitioning to coding
- Transforming values within a table
- Working with lists
- Working with records
- Working with tables
- Working with mixed structures

To get the most out of this chapter, it is important to understand the concepts covered in *Chapter 6, Structured Values*, which introduced structured values in the M language. Furthermore, we encourage you to open your favorite Power Query editor and try out the provided samples. By executing and exploring these scripts, you will gain a deeper understanding.

Transitioning to coding

Throughout the book so far, we have progressively developed an understanding of the Power Query M language. That knowledge is paramount for achieving more advanced data manipulation and transformation tasks. Many common operations can be executed via Power Query's **user interface** (**UI**), enabling users to modify values by interacting with menus and buttons.

However, there are many cases where transforming nested structures cannot be done through the UI and manual coding is required. In this section, we are going to cover some fundamentals, share a trick to getting the most out of the UI, and set you up with the basic skills you need to start coding M.

Getting started

Tables are the primary data structure in Power Query. They offer an intuitive way to represent data, making it easier for the user to understand and work with that data. Moreover, the Power Query editor is specifically tailored to work with tables, providing a wide range of table transformation operations directly from the UI. Whether you need to filter, sort, aggregate, or reshape your data, what you need is usually only a few clicks away.

Interaction with a query through the UI generates M code, which can be viewed in both the formula bar and the **Advanced Editor**. Every action a user executes is assigned to an identifier or variable within a let expression. However, the UI has limitations. First, it does not provide access to all transformation functions available in the M language, and second, it cannot assist with transforming nested structures. Does this mean you have to start coding extensively? Not necessarily: we will share a technique that can overcome this caveat in several cases. But first, you will need to understand Drill Down in M.

Understanding Drill Down

Drill Down is a feature that allows users to access or extract a specific element from another complex data structure. This operation is particularly useful when dealing with nested data, such as fields within a record, elements within a list, or cells within a table. Consider the following query:

```
let
    t = Table.FromRows(
        {
            {"Question", "Response1", "Response2", "Response3"},
            {"Overall quality?", "High", "Medium", "Low"},
            {"Ease of use?", "Good", "Average", "Poor"},
            {"Would you recommend?", "Yes", "No", "No"}
        }
    ),
    Source = Table.FromRecords(
        {
            [Survey = "a", Results = t],
            [Survey = "b", Results = t],
            [Survey = "c", Results = t]
        }, type table [ Survey = text, Results = table]
    )
in
    Source
```

Just like any other query interaction, **Drill Down** will automatically generate the necessary code to access that specific value.

When working with a table, the Power Query editor provides two simple ways you can dive deeper into your data:

1. Obtain all values from a column:

   a. **Right-click method:**

   First, find the column you're interested in. Let's say it's the *Results* column; see *Figure 8.1*. Now, right-click on the header of that column (1). A context menu pops up and you will see an option that says **Drill Down**; go ahead and click on it. This adds a new step to your query.

   You can remove this step by clicking the **x** in front of the step name in the **Applied Steps** section of the **Query Settings** pane. If that is not visible, go to the **View** tab to toggle it on.

   b. **Using the ribbon:**

   Click the header of the column you're interested in (1) to select it. Now navigate to the **Transform** tab. Here, you'll see an option that says **Convert to List** (2). When you click that, it adds a new step to your query, and your column is converted into a list. This process is shown in the following screenshot. When applied, you can remove this step:

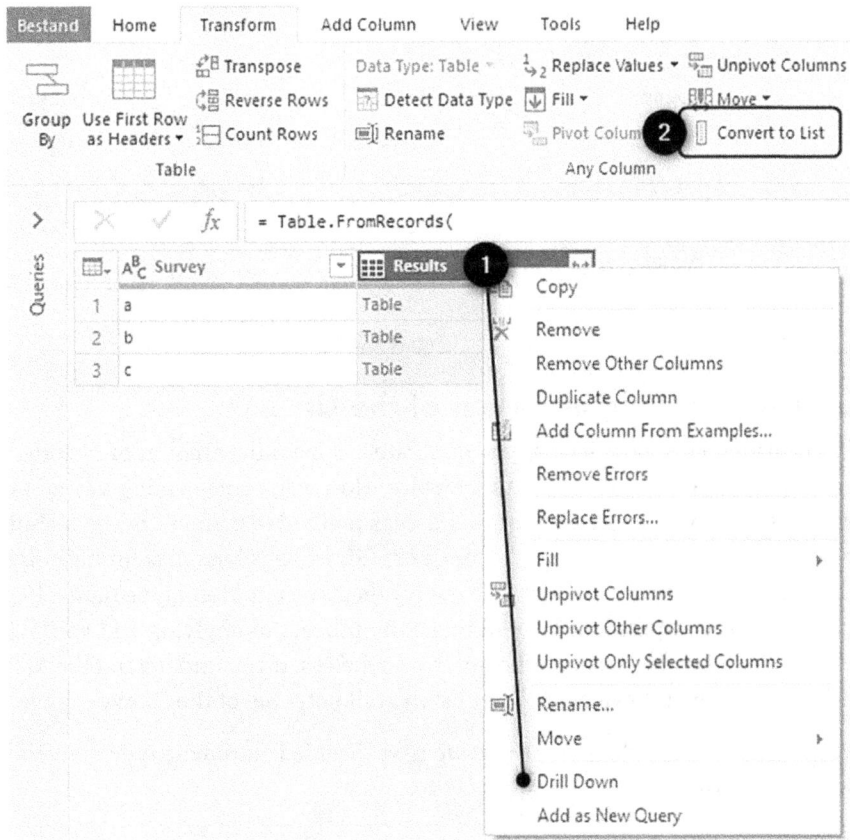

Figure 8.1: Drill down into a table column

2. Obtain the value from a cell:

    a. **Right-click method:**

First, find the cell you're interested in. Let's say the Results column for Survey a; see *Figure 8.2*. Right-click on the whitespace of that column (1). A context menu will pop up and you will see an option that says **Drill Down**. When applied, you can remove this step.

    b. **Click a structured value:**

To do this, you need to click on a structured value (2), if a cell contains such a value. This will yield that cell's value as a result. The code produced by the **drill-down** action is no different than item and/or field selection, explained in *Chapter 6, Structured Values*. This is shown in the following figure. When applied, you can remove this step.

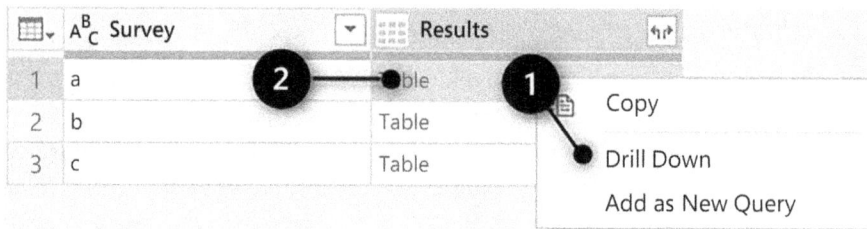

Survey	Results
1 a	Table
2 b	Table
3 c	Table

Copy
Drill Down
Add as New Query

Column1	Column2	Column3	Column4
Question	Response1	Response2	Response3
Overall quality?	High	Medium	Low
Ease of use?	Good	Average	Poor
Would you recommend?	Yes	No	No

Figure 8.2: Drill down into a table cell

The trick to getting more out of the UI

The UI provides a very efficient way to generate a substantial amount of M code. Even the most proficient M coders take advantage of this feature. However, transforming nested tables within a table requires a shift from the intuitive point-and-click method to manual coding techniques. That manual approach is essential because the Power Query UI, while robust, has limitations. Specifically, when dealing with nested structures, the UI can only display their literal type name, like Table, Record, or List. This generic representation can make the process of applying and verifying transformations step by step cumbersome and inefficient. Nevertheless, if you understand the M language's flow, let expression, and **Drill Down**, you can enlist the full potential of the UI once more.

When following along, please note that we have disabled automatic type detection in Power Query's **Options and Settings:**

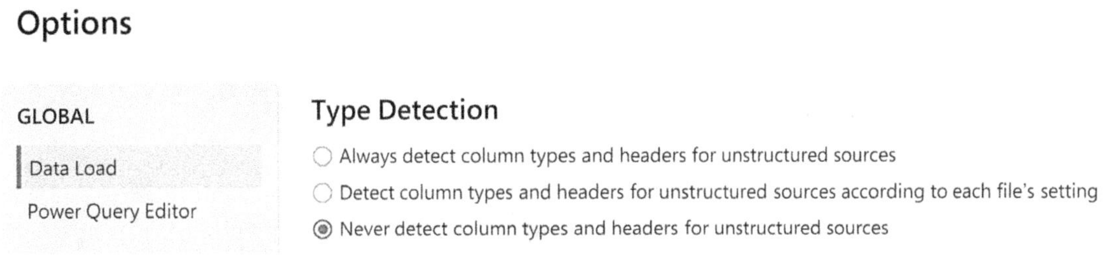

Options

GLOBAL

| Data Load

Power Query Editor

Type Detection

◯ Always detect column types and headers for unstructured sources

◯ Detect column types and headers for unstructured sources according to each file's setting

◉ Never detect column types and headers for unstructured sources

Figure 8.3: Power Query Options and Settings

The sample we have been exploring has two columns. The column Results contains nested tables with survey responses, as shown in *Figure 8.2*. Clicking on the whitespace (1) displays a secondary preview at the bottom of your screen in the **Preview** pane, offering a limited view of the contents within that nested structure. Suppose we want to transform all the nested tables in this column. You can follow these instructions; they demonstrate a low-code approach that will enable you to leverage the UI again:

1. Right-click the whitespace (1), as shown in *Figure 8.2*, and select **Add as new query** from the context menu. This action adds a new query called Results to the **Queries** pane on the left-hand side, which outputs the table value from that cell.

2. Right-click this new query's name in the **Queries** pane, and in the context menu, disable the **Enable load** option; this query will only be used as a staging area to develop and generate M code to transform all of the nested tables.

3. Navigate to the **Transform** tab and select **Transpose.**

4. Choose **Use First Row as Headers.**

5. Double-click the header of the first column and rename it Respondents.

6. *Steps 3* to *5* added new steps to the query, which are visible in the **Applied Steps** pane. The first is labeled Transposed Table. It's time to examine the M code and open the **Advanced Editor**. Since this variable contains a space, a quoted identifier has been used: #"Transposed Table" (line *18* in the following screenshot):

```
17        Results1 = Source{0}[Results],
18        #"Transposed Table" = Table.Transpose(Results1),
19        #"Promoted Headers" = Table.PromoteHeaders(#"Transposed Table", [PromoteAllScalars=true]),
20        #"Renamed Columns" = Table.RenameColumns(#"Promoted Headers",{{"Question", "Respondents"}})
21   in
22        #"Renamed Columns"
```

Figure 8.4: Part of the M code script taken from the Advanced Editor

7. We need to copy this identifier and everything that follows it, all the way to the end. Once done, close the **Advanced Editor** and return to our original query. Navigate to the **Add Column** tab and select **Custom Column**. In the **Custom Column Formula** area of the dialog box, enter the let clause because we did not copy that earlier, then paste in the copied code.

8. The final step is the most crucial: replacing the input table or value to transform. It is helpful to know that most table functions take a table as the first argument. Upon examining the code in *Figure 8.5*, we see that Results1 needs to be replaced. Highlight Results1 or delete it and inject **Results** from **Available Columns** by double-clicking it:

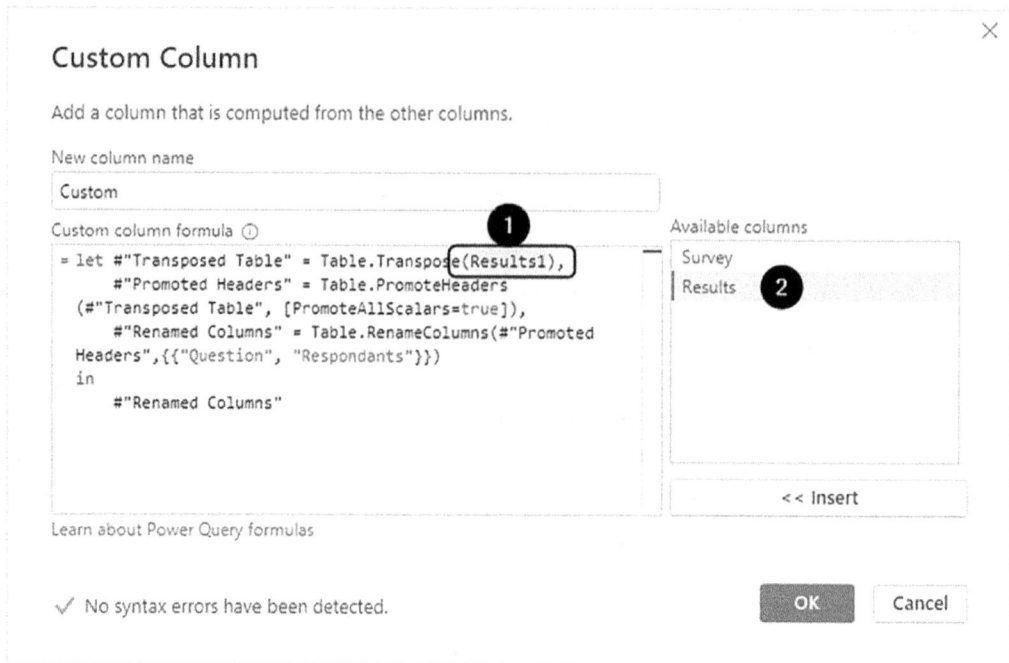

Figure 8.5: Replacing the table reference in the initial transformation step

Reviewing the preview for each of the nested tables, we see they all have successfully been transformed, like the one depicted here:

ABC Survey	Results	Custom
1 a	Table	Table
2 b	Table	Table
3 c	Table	Table

Respondants	Overall quality?	Ease of use?	Would you recommend?
Response1	High	Good	Yes
Response2	Medium	Average	No
Response3	Low	Poor	No

Figure 8.6: Preview of one of the transformed nested tables

Using this trick saves you from a lot of complex coding, at least for a while, when dealing with intricate nested table transformations. However, it's important to keep in mind that despite this newfound flexibility, your transformation options are still subject to the UI's limitations.

Alternatively, you could create your own custom transformation function from the helper query. That process is covered in *Chapter 9, Parameters and Custom Functions*.

Methods for multistep value transformation

When transforming data, you will often need to apply multiple transformations to get a value just right. What options are available to best manage that? It's time to highlight four different methods that handle multistep value transformation; each has its pros and cons.

Nesting functions

Similar to Excel worksheet functions, M functions can be nested. Nesting refers to the process of using a function to produce an argument value as input for another function. This requires knowledge about functions and their arguments. When creating this type of logic, you typically start from the inside and work your way out, adding more functions around the existing syntax. Keep in mind that this can quickly lead to complex, hard-to-read, and difficult-to-debug code.

Using a let expression

This method was illustrated in the previous example. It enables you to break down complex transformations into smaller, more manageable pieces or create variables to store values that are needed multiple times. This modularity makes the code more organized and often easier to understand. Remember that after the in clause, you can return one of the variables or another expression.

Using a record expression

Very similar to a let expression, the main difference between let and record is that record is more flexible. This makes a record expression extremely valuable for adoption, validation, troubleshooting, and debugging, since you can quickly change its return value to the entire record, a selection of fields, or a single field value. All of this is covered in depth in *Chapter 6, Structured Values*.

Using a custom function

Free-form coding, as well as creating custom functions from scratch, requires an understanding of the M language; however, when you create a custom function from another query, the need for in-depth M knowledge is reduced substantially. More importantly, the **Create function** option available in the context menu of a query will provide a helper query to develop and troubleshoot your function should that need arise. This, and more, is covered in *Chapter 9, Parameters and Custom Functions*. The main advantages of custom functions are reusability, standardization, and cleaner code through delegation.

Transforming values in tables

Transforming values is a fundamental skill and often a critical part of the process when cleaning, preparing, and reshaping data for analysis. The M language includes functions to transform table columns, rows, record fields, and lists, among others. When it comes to transforming structured values within a table, you will most likely encounter `Table.AddColumn`, `Table.TransformColumns`, and `Table.ReplaceValue`. Each has its own set of advantages and use cases.

> Many standard library functions take functions as arguments. Often these functions are unary – that means they accept a single argument. The each expression falls into this category; it's shorthand for declaring an untyped function that takes a single parameter, the underscore (_). When you come across each, it's helpful to know that a formula following it will be executed on every item in a list or a row in a table, for example, and the underscore provides access to the current item. For a more comprehensive understanding, please refer to *Chapter 9, Parameters and Custom Functions*.

Table.AddColumn

Selecting **Add Column | Custom Column** calls the Table.AddColumn M function. This offers a convenient way to gradually build more complex logic, creating new values based on existing ones. This means that while you create additional columns, any input values from other columns in the table remain intact. This ensures you can always trace back and compare your results with the original data, a crucial aspect for validation and auditing. However, sometimes, you may create custom columns for intermediate calculations not needed in the final output. As a best practice, it is advisable to remove all unnecessary columns before loading a query to a data model.

Consider this simple example: our table contains two rows with text values. To familiarize ourselves with and practice the use of M functions, we will combine these values in two steps. Step1 is already in place and generates a list for each row, as shown in the following code snippet, containing all the values from that row:

```
let
    Source = Table.FromRows(
        {
            {"Power", "BI"},
            {"Power", "Query"}
        }
    ),
    getAllRowValues = Table.AddColumn(
        Source,
        "Step1",
        each Record.ToList(_)
    )
in
    getAllRowValues
```

This and other techniques are discussed in the *Working with records* section later in this chapter.

Navigate to the **Add Column** tab and select **Custom Column**. The **Custom Column** dialog box (*Figure 8.7*) is shown and this enables you to do the following:

1. Specify a new column name.
2. Leverage the **Available columns** section on the right, to conveniently input values from other columns as argument(s) by simply double-clicking them.

3. Use the **Custom column formula** area to write an expression, such as:

```
Text.Combine( [Step1], " ")
```

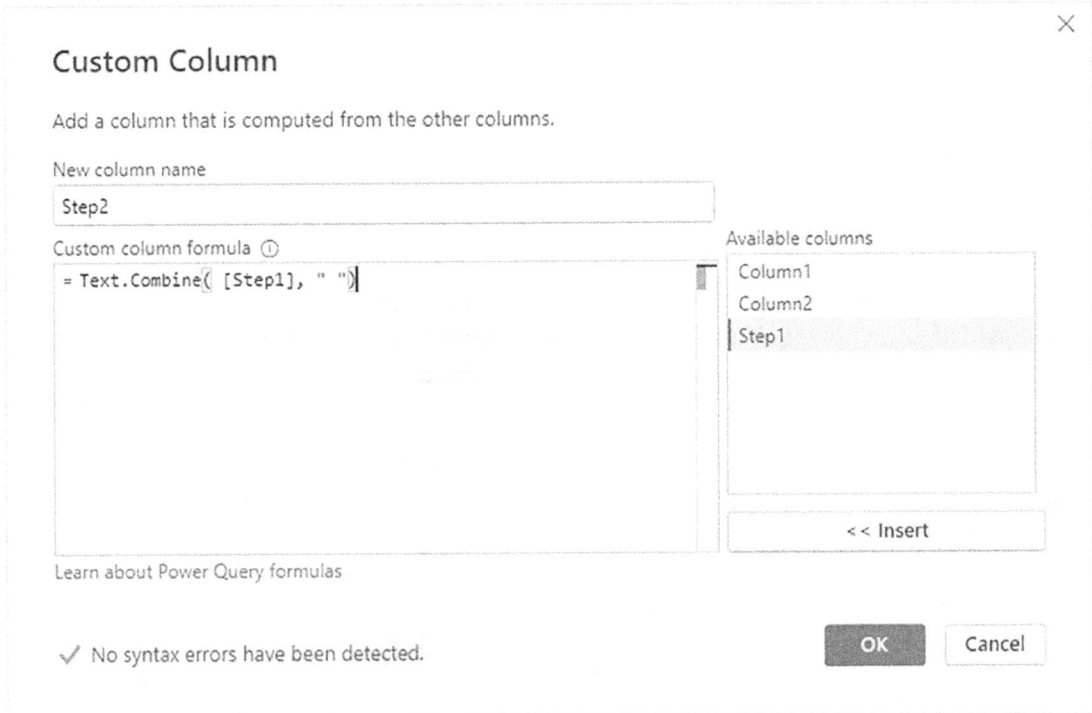

Figure 8.7: The Custom Column dialog box with the formula area and Available columns

Once confirmed, the expression is applied to each row of the table. This step-by-step approach is helpful when designing complex transformations. However, it's important to be mindful of potential performance implications, especially when dealing with large datasets. Adding numerous columns to a sizable dataset can impact preview loading, query execution times, and overall performance. Therefore, removing *Step1*, which is now redundant, is considered a best practice. Keep in mind that even though the column is not a part of the final output, you can still review it by selecting a previous step in the **Applied Steps** pane.

Table.TransformColumns

The versatile `Table.TransformColumns` function can be invoked from the UI, for example, when applying a text format function. Consider this `EmployeeData`:

```
let
    Source = Table.FromRows(
        {
            {101, "john", "prince", 50000},
            {102, "alice", "wonder", 60000},
            {103, "bob", "bever", 55000}
```

```
        },
        type table [
            EmployeeID=number,
            FirstName=text,
            LastName=text,
            Salary=number
        ]
    )
in
    Source
```

Select both the `FirstName` (1) and `LastName` (2) columns within the `EmployeeData` table while holding down the *CTRL* key (or the *Shift* key, since they are adjacent). Next, navigate to the **Transform** tab (3) and choose the **Format** option (4), and then select **Capitalize Each Word**, as follows:

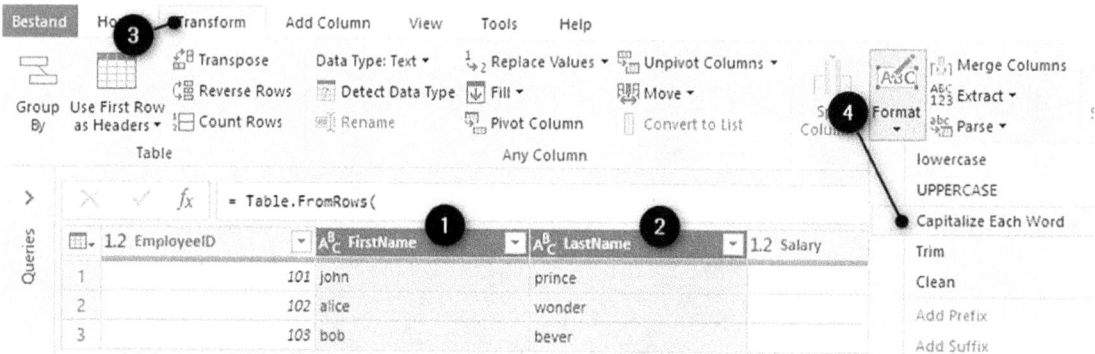

Figure 8.8: Actions to initiate a transformation that leverages Table.TransformColumns

These actions initiate a transformation that makes use of the `Table.TransformColumns` function. You can find the corresponding M code inside the formula bar, although it's formatted here for clarity. Source is the table to transform, followed by the second parameter of this function, `transformOperations`, as a list:

```
Table.TransformColumns(Source,
    {
        {"FirstName", Text.Proper, type text},
        {"LastName", Text.Proper, type text}
    }
)
```

The `transformOperations` list contains a list for each column to be transformed in the following format: `{ column name, transformation }` or `{ column name, transformation, new column type }`.

However, when you're dealing with a very wide table and need to apply a single transformation to all columns, managing a lengthy `transformOperations` list can become cumbersome. Instead, you can specify a `defaultTransformation` to be applied to all columns of the table.

Simply empty the `transformOperations` list, insert a comma directly after it, and specify a default transformation function to convert all columns to text with a proper format, as demonstrated here:

```
Table.TransformColumns(Source,
    {},
    each Text.Proper( Text.From(_))
)
```

But what if you need to apply a single transformation to all columns except a few specific ones? In such cases, you can include a `transformOperations` list for each column you want to exclude from a default transformation. Here, we're excluding `EmployeeID` and `Salary` from the default `Text.Proper` transformation, ensuring we retain the current value:

```
Table.TransformColumns(Source,
    {
        {"EmployeeID", each _, type number},
        {"Salary", each _, type number}
    },
    Text.Proper
)
```

Additionally, there are two more advanced methods that we will briefly mention here for completeness. The first allows you to transform a selection of columns with `List.Accumulate`; this function is covered in detail in *Chapter 13*, *Iteration and Recursion*, of this book. For each column where the name ends with `Name`, its contents will be transformed into proper text:

```
List.Accumulate(
    List.Select(
        Table.ColumnNames(Source),
        each Text.EndsWith(_, "Name")
    ),
    Source,
    (s, a) => Table.TransformColumns( s,
        {a, each Text.Proper(_), type text}
    )
)
```

The final advanced method enables you to transform one or more column selections using `List.Transform`. This provides a concise way to generate multiple `transformOperations` lists for one or more column selections, whether they are static, as in this example, or dynamic, as shown in the previous example. This will transform the contents of the `FirstName` and `LastName` columns into proper text and that of the `Salary` column into text:

```
Table.TransformColumns(Source,
    List.Combine({
```

```
            List.Transform({"FirstName", "LastName"},
                each {_, each Text.Proper(_), type text}
            ),
            List.Transform({"Salary"},
                each {_, each Text.From(_), type text}
            )
    })
)
```

It's important to note that when you specify more than one `transformOperations` list for any column, an error will be raised. Additionally, you cannot access another column other than the one that's undergoing transformation.

Table.ReplaceValue

The `Table.ReplaceValue` function is highly customizable and enables you to manipulate data with precision. It can be invoked through the UI. We will reuse the same sample data, `EmployeeData`, making sure it is in its original state by keeping only the `Source` step. Say we want to replace the `LastName` `bever` with `brown`. Select the `LastName` column, navigate to the **Transform** tab, and choose **Replace Values**. Then select **Replace Values**; a dialog box is shown where you can enter a value to find and a value to replace it with, and optionally set **Advanced options**, such as **Match entire cell contents**:

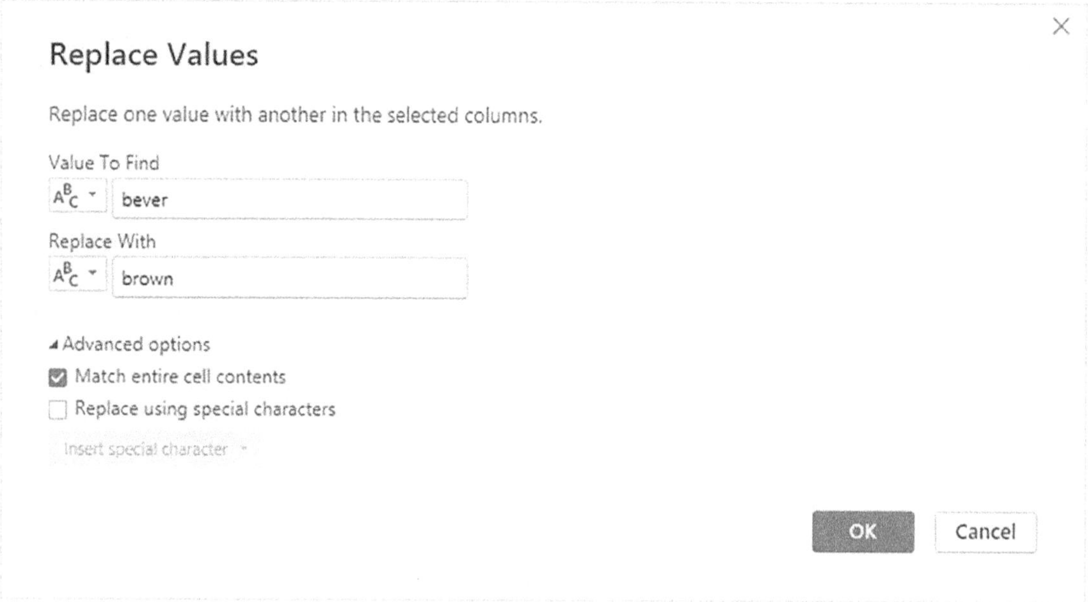

Figure 8.9: Replace Values dialog box

When the transformation is confirmed, it generates M code. You can review that code inside the formula bar:

```
Table.ReplaceValue(
    Source,
    "bever",
    "brown",
    Replacer.ReplaceValue,
    {"LastName"}
)
```

The `Table.ReplaceValue` function is invoked with these arguments:

- `Source` represents the table to be transformed
- `bever` is the `oldValue` to search for and replace
- *brown* is the `newValue` that will replace it
- `Replacer.ReplaceValue` is a replacer function from the standard library that replaces the entire cell content with a new value, but only if the current cell value matches the specified `oldValue` exactly
- Lastly, `columnsToSearch` is a list of column names in which to look for the `oldValue` and where the transformation will be applied if a match is found

However, instead of providing a constant as an argument, you may also use expressions. The following example illustrates a method for executing replacements in a more targeted and controlled manner by using specific conditions:

```
Table.ReplaceValue(
    Source,
    each [LastName],
    each if [EmployeeID]=103 then "brown" else [LastName],
    Replacer.ReplaceValue,
    {"LastName"}
)
```

When looking to replace values across multiple columns, you can expand the `columnsToSearch` list with additional column names. However, it is important to understand that values in those columns need to match the specified `oldValue` or condition in order for a replacement to occur. Consider this modification, where the `FirstName` column has been included in the columns list:

```
Table.ReplaceValue(
    Source,
    each [LastName],
    each if [EmployeeID]=103 then "brown" else [LastName],
    Replacer.ReplaceValue,
    {"FirstName", "LastName"}
)
```

The FirstName column and LastName column contain different values; therefore, the value in the FirstName column will not be replaced. However, if the FirstName column had contained bever, identical to the LastName column, it would have been altered to brown.

While this may not be the most practical example, let's proceed with it. Suppose we do need to replace both FirstName and LastName with brown for EmployeeID 103. Then, you could create a custom replacer as demonstrated here:

```
Table.ReplaceValue(
    Source,
    each [EmployeeID]=103,
    "brown",
    (x, y, z)=> if y then z else x,
    {"FirstName", "LastName"}
)
```

In the provided code, the fourth argument of the Table.ReplaceValue function is a custom function defined with three parameters: these represent currentValue, oldValue, and newValue. These parameters, while arbitrarily named, are crucial in determining the behavior of the replacement operation.

The function operates by evaluating whether the condition specified by oldValue (y) holds true. If this condition is met, indicating the criterion is satisfied, the function returns the newValue (z). Otherwise, it retains the currentValue (x) of the cell. This conditional approach allows precise control over the replacement process, ensuring that changes are made only when certain criteria are met. For a more detailed exploration of replacers and how they operate, refer to *Chapter 11, Comparers, Replacers, Combiners, and Splitters.*

Understanding the strengths and limitations of the functions highlighted here aids in effectively selecting one that fits the specific requirements of your data transformation task. The M language offers a wide range of functions. While there are more functions available, the ones covered here are most commonly used and provide a solid foundation for exploring other functions on your own.

As you become more and more familiar with the M language, you'll quickly notice that lists are frequently used as arguments within functions or returned as output. This underscores their importance; therefore, we'll explore how to work with lists next.

Working with lists

Considering the numerous functions designed to work with lists, their significance is evident. You can think of lists containing primitive values as similar to one-dimensional arrays: a flexible structure that allows for the easy storage and manipulation of data, including adding, removing, and modifying items. This section focuses solely on working with lists; lists that contain other value types, like records or tables, are covered later on in this chapter.

Transforming a list

Every element within a list can be referred to by its positional index – a number that reflects its ze-ro-based position within a list. The first element has a positional index of 0, followed by the second element with an index of 1, and so on. A method called item access provides access to each list element by using this zero-based index position within a set of curly brackets, { }.

List.Transform

List.Transform provides a wealth of possibilities. Much like the name suggests, it enables the application of a transformation function to every list element contained within the list provided as the first argument. The result or output is a list with newly transformed values. For example, this will return the square root of each number present within the input list:

```
List.Transform( {1, 4, 9}, Number.Sqrt )
// result: {1, 2, 3}
```

This illustrates its fundamental application perfectly. Another typical use case to employ List.Transform is iteration, particularly in a lookup operation. This usually involves passing a list of indices to extract associated values from another list based on their respective zero-based index position.

Obtaining column names by their position becomes straightforward. In a scenario like that, the input or list to be transformed comprises indices that represent the items to be retrieved. The transformation function then applies item access to a list of column names and replaces each index number with the corresponding column name. Let's try this with the **EmployeeData** table that featured in the Table.TransformColumns section of this chapter. Note that the query should also be named EmployeeData, so it can be referenced as shown here:

```
let
    colNames = Table.ColumnNames( EmployeeData ),
    requestPositions = { 1, 2 },
    getColNames = List.Transform(
        requestPositions,
        each colNames{_}
    )
in
    getColNames // result: FirstName, LastName
```

This returns the column names for the second and third columns of the table, FirstName and LastName. *Chapter 6* offers a more in-depth exploration of the *item access* process, while *Chapter 13* provides a deep dive into iteration and recursion.

List.Zip

Another useful function when working with lists is `List.Zip`. This function cannot be invoked from the UI side. It takes a list of lists as a single argument and returns a new list with lists where elements from all input lists have been combined based on their shared index position:

```
let
    list1 = {"A", "B", "C"},
    list2 = {1, 2, 3, 4, 5},
    zippedList = List.Zip({list1, list2})
in
    zippedList
```

Refer to *Figure 8.10* for an illustration of how `List.Zip` operates. In this example, the first elements of the given lists are "A" from `list1` and 1 from `list2`, both at index position 0. `List.Zip` combines them by sequentially selecting an element from `list1` and then from `list2`. This process adheres to the order in which the lists are provided to its argument, thereby creating a newly paired item: `{"A", 1}`:

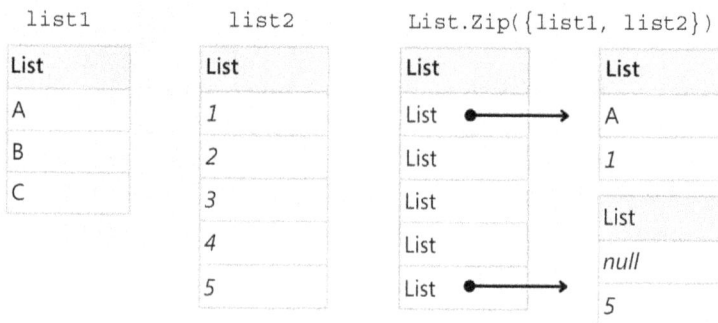

Figure 8.10: Examining List.Zip input lists and result list

It's important to note that the input lists in this example are of unequal lengths. To address this, the M engine automatically fills in a `null` for each missing corresponding position. As a result, the last two nested list items will contain a `null`. The `zippedList` variable returns a list with five nested lists, the contents of which are depicted in the following table:

INDEX POSITION	VALUE
0	{"A", 1}
1	{"B", 2}
2	{"C", 3}
3	{null, 4}
4	{null, 5}

Table 8.1: Contents of the nested lists

A practical use case for List.Zip involves creating replacement lists that act as arguments to other M functions. An illustrative example is when you need to rename multiple columns in a table, as demonstrated here:

```
let
    myTable = Table.FromRecords({
        [ID=1, Name="Alice"], [ID=2, Name="Bob"]
    }),
    oldNames = Table.ColumnNames(myTable),
    newNames = {"Identifier", "FullName"},
    zippedNames = List.Zip({oldNames, newNames}),
    renamedCols = Table.RenameColumns(myTable, zippedNames)
in
    renamedCols
```

The zippedNames step takes an item from oldNames and an item from the newNames input list and forms a new list of lists, each of which contains an old column name followed by a new column name.

The process of renaming columns within a nested table is similar. We will leverage Table.TransformColumns to alter the values in the Value column. This transformation, which occurs row by row, is directed by the each expression, enabling us to reference the nested table from the current row by passing the underscore:

```
let
    myTable = Table.FromRecords({
        [Type = "nested table", Value=
            Table.FromRecords({
                [ID=1, Name="Alice"], [ID=2, Name="Bob"]
            })
        ]}),
    NestedRename = Table.TransformColumns( myTable, {{"Value", each
        let
            oldNames = Table.ColumnNames(_),
            newNames = {"Identifier", "FullName"},
            zippedNames = List.Zip({oldNames, newNames}),
            renamedCols = Table.RenameColumns(_, zippedNames)
        in
            renamedCols, type table}}
    )
in
    NestedRename
```

In the nested let expression, the variables from the previous example are reused to transform all of the nested tables in the Value column.

Extracting an item

Apart from item access, there are only a few M functions available that can extract elements from a list, and their reach is limited. They include `List.First`, `List.Last`, `List.Single`, and `List.SingleOrDefault`. What makes all except one of them user-friendly is that with the exception of `List.Single`, they do not raise an error when their input list is empty; instead, they simply return `null` or, in the case of `List.SingleOrDefault`, a default value if one is specified. Examine this record expression:

```
[
    myEmptyList = {},
    listFirst = List.First(myEmptyList),
    listLast = List.Last(myEmptyList),
    listSingle = List.Single( myEmptyList ),
    singleOrDefault = List.SingleOrDefault(myEmptyList),
    singleOrDefault2 = List.SingleOrDefault(myEmptyList, 99),
    myNonEmptyList = {1, 2, 3},
    listFirst2 = List.First(myNonEmptyList),
    listLast2 = List.Last(myNonEmptyList),
    listSingle2 = List.Single(myNonEmptyList),
    singleOrDefault3 = List.SingleOrDefault(myNonEmptyList, 99)
]
```

The return values for all expressions within this record are shown in the following figure::

myEmptyList	List
listFirst	null
listLast	null
listSingle	Error
singleOrDefault	null
singleOrDefault2	99
myNonEmptyList	List
listFirst2	1
listLast2	3
listSingle2	Error
singleOrDefault3	Error

Figure 8.11: Accessing list items with M functions

Please note that supplying a list with more than a single element will raise an error in both `List.Single` and `List.SingleOrDefault`. Furthermore, it's good to know that the effectiveness of these value extraction functions will increase significantly when combined with other M functions that resize or filter lists.

Resizing a list

Various functions can adjust a list's size without altering the elements contained within; instead, they create a new list with fewer or more elements based on an offset or count. These include `List.FirstN`, `List.RemoveLastN`, `List.Skip`, and `List.Repeat`. In this section, we will highlight two of them: `List.Range` and `List.Alternate`.

List.Range

The `List.Range` function is helpful to obtain a subset of list elements. Like most list functions, it cannot be invoked from the UI. This function requires two parameters: a list and a numerical offset. Optionally, you can specify a count. It's important to note that the second argument, known as the offset, should be passed as a zero-based starting index position, whereas the optional third argument, known as the count, should be passed as a one-based item count. We will create a series of examples leveraging this query:

```
let
    Source = Table.FromColumns(
        {
            {1..5},
            {987, 645, 843, 754, 398}
        }, type table
        [i = number, Amount = number]
    ),
    listAmount = Source[Amount]
in
    listAmount
```

You might recognize we have drilled down into the Amount column, as shown in *Figure 8.12*. Even though this identifier is named `listAmount`, it may show as **Navigation** in the **Applied Steps** pane. It has been prepared to create a simple running total:

List
987
645
843
754
398

Figure 8.12: listAmount

Though *Chapter 13, Iteration and Recursion*, introduces a more efficient technique for calculating running totals, `List.Range` can be a viable option in certain scenarios. It provides a straightforward method to generate a list for summation.

Let's explore:

1. Click on the **fx** next to the formula bar to insert a manual step.
2. Replace the expression inside the formula bar with `Source`.
3. Navigate to the **Add column** tab and choose **Custom column**.
4. Enter `List.Range( )` into the formula area and input the `listAmount` variable as the first argument. Always start from the first item, which is at index position 0, and include the number of elements up to the current row of the table `[i]`, or copy the following code into the formula bar without `simpleRunningTotal =`

```
simpleRunningTotal = Table.AddColumn(
    Source,
    "simple RT prep",
    each List.Range( listAmount, 0, [i] ), type list
)
```

As you can see in *Figure 8.13*, the value in column i corresponds to the number of elements contained within each list. The top row has a list with one element, whereas the bottom row has a list containing all elements:

1.2 i	1.2 Amount	simple RT prep
1	1	987 List
2	2	645 List
3	3	843 List
4	4	754 List
5	5	398 List

List
987
645

Figure 8.13: The second row list contains the first two values from listAmount

Let's turn that around and create a reversed running total, if you will – here's how:

1. Click on the **fx** next to the formula bar to insert a manual step.
2. Replace the expression inside the formula bar with **Source**.
3. Navigate to the **Add column** tab and choose **Custom column**.

4. Enter List.Range( ) into the formula area and input the listAmount variable as the first argument. Start from the item, which is at index position [i]-1, or copy the following code into the formula bar without reverseRunningTotal =

```
reverseRunningTotal = Table.AddColumn(
    Source,
    "reverse RT prep",
    each List.Range( listAmount, [i]-1 ), type list
)
```

The initial part remains the same; however, we needed to make the second argument dynamic by referencing the first column, [i], which is an index starting from 1. To obtain a zero-based value, subtract 1. There's no need to specify a third argument since we aim to retrieve all remaining list items from that point on, as shown in *Figure 8.14*:

⊞▾ 1.2 i	1.2 Amount	reverse RT prep
1	1	987 List
2	2	645 List
3	3	843 List
4	4	754 List
5	5	398 List

List
645
843
754
398

Figure 8.14: The second row list contains everything except the first value from listAmount

Alright, let's see how easy it is to return the current and next row's value. Basically, all that will change is adding a count of 2 as the third argument – here's how:

1. Click on the **fx** next to the formula bar to insert a manual step.
2. Replace the expression inside the formula bar with **Source**.
3. Navigate to the **Add column** tab and choose **Custom column**.

4. Enter `List.Range( )` into the formula area as the first argument and input the `listAmount` variable. Start from the item, which is at index position `[i]-1`, and a count of 2, or copy the following code into the formula bar without `getCurrentAndNext =`:

```
getCurrentAndNext = Table.AddColumn(
    Source,
    "current and next",
    each List.Range( listAmount, [i]-1, 2 ), type list
)
```

Figure 8.15 shows the result:

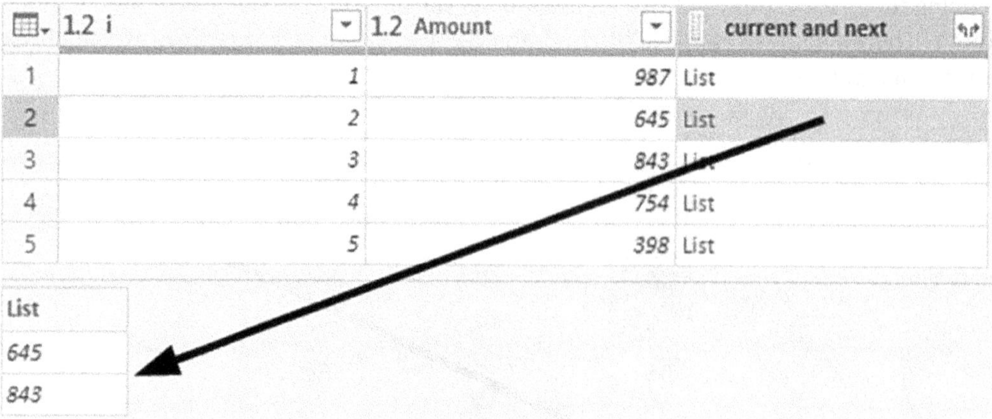

1.2 i	1.2 Amount	current and next
1	1	987 List
2	2	645 List
3	3	843 List
4	4	754 List
5	5	398 List

List
645
843

Figure 8.15: Get current and next amount

Obtaining the previous and current rows' values instead can also be achieved. This requires error handling; you can learn all about that in *Chapter 12* of this book:

1. Click on the **fx** next to the formula bar to insert a manual step.
2. Replace the expression inside the formula bar with **Source**.
3. Navigate to the **Add column** tab and choose **Custom column**.
4. Enter `List.Range( )` into the formula area and input the `listAmount` variable as the first argument. Start from the item, which is at index position `[i]-2`, seeing as the index starts from 1 with a count of 2.
5. Insert a `try` clause between the each expression and the `List.Range` function; after the function, insert an `otherwise` clause. This allows us to specify a default value in case an error is raised; we will provide a list: `{null, [Amount]}`. Or, you can copy the following code into the formula bar without `getPrevAndCurrent =`:

```
getPrevAndCurrent = Table.AddColumn(
    Source,
    "previous and current",
    each try List.Range( listAmount, [i]-2, 2 )
        otherwise {null, [Amount]}, type list
)
```

The result can be seen in the following screenshot:

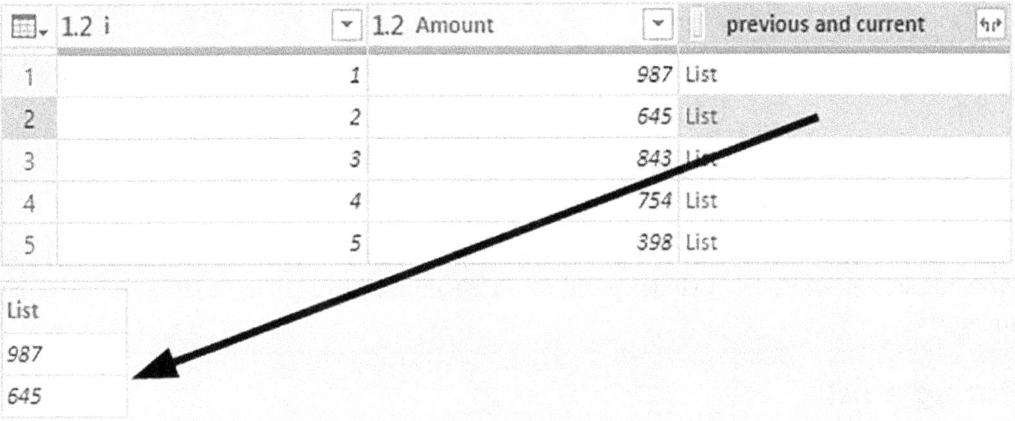

Figure 8.16: Get previous and current amount

When using List.Range within a table space, you require an index column to make either or both the offset and count parameters dynamic. Two functions closely related to List.Range are List.RemoveRange and List.InsertRange. The parameters of List.RemoveRange work identically to those of List.Range. However, List.InsertRange requires a list of values as the third argument instead of an optional count.

List.Alternate

List.Alternate, on the other hand, takes a list, a skip count, an optional extract count, and an optional offset that specifies the index position from where to start skipping values. Both counts are one-based and the offset is zero-based. Take a look at this record:

```
[
    myList = {"a", 1, "b", 2, "c", 3},
    numerals = List.Alternate( myList, 1, 1 ),
    letters = List.Alternate( myList, 1, 1, 1 )
]
```

See *Figure 8.17* to extract the numerals from myList. We alternate between skipping and extracting one item from the top of the list:

myList	numerals	letters
List	List	List
a	1	a
1	2	b
b	3	c
2		
c		
3		

Figure 8.17: Return values for each variable within the record

However, to extract the letters, we alternate between skipping and extracting one item starting from the second list item, which has an index position of 1, retaining the initial list item before the skipping commences.

Filtering a list

Similar to resizing lists, select and filter operations reduce the number of elements within a list – not by position, but based on the value of a list item. Some examples are List.RemoveNulls, List.FindText, and List.Select.

List.FindText

The List.FindText function offers a straightforward method for selecting all list items that contain a specific substring, provided as a second argument. Please note that this second argument only accepts a value of type text, and the function conducts a case-sensitive match:

```
let
    myList = {"a", 1, "b", 2, "c", 3, "ba"},
    findText = List.FindText( myList, "a")
in
    findText   //output: {"a", "ba"}
```

List.Select

List.Select, on the other hand, accepts a list and a selection function as its parameters, offering more control over the selection process. For instance, consider this record, which demonstrates how you can select items based on type, value, or text length:

```
[
    myList = {"a", 1, "b", 2, "c", 3, "ba"},
    selectByType = List.Select( myList, each _ is number),
```

```
    selectIsOdd = List.Select( myList, each
        try Number.IsOdd(_) otherwise false),
    selectByLen = List.Select( myList, each
        try Text.Length(_) >=2 otherwise false)
]
```

Figure 8.18 shows that items are only retained when the selection function returns true:

myList	ByType	IsOdd	ByLen
List	List	List	List
a	1	1	ba
1	2	3	
b	3		
2			
c			
3			
ba			

Figure 8.18: Return values for each variable within the record

It's important to remember that lists can contain values of any type. Therefore, if you cannot guarantee each list item's value type, it is wise to incorporate error handling. In this case, including a `try-otherwise` statement is effective. More information about errors and error handling can be found in *Chapter 12*, *Handling Errors and Debugging*.

A more advanced `List.Select` scenario is covered in the practical examples of *Chapter 11*, *Comparers, Replacers, Combiners, and Splitters*, such as selecting items based on another list of values.

To-list conversions

Up to this point, we have built a foundation to enhance your comfort level in working with lists. While the M language offers numerous list functions, our focus has been on those that transform, extract, resize, and select items. To understand why, it's important to know what structured value-to-list conversions are at your disposal, considering the anatomy of tables and records. We will use the **EmployeeData** query for illustration purposes. Here is the code once again, for your convenience. Please make sure to name this query **EmployeeData**, as we will be referring to it by this name from now on:

```
let
    Source = Table.FromRows(
        {
            {101, "john", "prince", 50000},
            {102, "alice", "wonder", 60000},
            {103, "bob", "bever", 55000}
        },
```

```
        type table [
            EmployeeID=number,
            FirstName=text,
            LastName=text,
            Salary=number
        ]
    )
in
    Source
```

Looking at a table, the main building blocks are easy to identify:

- Headers, such as column or field names
- The data section, which is everything below the headers, divided into either columns or rows

Each collection of items can be transformed into a list. We will examine them in the next sections.

Column or field names

This record expression shows three common functions that will obtain column or field names; each of them produces a list:

```
[
    tblColNames =  Table.ColumnNames( EmployeeData ),
    recFieldNames = Record.FieldNames( EmployeeData{0} ),
    tblColumnsOfType = Table.ColumnsOfType( EmployeeData, {Text.Type})
]
```

Figure 8.19 shows the output of these expressions:

tblColNames	recFieldNames	tblColumnsOfType
List	**List**	**List**
EmployeeID	EmployeeID	FirstName
FirstName	FirstName	LastName
LastName	LastName	
Salary	Salary	

Figure 8.19: Obtained column or field names

A single column

This record expression shows five common methods and functions to obtain all values from a column as a list:

```
[
    drilldown = EmployeeData[FirstName],
    tblColumn1 = Table.Column( EmployeeData, "FirstName" ),
    tblColumn2 = Table.Column( EmployeeData,
        Table.ColumnNames( EmployeeData ){1} ),
    tblToColumns1 = Table.ToColumns( EmployeeData){1},
    tblToList1 = Table.ToList( EmployeeData[[FirstName]] )
]
```

Figure 8.20 shows the output of these expressions; they all return the same value. It's important to note that the sequence of values aligns with the row order in the table:

List
john
alice
bob

Figure 8.20: Obtained single-column values

All columns

Obtaining all columns of the table will return a list of lists, as this record illustrates:

```
[
    tblToColumns = Table.ToColumns( EmployeeData )
]
```

Figure 8.21 shows the output of this expression. It's important to note that the sequence of nested lists aligns with the column order of the table:

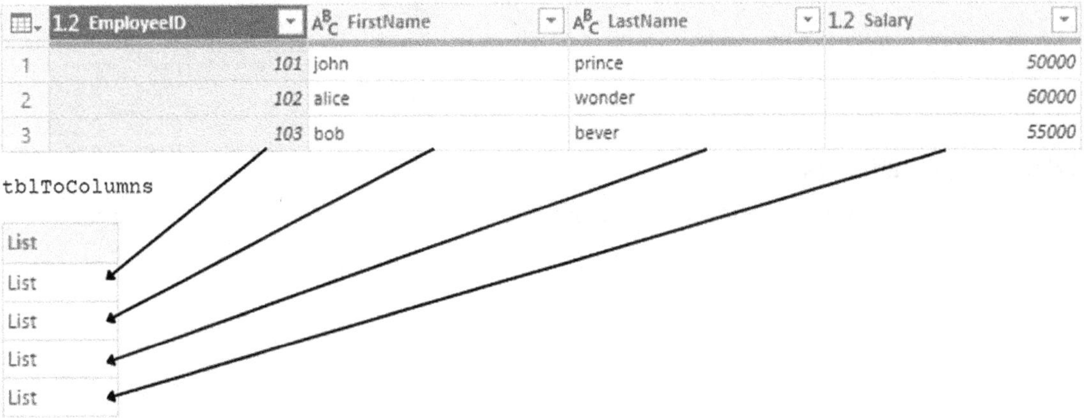

Figure 8.21: Obtained columns values

All rows

The methods and functions to obtain values from rows are illustrated here:

```
[
    tblToRows = Table.ToRows( EmployeeData ),
    tblToList = Table.ToList(
        Table.TransformColumnTypes( EmployeeData,
            List.Transform(
                Table.ColumnNames(EmployeeData),
                each {_, type text }
            )
        )
    ),
    tblToRecords = Table.ToRecords( EmployeeData ),
    recFieldValues = Record.FieldValues( EmployeeData{0} ),
    recToList = Record.ToList( EmployeeData{0} )
]
```

Figure 8.22 shows the output of these expressions. It's important to note that the sequence of (nested) values aligns with the row order of the table. Record expressions can be applied row by row and return values in sequence of the column or field order.

tblToRows	tblToList	tblToRecords	recFieldValues, recToList
List	List	List	List
List	101,john,prince,50000	Record	101
List	102,alice,wonder,60000	Record	john
List	103,bob,bever,55000	Record	prince
			50000

Figure 8.22: Obtained row values

Other operations

There are other relevant and common operations, like split and combine, as shown in the following code:

```
[
    tblSplit = Table.Split( EmployeeData, 1),
    lst = Table.ToRows( EmployeeData),
    lstCombine = List.Combine( lst ),
    lstSplit = List.Split( lstCombine, Table.ColumnCount(EmployeeData))
]
```

Figure 8.23 shows the output of these expressions:

tblSplit	lst	lstCombine	lstSplit
List	**List**	**List**	**List**
Table	List	*101*	List
Table	List	john	List
Table	List	prince	List
		50000	
		102	
		alice	
		wonder	
		60000	
		103	
		bob	
		bever	
		55000	

Figure 8.23: Obtained row values

All these operations yield a list value containing either primitive or structured values, such as lists, records, or tables, as shown in *Figure 8.23*. Understanding the various conversion methods at your disposal provides considerable flexibility, paving the way for a broad range of advanced data transformations. From this section forward, numerous examples leveraging one or more of these techniques will be presented.

Let's round off this section on working with lists with two practical examples.

Expanding multiple list columns simultaneously

When you come across data stored in several list columns, as shown in *Figure 8.24*, individually expanding each one at a time often leads to unwanted value duplication.

	ABC 123 Type	ABC 123 ID	ABC 123 Name
1	set 1	List	List
2	set 2	List	List

Figure 8.24: A table containing multiple list columns

To avoid this, these list columns can be transformed into a single structure, in the form of a table. By subsequently expanding that table, all former list columns are expanded at once. Consider this query:

```
let
    myTable = Table.FromRecords({
        [   Type = "set 1",
            ID = {1, 2},
            Name = {"Alice", "Bob"}
        ],
        [   Type = "set 2",
            ID = {3, 4},
            Name = {"Sam", "Kate"}
        ]}),
    combinedLists = Table.AddColumn(myTable, "Combined", each
        Table.FromColumns( {[ID], [Name]}, {"ID", "Name"}),
        type table [ID=Int64.Type, Name=text]
    ),
    cleanUpColumns = Table.SelectColumns( combinedLists,
        {"Type", "Combined"},
        MissingField.UseNull
    ),
    ExpandAllLists = Table.ExpandTableColumn(cleanUpColumns,
        "Combined",
        {"ID", "Name"}, {"ID", "Name"}
    )
in
    ExpandAllLists
```

Let's break down the code and the process together:

1. myTable generates a three-column-wide table. The "Type" column contains a text value, and the "ID" and "Name" columns contain lists, as shown in *Figure 8.24*. To avoid unwanted duplication when expanding both list columns, we will treat those lists as column values and join them together to form a table.

2. combinedList adds a column named "Combined" to myTable using the **Custom Column** option on the **Add Column** tab. This invokes the Table.AddColumn function and will show the **Custom Column** dialog box.

3. This allows us to specify the new column name, "Combined", and insert a formula. We will use the Table.FromColumns function and pass the list values from the "ID" and "Name" columns as a list by wrapping a set of curly brackets around them and separating them with commas, like so: {[ID], [Name]}, to output a two-column-wide table; as a second argument, we will provide a list with new column names: {"ID", "Name"}, as shown in *Figure 8.25*:

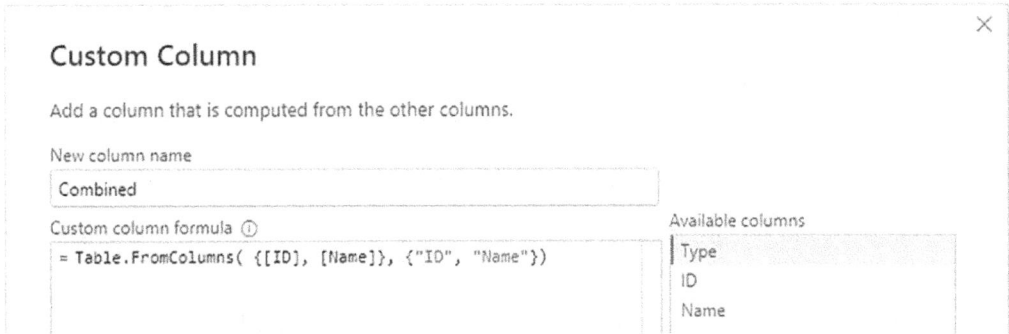

Figure 8.25: Custom Column dialog box

4. After clicking the **OK** button, we can review the code that has been generated inside the formula bar. We can update this code by ascribing a type to the value we have just created. First, enter a comma between the last two parentheses, and then a type, like so: type table [ID=Int64.Type, Name=text], as shown in *Figure 8.26*:

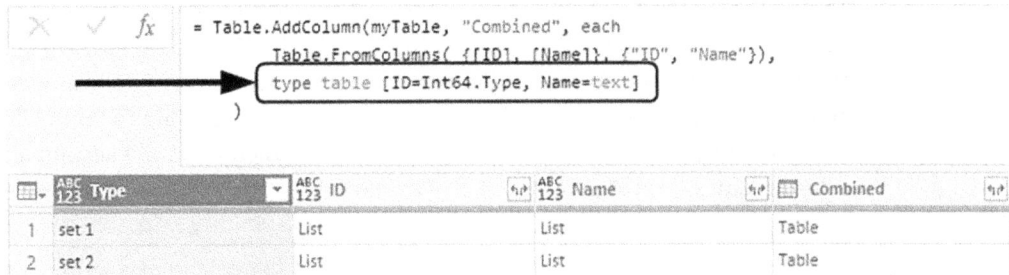

Figure 8.26: Ascribing a type to the table inside the Combined column

5. Now for cleanUpColumns. All list columns have become redundant: to remove them, we select **Choose Columns** on the **Home** tab. This invokes the Table.SelectColumns function to keep the Type and Combined columns. Manually inserting the optional MissingField type, MissingField.UseNull, will protect the structure of the outer table by inserting null values for any missing fields.

6. ExpandAllLists subsequently extracts all values through the expand column option available in the column header, which you can find to the right of the column name, indicated by two sideways arrows.

Alternatively, there's a more advanced method that can optimize this process by eliminating the need to add a custom column to the table. It involves reshaping the table as part of the workflow. To examine that approach, open the **Advanced Editor**, insert a comma at the end of the ExpandAllLists expression, go to a new line, and copy and paste the following code:

```
fxToTable = ( twoCols as list ) as table =>
    Table.FromColumns( twoCols, {"ID", "Name"}),
NoAddCols = Table.FromList(
```

```
     Table.ToList( myTable, each {_{0}} & {fxToTable({_{1}, _{2}})}),
     each _,
     type table [Type=text, Combined=table [ID=Int64.Type, Name=text]]
)
```

Update the variable after the in clause by replacing ExpandAllLists with NoAddCols, and click **Done**.

Although at this time you are not expected to fully understand this code, we will break it down for future reference:

1. A custom function known as fxToTable is created that is tailored to be invoked on values from columns 2 and 3, which correspond to the ID and Name column from myTable. Its syntax corresponds to the **Custom Column** expression defined (3) in the previous breakdown.

2. NoAddCols is more complex and performs several operations. We will start with this inner expression:

    a. `Table.ToList( myTable, each {_{0}} & {fxToTable({_{1}, _{2}})})`

        This transforms myTable into a list of row-value lists by applying a function to each row's values. From the table shown in *Figure 8.24*, you can see that we are taking the value from the first column and placing that inside a list: {_{0}}. The ampersand, &, allows us to combine this list with another list, a list that contains a table. That table was generated by invoking the custom fxToTable function on the second and third column values: {fxToTable({_{1}, _{2}})}.

    b. `Table.FromList( …, each _ )`

        This transforms the list of lists (a) into a table by applying a function that, by default, splits by commas. Since each list item is a list containing two items, this yields a two-column-wide table.

    c. `type table [Type=text, Combined=table [ID=Int64.Type, Name=text]]`

        Table.FromList also allows us to specify the columns for the new table; we provided a type table to define both column names and ascribe column types.

This process not only eliminates the need to add a custom column to the table but also removes the need to clean up redundant columns afterward.

Flattening inconsistent multi-level nested lists

Nested lists can contain valuable data that requires unpacking or flattening for further analysis. Often, you'll see recursion used to flatten inconsistent multi-level nested lists. However, we will present an alternative to achieve the same result. This involves using functions like Json.FromValue and Text.FromBinary to produce a string for manipulation, as demonstrated in the flattenList custom function in the following code. Don't worry if you are currently unfamiliar with custom functions, as they will be covered in depth in the next chapter of this book.

```
let
  inputList =
    {
      {"Product A", {"Product A1", "Product A2"}},
      {{"Product A1", "Product A2"}, {{"Product B"}}},
      {"Product C", {"Product C1", "Product C2",
        {"Product C2a", {{"Product C2b"}}}}, "Product D"},
      {"Product B", {{{"Product A", {
        {"Product A1", "Product A2"}}}}}},
      {"Product C", {"Product C1", "Product C2"}, {}}
    },
  myTable = Table.FromColumns({inputList},
    type table[to flatten = list]
  ),
  flattenList = (myList as list) as list =>
  let
    string = Text.FromBinary( Json.FromValue( myList )),
    cleanString = Text.Trim(
      Text.Remove( string, {"[", "]"}), "," ),
    convertToList = Splitter.SplitTextByDelimiter(",")(cleanString)
  in
    convertToList,
  InvokedOnList = flattenList( inputList ),
  InvokedOnTable = Table.TransformColumns( myTable,
    {{ "to flatten", flattenList, type list }}
  )
in
  InvokedOnTable
```

We will break this code down for future reference:

1. flattenList is a custom function that takes a list-type input and produces a list-type output value. The function body contains a let expression that we can explore:

    a. string uses the Json.FromValue function to generate a JSON representation of the list input value, which translates each list value into a JSON array, surrounding it with a set of square brackets, [ ]. The Text.FromBinary function converts that JSON into a text-type value.

    b. cleanString uses the expression Text.Remove(string, {"[", "]"}) to strip away all square brackets, basically removing all list levels. The output string may end with a comma in cases where a final nested list was empty. To protect our function, this possible trailing comma should be removed: Text.Trim(…, ",").

    c.   convertToList calls `Splitter.SplitTextByDelimiter(",")` to yield a function that is invoked on the `cleanString` variable to produce a list-type value.

2.   `InvokedOnList` illustrates how the `flattenList` custom function can be invoked on the `inputList` variable.

3.   `InvokedOnTable` illustrates how the `flattenList` custom function can be used within `Table.TransformColumns` to transform each row value in the "`to flatten`" column.

Once the `flattenList` function is invoked, only a single list containing text values remains. However, if any text values within these multi-level nested lists contain square brackets, the `cleanString` operation will remove them; that is a limitation you should be aware of.

The M language includes a wide array of list functions. This section aimed to highlight a select few to shed light on and provide a glimpse of their capabilities. Our main focus has been demonstrating techniques for transforming, extracting, resizing, and selecting list items, all of which have been illustrated through executable code samples. Next, we'll explore how to work with records.

Working with records

Records are a structure that allows for the organization of data in fields; each field is a name-value pair. Similar to lists, records can store various data types and offer capabilities for data manipulation, extraction, and modification.

While there is only a modest collection of record functions available in the M language compared to lists or tables, there are functions that accept a record as an argument or return a record as output. This section will cover common aspects of working with records. Again, it's important to mention that our focus is on working with records, and we will discuss working with mixed data structures later in this chapter.

Transforming records

Every field value within a record can be referred to by its field name – a unique identifier within the record. A method known as `field access` provides access to each field value by using that name within a set of square brackets, [ ].

The M language includes a function called `Record.TransformFields`, which can be used to modify record field values. However, it only plays a modest role when compared to `Table.TransformColumns`, which is covered extensively in the section *Transforming values in tables*. Transforming values by column is more common than modifying fields by row. As a result, the use of the `Record.TransformFields` function is more exclusive and often reserved for edge cases.

Moreover, the same result can be achieved through a record merge operation. During a record merge, fields on the left are overwritten by like-named fields from the right. Consider this example that illustrates both techniques:

```
let
    rec = [
        EmployeeID = "102",
```

```
            FirstName = "Alice",
            LastName = "Wonder",
            Salary = "6000.0"
        ],
    recTransformFields = Record.TransformFields( rec,
        {
            {"EmployeeID", Number.FromText},
            {"Salary", each Number.FromText(_, "en-US")}
        }
    ),
    recMerge = rec &
        [
            EmployeeID = Number.FromText(rec[EmployeeID]),
            Salary = Number.FromText(rec[Salary], "en-US")
        ],
    recCombine = Record.Combine(
        {
            rec,
            [
                EmployeeID = Number.FromText(rec[EmployeeID]),
                Salary = Number.FromText(rec[Salary], "en-US")
            ]
        })
in
    recCombine
```

Figure 8.27 shows the rec value:

EmployeeID	102
FirstName	Alice
LastName	Wonder
Salary	6000.0

Figure 8.27: rec value before modification

The recTransformFields, recMerge, and recCombine variables yield the same outcome (seen in *Figure 8.28*), although they use different methods. The recTransformFields step uses the standard library function Record.TransformFields, which is less versatile than Table.TransformColumns. For example, the transformOperations list consists of lists in the format {field name, transformation}, one for each field to be transformed, without the option to specify a type.

Understandably, it does not have a defaultTransformation; instead, it comes equipped with an optional missingField parameter.

EmployeeID	102
FirstName	Alice
LastName	Wonder
Salary	6000

Figure 8.28: rec value after modification

In the recMerge and recCombine step, the original record is referenced first, making it the left operand, followed by a newly constructed record as the right operand. The new record has two fields with corresponding field names in the original record, effectively overwriting those field values during the combination or merge operation to yield the same outcome.

Extracting a field value

Apart from field access, there are two functions, Record.Field and Record.FieldOrDefault, that can extract a field value from a record. Neither of these functions includes a missingField parameter. The Record.Field function will raise an error if the text string passed and the second argument does not match any of the field names within the record. On the other hand, Record.FieldOrDefault will return null or a default value if that was specified:

```
[
    rec = [
        EmployeeID = "102",
        FirstName = "Alice",
        LastName = "Wonder",
        Salary = 6000
    ],
    recField = Record.Field( rec, "FirstName"),
    recField2 = Record.Field( rec, "FirstNames"),
    recFieldOrDefault = Record.FieldOrDefault( rec, "FirstName"),
    recFieldOrDefault2 = Record.FieldOrDefault( rec, "FirstNames"),
    recFieldOrDefault3 = Record.FieldOrDefault( rec, "FirstNames", "Unknown")
]
```

Figure 8.29 shows the output of these expressions:

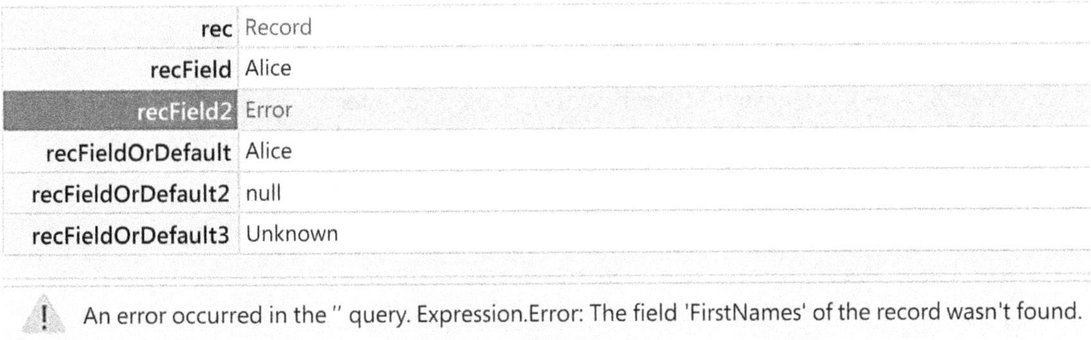

rec	Record
recField	Alice
recField2	Error
recFieldOrDefault	Alice
recFieldOrDefault2	null
recFieldOrDefault3	Unknown

⚠ An error occurred in the " query. Expression.Error: The field 'FirstNames' of the record wasn't found.

Figure 8.29: Output for the Record.Field value expressions

In the initial section of this chapter, we explained that a record expression is similar to a let expression. That process is demonstrated here. This is a simplified example of a multistep transformation process for content within the Value column:

```
let
    tbl = #table(type table[Value=number], {{100}}),
    transform = Table.TransformColumns( tbl,
        {
            { "Value", each
                [
                    a = Number.E,
                    b = Number.RoundAwayFromZero(a, 0),
                    c = _ * b
                ][c], type number
            }
        }
    )
in
    transform
```

The specific calculation or transformation is not important; what matters is the process of generating a value and passing that newly created value on to be used in other expressions. Field access is ultimately applied to the record expression yielding the final result by adding a field name in a set of square brackets; here, the value for the field c is returned: [c].

Troubleshooting a nested record expression is easy. Just return the entire record by commenting out *field access* and, if present, the *ascribed type*; here are the steps:

1. Start by highlighting that section of the code: `[c], type number`.
2. Press *Alt + Shift + A* on your keyboard to turn it into a comment.

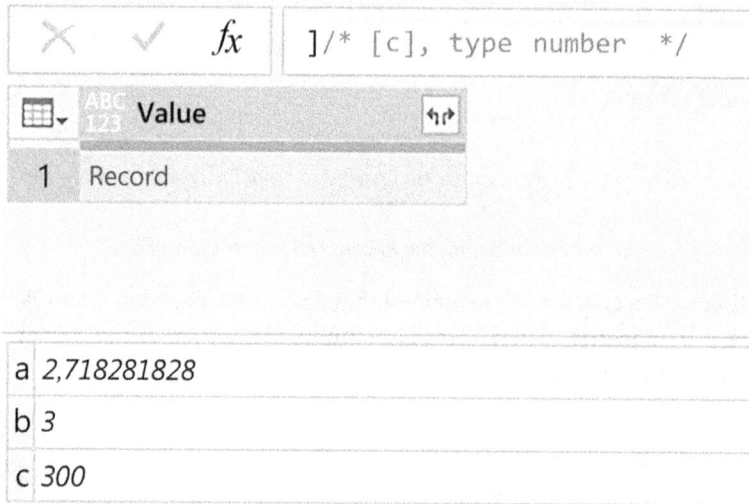

	ABC 123	Value	↕↔
1		Record	

a	*2,718281828*
b	*3*
c	*300*

Figure 8.30: Eliminate field access and ascribed type to return the entire record

That will return a full view of the record, which is extremely useful when you need to troubleshoot or review intermediate values, as shown in *Figure 8.30*.

Resizing records

In addition to the combination operator and projection, there are four functions that can resize a record: `Record.RemoveFields`, `Record.AddField`, `Record.SelectFields`, and `Record.Combine`. We will use these to create a new record and change the number of fields:

```
[
    rec = [
        EmployeeID = "102",
        FirstName = "Alice",
        LastName = "Wonder",
        Salary = "6000.0"
    ],
    recRemoveFields = Record.RemoveFields( rec, {"LastName"}),
    recRemoveFields2 = Record.RemoveFields( rec, {"LastNames"},
        MissingField.Ignore ),
    recAddField = Record.AddField( rec, "fxGreeting", ()=> "Hi!" ),
    recAddField2 = Record.AddField( rec, "fxGreeting", ()=> "Hi!",
        true ),
```

```
    recCombine = Record.Combine({rec, [fxGreeting = ()=> "Hi!"]}),
    recSelectFields = Record.SelectFields( recAddField2,
        {"fxGreeting"} ),
    recSelectFields2 = Record.SelectFields( recAddField2,
        {"fxGreetings"}, MissingField.UseNull )
]
```

Record.RemoveFields and Record.SelectFields come with an optional missingField parameter. Record.AddField comes with an optional delayed parameter. When passing a zero-parameter function as the third argument value, the definition of that function is evaluated and returns a function value. However, when you set the optional fourth argument to true, that function value is invoked to produce its return value, as shown in the following figure:

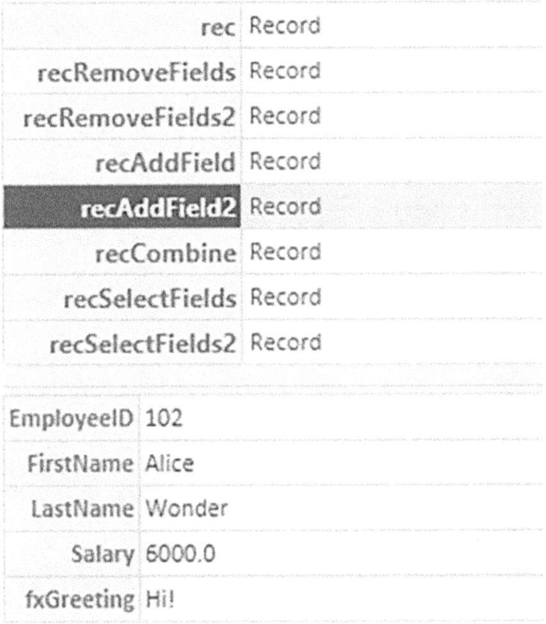

rec	Record
recRemoveFields	Record
recRemoveFields2	Record
recAddField	Record
recAddField2	Record
recCombine	Record
recSelectFields	Record
recSelectFields2	Record

EmployeeID	102
FirstName	Alice
LastName	Wonder
Salary	6000.0
fxGreeting	Hi!

Figure 8.31: New record values containing fewer or more fields

Filtering records

There are no standard library functions that filter records, but you can create your own. We share two custom function examples in the following code to give an idea of what is possible; don't worry if you don't understand how it all works at this time. Custom functions are discussed in depth in *Chapter 9, Parameters and Custom Functions*.

```
[
    rec = [
        EmployeeID = "102",
        FirstName = "Alice",
        LastName = "Wonder",
```

```
            Salary = 6000
    ],
    fxFieldsOfType =
        (
            r as record,
            t as type
        ) as record => [
            findFields = List.Select(
                Record.FieldNames(r),
                each Value.Is(Record.Field(r, _), t)
            ),
            getRecord = Record.SelectFields(
                r,
                findFields
            )
        ][getRecord],
    invokedCF1 = fxFieldsOfType(rec, Number.Type ),
    fxFieldNameStartsOrEndsWith =
        (
            r as record,
            t as text,
            optional startsWith as logical,
            optional ignoreCase as logical
        ) as record => [
            lookAtFunction = if startsWith ?? true
                then Text.StartsWith
                else Text.EndsWith,
            ignoreCase = if ignoreCase ?? true
                then Comparer.OrdinalIgnoreCase
                else Comparer.Ordinal,
            findFields = List.Select(
                Record.FieldNames(r),
                each lookAtFunction(_, t, ignoreCase)
            ),
            getRecord = Record.SelectFields(
                r,
                findFields
            )
        ][getRecord],
    invokedCF2 = fxFieldNameStartsOrEndsWith(rec, "name", false )
]
```

The custom function fxFieldsOfType lets you select field values of a specified type:

1. fxFieldsOfType is a custom function that takes a record-type value and a type-type value as input to yield a *record-type* value. The function body contains a record expression that we can explore further:

    a. findFields uses Record.Field to obtain the values from each field within a record and supply them to the Value.Is function, one by one. This evaluates whether the value type is compatible with the input type (t). If true, List.Select retains that field name that was provided by the Record.FieldNames(r) function, else it omits the field name.

    b. getRecord uses the Record.SelectFields function to select all fields from the record (r) that survived the compatibility check and whose names are listed in the findFields list.

    c. [getRecord] applies *field access* to the record expression to return the value from the field getRecord.

2. invokedCF1 illustrates how the fxFieldsOfType custom function can be invoked on a record by providing the record value and a *record-type* value as arguments.

On the other hand, fxFieldNameStartsOrEndsWith lets you select field names starting or ending with a specified substring, ignoring the case by default:

1. fxFieldNameStartsOrEndsWith is a custom function that has four parameters and will yield a *record-type* value. Two of these parameters are required and two are optional:

    a. r as record is required and accepts a record-type value

    b. t as text is required and accepts a text-type value

    c. Optional startsWith as logical is optional and defaults to true

    d. Optional ignoreCase as logical is optional and defaults to true

    The function body contains a record expression that we can explore further.

    a. lookAtFunction is a conditional statement that takes the startsWith input, to which it applies coalesce: ??, defaulting to true, and Text.StartsWith when no value is specified. When false, it is set to Text.EndsWith.

    b. ignoreCase works in a similar manner, defaulting to true and Comparer. OrdinalIgnoreCase. When false, it is set to Comparer.Ordinal.

    c. findFields uses the List.Select function to keep all field names from the list supplied by the Record.FieldNames function for which the applied lookAtFunction(_, t, ignoreCase) returns true.

2. invokedCF2 illustrates how the fxFieldNameStartsOrEndsWith custom function is invoked on a record by providing a record (rec) and a string ("name") and setting the optional startsWith (false).

To-record conversions

We have explored ways of transforming, extracting, resizing, and selecting records. From the perspective of a table, every table can be turned into a list of records. Each row in a table represents a unique record or entry, with its properties organized across the columns. These columns correspond to fields that store values for each property of a record. Now, let's explore structured value-to-record conversions.

Table row to record

Accessing a single row in a table returns a record. This can actually be demonstrated without using M code. Create a new blank query and reference the EmployeeData table by entering "= EmployeeData" directly into the formula bar. The table shows row numbers at the beginning of each row in the table; these numbers are not part of the data and cannot be accessed or requested. However, when you click on a row number, such as 2, a preview of that row is shown as a record at the bottom of the preview pane.

To obtain that row, it's important to restate that positional indices in M are zero-based. Therefore, to acquire the second record, you will need to apply the positional index operator and include a 1 (shown in *Figure 8.32*), like this: EmployeeData{1}:

EmployeeID	102
FirstName	alice
LastName	wonder
Salary	60000

Figure 8.32: Accessing a single row from a table returns a record

To create a record for each table row, you can add a **Custom Column** and reference the current row (or record) by inserting an underscore in the formula section of the dialog box. This will generate an expression similar to the following:

```
Table.AddColumn( EmployeeData, "rec", each _ )
```

A new column has been added to the table, containing a nested record for each row. This, and more, is addressed in *Chapter 6, Structured Values*.

Record from table

We have discussed the process of retrieving a single record from a table and creating records for each row in a table, both of which are common transformations. However, converting an entire table into a single record is quite uncommon. This is due to the requirement that field names within a record are unique and of the text type. Therefore, a table-to-record conversion is not only restricted to two-column-wide tables, but the first column also has to contain a unique textual key.

A practical application for this process is creating a lookup record that can be used in exact-text-match replacements, where cell contents are conditionally replaced by another value. Consider this query:

```
let
    Attributes = Table.FromRows(
        {
            {"Colour", "Red", "X1"},
            {"Colour", "White", "X2"},
            {"Colour", "Blue", "X3"},
            {"Colour", "blue", "X3"}
        }, type table[Attribute=text, Value=text, Name=text]
    )
in
    Attributes
```

To create a lookup record from a table, follow these steps:

1. We need to ensure that this table has two columns. The first column must contain unique text values, which will be used as record field names: this will be the Name column. The second column should contain the field values; they can be of any type – this will be the Value column. In a lookup record, a field name acts as the text to match and the field value as the corresponding replacement value.

2. Hold down the *CTRL* key and select the columns in this order: the Name column first (1), then the Value column (2). Now select **Remove Columns** (3), then click **Remove Other Columns** (4), as shown in *Figure 8.33*:

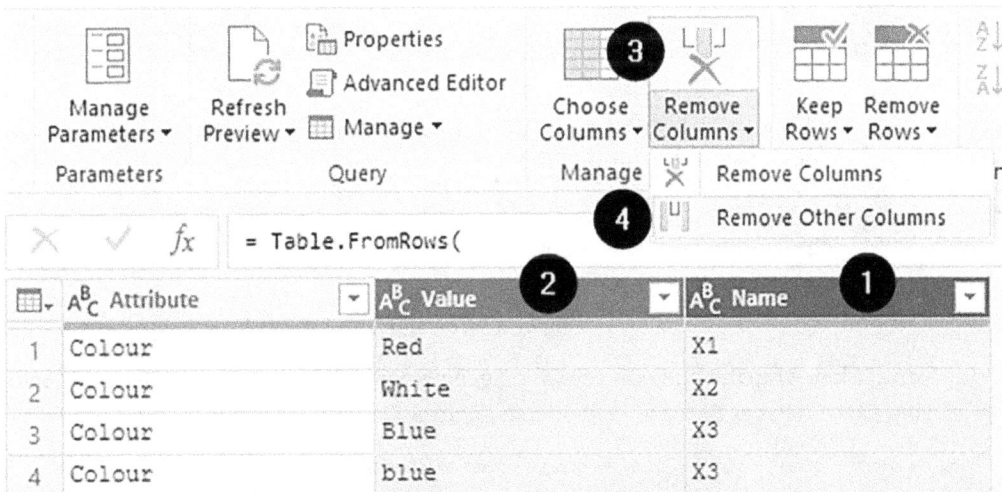

Figure 8.33: Column selection order and removing other columns

3. Make sure the first column (Name) is selected (**1**), navigate to the **Transform** tab, and choose **Pivot Column** (**2**). In the dialog box, the second column will be automatically set as Value (**3**). Open the **Advanced options** section and set the aggregation to **Don't Aggregate** (**4**), as shown in *Figure 8.34*.

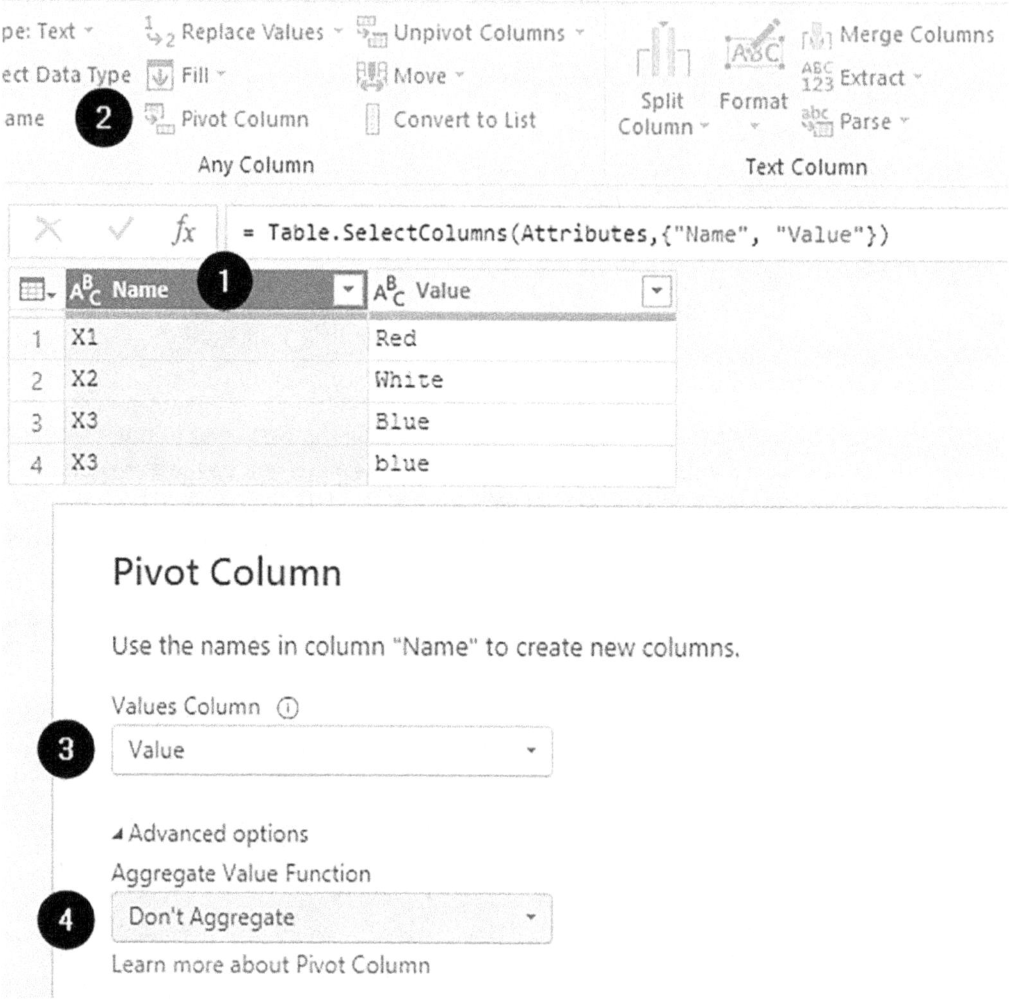

Figure 8.34: Pivot column steps

In the formula bar, wrap the function Table.ToRecords around the expression; don't forget to include the closing parenthesis at the end, as shown in *Figure 8.35*:

```
= Table.ToRecords( Table.Pivot(#"Removed Other Columns", List.Distinct(#"Removed Other Columns"[Name]), "Name", "Value"))
```

Figure 8.35: Wrapping a function around the outermost expression in the formula bar

This returns a list containing one record. To access that value, you can *drill down* by clicking on Record and using item access by adding {0} after the closing parenthesis of the outermost function or wrapping another function around it, such as List.First.

When encountering the error message *Expression.Error: There were too many elements in the enumeration to complete the operation.* in any of the fields, this indicates that the first column of your table contains duplicate values and is not distinct; see *Figure 8.36*:

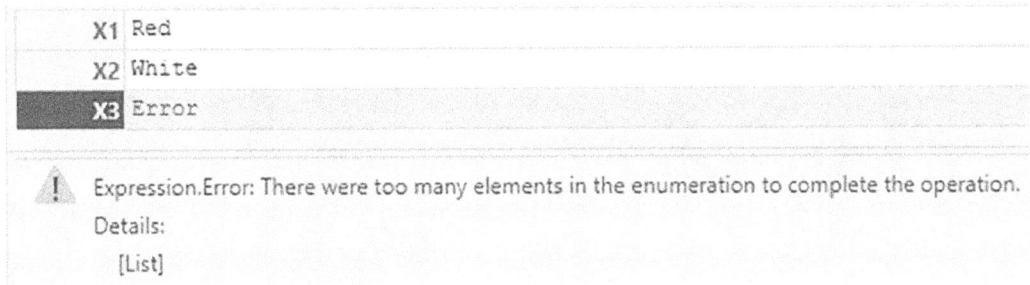

X1 Red

X2 White

X3 Error

⚠ Expression.Error: There were too many elements in the enumeration to complete the operation.

Details:

[List]

Figure 8.36: Showing the field- or cell-level error

To resolve that issue, follow these steps:

1. Go back to your query and select the variable associated with *step 1* in the **Applied Steps** pane on the right-hand side. Here, that's **Removed Other Columns**.

2. Check your data for duplicates and determine the appropriate action to remove them; see *Figure 8.37*:

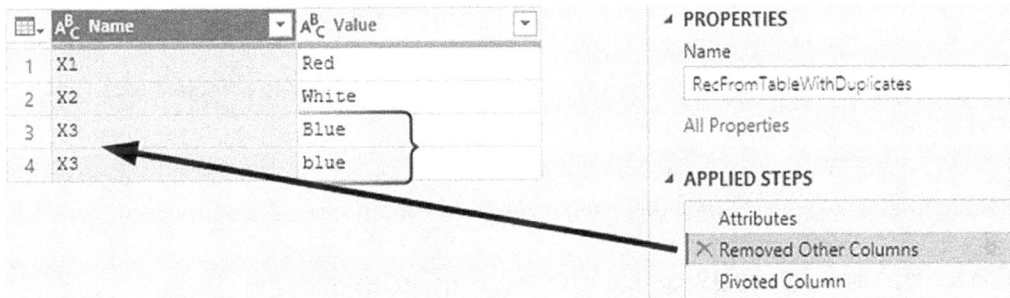

Figure 8.37: Column selection order and removing other columns

3. The IDs in the Name column are identical; you can filter out blue in the Value column or navigate to the **Home** tab and choose **Remove Rows**, followed by **Remove Duplicates**. Confirm when prompted to insert a step. This will remove duplicate values by removing entire rows, resolving this specific type of cell-level error.

The M language includes a Record.FromTable function, which requires a table with two columns, one containing a unique textual key. The columns should be named Name and Value. If table column names differ or the Name column does not contain distinct values, an error will be raised. To illustrate, when you remove the Pivoted Column step, insert a manual step and wrap this function around the variable, like so:

```
Record.FromTable( #"Removed Duplicates" )
```

It produces the exact same result as output.

Record from list

Another method to construct a record is using the `Record.FromList` function. This function takes a list of values and a list of field names or a record type, as illustrated here:

```
let
    Rec1 = Record.FromList(
        {102, "alice", "wonder", 60000},
        { "EmployeeID", "FirstName", "LastName", "Salary" }
    ),
    Rec2 = Record.FromList(
        {102, "alice", "wonder", 60000},
        type [
            EmployeeID=number,
            FirstName=text,
            LastName=text,
            Salary=number
        ]
    )
in
    Rec2
```

This function is useful when you have a list of values and you want to associate each list item with a specific name.

Let's conclude this section on working with records by examining a practical example that uses a lookup to execute a conditional replacement or gather additional information.

Conditional lookup or value replacement

The capability to leverage a lookup record is powerful. This technique can substitute complex joins, Excel vlookup, and xlookup, and it can be used to produce intermediate values in more complex calculations or transformations.

For instance, replacing IDs with actual descriptions will make it easier to analyze this data in Excel, enriching and making the data more understandable for end users:

```
let
    Attributes = Table.FromRows(
        {
            {"Colour", "X1", "Red"},
            {"Colour", "X2", "White"},
            {"Colour", "X3", "Blue"},
            {"Size", "X1", "S"},
            {"Size", "X2", "M"},
```

```
                    {"Size", "X3", "L"},
                    {"Size", "X4", "XL"},
                    {"Size", "X5", "XXL"}
            }, type table[Attribute=text, ID=text, Value=text]
        ),
        toRecord = Table.Group(Attributes, {"Attribute"},
            {{"lookup", each Record.FromList( [Value], [ID] )}}),
        lookup = Record.FromList( toRecord[lookup], toRecord[Attribute] ),
        Source = Table.FromRows(
            {
                {"345-6245", "X5", "X1"},
                {"645-1366", "X3", "X2"},
                {"824-9206", "X4", "X3"},
                {"627-2078", "X3", "X3"},
                {"273-7134", "X4", "X2"}
            }, type table[Item=text, Size ID=text, Colour ID=text]
        ),
        AddDescription = Table.AddColumn( Source, "Description", each
            Record.FieldOrDefault( lookup[Size], [Size ID], "Unknown" )
            & ", " &
            Record.FieldOrDefault( lookup[Colour], [Colour ID], "Unknown" ), type
text
        ),
        ReplaceWithDescription = Table.TransformColumns( Source,
            {{"Size ID", each Record.FieldOrDefault( lookup[Size], _, "Unknown" ),
type text},
            {"Colour ID", each Record.FieldOrDefault( lookup[Colour], _, "Unknown"
), type text}}
        )
in
    ReplaceWithDescription
```

Let's examine what each variable in this code represents:

- `Attributes` is a table that holds the attributes of items, like their color and size.

- `toRecord` groups the `Attributes` table by the `Attribute` column to ensure unique IDs for each group. A record is created where `ID` is the field name and `Values` is the field value. A more detailed explanation of the `Group By` operation is covered in the next section, *Working with tables*.

- The grouped records are then used to create a single record, named `lookup`, which serves as a dictionary. `Attribute` values are keys, and the associated records (created in the previous step) are values.

- Source is a table containing item codes with their size and color IDs.

- AddDescription illustrates how to add a new column named Description to the Source table. This looks up size and color in a lookup record. If an ID is not found, it will return the value specified as default: "Unknown".

- ReplaceWithDescription illustrates how to replace the size ID and color ID values in the Source table with their matching size and color descriptions using the lookup record.

Records in the M language are a foundational structure. Our exploration has been centered on demonstrating techniques for manipulating records. These techniques include transforming, extracting, resizing, and selecting fields from records; all have been illustrated through executable code samples.

After examining lists and records, we now turn our attention to the main remaining structured value: the table. This section will cover the essentials of working with nested tables.

Working with tables

Tables are structured collections of rows and columns, where each cell can hold data of any type. They are the predominant structure in Power Query, as evidenced by the way the UI has been designed to operate on them. Now it's time to explore the basics of nested tables and see examples of how to create, access, and manipulate them. Our primary focus is on understanding the nuances of working with a nested table structure.

Here's our sample dataset. Call this query SurveysData; we will refer to it using that name from now on:

```
let
    Source = Table.FromRows( List.Zip( { List.Transform( {"1".."5"}, each "Wave
"& _ ),
        Table.Group( Table.FromRows(
            {
                {456, 30, "Female", "Intermediate", "High", "Good", "Yes", "Well
organized content", #date(2023,3,1), #date(2023,3,10), 5, 8},
                {457, 52, "Male", "Expert", "Medium", "Good", "Yes",
"Requires frequent updates", #date(2023,3,1), #date(2023,3,10), 3, 6},
                {458, 24, "Female", "Beginner", "High", "Excellent", "Yes", "Very
engaging and easy to follow", #date(2023,3,1), #date(2023,3,10), 7, 9},
                {459, 43, "Male", "Intermediate", "Low", "Average", "No", "The
interface is not user-friendly", #date(2023,3,1), #date(2023,3,10), 2, 4},
                {460, 28, "Non-binary", "Expert", "High", "Good", "Yes", "Feature-
rich and versatile", #date(2023,3,1), #date(2023,3,10), 6, 8},
                {461, 37, "Female", "Beginner", "Medium", "Poor", "No",
"Overwhelming for beginners", #date(2023,3,11), #date(2023,3,20), 1, 5},
                {462, 46, "Male", "Intermediate", "High", "Excellent", "Yes", "High
performance and reliability", #date(2023,3,11), #date(2023,3,20), 4, 8},
                {463, 21, "Female", "Beginner", "Low", "Poor", "No", "Too complex
for novices", #date(2023,3,11), #date(2023,3,20), 1, 3},
```

```
                    {464, 55, "Male", "Expert", "Medium", "Average", "Yes", "Solid but
could be more intuitive", #date(2023,3,11), #date(2023,3,20), 3, 6},
                    {465, 33, "Non-binary", "Intermediate", "High", "Good", "Yes",
"Adaptable to various tasks", #date(2023,3,11), #date(2023,3,20), 5, 7},
                    {466, 40, "Female", "Beginner", "Medium", "Average", "No", "Lacks
in-depth tutorials", #date(2023,3,21), #date(2023,3,30), 2, 5},
                    {467, 26, "Male", "Expert", "High", "Excellent", "Yes",
"Efficient in processing large datasets", #date(2023,3,21), #date(2023,3,30),
6, 9},
                    {468, 48, "Female", "Intermediate", "Low", "Poor", "No",
"Unreliable with frequent downtime", #date(2023,3,21), #date(2023,3,30), 1, 3},
                    {469, 23, "Non-binary", "Beginner", "Medium", "Good", "Yes",
"Good for beginners, but lacks advanced features", #date(2023,3,21),
#date(2023,3,30), 3, 6},
                    {470, 39, "Male", "Expert", "High", "Excellent", "Yes",
"Supports a wide range of functions", #date(2023,3,21), #date(2023,3,30), 5,
8},
                    {471, 34, "Female", "Intermediate", "High", "Good", "Yes", "User
community is very helpful", #date(2023,3,21), #date(2023,3,30), 4, 7},
                    {472, 50, "Male", "Beginner", "Low", "Average", "No",
"Difficult to get started without assistance", #date(2023,4,1),
#date(2023,4,10), 2, 4},
                    {473, 22, "Female", "Expert", "Medium", "Good", "Yes",
"Impressive analytics capabilities", #date(2023,4,1), #date(2023,4,10), 6, 7},
                    {474, 41, "Non-binary", "Intermediate", "High", "Excellent", "Yes",
"Meets professional standards", #date(2023,4,1), #date(2023,4,10), 4, 8},
                    {475, 29, "Male", "Beginner", "Medium", "Average", "No", "Features
are not well explained", #date(2023,4,1), #date(2023,4,10), 2, 5}
            }, {"RespondentID", "Age", "Gender", "ExperienceLevel",
"OverallQuality", "EaseOfUse", "WouldRecommend", "SpecificFeedback",
"SurveyStartDate", "SurveyEndDate", "UsageFrequency",
"SatisfactionScore"}
        ), {"SurveyStartDate"}, {{"Results", each _ , type table }})[Results] &
{#table({"RespondentID", "Age", "Gender", "ExperienceLevel",
"OverallQuality", "EaseOfUse", "WouldRecommend", "SpecificFeedback",
"SurveyStartDate", "SurveyEndDate", "UsageFrequency",
"SatisfactionScore"}, {})} }),
    type table [Survey=text, Results= table [RespondentID=number, Age=number,
Gender=text, ExperienceLevel=text, OverallQuality=text,
EaseOfUse=text, WouldRecommend=text, SpecificFeedback=text,
SurveyStartDate=date, SurveyEndDate=date, UsageFrequency=number,
SatisfactionScore=number]]
    )
in
    Source
```

The SurveysData query is depicted in *Figure 8.38*, along with a preview of Wave 1's nested results. Note only the first five columns are visible. To preview nested structures, select a cell by clicking anywhere on the whitespace; you can change the selection by using the up and down arrow keys on your keyboard. Quickly review these nested tables to understand the data we are dealing with:

	A^B_C Survey	Results
1	Wave 1	Table
2	Wave 2	Table
3	Wave 3	Table
4	Wave 4	Table
5	Wave 5	Table

RespondentID	Age	Gender	ExperienceLevel	OverallIQ
456	30	Female	Intermediate	High
457	52	Male	Expert	Medium
458	24	Female	Beginner	High
459	43	Male	Intermediate	Low
460	28	Non-binary	Expert	High

Figure 8.38: SurveysData and the first five columns visible in the secondary preview

Transforming tables

Nested tables are tables contained within another table that enable the storage, manipulation, addition, removal, and selection of data. As explained at the start of this chapter, even though many table transformations are available from within the UI, they cannot be invoked on a nested table structure. To overcome this limitation, we have provided *strategies for transitioning to code, methods for complex multistep value transformation,* and *techniques for transforming values within a table*; these sections are prerequisites for what comes next. Let us emphasize that although the add-custom-column method is often applied for demonstration, validation, and the enhancement of your learning experience, it is not necessarily the best approach.

Extracting a cell value

The drill-down action into a single cell of a table will produce one of two syntax variants, depending on whether or not your table has keys. Regardless, to obtain a value from a specific intersection within a table, the following method will always work. First, select the row (1) by applying *item access*. Then, look up the column (2), applying *field selection*. This method is demonstrated in *Figure 8.39*. To safeguard the expression, you can make these selections optional by appending a question mark, ?.

For example, to extract the survey start date for each wave without expanding the full nested table, follow these steps:

1. Create a new blank query or reference the SurveysData query: = SurveysData

2. Select **Add custom column** from the menu that appears when you click on the mini table icon in the top-left corner of the table (3)

3. Enter this code into the formula section: `[Results]{0}?[SurveyStartDate]?`

The result is shown in the following screenshot:

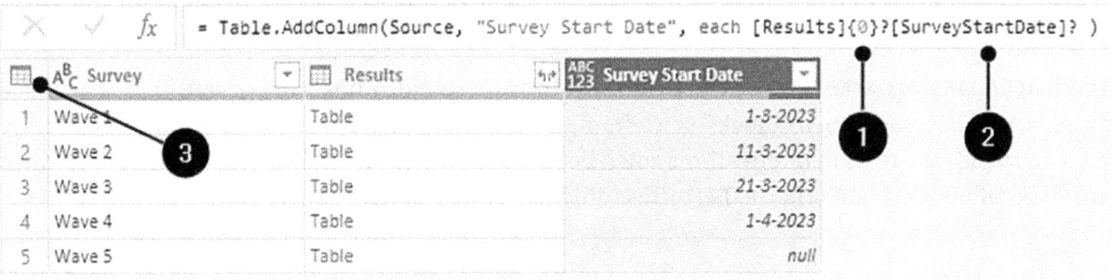

Figure 8.39: Applying item and field access to a table

What is happening here? `[Results]{0}` is the initial part of the code. It attempts to retrieve the first row (index 0) from the table in the `Results` column. However, if the table is empty, as in the case with the row corresponding to `Wave5`, this operation results in an error because there's no row to access. By adding a question mark (?) like so: `[Results]{0}?`, the selection becomes optional. If the requested row is missing, instead of an error, a `null` value is returned. This is crucial for ensuring the code doesn't fail when encountering null values or empty tables.

The next part, `[Results]{0}?[SurveyStartDate]`, builds upon the previous operation. It tries to access a field named `SurveyStartDate` from the row retrieved by `[Results]{0}?`. However, if `[Results]{0}?` returns `null` (indicating an empty table or missing row), attempting to access `SurveyStartDate` would lead to an error. This is because the operation tries to extract a field from a `null` value instead of a record. Hence, the inclusion of the second question mark (?) at the end makes accessing the `SurveyStartDate` field optional as well, thereby preventing errors if the initial part yields a `null` or the field is not present in the record. This methodical approach ensures the query remains error-free even when dealing with missing, incomplete, or mismatching data.

This technique for extracting a cell's value can be useful in certain data transformation scenarios. Imagine your raw data comes with a page header that contains an element that needs to be included in the final output. This allows you to do so. A practical example of such a requirement is included in *Chapter 14, Troublesome Data Patterns*.

There is one M function that can extract a cell's value, `Table.FirstValue`; however, it can only obtain the value in the first column and row of a table or return a specified default. Of course, there are functions that can return a single record from a table, such as `Table.First` or `Table.Last`. When combined with field access, they also allow you to obtain a specific cell value. Moreover, it's important to keep in mind that the effectiveness of these functions increases when combined with other functions that resize or filter tables.

Resizing a table in length

List and table functions share many similarities, and so there are also table functions with the ability to modify the size of a table without accessing or changing values in each row. They achieve this by returning a new table with fewer or more rows based on an offset or count. Among them are Table.Skip, Table.FirstN, Table.Range, Table.RemoveLastN, and Table.Repeat. In this section, we will focus on Table.RemoveFirstN and Table.AlternateRows. These functions help to manipulate a table's size.

The functions Table.RemoveFirstN and Table.Skip are essentially interchangeable. Both are useful for eliminating unwanted, or "junk," rows from the top of a table. These functions offer flexibility; you can specify the rows to remove. This could be just the first row, a predetermined number of rows, or rows that meet certain criteria. Let's illustrate this with an example query:

```
let
    Source = SurveysData,
    Step1 = Table.AddColumn(Source, "NoCountOrCondition",
        each Table.RemoveFirstN([Results])),
    Step2 = Table.AddColumn(Step1, "Count",
        each Table.RemoveFirstN([Results], 2)),
    Step3 = Table.AddColumn(Step2, "Condition",
        each Table.RemoveFirstN([Results], each [Age] < 45 ))
in
    Step3
```

Figure 8.40 presents the first two columns of the results from Wave 1, shown on the far left of the figure. To remove only the top row, you can omit the countOrCondition parameter, which is the second argument in this function. This approach is illustrated in the second example from the left. Alternatively, when you need to remove a specific number of top rows, you can pass a one-based count as a second argument. For instance, to remove the first two rows, you would pass the number 2. This scenario is depicted in the third example from the left. Another option is to use a condition-based approach. Here, you can specify a condition, such as age < 45, to remove rows that meet this criterion until a row does not satisfy the condition. The first row that fails to meet the condition becomes the new top row of the table. This method is demonstrated in the example on the far right:

Wave 1, first 2 cols

RespondentID	Age
456	30
457	52
458	24
459	43
460	28

NoCountOrCondition

RespondentID	Age
457	52
458	24
459	43
460	28

Count

RespondentID	Age
458	24
459	43
460	28

Condition

RespondentID	Age
457	52
458	24
459	43
460	28

Figure 8.40: Wave 1 return values for the RespondentID columns

Table.AlternateRows is another useful function, similar to List.Alternate in functionality but differing in the type of values it processes. One aspect to be aware of is the fact that their parameter order is not the same, an inconsistency worth noting.

Like its list counterpart, Table.AlternateRows filters data according to a repetitive row pattern. Practical use cases include:

- **Sampling or data reduction:** In large datasets, it can be used to obtain a representative sample for initial query development or preliminary analysis.
- **Removing redundant headers after combining data:** Limited to cases where headers are repeated at fixed intervals.
- **Filtering out noise:** When encountering periodic interference in data, like when every nth row is a maintenance or calibration check.

Table.AlternateRows takes a table, an offset, a skip count, and an extract count, which indicates how many rows to take or keep each time. The offset is zero-based and both counts are one-based; all arguments are required. Let's apply this function to our survey data to gain a better understanding of what that means. Consider this query:

```
let
    Source = SurveysData,
    Step1 = Table.AddColumn(Source, "V1",
        each Table.AlternateRows([Results], 0, 1, 1)),
    Step2 = Table.AddColumn(Step1, "V2",
        each Table.AlternateRows([Results], 1, 0, 1)),
    Step3 = Table.AddColumn(Step2, "V3",
        each Table.AlternateRows([Results], 1, 1, 0 )),
    Step4 = Table.AddColumn(Step3, "V4",
        each Table.AlternateRows([Results], 1, 1, 1 ))
in
    Step4
```

It generates the output depicted in the following figure for the first record of the table, which is Wave 1. This time, the view is restricted to only showing the initial column:

Wave 1, col1	Step1, col V1	Step2, col V2	Step3, col V3	Step4, col V4
RespondentID	RespondentID	RespondentID	RespondentID	RespondentID
456	457	456	456	456
457	459	457		458
458		458		460
459		459		
460		460		

Figure 8.41: Wave 1 return values for like-named steps and columns. View limited to the first column

To understand each output depicted in *Figure 8.41*, let's examine Step 1: Table.AlternateRows([Results], 0, 1, 1). Apply this pattern for each argument value in the input table ([Results]): begin at the top row (offset position 0), skip 1 row, keep 1 row, and repeat this pattern for all remaining rows in the table. Now apply this pattern and fill in the argument values to understand the return values for the other columns on your own.

Resizing a table in width

Resizing a table can involve adjusting both its rows and columns. For instances where you need a specific number of columns – let's say the first three – projection is a useful technique. It allows you to create a table with fewer columns. This method is efficient and comes with the ability to make column or field selection optional, protecting the expression as demonstrated in *Chapter 6, Structured Values*.

The UI-invoked operation **Remove Columns** triggers the Table.RemoveColumns function. Meanwhile, **Choose Columns** and **Remove Other Columns** both call the Table.SelectColumns function. These functions are all equipped with a MissingField.Type as an optional third parameter. This enumeration dictates how the function behaves when a column listed in its second parameter, columns, is missing or does not exist.

Choosing between these functions depends on the specific requirements of your data transformation task and the nature of your data source. For instance, the likelihood of changing columns is far greater in an Excel data source than in a database. Therefore, it's important to consider if column changes are to be expected over time and how they should be handled. Do new columns have to be included automatically? What impact would that have on subsequent transformations or even further downstream?

Let's explore both methods; consider this query:

```
let
    Source = SurveysData,
    Step1 = Table.AddColumn(Source, "V1", each
    Table.SelectColumns(
        [Results],
        {"RespondentID", "Age", "Gender", "Country"} )),
    Step2 = Table.AddColumn(Source, "V2", each
    Table.SelectColumns(
        [Results],
        {"RespondentID", "Age", "Gender", "Country"},
        MissingField.Ignore )),
    Step3 = Table.AddColumn(Source, "V3", each
    Table.SelectColumns(
        [Results],
        {"RespondentID", "Age", "Gender", "Country"},
        MissingField.UseNull ))
in
    Step3
```

To limit a table to a specific subset of columns, `Table.SelectColumns` can be leveraged. It explicitly lists columns to retain; note that newly added columns in the data source won't be included without manually updating the query (see *Step1*). Furthermore, by default, an error will be raised if any of the listed column names do not correspond to actual column names in the table:

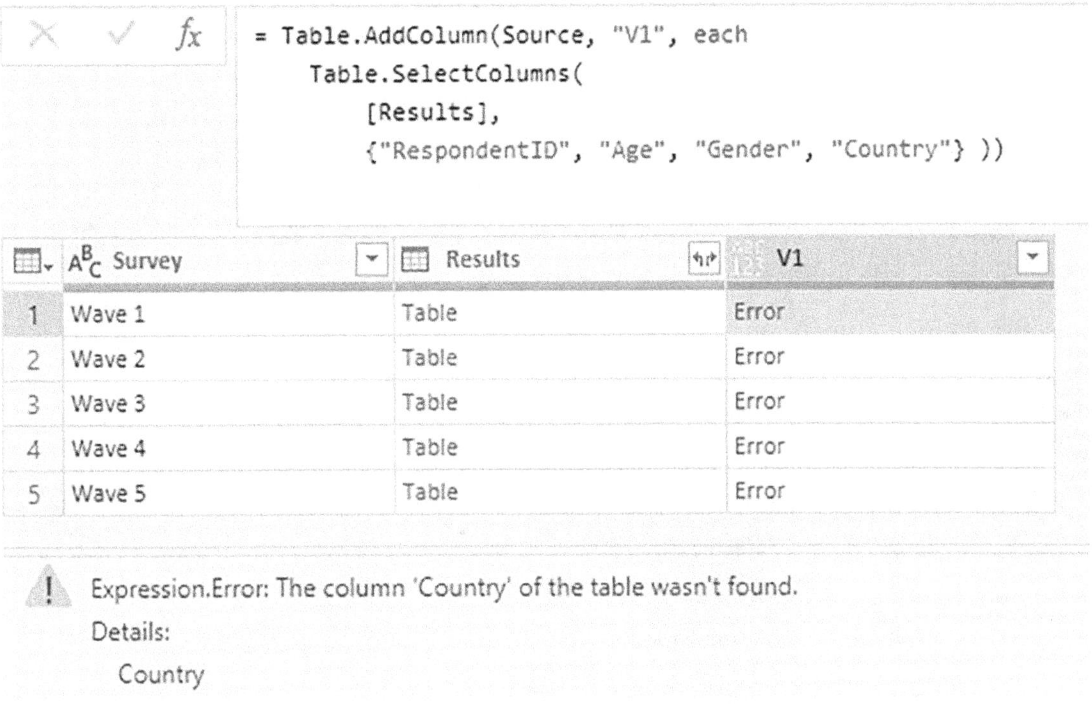

```
= Table.AddColumn(Source, "V1", each
      Table.SelectColumns(
          [Results],
          {"RespondentID", "Age", "Gender", "Country"} ))
```

	A^BC Survey		Results		V1	
1	Wave 1		Table		Error	
2	Wave 2		Table		Error	
3	Wave 3		Table		Error	
4	Wave 4		Table		Error	
5	Wave 5		Table		Error	

⚠ Expression.Error: The column 'Country' of the table wasn't found.

Details:

Country

Figure 8.42: Selecting a column that does not exist raises an error

When you use `Table.SelectColumns` together with the `MissingField` type set to `MissingField.Ignore` (refer to *Step2* and *Figure 8.43*), the function behaves differently. If any column names specified in the list do not match the columns in the table, they will be silently excluded without generating an error. However, this approach can lead to issues in subsequent query steps, especially if they rely on a field that is unexpectedly missing.

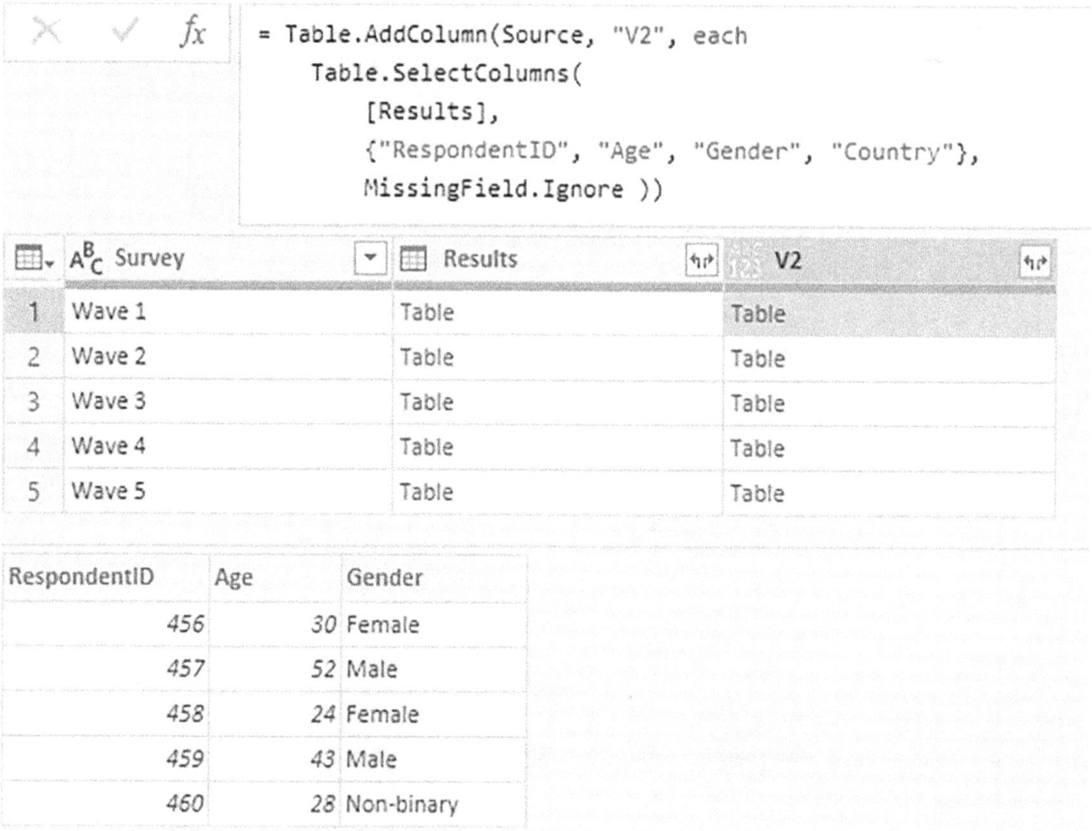

```
    ×    ✓    ƒx        = Table.AddColumn(Source, "V2", each
                            Table.SelectColumns(
                                [Results],
                                {"RespondentID", "Age", "Gender", "Country"},
                                MissingField.Ignore ))
```

	ABC Survey	▾	Results	⯇⯈	V2	⯇⯈
1	Wave 1		Table		Table	
2	Wave 2		Table		Table	
3	Wave 3		Table		Table	
4	Wave 4		Table		Table	
5	Wave 5		Table		Table	

RespondentID	Age	Gender
456	30	Female
457	52	Male
458	24	Female
459	43	Male
460	28	Non-binary

Figure 8.43: MissingField.Ignore prevents the error and returns all valid columns

When the `MissingField` type is set to `MissingField.UseNull` within `Table.SelectColumns` (refer to *Step3* and *Figure 8.44*), the function includes all specified columns in the output. This includes those that do not correspond to an actual column in the table. In such cases, non-existent columns are included and will contain `null` values, without causing an error. However, be aware that this could lead to complications in later stages of the query, especially in calculations or transformations that depend on the values of these fields.

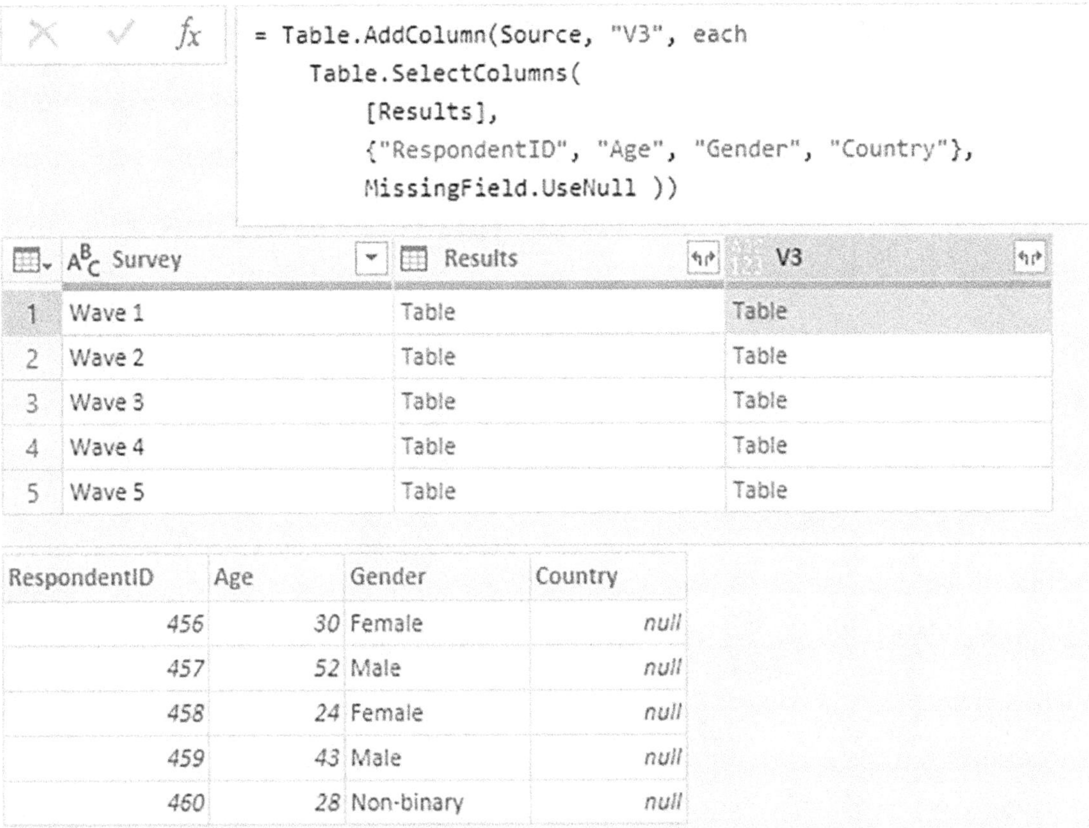

```
  ✕    ✓    fx     = Table.AddColumn(Source, "V3", each
                        Table.SelectColumns(
                           [Results],
                           {"RespondentID", "Age", "Gender", "Country"},
                           MissingField.UseNull ))
```

⊞▾	A^BC Survey	▾ ⊞ Results	⇥	⊞ V3	⇥
1	Wave 1	Table		Table	
2	Wave 2	Table		Table	
3	Wave 3	Table		Table	
4	Wave 4	Table		Table	
5	Wave 5	Table		Table	

RespondentID	Age	Gender	Country
456	30	Female	null
457	52	Male	null
458	24	Female	null
459	43	Male	null
460	28	Non-binary	null

Figure 8.44: MissingField.UseNull prevents the error and returns all selected columns

Finally, you can opt to remove a specific subset of columns with Table.RemoveColumns, as shown in the following code. This function explicitly lists columns to remove; any new columns coming from the data source are automatically included in the output. Needless to say, this can result in retaining unnecessary columns unless the query is manually updated. Using this function with MissingField types like MissingField.UseNull or MissingField.Ignore prevents errors when specified columns in the second parameter are absent.

Of course, depending on transformations further downstream, automatically including new columns may cause problems.

```
let
    Source = SurveysData,
    Step1 = Table.AddColumn(Source, "V1", each
    Table.RemoveColumns(
        [Results],
        {"Age", "Gender", "Country"} )),
    Step2 = Table.AddColumn(Source, "V2", each
    Table.RemoveColumns(
        [Results],
        {"Age", "Gender", "Country"},
        MissingField.Ignore )),
    Step3 = Table.AddColumn(Source, "V3", each
    Table.RemoveColumns(
        [Results],
        {"Age", "Gender", "Country"},
        MissingField.UseNull ))
in
    Step3
```

Of course, there are dynamic approaches to selecting columns. In some scenarios, such techniques can significantly enhance the robustness of your queries and minimize maintenance needs.

Filtering tables

Select or filter operations can reduce the number of rows in a table based on their field value, such as `Table.SelectRowsWithErrors`, `Table.FindText`, and `Table.SelectRows`. The latter is one of the most used functions in the M language and is commonly invoked through the UI. The second parameter is a condition as a function; however, before we get ahead of ourselves, it's time to cover the basics.

Filtering a table using the UI is generally straightforward, but it's important to remember that you're likely not seeing the full picture. That is because the UI displays the top 1,000 rows in the preview pane. As a result, the variety within a column can be greater than depicted inside the filter selection area. *Figure 8.45* illustrates this; you can enter the following code directly into the formula bar of a new blank query to generate the sample data:

```
= Table.FromColumns(
        {List.Repeat({"High"}, 999) & {"Medium", "Low"}}
    )
```

When looking at the column header drop-down menu from Column1, it displays two distinct values (**High** and **Medium**), even though three (**High**, **Medium**, and **Low**) are present, as shown in *Figure 8.45*. When you deselect **High** and press **OK** to review all other remaining values, only **Medium** shows up and not **Low**. That's because the M code generated by this action was translated to: ([Column1] = "Medium") contrary to what you might have expected, something like ([Column1] <> "High").

In all honesty, we were warned: a message saying *List may be incomplete.* and a *Load more* option were displayed. Keep in mind that depending on the amount of data, you may see that message more than once.

However, the UI also provides filters specific to the type of data within that column. For text columns, placing your cursor on **Text Filters** will reveal options such as **Equals, Begins With, Ends With, Contains**, and their negations. These options vary for number and date type columns, offering a set of filter choices appropriate for those data types.

To further explore filtering, first remove the **Filtered Rows** step by clicking the **x** in front of its name in the **Applied Steps** pane. Now let's apply a **Text Filter** instead, by selecting **Does Not Equal** from the options. This opens the **Filter Rows** dialog box. Here, you can enter **High** and click **OK**; now the result aligns with our expectations, and moreover, the M code accurately reflects that: ([Column1] <> "High").

The **Filter Rows** dialog box features an **Advanced** setting that allows you to define complex combined filter conditions. However, it does not provide control over operator precedence, which determines the order in which individual operators are evaluated.

In the M language, logical and is evaluated before logical or, but a parenthesized expression can be used to alter this default precedence:

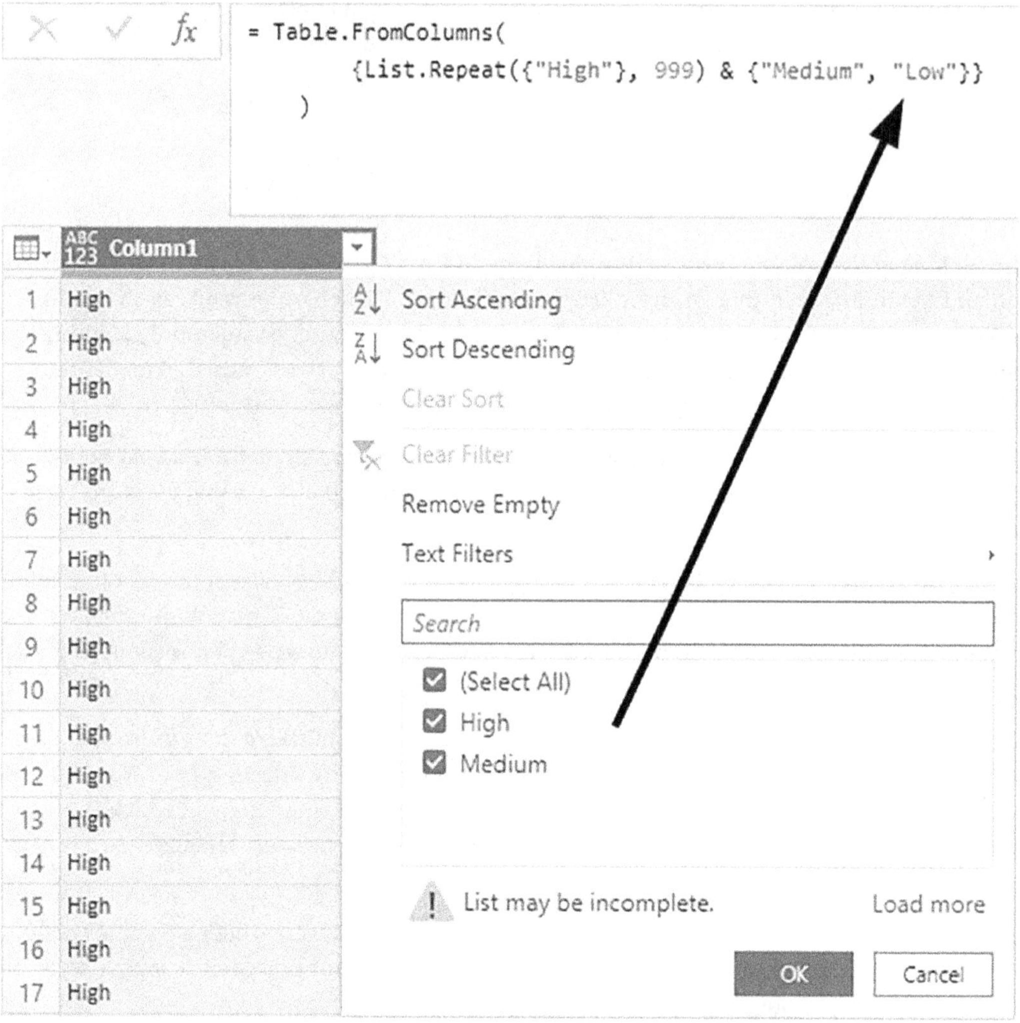

Figure 8.45: The List may be incomplete. message, indicating that not all distinct values within the column are shown

Now that we know this, let's examine the second parameter of the Table.SelectRows function. That parameter expects a condition, essentially a logical test, as a function. When that expression evaluates to true, the row passes the criteria and is kept; if it returns false, the row is excluded from the output.

Take a look at the criteria in *Figure 8.46*. We will apply direct comparisons to specific column values, meaning the ExperienceLevel column should only include rows with the values Intermediate or Expert. Similarly, the OverallQuality, EaseOfUse, and WouldRecommend columns should correspond to the values High, Good, and Yes, respectively. To begin, create a reference to the SurveysData query:

ExperienceLevel	OverallQuality	EaseOfUse	WouldRecommend
Intermediate	High	Good	Yes
Expert	High	Good	Yes

Figure 8.46: Multiple filter criteria

Here is the M code used to transform each nested table. Notice how the parenthesized expression is used to modify the evaluation of the default operator precedence:

```
let
    Source = SurveysData,
    SelectRows = Table.TransformColumns( Source, {{"Results", each
        Table.SelectRows( _, each
            (
                [ExperienceLevel] = "Intermediate"
                or [ExperienceLevel] = "Expert"
            )
            and [OverallQuality] = "High"
            and [EaseOfUse] = "Good"
            and [WouldRecommend] = "Yes"
        ) }} )
in
    SelectRows
```

To eliminate the possibility of bias and ensure the accuracy of complex filters, incorporating a validation step can be considered. Although adding a column may seem contrary to best practices, it offers significant benefits as a development aid, enabling the fine-tuning of filter criteria and the verification of results before transferring the filter logic to a SelectRows step. Furthermore, you can prevent this ValidateFilter step from being executed at runtime by ensuring that it is not referenced by any other step and is not the last step in your query. When you adhere to this, there is no impact on performance. Follow these steps:

1. Open the **Advanced Editor** window.
2. Copy the SelectRows step, including its identifier.
3. Go to the Source step and move the cursor to the end of the line.
4. Press *Enter*.
5. Paste the code.
6. Add a comma after the closing parenthesis.
7. Change the step identifier to ValidateFilter.
8. Replace Table.SelectRows with Table.AddColumn.

9. After the table input, which is the underscore, enter a comma and provide a new column name: "Validation". Click **Done**.

```
let
   Source = SurveysData,
   ValidateFilter = Table.TransformColumns( Source, {{"Results", each
     Table.AddColumn( _, "Validation", each
          (
              [ExperienceLevel] = "Intermediate"
              or [ExperienceLevel] = "Expert"
          )
          and [OverallQuality] = "High"
          and [EaseOfUse] = "Good"
          and [WouldRecommend] = "Yes"
     ) }} ),
   SelectRows = Table.TransformColumns( Source, {{"Results", each
     Table.SelectRows( _, each
          (
              [ExperienceLevel] = "Intermediate"
              or [ExperienceLevel] = "Expert"
          )
          and [OverallQuality] = "High"
          and [EaseOfUse] = "Good"
          and [WouldRecommend] = "Yes"
     ) }} )
in
   SelectRows
```

10. Select the `ValidateFilter` step and inspect the outcome for each nested table; *Figure 8.47* shows the criteria and `Validation` columns for `Wave 1`.

ExperienceLevel	OverallQuality	EaseOfUse	WouldRecommend	Validation
Intermediate	High	Good	Yes	*TRUE*
Expert	Medium	Good	Yes	*FALSE*
Beginner	High	Excellent	Yes	*FALSE*
Intermediate	Low	Average	No	*FALSE*
Expert	High	Good	Yes	*TRUE*

Figure 8.47: The ValidateFilter step shows a Validation column

In addition, nested tables are not exclusively provided by external sources; they can also be the result of another transformation to solve more complex data transformation scenarios. For example, they can be used when looking for an approximate match, a common requirement when dealing with volume or price discounts. What makes these types of transformations more intricate is the need to access fields from both the outer and inner tables, which introduces scope, covered in *Chapter 7, Conceptualizing M*, of this book.

Approximate match

Let's examine the data in *Figure 8.48*. It shows two tables: SalesData, which contains sales orders, and DiscountRates. Depending on an order's total value, a discount may be applicable. These tables cannot be merged because there is no shared key between them. Consider this query:

```
let
    SalesData = Table.FromRows(
        {
            {"ORD-123", 149},
            {"ORD-124", 650},
            {"ORD-125", 749},
            {"ORD-126", 543},
            {"ORD-127", 324},
            {"ORD-128", 1685},
            {"ORD-129", 750},
            {"ORD-130", 999}
        },
        type table [OrderID=text, Total Value=number]
    ),
    DiscountRates = Table.Buffer( Table.FromColumns(
        {
            {750, 1500},
            {0.02, 0.05}
        },
        type table [Value=number, Discount=number]
    )),
    AddNetValue = Table.AddColumn( SalesData,
        "Net Value",
        each [Total Value] * ((1-List.Last(Table.SelectRows(DiscountRates,
 (row)=> row[Value] <=[Total Value])[Discount])) ?? 1), type number
    )
in
    AddNetValue
```

Here, we add a new column named Net Value to the SalesData table. For audit reasons, we will keep the Total Value column unchanged. That new column value will be calculated by finding the relevant discount rate in the DiscountRates table for each row in SalesData and applying that to Total Value. This calculation will yield Net Value after discount. If no discount is applicable, Net Value will be the same as the original Total Value.

SalesData

	A^B_C OrderID	1.2 Total Value
1	ORD-123	149
2	ORD-124	650
3	ORD-125	749
4	ORD-126	543
5	ORD-127	324
6	ORD-128	1685
7	ORD-129	750
8	ORD-130	999

DiscountRates

	1.2 Value	1.2 Discount
1	750	0,02
2	1500	0,05

Figure 8.48: SalesData and DiscountRate sample

This is demonstrated in the AddNetValue step; here's a breakdown:

- each [Total Value] refers to the value in the Total Value column of the outer SalesData table, applicable to the current row.
- Table.SelectRows(DiscountRates, (row)=> row[Value] <= [Total Value]) filters the inner DiscountRates table to keep rows where the value is less than or equal to Total Value for the current row in the outer SalesData.
- [Discount] extracts the Discount column from the filtered table, as a list.
- List.Last() retrieves the last value from this Discount list.
- (1 -) ?? 1 subtracts the Discount value from 1; when there is no discount (i.e., if the Discount value is null), it defaults to 1 (meaning no discount).

To-table conversions

We have laid the groundwork for you to become more familiar with functions and transformations in M. Our aim is to encourage a transition from relying solely on the UI to being able to read, understand, modify, and write expressions independently. Many table transformation functions are accessible through the UI and ready for you to explore. Specifically, we have focused on functions that transform, extract, resize, and select data within nested tables, using various methods.

To benefit even more from these techniques, it's important to understand the available conversions from structured values to tables. These conversions allow more sophisticated and complex transformations, providing you with the capability to construct tables from different types of values. In the following section, we'll highlight some of the most commonly used conversions.

Record-to-table conversion

Our first focus is on the conversion of a table row. Each row in a table is essentially a record, and this record can be transformed into a two-column table. In this new table, the first column is called Name and contains all field names from the record. The second column, named Value, contains the corresponding field values from the record. The following screenshot illustrates this:

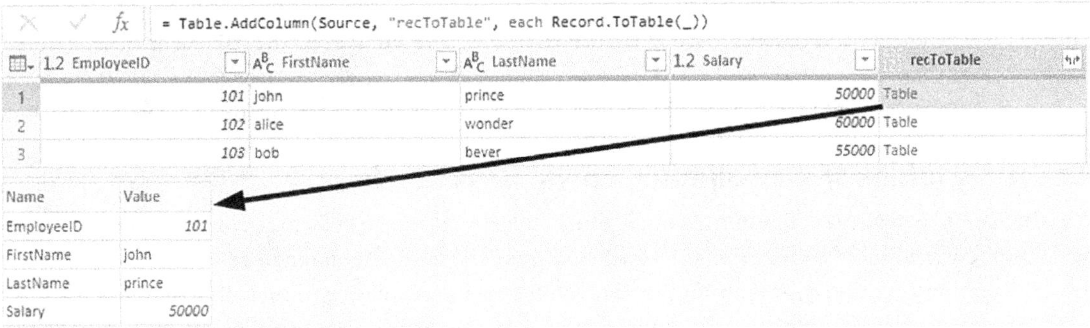

Figure 8.49: Preview of the Record.ToTable output when applied to each row in a table

This transformation is particularly useful when you need the standard functionality that a table function provides, but there's no similar function for lists or records. Take, for instance, the table functions that fill values vertically, up or down a column. There's no direct equivalent for spreading values horizontally, across a row, from left to right or vice versa. But, by converting each row (a record) into a table with Record.ToTable (as shown in *Figure 8.49*), you can work around that limitation.

Have a look at the following code:

```
let
    Source = Table.FromRows({
        {null, 2023, null, null, null, 2024},
        {"Branch", "Q1", "Q2", "Q3", "Q4", "Q1"},
        {"BU1", 463, 582, 325, 487, 582},
        {"BU2", 264, 384, 201, 298, 275}
    }),
    FillRight = Table.AddColumn(Source, "Rec to tbl", each
        if [Column1] is null
        then Record.FromTable( Table.FillDown( Record.ToTable(_), {"Value"}))
        else _),
    ToTable = Table.FromRecords( FillRight[Rec to tbl] )
in
    ToTable
```

This query shows a creative method to fill values horizontally, spreading them across a row inside the table, a functionality not directly available in standard table functions.

This process begins by creating a table, Source, with various data points, including null values that need to be filled. The key part of the query is the FillRight step, where we add a new column, Rec to tbl. In this column, for each row, we check if the first column (Column1) is null. It's only for this row that we need to use a fill-right operation. If it is null, we convert the row into a table using Record. ToTable, and then apply the Table.FillDown function to the Value column. This action fills the null values horizontally across the row.

In rows where Column1 is not null, we leave the row as is. The final step, ToTable, transforms these table objects back into a single table. The result is a table where horizontal gaps (null values) in each row are filled with the value from the left, replicating the fill-down functionality in a horizontal manner.

Creating tables from columns, rows, or records

Another useful category of functions is those that convert a table into columns, rows, or records, along with their counterpart "to" functions. These functions are among the most used in custom advanced transformation scenarios. A common pattern you'll encounter involves converting a table into a list of columns, rows, or records, applying some transformative techniques, and then reassembling these elements back into a table format.

There are numerous examples within this book that use these functions and follow this pattern. To avoid repetition, detailed demonstrations are not included in this section. However, the next section, titled *Working with mixed structures*, will comprehensively cover applications for each of the Table.From functions.

Here's a brief description of the functions in the Table.From group:

- Table.FromColumns: This constructs a table from a list of column-value lists. An optional columns parameter can be included. The order of the list items determines the column order from the beginning to the end of the table. When column-value lists have varying lengths, null values are used to bridge the gap. Its counterpart is the Table.ToColumns function.

- Table.FromRows: This uses a list of single-row-value lists and an optional columns parameter. The value order within each nested list determines the value order across the columns of the table. All row-value lists must contain the same number of elements, if lists are of unequal length or an error is raised. Its counterpart is the Table.ToRows function.

- Table.FromRecords: This takes a list of records, and can include optional columns and missingField parameters. The order of records in the list defines the order of rows in the table. Its counterpart is the Table.ToRecords function.

Table information

The M language includes a set of functions specifically designed to provide information about a table's structure and contents. These functions include Table.ColumnCount, Table.RowCount, Table.IsEmpty, Table.Keys, Table.Profile, and Table.Schema. These can be helpful for certain data assessment and manipulation tasks.

For instance, to prevent errors and avoid unnecessary processing, you might need to confirm the presence of data in a table before performing complex transformations. Or, when integrating data from multiple sources, it's often important to compare the structures of different tables. There are situations where an append operation should only proceed if the schemas of the tables meet specific criteria, such as having matching column names, an identical number of columns, or columns of a particular type, while excluding or flagging others.

In this section, our primary focus will be on the Table.Profile function. But before delving into that, let's briefly explore Table.Schema. This function returns a schema of the input table, generating a row for each column in the input table. Each row provides detailed properties of a column, like the column's name, position, type, and other metadata. The following figure illustrates the first five columns of the output from Table.Schema, providing key information about the data:

	Name	Position	TypeName	Kind	IsNullable
1	RespondentID	0 Int64.Type	number		TRUE
2	Age	1 Int64.Type	number		TRUE
3	Gender	2 Text.Type	text		TRUE
4	ExperienceLevel	3 Text.Type	text		TRUE
5	OverallQuality	4 Text.Type	text		TRUE
6	EaseOfUse	5 Text.Type	text		TRUE
7	WouldRecommend	6 Text.Type	text		TRUE
8	SpecificFeedback	7 Text.Type	text		TRUE
9	SurveyStartDate	8 Date.Type	date		TRUE
10	SurveyEndDate	9 Date.Type	date		TRUE
11	UsageFrequency	10 Int64.Type	number		TRUE
12	SatisfactionScore	11 Int64.Type	number		TRUE

Figure 8.50: Partial view of the Table.Schema return values, providing insight into column properties

Table.Profile, on the other hand, generates a profile of the input table. For each column in the input table, a row is generated in the output table that provides information to assess the data in that column, such as its name, minimum and maximum values, count of unique values, and so on (see *Figure 8.51*), which is useful for summary statistics.

	Column	Min	Max	Average	StandardDeviation	Count	NullCount	DistinctCount
1	Age	24	52	35.4	11.69615321	5	0	5
2	EaseOfUse	Average	Good	null	null	5	0	3
3	ExperienceLevel	Beginner	Intermediate	null	null	5	0	3
4	Gender	Female	Non-binary	null	null	5	0	3
5	OverallQuality	High	Medium	null	null	5	0	3
6	RespondentID	456	460	458	1.58113883	5	0	5
7	SatisfactionScore	4	9	7	2	5	0	4
8	SpecificFeedback	Feature-rich and versatile	Well organized content	null	null	5	0	5
9	SurveyEndDate	10-3-2023	10-3-2023	10-3-2023	null	5	0	1
10	SurveyStartDate	1-3-2023	1-3-2023	1-3-2023	null	5	0	1
11	UsageFrequency	2	7	4.6	2.073644135	5	0	5
12	WouldRecommend	No	Yes	null	null	5	0	2

Figure 8.51: View of Table.Profile's return values, which help to assess column data

More importantly, data validation can accommodate specific needs not included in the default output. This is possible by expanding Table.Profile with additional aggregates through its optional second parameter.

This parameter is a list containing nested lists, one for each column to be added to its output. Each of these nested lists should in sequence contain these three elements:

1. **New column name:** This is the name of the additional column to be added to the default output. It's advisable to provide a name that is descriptive and helps users understand the metric it represents.

2. **Type check function:** A simple expression like each true ensures that the aggregation function will be applied to all columns, regardless of type. However, if you want to limit the aggregation function to columns of a specific type, you need to supply a function that tests each value. For instance, Type.Is(_, type number) will identify columns of type number.

3. **Aggregation function:** When a column fails the type check (2), this returns a null, and the evaluation of the aggregation function is skipped. For columns that pass the type check, this aggregation function is invoked.

The following query incorporates three such aggregate columns:

```
let
  Source = Table.FromColumns(
    {List.Numbers(1, 200, 1) & {null, "text", null, null}},
    type table [myNumber = number] // ascribing a type
  ),
  getProfile = Table.Profile( Source,
    {
      {
        "count of Elements",
        each Type.Is(_, type number),
        each List.Count(_)
      },
      {
        "count No Nulls",
        each Type.Is(_, type number),
        each List.NonNullCount(_)
      },
      {
        "raise Type Error",
        each Type.Is(_, type number),
        each List.NonNullCount(List.Transform(_, Number.From))
      },
      {
        "count of Numbers",
        each Type.Is(_, type number),
        each List.Count(List.Select(_, (x) =>
          Type.Is(Value.Type(x), type number)))
```

```
      )
    }
  }
),
demoteHeaders = Table.DemoteHeaders(getProfile),
transposeTable = Table.Transpose(demoteHeaders)
in
transposeTable
```

This query produces a one-column-wide table; we transposed its output, as you can see in *Figure 8.52*. The added aggregations contain a condition that checks whether or not a column is of type number. Since the myNumber column has been ascribed the number type, it passes the type check function and the aggregation function is executed.

Understanding the value an aggregation returns is important, as it influences how functions handle data. To make validating the results easy, we will only count items. Take List.Count, for example: this function does not have to access any of the list items to determine the number of elements within a list. It returns the same number as the table row count, 204, as seen on line 9 in the following figure:

	ABC 123 Column1	ABC 123 Column2
1	Column	myNumber
2	Min	1
3	Max	text
4	Average	Error
5	StandardDeviation	Error
6	Count	204
7	NullCount	3
8	DistinctCount	202
9	count of Elements	204
10	count No Nulls	201
11	raise Type Error	Error
12	count of Numbers	200

Figure 8.52: Additional aggregates to Table.Profile

On the other hand, List.NonNullCount accesses all of the list items as it needs to determine whether a list item is something other than null. This returns a count of 201, as seen on line 10 of *Figure 8.52*. But was that number expected?

It depends on whether we should or should not consider the type of value counted in the list. After all, the list contains a text value, even though the column has been ascribed a number type. Knowing that the base query (in the Source step) will raise a type conversion error at query execution time if loaded separately into the data model, you can choose to raise the error in the profile as well, as seen on line *11*, or only count list items that convert to a number, as shown on line *12* of *Figure 8.52*.

These are important considerations and distinctions when adding additional aggregates to the `Table.`
`Profile` function.

Generally speaking, there is a significant degree of similarity between list and table functions, and
most are named in an easy-to-understand and consistent manner. This means you can quickly expand
your knowledge of M functions by familiarizing yourself with the naming convention and syntax. The
substantial overlap also means there is no need to learn all available functions by heart.

Working with mixed structures

This section focuses on structured values that contain structures of a different type. Although a wide
range of scenarios is possible, we cannot possibly illustrate them all; however, this section should
provide enough insight into how to tackle the most common challenges you are likely to encounter.

Lists of tables, lists, or records

As demonstrated earlier, handling a list of items that share a consistent structure and are grouped
together can easily be managed and converted to a table. This approach is incredibly powerful and
applies equally to working with a single column in a table or converting lists in every table row in a
table to reshape the data.

Let's explore the first scenario, dealing with columns that contain structured values. Imagine a table
organized in the following manner:

- Table values
- List of lists, where each inner list represents column values
- List of lists, where each inner list represents row values
- List of records, where each record represents a table row

Consider this query, which will generate such a table:

```
let
  Source = #table(
    {"Tables", "ColumnLists", "RowLists", "Records"},
    {
      {
        #table(2, {{1, 2}, {3, 4}}),
        {{1, 3}, {2, 4}},
        {{1, 2}, {3, 4}},
        {[C1 = 1, C2 = 2], [C1 = 3, C2 = 4]}
      },
      {
        #table(3, {{5, 6, 7}, {8, 9, 0}}),
        {{5, 8}, {6, 9}, {7, 0}},
        {{5, 6, 7}, {8, 9, 0}},
        {[C1 = 5, C2 = 6, C3 = 7], [C1 = 8, C2 = 9, C3 = 0]}
```

```
        }
      }
   )
 in
   Source
```

In most scenarios, a generic pattern can be applied to convert a column containing structured values into a single table. Here's what that base pattern entails:

- Drill down into the column containing the structured value, to extract it as a list.
- Transform each list item into a table using the appropriate `Table.From` function.
- Use `Table.Combine` to combine all tables in the list into a single table.

The exception to this pattern is when you are dealing with a column of tables. In such a case, a combine operation suffices, bypassing the need for a conversion step.

Let's put theory into practice and apply these steps to the sample data:

1. Drill down into the `Tables` column. This yields a list of tables; inside the formula bar, you'll find this expression: `Source[Tables]`

2. This list of tables can be combined, stacking all of the tables on top of each other to form a single table by wrapping `Table.Combine` around it, as illustrated here:

   ```
   listOfTables = Table.Combine(Source[Tables])
   ```

   To continue practicing, you can either remove the step to revert back to `Source`, or insert a manual step by clicking the **fx** next to the formula bar and replacing the variable that is returned by the `Source` variable, like so: `= Source`

3. Drilling down into any of the other columns will yield a list of lists. These can be transformed into tables. For the `ColumnLists` column, that means transforming each list item with the `Table.FromColumns` function first to place the column lists side by side, forming a table, before combining them, as demonstrated here:

   ```
   listOfColumnLists = Table.Combine(
       List.Transform(Source[ColumnLists], each Table.FromColumns(_)))
   ```

4. Similarly, the `listOfRowLists` and `listsOfRecords` variables transform list items by stacking them on top of each other to form rows in a table, before combining the tables:

   ```
   listOfRowLists = Table.Combine(
       List.Transform(Source[RowLists], each Table.FromRows(_))),
   listsOfRecords = Table.Combine(
       List.Transform(Source[Records], each Table.FromRecords(_)))
   ```

In these examples, we have consequently extracted a single column; basically, that means that all other data from the primary table is lost. Of course, there are cases where this is perfectly fine and just what is needed, but you are also likely to encounter scenarios where data from the primary table has to be retained. In such cases, you can apply the transform operation to each row of the table and follow that with an expand column operation. That will widen and expand the primary table to include new columns and rows for the selected fields from the nested table. This may lead to the duplication of primary table fields.

We will reuse ColumnLists from the previous example to illustrate how the base pattern changes in these types of scenarios:

- Selecting a method to transform values in a table. We will demonstrate using the Table.TransformColumns function to transform the ColumnLists column.
- Passing the function to the Source table as the first argument and transformOperations as a list. {{"ColumnLists", each Table.FromColumns(_) }} specifies the column name as well as the transformation to apply to each row in the table.
- Using the expand column option, depicted by sideways arrows, in the ColumnLists column header and select all columns; optionally check or uncheck **Use original column name as prefix**.

The following query reflects the steps described earlier:

```
let
    Source = Table.FromColumns(
        {
            {"A", "B"},
            {"a", "b"},
            {{{1, 3}, {2, 4}}, {{5, 8}, {6, 9}, {7, 0}}}
        }, {"Field1", "Field2", "ColumnLists"}
    ),
    Transform = Table.TransformColumns( Source,
        {{"ColumnLists", each Table.FromColumns(_) }}
    ),
    ExpandColumnLists = Table.ExpandTableColumn( Transform,
        "ColumnLists",
        {"Column1", "Column2", "Column3"},
        {"Column1", "Column2", "Column3"}
    )
in
    ExpandColumnLists
```

By default, an Expand Column operation will hard-code both the selected field names (the third argument) and the optional new column names (the fourth argument). Know that there are methods to make this dynamic.

Tables with lists, records, or tables

Table columns containing table, list, or record values usually show an **Expand Column** option in the column header. By default, this allows users to select fields from a table or record. For list columns, it provides the option to expand to new rows or to extract and concatenate all of the list items into a (delimited) string, as shown in *Figure 8.53*. That optional delimiter may be used in a subsequent step to split that column if required.

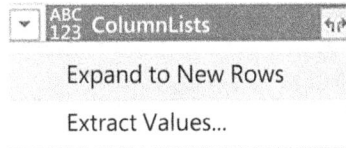

Figure 8.53: Showing list Expand Column options

These actions can all be performed through the UI and won't be covered in detail here. For scenarios that require a single item to be retrieved, optional field and item access can be applied as explained in detail in *Chapter 6, Structured Values*. Alternatively, functions can be used to obtain a value based on its position or on criteria, as demonstrated in previous sections of this chapter.

Expanding multiple list columns simultaneously was demonstrated in the *Working with lists* section. This involves joining them together to form a table. Multiple record columns may be expanded one by one; this will only widen the primary table by adding additional columns, but it will not expand the table by increasing the number of rows. Alternatively, records can be merged into a single record. Remember that if you opt for a merge, field names must be unique; otherwise, an overwrite operation will occur. This means field values from the left operand will be overwritten by like-named fields from the right operand, as illustrated in *Figure 8.54*:

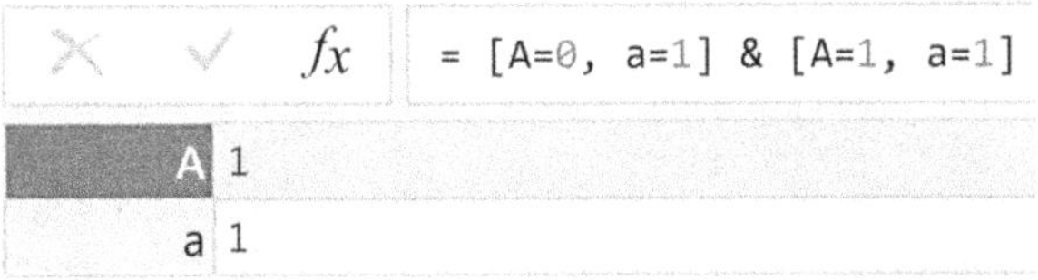

Figure 8.54: This record merge illustrates an overwrite operation

Expanding multiple table columns simultaneously is rare and may apply to cases where tables can be merged on a common index or key. Even more unique are cases where data aligns perfectly on a row-by-row basis and tables need to be stitched or joined together, side by side. A pattern to achieve this is illustrated here:

```
let
    allTables = {
        #table({"A", "B"}, {{1, 2}}),
        #table({"a", "b"}, {{3, 4}, {5, 6}}),
        #table({"x", "y"}, {{null, null}, {9, 0}})
    },
    allCols = List.Combine(
```

```
        List.Transform( allTables, Table.ToColumns )),
    allNames = List.Combine(
        List.Transform( allTables, Table.ColumnNames )),
    result = Table.FromColumns( allCols, allNames )
in
    result
```

It creates a single list, allCols, containing all column lists, and another list, allNames, with all column names. These are fed into the Table.FromColumns function to produce a table. Note that column names must be unique or an error will be raised.

Mixed structures

There is a wide range of data transformation needs; this next part introduces patterns that can aid in flattening and extracting data from structured data types.

Flatten all

Imagine you come across a table, or maybe one or a few columns in a table, where you find a jumble of different data types, kind of like what you see in *Figure 8.55*. It's not something you see every day. So, how would you go about extracting all the different values from these nested structures?

	ABC 123 Column1	ABC 123 Column2	ABC 123 Column3	ABC 123 Column4
1	List		List	List
2	List	List	Record	Record
3	21-1-2024		List	List
4	7-3-2024		List	List
5	List	List	Record	Record

Figure 8.55: Table with mixed types

Understanding methods to determine type and transform and convert values will go a long way. Essentially, this query transforms all cells within the table, depending on whether it's a list, a record, or another type of value:

```
let
    Source = #table(4, {
        {{"Let's", "go"}, "", {1, 2}, {"3".."9"}},
        {{null}, {true, true, false}, [a=1, b=2], [a=1, b=2]},
        {#date(2024, 1, 21), "", {1, 2}, {"3".."9"}},
        {#date(2024, 3, 7), "", {1, 2}, {"3".."9"}},
        {{null}, {true, true, false}, [a=1, b=2], [a=1, b=2]}
    }),
    getValues = Table.TransformColumns( Source, {}, each
        if Value.Is(_, type list)
        then Text.Combine( List.Transform(_, Text.From), ", ")
```

```
            else if Value.Is(_, type record)
            then Text.Combine( List.Transform(
                List.Zip({ Record.FieldNames(_), Record.ToList(_) }),
                    (x)=> Text.Combine({ x{0}, " = ", Text.From(x{1}) })
                ), ", ")
            else _ )
    in
        getValues
```

By leveraging the `Table.TransformColumns` default transformation, logic is applied to all columns of the `Source` table. We are providing three methods to handle a value:

- If the value is a list, it converts each item into text and combines them into a single text string separated by commas.
- If the value is a record, it converts each field in to a text string in the format "`field name = field value`" and combines these strings, separated by commas.
- However, when the value is neither a list nor a record, it leaves the value as is.

The output is shown in the following figure:

■▾	ABC 123 Column1 ▾	ABC 123 Column2 ▾	ABC 123 Column3 ▾	ABC 123 Column4 ▾
1	Let's, go		1, 2	3, 4, 5, 6, 7, 8, 9
2		true, true, false	a = 1, b = 2	a = 1, b = 2
3	21-1-2024		1, 2	3, 4, 5, 6, 7, 8, 9
4	7-3-2024		1, 2	3, 4, 5, 6, 7, 8, 9
5		true, true, false	a = 1, b = 2	a = 1, b = 2

Figure 8.56: The return value for the getValues step shows all data

Of course, there are many variants that can be derived from this pattern, such as extracting each initial or final item from a list or record, or selecting a number of record fields or list items based on a condition. Those techniques have all been illustrated in this chapter and can be incorporated here to meet your specific requirements, however exotic they may be.

Unpacking all record fields from lists

Often, data comes in nested formats, like records within lists. We have already seen how a list of records can be converted to a table, but what if you require a structured approach to extract and flatten this data, adding a new column to the outer table for each nested record field? Consider this pattern:

```
let
    Source = Table.FromColumns(
        {
            {1, 2},
            {
                {
                    [Tag = 2, Other = "text1"],
```

```
                    [Tag = 3, Other = "text2"],
                    [Tag = 4, Other = "text3"],
                    [Tag = 5, Other = "text4"]
                },
                {
                    [Tag = 9, Other = "textA"],
                    [Tag = 8, Other = "textB"],
                    [Tag = 7, Other = "textC"],
                    [Tag = 6, Other = "textD"]
                }
            }
        },
        type table [Key = number, Changes = list]
    ),
    PrefixNewColumnNamesWith = "Change ",
    ExtractRecords = List.Accumulate(
        Record.FieldNames(Source[Changes]{0}{0}),
        Source,
        (s, a) =>
            Table.AddColumn(
                s,
                PrefixNewColumnNamesWith & a,
                (x) => Text.Combine(List.Transform(x[Changes],
                    (y) => Text.From(Record.Field( y, a))), ", "),
                type text
            )
    )
in
    ExtractRecords
```

This is an advanced scenario; therefore, don't worry if you do not fully understand how it works at this time. You can always return to it at a later stage of your learning. Let's take a closer look at what's being done here:

- The `PrefixNewColumnNamesWith` variable is set to `Change`, a string that will be used to prefix existing field names, extracted from the records, to help avoid potential name conflicts with existing columns in the outer `Source` table.

- The `ExtractRecords` step uses the `List.Accumulate` function, which is essential for processing each field name in these records. You can learn more about this function in *Chapter 13, Iteration and Recursion*, but we'll provide a brief overview here.

The `List.Accumulate` function iterates over the field names of the records (obtained by `Record.FieldNames(Source[Changes]{0}{0})`). The field names refer to the first row of the `Changes` column in the `Source` table. The function accesses the first list item, which is a record to retrieve all field names:

- For each iteration, it applies a function to add a new column to the table (s), which refers to the second argument in `List.Accumulate`, the `Source` table.
- The new column name is created by concatenating `PrefixFieldNamesWith` with the current iterated field name (a), which refers to the first argument in `List.Accumulate`.
- Then a function is applied to each list in the `Changes` column to transform each record in the list by extracting the value of the current field (a) and converting it to text. Finally, it combines these text values into a single string, separated by commas.

This code is more robust in handling potential field name conflicts. Prefixing the new column names with `Change` ensures that new columns added to the table are less likely to clash with any existing column names. This is an essential consideration for scenarios where field names inside records might match the names of existing columns in the outer table. When this is not required, you can simply pass an empty text string instead.

Extracting data through lookup

These last examples focused on flattening data, but there are many scenarios that require a more targeted approach to extract a value. As tables are the dominant structure, we will illustrate how to look up rows that match criteria in a nested table, which is a common requirement. In this example (see *Figure 8.57*), the outer table includes a single row per project, and the `Details` column contains a record with two fields: `Version`, a list with change log data where the final list item represents the "active" version (for `Project` 98731 that's 1,01); and `Details`, a nested table providing notes for each version.

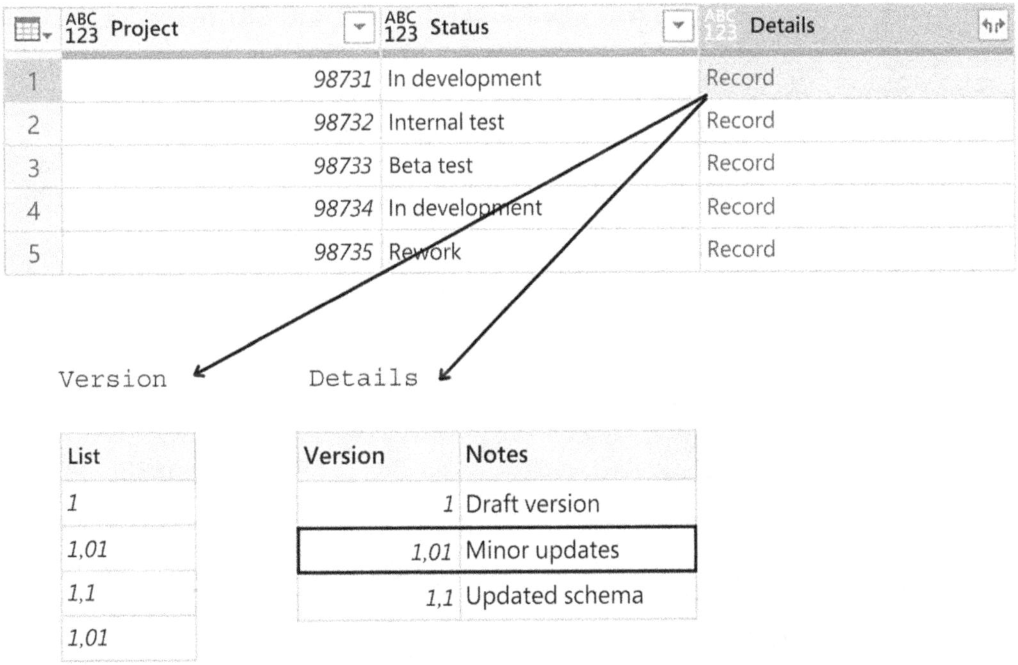

Figure 8.57: Project data and a view of the contents within a nested record

The task is to extract the active version and use that to perform a lookup in the corresponding nested `Details` table to retrieve the notes associated with that version. This involves matching the version number and extracting the relevant notes.

In all lookup scenarios, `Table.SelectRows` will do the trick. However, because there will only ever be one matching row in the `Details` table, we can use a `lookup` as well in this special case. However, keep in mind that when a `lookup` returns more than a single row, an error is raised. Consider this query:

```
let
    Source = Table.FromRows(
        {
          { 98731, "In development",
            [
              Version = {1.00, 1.01, 1.10, 1.01},
              Details = #table(
                {"Version", "Notes"},
                {
                  {1.00, "Draft version"},
                  {1.01, "Minor updates"},
                  {1.10, "Updated schema"}
                }
              )
            ]
          },
          { 98732, "Internal test",
            [
              Version = {1.00, 2.00, 2.50},
              Details = #table(
                {"Version", "Notes"},
                {
                  {1.00, "Beta version"},
                  {2.00, "Major overhaul"},
                  {2.50, "Performance improvements"}
                }
              )
            ]
          },
          { 98733, "Beta test",
            [
              Version = {2.00, 2.01},
              Details = #table(
                {"Version", "Notes"},
```

```
            {
              {2.00, "New release"},
              {2.01, "Minor Bug fixes"}
            }
          )
        ]
      },
      { 98734, "In development",
        [
          Version = {1.00, 1.20},
          Details = #table(
            {"Version", "Notes"},
            {
              {1.00, "Initiated from template"},
              {1.20, "Feature additions"}
            }
          )
        ]
      },
      { 98735, "Rework",
        [
          Version = {1.00, 2.00, 3.00, 3.50, 4.00, 3.50},
          Details = #table(
            {"Version", "Notes"},
            {
              {1.00, "Draft version"},
              {2.00, "New release"},
              {3.00, "Major overhaul"},
              {3.50, "Beta version"},
              {4.00, "To Production environment"}
            }
          )
        ]
      }
    }, {"Project", "Status", "Details"}
  ),
    ReplaceValue = Table.ReplaceValue( Source,
      each [Details],
      each [
        Version=List.Last([Details][Version]),
        Notes=[Details][Details]{[Version=Version]}[Notes] ],
```

```
          Replacer.ReplaceValue,
          {"Details"}
     ),
     ExpandDetails = Table.ExpandRecordColumn( ReplaceValue,
        "Details",
        {"Version", "Notes"},
        {"Version", "Notes"}
     )
  in
     ExpandDetails
```

The `ReplaceValue` step performs a transformation on the `Details` column of the `Source` table. `Table.ReplaceValue` replaces specific values in a table column. It takes five arguments: the table to transform, the old value, the new value, a replacer, and columns where replacements should occur. Here's how it works:

- `OldValue: each [Details]` specifies that the old value to be replaced is the current value in the `Details` column.

- `NewValue`: This initializes a record with two fields: `Version` and `Notes`. Both fields are assigned an expression:

  - `Version=List.Last([Details][Version])`: This extracts the last item from the `Version` list within the current `Details` record.

  - `Notes=[Details][Details]{[Version=Version]}[Notes]`: This performs a lookup in the nested table of the current `Details` record and uses `{[Version=Version]}` to find the row where the `Version` column matches the last version number extracted previously (i), retrieving the `[Notes]` field from the matched row.

- Essentially, for each row in the `Source` table, the `Details` record is replaced with a new record containing the last list item from the `Version` list and the corresponding notes from the nested table.

- `Replacer.ReplaceValue` is one of the built-in replacers; this function will replace the entire cell content if the current value matches the specified `oldValue` precisely.

- `Columns to search: {"Details"}` specifies a list of columns to search in and replace the old value; any replacements will only occur in these columns.

As mentioned, in all cases where more than one single row is to be expected – or, rather, a single row cannot be guaranteed – `Table.SelectRows` should be used instead of a lookup. This means the third argument value specified within `Table.ReplaceValue`, `NewValue`, can also be specified like this:

```
each Table.SelectRows( [Details][Details],
    (row)=> row[Version] = List.Last([Details][Version])
)
```

Here, `Table.SelectRows` filters the nested `Details` table to keep only rows where the `Version` column matches the version retrieved from the `Version` list in the current `Details` record, which is the criterion for selecting rows. For each row in the `Source` table, the `Details` record is replaced with a filtered table containing only the rows that match the last item from the `Version` list.

Finally, an expand column operation is initiated through those sideways arrows in the column header, used to extract the data. You can expect the following behavior:

- When more than one field is selected, a record will widen the primary table.
- If a table contains more than one row and multiple fields are selected, it will both widen and expand the primary table.

Navigating mixed structures is all about recognizing values and knowing how to handle them. Although every scenario is different, there are many techniques at your disposal.

Summary

In this chapter, we've set the stage for you to confidently step beyond the confines of the UI, by introducing a low-code approach to kickstart that journey. This shift in your ability will provide access to a vast number of functions that will enhance your data transformation capabilities further.

We explored working with lists, records, and tables, including when nested inside other structures or when mixed. The aim has been to provide you with practical techniques for extracting, reshaping, and transforming these values, occasionally showcasing multiple methods that achieve the same outcome and thereby highlighting the flexibility of the M language.

Understanding each dataset comes with its unique challenges and requirements. We presented a variety of examples covering a wide range of scenarios. Whether straightforward, like selecting data, or more intricate, like selecting data, the goal has been to inspire and prepare you for a wide range of potential puzzles that might find their way to you.

In the next chapter, we will start to learn how you can write your own custom functions.

Learn more on Discord

Join our community's Discord space for discussions with the author and other readers:

`https://discord.gg/vCSG5GBbyS`

9

Parameters and Custom Functions

The M language is a functional language containing hundreds of functions suited for a great number of tasks. At first, the standard function library will likely meet most of your transformation needs. However, once you run into more challenging situations with the M language, you will find that being able to write your own custom functions opens up new possibilities; it can greatly simplify the data transformation process and make it so you can easily repeat complex logic. This is especially true when you leverage a feature like creating a function, which allows you to transform existing queries into dynamic, reusable functions. The biggest benefit here is that you can set up your logic once and apply it with ease everywhere else. If you need to modify your logic later, simply update your function. This change will automatically propagate to all queries using that function.

Accordingly, this chapter covers the following:

- Parameters
- What are custom functions?
- Transforming a query into a function
- Invoking custom functions
- The Each expression
- Refining function definitions
- Referencing column and field names
- Debugging custom functions
- Function scope

Parameters

Parameters in Power Query play an important role in making queries dynamic. Think of them as variables that you can tweak to change the behavior of your queries. As you go through this chapter, you'll discover how parameters are a useful building block for storing and managing values. We will delve into what they are, how you can create one, and look at where and how to use them.

Understanding parameters

Parameters are placeholders that make it easy to adapt and manage your queries. They allow for the input of scalar values like dates, numbers, or text, without the need to hardcode these values directly into the queries. This design enables you to make external modifications to a single parameter, which then automatically propagates updates across multiple queries or steps within a query.

Typical use cases for using parameters provide flexibility by allowing a user to:

*   Choose a server and database name. This allows users to switch between development, test, and production servers.
*   Limit the number of rows that are imported into a dataset. During development, the user can then work with a small dataset. After uploading the report, a simple change of parameters then causes the next refresh to import the remaining data.

In these scenarios, parameters provide both flexibility and ease of use, and make it much easier to maintain your queries. Another benefit of using parameters is that you can change their values outside of the Power Query editor. So how does that work?

The frontend of Power BI Desktop provides an option to change parameters without opening Power Query. To do that, you navigate to the **Home** tab of the ribbon, click on the dropdown below the **Transform data** button, and select **Edit parameters**, as shown in the following screenshot. Remember that you will need to refresh your dataset to see the changes in your parameter take effect.

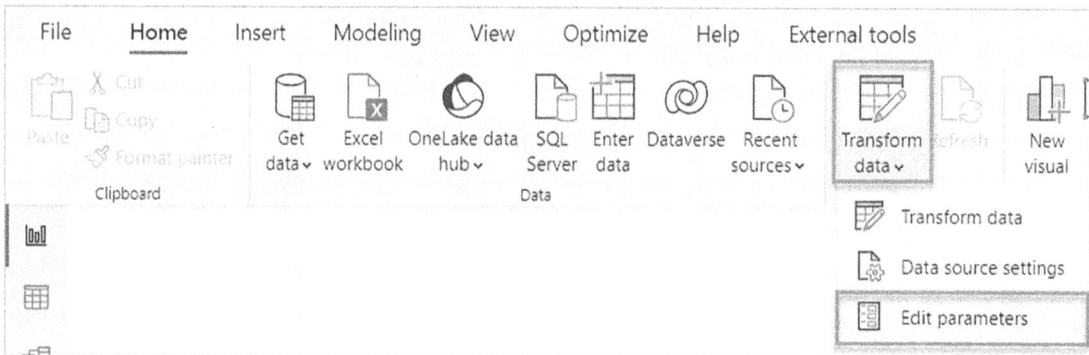

Figure 9.1: Changing parameters in Power BI Desktop

After including the parameters, users can upload their dataset to the Power BI service. When that a dataset contains parameters, users are able to change any parameters they have set comfortably from the workspace. To do that, users can:

1. Go to `https://app.powerbi.com`.
2. Navigate to the relevant **workspace** and select the dataset's **Settings** option.
3. Go to the **Parameters** section.

The resulting screen is shown in the following image:

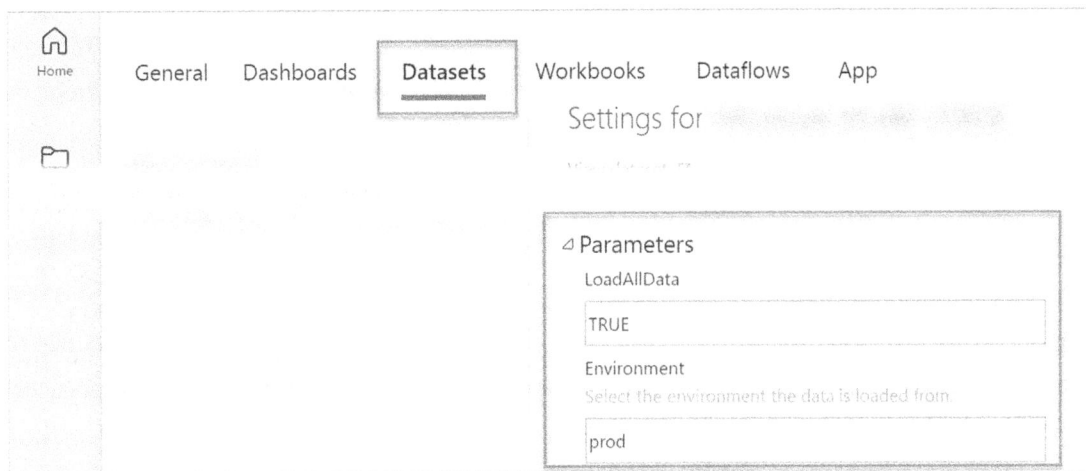

Figure 9.2: Changing parameters from the Datasets settings in the Power BI service

Users can then change the defined parameters. For parameters in the Power BI service, the same applies here as it does for desktop files; changes only become visible after refreshing the dataset.

It's much easier to change a parameter in the query pane than to search through the entire query steps to find the relevant code to change. Now that you know what parameters are for, let's look at how to create them.

Creating parameters

Creating a parameter in Power BI is easy. Users can create one by opening the Power Query editor and by performing the following steps:

1. Navigate to the **Home** tab.
2. Select **Manage Parameters**.
3. Click on **New Parameter**.

This operation opens the menu shown in the following screenshot, where they can create or modify parameter properties:

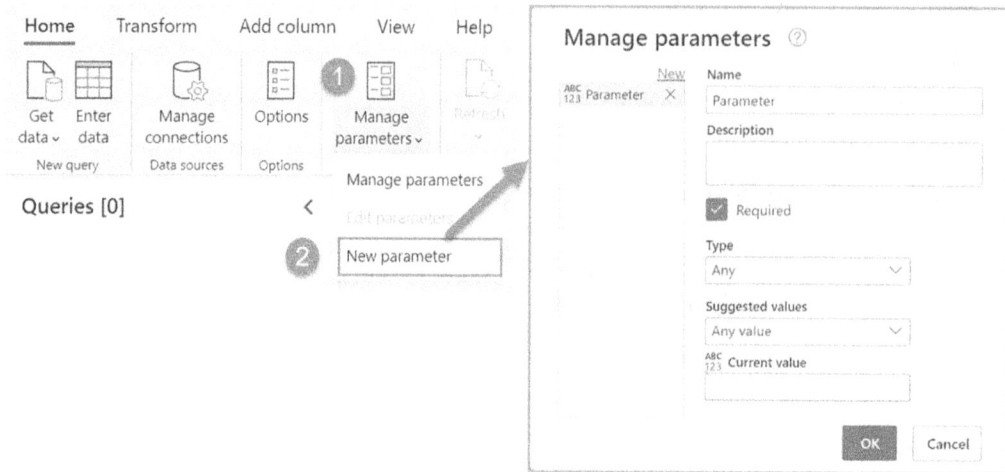

Figure 9.3: Creating a parameter using Manage parameters

The **Manage parameters** pane allows users to provide additional information about the parameters, but it also provides ways to enforce a particular type of value. The following is an explanation of each of the properties:

- **Name:** This is the identifier for your parameter. It's the name you'll use to refer to this parameter throughout your query. Just like naming a variable in programming, it should ideally be descriptive enough to understand its purpose at a glance.

- **Description:** With this property, you can add a brief note or explanation about the purpose and use of the parameter. It serves as a reminder or guide to understand why the parameter was created and what it's intended for.

- **Required:** This one determines whether a value must be provided for this parameter for the query to run.

- **Type:** It lets you set the expected data type for the parameter. By specifying a type (like text, number, or date), you ensure that the parameter accepts only values of that specific type. This is important for data integrity and avoiding unexpected errors during query execution.

- **Suggested values:** This property provides guidance about the values that the parameter can accept. There are three options:

  - **Any value:** This indicates that it can accept any value of its specified type without restrictions.

  - **List of values:** This lets you define a predetermined set of values that the parameter can take. For instance, if you have a parameter that should only take the values Low, Medium, or High, you'd use this.

  - **Query:** This allows values based on the result of a query. It's useful when the allowed values for a parameter are dynamic and might change, based on another data source or logic. You could for example provide a unique list of product categories from a database.

- **Current value:** This is the currently assigned value of the parameter. It's the value that the parameter will use by default when the query runs unless it is overridden. If the parameter is marked as **Required** but doesn't have a **Current value** set, then the query won't run until a value is provided.

After configuring the settings, your parameter is added to the **Queries** pane. The user interface automatically adds three metadata fields:

- IsParameterQuery: Set to true to indicate that this is a parameter.
- IsParameterQueryRequired: Indicates whether the parameter is required.
- Type: Specifies the data type of the parameter.

For example, when entering a required date value of January 1st 2024, Power Query creates the parameter as a new query. When you open the Advanced editor for that query, it shows the following code and metadata:

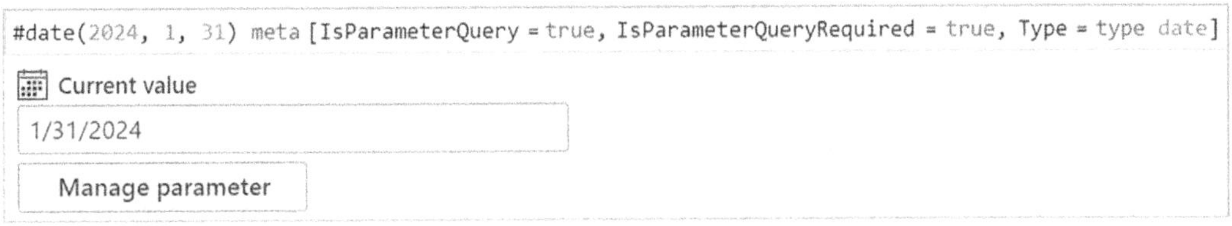

```
#date(2024, 1, 31) meta [IsParameterQuery = true, IsParameterQueryRequired = true, Type = type date]
```

Current value

```
1/31/2024
```

Manage parameter

Figure 9.4: Metadata when adding a parameter

You can inspect the above code in the provided exercise file of this chapter, which you can find on GitHub. While you can make use of the user interface to create and edit parameters, you can also create and edit parameters using the **Advanced editor**. Knowing the syntax would allow you to programmatically add M parameters (for instance, by using Tabular Editor 3), or to manually paste the parameter code into the **Advanced editor** for your query. You can read more on metadata in *Chapter 7, Conceptualizing M*.

Now you know how to create parameters, let's delve into how you can use parameters in your queries.

Using parameters in your queries

You can integrate parameters into your M code by referencing them, much like how you would reference a table or a specific step in your query. Let's work through an example to clarify this.

We will work with a simple dataset, as illustrated in *Figure 9.5*:

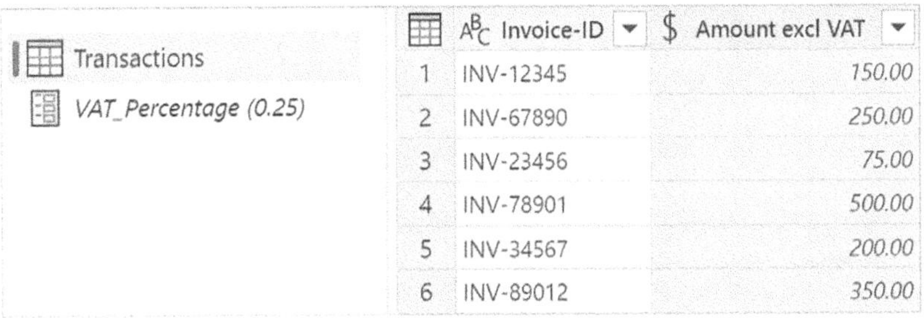

	A^B_C Invoice-ID ▼	$ Amount excl VAT ▼
Transactions	1 INV-12345	150.00
VAT_Percentage (0.25)	2 INV-67890	250.00
	3 INV-23456	75.00
	4 INV-78901	500.00
	5 INV-34567	200.00
	6 INV-89012	350.00

Figure 9.5: Sample invoice data

To follow along, you can download the provided PBIX file from GitHub for this chapter.

The above dataset has a column with invoices and an amount excluding VAT. Our goal is to create a new column that contains the amount including VAT, but the user should be able to easily change the VAT value using a parameter.

To do that, you will first need to create the desired parameter as learned in the previous section. That means you need to do the following:

1.   Open the **Manage Parameters** menu.
2.   Name the parameter VAT_Percentage.
3.   Set the type to **Decimal Number**.
4.   Set a current value of 0.25 (representing 25% VAT).

That looks as follows:

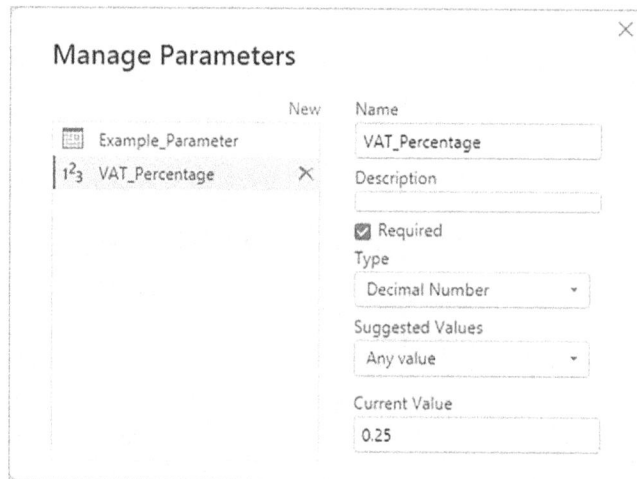

Figure 9.6: Properties for creating the VAT_Percentage parameter

With the parameter in place, you can now create a custom column. To do that, navigate to **Add Column** in the ribbon, and select **Custom Column**. On the pop-up screen, name the column Amount incl VAT.

So how do you include the parameter in your expression? You can reference it just like you would reference any other table or step name. This process is illustrated here:

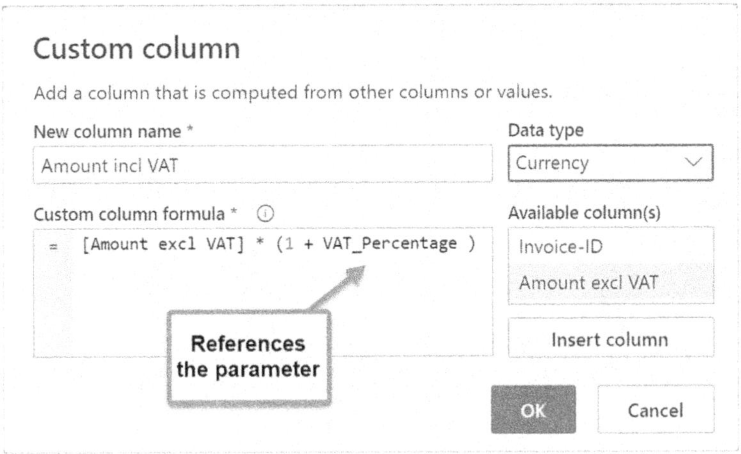

Custom column

Add a column that is computed from other columns or values.

New column name *

Amount incl VAT

Data type

Currency

Custom column formula * ⓘ

= [Amount excl VAT] * (1 + VAT_Percentage)

References the parameter

Available column(s)

Invoice-ID

Amount excl VAT

Insert column

OK   Cancel

Figure 9.7: Referencing a parameter in a custom formula

When your parameter name includes special characters or spaces, be careful. In those cases, it's important to use a particular notation to ensure the M language interprets it correctly. You would use the #"<Your Parameter Name>" format. For instance, if your parameter is named VAT Rate %, you would reference it as #"VAT Rate %".

> **Pro Tip:** To maintain clean code, we recommend using variable names consisting of only letters, numbers, and underscores, and ensuring they don't begin with a number. By following this convention, there's no need for special notation.

Since you now know how to reference a parameter, let's look at a few practical examples that make use of a parameter in the *Putting It All Together* section.

Putting it all together

Parameters can be convenient in different scenarios. This section delves into three commonly seen scenarios and how they make use of parameters.

Parameterizing connection information

Working with databases often means juggling between development, testing, and production environments. And changing different servers and their respective names can be a tedious task. In these cases, parameters offer an elegant solution that simplify the switch between different servers and databases. Let's delve into an example.

This example is meant to be read along with. Yet, if you have access to a database, feel free to also try this at your end.

Connecting to a SQL database requires specifying both a server and a database. The typical code to connect to a SQL database looks something as follows:

```
Sql.Database(
  "localhost\sql-dev.database.windows.net",
  "db-staging-dev-westeu-001" )
```

We can break these down as:

- **Server:** `localhost\sql-dev.database.windows.net`
- **Database:** `db-staging-dev-westeu-001`

Notice the text dev in both components. When setting up databases, administrators try to streamline the transition between environments. You only need to replace dev with `test` for a testing environment or `prod` for a production environment.

Instead of hardcoding the environment of the server, we can incorporate parameters in this scenario. That would work as follows:

1. Navigate to **Manage Parameters** and create a new parameter.
2. Name it `Environment`, ensure that **Required** is checked, and define its **Type** as **Text**. Click the **List of values** dropdown for suggested input.
3. Use the **List of values** feature to configure the selectable options in the dropdown menu. Populate it with `dev`, `test`, and `prod`.

After configuring these settings, the parameter properties will look as follows:

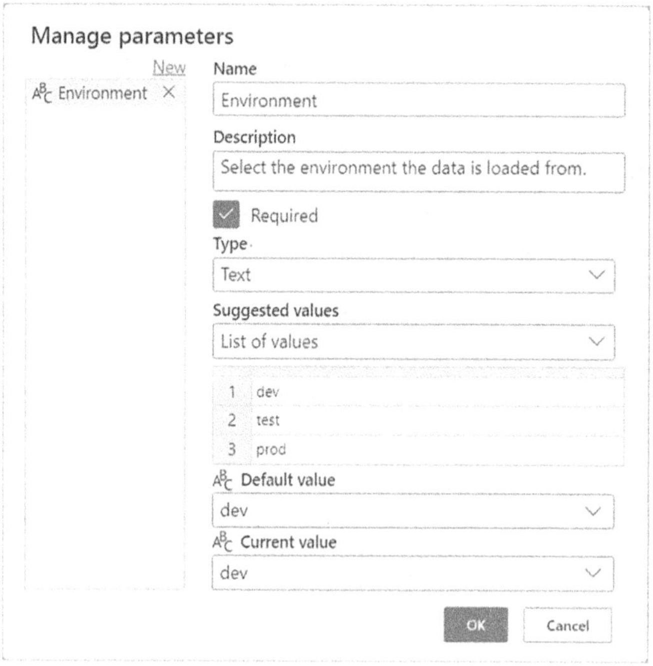

Figure 9.8: Define database connection parameters

Remember the database code we looked at earlier? We now have the parameter in place to adjust the database environment as we like, whether we need dev, test or prod. To do that, a user can select the query step that contains the database connection expression. The formula bar then shows:

```
Sql.Database(
  "localhost\sql-dev.database.windows.net",
  "db-staging-dev-westeu-001" )
```

To incorporate the parameter, the user can replace dev with the Environment parameter:

```
Sql.Database(
 "localhost\sql-" & Environment & ".database.windows.net",
 "db-staging-" & Environment & "-westeu-001" )
```

In this example, the Environment parameter functions as a placeholder that allows you to easily change the connection string. After saving this change and uploading the file to the Power BI service, you gain the flexibility to alter the parameter value directly from the dataset settings menu. This means you can switch your database connection without even opening Power BI Desktop. Now that you've seen the first common scenario for parameters, let's look at the second one, dynamic file paths.

Dynamic file paths

When working with queries that include file paths, it's important to consider that these paths might work well for the original creator but not necessarily for others. If you anticipate that your file will be used by multiple people, and it contains file paths, thoughtful query design becomes important. Providing an easy way for users to modify the file path is valuable in particular, and parameters are a great way to achieve this flexibility. Let's explore how to implement this. You can follow along by downloading the Avocado Prices.csv file included in the exercise files.

Suppose you're creating training materials that incorporate the Avocado Price.csv file provided with this book. To keep things organized, you decide to store this file on your C drive, within a folder named data. To connect to this file through Power Query, you:

1. Choose **Get Data** and select **Text/CSV**.
2. Browse to C:\Data and select the CSV file.
3. The CSV import menu will pop up; hit **OK**.

This sequence will produce the following M code:

```
Csv.Document(
   File.Contents("C:\Data\Avocado Prices.csv"),
   [Delimiter=",", Columns=14,
    Encoding=1252, QuoteStyle=QuoteStyle.None] )
```

Notice the direct file path, C:\Data\Avocado Prices.csv, embedded within. While this might be convenient for you, it may not be for everyone. What if your trainees have stored their files in different locations? What if you've created other queries that also use this file path as a reference?

Hardcoding the file path then quickly becomes a stumbling block, requiring tedious, manual updates by each person. Luckily, you can use parameters to introduce flexibility in your file paths. Here's how to implement this solution.

Start out by creating a **text type** parameter. Let's name it CSVFilePath and set the **Current value** field to C:\Data\Avocado Prices.csv. The properties of this parameter are shown in the following screenshot:

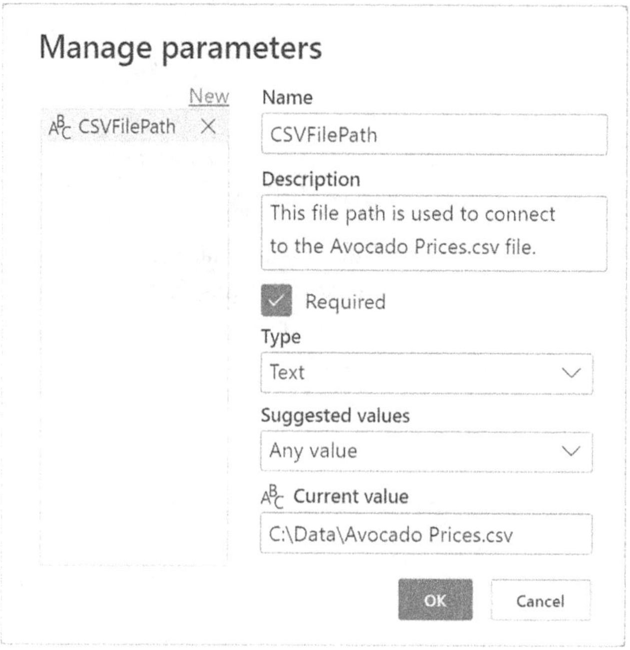

Figure 9.9: Create a parameter called CSVFilePath

With the parameter in place, now it's time to include it in the code. When you initially linked the CSV, a step titled **Source** was formed in the **Applied Steps** pane, located on the right side of the Query editor.

Here's a straightforward method to integrate your parameter:

1. Click the gear icon adjacent to the **Source** step.
2. For **File Path**, drop down the menu and select **Parameter**.
3. To finish, pick the **CSVFilePath** parameter.

The steps to do this are shown in the following image:

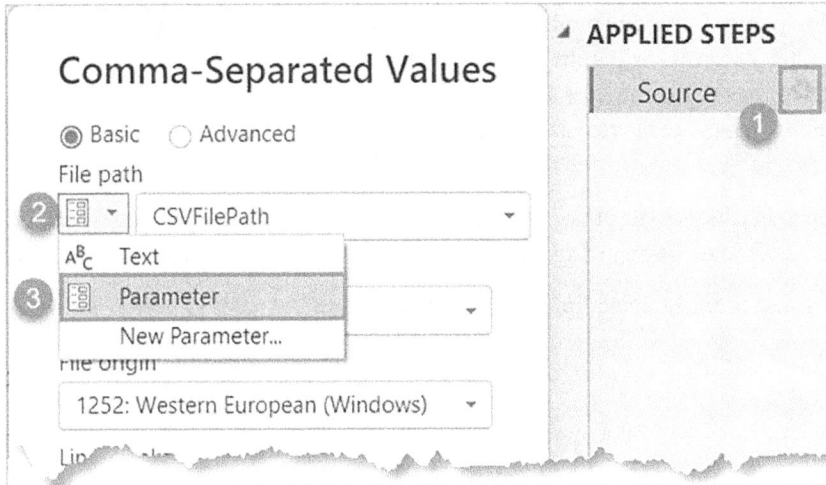

Figure 9.10: You can use a parameter as the file path

With this modification, your M code now looks like:

```
Csv.Document(
  File.Contents( CSVFilePath ),
  [Delimiter=",", Columns=14,
    Encoding=1252, QuoteStyle=QuoteStyle.None]
)
```

You'll notice that where the hardcoded file path once was, the **CSVFilePath** parameter now stands. This change brings your query flexibility.

By merely adjusting the parameter values, your query now becomes flexible without rewriting or modifying the core query. If you or someone else needs to change the folder path in the future, they only need to update the parameter at the front.

> **Pro Tip:** Feeling confident with M code? Bypass the interface and modify the code directly to reference **CSVFilePath**. Moving from hardcoded paths to parameter values simplifies your work process immensely.

Now that you know how to connect to file paths dynamically, let's have a look at our third scenario where we filter date ranges.

Filtering a date range

Date values are included in many models, whether you're creating monthly sales reports, diving into historical weather patterns, or identifying financial trends. However, working with a query's entire date history often makes your queries slow. This is a scenario where parameters can help. Parameters provide flexibility when it comes to managing date ranges, capable of handling both fixed and rolling date spans.

Consider a scenario where, to improve performance, you wish to work with data from only the last few quarters. Instead of manually adjusting the start and end dates for each quarter, you can use parameters.

If you have a transactions table equipped with a date column, you could use an expression like:

```
Table.SelectRows(
  DataTable,
  each [Date] >= StartDate and [Date] <= EndDate )
```

In this code, the first argument references the `DataTable` table to filter, while the second argument filters the `Date` column.

Whenever your focus shifts to a new quarter, all you'd need to modify are the `StartDate` and `EndDate` parameters. However, there's a catch: while the above method allows you to easily adjust the parameter values, you must still manually set the `StartDate` and `EndDate` for each quarter. Wouldn't it be nice to supply a parameter with a dynamic value?

Unfortunately, the ribbon's built-in parameters do not support dynamic values based on expressions, but that doesn't mean you're out of options. You can include the output of an expression in your queries, even if it isn't formally labeled as a parameter.

For instance, think of the situation where you're aiming to filter data from the recently concluded quarter. Creating a blank query allows you to incorporate the following expression, determining the `EndDate`:

```
Date.AddDays(
  Date.StartOfQuarter( Date.From( DateTime.LocalNow() ) ),
  -1 )
```

This function retrieves today's datetime value, converts it into a date, and then rolls it back to the start of the current quarter, and subtracts one day. Thus, it consistently lands you on the final day of the preceding quarter.

For the `StartDate`, you can simply reference the `EndDate` and shift it to the start of the quarter:

```
Date.StartOfQuarter( EndDate )
```

Although these queries are not part of the official parameter screen within the ribbon, they function similarly and can be referenced accordingly.

Custom functions

Custom functions play an important role in the M language. They allow you to consolidate your logic, making your code modular, reusable, and efficient. Think of a custom function as a tool designed for a specific task.

And while there are hundreds of standard library functions available, sometimes creating your own function is useful. They allow you to create solutions specific to your data challenges that consolidate multiple custom steps or address data transformation issues that built-in functions do not handle.

For instance, consider complex tasks like creating running totals, retrieving the previous row value, or computing an ISO week number. Manually writing the code for these transformations can be complicated and error-prone. Yet, by providing a custom function, you can now achieve the desired outcome with a reusable function call that you only need to set up once. Once created, these functions can easily be reused, making it easier for team members with lower levels of expertise to leverage your custom solutions.

The following pages will guide you through understanding what functions are, how to create your own, and how to use them effectively. Along the way, you'll also learn about refining function definitions, debugging, and managing function scope.

What are custom functions?

You can think of custom functions as mini queries. They accept inputs, which we call parameters, and they perform an action based on those parameters to return a result. To be able to create custom functions, it's important to know which elements they consist of.

You can define a custom function by providing parameters inside a set of parentheses, followed by =>, and concluding with an expression to evaluate. The expression defines how the function should compute its result. Let's look at an example.

A simple function that adds 10 to a value can be written as:

```
(parameter) => parameter + 10
```

Here's how to interpret it:

- `(parameter)`: This denotes the input or parameter our function takes as input. You can name the parameter as you like.
- `Goes-to symbol`: the => symbol separates the function's parameters from its expression.
- `parameter + 10`: This is the expression (or function body) that instructs how the function should process the input to produce an output value.

You can design a function to work with more than one input. For instance, if you wish to create a function that multiplies two numbers, you can do it as:

```
(a, b ) => a * b
```

While a and b are the chosen names for parameters in the above function, you have the freedom to name them as you see fit. For instance, the following function definition is no different from the one above:

```
(left, right ) => left * right
```

> **Pro Tip:** While you are free to choose the names of your function parameters, it's often a good idea to use meaningful names for your parameters, especially when your code is intended for a broader audience. It makes the parameter's purpose clear right from the start.

The examples so far write the entire function expression without using any variables. However, if you want to add additional clarity to your functions, consider integrating the let expression.

Here's how you could do that:

```
( MyText ) =>
let
  TextToNumber = Number.FromText( MyText ),
  MultiplyBy3  = TextToNumber * 3,
  NumberToText = Number.ToText( MultiplyBy3 ),
  OutputString = "3 times "& MyText & " is " & NumberToText
in
  OutputString
```

This function transforms a text string into a number, multiplies it by 3, and provides a custom string as output. So if you name this function fxMultiplyText and call it with fxMultiplyText("5"), it would return the string: "3 times 5 is 15".

Depending on how you invoke this function, it may or may not throw an error. If you run into an error, make sure the resulting code in the formula bar uses fxMultiplyText("5"), where the number 5 is enclosed by a single pair of parenthesis.

Some functions don't require any input parameters. An example from the standard function library is DateTime.LocalNow. You can invoke it by simply opening and closing parenthesis behind the function name:

```
DateTime.LocalNow()
```

This would return a datetime value corresponding to the local datetime on your machine. You can also create a custom function without parameters. For instance, you can return the value of the earth's radius by writing:

```
() => 6371
```

This statement does not take any parameters and returns a number value. However, such usage is rare. Instead of creating a function like this, it's often more practical to store the output value as a parameter or variable in your code.

This section covered the basics of making custom functions, including defining parameters and creating the function body. It required you to write the function definition manually. If you want to automatically generate custom function code, Power Query also offers a convenient alternative. You can transform a query into a function.

Transforming queries into a function

Power Query has a functionality that allows you to transform your query into a function. And unlike manually written custom functions, this method keeps all query steps visible and editable. The following section explores how to use this feature to create flexible, reusable functions from your queries.

What is the "create function" functionality?

In Power Query, the **Create Function** feature enables you to convert any query into a reusable function. If your query has no parameters, it will create a parameter-less function. For more advanced functions, this feature makes use of the parameters in your code to form the function's arguments.

Let's say you want to add parameters to your function. To do that, you should identify the variable elements in your query and link them to the corresponding parameters in your report. The **Create Function** feature then automatically integrates the necessary code for these input parameters into your custom function.

If you choose not to use parameters, the function will simply return the result of your original, unaltered query. However, creating a function without parameters is less common, as you could simply use the original query directly.

This `Create Function` functionality has three main advantages:

- **Visibility of the query:** The original query remains visible in your project. That means you can still inspect, modify, and run your logic as a standalone query.
- **Function updates:** Changes to the original query automatically reflect in the linked function. This means you can easily refine your logic without having to update the function.
- **Ease of creating functions:** Users can create custom functions without writing M code, simply by using parameters.

So how can we create a function using the **user interface (UI)**? To create a function from a query, you can follow these steps:

1. If you want parameters, incorporate them in your query. This could be something as simple as a filter criterion or a value that contributes to a calculation.
2. Go to the **Queries** pane located on the left, and right-click on your query.
3. Click on the **Create Function** button. This will bring up a dialog box.
4. Make your function name descriptive so that it's easy to recognize what it does.
5. Click **OK** to create the function.

Following these steps, your new function will appear in the **Queries** pane, and you can use it just like any other function in Power Query. Let's continue and find out how we can apply these steps with a practical example.

Suppose you're creating logic for a calendar table. Before making a function, you prepare a query called CalendarLogic, which looks like this:

```
1   let
2     Source = List.Dates(
3             #date(2023,1,1),
4             Duration.Days( #date(2023,10,1) - #date(2023,1,1) ) + 1,
5             #duration( 1, 0, 0, 0 )
6           ),
7     ToTable = Table.FromList(Source, Splitter.SplitByNothing(), type table [Date = date], null, 1),
8     AddYear = Table.AddColumn(ToTable, "Year", each Date.Year([Date]), Int64.Type),
9     AddMonth = Table.AddColumn(AddYear, "Month", each Date.Month([Date]), Int64.Type)
10  in
11    AddMonth
```

Figure 9.11: CalendarLogic query

This query generates a column with dates and adds a **Year** and a **Month** column. You want your users to be able to adjust how long the calendar should run. You therefore decide to include a startDate and an endDate parameter of type date. The adjusted CalendarLogic query now looks like this:

```
1   let
2     Source = List.Dates(
3             startDate,
4             Duration.Days( endDate - startDate ) + 1,
5             #duration( 1, 0, 0, 0 )
6           ),
7     ToTable = Table.FromList(Source, Splitter.SplitByNothing(), type table [Date = date], null, 1),
8     AddYear = Table.AddColumn(ToTable, "Year", each Date.Year([Date]), Int64.Type),
9     AddMonth = Table.AddColumn(AddYear, "Month", each Date.Month([Date]), Int64.Type)
10  in
11    AddMonth
```

Figure 9.12: CalendarLogic query with parameters

With these parameters in place, we are now ready to transform the query into a function. To do that, simply right-click your query and select **Create Function**, as shown in the following image:

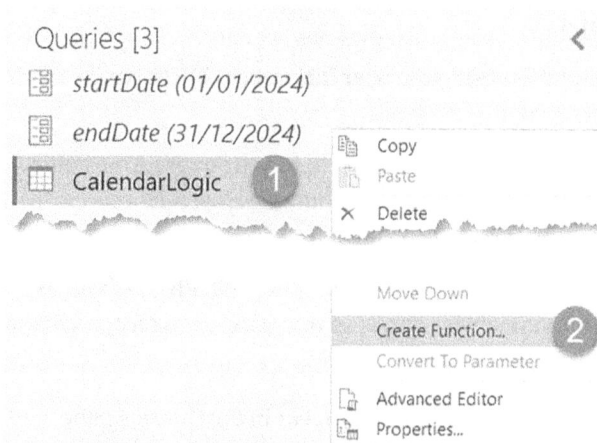

Figure 9.13: The 'Create Function' menu in the Queries pane

You can then define the name of your function in the pop-up message that appears:

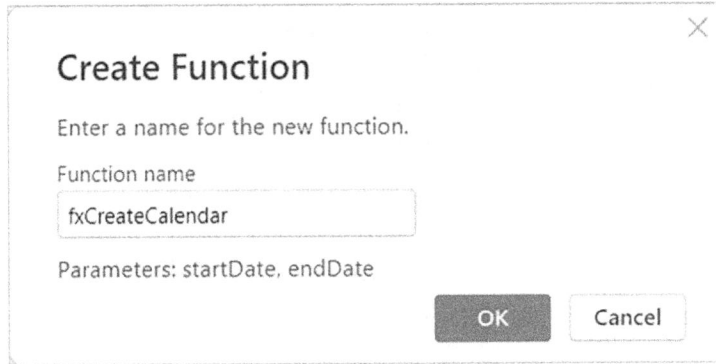

Create Function   ✕

Enter a name for the new function.

Function name

fxCreateCalendar

Parameters: startDate, endDate

OK   Cancel

Figure 9.14: The Create Function menu

Since this function creates a calendar table, we call this function fxCreateCalendar. After pressing **OK**, Power Query turns your query into a function with the name you just specified.

After performing these operations, you end up with four queries:

- The startDate and endDate parameters
- The CalendarLogic query with your calendar logic
- The fxCreateCalendar function that links with the CalendarLogic query

Your query panel will look like the following image:

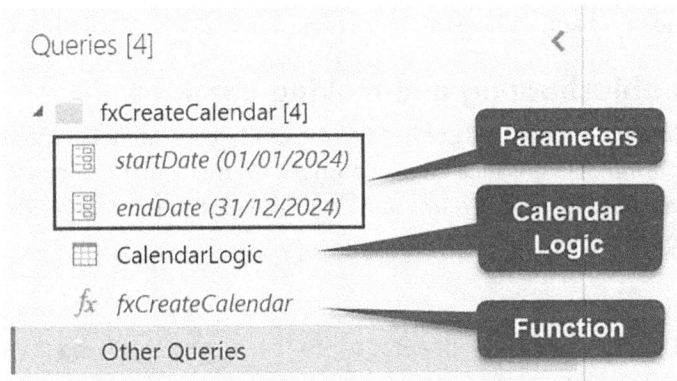

Queries [4]   ‹

▲ fxCreateCalendar [4]
        startDate (01/01/2024)   **Parameters**
        endDate (31/12/2024)
                                                        Calendar
                                                        Logic
     CalendarLogic

fx fxCreateCalendar
                                                        Function
     Other Queries

Figure 9.15: Components used in the 'Create Function' operation

Now that the function is set up, let's explore how to use it effectively. To do so, open a new blank query, rename it Calendar, and input the following code:

```
fxCreateCalendar( #date( 2024,1,1), #date( 2024,12,31 ) )
```

This produces the table displayed in the following screenshot:

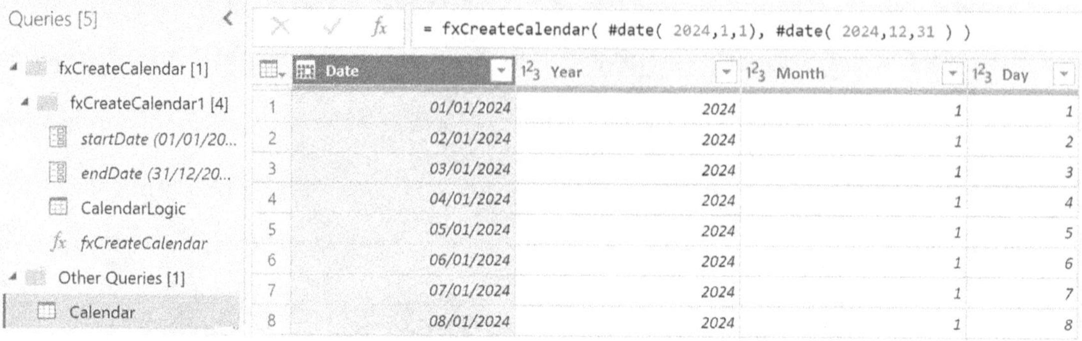

Figure 9.16: Use a function to create a Calendar table

So with a single line of code that uses your custom function, you end up with a calendar table that includes your custom logic; isn't that great? You can find the finished solution in the exercise files provided with the book.

So far, you might think the primary advantage of using the **Create Function** feature is the automation of function creation, but its advantages extend beyond that. This feature is also useful in scenarios that require changes or troubleshooting.

It's a common experience to run into errors while working with custom functions, often due to input errors or unforeseen edge cases that the function doesn't account for. The **Create Function** functionality makes your life easier here, as it offers a systematic way to inspect each step of your function. This allows you to easily identify and resolve the cause of any errors, which we will show next.

Simplifying troubleshooting and making changes

The beauty of the **Create Function** feature lies in how easily you can make modifications. Let's say you need to add a column that specifies the day number. To make that change, all you need to do is navigate to the original `CalendarLogic` query and insert the new column there. This process is shown in the following image:

Figure 9.17: Dynamic link: a query and custom function update together

You can now see the newly created step called Inserted Day in the CalendarLogic query. This dynamic link between the fxCreateCalendar function and the CalendarLogic query means any updates you apply—be it adding columns or tweaking formulas—immediately sync, saving you from manual edits and reducing the chance for errors. This not only simplifies the troubleshooting process—allowing you to inspect each step of the query—but also makes it straightforward to incorporate new logic as requirements change.

When you try to open the **Advanced editor** of this linked function, a message will appear. This message indicates that any modification of the function will break the link between the queries, as shown in this screenshot:

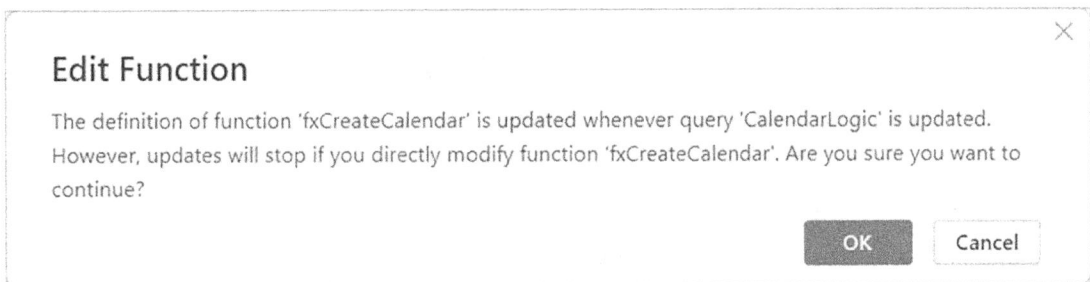

Figure 9.18: Warning message when trying to edit the created function

If you just want to inspect the data, it's safe to click **OK** and have a look. Just make sure to not save any changes and the link will stay in place.

If you want to stop the updates between the query and the function, you can also right-click the function and select **Properties….** This screen contains a **Stop Updates** button, as shown:

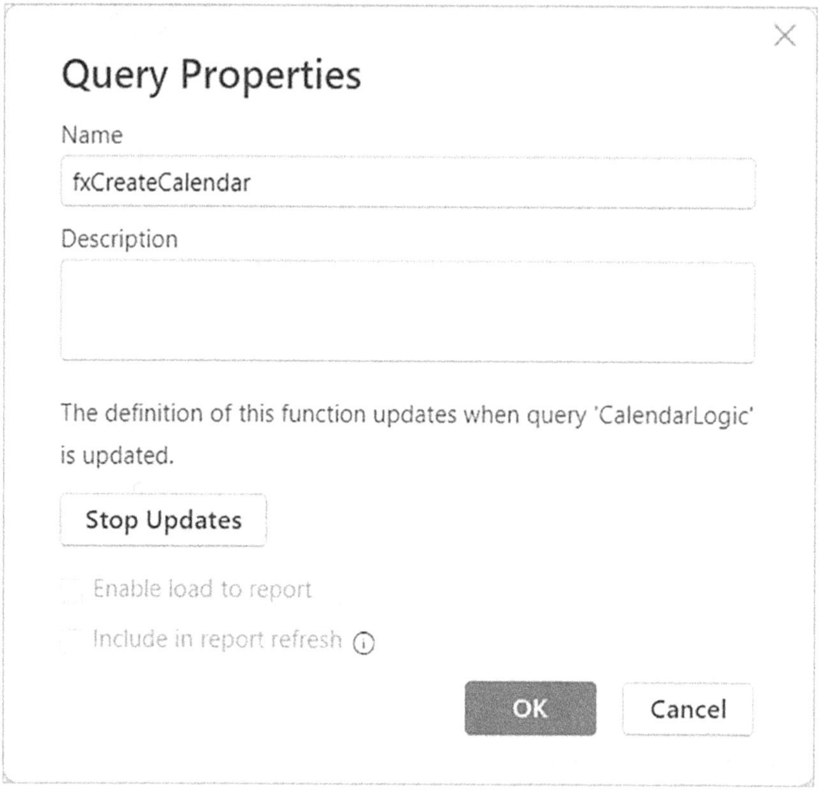

Query Properties

Name

fxCreateCalendar

Description

The definition of this function updates when query 'CalendarLogic' is updated.

Stop Updates

Enable load to report

Include in report refresh ⓘ

OK   Cancel

Figure 9.19: Properties screen of a function that updates with query changes

Pro Tip: Be very careful here. After you click **Stop Updates**, there is no way to restore the updates to the current function. You will have to set up a new function by using the **Create Function** operation, as explained earlier in this chapter.

As we've seen, the **Create Function** feature offers a convenient way to transform queries into reusable, easily adjustable functions. But once these custom functions are created, how do you actually put them to use in your reports? The next section will delve into the methods to invoke these custom functions.

Invoking custom functions

Once you create a function, you can invoke it in different ways. You can either invoke it:

- Manually in the **Advanced editor** or formula bar
- Using the UI

So how does that work?

Manually in the advanced editor or formula bar

Most advanced users invoke a function by referencing it directly. Suppose you have created a function called MyFunction that takes a single numeric value and returns that number plus 10. You create a blank query and paste MyFunction(20) in the formula bar, as illustrated in the following screenshot:

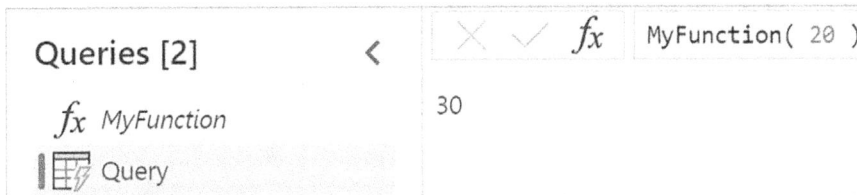

Figure 9.20 – Invoke a function in the formula bar

This invokes the function and returns 30. Depending on your function expression, the outcome referencing a function can be almost anything, be it a list, a table, or a new column in your table—you name it. If you want to invoke a custom function within a new column, there's another way to go about, which we will cover next.

Using the UI

Power Query also provides a way to create a column that invokes a function through the UI. To do that, you can:

1. Go to the **Add Column** tab in the ribbon.
2. Select **Invoke Custom Function**.

You can find the **Invoke Custom Function** option in the following image:

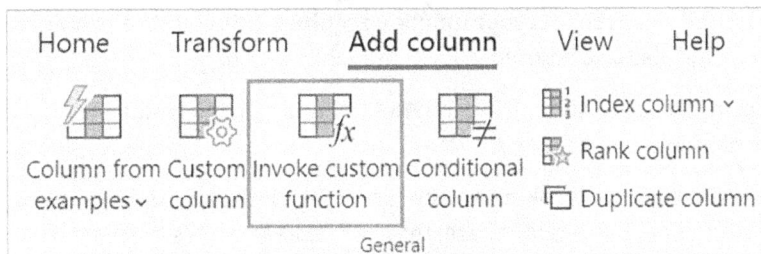

Figure 9.21: UI button to invoke a custom function

This launches a pop-up menu that displays the custom functions available in your file. It also allows you to specify the input parameters for your custom function. Since the custom function used as follows has a single argument, the menu requires information about a single parameter:

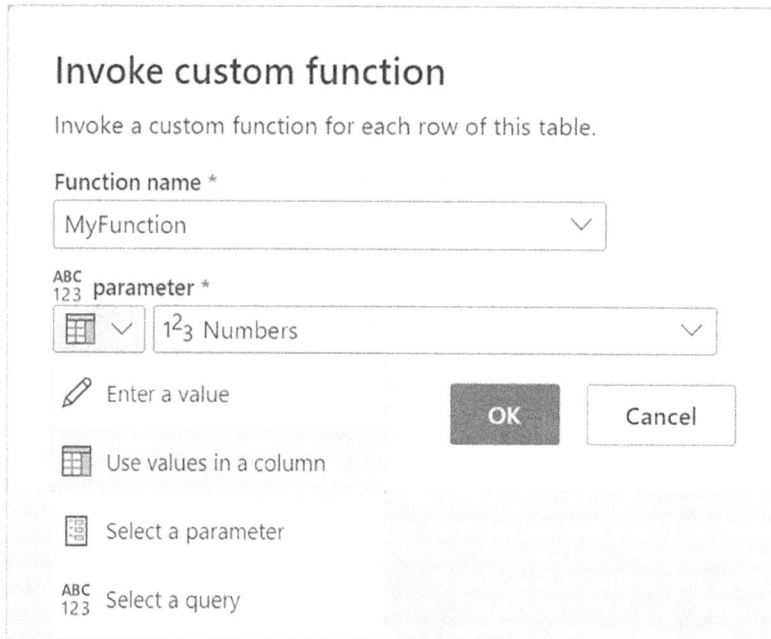

Invoke custom function

Invoke a custom function for each row of this table.

Function name *

| MyFunction | ⌄ |

ABC 123 **parameter** *

| ⊞ ⌄ | 1²3 Numbers | ⌄ |

✏ Enter a value | **OK** | | Cancel |

⊞ Use values in a column

▤ Select a parameter

ABC 123 Select a query

Figure 9.22: The invoke custom function menu

In the **parameter** dropdown, you have several options:

- **Enter a value:** Allows you to manually input a value. This is the least dynamic option.
- **Use values in a column:** Lets you select a column to apply the function on. The dropdown suggests any column in your table.
- **Select a parameter:** Allows you to reference a parameter. Parameters allow for an easy way to reference or adjust a value that can be used throughout your queries.
- **Select a query:** Allows you to reference the output of a query. Just beware that a function may require specific input data types. By referencing another query, the output value of that query should have the data type that your function requires. This could be primitive values like text or numbers, but also a structured value like a table, record or list.

Since this method invokes a function using the **Add Column** tab, the result of performing your function is added to a new column.

Now that you know the basics of invoking a custom function, let's have a look at the most used expression that creates a function in the M language: the each expression. It's the most used because Power Query automatically inserts it in a great range of functions when performing operations through the UI.

The each expression

The each expression in the Power Query M language is a shorthand syntax that allows you to define unary (single argument) functions without the complexities of function declarations.

So why is the each expression part of the M language, when we can define our own functions? The most important reasons are that this expression is more user-friendly and makes your code easier to read.

Let's start with a basic example to understand why. Imagine you want to create a function that accepts a number and adds 5 to it. Here's how you'd typically write it:

```
( MyValue) => MyValue + 5
```

In this function, `MyValue` is the single parameter. Now, let's simplify this:

```
(_) => _ + 5
```

The function still has a single parameter, now represented by the underscore. This is very similar to what the each construct does. The each construct is syntax sugar for a function that takes a single parameter, with the underscore as its name.

What that means is that the following expression is an even more simplified version of the one above:

```
each MyValue + 5
```

The simplified each declaration is used to improve the readability of higher-order function invocation. This is useful because it makes writing code quicker and often decreases the length of your code. To understand what that means, let's look at some common use cases.

Common usecases

You will find the each expression used in various functions. Some common ones are `Table.AddColumn`, `Table.SelectRows` and `List.Transform`. In the following text, we will incorporate these functions in some examples. We will look at:

- Automatic addition of each in custom columns
- Using each in `Table.TransformColumns`
- Skipping underscores in field or column references
- Simplifying single-argument function calls

Let's find out how these work.

Automatic addition of each in custom columns

Imagine you have a column called `Numbers` and you want to add 5 to each value. You can go to **Add Column**, select **Custom Column**, and add the formula:

```
[Number] + 5
```

The **Custom column** pop-up that appears this looks like:

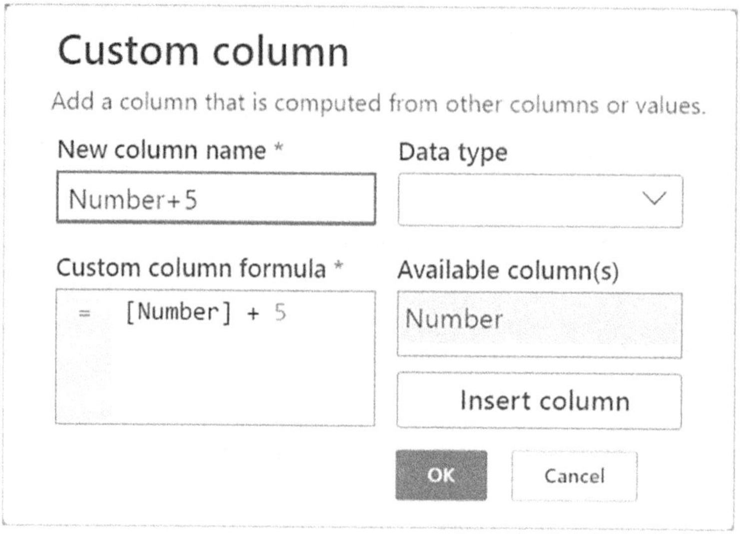

Custom column

Add a column that is computed from other columns or values.

New column name *

```
Number+5
```

Data type

Custom column formula *

```
=   [Number] + 5
```

Available column(s)

```
Number
```

Insert column

OK   Cancel

Figure 9.23: Customizing a column

After clicking **OK**, the following expression appears in the formula bar:

```
Table.AddColumn(
    Source,
    "newColumn",
    each [Number] + 5 )
```

Hold on—the above code includes the each keyword on line 4. How did it appear there when we did not provide it in the custom column formula box?

Here's why: when you add a custom column using Power Query's UI, the software does some of the work for you. It automatically calls the Table.AddColumn function and adds the each keyword as prefix to your formula. You don't need to insert it manually. This is helpful because the concept of each is often confusing for beginners. Let's have a look at how this same concept applies to the Table.TransformColumns function.

Using each in Table.TransformColumns

The Table.TransformColumns function is used to manipulate column values. When you use this function via the Power Query interface, you'll often see the each keyword in action.

Imagine you want to add the prefix Miss to the value in a column called Name. To do that, you select the column, go to the **Transform** tab, click on **Format**, select **Add Prefix**, and type in Miss. The generated code will appear as follows:

```
Table.TransformColumns(
    Source, {{"Name", each "Miss " & _, type text}} )
```

This expression is functionally equivalent to:

```
Table.TransformColumns(
    Source, {{"Name", (_) => "Miss " & _, type text}} )
```

Notice how the two code examples differ. The key lies in understanding how the Table.TransformColumns function works. It needs a specific way to define how each value in a column should be changed. This is where the function parameter comes into play, representing each value in the column we're modifying.

In the first approach, we use each, a shorthand method. The second approach employs (_) =>, a more explicit function definition. Both methods achieve the same result: they prepend the word Miss to every entry in the Name column.

As you've seen in these examples, the underscore is often used to refer to the value being transformed. Let's move on and explore another example to find out when we can omit the underscore.

Skipping underscores in field or column references

In specific situations, it's okay to leave out the underscore character when you're dealing with records or table fields. Let's say you want to add a new column that subtracts 10 from the values in an existing Sales column. The long form to write this would be:

```
Table.AddColumn(Source, "Custom", (_) => _[Sales] - 10 )
```

The underscore then refers to the entire table row, represented by a record.

When we access a field directly using square brackets—a process known as field selection—it's not necessary to precede the field name with an underscore. This lets us write a more concise version:

```
Table.AddColumn(Source, "Custom", (_) => [Sales] - 10 )
```

The Power Query UI simplifies this further with the each construct:

```
Table.AddColumn(Source, "Custom", each [Sales] - 10 )
```

All three expressions achieve the same result, which is subtracting 10 from each value in the [Sales] column.

We've just looked at simplifying our code by leaving out underscores. Yet you can simplify your code even further when calling a function that has just a single argument, let's find out how.

Simplifying single-argument function calls

Many functions allow you to incorporate another function as a parameter. The way you do this depends on the number of arguments the nested function requires. When dealing with a single-argument function, things can be quite simple. You can omit the parentheses and directly reference the function's name.

For instance, consider the following example where we add 10 to every element in a list:

```
let
    fxAddTen = (MyValue) => MyValue + 10,
    MyList = { 1 .. 5 },
    TransformList = List.Transform( MyList, fxAddTen )
  in
    TransformList
```

In this instance, we called the `fxAddTen` function inside the `List.Transform` function without using parentheses. But there's another way to do this that is just as valid. We can replace the `TransformList` step with:

```
    TransformList = List.Transform( MyList, each fxAddTen(_))
```

The examples above illustrate how you can simplify functions with a single argument. They have the option to leave out the each keyword and the parenthesis.

However, when a function requires more than one argument the approach changes. A function with multiple parameters requires you to either:

- Use the each construct
- Formally write out a function definition

Here is an example:

```
    TransformList = List.Transform( MyList, each fxAddTen( _, 10) )
```

The following is the manual approach:

```
    TransformList = List.Transform( MyList, (_)=> fxAddTen( _, 10) )
```

In summary, single-argument functions can be invoked by simply stating the function names, without parentheses. For multi-argument functions, a more detailed syntax is necessary, involving either the each keyword or a custom function definition.

So far, we've looked at how we can create and invoke functions at the most basic level. However, there are ways in which we can refine our functions to make them more robust and prevent errors up front. That's what we'll look at next.

Refining function definitions

When working toward your ideal custom function, it's not just about creating them—it's about perfecting them. It's important to note that a well-defined function is clear in its purpose, flexible in its use, and robust against errors.

Building the custom function often starts out with basic logic, and through multiple iterations, more steps are included in the function until we reach the desired outcome. It's usually at this stage that we refine our function, so that they are even more robust.

In the following section, we explore two methods to refine custom functions:

- **Defining data types:** This ensures the data remains consistent and accurate so that the function input is as expected.
- **Adding optional parameters:** This allows users flexibility in how the function is used, addressing diverse needs without rigid constraints.

These strategies not only improve the usability of custom functions but also make them more resilient and adaptable to different scenarios. Let's have a look at how these methods can improve your queries.

Specifying data types

When creating custom functions, our goal is not just to make them operate but to also make them reliable and less prone to errors. One way to do this is by clearly stating what kind of data each parameter accepts. This way, we make sure our functions only accept certain types of values, which prevents surprises. For instance, if your query expects a date but you instead provide a list value, your function will likely return an error.

For both input parameters and function outputs, you can define data types. A parameter without a defined data type is referred to as an **implicit parameter**. This means it can accept values of any type. Specifying a data type for a parameter turns it into an **explicit parameter**.

Once you define a data type for your input parameter, the custom functions only accept values of the specified type. In *Chapter 5*, when discussing data types, we learned about both primitive types and nullable primitive types. We will now delve into how the difference between these becomes relevant when refining custom functions.

Primitive types

Let's first have a look at how we can assign a primitive data type to a parameter. The data used to apply the following custom function is available in the exercise files provided with the book.

Imagine we have a column with the ages of people, and you want to create a function named fxValidAge. The function checks if the ages are realistic, where we assume they should be between 0 and 125. Here's how you can do it:

```
(age as number) as logical =>
  age >= 0 and age <=  125
```

In this example, age as number is an explicit parameter. It indicates that the function requires a number value for the age argument. After the parenthesis, you find the text as logical, which means the function will provide a result that's either true (valid age) or false (not valid).

In the following screenshot, you can see a table with two columns. The `fxValidAge` column applies the above function to the `Age` column and returns its result:

1²3 Age	ABC 123 fxValidAge
1	23 TRUE
2	105 TRUE
3	5 TRUE
4	71 TRUE
5	-20 FALSE
6	195 FALSE

Figure 9.24: Function tests whether ages are valid

The newly created column now shows a true or false value to indicate whether an age is valid. When we specified the data type for our input parameter, it forced the engine to verify whether the input values match the data type. At this point, all of the rows return a valid value because the input ages are of a number type. However, if you try to provide text (like "20") or any non-number, Power Query will return the following error:

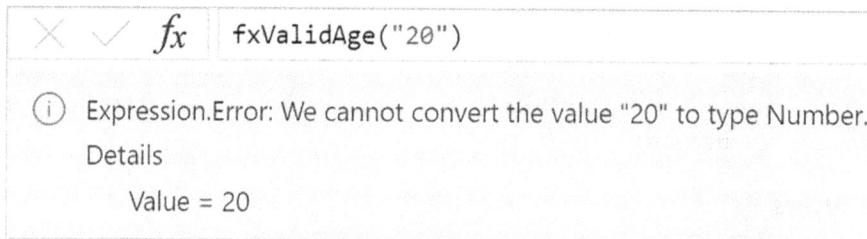

```
fx    fxValidAge("20")
```

Expression.Error: We cannot convert the value "20" to type Number.
Details
    Value = 20

Figure 9.25: Providing a non-number results in an error

This error message appears because our explicit parameter instructs the function to only accept values of type number, yet it receives a text value. The explanation so far has been about the function input; however, we can also instruct data types for the output of the function.

As output, the function currently expects a logical value (`true` or `false`). This is defined by `as logical` in the function definition. If you changed `as logical` to `as text`, but the result remains a Boolean value (`true` or `false`), an error will pop up saying the data type is not as expected.

Another important aspect of building a robust function is dealing with null values. It is very common for your columns to contain both null values and numbers. They have very specific behavior and can easily break your queries. Since the above custom function does not currently handle null values, using it in your queries is risky and can cause errors when running into nulls. Fortunately, we can add support for null values by using nullable data types when defining your function parameters, which we will discuss next.

Nullable primitive types

Sometimes, your data may include missing or unknown values, referred to as null values. In scenarios where a column could contain such null values alongside a primitive value, nullable primitive types become invaluable. These types are designed to accept both a specific primitive value and null values. We first discussed nullable types in *Chapter 5, Understanding Data Types*, which can be a complex topic. For a better understanding, we recommend revisiting that chapter before proceeding.

Using a strict primitive type (like text) for a column that might encounter null values can lead to errors in your queries when null values occur. On the other hand, specifying a column as type any is often too broad a classification. To address this, it's good practice to use a nullable primitive type. The term 'nullable' here means that the column can contain either a value of the specified primitive type or a null value. So how can we apply this?

Remember our age-checking function from the previous page? Suppose you have a dataset of customer ages, but some entries are missing. Let's see how you can use nullable types to handle this. If you use the function as-is on this dataset, you get an error that looks like the following screenshot:

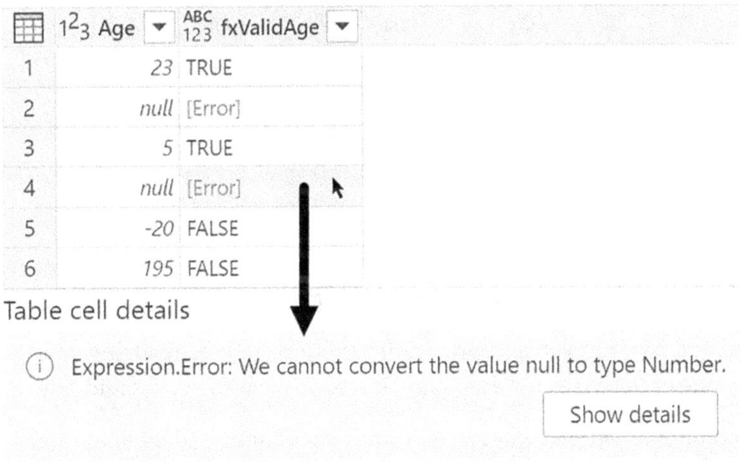

Figure 9.26: An error occurs when a function meets an unexpected null value

Your function checks if each input value matches its expected data type. Right now, the function is set to accept numbers only. If it encounters a value it doesn't recognize, like a null value, it gets confused and generates an error.

Learning how to manage situations with null values is, therefore, valuable. It allows you to handle the imperfect data that is often present in data sources. To address this issue, we'll change the parameter type to a `nullable number`:

```
(age as nullable number) as logical =>
    if age >= 0 and age <=  125 then true else false
```

The function now only accepts an age value with a nullable number type. With this modification, your function will attempt to return null whenever it encounters an unaccounted null value within the function expression. Unfortunately, the changed code still returns the error `Expression.Error: We cannot convert the value null to type Logical.`

The reason is that our function also enforces a logical value as output. And since the function tries to return null when it encounters null in one of the parameters, we get the error.

We can fix this by changing the function output to a nullable type, as shown here:

```
(age as nullable number) as nullable logical =>
        if age >= 0 and age <=  125 then true else false
```

With the change we made to the above code, the output of the function now accepts Boolean values and nulls. The following screenshot illustrates the result of applying this function to the Age column:

	1²₃ Age	ABC 123 fxValidAge
1	23	TRUE
2	null	null
3	5	TRUE
4	null	null
5	-20	FALSE
6	195	FALSE

Figure 9.27

When we apply this new function to the column with ages (including the nulls), it works smoothly.

In short, by defining data types you add precision to your function, ensuring valid input and making sure it returns a value of the expected data type. It knows what to expect and how to respond.

You may also encounter situations where you want your function to be able to handle different scenarios. Suppose some scenarios would require more variables than others. In those cases, you could resort to making some arguments optional. That way, you can have just a few required arguments to keep things simple, yet provide more functionality by offering one or more optional arguments. In the upcoming section, we'll explore how you can make arguments optional.

Making parameters optional

By default, a value must be provided for each parameter when a function is invoked. Yet, when working with custom functions, flexibility can be an important feature. An effective way to introduce flexibility is by allowing certain parameters to be optional. This means that when invoking a function, it's not always necessary to provide a value for every parameter. For instance, the Date.StartOfWeek function by default requires a single argument. An optional second argument allows you to specify which day you expect as start of the week. So how does that work?

When you define your function parameters, you can make them optional by proceeding them with the text optional. They often come with a default value, ensuring that the function can still run even if no value is provided for that specific parameter. Let's look at an example.

In our earlier example, we tested whether an age is valid. Imagine we want to provide our users with the option to set a maximum valid age. We can introduce an optional parameter, as follows:

```
(age as nullable number, optional maxAge as nullable number)
  as nullable logical =>
    age >= 0 and age <=  (maxAge ?? 125)
```

The code now includes an optional maxAge parameter that expects a nullable number as input. Let's examine what this code does:

- The preceding custom function has two arguments. The first argument requires an Age, but the maxAge argument is optional.
- The second argument is made optional by prefixing it with the word optional. Given this, whenever a user calls the function, it will not require the second argument to be filled in.
- Both arguments use a nullable type, implying that they support both the primitive type and null values.
- The coalesce operator (??) is used together with maxAge to provide a fallback value, as we will discuss next.

So what happens when you invoke the function without providing the optional argument? If the optional argument is omitted, the function defaults to using a null value. Given this, it's important to anticipate and handle this potential null value. This is where the coalesce operator comes in handy. This operator allows you to provide a fallback value. It first checks the primary value to the left of the operator. If it's non-null, it returns it; if it's null, it returns the fallback value on the right. In the context of the function's second argument, the coalesce operator would return 125 when faced with a null.

> **Pro Tip:** Power Query requires optional parameters to be positioned after the required arguments. That means that once you define an optional parameter, all parameters that follow must also be optional.

You can now invoke this function with either one or two parameters:

```
fxValidAge( 100 )     // Output: true
fxValidAge( 100, 90 ) // Output: false
```

In the first case, only the mandatory parameter is provided. In the second, the optional parameter is included. It checks whether the age of 100 is within the range of 0 to 90. Since it's not, it returns false. Knowing this would allow a user to take alternative action for outliers. For instance, they may return an error, or assume the input is wrong and provide a fallback value instead.

Now that you know how to create functions, define their data types, and even how to make parameters optional, let's have a look at how we can reference column and field names within functions. You might want to reference the field name using field selection (using square brackets), but surprisingly, that won't work. Let's find out why.

Referencing column and field names

Creating custom functions in Power Query involves an important step: defining parameters. These parameters are crucial, as they enable users to influence the function's output. However, referencing objects required for your function's logic isn't always straightforward. For example, in a standard formula, you might reference a column simply as `Column1`. But this direct approach doesn't work when a user inputs a column name as a parameter in your function; the typical square bracket notation isn't applicable in this context.

The upcoming section addresses scenarios where direct object referencing in the Query editor poses challenges. It guides you through alternative methods, focusing on the use of functions to make your references. This approach is required when standard referencing techniques fall short. By mastering these techniques, you'll improve your ability to create effective custom functions.

Referring to field names in a record

Suppose you want to filter a table's rows. The default function to filter rows in a table is `Table.SelectRows`. For example, to return the rows where the Sales amount is less than `1,000`, you write:

```
Table.SelectRows( Source, each [Sales] < 1000 )
```

But what if you want a function that lets the user pick which column to filter? You might try this, but it won't work:

```
( table as table, columnName as text ) as table =>
   Table.SelectRows( table, each [columnName] < 1000 )
```

When you run this, it filters the table in the first argument just fine. But it doesn't do what you would expect with the second argument. Instead of retrieving the user input from the `columnName` argument, the engine looks for a column named `columnName`.

So how do we fix this? First, understand what `[Sales]` means in the initial formula. It could be a column name in a table or a field name in a record.

If you are not sure, here's an easy way to test this. Try replacing the condition with an underscore; you'll get an error, but this error helps us. It says, `We cannot convert a value of type Record to type Logical`. This confirms we're dealing with a record.

To dynamically refer to a column, you can then use the `Record.Field` function. This function takes two inputs: the record and the column name as text. Here's how you can rewrite the function:

```
( table as table, columnName as text ) as table =>
Table.SelectRows( table,
  each Record.Field(_, columnName) < 1000)
```

This way, the function will filter rows based on the column name that your user provides, achieving the dynamic behavior we wanted. The provided solution works for a record, but how can you proceed when selecting columns from a table?

Referring to columns in a table

Another object with a similar issue is a table column. Suppose you want to check if a value in the current row also exists in a column from another table. For this example, let's consider a table named Bonus with a column called Products.

If you do not need the column as a parameter, the formula could look like this:

```
Table.AddColumn(
  Source,
  "IsBonusProduct",
  each if List.Contains(Bonus[Products], [Product]) then true
    else false )
```

Here, we add a new column called IsBonusProduct to the source table. The output tells us if the corresponding Product also exists in the Bonus[Products] list.

But what if you want to make this more flexible? For instance, you might want to let the user specify the lookup table and column. That would allow them to maintain a simple table of replacement values. For instance, they could have a calendar table and want to specify the column names for each of the languages they use. Storing these in a table is much easier than hardcoding them.

Unfortunately, a direct reference to a column isn't possible. To achieve this, you should instead use the Table.Column function, which returns a list from a specific table and column.

Here's how you can write a custom function to handle this:

```
( table as table, newColumnName as text, lookupTable as table, lookupColumnName
as text ) as table =>
Table.AddColumn(
  table,
  newColumnName,
  each if List.Contains(
    Table.Column( lookupTable, lookupColumnName),
      Record.Field( table, "Product" ) )
    then true else false )
```

In this function, you have four parameters:

- table: The main table you're working on
- newColumnName: The name of the new column you're adding
- lookupTable: The table containing the list you're checking against
- lookupColumnName: The specific column in lookupTable that has the list

To make this work effectively, you need to use two specific functions: `Table.Column` for targeting columns and `Record.Field` for targeting fields.

First, `Table.Column` fetches the list of values from the designated lookup table and column. Next, the function checks whether the current `Product`, identified by the `Record.Field` function, exists in that list. It then returns either true or false, based on this check.

The important part here is that users can now provide a text value for both the `lookupTable` and `thelookupColumnName`, and the function will pick up the actual column values. Later in this chapter, we will explore a project that illustrates how you can use this in a practical example.

Custom functions can add complexity to your code. As you introduce more iterations, your code lengthens, sometimes extending over several pages. This added complexity is manageable until you encounter an error in your custom function. At this point, a step-by-step examination of your code becomes useful to pinpoint where the error occurs. Unlike regular queries, functions don't inherently provide a simple way to perform this detailed examination. Mastering debugging techniques for custom functions is, therefore, essential. The next section will guide you through effective methods to tackle these challenges.

Debugging custom functions

The process of creating custom functions is straightforward once you understand the basics. It involves defining parameters and integrating them into your code, transforming your query into a function. But what happens when you encounter an error in a custom function? Or maybe you're adapting code you found online and run into issues? You have now lost the steps from the query pane that normally help you troubleshoot your code. Well, this is where understanding how to debug custom functions comes into play.

Let's say you're working with a specific function like the following:

```
1   ( numberList as list, minValue as number, maxValue as number ) as text =>
2     let
3       List       = List.Select ( numberList, each _ >= minValue and _ <= maxValue ),
4       ListToText = List.Transform ( FilteredList, each Text.From ( _ ) ),
5       CombineText = Text.Combine ( ListToText, ", " )
6     in
7       CombineText
```

Figure 9.28: You recognize a custom function by the function parameters on the first line

The above code shows up in the query pane as a function. And whenever you execute the function, you only see the final output. But if you are new to custom functions or you run into an error, you might want to see how each step works.

Luckily, there's an easy way to return a function into a query. To do that, you:

1. Create a variable for each parameter in your query definition.
2. Comment out the function definition.

Here's what that looks like:

```
1   // ( numberList as list, minValue as number, maxValue as number ) as text =>
2   let
3       numberList  = { 1 .. 10 },
4       minValue    = 2,
5       maxValue    = 8,
6       List        = List.Select ( numberList, each _ >= minValue and _ <= maxValue ),
7       ListToText  = List.Transform ( List, each Text.From ( _ ) ),
8       CombineText = Text.Combine ( ListToText, ", " )
9   in
10      CombineText
```

Figure 9.29: A custom function turns into a regular query when adding the relevant parameters

Each parameter that we defined in line 1 now has its own definition in the `let` expression on lines 3–5. This means that the rest of the query can still reference the parameter names, but this time, it retrieves the values from within the code.

By doing this, you turn the function back into a query. This allows you to examine each step of the logic closely. Once you've finished debugging, you can return your logic to a function by undoing the changes: comment out the debugging variables and uncomment the function definition line.

Up to this point, we've saved functions as distinct queries. This is done either by manually writing the function or by converting an existing query into one. It's important to note, however, that defining a function directly within a query is also a valid approach. You can then use this function later in the same query. The upcoming section will delve into the concept of function scope. We'll explore how understanding scope enables you to effectively call functions within a single query.

Function scope

Similar to creating parameters and queries, there are scopes in which you can define a function. You can either define one as:

- Top-level expression
- In-line in a query

So how do those two ways differ, and what can you use them for?

Top-level expression

The way most people use custom functions is as a top-level expression. To create a top-level function, you can paste the function code into the **Advanced editor** and press **OK**. Power Query automatically creates the function and adds it between your queries in the **Queries** pane. From here, it can be referenced from other queries or functions.

The following image illustrates what a simple function named **MyFunction** looks like and how it is defined:

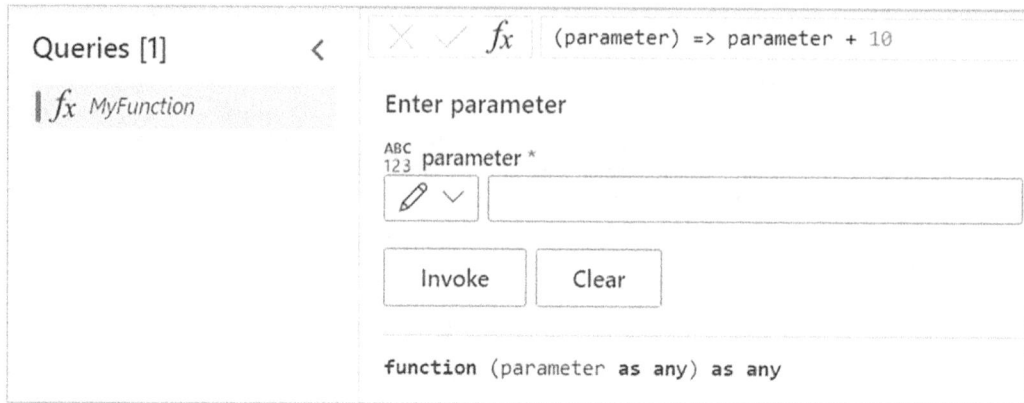

Figure 9.30: Creating a custom function

You can recognize a function by its prefix with the **fx** symbol in the **Queries** pane. Whatever name you give to the query will be the name of your function. For example, the above function is called MyFunction. The benefit of defining a function at this level is that you can call it from other queries by referencing its name. So far, this is also how we've looked at custom functions throughout the chapter. However, you can also create custom functions in line within a query, which we will cover now.

In line within a query

Defining a function in line within one of your queries is a useful technique. Think of it like this; a function is an expression, and your query consists of a series of expressions. And just like any other expression, you can include your custom function definition within your query.

For instance, suppose you created the following logic in a query called SquareRoots:

```
let
    Value1 = 5,
    Value2 = 10,
    sqrtDivide = ( Number1, Number2 ) =>
      let
        SqrtNumber1 = Number.Sqrt( Number1 ),
        SqrtNumber2 = Number.Sqrt( Number2 ),
        Result = SqrtNumber1 / SqrtNumber2
      in
        Result,
    Applyfunction = sqrtDivide( Value1, Value2 )
in
    Applyfunction
```

What we see here is a let expression as you know it from any of your queries. The third query step defines a custom function named `sqrtDivide`. Later, we invoke that function by calling it in the `Applyfunction` step. What this shows is that you can use a custom function even if it is not stored as a single query.

It's important to know that functions created within a query are only usable in the scope of that specific query. For instance, `sqrtDivide` can be used in the `ApplyFunction` step because it's part of the same query. If you navigate to a different query, like `Calendar`, you won't be able to use the `sqrtDivide` function. This is because it's limited to where it was created, which is outside of `Calendar`.

When deciding how to set up your function, think about how you'll use it. If you need to use the custom function in several queries, make it a top-level expression. If you only need it in one query, an inline function reduces the number of items in the query pane and keeps it organized. Ultimately, it's up to you to decide. So with all this freshly gained knowledge, how can you use this in some practical scenarios? Let's find out.

Putting it all together

So far, we have learned various ways to create custom functions and make use of parameters. We have explored the components of a custom function and learned that the each expression is syntax sugar for a unary function. We then delved into defining data types for both input parameters and the output of your function. And then we looked at how making parameters optional includes an additional level of flexibility.

We encourage you to apply these concepts in your own projects. Whenever you need the logic in multiple places, try covering some of your query logic in custom functions. Practical application is key to understanding these concepts. Next, we will reinforce what we have learned by looking at some practical examples that bring these ideas together.

Turning all columns into text

The first scenario we will look at is turning columns into a desired data type.

Introduction to the column type problem

For our first scenario, we're going to look at a situation where new data may come in from an unstructured file. The challenge with unstructured files like CSV, Excel, or JSON is that they don't provide metadata, with information about the data types in the file. This can, therefore, lead to recurring work with regards to setting data types. To make this process easier, let's focus on creating a custom function to deal with our requirements. You can follow along by navigating to this dataset in the exercise file accompanying this book.

Here's the situation that our function needs to address. You have a file with more than 20 queries. Most of these queries have columns containing text. New columns are added from time to time, and they're also text. You want to avoid manually setting the column types each time. Some columns should remain unchanged and not be converted to text.

Your task is to create a function that transforms all columns in your query to the type text. With such a function in place, we can simply call that function as the final step of each query. And regardless of any columns added later, the function will transform your columns into text. So how can we do that?

Understanding data type transformation

Suppose we work with the following table:

ABC 123 Destination	ABC 123 Country	ABC 123 Popular Attractions	ABC 123 Best Time to Visit	ABC 123 Description
Paris	France	Eiffel Tower, Louvre, Notre-Dame	Spring and Fall	Known as the "City of Love," fam
Tokyo	Japan	Tokyo Disneyland, Senso-ji Temple	Spring and Autumn	A bustling metropolis with a rich
Venice	Italy	Grand Canal, St. Mark's Square	Spring and Summer	Renowned for its romantic canals
New York City	USA	Times Square, Central Park	Spring and Fall	The city that never sleeps, offerir
Sydney	Australia	Sydney Opera House, Bondi Beach	Spring and Summer	Home to iconic landmarks like th
Santorini	Greece	Oia, Fira	Summer	A stunning island in the Aegean
Cairo	Egypt	Pyramids of Giza, Egyptian Museum	Fall and Winter	Explore ancient history, including
Rio de Janeiro	Brazil	Christ the Redeemer, Copacabana Beach	Summer	Famous for its Carnival, Christ the

Figure 9.31: Table with columns of type any

Each of the columns is currently of type any. When you set the first two columns to type text, Power Query uses the `Table.TransformColumnTypes` function:

```
Table.TransformColumnTypes(
    Source,
    {{"Destination", type text}, {"Country", type text}} )
```

The generated code shows that the function requires two things. First, it needs a table as its starting point—in this case, `Source`. Then, it requires an outer list that holds multiple inner lists. Each inner list contains two things: the name of the column to change and what type to change it to. In this example, that is:

```
{{"Destination", type text}, {"Country", type text}}
```

While this example shows the format we want, it's not very flexible. After all, it hardcodes the column names into the expression. That means it could cause errors when column names change or are deleted, but it also excludes any new columns that may be added to the data in the future.

That means that this automatically generated code would require constant manual adjustment. That's not the work a smart developer wants to spend their time on. Let's see if we can create a function for this.

Building the initial function

To build the first version of this function, we will:

1. Retrieve the *names of all columns* in the table and put them in a list.
2. Change each column name in the list to a pair: the name and its data type.
3. Use this updated list as input for `Table.TransformColumnTypes`.

To retrieve all column names from a table, you can make use of the `Table.ColumnNames` function. The following statement returns all column names from the table in a step called `Source`:

```
Table.ColumnNames( Source )
```

This returns the following:

```
{ "Destination", "Country", "Popular Attractions", "Best Time to Visit",
"Description" }
```

We end up with a list of column names. Ideally, we would turn each text value in the list into a list that contains the column name and the data type. To achieve this, you can use the `List.Transform` function, as shown:

```
List.Transform(
    Table.ColumnNames( Source ),
    each {_ , type text } )
```

In this code, the first argument retrieves a list of all column names from the source table, whereas the second argument provides the logic to transform each item in the list into the correct format.

The underscore in the second argument represents each column name in the list. The expression adds `", type text"` after the column names and surrounds the output with curly brackets. The output of the above expression is:

```
{ {"Destination", type text }
  {"Country", type text }
  {"Popular Attractions", type text }
  {"Best Time to Visit", type text }
  {"Description", type text }
}
```

What's left for us to do is to pass this argument to the `Table.TransformColumnTypes` argument. So far, the steps we performed are:

```
1  let
2      Source = MyTable,
3      Columns = Table.ColumnNames( Source ),
4      TransformTypes = List.Transform( Columns, each { _, type text } ),
5      TypeToText =  Table.TransformColumnTypes( Source, TransformTypes )
6  in
7      TypeToText
```

Figure 9.32: Query that transforms columns to type text

To turn this code into a function, the first step is to identify the parameters that your function requires. In this situation, the function aims to change all column types to text. Therefore, you mainly need an input table. Let's create a parameter for the table name and incorporate the parameter on line 3.

Doing that gives us the following code:

```
1   ( InputTable as table ) as table =>
2   let
3       Source = InputTable,
4       Columns = Table.ColumnNames( Source ),
5       TransformTypes = List.Transform( Columns, each { _, type text } ),
6       TypeToText =  Table.TransformColumnTypes( Source, TransformTypes )
7   in
8       TypeToText
```

Figure 9.33: Function that transforms columns to type text

After creating our first version of the function, let's name it fxToText. Now, whenever you want to turn all your columns to text, all you have to do is add a step with the code:

```
FxToText ( <previousStep> )
```

Applying this to the Source step turns all our columns into text, as illustrated here:

```
X  ✓   fx    fxToText( Source )
```

	A%C Destination ▼	A%C Country ▼	A%C Popular Attractions ▼	A%C Best Time to Visit ▼	A%C Description
1	Paris	France	Eiffel Tower, Louvre, Notre-Dame	Spring and Fall	Known as the "City
2	Tokyo	Japan	Tokyo Disneyland, Senso-ji Temple	Spring and Autumn	A bustling metrop
3	Venice	Italy	Grand Canal, St. Mark's Square	Spring and Summer	Renowned for its r

Figure 9.34: The fxToText function turns all columns into text

This is a great start. Let's see if we can refine our function with functionality that allows you to exclude columns from the conversion to text.

Enhancing the function with optional parameters

The above code works, and you can now use it. However, the last requirement of this case is to be able to exclude specific columns so that they are not converted to text. Since this feature won't be used on every query, it makes sense to make this parameter optional. That way, our function does not overcomplicate simple uses but can still cover exclusions when necessary.

So what should we do to build this requirement into the function?

1. Start by adding an optional parameter that takes a list of columns you want to exclude.
2. Then, modify the code so it excludes these specified columns from the conversion.

First, let's add an optional parameter named Exclusions. When a function requires multiple items, it's often useful to request them in the form of a list. This lets users either manually enter a list or refer to columns for values. Update your input parameters like this:

```
( InputTable as table, optional Exclusions as list ) as table
```

Remember what happens if the user doesn't provide a value for an optional parameter? The function by default provides a null value for this parameter. To make the function work properly, it needs to handle this null value.

To manage the null, consider how the rest of your function will use `Exclusions`. A straightforward way to exclude specific columns is with the List.RemoveItems function. You can use it like this:

```
List.RemoveItems( AllColumns, Exclusions )
```

However, if `Exclusions` is null, the `List.RemoveItems` operation fails. To prevent this, you can use an empty list as a fallback. An easy way to achieve this is by using the coalesce operator:

```
Exclusions ?? {}
```

This expression returns an empty list whenever the `Exclusions` parameter is null. Since removing an empty list doesn't change the original list, this solution fits our needs. Putting this together in our final function then gets us:

```
1   ( InputTable as table, optional Exclusions as list ) as table =>
2   let
3       Source = InputTable,
4       AllColumns = Table.ColumnNames( Source ),
5       Exclusions = Exclusions ?? {} ,
6       RelevantColumns = List.RemoveItems( AllColumns, Exclusions ),
7       TransformTypes = List.Transform( RelevantColumns, each { _, type text } ),
8       TypeToText =  Table.TransformColumnTypes( Source, TransformTypes )
9   in
10      TypeToText
```

Figure 9.35: Incorporating an optional parameter

Since removing an empty list doesn't change the original list, this solution fits our needs. We can apply it to our table as follows:

ABC 123 Destination	ABC 123 Country	ABC Popular Attractions	ABC Best Time to Vi...	ABC Description
1	Paris	France	Eiffel Tower, Louvre, Notre-Dame	Spring and Fall	Known as the "City of Lov
2	Tokyo	Japan	Tokyo Disneyland, Senso-ji Temple	Spring and Autumn	A bustling metropolis wit
3	Venice	Italy	Grand Canal, St. Mark's Square	Spring and Summer	Renowned for its romant

Figure 9.36: A function that turns all except a few columns to text

Notice how the **Destination** and **Country** columns are not converted to type text. Mission accomplished. We've successfully built a function that converts your columns to text. All you have to do is add this function as the final step of your query and reference the previous step. The function's text conversion will then work on both existing and future columns. And if you wish to exclude certain columns, you can do so using the optional second argument.

Next, we'll look at a useful example that takes a different angle. It requires knowing how to reference different objects within your table, but it also challenges your knowledge of scope.

Merging tables based on date ranges

In this section, we'll tackle the challenge of merging tables based on a range of dates. We will incorporate the different concepts we've learned throughout the chapter. You will need to be aware of the each construct and the scope in which we perform our code. We'll use this to make references to different values. At the same time, the custom function requires you to know how to reference columns and fields so that they can be used as input parameters. The data is available in the exercise files that you can find on the GitHub page for the book.

Imagine you're dealing with customer transactions tied to specific contracts, but there's no unique contract ID to connect them. While Power Query offers various types of joins, it falls short when you need to join tables based on a range of dates. The good news is that this is a great opportunity to hone your problem-solving skills, to find out if you can solve the scenario by building a custom function.

Our custom function will address these requirements:

- The main table has a column containing dates.
- The Contracts table includes both start and end dates for each contract.
- The data types of all columns should remain intact after the join.

We'll start by creating a formula to perform this specialized join. After that, we'll transform it into a reusable function.

Performing a join based on date ranges

For this example, consider a simplified dataset. We have a Transactions table with five transactions, each with a corresponding date. There's also a Contract table, listing each contract's start and end dates:

Table: Transactions				Table: Contract		
A^B_C Id	Date	1^2_3 Amount		A^B_C ContractID	Start	End
SI-1401	2/7/2023	237		VI-2023-A1	1/1/2023	3/31/2023
SI-1402	11/3/2023	489		VI-2023-B2	4/1/2023	6/30/2023
SI-1403	9/22/2023	712		VI-2023-C3	7/1/2023	8/31/2023
SI-1404	5/9/2023	56		VI-2023-D4	9/1/2023	12/31/2023
SI-1405	12/29/2023	901				

Figure 9.37: Dataset for a range-based join

Our objective is to enrich the Transactions table with data from the Contract table. A straightforward way to do this is by adding a new column and using the Table.SelectRows function.

For the first step:

1. Go to **Add Column** in the ribbon and select **Custom Column**.

2. Name the new column `Contracts`.

3. Add the formula: `Table.SelectRows( Contract , each true )`.

Using this setup, the entire Contracts table will appear in each row of the new column. The code will look like this:

```
Table.AddColumn(
    Source,
    "Contracts",
    each Table.SelectRows( Contract, each true ) )
```

In this code, we add a new column called `Contracts` to the table called `Source`. The newly added column contains a copy of the `Contract` table and returns all rows. This sets the stage for us placing all contract data within reach for each transaction. Since we now have access to the data of the Contract table, our next task is to filter the table down to a specific date.

Adjusting the formula for a specific date

In the `Table.SelectRows` function, the condition you specify affects only the rows in the Contract table. To filter out only those contracts that start on July 1st, 2023, you can use the following code:

```
Table.AddColumn(
    Source,
    "Contracts",
    each Table.SelectRows( Contract,
        each [Start] = #date(2023,7,1) )
)
```

Notice the change of code in the second argument of the `Table.SelectRows` function. It specifies that we only want rows of a particular date.

The above code shows a necessary step to filter down rows, but it still hardcodes the date. To make our custom function work, it's important that the date filters a date range and does so dynamically. Let's find out how we can do that.

Making the date filter dynamic

Next, we aim to replace the hardcoded date with a dynamic reference to the Date column in the Transactions table. This introduces a complex issue, scope, a topic we touched upon in *Chapter 7, Conceptualizing M*.

If you try to replace `#date(2023, 7, 1)` with `[Date]`, Power Query will return an error. It can't find the `Date` field in the current record context.

The key lies in understanding the role of the `each` keyword. The first instance of `each` is in `Table.AddColumn`, where the Date column from the Transactions table is still in scope. However, another `each` keyword appears in `Table.SelectRows`. This introduces a conflict.

Remember, each is essentially shorthand for a single-argument function, represented as (_) =>. That means the code contains two variables with the underscore (_) as their name. And whenever you reference a variable name that appears multiple times, the one in the inner scope is prioritized over the one in the outer scope.

To access both an internal column (Start from Contracts) and an external one (Date from Transactions), we need to turn one of the each expressions into a custom function of our own. This will allow us to provide a different variable name and, with that, manage the different scopes involved. Let's find out how we can incorporate this into our code.

Dealing with scopes using a custom function

The Table.AddColumn function can accept a custom function parameter to handle the scope issue. The custom function allows access to both the Transactions and Contracts tables:

```
Table.AddColumn(
  Source,
  "Contracts",
  (x) => Table.SelectRows( Contract,
    each x[Date] <= [Start] )
)
```

Here, the parameter x helps to access the outer context where the Transactions table is visible. It is available within the scope of the Table.AddColumn function. Using the same concept, we can also include the criteria for the end date, which results in:

```
Table.AddColumn(
  Source,
  "Contracts",
  (x)=> Table.SelectRows( Contract ,
    each x[Date] >= [Start] and x[Date] <= [End] )
)
```

The filtering condition now refers to the x[Date] column, which refers to the Date column in the Transaction table. Great, so the scope issue is solved here. However, when we expand columns after performing the above operation, we lose data types. Let's see how we can keep those intact.

Addressing data type issues

We now have the relevant filtered rows in each line of the new column. However, there's one remaining problem: the column lacks a specified data type, as shown in the following image:

	Id	Date	Amount	Contracts
1	SI-1401	2/7/2023	237	[Table]
2	SI-1402	11/3/2023	489	[Table]
3	SI-1403	9/22/2023	712	[Table]
4	SI-1404	5/9/2023	56	[Table]
5	SI-1405	12/29/2023	901	[Table]

Figure 9.38: Join column misses a data type

What can we do to specify the correct data types here? Manually inputting them would take away the purpose of a custom function. Yet the Contracts table already has the correct data types. Perhaps we can refer to those and provide them to the new column?

Retrieving data types from another table using the `Value.Type` function is the simplest solution. You can use the function to simply reference the Contracts table and retrieve the data type definition.

The code, which also sets the data type for the new column, looks like this:

```
Table.AddColumn(
  Source,
  "Contracts",
  (x)=> Table.SelectRows( Contract ,
    each x[Date] >= [Start] and x[Date] <= [End] ),
  Value.Type( Contract )
)
```

The above example now includes the fourth argument of `Table.AddColumn`. It dynamically picks up the data types from the contracts table. Now, the new column not only filters the data correctly but also carries the appropriate data type from the Contract table.

With this logic in place, our query performs the join with all our requirements. Next, you need to transform this logic into a function.

Turning logic into a function

To make our code reusable, we'll turn it into a custom function. We aim to closely resemble the `Table.NestedJoin` function. Initially, we'll introduce two parameters:

- The table to add a column to (Table)
- The column to use for the date comparison (Date)

As discussed earlier in this chapter, by using the `Record.Field` function, we are able to take a text value as input for the date column and still reference the column. Incorporating this into our M code looks as follows:

```
( Table as table, Date as text ) as table =>
Table.AddColumn(
  Table,
  "Contracts",
  (x)=> Table.SelectRows( Contract,
    each Record.Field(x, Date) >= [Start]
      and Record.Field(x, Date) <= [End] ),
  Value.Type( Contract )
)
```

While the code gets more verbose, it successfully references the date field from your transactions table. Next, we add parameters for:

- The table to join (`joinTable`)
- The name of the new join column (`newColumnName`)
- The start and end dates used in the join (`startDate` and `endDate`)

To do that, we expand the parameter list and incorporate the parameter references:

```
(Table as table, Date as text, joinTable as table, startDate as text, endDate
as text, newColumnName as text) as table =>
Table.AddColumn(
  Table,
  newColumnName,
  (x)=>
  Table.SelectRows( joinTable, each
    Record.Field(x, Date) >= Record.Field(_, startDate) and
    Record.Field(x, Date) <= Record.Field(_, endDate) ),
  Value.Type( joinTable )
)
```

You can see how the `joinTable` parameter replaces the hardcoded Contract table, and the `newColumnName` replaces the hardcoded name. Lastly, the `startDate` and `endDate` now also use `Record.Field` to reference a column.

We now have a complete custom function—`fxDateRangeJoin`. When you apply it to the Transactions table, you end up in the following situation:

```
fxDateRangeJoin( Source, "Date", Contract, "Start", "End", "Contracts" )
```

	ABC Id	Date	123 Amount	Contracts
1	SI-1401	2/7/2023	237	[Table]
2	SI-1402	11/3/2023	489	[Table]
3	SI-1403	9/22/2023	712	[Table]
4	SI-1404	5/9/2023	56	[Table]
5	SI-1405	12/29/2023	901	[Table]

Figure 9.39: Custom function for date range joins

What remains for us to do is expand the Contracts column and include the three fields from the other table. Doing that gives us:

	ABC Id	Date	123 Amount	ABC ContractID	Start	End
1	SI-1401	2/7/2023	237	SI-1401	1/1/2023	3/31/2023
2	SI-1402	11/3/2023	489	SI-1404	9/1/2023	12/31/2023
3	SI-1403	9/22/2023	712	SI-1404	9/1/2023	12/31/2023
4	SI-1404	5/9/2023	56	SI-1402	4/1/2023	6/30/2023
5	SI-1405	12/29/2023	901	SI-1404	9/1/2023	12/31/2023

Figure 9.40: Expanding fields after performing the date range join to include the relevant fields

And that's it—we have achieved our goal. From now on, whenever you need to join tables based on a range of dates, instead of a complex formula, you can use this simplified function.

As you've seen through these two projects, turning a query into a robust custom function is an iterative process. You start by building your query logic. Once satisfied, you analyze which parts should be dynamic. With that in mind, you introduce the parameters and incorporate them throughout your code. This process can be daunting at first, but with experience, it becomes a very powerful concept to use in your queries.

Summary

This chapter introduced parameters. Parameters, as you've seen, are more than mere placeholders in Power Query. They provide you with flexibility and cater to varied scenarios. As you progress in your Power Query journey, you will find yourself reaching out to parameters more and more to make your queries easier to adjust.

We also took a deep dive into the world of custom functions in Power Query M. They allow you to turn your custom queries into reusable logic. You learned how to transform a query into a function without having to write it yourself. We then covered the ins and outs of invoking functions and highlighted the role of the each expression in simplifying the creation of functions.

We also explored how the syntax varies when calling single- versus multi-argument functions. In more intricate situations, where scope becomes a concern, working with the each keyword does not suffice. For these cases, creating your own custom function is required. Beyond that, we touched on data types and the flexibility that optional parameters provide. And when you run into errors, you now know how to debug your functions.

With this new knowledge of how to build custom functions, you now have the ability to reuse logic throughout multiple queries, while keeping your code organized. And with your custom functions in hand, you just gained another way to provide more junior colleagues with an easy way to perform complex transformations.

In the upcoming chapter, we delve into another essential topic. You'll learn how to work with dates, times, and durations. These types of values not only appear commonly in the data you import; virtually every Power BI model also requires a good data table. Learning how to work with these types of values is, therefore, invaluable and will prove useful in a great range of scenarios.

Learn more on Discord

Join our community's Discord space for discussions with the author and other readers:

```
https://discord.gg/vCSG5GBbyS
```

10

Dealing with Dates, Times, and Durations

Given the importance of dates in reporting, understanding how to handle dates, times and durations in Power Query is a critical skill to master. Indeed, nearly every Power BI data model has, or should have, a date table dimension. This is because while knowing the value of a KPI or metric is important, it is much more important to know the value of that KPI or metric at specific dates or at specific times and even more valuable to understand the trend of that KPI or metric over the span of days, months, or even years.

Luckily, the M language includes well over 100 standard functions for dealing with dates, times, durations, date/times, and date/time/time zone calculations and transformations. With these functions, it is relatively simple to perform most standard temporal calculations. In this chapter, we will explore many of these functions as well as practical applications that will increase your depth of knowledge and understanding of the M language.

Specifically, this chapter covers the following topics:

- Dates
- Time
- Dates and times
- Time zones
- Duration

Technical requirements

The Power Query editor within Power BI Desktop can be used to complete the examples in this chapter. For a review of using the Power Query editor, see *Chapter 2*.

Dates

Dates are the backbone of temporal analysis, forming the foundation upon which we generate meaningful insights about data. There are almost 60 M functions specific to working with dates. But dates have a secret – they are really just numbers that represent the number of days prior to or after a particular reference date.

We can demonstrate this with a simple example by creating a blank query and using the advanced editor with the following code:

1. Create the following query in the Power Query editor:

    ```
    let
        Source = List.Generate(() => -10, each _ <= 10, each _ + 1)
    in
        Source
    ```

2. In the **List Tools | Transform** tab of the ribbon, click the **To Table** button:

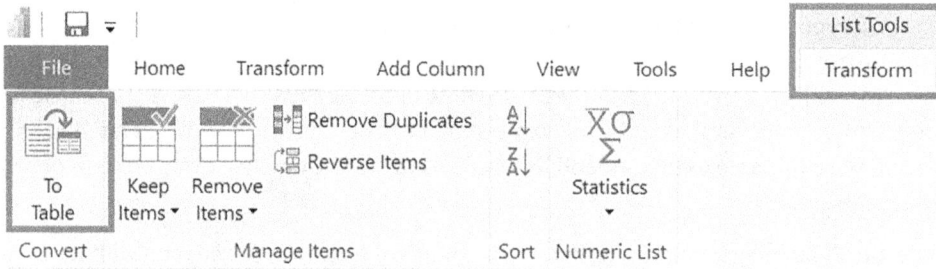

Figure 10.1: Convert list to table

3. On the **To Table** dialog, simply click the **OK** button.
4. Right-click the header for **Column1** and choose **Duplicate Column**.
5. Right-click the header for **Column1**, choose **Change Type**, and then **Date**:

```
 ×   ✓   fx   = Table.FromList(Source, Splitter.SplitByNothing(), null, null, ExtraValues.Error)
```

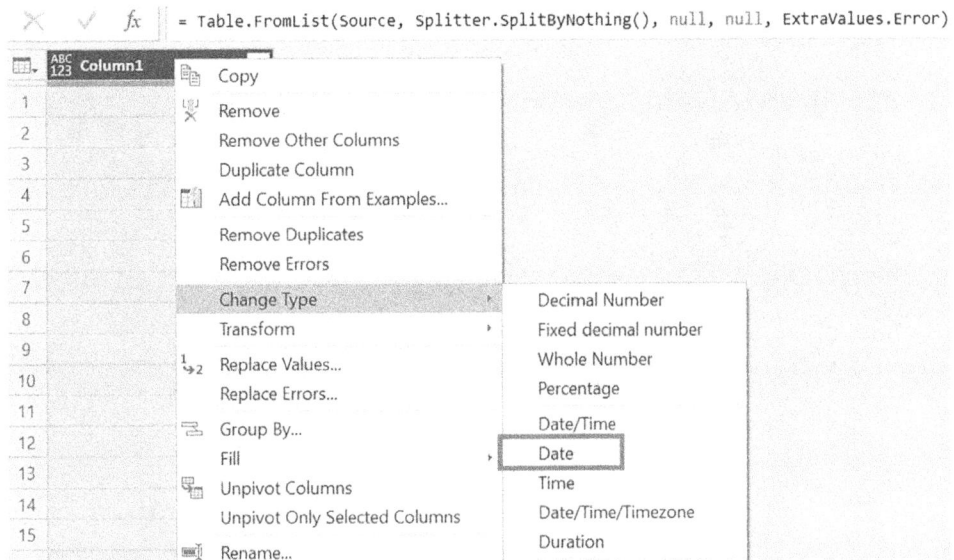

Figure 10.2: Convert column to Date

Once the column is converted to a date, we can see that the number 0 corresponds to a reference date of 12/30/1899. Each positive or negative increment of 1 will increase or decrease the date by one day, respectively.

There are limits to M's ability to handle certain dates. For example, dates prior to 1/1/1 and after 12/31/9999 are not possible to represent in M. Perhaps oddly, converting from a number to a date has different restrictions. While the same maximum date of 12/31/9999 applies (2,958,465), the minimum number that can be converted is -657,434, which corresponds to a date of 1/1/100.

These limitations appear quite arbitrary, as they do not correspond to such things as the number of bytes for storing the number, neither are the limits balanced between positive and negative days after or before the reference date. But, for most practical applications, these limitations are not a concern. That said, these limitations can impact calculating things such as past and future astronomical events, such as solstices and equinoxes (see the *Julian days* example later in this section).

The fact that dates are represented as numbers is perhaps not as important in M as, for example, DAX. In DAX, the fact that dates are numbers allows the full range of arithmetic operations, such as using simple addition or subtraction to calculate dates.

However, in M, if we attempt this, we receive an error, such as that shown in *Figure 10.3*:

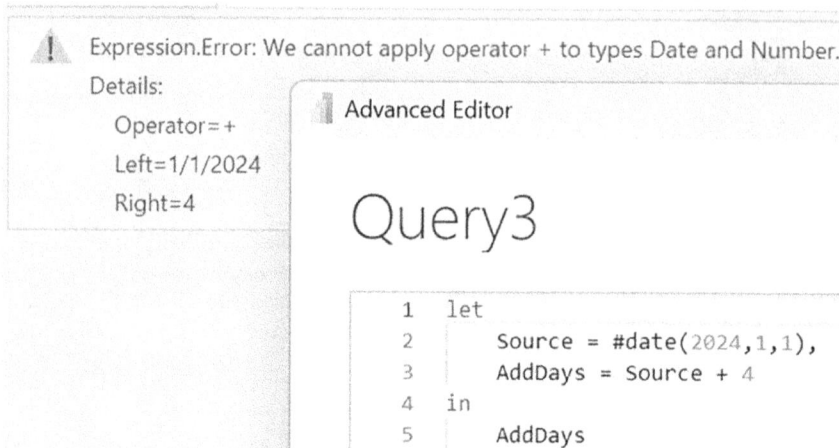

> ⚠ Expression.Error: We cannot apply operator + to types Date and Number.
> Details:
>   Operator=+
>   Left=1/1/2024
>   Right=4

> ▌ Advanced Editor
>
> # Query3
>
> ```
> 1  let
> 2      Source = #date(2024,1,1),
> 3      AddDays = Source + 4
> 4  in
> 5      AddDays
> ```

Figure 10.3: Error adding a number to a date

Instead, we must specifically convert the date to a number and the number to a date, by using the following code in a new (blank) query:

```
let
    Source = #date(2024,1,1),
    AddDays = Number.From(Source) + 4,
    NewDate = Date.From(AddDays)
in
    NewDate
```

This code returns a date of January 5th, 2024. This may appear as 1/5/2024 or 5/1/2024, depending on your culture settings.

We first construct the date using the #date function, which takes the year, month, and day as the first, second, and third parameters, respectively. The Number.From function is used to cast the date data type to a number, and then the Date.From function is used to cast the number back to a date data type. The Date.From function takes any text, datetime, datetimezone, or number value as its first parameter and attempts to convert that value to a date. If any other data type is provided or the Date.From function is unable to parse the value and determine the date, an error is returned.

An optional second parameter, **Culture**, allows the specification of a culture when converting the value to a date. For example, if you are running Power BI Desktop on a computer with the local culture being United States English, en-US, and receive a date as text in the culture of the United Kingdom, en-GB, then the following expression could be used to properly parse the date and return February 14th, 2024 (2/14/2024):

```
Date.From("14/2/2024", "en-GB")
```

Certain arithmetic operations are allowed. For example, consider the following code:

```
let
    Date1 = #date(2024, 1, 1),
    Date2 = #date(2024, 1, 5),
    Diff = Date2 - Date1
in
    Diff
```

This returns a `Duration` type with a value of `4.00:00:00` or, essentially, 4 days.

Let's next take a look at some of the various functions available for dates within M, starting with a simple query to display a list of dates for the years 2024, 2025, and 2026:

```
let
    Source = List.Generate( () => #date(2024, 1, 1), each _ <= #date(2026, 12,
31), each Date.AddDays( _, 1)),
    Table = Table.FromList(Source, Splitter.SplitByNothing(), null, null,
ExtraValues.Error),
    RenameColumn1 = Table.RenameColumns(Table,{{"Column1", "Date"}})
in
    RenameColumn1
```

Here, we see that in our `Source` statement, we use the `Date.AddDays` function within the `List.Generate` function to increment the date by 1 until we reach `December 31st, 2026`. There are also related functions for other standard temporal units, including `Date.AddWeeks`, `Date.AddMonths`, `Date.AddQuarters`, and `Date.AddYears`.

There are a number of functions for extracting the components of a date, as shown in the following code, that we can add to our original query of dates for the years 2024–2026:

```
    AddYearColumn = Table.AddColumn( RenameColumn1, "Year", each Date.
Year([Date])),
    AddMonthColumn = Table.AddColumn( AddYearColumn, "Month", each Date.
Month([Date])),
    AddDayColumn = Table.AddColumn( AddMonthColumn, "Day", each Date.
Day([Date]))
```

You can modify the preceding code and add this code by doing the following:

1. Add a comma to the end of the last line above the `in` keyword.
2. Paste the three lines of code after the comma that you just added and prior to the `in` keyword.
3. Change the statement after the `in` keyword from `RenameColumn1` to `AddDayColumn`.

Here, the `Date.Year`, `Date.Month`, and `Date.Day` functions are used to extract the respective components of the date. Another way that you can extract date components is via the `Date.ToRecord` function. For example, the following expression returns a record that includes a field/value pair for year, month, and date:

```
Date.ToRecord(#date(2024, 2, 14))
```

There are also functions to infer additional information from a date, such as the quarter of the year, week of the year, week of month, day name, and so on:

```
    AddQuarterColumn = Table.AddColumn( AddDayColumn, "Quarter", each Date.
QuarterOfYear([Date])),
    AddWeekOfYearColumn = Table.AddColumn( AddQuarterColumn, "Week of Year",
each Date.WeekOfYear([Date])),
    AddWeekOfMonthColumn = Table.AddColumn( AddWeekOfYearColumn, "Week of
Month", each Date.WeekOfMonth([Date])),
    AddDayOfWeekColumn = Table.AddColumn( AddWeekOfMonthColumn, "Day of Week",
each Date.DayOfWeek([Date])),
    AddDayOfWeekNameColumn = Table.AddColumn( AddDayOfWeekColumn, "Day of Week
Name", each Date.DayOfWeekName([Date])),
    AddMonthNameColumn = Table.AddColumn( AddDayOfWeekNameColumn, "Month Name",
each Date.MonthName([Date])),
    AddDaysInMonthColumn = Table.AddColumn( AddMonthNameColumn, "Days In
Month", each Date.DaysInMonth([Date])),
    AddLeapYearColumn = Table.AddColumn( AddDaysInMonthColumn, "Is Leap Year",
each Date.IsLeapYear([Date]))
```

You can modify the preceding code and add this code by doing the following:

1. Add a comma to the end of the last line above the `in` keyword. This code assumes that the last step prior to the `in` keyword is a step called `AddDayColumn`.
2. Paste the eight lines of code after the comma that you just added and prior to the `in` keyword.
3. Change the statement after the `in` keyword to `AddLeapYearColumn`.

Also included in the standard M library are the `Date.StartOf` and `Date.EndOf` families of functions. M functions exist for each of these families for the standard temporal units of day, week, month, quarter, and year and return a `datetime` value, indicating the start or end of the temporal unit, respectively. For example, the following query returns 2/29/2024:

```
let
    Source = Date.EndOfMonth(#date(2024, 2, 14))
in
    Source
```

Here, the `Date.EndOfMonth` function is used to retrieve the date of the end of the month for the date `February 14th, 2024`.

The `Date.StartOf` and `Date.EndOf` families of functions are perhaps a bit peculiar in that their output depends on the data type passed into the function. Passing in a `date`, `datetime`, or `datetimezone` data type produces the corresponding data type as output. For example, let's change the `Source` line for the query to:

```
Source = Date.EndOfMonth(#datetime(2024, 2, 14, 0, 0, 0))
```

This produces the output 2024-02-29T23:59:59.9999999, a datetime data type. Now let's change the Source line to:

```
Source = Date.EndOfMonth(#datetimezone(2024, 2, 14, 0, 0 , 0, -5, 0))
```

This produces the output 2024-02-29T23:59:59.9999999-05:00, a datetimezone data type with a time zone of **Eastern Standard Time (EST)** or **-5 Coordinated Universal Time (UTC)**.

Three additional families of functions exist for the date data types: IsInCurrent, IsInNext, and IsInPrevious. Again, each of these families include functions for the standard temporal units of day, week, month, quarter and year.

These functions return a logical output depending upon whether the input date is, for example, within the current year for the IsInCurrentYear function. This determination is based upon the current date and time on the system, and thus, different results may be returned when running Power BI Desktop on a local computer versus in the Power BI service, with a tenant that exists in a different time zone.

The IsInNext and IsInPrevious function families include additional *N* variants, such as IsInNextNDays, IsInNextNWeeks, IsInNextNMonths, IsInNextNQuarters, and IsInNextNYears. In addition to the first parameter of a date data type, these functions include a second parameter specifying the number of temporal units (positive or negative) to determine whether the date is within the specified date range, such as within the next 2 weeks: Date.IsInNextNWeeks(#date(2024, 2, 14), 2).

An additional IsIn function for the current year to date is available, Date.IsInYearToDate. This function returns true or false, depending upon whether the date passed into the function is within the current year to date.

Finally, there is the Date.ToText function. As one might expect, this function converts the date data type to a text data type. However, this function includes two optional arguments, a Format parameter and a Culture parameter. Rick de Groot maintains a list of different codes that can be used within the Format parameter here: https://powerquery.how/date-totext/. *Table 10.1* displays the table of format codes for dates from the powerquery.how website:

Format	Description	December 31, 2023	February 1, 2003
%d	Single Digit Day (1–31)	31	1
dd	Double Digit Day (01–31)	31	01
ddd	Short Weekday Name	Sun	Sat
dddd	Full Weekday Name	Sunday	Saturday
%M	Single Digit Month (1–12)	12	2
MM	Double Digit Month (01–12)	12	02
MMM	Short Month Name	Dec	Feb

MMMM	Full Month Name	December	February
%y	Year (0–99)	23	3
yy	Year (00–99)	23	03
yyy	Year with at least three digits	2023	2003
yyyy	Four-Digit Year	2023	2003
yyyyy	Five-Digit Year	02023	02003
m, M	Day followed by Full Month Name	December 31	February 1
y, Y	Standard Long Date	December 2023	February 2003
d	Standard Short Date	12/31/2023	2/1/2003
D	Full Long Date	Sunday, December 31, 2023	Saturday, February 1, 2003
%g, gg	The Period of an Era	A.D.	A.D.

Table 10.1: Format codes for date data types

Thus, using `Date.ToText`, as in the following expression:

```
Date.ToText( #date(2024, 2, 14), "dddd, MMMM %d yyyy gg")
```

returns `Wednesday, February 14, 2024 A.D.` This may vary depending on your `Culture` settings.

The `Culture` parameter can further influence this. For example, the following expression:

```
Date.ToText( #date(2024, 2, 14), "dddd, MMMM %d yyyy gg", "uk")
```

returns the same format but for the Ukrainian culture: середа, лютого 14 2024 н.е.

As one might expect, the `Date.FromText` function essentially does the opposite of the `Date.ToText` function, converting the text representation of a date to a date data type.

> While one might think that `Date.FromText` is just syntax sugar for `Date.From`, the `Date.FromText` function supports the same `Format` and `Culture` parameters as `Date.ToText`.

This completes our exploration of dates within Power Query M. We now move on to exploring time.

M calendar table

As mentioned earlier in this chapter, nearly all Power BI data models have or should have a date dimension table. Often, these date dimension tables come from a data warehouse. However, in many circumstances, there is no data warehouse from which to pull a date dimension table.

In these cases, Melissa de Korte's famous M **Extended Date Table** function can be used. The code for this function is too long to include as text in a book but is included in the GitHub repository for this book both in a text file and within the PBIX file for this chapter. The code is also available at the following link: `https://bit.ly/484rXxi`.

To use the Extended Date Table, simply create a blank query in the Power Query editor. Open the query with the advanced editor, remove all existing code, and paste in the code for the Extended Date Table.

Once created, the function displays the following:

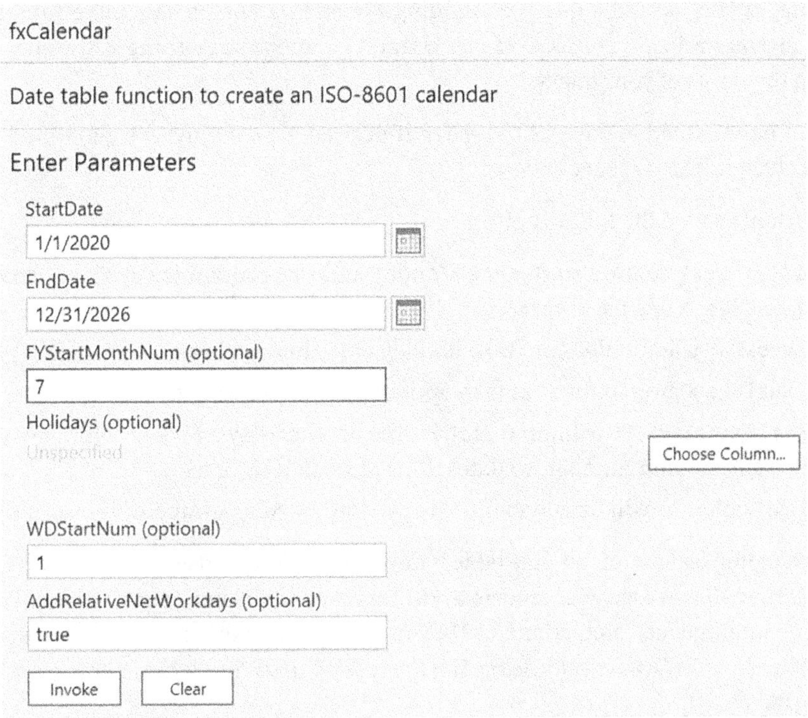

Figure 10.4: Extended Date Table

The function requires two parameters, `StartDate` and `EndDate`, as shown in *Figure 10.4*. In addition, there are four optional parameters:

- `FYStartMonthNum`: The month number the fiscal year starts; January if omitted
- `Holidays`: Select a query (and column) that contains a list of holiday dates
- `WDStartNum`: Switch default weekday numbering from 0–6 to 1–7 by entering a 1
- `AddRelativeNetWorkdays`: If true, adds a `Relative Networkdays` column to the date table

Thus, *Figure 10.4* displays a configuration for generating a date table between the years 2020 and 2026, where the fiscal year starts in July, weekdays are numbered 1–7, and the Relative Networkdays column will be included in the date table. Also, no `Holidays` column is specified.

Pressing Invoke on this configuration creates an Invoked Function query, containing the following expression:

```
let
    Source = fxCalendar(#date(2020, 1, 1), #date(2026, 12, 31), 7, null, 1,
true)
in
    Source
```

Please note that in this case, the query containing Melissa de Korte's date table function is named fxCalendar, as shown in *Figure 10.4*. If you name the query something different, then change fxCalendar to the name of your query.

This query can be renamed to Date or Calendar if desired. 61 columns are generated for the dates spanning 1/1/2020 to 12/31/2026.

It is also important to note the following:

*   The Fiscal Week column starts on a Monday and can contain fewer than 7 days in the First and/or Last Week of a fiscal year.
*   The IsWeekDay column does not take holiday dates into account.
*   The IsBusinessDay column does take optional holiday dates into account.
*   The IsPYTD and IsPFYTD columns compare the previous Day of Year column with the current Day of Year column number, so dates don't align in leap years.
*   No Fiscal columns will be added if the FYStartMonthNum parameter is omitted.

One of the outstanding features of this date table is implementation of offsets such as the CurrYearOffset, CurrQuarterOffset, CurrMonthOffset, CurrWeekOffset, and CurrDayOffset columns. These columns make date/time intelligence calculations in DAX much easier as this excellent blog article, *Time Intelligence In DAX: How To Dynamically Select Starting Period*, by *Brian Julius*, demonstrates: https://bit.ly/47OBQ1W.

Other date formats

The dates covered here are used in most parts of the world and are based on what is known as the Gregorian calendar. The Gregorian calendar was introduced in the year 1582 by Pope Gregory XIII as a replacement for the Julian calendar. However, there are other calendars and date formats used throughout the world and within certain scientific domains. We will take a look at two such systems, starting with Julian days.

Julian days

Julian days are a continuous count of whole solar days, since a 0 reference date of noon UTC, Monday January 1st, 4713 BC. The equivalent date in the Gregorian calendar is November 24, 4714 BC. The **Julian Day Number (JDN)** is a way to uniquely identify each day by assigning it a single number. The JDN is used in a variety of different scientific and computing domains, including:

- **Time measurement:** Julian Days provide a continuous and uniform time measurement system that is widely used in astronomy and astrophysics for specifying the date and time of observations, calculations, and events. It simplifies calculations involving intervals between two dates.

- **Ephemerides:** Astronomical ephemerides, which provide the positions of celestial objects over time, often use Julian Days for their time scale.

- **Uniform dating system:** Julian Days offer a uniform and continuous dating system that is useful in historical chronology. It allows for easy calculation of time intervals and is particularly valuable for historical events that span long periods.

- **Time-stamped data:** In geophysics and earth sciences, data collected over time, such as seismic events or environmental observations, are often recorded with JDNs. This allows for precise chronological ordering of events.

- **Computational efficiency:** Julian Days are convenient for computer algorithms and programming because they provide a single, continuous number that simplifies date and time calculations. This is especially useful when dealing with large datasets or performing calculations involving time intervals.

- **Navigation calculations:** In navigation, Julian Days are used for calculating positions of celestial bodies and determining the time of celestial events. They provide a standardized way to represent time for navigation purposes.

- **Consistency in data:** Julian Days provide a consistent and unambiguous way to represent dates and times across different datasets and disciplines. This consistency is crucial for research, data analysis, and communication between scientific communities.

- **Leap day and year calculations:** Julian Days simplify calculations involving leap days and leap years because they are a continuous count of days, unaffected by variations in the lengths of months or years.

In summary, Julian days play a crucial role in various scientific and computational contexts, providing a standardized and continuous time measurement system that is particularly useful in disciplines where precise chronological ordering and consistent time intervals are important.

We can construct an M function to convert Gregorian dates to Julian dates as follows:

```
let fnJulianDay = ( GregorianDate as date) as number =>
    let
        GregorianYear = Date.Year( GregorianDate ),
        GregorianMonth = Date.Month( GregorianDate ),
        GregorianDay = Date.Day( GregorianDate ),
        Y = if GregorianMonth > 2 then GregorianYear else GregorianYear - 1,
        M = if GregorianMonth > 2 then GregorianMonth else GregorianMonth + 12,
        D = GregorianDay,
        A = Number.IntegerDivide( Y, 100),
        B = 2 - A + Number.IntegerDivide( A, 4),
        JulianDay = Number.IntegerDivide( 365.25 * ( Y + 4716), 1) + Number.
IntegerDivide( 30.6001 * ( M + 1), 1) + D + B - 1524.5
    in
```

```
        JulianDay,
        Documentation = [
        Documentation.Name =  " fnJulianDay",
        Documentation.Description = " Converts Gregorian date to Julian day",
        Documentation.LongDescription = " Converts Gregorian date to Julian
day",
        Documentation.Category = " Number",
        Documentation.Version = " 1.0",
        Documentation.Source = " local",
        Documentation.Author = " Gregory J. Deckler",
        Documentation.Examples = { [Description =  " fnJulianDay( #date( 1987,
1, 1 ) )",
        Code = " Based on Jean Meeus' Astrological Algorithms",
        Result = " " ] }
        ]
in
    Value.ReplaceType( fnJulianDay, Value.ReplaceMetadata( Value.Type(
fnJulianDay ), Documentation ))
```

Name this query fnJulianDay. Next, create the following query:

```
let
    Source = List.Generate( () => #date(1987, 1, 1), each _ <= #date(1987, 12,
31), each Date.AddDays( _, 1)),
    Table = Table.FromList(Source, Splitter.SplitByNothing(), null, null,
ExtraValues.Error),
    RenameColumns = Table.RenameColumns(Table,{{"Column1", "Date"}}),
    AddJDNColumn = Table.AddColumn(RenameColumns, "Julian Day", each
fnJulianDay([Date]))
in
    AddJDNColumn
```

This expression returns a table for the year 1987 that includes a column for the Julian Day equivalent.

Similarly, we can create a fnGregorianDate function to convert Julian Days to their Gregorian calendar equivalent dates:

```
let fnGregorianDate = ( JulianDay as number) as date =>
    let
        Z = Number.IntegerDivide( JulianDay + .5, 1 ),
        F = JulianDay + .5 - Z,
        alpha = Number.IntegerDivide( Z - 1867216.25, 36524.25),
        A = if Z < 2299161 then Z else Z + 1 + alpha - Number.IntegerDivide(
alpha, 4 ),
        B = A + 1524,
```

```
            C = Number.IntegerDivide( B - 122.1, 365.25 ),
            D = Number.IntegerDivide( 365.25 * C, 1),
            E = Number.IntegerDivide( B - D, 30.6001),
            Day = B - D - Number.IntegerDivide( 30.6001 * E, 1),
            Month = if E < 14 then E - 1 else E - 13,
            Year = if Month > 2 then C - 4716 else C - 4715,
            GrgorianDate = #date( Year, Month, Day )
        in

        GrgorianDate,
        Documentation = [
        Documentation.Name =   " fnGregorianDate",
        Documentation.Description = " Converts Julian day to Gregorian date",
        Documentation.LongDescription = " Converts Julian day to Gregorian
date",
        Documentation.Category = " Date",
        Documentation.Version = " 1.0",
        Documentation.Source = " local",
        Documentation.Author = " Gregory J. Deckler",
        Documentation.Examples = { [Description =   " fnGregorianDate( 2446796.5
)",
        Code = " Based on Jean Meeus' Astrological Algorithms",
        Result = " " ] }
        ]
    in
    Value.ReplaceType( fnGregorianDate, Value.ReplaceMetadata( Value.Type(
fnGregorianDate ), Documentation ))
```

Name this query fnGregorianDate. We can then modify our example query as follows to return both a Julian Day column and a Gregorian Date column:

```
let
    Source = List.Generate( () => #date(1987, 1, 1), each _ <= #date(1987, 12,
31), each Date.AddDays( _, 1)),
    Table = Table.FromList(Source, Splitter.SplitByNothing(), null, null,
ExtraValues.Error),
    RenameColumns = Table.RenameColumns(Table,{{"Column1", "Date"}}),
    AddJDNColumn = Table.AddColumn(RenameColumns, "Julian Day", each
fnJulianDay([Date])),
    AddGregorianDateColumn = Table.AddColumn(AddJDNColumn, "Gregorian Date",
each fnGregorianDate([Julian Day]))
in
    AddGregorianDateColumn
```

Alternate date formats

Certain systems store dates in different formats. An example of this is some versions of the popular J. D. Edwards **Enterprise Resource Planning** (ERP) software system, now owned by Oracle. This system stores dates using a century flag, with the following format: cyyddd. Here, c is a century flag where 0 equals 1900 and 1 equals 2000. The year within that century is stored as a two-digit number between 0 and 99. Finally, the day is stored as the numeric day of the year.

To convert this date format to a date data type in Power Query, we can use the following function in a query named fnJDEToDate:

```
let fnJDEToDate = ( JDEDate as any) as date =>
    let
        c = Number.From(Text.Start(Text.From( JDEDate ), 1)),
        yy = Number.From(Text.Middle(Text.From( JDEDate ), 1, 2)),
        ddd = Number.From(Text.End(Text.From( JDEDate ), 3)),
        Year = 1900 + c * 100 + yy,
        tmpDateList = List.Generate( () => #date( Year, 1, 1 ), each _ < #date(
Year + 1, 1, 1), each Date.AddDays( _, 1 )),
        tmpDateTable = Table.FromList(tmpDateList, Splitter.SplitByNothing(),
null, null, ExtraValues.Error),
        AddDayOfYear = Table.AddColumn( tmpDateTable, "Day of Year", each Date.
DayOfYear([Column1])),
        DateTable = Table.SelectColumns( Table.SelectRows( AddDayOfYear, each
[Day of Year] = ddd), "Column1" ),
        Date = DateTable[Column1]{0}
    in
        Date,
        Documentation = [
        Documentation.Name =  " fnJDEToDate",
        Documentation.Description = " Converts cyyddd to date",
        Documentation.LongDescription = " Converts cyyddd to date",
        Documentation.Category = " Date",
        Documentation.Version = " 1.0",
        Documentation.Source = " local",
        Documentation.Author = " Gregory J. Deckler",
        Documentation.Examples = { [Description =  " fnJDEToDate( 124045 )",
        Code = " ",
        Result = " " ] }
        ]
in
    Value.ReplaceType( fnJDEToDate, Value.ReplaceMetadata( Value.Type(
fnJDEToDate ), Documentation ))
```

By way of explanation, we grab the individual components of the century (c), the two-digit year (yy) and the three-digit day of year (ddd), using the `Text.Start`, `Text.Middle` and `Text.End` functions, respectively. We can then calculate the year with the formula `1900 + c * 100 + yy`. Once we have the year, we can generate a list of dates for that year, convert the list to a table, add a `Day of Year` column using the `Date.DayOfYear` function, and finally, filter down to the correct row in the table, convert that table to a list, and extract the first value in the list, `{ 0 }`.

We can use this function to quickly convert a table of dates in the cyyddd format, such as the following expression:

```
let
    Source = List.Generate( () => 124001, each _ < 124367, each _ + 1),
    #"Converted to Table" = Table.FromList(Source, Splitter.SplitByNothing(),
null, null, ExtraValues.Error),
    #"Duplicated Column" = Table.DuplicateColumn(#"Converted to Table",
"Column1", "Column1 - Copy"),
    #"Removed Columns" = Table.RemoveColumns(#"Duplicated Column",{"Column1 -
Copy"}),
    #"Invoked Custom Function" = Table.AddColumn(#"Removed Columns", "Date",
each fnJDEToDate([Column1]))
in
    #"Invoked Custom Function"
```

This expression returns a table for all dates in the year 2024.

Additional custom date functions

Creating custom functions for working with dates can save a great deal of time. Here, we discuss a number of practical custom functions for dates.

Working days

As demonstrated thus far, there are many different ways to express dates within society as well as within **information technology (IT)** systems. Similarly, there are numerous ways to consider the passage of time. An example of this is that many business organizations track the passage of time in working days (Monday–Friday) and do not count weekend days.

Two custom functions can help when dealing with working days. The first can help classify working and non-working days:

```
let CategorizeDay = (date as date) =>
    let
        Category = if Date.DayOfWeek(date, Day.Monday) <= 4 then "Weekday" else
"Weekend"
    in
        Category
in
    CategorizeDay
```

The `CategorizeDay` function takes a single date parameter as input. The `DayOfWeek` function is used to return a numeric value from 0 to 6, with 0 being Monday. The second, optional parameter of the `DayOfWeek` function is used to switch the output from the default of 0 for Sunday to 0 for Monday. `Day.Monday` is a built-in enumeration. Thus, the weekdays are numbered 0, 1, 2, 3, and 4 for Monday, Tuesday, Wednesday, Thursday, and Friday, respectively. Thus, any value less than 4 means that the date is a weekday and values greater than 4 are weekends.

The second custom function can help determine the number of working days between two dates, including handling holidays:

```
let WorkingDaysBetweenDates = (startDate as date, endDate as date, optional
holidays as list) =>
    let
        holidayDates = if holidays = null then { } else holidays,
        days = Number.From(Duration.From(endDate - startDate)) + 1,
        allDates = List.Dates(startDate, days, #duration(1, 0, 0, 0)),
        workingDays = List.Select(allDates, each Date.DayOfWeek(_, Day.Monday)
<= 4 and not List.Contains(holidayDates, _))
    in
        List.Count(workingDays)
in
    WorkingDaysBetweenDates
```

Here, the `WorkingDaysBetweenDates` custom function takes three parameters: a start date, an end date, and an optional list of holiday days. We first check to see if the optional third parameter is included and, if not, create an empty list. Next, we calculate the number of days to include in our date range, from the `startDate` to the `endDate`, by subtracting the two dates, converting the resulting duration to a number, and adding 1. We then use the `List.Dates` function to generate a list of the dates included in our range. Note that we could also have used the `List.Generate` function for this purpose. The next expression selects the generated list items, using the same logic as our `CategorizeDay` function, but it also does not select any dates that are in the `holidayDates` list. Finally, we simply need to count the items in the filtered list.

Moving average

A common scenario in data analytics is to provide the moving or rolling average of a particular metric. While this can be achieved in DAX, Power Query M can also be used to add this information to a table. The following custom function adds a moving average column (`MovingAvg`) to a table:

```
let MovingAverage = (sourceTable as table, valueColumn as text, windowSize as
number) =>
    let
        BufferedValues = List.Buffer(
            Table.ToColumns(
```

```
                    Table.SelectColumns(sourceTable, valueColumn)
            ){0}
        ),
        addIndex = Table.AddIndexColumn(sourceTable, "Index", 1, 1, Int64.
    Type),
        movingAvg = Table.AddColumn(
            addIndex,
            "MovingAvg",
            each
                if [Index] >= windowSize then
                    List.Average(
                        List.Range(
                        BufferedValues,
                        _[Index] - windowSize,
                        windowSize
                    )
                ) else null, type number
        ),
        removeIndex = Table.RemoveColumns(movingAvg, {"Index"})
    in
    removeIndex
 in
 MovingAverage
```

This function takes three parameters for the table, the name of the column to calculate a moving average on, and a specified window size for the moving average. The function first buffers the specified moving average value column of the table into memory. An index column is added, starting with a value of 1 and each row incremented by 1. Next, the moving average column, MovingAvg, is added to the table, with the windowSize parameter specifying how many rows to include in the moving average. Finally, the entire original table plus the MovingAvg column is returned as a table.

As an example, assuming this function is used on a fact table that includes daily sales information with a window size of 30, calling this function would return that fact table with a moving average calculated for each row for the last 30 days.

The pattern used here can be easily adapted to a rolling sum or similar calculation by simply replacing the List.Average function with the List.Sum function, or a similar function.

Let's now move on to discussing time.

Time

While perhaps not as frequently used in reporting as much as dates, time can also be an important reporting element, particularly when reporting on metrics such as employee performance or supply chain productivity.

Similar to dates, time is also represented in numeric form as fractions of a day. To observe this, create a new query with:

```
let
    Source = List.Generate(() => 0, each _ <= 24, each _ + 1),
    Table = Table.FromList(Source, Splitter.SplitByNothing(), null, null,
ExtraValues.Error),
    AddMultiplicationColumn = Table.AddColumn(Table, "Multiplication", each
[Column1] / 24, type number),
    DuplicateColumn = Table.DuplicateColumn(AddMultiplicationColumn,
"Multiplication", "Multiplication - Copy"),
    ChangeType = Table.TransformColumnTypes(DuplicateColumn,{{"Multiplication -
Copy", type time}}),
    RenameColumns = Table.RenameColumns(ChangeType,{{"Multiplication - Copy",
"Time"}})
in
    RenameColumns
```

The table shown in *Figure 10.5* is displayed:

	ABC 123 Column1	1.2 Multiplication	Time
1	0	0	12:00:00 AM
2	1	0.041666667	1:00:00 AM
3	2	0.083333333	2:00:00 AM
4	3	0.125	3:00:00 AM
5	4	0.166666667	4:00:00 AM
6	5	0.208333333	5:00:00 AM
7	6	0.25	6:00:00 AM
8	7	0.291666667	7:00:00 AM
9	8	0.333333333	8:00:00 AM
10	9	0.375	9:00:00 AM
11	10	0.416666667	10:00:00 AM
12	11	0.458333333	11:00:00 AM
13	12	0.5	12:00:00 PM
14	13	0.541666667	1:00:00 PM
15	14	0.583333333	2:00:00 PM
16	15	0.625	3:00:00 PM
17	16	0.666666667	4:00:00 PM
18	17	0.708333333	5:00:00 PM
19	18	0.75	6:00:00 PM
20	19	0.791666667	7:00:00 PM
21	20	0.833333333	8:00:00 PM
22	21	0.875	9:00:00 PM
23	22	0.916666667	10:00:00 PM
24	23	0.958333333	11:00:00 PM
25	24	1	Error

Figure 10.5: Time table of hours

We can see from the table that a numeric value of 0 corresponds to midnight (`12:00:00 AM`). In the **Multiplication** column, we have divided **Column1** by 24 to get the hours fraction of the day. This value, when converted to a time value, returns the corresponding hour of the day. Note that values equal to or greater than 1 return an error.

Time values have similar restrictions regarding arithmetic operations as date data types. This means that you can add or subtract time values from one another, but you cannot perform arithmetic operations involving numbers without specifically converting the values between data types.

Similar to dates, we have a number of functions for extracting the `Hour`, `Minute`, and `Second` time components, such as the following:

```
    AddHourColumn = Table.AddColumn(RenameColumns, "Hour", each Time.
Hour([Time])),
    AddMinuteColumn = Table.AddColumn(AddHourColumn, "Minute", each Time.
Minute([Time])),
    AddSecondColumn = Table.AddCvvv(AddMinuteColumn, "Second", each Time.
Second([Time]))
```

Also similar to dates, there is a `Time.Record` function that also extracts these same time components into a record.

Similar to the date data type, the `time` data type also has a constructor, the `#time` function. The `#time` function takes three parameters: `Hour`, `Minute` and `Second`. While you might think that you could use addition to add time to a date and return a `datetime` data type, doing so results in an error:

```
#date(2024, 2, 14) + #time(17, 0, 0)
```

```
Error: We cannot apply operator + to types Date and Time.
```

However, the concatenation operator does work. Thus, the following expression returns a `datetime` data type of February 14th, 2024 at 5 PM (`2/14/2024 5:00:00 PM`):

```
#date(2024, 2, 14) & #time(17, 0, 0)
```

Two additional functions, `Time.StartOfHour` and `Time.EndOfHour`, return datetime data types representing the start and end of the hour, given a time, datetime, or datetimezone input value data type. For example, the following expression returns `13:59:59.9999999`:

```
Time.EndOfHour(#time(13,10,5))
```

In this example, the `#time` function is used to create a time data type value. The `#time` function takes hours, minutes, and seconds as the first, second, and third parameters, respectively.

The `Time.From` and `Time.FromText` functions convert an input value to a time data type. The `Time.From` function accepts an input value of text, datetime, datetimezone, or number. Both of these functions also include an optional `Culture` parameter similar to their equivalent date functions.

Finally, the `Time.ToText` function converts a time data type to a text data type. The representation of this text time can be controlled via an optional second parameter, the `Format` parameter. More information about the various formatting options can be found on the *Gorilla BI* website operated by Rick de Groot here: `https://gorilla.bi/power-query/custom-format-strings/`. Similar to the equivalent data function, `Date.ToText`, a third, optional parameter, `Culture`, can also be specified.

Creating a time table

Certain reporting applications require a proper time dimension at either the minute or second granularity. This can be achieved via the following M code:

```
let
    Source = List.Generate( () => 0, each _ < 24 * 60, each _ + 1 ),
    Table = Table.FromList(Source, Splitter.SplitByNothing(), null, null,
ExtraValues.Error),
    Divide = Table.TransformColumns(Table, {{"Column1", each _ / 24 / 60, type
number}}),
    ChangeType = Table.TransformColumnTypes(Divide,{{"Column1", type time}}),
    RenameColumns = Table.RenameColumns(ChangeType,{{"Column1", "Time"}}),
    AddHourColumn = Table.AddColumn(RenameColumns, "Hour", each Time.
Hour([Time])),
    AddMinuteColumn = Table.AddColumn(AddHourColumn, "Minute", each Time.
Minute([Time])),
    AddSecondColumn = Table.AddColumn(AddMinuteColumn, "Second", each Time.
Second([Time])),
    AddStartOfHourColumn = Table.AddColumn(AddSecondColumn, "Start of Hour",
each Time.StartOfHour([Time])),
    AddEndOfHourColumn = Table.AddColumn(AddStartOfHourColumn, "End of Hour",
each Time.EndOfHour([Time]))
in
    AddEndOfHourColumn
```

This M expression returns a time table at the minute level of granularity. A couple of small modifications will return a time table at the second level of granularity:

```
let
    Source = List.Generate( () => 0, each _ < 24 * 60 * 60, each _ + 1 ),
    Table = Table.FromList(Source, Splitter.SplitByNothing(), null, null,
ExtraValues.Error),
    Divide = Table.TransformColumns(Table, {{"Column1", each _ / 24 / 60 / 60,
type number}}),
    ChangeType = Table.TransformColumnTypes(Divide,{{"Column1", type time}}),
    RenameColumns = Table.RenameColumns(ChangeType,{{"Column1", "Time"}}),
    AddHourColumn = Table.AddColumn(RenameColumns, "Hour", each Time.
Hour([Time])),
```

```
    AddMinuteColumn = Table.AddColumn(AddHourColumn, "Minute", each Time.
Minute([Time])),
    AddSecondColumn = Table.AddColumn(AddMinuteColumn, "Second", each Time.
Second([Time])),
    AddStartOfHourColumn = Table.AddColumn(AddSecondColumn, "Start of Hour",
each Time.StartOfHour([Time])),
    AddEndOfHourColumn = Table.AddColumn(AddStartOfHourColumn, "End of Hour",
each Time.EndOfHour([Time]))
in
    AddEndOfHourColumn
```

Shift classification

We can create a simple function to classify times into first, second, and third shifts. Assuming that shift one runs from 8 AM to 4 PM, the second shift from 4 PM to midnight, and the third shift from midnight to 8 AM, the following function classifies a time passed in as a parameter as falling within a particular shift:

```
let ShiftClassification = ( actualTime as time ) =>
    let
        hourEndShift3 = Time.Hour(#time(8, 0, 0)),
        hourEndShift1 = Time.Hour(#time(16, 0, 0)),
        hour = Time.Hour(Time.StartOfHour( actualTime )),
        shift = if hour < hourEndShift3 then "Third" else if hour <
hourEndShift1 then "First" else "Second"
    in
        shift
in
    ShiftClassification
```

The completes our exploration of time within the M language. We now move on to dates and times.

Dates and times

As one might anticipate, the representation of both a date and a time is possible within the M language. This data type is a datetime data type and exhibits similar properties to both date data types and time data types. In fact, since dates are simply whole numbers based upon a reference date and time is a decimal number reflecting the fractions of a day, a datetime data type can be represented as a decimal number, where the whole number portion represents the date and the decimal portion represents the time. For example, the following expression returns noon on February 14th (2/14/2024 12:00:00 PM):

```
DateTime.From(45336.5)
```

The individual components of date and time can be extracted from a datetime data type using the DateTime.Date and DateTime.Time functions. Alternatively, the DateTime.ToRecord function returns a record with field/value pairs for Year, Month, Day, Hour, Minute, and Second.

Similar to dates and times, a constructor is available for the datetime data type: the #datetime function. The following returns February 14th, 2024 at 5 PM:

```
#datetime(2024, 2, 14, 17, 0, 0)
```

Two additional functions, DateTime.LocalNow and DateTime.FixedLocalNow, return the current date and time of the system. The only difference between these two functions is that DateTime.LocalNow may return different values when executed multiple times during the evaluation of an M expression. DateTime.FixedLocalNow does not exhibit this behaviour and will only return a single datetime value over the course of multiple executions within an M expression.

Prior to improvements in the Power BI service, these two functions were often used within a separate query in order to return the time of the last refresh of a dataset. This date and time could then be displayed within a Card visual on report pages.

Similar to dates, there are IsInCurrent, IsInNext, and IsInPrevious families of functions. These families each include individual functions for the time components of Hour, Minute, and Second. The IsInNext and IsInPrevious families also include N variants, such as IsInNextNHours, IsInNextNMinutes, and IsInNextNSeconds. All of these functions return a logical Boolean value of true or false, depending on whether or not the datetime value meets the specified conditions.

The DateTime.FromFileTime function is rather obscure; it converts Windows file time into a standard datetime format. Windows file time is recorded as the total number of 100-nanosecond intervals since 12:00 AM, January 1, 1601 AD (also referred to as 1601 CE), in **Coordinated Universal Time (UTC)**. This specific starting point is used as a reference to ensure consistency in file time records across Windows systems. The DateTime.FromFileTime function simply converts Windows file times to a datetime data type value. Thus, the expression DateTime.FromFileTime(133524036000000000) returns a datetime value of February 14th (2/14/2024 12:00:00 PM) if you are in the United States Eastern Time Zone (Standard not Daylight Savings Time). Finally, the function DateTime.AddTimeZone adds time zone information to a datetime data type, returning a datetimezone data type. Continuing with our previous example, the following M expression returns a datetimezone data type that adds time zone information for **Eastern Time (US)**:

```
= DateTime.AddZone(DateTime.From(45336.5), -5, 0)
```

The value returned from this expression is 2/14/2024 12:00:00 PM -05:00.

Speaking of time zones, let's next move on to exploring the functions related to datetimezone data types.

Time zones

While eminently practical and relatively easy to understand, time zones have caused issues with software systems and programming from the very dawn of computing. Fortunately, the M language includes the datetimezone data type, with an array of supporting functions that ease the burden of dealing with dates and times that include time zones.

Unlike date, time, and datetime data types, datetimezone data types cannot be represented solely as decimal numbers. In fact, creating a datetimezone value using `DateTimeZone.From(45336.5)` adds the additional time zone information of the local system, returning `2/14/2024 12:00:00 PM -05:00`, for example, for a system running in the United States EST time zone.

There are actually two additional elements for a datetimezone data type: `ZoneHours` and `ZoneMinutes`. These additional elements can be retrieved using the `DateTimeZone.ZoneHours` and `DateTimeZone.ZoneMinutes` functions, respectively. Additionally, the `DateTimeZone.ToRecord` function returns a record consisting of the following fields:

- Year
- Month
- Day
- Hour
- Minute
- Second
- ZoneHours
- ZoneMinutes

As with dates, times, and datetime data types, the datetimezone data type includes a constructure, the `#datetimezone` function. This function takes up to eight parameters – year, month, day, hour, minute, second, offset hours and offset minutes. For example, the following returns `February 14th, 2024 at 5 PM EST`:

```
#datetimezone(2024, 2, 14, 17, 0, 0, -5, 0)
```

Similar to the `DateTime` family of functions, the `DateTimeZone` family of functions includes functions for returning the current local system time, `DateTimeZone.LocalNow` and `DateTimeZone.FixedLocalNow`. These functions work the same as their `DateTime` counterparts but include the local time zone information as well.

In addition, two additional functions are provided for retrieving the current UTC time. These functions are `DateTimeZone.UtcNow` and `DateTimeZone.FixedUtcNow`. Again, the difference between these functions is that multiple calls within an expression to `UtcNow` may return different times, while multiple calls to `FixedUtcNow` will return the same time.

An additional function, `DateTimeZone.ToUtc`, converts a datetimezone value to UTC time. Continuing with our example, the expression `DateTimeZone.ToUtc(DateTimeZone.From(45336.5))` returns `2/14/2024 5:00:00 PM +00:00` when evaluated on a system in the United States EST time zone. Here, the original value of noon on February 14th, 2024 is moved ahead 5 hours to 5PM. This makes sense considering that EST has a `ZoneHours` of `-5`, meaning that the EST time zone is 5 hours behind UTC time.

Similar to the `ToUtc` function, the `DateTimeZone.ToLocal` function converts a datetimezone value to the local system time of the computer evaluating the expression. Thus, the expression `DateTimeZone.ToLocal(DateTimeZone.From("2/14/2024 5:00:00 PM +00:00"))` returns `2/14/2024 12:00:00 PM -05:00` when evaluated on a computer running in the EST time zone.

Time zone information can also be manipulated with the DateTimeZone.RemoveZone and DateTimeZone.SwitchZone functions. The DateTimeZone.RemoveZone function removes the time zone information, returning a datetime data type. The DateTimeZone.SwitchZone function replaces the time zone information with the time zone specified by the second and third parameters of that function.

Note that the SwitchZone function does not simply replace the time zone but, rather, converts the datetimezone value to the new time zone. Thus, the expression DateTimeZone.SwitchZone(DateTimeZone.From(45336.5), 0, 0) is equivalent to our previous example using the ToUtc function and returns the exact same value, 2/14/2024 5:00:00 PM +00:00. Thus, the SwitchZone function can be seen as a more general use function than the more specific ToUtc and ToLocal functions.

Finally, the DateTimeZone.FromFileTime works identically to its DateTime function counterpart but, as expected, adds in the time zone information pulled from the local system evaluating the expression.

Correcting data refresh times

A common scenario in reporting is to include the last time the data was refreshed. However, the Power BI service records the refresh time in the time zone of the Power BI tenant's region. This may or may not correspond to the time zone of the country in which users view the report.

This issue can be fixed by using a custom function for calculating the refresh time, storing the date and time as a single row table in the data model, and then displaying this date and time on report pages. The following custom function adjusts the refresh time to account for such issues and also includes the ability to handle daylight savings time:

```
(Summer_GMT_Offset as number, Winter_GMT_Offset as number) =>
let
    UTC_DateTimeZone = DateTimeZone.UtcNow(),
    UTC_Date = Date.From( UTC_DateTimeZone ),
    StartSummerTime = Date.StartOfWeek( #date( Date.Year( UTC_Date ) , 3 , 31
), Day.Sunday ),
    StartWinterTime = Date.StartOfWeek( #date( Date.Year( UTC_Date ) , 10, 31
), Day.Sunday ),
    UTC_Offset = if UTC_Date >= StartSummerTime and UTC_Date < StartWinterTime
then Summer_GMT_Offset else Winter_GMT_Offset,
    CET_Timezone = DateTimeZone.SwitchZone( UTC_DateTimeZone, UTC_Offset)
in
    CET_Timezone
```

This function comes from Rick de Groot and takes two parameters: the summer offset and winter offset from UTC time for the desired time zone with which to display the desired time. First, the DateTimeZone.UtcNow function is used to get the date, time and time zone. Next, the Date.From function is used to store just the date portion. Assuming that summer (standard time) starts on the last Sunday in March and winter (daylight savings time) starts on the last Sunday in October, the next two lines determine the dates of summer and winter times.

The desired offset is then calculated based on the current date compared with the summer and winter dates. The time is then adjusted using the `DateTimeZone.SwitchZone` function.

Let's now discuss duration.

Duration

Unlike the **Analysis Services** tabular data model, the M language includes a data type for duration. The unfortunate omission of a duration data type in Analysis Services means that calculations involving duration are perhaps better handled in Power Query rather than with DAX columns or measures. However, it is also important to realize that `duration` data type columns in Power Query are converted to decimal numbers when loaded into the data model. Consider the following expression:

```
let
    Source = Duration.From("0.01:00:00"),
    #"Converted to Table" = #table(1, {{Source}}),
    #"Changed Type" = Table.TransformColumnTypes(#"Converted to
Table",{{"Column1", type duration}})
in
    #"Changed Type"
```

This single row table, containing a duration data type column with a value of 1 hour, when loaded into the data model becomes the value `0.0416666666666667`, which is the fractional amount of a day (1 hour/24 hours). Thus, in order to display a duration format in reports, you must perform conversions on the data and either finally convert the value to text, using the `FORMAT` DAX function, or utilize Custom Format Strings in order to keep the value as a number.

The duration data type includes a constructor, the `#duration` function. The `#duration` function takes four parameters – days, hours, minutes, and seconds. The following expression returns a duration of `05.02:15:33`:

```
#duration(5, 2, 15, 33)
```

A duration data type can be added to a date, time, datetime, or datetimezone data type using the addition operator (+). Thus, the following expression returns a date of February 14, 2024 as `2/14/2024`:

```
#date(2024, 2, 9) + #duration(5, 2, 15, 33)
```

While the following expression returns a time of 7:15:33 PM:

```
#time( 17, 0, 0) + #duration(5, 2, 15, 33)
```

The individual components of the duration can be extracted with the `Duration.Days`, `Duration.Hours`, `Duration.Minutes`, and `Duration.Seconds` functions. Alternatively, the `Duration.ToRecord` function returns a record with these same values, as fields labeled `Days`, `Hours`, `Minutes`, and `Seconds`.

Four additional functions make calculating the total number of days, hours, minutes, and seconds for a duration trivial. These functions are `Duration.TotalDays`, `Duration.TotalHours`, `Duration.TotalMinutes`, and `Duration.TotalSeconds`. Thus, an expression such as `Duration.TotalSeconds(Duration.From("1.2:10:12"))` returns the value 94,212, which is 3,600 seconds in an hour multiplied by 26 hours (1 full day plus 2 hours), plus 10 minutes times 60 seconds per minute, plus 12 seconds, equaling 94,212 total seconds.

As mentioned, because the Analysis Services tabular engine does not support a true duration data type, it is advisable to perform duration calculations within Power Query and then use one of the `Total` functions in Power Query, such as `Duration.TotalSeconds`, to convert the duration column to a numeric total number of seconds prior to loading into the data model. Once stored as seconds, there are many standard DAX methods of converting the value to a duration, coupled with the use of Custom Format Strings to display the numeric number in duration format. Once such example is Chelsie Eiden's `Duration` in the Power BI Community site's *Quick Measure Gallery*: https://bit.ly/47JMPJR.

Working duration

Similar to calculating working days between two dates, a simple custom function can be created to calculate the work duration between two times:

```
( startTime as time, endTime as time, workStartTime as time, workEndTime as
time) =>
    let
        actualStartTime = if startTime < workStartTime then workStartTime else
startTime,
        actualEndTime = if endTime > workEndTime then workEndTime else endTime,
        workDuration = actualEndTime - actualStartTime
    in
        workDuration
```

This function takes four parameters, the actual start and end times as well as the start and end times of the working day. Simple `if` statements are used to determine whether the input starting time is less than the work start time and whether the input end time is greater than the work end time. The duration is then calculated by simply subtracting the modified start and end times.

An even simpler function can be used to convert the number of days and working hours per day to a duration:

```
(days as number, hoursPerDay as number) =>
    days * hoursPerDay * #duration(0, 1, 0, 0)
```

Summary

In this chapter, we covered the topics of dates, times, dates and times, time zones and durations. The majority of the functions dealing with these data types were covered, and we explored some practical applications of using these functions, including Melissa de Korte's famous Extended Date Table, the creation of functions for converting between Gregorian dates and Julian days, and handling alternate date formats. We also covered examples of calculating the number of working days between two dates and how to calculate a moving average. With respect to time, we demonstrated the creation of a time dimension table at both the minute and second level of granularity and how to classify time into first, second, and third shifts. Dates and times were also covered and included an example for correcting data refresh times. Finally, durations were discussed, with examples of calculating work duration and converting work days to durations.

In the next chapter, we continue our exploration of M by discussing several techniques for manipulating and refining data. This includes a detailed look at comparing, replacing, combining and splitting values.

Learn more on Discord

Join our community's Discord space for discussions with the author and other readers:

https://discord.gg/vCSG5GBbyS

11

Comparers, Replacers, Combiners, and Splitters

Data preparation within Power Query involves several techniques aimed at manipulating and refining data. These techniques include splitting, combining, comparing, and replacing values to achieve the desired data structure and quality. Here's a brief overview of each technique:

Technique	Purpose	Example
Comparers	Determine equality and order	Identifying duplicates, ranking, and sorting data
Replacers	Substitute values	Correcting misspellings or irregularities to ensure uniformity
Combiners	Concatenate values	Concatenating strings, merging columns
Splitters	Separate values	Dividing strings, splitting columns

Table 11.1: Brief overview of the techniques used to manage data

This chapter provides an overview of the splitting, combining, comparing, and replacing capabilities in the Power Query M language. It aims to equip you with the necessary knowledge to effectively apply these transformations in your workflows. This chapter covers the following topics:

- Key concepts
- Comparers
- Comparison criteria
- Equation criteria
- Replacers
- Custom replacers
- Combiners
- Splitters
- Practical examples

Technical requirements

To get started, visit the GitHub repository and download the PBIX file that accompanies this chapter. That file is prepared for you to follow along and apply the techniques discussed here, offering a hands-on approach that enhances your understanding. By following along, you're not just learning theoretically; you're also gaining practical experience that solidifies your knowledge and skills.

Key concepts

Before we delve into the main subject of this chapter, it's beneficial to briefly review some related topics. First, almost all comparers, combiners, and splitters yield a function value. These values are then used as arguments for other M functions. Therefore, understanding concepts related to functions and their invocation is essential. Second, what do comparer functions and the enumeration Order.Type have in common?

Function invocation

To effectively use functions within our code, understanding the invoke expression is key. The invoke expression consists of a set of parentheses that can optionally contain a list of arguments. It triggers the execution of the function body, which either returns a value or produces an error. For a more in-depth understanding of functions, please refer to *Chapter 9, Parameters and Custom Functions*.

The most straightforward way to call a function is to use its full name. After the name, you include an invoke expression that lists an argument for all required parameters. For example, with the Text.Contains function, you can check if hello is part of Hello World. Both of these text inputs meet the function's required parameters:

```
let
    Result = Text.Contains("Hello World", "hello")
in
    Result
```

When a function invocation generates a new function, the process of fully qualifying it can be continued by adding invoke expressions that list all required arguments, as needed. For example, this discountFunction will generate a new function that subsequently needs a numerical argument as input. A completely qualified invocation is shown in the Result step:

```
let
    discountFunction = (discountRate as number) as function =>
        (sales as number) as number => sales * (1 - discountRate),
    Result = discountFunction(0.1)(100)
in
    Result
```

Some common errors

Some commonly found errors that you should be mindful of are as follows:

- **Missing closing parenthesis?**

  Most IDEs support the highlighting of matching parentheses. Use this feature to quickly identify the location of a missing parenthesis.

- **Incorrect number of arguments?**

  Refer to **IntelliSense** or the function documentation to ensure you're passing the correct number of arguments.

- **Mismatched argument types?**

  The argument type must be compatible with its corresponding parameter type. Refer to **IntelliSense** or the documentation to ensure you're passing the correct type for each argument.

- **Misspelling a function's name or incorrect letter casing?**

  Use **IntelliSense** and select the function from the list of suggestions to avoid such errors.

Closures

Closures may sound technical or like a term reserved for experts and developers, but we promise you, they're not as daunting as they seem. Let us show you how they can make your code smarter. A closure is a function that is able to retain the argument value for a parameter from its outer (parent) scope, even after that outer function has completed execution. This ability to "remember" sets a closure apart from a regular function, preserving a value for future invocations, regardless of the environment the closure is called from. See the following code example, as well as *Figure 11.1*. You can gain a deeper understanding of closures, scope, context, and environments in *Chapter 7, Conceptualizing M*.

```
let
    makeMultiplier = (x) => (y) => x * y,
    multiplyBy2 = makeMultiplier(2),
    multiplyBy3 = makeMultiplier(3),
    Result1 = multiplyBy2(4),  // Result will be 8
    Result2 = multiplyBy3(4)   // Result will be 12
in
    [Result1=Result1, Result2=Result2]
```

Let's break down this code sample to gain a better understanding of what it means:

- makeMultiplier is a function that accepts a single argument, x. This function, makeMultiplier, returns another function. When initialized, it returns this new function: (y) => x * y.
- Both multiplyBy2 and multiplyBy3 are closures generated by invoking the makeMultiplier function with arguments 2 and 3, respectively. Each of these closures is a function that "remembers" the value of x from its creation, a 2 for multiplyBy2 and a 3 for multiplyBy3. This ability to remember variables from the environment where they were created is the fundamental concept of a closure.

- Finally, these closures can be invoked. For instance, when `multiplyBy2(4)` is called, it uses the value of x it "remembered" (2) and the new value for y (4) to return 8. Similarly, the function `multiplyBy3(4)` returns 12:

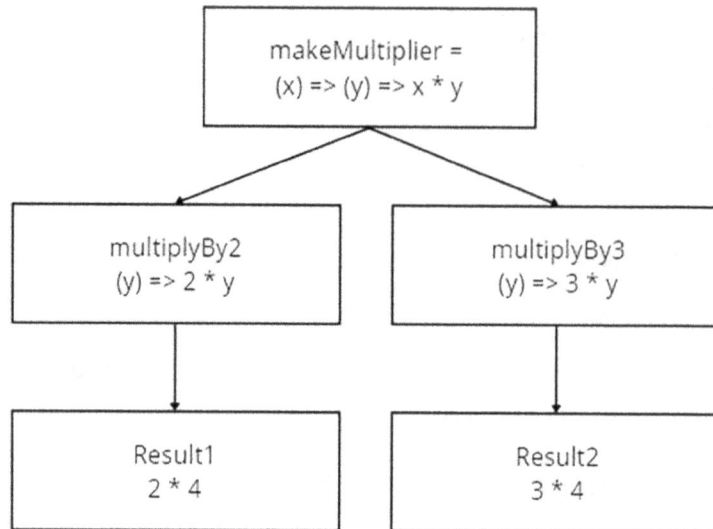

Figure 11.1: Diagram view of our code

By understanding closures, you can create more modular, reusable, and dynamic code. This enables you to design solutions and custom functions that come with a set level of adaptability, capable of dealing with a wider range of requirements.

Higher-order functions

Diving deeper into the M language's capabilities, we encounter the concept of higher-order functions, widely used across multiple programming languages. M is described as a functional language and exhibits certain traits; for example, functions are considered first-class citizens, meaning they can be assigned to variables, passed as arguments to other functions, and returned as results. This enables them to be manipulated and circulated like any other value. The term **"higher-order function"** is used to describe functions that can accept other functions as arguments or return functions as a result, like the `makeMultiplier` from the previous example.

Many standard library functions have a function type parameter, qualifying them as higher-order functions, like `List.Transform`, for example, which takes a list and a transform function as its parameters. `List.Transform` applies the transform function to each element of the list, resulting in a list with newly formed elements:

```
let
    defaultDiscount = 0.1,
    discountFunction = (discountRate as number) as function =>
        (sales as number) as number => sales * (1 - discountRate),
```

```
        applyDefaultDiscount = discountFunction(defaultDiscount),
        myList = {100, 900, 200, 500},
        Result = List.Transform( myList, applyDefaultDiscount )
    in
        Result
```

How does this code work? Let's break it down:

- The variable defaultDiscount is set to 0.1 or 10%.
- discountFunction accepts a single argument, discountRate. It is a function that returns the function (sales as number) as number => sales * (1 – discountRate).
- The applyDefaultDiscount variable is a closure generated by invoking the discountFunction function with the argument value, defaultDiscount. This function will apply the value for defaultDiscount from its creation.
- The myList variable is a list that contains four values: 100, 900, 200, and 500.
- Finally, the List.Transform function invokes the closure, applyDefaultDiscount, to each element in myList. It returns a new list with transformed values.

Functions can modify individual elements of a list or table, and higher-order functions enable these transformations to be applied to all elements efficiently and succinctly. In this case, List.Transform automatically passes the required argument to the applyDefaultDiscount closure at the time of invocation. In computer science terminology, this behavior is often referred to as a **"callback function invocation"** or simply a **"callback invocation"**. However, the Power Query M language documentation does not officially designate this process with a specific term.

Here's an example that shows how higher-order functions can make code easier to read by simplifying how argument values are passed, even when there are multiple arguments:

```
    let
        Result = Text.Contains(
                "Hello World", "hello",
                Comparer.OrdinalIgnoreCase
            )
    in
        Result
```

A comparer is used as an argument for the higher-order Text.Contains function. This function automatically provides its two input parameters to the comparer, eliminating the need to qualify them as arguments explicitly. We will explore various comparers available in the M language in more depth. Before we do, let's first explore anonymous functions or user-defined custom functions. These are not native to the M language but can be created by the user on the fly.

Anonymous functions

Anonymous functions are unnamed functions that can be defined inline within other functions. They are useful when custom function logic is required for a specific purpose and doesn't need to be reused elsewhere. Here is an example:

```
let
    Result = ((x, y) => x + y)(3, 4)
in
    Result
```

Anonymous functions can look daunting, especially when their parameters have non-descriptive names. Let's break the preceding example down:

- The function (x, y) => x + y requires two values (x, y) and will apply the + operator to them, in order to produce a single value or raise an error.
- The function is enclosed in a set of parentheses, for precedence ordering, and will evaluate the function expression to produce a function value.
- The invocation operator containing the argument list, (3, 4), is added. It evaluates the function body to yield the value 7.

Know that in most cases, the evaluation of a function expression is separated from a function's invocation. You can learn all there is to know about functions in *Chapter 9, Parameters and Custom Functions*.

So far, we have touched on concepts such as function invocation, closures, and higher-order functions. Now it's time to take a look at what the Order.Type enumeration and comparer functions have in common.

Ordering values

Do you sort the books on your shelf by one or more criteria, such as title, author, genre, and maybe size or color? Similarly, in Power Query, the Order.Type enumeration and comparer functions allow us to order data based on specific criteria.

In the M language, comparer functions and the Order.Type enumeration are used to order values. However, they are not the same:

- Enumerations define a set of named values, organizing related constants for more readable and maintainable code. These named values clarify their purpose, simplifying the process of setting options or states in your code. Enumerations are introduced in *Chapter 4* of this book. The Order.Type enumeration is a predefined set of values representing different types of ordering. A convenient method to specify the desired order of values is as follows:

Order.Type	Value	Direction
Order.Ascending	0	Numerically from low to high, or alphabetically ascending
Order. Descending	1	Numerically from high to low, or alphabetically descending

Table 11.2: Specifying the order of values

- Comparer functions, on the other hand, are utilized to evaluate two values and return an integer indicating their relative order. These functions give you control over how items are compared when sorting a table or list. This feature is highly customizable, allowing you to set specific sorting rules and criteria.

In summary, comparer functions offer a comprehensive and customizable method for comparing and sorting values, while the Order.Type enumeration makes it easy to set the sorting direction. While both are used to arrange values, they serve different roles and cannot be used interchangeably in the M language.

Comparers

Comparer functions play a crucial role in data processing, providing a means to evaluate and establish relative order or determine equality. Take, for instance, the strings Hello, hello, and HELLO. You might question if they are identical. However, it's comparer functions that can dictate the rules – such as case sensitivity – for how strings are interpreted and compared.

The role of comparer functions is to provide a method to compare values and determine their relative order or equality. Comparer functions are used in various scenarios, such as sorting or performing comparisons, for example, in conditional expressions.

In Power Query, these functions are mostly used as optional arguments to higher-order functions that require a comparison or equation operation. Some of them are listed here, but there are more functions equipped with a comparer or equationCriteria or comparisonCriteria parameter:

Text functions	List functions	Table functions
Text.Contains	List.Sort	Table.Sort
Text.StartsWith or EndsWith	List.Max or Min	Table.Max or Min
Text.PositionOf	List.RemoveMatchingItems	Table.Group

Table 11.3: Comparer functions

In the M language, there are four default comparer functions. Except for Comparer.Equals, all of them return a function value.

Comparer.Equals

`Comparer.Equals` returns a logical value after evaluating the equivalence between two values. This function requires three arguments: a comparer to guide the evaluation and the two values to be compared. You can specify a built-in comparer, such as `Comparer.Ordinal`, `Comparer.OrdinalIgnoreCase`, or `Comparer.FromCulture`:

```
let
    myTable = Table.FromRows(
        {
            { "APPLE", "apple" },
            { "apple", "apple" },
            { "42", 42.0 },
            { 42, 42.0 }
        }
    ),
    equivalenceChecks = Table.AddColumn( myTable,
        "equivalenceCheck",
        each Comparer.Equals(
            Comparer.FromCulture("en-US"),
            [Column1],
            [Column2]
        ), type logical
    )
in
    equivalenceChecks
```

Here's a breakdown of the code for which *Figure 11.2* depicts the outcome:

- The `myTable` variable yields a table from a list with row value lists.
- The `Table.AddColumn` function is used to add a new column to `myTable`.
- That new column is named `equivalenceCheck`.
- The each keyword tells Power Query to apply the function that follows to each row in `myTable`.
- To determine value equality, we provided `Comparer.FromCulture("en-US")`, which will compare the value in `Column1` with the value in `Column2` according to the rules of the English (United States) culture and yield a Boolean value:

	Column1	Column2	equivalenceCheck
1	APPLE	apple	FALSE
2	apple	apple	TRUE
3	42	42	FALSE
4	42	42	TRUE

Figure 11.2: Illustrating a Comparer.Equals equivalence check

Comparer.Ordinal

Comparer.Ordinal returns a comparer function that takes two argument values. It then applies ordinal rules for comparison, which rely on the Unicode code values of the characters involved. To illustrate, this query produces a two-column-wide table:

```
let
    myTable = Table.FromRows(
        {
            { "A" },
            { "APPLE" },
            { "Apple" },
            { "B" },
            { "a" },
            { "apple" }
        },
        type table[ Value1=text]
    ),
    unicodeValue = Table.AddColumn( myTable,
        "Unicode code value",
        each Text.Combine(
            List.Transform( Text.ToList( [Value1] ),
                (v)=> Text.From( Character.ToNumber(v))
            ), ", "
        ), type text
    )
in
    unicodeValue
```

Here's a breakdown of the code for which *Figure 11.3* depicts the outcome:

- The myTable variable yields a table from a list with row value lists.
- The Table.AddColumn function is used to add a new column to myTable. This new column is named Unicode code value.
- Text.ToList([Value1]) takes the text from the Value1 column and converts that string into a list where each list item is a single character from the original text.
- This list of characters is inserted into the List.Transform function, allowing us to apply a specific operation to every character in the list.
- (v)=> Text.From(Character.ToNumber(v)) is where the magic happens. Each character (v) in the list is passed to Character.ToNumber(v), yielding its Unicode code value, a number. Then, Text.From converts that number back into a text value.

- After transforming each character, we're left with a list of text values. `Text.Combine` takes these pieces and assembles them into a single string, separating each value with a comma and a space:

	Value1	Unicode code value
1	A	65
2	APPLE	65, 80, 80, 76, 69
3	Apple	65, 112, 112, 108, 101
4	B	66
5	a	97
6	apple	97, 112, 112, 108, 101

Figure 11.3: Unicode code value for each character in Value1

The first column contains a textual value and the second column depicts the Unicode code value that makes up the characters in the string. Through this, a relative ranking between text values can be established.

This query illustrates how the ordering process of ranked values is performed, placing them in ascending order (from lowest to highest):

```
let
    myTable = Table.FromRows(
        {
            { "APPLE", "apple" },
            { "apple", "apple" },
            { "apple", "APPLE" }
        },
        type table[ Value1=text, Value2=text]
    ),
    myComparer = Comparer.Ordinal,
    sortValue2 = List.Sort( myTable[Value2], Comparer.Ordinal ),
    equivalenceChecks = Table.AddColumn( myTable,
        "equivalenceCheck",
        each myComparer(
            [Value1],
            [Value2]
        ), Int64.Type
    )
in
    equivalenceChecks
```

Here's a breakdown of the code for which *Figure 11.4* shows the outcome:

1. The `myTable` variable yields a table from a list with row value lists.

2. Comparer.Ordinal is assigned to the myComparer variable.

3. sortValue2 produces a sorted list of the Value2 column values after applying ordinal rules to rank and order them.

   To understand the list item order in sortValue2, we will compare the two values on each row and show the ranking value that is assigned in a new column: equivalenceCheck.

4. each myComparer([Value1], [Value2]) will evaluate the two values on each row, establishing a relative rank when applying ordinal rules. This returns an integer indicating the relative order between them, enabling ordering them from lowest to highest:

	ABC Value1	ABC Value2	1²3 equivalenceCheck
1	APPLE	apple	-1
2	apple	apple	0
3	apple	APPLE	1

Figure 11.4: Comparison with ordinal rules

The myComparer function returns an integer value of -1, 0, or 1.

- If the returned value is negative (-1), it means that the first value should come before the second value in the sorted result as it has a lower rank or position, compared to the second value.
- If the returned value is zero (0), it means that the first value is considered to be equal to the second value in the sorted result as it has an equal rank or position, compared to the second value. Therefore, their order is not rearranged.
- If the returned value is positive (1), it means that the first value should come after the second value in the sorted result as it has a higher rank or position, compared to the second value.

In the **Query Settings** pane, go to the **Applied Steps** section and select the sortValue2 step. This displays a list of sorted values based on the input from the table's second column. The output retains the same order as the table's first column, aligned with their respective ranks as indicated in the equivalenceCheck column.

Comparer.OrdinalIgnoreCase

Comparer.OrdinalIgnoreCase returns a comparer function that takes two argument values. It applies ordinal comparison rules but ignores character casing. The function ranks these values, determining their relative position in an ascending sort order. Items with the same rank maintain their original order from the input:

```
let
    myTable = Table.FromRows(
        {
            { "APPLE", "apple" },
            { "apple", "Apple" },
            { "apple", "APPLE" }
```

```
        },
        type table[ Value1=text, Value2=text]
    ),
    myComparer = Comparer.OrdinalIgnoreCase,
    sortValue2 = List.Sort( myTable[Value2],
        Comparer.OrdinalIgnoreCase ),
    equivalenceChecks = Table.AddColumn( myTable,
        "equivalenceCheck",
        each myComparer(
            [Value1],
            [Value2]
        ), Int64.Type
    )
in
    equivalenceChecks
```

The process and code structure are equivalent to that of the previous example, with the exception that we are now applying ordinal rules while ignoring character casing. Therefore, the breakdown only highlights these differences:

- `Comparer.OrdinalIgnoreCase` is assigned to the `myComparer` variable.
- `sortValue2` produces a sorted list of the `Value2` column values after applying ordinal rules and ignoring case to rank and order them:

A^B_C Value1	A^B_C Value2	1^2_3 equivalenceCheck
1	APPLE	apple	0
2	apple	Apple	0
3	apple	APPLE	0

Figure 11.5: Comparison with ordinal rules while ignoring case

In a case-insensitive setting, different capitalizations of the same word, such as "apple," "Apple," and "APPLE," are considered to be equal. Consequently, their order remains the same in the sorted list, as shown in the `sortValue2` step illustrated in *Figure 11.5*.

Comparer.FromCulture

`Comparer.FromCulture` returns a comparer function that takes two arguments. The first is a culture, represented by a well-known language tag like `en-US` for English in the United States. This tag is used to specify locale settings in the .NET framework. The second argument is an optional `ignoreCase` Boolean, a `true` or `false` value to specify if character casing should be ignored; when omitted, its default is `false`:

```
let
    myTable = Table.FromRows(
```

```
        {
            { "APPLE", "apple" },
            { "apple", "apple" },
            { "apple", "APPLE" }
        },
        type table[ Value1=text, Value2=text]
    ),
    myComparer = Comparer.FromCulture("en-US"),
    equivalenceChecks = Table.AddColumn( myTable,
        "equivalenceCheck",
        each myComparer(
            [Value1],
            [Value2]
        ), Int64.Type
    )
in
    equivalenceChecks
```

To highlight the difference between earlier code samples, here `Comparer.FromCulture` is assigned to the `myComparer` variable. *Figure 11.6* shows the result:

	A^B_C Value1		A^B_C Value2		1^2_3 equivalenceCheck	
1	APPLE		apple			1
2	apple		apple			0
3	apple		APPLE			-1

Figure 11.6: Comparison with culture-sensitive rules

This performs a culture-sensitive comparison of two values based on the rules defined by the specified culture. It takes into account cultural conventions such as language-specific sorting rules and case sensitivity. Notably, in this example, the lowercase word is ranked and ordered before uppercase, in contrast to the ordinal comparison seen earlier. That is because of the way .NET's culture-aware comparers work.

The impact of applying language-specific rules becomes even more evident when comparing the Danish word `Færdig` with `Faerdig`, for example:

```
let
    Danish = Comparer.FromCulture("da-DK")(
        "Færdig",
        "Faerdig"
    ),
    English = Comparer.FromCulture("en-US")(
        "Færdig",
```

```
        "Faerdig"
    )
in
    [DK = Danish, US = English]
```

This record indicates that in English, the characters æ and ae are considered to be identical, resulting in a US field value of 0. However, in Danish (da-DK), these characters are regarded as distinct, leading to a DK field value of 1:

DK	1
US	0

Figure 11.7: Illustrating culture differences comparing "æ" and "ae" characters

Comparison criteria

Now examine the books on your shelf; do you notice one that is out of place? Take it. Determining its proper location requires comparison. You will compare the book in your hands to others on the shelf by applying specific criteria, repeating that process until you find its rightful place. The same holds true for data. By setting relevant criteria, you can order it in meaningful ways, such as ordering month names from January to December, weekdays from Monday to Sunday, and so on.

Comparison criteria can be used to arrange data according to specific logic. In this section, we will explore various methods provided by the Power Query M language for defining comparison criteria to order values. We'll use the List.Sort and Table.Sort functions as examples to show how you can create custom rules and gain exact control over the ordering of data.

Numeric value

When sorting data using Table.Sort, you can designate any numerical value to signify a desired sort order. Lower values take precedence over higher ones, with the data arranged in ascending order. This method is straightforward and suits cases where the sort order can be directly linked to numeric values. The following is an example of this:

```
let
    myTable = Table.FromRecords(
        {
            [Label="Moderate", Order=1],
            [Label="Low", Order=2],
            [Label="High", Order=0]
        },
        type table[Label=text, Order=Int64.Type]
    ),
    sortData = Table.Sort( myTable, each [Order] )
in
    sortData
```

`Table.Sort( myTable, each [Order] )` will order rows based on the value in the `Order` column. By default, this sorting is done in ascending order. This means rows will be arranged from the lowest value in the `Order` column to the highest, as illustrated here:

	AᴮC Label	1²₃ Order
1	High	0
2	Moderate	1
3	Low	2

Figure 11.8: Outcome of the sortData step

Computing a sort key

For more complex scenarios, you can use a function to calculate a key for each element. That key becomes the basis for sorting. This method is especially beneficial when the desired sort key cannot be directly derived from the original values and requires some sort of computation. Consider this expression:

```
List.Sort(
    { "April", "February", "January", "March" },
    each Date.From( _ & " 2020" )
)
```

There's a list with month names in alphabetical order: `April`, `February`, `January`, and `March`. To place them in chronological order, we could derive a date type value. Here, the sort key is computed by appending a year to each month name and leveraging the `Date.From` function to convert that string into a date type value. `List.Sort` will then order the month names in chronological order, instead of alphabetical order, as shown in *Figure 11.9*:

	List
1	January
2	February
3	March
4	April

Figure 11.9: Ordering month names chronologically

You may come across situations where ordinal values cannot be calculated directly. In such instances, a lookup may be necessary to establish a specific order. Consider this query, which returns a one-column-wide table, `myTable`, showing the values `Moderate`, `Low`, and `High`:

```
let
    myTable = Table.FromColumns({
        { "Moderate", "Low", "High" }
        }, type table[Label=text]
```

```
    ),
    sortData = Table.Sort( myTable,
        each Record.FieldOrDefault(
            [High=0, Moderate=1, Low=2], [Label]
        )
    )
in
    sortData
```

Even if this column were a part of a very large table, the variance within that column is limited to these three values. That means we can easily create a record on the fly to specify a preferred order:

1. Ensure each label matches a field name within the record.
2. Assign each field a numerical value; keep in mind that numbers are ordered from low to high. We will use 0, 1, 2, but 100, 200, 300 would achieve the same result.
3. Use the record initializer, a set of square brackets, to create the record and separate each field with a comma. The record expression should look like this:

```
    [High=0, Moderate=1, Low=2]
```

Note that if you want to use this record expression in more than one query, you should store it as a separate query within your file. That will allow you to use it repeatedly without duplicating its code. However, in this example, we will leverage it only once; therefore, we will insert the record directly into the sorting operation:

1. Invoke Table.Sort to change the row order within myTable.
2. Apply the following function:

```
    each Record.FieldOrDefault( [High=0, Moderate=1, Low=2], [Label] )
```

This record function will attempt to map field names within the record, provided as its first argument, to the (text) label provided as the second argument, to obtain its field value. Since that is a number, it will determine the order, as illustrated in *Figure 11.10*.

	ABC Label
1	High
2	Moderate
3	Low

Figure 11.10: Ordering values with the help of a lookup record

Now that you understand how to compute sort keys, let's explore how to apply these keys along with sorting directions that enable us to fine-tune our data ordering to meet very specific requirements.

List with key and order

To simultaneously select a specific key for sorting and control the sort order, you can use a list of lists as your sorting criteria. Each nested list should contain two elements: the key to sort by and the desired sort direction, specified using Order.Type (Order.Ascending = 0 or Order.Descending = 1). This method provides flexibility when custom sorting logic is required. Let's look at an example:

```
let
    myTable = Table.FromRecords({
        [Category = "Category A", SubCategory = "SubCategory 11"],
        [Category = "Category C", SubCategory = "SubCategory 20"],
        [Category = "Category A", SubCategory = "SubCategory 1"],
        [Category = "Category B", SubCategory = "SubCategory 2"],
        [Category = "Category C", SubCategory = "SubCategory 9"],
        [Category = "Category B", SubCategory = "SubCategory 5"],
        [Category = "Category A", SubCategory = "SubCategory 10"]
    }, type table [Category=text, SubCategory=text]),
    sortedTable = Table.Sort( myTable,
        {
            {each Text.Lower( Text.AfterDelimiter([Category], " ")), 1},
            {each Number.From(Text.Select([SubCategory], {"0".."9"})), 0}
        })
in
    sortedTable
```

Let's break down the contents of each nested column sorting list:

```
{each Text.Lower( Text.AfterDelimiter([Category], " ")), 1}
```

- Text.AfterDelimiter([Category], " "): Use Text.AfterDelimiter to extract the text from the Category column after the first space character.
- Use Text.Lower to convert the Category string to lowercase.
- Order it as descending, by providing a 1 or Order.Descending:

```
{each Number.From(Text.Select([SubCategory], {"0".."9"})), 0}
```

- Use Text.Select to extract the numerals from the SubCategory column.
- Use Number.From to convert that string into a number.
- Order it as ascending, by providing a 0 or Order.Ascending.

The following screenshot shows the outcome:

	A^B_C Category		A^B_C SubCategory	
1	Category C		SubCategory 9	
2	Category C		SubCategory 20	
3	Category B		SubCategory 2	
4	Category B		SubCategory 5	
5	Category A		SubCategory 1	
6	Category A		SubCategory 10	
7	Category A		SubCategory 11	

Figure 11.11: Sorting names in descending order and subcategory numbers in ascending order

Custom comparer with conditional logic

To fully control the comparison process, you can create a custom comparer function that takes two arguments. This function should return -1, 0, or 1 depending on the relationship between the left and right inputs. Though the following example is simplified, it highlights how you can use conditional logic to handle more complex sorting scenarios:

```
let
    customComparer = (x, y) =>
        if Number.IsEven( x ) and x > y then -1
        else if x < y then 1
        else 0,
    listNumbers = {1..10},
    sortedList = List.Sort( listNumbers,
        customComparer
    )
in
    sortedList
```

The customComparer expression starts with (x, y) =>, indicating it is a function with two parameters, x and y, that will return a function value.

The function body will only be evaluated when it is invoked. That function body contains conditional statements that prioritize even numbers over odd ones, where x is greater than y, in the order in which list items are encountered. Cases where x is less than y are placed later in the sorting order. When applied to a list with sequential numbers that run from 1 up to 10, it returns the outcome depicted in *Figure 11.12*:

	List
1	10
2	8
3	6
4	4
5	2
6	1
7	3
8	5
9	7
10	9

Figure 11.12: Custom comparer with conditional logic to order values

Custom comparer with Value.Compare

However, you can also create a two-parameter custom comparer function to fully control the comparison process. Use the `Value.Compare` function to delegate custom comparison logic to yield a result of `-1`, `0`, or `1` as needed. This method is particularly beneficial when complex comparison rules are required. Consider the following example:

```
let
  weekdayComparer = (a, b) =>
    let weekstartDate = #date(2024, 1, 1),
        weekdayCulture = "en-US",
        weekdayRecord = Record.Combine(
          List.Transform(
            List.Dates( weekstartDate, 7, Duration.From(1)),
            each Record.FromList(
            {Date.DayOfWeek( _, Date.DayOfWeek( weekstartDate, 0 ))},
            {Date.DayOfWeekName( _, try weekdayCulture ?? "en-US"
                otherwise "en-US" )}
    ))) in
    Value.Compare(
      Record.Field( weekdayRecord, a[colName] ),
      Record.Field( weekdayRecord, b[colName] )
    ),
  myData = Table.FromColumns({
    {"Thursday", "Sunday", "Saturday", "Monday", "Tuesday", "Friday",
"Wednesday"}
    }, type table [colName=text]
  ),
```

```
    sortedData = Table.Sort(myData, weekdayComparer)
in
    sortedData
```

In this example, the weekdayComparer includes a nested function that generates a weekdayRecord, which is culture-aware and denotes the days of the week and their number. The culture defaults to en-US. If further exploration is desired, the M code for that part of the function is listed separately here as fxCreateWeekdayRecord:

```
let
    fxCreateWeekdayRecord = (
        weekstartDate as date,
        optional weekdayCulture as text
    ) as record =>
    Record.Combine(
      List.Transform(
        List.Dates( weekstartDate, 7, Duration.From(1)),
        each Record.FromList(
        { Date.DayOfWeek( _, Date.DayOfWeek( weekstartDate,
            Day.Sunday )) },
        { Date.DayOfWeekName( _, try weekdayCulture ?? "en-US"
            otherwise "en-US" ) }
        )
      )),
    fxDocumentation = [
      Documentation.Name = " fxCreateWeekdayRecord ",
      Documentation.Description = " Returns a record where
      Fieldnames correspont to the weekday name,
      Fieldvalues correspont to the weekday number.
      'weekstartDate' is considered to be the first day of the week
      'weekdayCulture' is optional and defaults to 'en-US'. ",
       Documentation.Author = " Melissa de Korte ",
       Documentation.Version = " 1.0 "
    ]
in
   Value.ReplaceType( fxCreateWeekdayRecord, Value.ReplaceMetadata(
       Value.Type( fxCreateWeekdayRecord ),
       fxDocumentation
     )
   )
```

As seen in *Figure 11.13*, all this fxCreateWeekdayRecord function requires is a single date value that marks the first day of the week and optionally a culture:

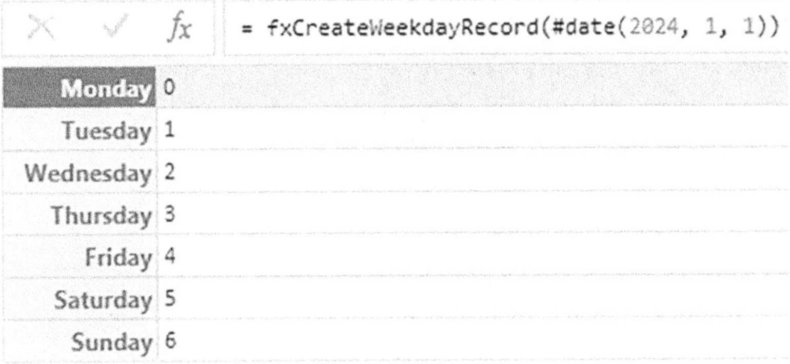

Figure 11.13: fxCreateWeekdayRecord's output, a record

When working with comparison criteria to arrange data, it's important to understand their adaptability to various situations. The techniques explored here, such as simply using numeric values for sorting or leveraging more advanced functions to compute sort keys, highlight the diverse toolbox at our disposal.

The ability to create custom comparer functions, to provide a method to compare values and determine their relative order or equality, allows for intricate comparisons and adds another layer of sophistication to the process.

Equation criteria

In the world of data, determining equality isn't always straightforward. Equation criteria enable us to identify differences or commonalities between two values.

Equation criteria are used to determine equality and match data in tables or lists according to specific logic. In this section, we will explore various ways to specify equation criteria in the M language. We will use the List.Contains function to illustrate how these methods help to establish control over equality testing.

Default comparers

In this chapter, we have already covered the role of comparer functions at length, which is to provide a method to compare values, determining their relative order and equality. Therefore, you can simply pass a default comparer as equationCriteria. Here, the selected comparer acts like a built-in rulebook that List.Contains follows when comparing values. By ignoring case sensitivity, New York and new york are considered to be equal:

```
List.Contains(
    {"New York", "London", "Tokyo"},
    "new york",
    Comparer.OrdinalIgnoreCase
)
//Result: TRUE
```

Custom comparer

For more intricate scenarios, you can create a two-parameter custom comparer. This allows full control over the comparison process by establishing your own equality rules. For instance, this function verifies if a list item (x) contains a specific substring (y):

```
List.Contains(
    {"New York", "London", "Tokyo"},
    "yO",
    (x, y)=> Text.Contains( x, y, Comparer.OrdinalIgnoreCase)
)
//Result: TRUE
```

Key selectors

Key selectors allow you to focus on a specific field or selection of fields, directing the function's attention to these specified areas. For instance, if you're working with a list of records and are only interested in matching the 'ID' field, a key selector will enable focus solely on that field, ignoring all the other field values:

```
List.Contains(
    {
        [ID=1, Name="John", Role="Manager"],
        [ID=2, Name="Jane", Role="Developer"],
        [ID=3, Name="Sam", Role="Designer"]
    },
    [ID=1, Name="Anne", Role="Analyst"],
    each [ID]
)
//Result: TRUE
```

Combining key selectors and comparers

When you combine key selectors and comparers, you can focus on specific fields (thanks to the key selector) and apply specific comparison rules (thanks to the comparer). Here we're performing a case-insensitive match over two record fields:

```
List.Contains(
    {
        [ID=1, Name="John", Role="Manager"],
        [ID=2, Name="Jane", Role="Developer"],
        [ID=3, Name="Sam", Role="Designer"]
    },
    [ID=1, Name="Anne", Role="manager"],
    {
```

```
        each Record.SelectFields(_, {"ID", "Role"}),
        Comparer.OrdinalIgnoreCase
    }
)
//Result: TRUE
```

Equation criteria are useful to match data in tables or lists. We've showcased several techniques that enable you to manage equality testing within M functions. Similar to comparisonCriteria, the capability to define and pass custom comparers as equationCriteria offers significant flexibility in determining equality.

Ever wanted the ability to correct a mistake in an instant? Replacers provide that means for your data, allowing you to substitute values in part or in full.

Replacers

Replacer functions are used by other functions in the Power Query M language. There are two default replacers, Replacer.ReplaceText and Replacer.ReplaceValue, which are used as arguments to either List.ReplaceValue or Table.ReplaceValue to substitute a value. This enables users to replace specific substrings or values with new strings, new values, or expressions. These functions are commonly used in data transformation scenarios where it is necessary to modify and clean inconsistent data to obtain uniformity.

For instance, let's take a look at this table (*Figure 11.14*) where we want to replace HR with Human Resources in the Department column:

	A^B_C Employee name		Department	
1	John		Sales	
2	Lisa		Marketing	
3	David		Finance	
4	Sarah		HR	
5	Alex		Operations	

Figure 11.14: Sample data

Here's how to do it using the **User Interface (UI)**:

- Select the Department column of the table.
- Navigate to the **Transform** tab on the ribbon and choose **Replace values.**
- A dialog box will appear. Input HR in the field for value to find.
- Enter Human Resources in the field for value to replace it with.
- Under **Advanced Options**, set **Match entire cell contents** and confirm.

A **Replaced Value** step is added to the query, resulting in a modified table (*Figure 11.15*) where HR has been replaced with Human Resources in the Department column:

	A^B_C Employee name	A^B_C Department
1	John	Sales
2	Lisa	Marketing
3	David	Finance
4	Sarah	Human Resources
5	Alex	Operations

Figure 11.15: Result of the Replaced Value operation

When you look at the M code in the formula bar, you'll notice the higher-order function Table.ReplaceValue is called. This function provides all the necessary arguments to the inner function, Replacer.ReplaceValue:

```
let
    Example = Table.FromColumns(
        {
            {"John", "Lisa", "David", "Sarah", "Alex"},
            {"Sales", "Marketing", "Finance", "HR", "Operations"}
        }, type table [Employee name=text, Department=text]
    ),
    #"Replaced Value" = Table.ReplaceValue(Example,"HR",
        "Human Resources",Replacer.ReplaceValue,{"Department"})
in
    #"Replaced Value"
```

Now, it's time to examine replacers in more detail. There are two default replacer functions in the M language.

Replacer.ReplaceText

The function Replacer.ReplaceText facilitates the substitution of a specific text pattern with another within a provided string. It has three parameters of the text type: the input or curText where the replacement will occur, the oldText – a pattern to be identified and replaced – and finally, the newText that will replace it.

The function scans for all occurrences of the oldText within the curText and substitutes them with the newText. Here is an example query:

```
let
    String1 = "The sun shines, shines brightly.",
    String2 = "A sudden rattle noise startled birds.",
```

```
    Example = Table.FromRecords({
      [ curText=String2, oldText="t", newText="f",
        ReplaceText=Replacer.ReplaceText(curText, oldText, newText) ],
      [ curText=String2, oldText="tt", newText="ff",
        ReplaceText=Replacer.ReplaceText(curText, oldText, newText) ],
      [ curText=String1, oldText="shines", newText="radiates",
        ReplaceText=Replacer.ReplaceText(curText, oldText, newText) ],
      [ curText=String1, oldText="shines,", newText="radiates",
        ReplaceText=Replacer.ReplaceText(curText, oldText, newText) ]
      }, let t = type text in type table
      [curText=t, oldText=t, newText=t, ReplaceText=t]
    ),
    ReplaceValue = Table.ReplaceValue( Example, ".", "!",
      Replacer.ReplaceText, {"curText", "ReplaceText"}
    )
  in
    ReplaceValue
```

The function `Replacer.ReplaceText` replaces each occurrence of the `oldText` with the `newText` within the provided text string or `curText`, supporting partial text replacements. The syntax is as follows: `Replacer.ReplaceText(curText, oldText, newText)`.

This process is illustrated in the example step of the query, as shown in *Figure 11.16*. The first three columns of the table present the input values, and the final column displays the output after a fully qualified `Replacer.ReplaceText` function is executed:

	A^B_C curText	A^B_C oldText	A^B_C newText	A^B_C ReplaceText
1	A sudden rattle noise startled birds.	t	f	A sudden raffle noise sfarfled birds.
2	A sudden rattle noise startled birds.	tt	ff	A sudden raffle noise startled birds.
3	The sun shines, shines brightly.	shines	radiates	The sun radiates, radiates brightly.
4	The sun shines, shines brightly.	shines,	radiates	The sun radiates shines brightly.

Figure 11.16: Replace text examples

When you select **Replace Values** from the **Transform** tab in the UI, the transformation is applied to all selected columns. Those column names are listed in the final argument of `Table.ReplaceValue`, as depicted here in *Figure 11.17*:

```
× ✓ fx   = Table.ReplaceValue( Example, ".", "!", Replacer.ReplaceText, {"curText", "ReplaceText"} )
```

	A^B_C curText	A^B_C oldText	A^B_C newText	A^B_C ReplaceText
1	A sudden rattle noise startled birds!	t	f	A sudden raffle noise sfarfled birds!
2	A sudden rattle noise startled birds!	tt	ff	A sudden raffle noise startled birds!
3	The sun shines, shines brightly!	shines	radiates	The sun radiates, radiates brightly!
4	The sun shines, shines brightly!	shines,	radiates	The sun radiates shines brightly!

Figure 11.17: Implicit Replacer.ReplaceText invocation within Table.ReplaceValue

In both the curText and ReplaceText columns of the table, a period has been replaced with an exclamation mark.

Replacer.ReplaceValue

The Replacer.ReplaceValue function, on the other hand, is used to substitute specific values with other values or expressions. It has three parameters of the any type: the original input (or curVal) where the replacement will occur; the oldVal, which is the value to be identified and replaced; and the newVal that will take its place. The function compares the oldVal with the curVal and, if they match, replaces the curVal with the newVal. Here's an example query for better understanding:

```
let
  Value1 = "Make some noise.",
  Example = Table.FromRecords({
    [ curVal=Value1, oldVal="noise", newVal="love",
      ReplaceValue=Replacer.ReplaceValue(curVal, oldVal, newVal)],
    [ curVal=Value1, oldVal=Value1, newVal="You rock!",
      ReplaceValue=Replacer.ReplaceValue(curVal, oldVal, newVal)],
    [ curVal=10.1, oldVal=10, newVal=11,
      ReplaceValue=Replacer.ReplaceValue(curVal, oldVal, newVal)],
    [ curVal=10, oldVal=10, newVal=11,
      ReplaceValue=Replacer.ReplaceValue(curVal, oldVal, newVal)],
    [ curVal={1..3}, oldVal={3..5}, newVal=List.First({1..3}),
      ReplaceValue=Replacer.ReplaceValue(curVal, oldVal, newVal)],
    [ curVal={1..3}, oldVal={1..3}, newVal=List.First({1..3}),
      ReplaceValue=Replacer.ReplaceValue(curVal, oldVal, newVal)]
    },  let t = type text in
  type table [curVal=t, oldVal=t, newVal=t, ReplaceValue=any])
in
    Example
```

The function Replacer.ReplaceValue replaces the curVal with newVal, when the curVal matches the oldVal. This is illustrated in the example step of the query (seen in *Figure 11.18*). The first three columns of the table present the input values, and the final column displays the output after a fully qualified Replacer.ReplaceValue function has been invoked.

	curVal	oldVal	newVal	ReplaceValue
1	Make some noise.	noise	love	Make some noise.
2	Make some noise.	Make some noise.	You rock!	You rock!
3	10,1	10	11	10,1
4	10	10	11	11
5	List	List	1	List
6	List	List	1	1

Figure 11.18: Replace value examples

It's important to emphasize that `Replacer.ReplaceValue` requires an exact match. This operation can be performed on any type of value, primitive as well as structured.

To illustrate, here is an example that performs a conditional replacement. Consider a common scenario like this but keep in mind that there are multiple solutions to such challenges. You have a dimension table that changes slowly over time. Our sample displays employees and their respective departments during specific periods of employment:

▦▾	A^B_C Emp	▾	StartDate	▾	EndDate	▾	A^B_C Dept	▾
1	John		1-1-2020		5-11-2023		Operations	
2	Lisa		15-9-2015		10-12-2023		Sales	
3	David		1-3-2019		*null*		Finance	
4	John		6-11-2023		*null*		Sales	
5	Lisa		11-12-2023		*null*		Marketing	

Figure 11.19: Slowly changing dimension

Copy and paste this code into a new blank query to follow along:

```
let
  SCD = Table.FromColumns(
    {
      {"John", "Lisa", "David", "John", "Lisa"},
      {#date(2020, 1, 1), #date(2015, 9, 15), #date(2019, 3, 1), #date(2023,
11, 6), #date(2023, 12, 11) },
      {#date(2023, 11, 5), #date(2023, 12, 10), null, null, null },
      {"Operations", "Sales", "Finance", "Sales", "Marketing" }
    }, type table [Emp=text, StartDate=date, EndDate=date, Dept=text]
  ),
  MergedExample = Table.NestedJoin(
    Table.FromColumns(
      {
        List.Repeat( {#date(2023, 11, 1), #date(2023, 12, 1), #date(2024, 1, 1)
}, 3 ),
        List.Repeat( {"John"}, 3 ) & List.Repeat( {"Lisa"}, 3 ) & List.Repeat(
{"David"}, 3 )
      },  type table [Date=date, Employee=text]
    ), {"Employee"},
    SCD, {"Emp"},
    "Department", JoinKind.LeftOuter
  )
in
  MergedExample
```

This dimension has been merged with a fact table to yield a table with all departments where an employee was active as there was one merge key, the employee (*Figure 11.20*). For the initial record of John on November 1st, 2023, we aim to return `Operations`, and for subsequent records, we intend to return `Sales` from this nested table:

Date	Employee	Department
1	1-11-2023	John	Table
2	1-12-2023	John	Table
3	1-1-2024	John	Table
4	1-11-2023	Lisa	Table
5	1-12-2023	Lisa	Table

Emp	StartDate	EndDate	Dept
John	1-1-2020	5-11-2023	Operations
John	6-11-2023	null	Sales

Figure 11.20: The merge obtained all Department history for each employee

To help generate the code, select the `Department` column, go to the **Transform** tab on the ribbon, and select **Replace Values**. In the dialog box, leave everything as is and just confirm, as shown in *Figure 11.21*:

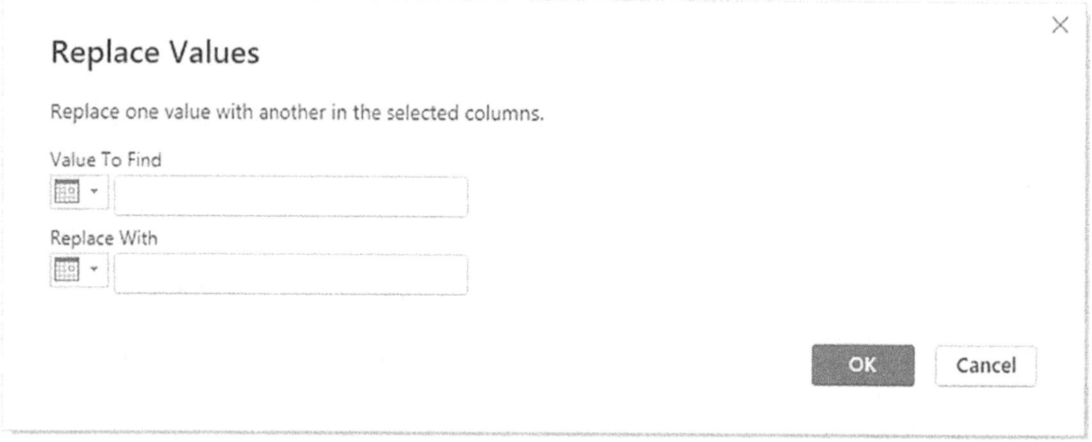

Replace Values

Replace one value with another in the selected columns.

Value To Find

Replace With

OK   Cancel

Figure 11.21: Leave the Replace Values dialog box empty

Inside the formula bar, you can see the code that was created:

```
Table.ReplaceValue(MergedExample,"","",Replacer.ReplaceValue,
    {"Department"})
```

The higher-order function, `Table.ReplaceValue`, has called the `Replacer.ReplaceValue` function. The remaining task is to specify the `oldValue`, which is what we are looking for, and the `newValue`, which is what we want to replace it with in the parent expression. This will allow these values to be passed to the replacer function, instead of the empty text strings provided there.

The first part is simple; we are in a table, and for each row of that table, we want to replace the value that is currently in that cell. Therefore, we need to replace the first, empty text string, which is a set of double quotes, with: `each [Department]`

```
Table.ReplaceValue(MergedExample, each [Department],"",
    Replacer.ReplaceValue,{"Department"})
```

The second set of double quotes is for the replacement value. Here we want to use `Table.SelectRows` to select a single row from the nested table, in order to extract the department:

```
Table.ReplaceValue( MergedExample, each [Department],
    each Table.SelectRows( [Department], (row) =>
        row[StartDate] <= [Date] and
        (row[EndDate] >= [Date] or row[EndDate] = null)
    )[Dept]?{0}?,
  Replacer.ReplaceValue, {"Department"})
```

Figure 11.22 shows the values obtained from the nested structure:

▦ ▾	▦ Date ▾	A^B_C Employee ▾	ABC 123 Department ▾
1	1-11-2023	John	Operations
2	1-12-2023	John	Sales
3	1-1-2024	John	Sales
4	1-11-2023	Lisa	Sales
5	1-12-2023	Lisa	Sales
6	1-1-2024	Lisa	Marketing
7	1-11-2023	David	Finance
8	1-12-2023	David	Finance
9	1-1-2024	David	Finance

Figure 11.22: Expected outcome

At this point, if you don't fully comprehend the M code, consider reviewing *Chapter 8*, which focuses on working with nested structures and will address these types of scenarios in more detail.

We've covered default "replacers" in the Power Query M language, which are particularly useful for data modification and data cleaning tasks. These tasks may include removing unwanted characters, correcting misspellings, or standardizing values.

`Replacer.ReplaceText` focuses on substring substitution within text, while `Replacer.ReplaceValue` is used to replace a cell's content. Both are used by higher-order functions such as `Table.ReplaceValue` and `List.ReplaceValue` to effortlessly manipulate and transform data to meet specific requirements. A perfect example is the `Replace Values` operation.

Custom replacers

Custom replacers enable users to extend beyond the limitations of default options, offering a flexible and powerful way to address issues in data. Unlike the one-size-fits-all approach of default replacers, custom replacers allow you to address anomalies with surgical precision, transforming your nearly perfect dataset into a flawless one. Whether it's replacing values entered as placeholders or correcting inconsistent naming conventions, you can tackle them all.

Replacer functions within `Table.ReplaceValue` or `List.ReplaceValue` play a crucial role in data transformation and manipulation. They allow users to replace specific values in a table column or list, respectively, with new values, based on defined rules or conditions. It's common to encounter inconsistencies or errors when working with data. Custom replacer functions offer a means to address these issues by enabling users to define their own replacement logic.

To manage the replacement process effectively, you can create an inline, anonymous replacer function on the fly that takes three parameters, as illustrated here:

```
Table.ReplaceValue(
    Source, //table to transform
    each true, // oldValue, logical condition
    null, // newValue
    (x, y, z) => if y then z else x, // custom replacer logic
    colList // columns as a list
)
```

Custom replacer logic, similar to default replacers, requires three parameters: `currentValue (x)`, `oldValue (y)`, and `newValue (z)`. Instead of the inline function `(x, y, z) => if y then z else x`, you can also define a custom function like this `customReplacer` expression, which is equivalent:

```
let
    customReplacer = (currentValue, oldValue, newValue) =>
        if oldValue then newValue else currentValue
in
    customReplacer
```

In this example, the `customReplacer` function is defined without a type and takes currentValue, oldValue, and newValue as parameters. It evaluates whether the oldValue returns true; if so, it replaces the currentValue with the newValue. Otherwise, it keeps the `currentValue` unchanged.

Custom replacer functions can be used within the higher-order `Table.ReplaceValue` and `List.ReplaceValue` functions to handle specific replacement requirements. It's important to note that custom replacer functions provide a high degree of flexibility.

Consider the table in *Figure 11.23*. It contains four date columns. These columns hold three specific date values that require a replacement by a null. To avoid multiple ReplaceValue transformations, we will devise a strategy to replace them all in a single step.

	A^B_C Label	Date Column1	Date Column2	Date Column3	Date Column4
1	Entry 1	1-11-2023	9-12-2023	21-1-2024	1-1-0001
2	Entry 2	9-9-2023	1-1-1900	1-1-0001	9-3-2024
3	Entry 3	2-2-2024	11-12-2023	9-9-9999	3-9-2023
4	Entry 4	25-5-2021	1-1-0001	1-1-1900	11-1-2024
5	Entry 5	9-9-9999	5-1-2024	9-10-2023	7-3-2024

Figure 11.23: Multiple date values need to be replaced

In fact, this M code illustrates three slightly different methods for you to explore. The first is Anonymous, an untyped inline function. The second is Typed, a typed inline function. Lastly, we have CF, a typed custom function assigned to the variable dateReplacer:

```
let
    datesToReplace = {#date(1, 1, 1),#date(1900, 1, 1),#date(9999, 9, 9)},
    dateReplacer = (x as nullable date, y as nullable logical, z as nullable
date) as nullable date =>
        if List.Contains( datesToReplace, x) then z else x,
    colsList = List.Select( Table.ColumnNames(Source), each
        Text.StartsWith(_, "Date")),
    Source = Table.FromColumns(
        {
            {"Entry 1", "Entry 2", "Entry 3", "Entry 4", "Entry 5"},
            {#date(2023, 11, 1), #date(2023, 9, 9), #date(2024, 2, 2), #date(2021, 5,
25), #date(9999, 9, 9)},
            {#date(2023, 12, 9), #date(1900, 1, 1), #date(2023, 12, 11), #date(1, 1,
1), #date(2024, 1, 5)},
            {#date(2024, 1, 21), #date(1, 1, 1), #date(9999, 9, 9), #date(1900, 1,
1), #date(2023, 10, 9)},
            {#date(1, 1, 1), #date(2024, 3, 9), #date(2023, 9, 3), #date(2024, 1,
11), #date(2024, 3, 7)}
        }, type table[Label=text, Date Column1=date, Date Column2=date,
Date Column3=date, Date Column4=date]
    ),
    Anonymous = Table.ReplaceValue( Source, null, null, (x, y, z) =>
        if List.Contains( datesToReplace, x) then z else x, colsList ),
    Typed = Table.ReplaceValue( Source, null, null, (x as nullable date, y as
nullable logical, z as nullable date) as nullable date =>
        if List.Contains( datesToReplace, x) then z else x, colsList ),
    CF = Table.ReplaceValue( Source, null, null, dateReplacer, colsList )
in
    CF
```

Here is an explanation of each variable within the M code:

- `datesToReplace`: A list with three date values to look for, which need to be replaced in multiple columns in the table.
- `dateReplacer`: A typed custom function that checks if the `currentValue` (x) is in the list of dates to replace. If it is, the function returns the `newValue` (z); if not, it returns the `currentValue` (x) unchanged.
- `colsList`: This selects only those columns from the source table whose name starts with `Date`. It's a dynamic way to identify all date columns within this table.
- `Source`: Specifies the table of data we've been provided.
- `Anonymous`: Illustrates how to apply an inline, untyped custom replacer.
- `Typed`: Illustrates how to apply an inline, typed custom replacer.
- `CF`: Illustrates how to apply the custom replacer assigned to the variable `dateReplacer`.

Default replacers have the ability to substitute values across multiple columns, but they rely on specified values for replacement and are therefore more limited. However, custom replacer functions offer a more versatile solution. They allow you to define your own conditions, effectively removing any limitations and providing a precise method tailored to your unique requirements.

We've introduced the concept of custom replacers, showcasing three different methods: an untyped inline function, a typed inline function, and a typed function assigned to a variable. These allow for dynamic value replacement based on specified conditions. Custom replacers must be defined as three-parameter functions that represent the `currentValue`, `oldValue`, and `newValue`, respectively. If you want to learn more about custom functions, see *Chapter 9, Parameters and Custom Functions*.

Combiners

Combiners merge text values from a list or columns within a table to form a single text value. Whether concatenating first and last names to create full names or joining address components into a complete address, combiners are essential in everyday scenarios where separate elements need to be brought together to create something more meaningful. The same principle applies to transformation scenarios, where merging columns before additional transformations, such as unpivoting, is crucial to ensure that related values remain together throughout the process. This provides the means to separate these combined values again, at a later stage in the transformation process.

In the Power Query M language, combiners join a list of text values into a single text. They are utilized by higher-order standard library functions such as `Table.ToList` and `Table.CombineColumns`, which use a combiner function to process each row in a table and produce a single value per row.

A common operation performed via the UI is **Merge Columns**. Located on the **Transform** tab of the ribbon (see *Figure 11.24*), it utilizes `Table.CombineColumns` and `Combiner.CombineTextByDelimiter`. To ensure successful operation, a nested `Table.TransformColumnTypes` is incorporated into the transformation when a type other than text is detected. This guarantees that either a single text value or a cell-level error is produced. This enables users to combine the various primitive values, including text, numbers, dates, and more. Consider the table this code generates:

```
let
    Source = Table.FromColumns({
        {"1", 1,  1, null, true, #time(12, 0, 0), #date(2024, 1, 1)},
        {"2", "2", 2, 2, false, #time(1, 0, 0), #date(2024, 2, 2) }
    })
in
    Source
```

When you select more than one column, in this case all (as seen in *Figure 11.24*), the **Merge Columns** option (2) is enabled on the **Transform** tab (1). This action will prompt the associated dialog box (3) to appear:

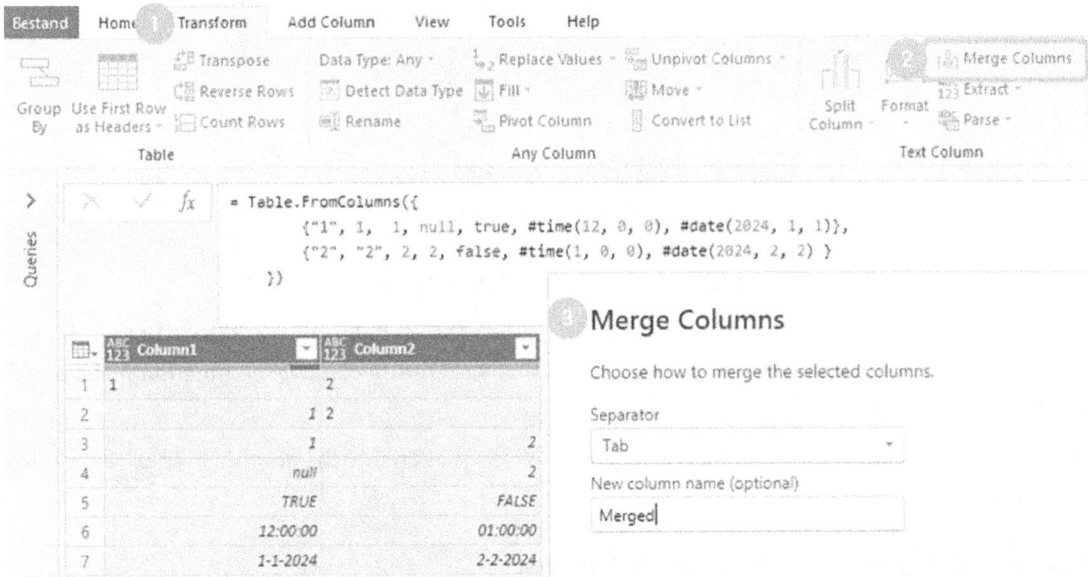

Figure 11.24: Merge Columns through the graphical UI

We have chosen Tab as the separator from the drop-down menu, but any separator that is not used as a character in the dataset will do. Upon confirmation of the operation, a new column named Merged will replace the input columns. This generates the following M code. Note that the culture may vary based on your locale:

```
let
    Source = Table.FromColumns({
        {"1", 1,  1, null, true, #time(12, 0, 0), #date(2024, 1, 1)},
        {"2", "2", 2, 2, false, #time(1, 0, 0), #date(2024, 2, 2) }
    }),
    MergedColumns = Table.CombineColumns(
        Table.TransformColumnTypes( Source,
            {{"Column1", type text}, {"Column2", type text}}, "en-US"
        ),  {"Column1", "Column2"},
```

```
        Combiner.CombineTextByDelimiter( "#(tab)", QuoteStyle.None ),
        "Merged"
    )
  in
    MergedColumns
```

It produces the outcome shown in *Figure 11.25*:

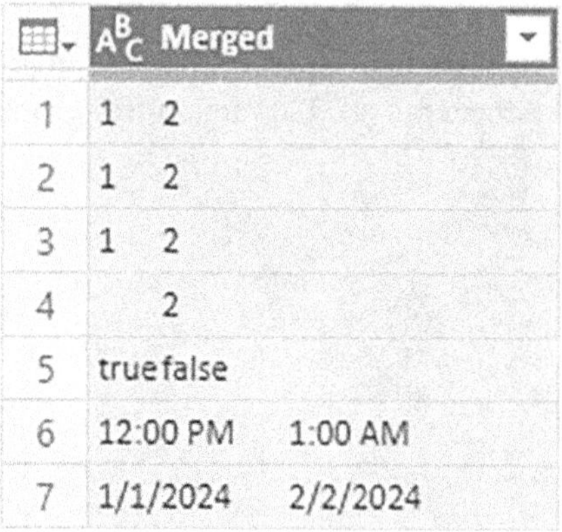

Figure 11.25: The result of combining these columns

Please note, if you want to keep the input columns, select **Merge Columns** from the **Add Column** tab on the ribbon. However, this will generate M code that uses the Text.Combine function instead of a combiner to produce a single value.

The M language features five default combiner functions that enable the combination of text values in various ways.

Combiner.CombineTextByDelimiter

Returns a function that combines a list of text values into a single text using the specified delimiter. The parameters include:

- Delimiter (text): Specifies the character(s) to use as a delimiter
- QuoteStyle (number): Governs how quotes are treated

Functionality

The delimiter requires a text type value that defines the character or characters used as separators between the combined text values. quoteStyle is an enumeration that controls how quotation marks are treated within a text string during operations, such as combining text.

Example

Here, the delimiter --- is provided to the combiner function. That is subsequently invoked on this list of text strings: {"a", "b", "c"}. This yields the result a---b---c, where each text string is separated by the delimiter provided to the combiner function:

```
Combiner.CombineTextByDelimiter("---")(
    {"a", "b", "c"}
)
//Result: a---b---c
```

When introducing quoted strings into the list with text values, QuoteStyle.None signifies that quote characters within a string have no special significance. They are treated like any other character in the text, as illustrated here:

```
Combiner.CombineTextByDelimiter("_", QuoteStyle.None)(
    {"This ", "is","a ""string in quotes"""}
)
//Result: This _is_a "string in quotes"
```

However, QuoteStyle.Csv signifies that quotation marks should be treated as special characters to indicate the beginning and end of a quoted string. Nested quotes within the string are indicated by two successive quote characters:

```
Combiner.CombineTextByDelimiter("_", QuoteStyle.Csv)(
    {"This ", "is","a ""string in quotes"""}
)
//Result: This _is_"a ""string in quotes"""
```

Combiner.CombineTextByDelimiter returns a function that can be applied to a list of text values, combining them into a single text using the specified arguments. If you omit the optional quoteStyle argument or pass a null, QuoteStyle.Csv will be applied by default.

Combiner.CombineTextByEachDelimiter

Returns a function that combines a list of text values into a single text using each specified delimiter in sequence. It includes the following parameters:

- Delimiters (list): Specifies the character(s) to use as delimiters
- QuoteStyle (number): Governs how quotes are treated

Functionality

The sequence of delimiters is determined by their number and order, provided as its first argument. If the number of text values to be combined exceeds the number of delimiters, the remaining text values are combined without a separator. The behavior of quoteStyle is equivalent to that of the Combiner.CombineTextByDelimiter function.

Example

To avoid exhausting the list with the available delimiters, you can calculate the minimum number of delimiters required and store them in a variable. This takes a modular approach, creating a function, a closure, and invoking that on the inputList:

```
let
    inputList = {"a", "b", "c", "d", "e", "f"},
    delimiterPattern = {"---", "_"},
    delimitersList = List.Repeat( delimiterPattern,
        Number.RoundUp(
            (List.Count(inputList)-1) /
            List.Count(delimiterPattern)
        )
    ),
    closure = Combiner.CombineTextByEachDelimiter(delimitersList),
    Result = closure(inputList)
in
    Result
//Output: a---b_c---d_e---f
```

Here's a breakdown of the code:

- inputList is a list containing six text values.
- delimiterPattern is a list containing two delimiters.
- delimitersList repeats the delimiterPattern a set number of times to ensure there are enough elements to separate each text value in the inputList.
- closure is a function produced by invoking the combiner function with the delimiterList provided.
- The result invokes that closure on the inputList, to yield a---b_c---d_e---f.

The Combiner.CombineTextByEachDelimiter function returns a function that merges a list of text values into a single text, using a specified number and order of delimiters.

Combiner.CombineTextByLengths

Returns a function that creates a single text string by combining a list of text values into a single text using the specified lengths. The parameters include:

- Lengths (list): Specifies the length of each text section.
- Template (text): Initial character sequence.

Functionality

The lengths list indicates the number of characters to be extracted from each corresponding text value. The optional template argument sets the initial characters for the combined output. When omitted or set to null, the function uses a string of spaces whose number matches the sum of specified lengths. If you provide a custom string, it replaces this default template.

Example

The template gets overwritten by extracted texts during the combining process. If a custom template falls short of the needed number of characters, it is padded with additional spaces. However, any surplus characters in a template will appear in the final output of the combined text:

```
Combiner.CombineTextByLengths(
    { 4, 4, 4, 4 }, "\\\\^^^^////****")(
    {"98", "DELTA", "19990110", "NO", "¯\_(ツ)_/¯"}
)
//Result: 98\\DELT1999NO**
```

Here's a breakdown of the code:

- The combiner is provided with a list of lengths, { 4, 4, 4, 4 }, and a template text consisting of 4x4=16 characters, "\\\\^^^^////****".
- It is subsequently invoked on this list of strings: {"98", "DELTA", "19990110", "NO", "¯_(ツ)_/¯"}. This list contains 5 strings.
- Based on the list of lengths, this combiner will obtain 4 characters from 4 strings to overwrite the 16-character template. When a string has fewer than 4 characters, the template value is shown, yielding this result: 98//DELT1999NO**.

Excess characters are disregarded, as are additional text values for which no corresponding length is provided. However, if a length exceeds the character count, the full text value is extracted and the template is not fully overwritten.

Combiner.CombineTextByPositions

Returns a function that concatenates text from specified positions out of a list of text values. The parameters include:

- Positions (list): Specifies the positions to extract
- Template (text): Initial character sequence

Functionality

The positions list represents a cumulative character count to be extracted from the corresponding text value. Each subsequent position should either match or exceed the previous one.

Example

The optional `template` is a string that defines a base pattern to be overwritten during the combination process. When the number of characters to extract surpasses the length of the corresponding text value, a part of that template is not overwritten and becomes part of the output. Any excess characters are ignored. However, if there are additional texts for which no positions are provided, only the first complete text is included, while any subsequent text values are excluded:

```
Combiner.CombineTextByPositions(
  { 0, 4, 6, 10, 12, 12 }, Text.Repeat( "*", 14))(
  {"98", "DELTA", "19990110", "NO", "¯\_(ツ)_/¯", "Wait", "What"}
)
//Result: 98**DE1999NOWait
```

Figure 11.26 illustrates how this process works:

Texts	98	DELTA	19990110	NO	¯_(ツ)_/¯	Wait	What
Positions	0	4	6	10	12	12	
Chars to extact	4	2	4	2	0		
explanation	= 4-0	= 6-4	= 10-6	= 12-10	= 12-12		
yield	98**	DE	1999	NO		Wait	

Figure 11.26: The Combiner.CombineTextByPositions process

Combiner.CombineTextByRanges

Returns a function that concatenates text segments using specified positions and lengths. Below are the parameters it uses:

- Ranges (`list`): Specifies the position and number of characters to extract
- Template (`text`): Initial character sequence

Functionality

The `ranges` list contains a nested list with two values: a starting position, indicating where characters will be placed in the output string and the number of characters to extract from the corresponding text, or a `null` indicating the entire string should be included. It's crucial to note that if a later extraction's position overlaps with an earlier one, the later extraction will overwrite the former. Any surplus items in the input list for which no range is specified are ignored.

Example

The optional `template` provides an initial string pattern that is overwritten. When a starting position surpasses the number of characters extracted at that specific point or the character count in the custom `template` exceeds the number of characters provided, template characters become part of the output:

```
Combiner.CombineTextByRanges(
    {{2, 2 }, {6, 4}, {10, 4}, {0, null}}, Text.Repeat( "*", 16))(
```

```
        {"98", "DELTA", "19990110", "NO", "¯\_(ツ)_/¯"}
    )
    //Result: NO98**DELT1999**
```

We've discussed combiners in the Power Query M language, which are essential for joining text values into a single string. These combiners are used by higher-order functions such as `Table.ToList` and `Table.CombineColumns`, which utilize a combiner to process table rows, yielding a single value per row. A perfect example of this is the **Merge Columns** operation offered by the UI. Furthermore, we have provided practical code snippets for effectively merging text values for each default combiner function in the M language. These examples are both informative and executable, providing a valuable reference for exploring their capabilities.

Splitters

On the other hand, splitters perform the task of dividing a single text value into multiple distinct components. Whether separating full names into first and last names or dissecting a complete address into individual elements, they can break a string apart into more granular pieces. This principle is also relevant in transformation scenarios where previously merged column values need to be separated. Splitters provide a means to reverse the merging process, separating values back into their original distinct components at a subsequent stage in the data transformation process.

In the Power Query M language, splitters are used to separate a string into a list of text values based on a specific delimiter or pattern. These are often utilized by higher-order standard library functions such as `Table.SplitColumn`, which is designed to divide a single column into multiple columns or rows. This is a common operation frequently used when handling strings that require parsing or transformation.

When you select a column containing text values, the **Split Column** button is enabled in the UI. You can find it on both the **Home** and **Transform** tabs of the ribbon. This invokes the `Table.SplitColumn` function, utilizing one of the default splitters based on the users selection, in this case **By Delimiter**.

For instance, let's take a look at the following table where we want to split `Column1` into columns:

Figure 11.27: Sample data

Here's how to do it using the UI.

1. Select the `Column1` column of the table.
2. Navigate to the **Home** or **Transform** tab on the ribbon and choose **Split Column**.
3. A dialog box will appear. Select **Custom**, then enter a comma followed by a space.
4. Open up **Advanced Options** and make sure split into **Columns** is selected and the number of columns to split into is 2. Confirm.

A Split Column by Delimiter step is added to the query, resulting in a modified table (*Figure 11.28*) where Column1.2 has been added with World in the first cell of this new column:

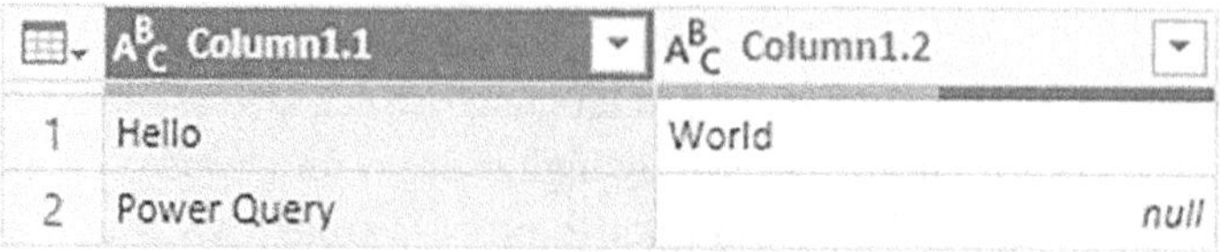

A^B_C Column1.1	A^B_C Column1.2
1 Hello	World
2 Power Query	null

Figure 11.28: Result of this Split Column operation

Upon the inspection of the M code within the formula bar, you'll find the expression assigned to the #"Split Column by Delimiter" step. The higher-order Table.SplitColumn function was invoked and supplied all required text arguments to the inner Splitter.SplitTextByDelimiter(", ", QuoteStyle.Csv) function:

```
let
    Source = Table.FromList(
        {"Hello, World", "Power Query"},
        Splitter.SplitByNothing()
    ),
    #"Split Column by Delimiter" = Table.SplitColumn(Source,
        "Column1",
        Splitter.SplitTextByDelimiter(", ", QuoteStyle.Csv),
        {"Column1.1", "Column1.2"}
    )
in
    #"Split Column by Delimiter"
```

Splitter functions are versatile, making them a powerful tool for text manipulation. Each one produces a function value when invoked. To use a splitter effectively, it's best to first define it by specifying the arguments, then call the returned function, also known as a closure, by passing the text string to be split.

The returned function, a closure, performs the actual splitting operation. This two-step process allows for greater flexibility as you can define the splitter once with specific arguments and reuse it multiple times with different text string inputs, making it efficient for batch text processing. Now, let's explore the specific traits of each splitter. The M language features 10 default splitter functions.

Four of them accept an optional quoteStyle parameter. They are:

- Splitter.SplitTextByDelimiter
- Splitter.SplitTextByAnyDelimiter
- Splitter.SplitTextByEachDelimiter
- Splitter.SplitTextByWhitespace

The quoteStyle parameter is an enumeration that governs the handling of quotation marks within a string during a splitting operation:

- quoteStyle.None indicates that quotation marks within a string hold no special meaning and are treated like any other character in the text.
- quoteStyle.Csv implies that quotation marks should be considered a special character to denote the start and end of a quoted string. Nested quotes within the string are represented by two consecutive quote characters. If you omit the optional quoteStyle argument or pass a null, the QuoteStyle.Csv will be used by default.

Splitter.SplitByNothing

Returns a function that prevents splitting by encapsulating its argument in a list. Notably, this function has no parameters.

Functionality

When invoked, Splitter.SplitByNothing returns a function specifically designed to manage the splitting behavior in Power Query operations, while preserving the intended data structure. This is accomplished by encapsulating its argument within a list, thus creating a single-element list that prevents a splitting operation. This ensures data remains unaffected by splitting behaviors from higher-order functions.

Example

Power Query, by default, uses commas as separators. For instance, if we have two elements in a list and wish to convert that into a single-column table, we can leverage the Table.FromList function. However, executing the code shown in *Figure 11.29* results in each string being split into columns, returning a two-column-wide table instead.

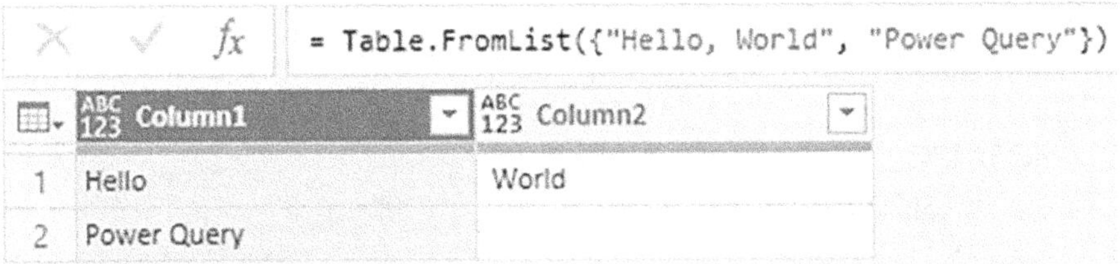

Figure 11.29: Default splitting by Table.FromList

To adjust the splitting behavior, `Splitter.SplitByNothing` can be passed as a second argument value. This will encapsulate each value within a list, ensuring every string is treated as an individual element, returning a single-column table, as seen in *Figure 11.30*:

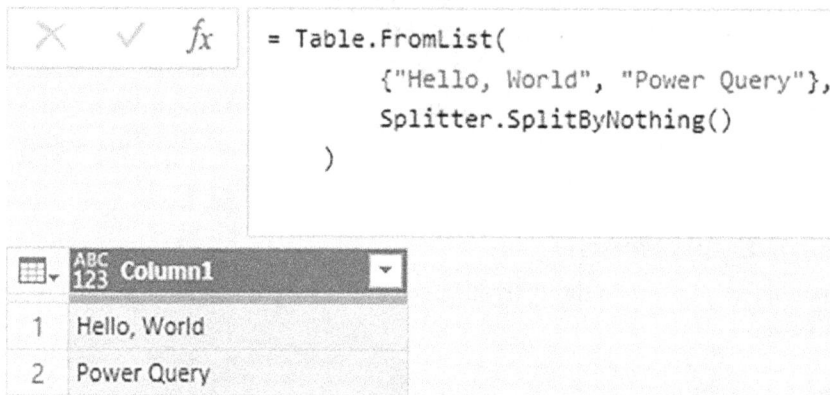

Figure 11.30: Overriding default splitting behavior

Here is the code for these examples, along with an additional one that demonstrates the encapsulation process by placing its argument within a list, creating a single-element list that prevents a splitting operation:

```
Let
    defaultBehaviour = Table.FromList(
        {"Hello, World", "Power Query"}
    ),
    modifiedBehaviour = Table.FromList(
        {"Hello, World", "Power Query"},
        Splitter.SplitByNothing()
    ),
    encapsulatingElements= List.Transform(
        {"Hello, World", "Power Query"},
        Splitter.SplitByNothing()
    )
in
    encapsulatingElements
```

Splitter.SplitTextByAnyDelimiter

Returns a function that divides a text into a list of text values using any of the specified `delimiters`. It utilizes the following parameters:

- `delimiters` (`list`): Specifies the characters to use as a delimiter
- `quoteStyle` (`number`): Governs how quotes are treated
- `startAtEnd` (`logical`): Determines the direction of splitting

Functionality

It returns a function that can be applied to a text value, splitting it into a list of text values based on the specified arguments. `delimiters` is a required argument and takes a list of text values that each act as a delimiter for the splitting operation. These delimiters can be a single character or multiple characters, and the function will split the text at any occurrence of a delimiter.

The `quoteStyle` is an optional argument and specifies how the function should handle quotes within the text. It is an enumeration and accepts two values, `QuoteStyle.None` and `QuoteStyle.Csv`, or their equivalent numerical value. The first includes quotes as part of the output, while the second ignores them.

`startAtEnd` is also an optional argument and takes a Boolean value. When set to `true`, the function reverses the splitting direction and starts the splitting operation from the end of the text string, which can yield a different result in certain cases.

Example

Here, the `startAtEnd` argument is valuable when a text string is asymmetrical or contains quotes that make the string non-uniform. In such cases, starting the split operation from the end can yield a different result, providing an additional layer of control over the text manipulation process, as illustrated in this example:

```
let
    string = "apple,""orange,banana;grape"",mango""",
    splitFunction = Splitter.SplitTextByAnyDelimiter(
        {",", ";"},
        QuoteStyle.Csv,
        true
    ),
    result = splitFunction(string)
in
    result
// startAtEnd true: {"apple,orange", "banana", "grape,mango"}
// startAtEnd false: {"apple", "orange,banana,grape, "mango"}
```

Splitter.SplitTextByCharacterTransition

Returns a function that splits a text into a list of text values at points where a character transition satisfies all conditions. The parameters it uses are:

- `before` (list or function): Evaluates a character to yield `true` or `false`
- `after` (list or function): Evaluates a character to yield `true` or `false`

Functionality

Like all other splitters, when invoked it will generate a new function, in this case, designed to segment text into a list based on the transition between characters. This enables you to divide text whenever there's a shift from a 'before' character to an 'after' character, implying that both conditions must be satisfied.

Example

The before parameter is set to return true for any character. The after parameter uses an isEven function to verify if a character represents an even number. When both conditions are fulfilled, the string is divided, guaranteeing that the input text string is separated before each character representing an even number. Evidently, the isEven function can be substituted with a list containing even numbers, such as {"0", "2", "4", "6", "8"}, to achieve the same outcome:

```
let
    string = "Abc1234Abc1234",
    isEven = (char) =>
        try Number.IsEven( Number.From(char)) otherwise false,
    splitFunction = Splitter.SplitTextByCharacterTransition(
        each true,
        isEven
    ),
    result = splitFunction(string)
in
    result
//Output: {"Abc1", "23", "4Abc1", "23", "4"}
```

When utilizing functions as arguments, it's important to handle exceptions. In this example, the try and otherwise keywords are used to prevent the function from failing when it attempts to convert a non-numeric character into a number.

This capability of using functions as parameters in Splitter.SplitTextByCharacterTransition significantly extends its useability. This allows for more intricate text-splitting scenarios tailored to meet specific requirements.

Splitter.SplitTextByDelimiter

This returns a function that divides a text into a list of text values using the specified delimiter. Here are the parameters:

- delimiter (text): Specifies the characters to use as a delimiter
- quoteStyle (number): Governs how quotes are treated

Functionality

The delimiter requires a text type value that defines the character or characters used as separators for dividing the text string. `quoteStyle` is an enumeration that determines how quotes within the text are handled during the splitting process.

Example

Unlike the `Splitter.SplitTextByAnyDelimiter` function, this function does not accept a list of delimiters or include a `startAtEnd` parameter, making it less flexible but more straightforward. When compared to the closely related `Text.Split` function, the distinguishing feature of `Splitter.SplitTextByDelimiter` is its ability to manage quote styles. However, if you do not require `QuoteStyle.Csv`, the simplicity and user-friendliness of `Text.Split` make it an ideal choice for basic text-splitting tasks:

```
Let
    string = "apple,""orange,banana;grape"",mango""",
    splitFunction = Splitter.SplitTextByDelimiter(
        ",",
        QuoteStyle.None
    ),
    result = splitFunction(string)
in
    result
//Output: {"apple", """orange", "banana;grape""", "mango"""}
```

In this case, the splitting process uses a comma as a delimiter. The enumeration `QuoteStyle.None` is used to indicate that quotes within the text should not be considered special characters during the split. As a result, the input string is divided at each comma, ignoring double quotes. However, if you alter the `quoteStyle` to `QuoteStyle.Csv`, any text enclosed in double quotes is considered a single unit; even if it includes the chosen delimiter, such a string will not be affected by the splitting process.

Splitter.SplitTextByEachDelimiter

Returns a function that splits a text into a list of text values in sequence, in the order in which the delimiters are specified. The parameters are as follows:

- `delimiters` (list): Specifies the characters to use as a delimiter
- `quoteStyle` (number): Governs how quotes are treated
- `startAtEnd` (logical): Determines the direction of splitting

Functionality

The sequence and number of delimiters provided as the first argument will dictate where and how many times a text string is split. The behavior of `quoteStyle` and `startAtEnd` is equivalent to that described before.

Example

In this case, `startAtEnd` is set to `true`, indicating that the function initiates the splitting operation from the end of the text string. It then follows the precise order and number of delimiters that are provided to direct the splitting process:

```
let
    string = "apple,""orange,banana;grape"",mango""",
    splitFunction = Splitter.SplitTextByEachDelimiter(
        {",", ";"},
        QuoteStyle.None,
        true
    ),
    result = splitFunction(string)
in
    result
//Output: {"apple,""orange,banana", "grape""", "mango"""}
```

Splitter.SplitTextByLengths

Returns a function that breaks down a text into a list of text values by specified lengths. The parameters include:

- `Lengths` (list): Specifies the length of each text section
- `StartAtEnd` (logical): Determines the direction of splitting

Functionality

`Lengths` is a list containing positive numbers that represent the length of each segment to split a text into. The `startAtEnd` parameter is an optional Boolean value that, if set to `true`, allows you to reverse the split direction to start from the end. The returned function can be applied to a text value. This divides its input in the specified direction and lengths to produce a list with text values.

Characters for which no corresponding length is provided are ignored. However, if the length exceeds the total character count, a list item with zero characters is added for each excess length item, without raising an error.

Example

The `Splitter.SplitTextByLengths` function is particularly useful when handling strings from databases or flat files with a pre-determined fixed-width length for each field or column. This guarantees each field occupies a consistent number of characters, simplifying the parsing process. Let's look at the following example:

```
let
    string = "apple,""orange,banana;grape"",mango""",
    lengths = {5, 1, 1, 6, 1, 6, 1, 5, 1},
    splitFunction = Splitter.SplitTextByLengths(
```

```
        lengths,
        false
    ),
    result = splitFunction(string)
in
    result
//Output: {"apple",",","""","orange",",","banana",";","grape",""""}
```

Identifying fixed-width data is straightforward. Navigate to the **View** tab and enable **Monospaced**; see *Figure 11.31*. This setting changes the typeface into one where each character occupies the same amount of horizontal space. If equal space has been assigned to fields or columns, it should now be clearly visible.

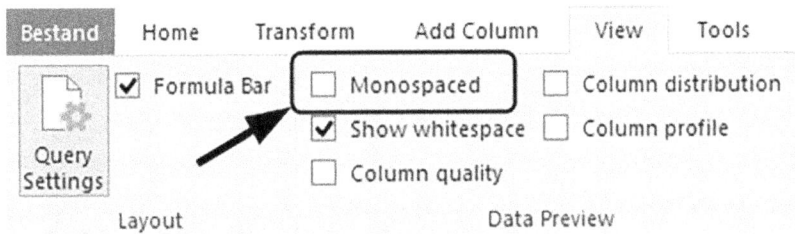

Figure 11.31: Monospaced option is located on the View tab

Splitter.SplitTextByPositions

This returns a function that divides text at specified positions to yield a list of text values. The parameters for this function are:

- positions (list): Specifies the position to split
- startAtEnd (logical): Determines the direction of splitting

Functionality

The positions list represents a cumulative character count for the split. Each item in the positions list should match or exceed the previous one and cannot be negative.

Example

When the last item in the positions list is less than the total character count, it will include all remaining characters from the string. However, for each item in the positions list that exceeds the total character count, an item with zero characters is added to the result list, without raising an error:

```
let
    string = "apple,""orange,banana;grape"",mango""",
    positions = {0, 5, 5, 6, 7, 13},
    splitFunction = Splitter.SplitTextByPositions(
        positions,
        false
```

```
    ),
    result = splitFunction(string)
in
    result
//Output: {"apple", "", ",", """"", "orange", ",banana;grape"",mango"""}
```

Splitter.SplitTextByRanges

This returns a function that devides a text according to specified ranges, defined by a starting position and length. It uses the following parameters:

- ranges (list): Specifies the position and number of characters to take
- startAtEnd (logical): Determines the direction of splitting

Functionality

The ranges list, which contains nested lists with two values, dictates the output order. These values represent a starting position and the number of characters to retrieve, or a null to include all remaining characters in the string. If splitting positions overlap with an earlier one, the function will re-retrieve that text segment.

Example

In the following example, for each item in the ranges list where the position exceeds the total character count, an item with zero characters is added to the result list, without raising an error:

```
let
    string = "apple,""orange,banana;grape"",mango""",
    ranges = {{14, null}, {0, 5}, {3, 2}, {7, 6}},
    splitFunction = Splitter.SplitTextByRanges(
        ranges,
        false
    ),
    result = splitFunction(string)
in
    result
//Output: {"banana;grape"",mango""", "apple", "le", "orange"}
```

Splitter.SplitTextByRepeatedLengths

Returns a function that splits a text into a list of text values by a given length, repeatedly. The parameters are as follows:

- lengths (number): Specifies the length of each text section
- startAtEnd (logical): Determines the direction of splitting

Functionality

Length is a positive number that represents the segment length to split a text into. The startAtEnd parameter is an optional Boolean value that, if set to true, allows you to reverse the split direction to start from the end.

Example

The returned function can be applied to a text value, dividing it based on the specified direction and length, to produce a list with text values. Unlike Splitter.SplitTextByLengths, this function does not take a list of lengths, making it less flexible but more user-friendly for splitting tasks with a consistent length:

```
let
    string = "apple,""orange,banana;grape"",mango""",
    splitFunction = Splitter.SplitTextByRepeatedLengths(
        10,
        false
    ),
    result = splitFunction(string)
in
    result
//Output: {"apple,""ora", "nge,banana", ";grape"""",ma", "ngo"""}
```

There is no padding capability; therefore, the final list item of the result list may consist of fewer characters than the specified length.

Splitter.SplitTextByWhitespace

Returns a function that separates a text into a list of text values based on the existence of whitespace characters, offering a straightforward method for dividing text. It includes the following parameter:

- quoteStyle (number): Governs how quotes are treated

Functionality

It returns a function that splits text into a list of text at each whitespace. Whitespace in the Power Query M language encompasses a variety of characters, including spaces and control characters such as carriage returns, line feeds, and tabs.

quoteStyle is optional and specifies how quotes within text are handled. QuoteStyle.None includes quotes and treats them like any other character, while QuoteStyle.Csv ignores them. A quoted section will not be separated.

Example

When working with text values, you need to use character escape sequences to embed control characters. Specifically, if you want to insert a carriage return, you have three alternatives: you can use its short 4-digit hexadecimal format #(000D), opt for the longer 8-digit hexadecimal Unicode representation #(0000000D), or use the simpler escape shorthand #(cr).

Generally, the escape shorthand is preferred. This means that for a tab, we use #(tab), and for a line feed, #(lf). Multiple escape codes can be included in one escape sequence, separated by commas, as in #(cr,lf), which is equivalent to #(cr)#(lf):

```
let
    string = "A#(000D) B#(tab) C#(lf)D#(cr,lf)
        E#(cr)F#(lf)1#(0000000D)",
    splitFunction = Splitter.SplitTextByWhitespace(),
    result = splitFunction(string)
in
    result
//Output: {"A",  "B","C",  "D","E",  "F","1",  ""}
```

Splitters are useful when you need to break a string into smaller parts based on a specific pattern, delimiter, length, or position. They are commonly used in scenarios that involve parsing strings containing combined values, such as in a CSV, in a delimited text file, or in strings that contain other values of interest, like dates or numbers, for example. The provided code snippets are intended to be used as a reference and for exploring their functionalities.

Practical examples

Thus far, you've gained an understanding of the different comparers, replacers, combiners, and splitters available in the M language. Now, with this foundational knowledge, it's time to solidify your learning through practical examples that demonstrate their use in real-world scenarios. These examples will enhance your understanding of how to integrate these functions into your own workflows.

Feel free to devise your own strategy for these scenarios before delving into them. If you're uncomfortable with translating this into M code at this time, that's perfectly fine. You can still formulate an outline and consider potential obstacles to overcome. This will enable you to compare your approach with the one suggested here. However, keep in mind that there are numerous solutions to any given problem; this book only presents one possible method.

Removing control characters and excess spaces

A common task in cleaning and transforming text strings is removing control characters and excess spaces. Unlike Excel's trim function, its Power Query equivalent, Text.Trim, only removes leading and trailing whitespace from a text value, although you can specify other characters to trim as well. Here's a sample table:

```
let
  Source = Table.FromColumns(
    {
      {
        "A#(000D) B#(tab) C#(1f)D#(cr,lf) E#(cr)F#(1f)1#(0000000D)",
        "       A   #(000D)   B#(tab)   C#(1f)D       "
      }
    }
  )
in
  Source
```

Goals

- Ensure user inputs conform to expected formats
- Ensure consistency by eliminating spacing variations and eliminating non-printable characters

A cleanTrim function

Let's create our own function, `cleanTrim`, that can do it all. Enhance `Text.Trim` to remove control characters and all excess spaces within a string as well. This is the domain of the `Splitter.SplitTextByWhitespace` function, splitting a text at each whitespace, returning a list of text values:

```
(string as text) as text =>
    Text.Trim(
        Text.Combine(
            Splitter.SplitTextByWhitespace()(
                string
            ), " "
        )
    )
```

Whitespace in M encompasses both spaces and control characters. When the splitter is invoked, it returns a list with text values, which can be combined with a single space, to convert back to a string. We can use functions like `Combiner.CombineTextByDelimiter` or `Text.Combine`, for example; both yield the same result. However, it's important to understand that if the list contains an empty text string as the initial or final item, a combine operation will insert a preceding or trailing space.

This can be resolved with `Text.Trim`. It's worth mentioning that, based on limited testing, a `trim` operation on the inner 'string' input doesn't exhibit a significant performance impact when compared to applying it to the combined output, as demonstrated here.

When the `cleanTrim` function is invoked on `Column1`, adding a column to the table, it yields the result shown in *Figure 11.32*:

Figure 11.32: Result of invoking cleanTrim on the sample data

Extract email addresses from a string

In addition to cleaning and transforming text strings, the ability to extract a specific part of a string is equally important. While there are numerous different types of scenarios and there is no "one-fits-all" solution, understanding splitters can be strategically beneficial. Our next task is extracting what appear to be valid email addresses from this sample data:

```
let
    Source = Table.FromRows(
        {
            {"Wendy Darling, UK, wendy.darling@nevergrowup.co.uk"},
            {"john.darling@nevergrowup.co.uk, UK;john.boy@abc.com"},
            {"michael; michael.darling@nevergrowup"},
            {"Peter Pan peter.pan@neverland.com"},
            {"tink@pixie@fairy.org Tinker Bell"},
            {"Captain Hook: captain.hook@piratescove.org"}
        }, type table [Contact info=text]
    )
in
    Source
```

Goals

- Isolate and retrieve email addresses from mixed text data
- Improve accuracy by identifying and analyzing patterns

Developing a getEmail function

Examining this sample, it is evident that rows three and five are structurally invalid due to either a missing domain or including more than one @ symbol within the address. Another important thing to note is that we require more than one separator to segment each string effectively.

Ultimately, we aim to create a custom getEmail function. However, we first need to develop a logic that enables us to exclude and extract email addresses from these entries. Click on the **mini table** icon located to the left of the Contact Info column header and select **Add Custom Column**. We will gradually construct a solution while reviewing intermediate results:

1. In the dialog box, you can optionally assign another name to this column. As this is just a temporary column, we will leave it as is.

2. Enter Splitter.SplitTextByAnyDelimiter() in the formula section because multiple separators are needed.

3. Within the parentheses, include a list with all distinguishable separators: {" ", ",", ";", ":"}.

4. To execute this function, add another set of parentheses after the closing one and choose the Contact Info field from the **Available columns** list.

5. It is important to note here that it has been formatted for readability, but in the formula bar, the code generated by these actions will look like this:

```
Table.AddColumn(Source, "Custom", each
        Splitter.SplitTextByAnyDelimiter(
            {" ", ",", ";", ":"}
        )([Contact info])
    )
```

6. Preview the contents of the output lists by clicking on the whitespace next to these nested list values. For instance, the second-row list values are { "john.darling@nevergrowup.co.uk", "", "UK", "john.boy@abc.com"}.

7. These lists require filtering. To do that, return to the **Custom Column** dialog box by clicking on the **gear wheel** icon located to the right of the step name in the **Applied Steps** section of the **Query Settings** pane.

8. In front of the formula, add List.Select(. Then, proceed to the end and enter a comma followed by a ')' closing parenthesis. You will see a warning indicating that a comma cannot precede a closing parenthesis. Next, specify the function that will define the selection criteria as an argument.

9. A structurally valid email address should include the at (@) symbol, followed by a period (.), in that order. Thus, we can attempt to split each list item again using Splitter. SplitTextByEachDelimiter with this argument: {"@", "."}. To invoke it, add a set of parentheses with the underscore (_).

10. Although this resolves the error warning, our expression is not complete. This splitter will yield a new list, but we are only interested in lists that contain three elements. Therefore, add `List.Count( … ) =3`. The code in the formula box should look like this:

```
List.Select(
    Splitter.SplitTextByAnyDelimiter(
        {" ", ",", ";", ":"}
    )([Contact info]),
    each List.Count(
        Splitter.SplitTextByEachDelimiter(
            {"@", "."}
        )(_)
    ) =3
)
```

11. Preview the contents once more by clicking on the whitespace next to the nested list values. Additional criteria are necessary to exclude structurally invalid email addresses. For example, cases that include more than one @ symbol, or instances where the @ symbol is immediately followed by a period (.) still need to be addressed.

12. To do this, return to the **Custom Column** dialog box by clicking on the **gear wheel** icon. Expand the selection as a function argument by entering the **and** keyword followed by this expression: `Text.Length( Text.Select(_, "@")) =1`. This resolves one potential issue. To address the other, enter another **and** keyword followed by not `Text.Contains(_, "@.")`, as shown here:

```
List.Select(
    Splitter.SplitTextByAnyDelimiter(
        {" ", ",", ";", ":"})(
    [Contact info]),
    each List.Count(
        Splitter.SplitTextByEachDelimiter(
            {"@", "."}
        )(_)
    ) =3 and
    Text.Length( Text.Select(_, "@")) =1 and
    not Text.Contains(_, "@.")
)
```

13. The final step involves extracting and combining the remaining list items. Open the dialog box and wrap `Text.Combine( …, ", ")` around it. Once you're satisfied with the result, you can copy the M code from here in its entirety.

14. Choose **New Source**, then **Blank Query**. Remove the default `let` expression and replace it with the copied code. To transform this code into a custom function query, we need to start this expression with a function initializer. Position your cursor before the code and add `(string as text) as text =>`.

15. This function takes a text type input and will yield a text type value: (string as text) as text. The input parameter is named `string`, not [Contact info]. Replace that, then close this query and give it an appropriate name like `getEmail`:

```
(string as text) as text =>
    Text.Combine(
        List.Select(
            Splitter.SplitTextByAnyDelimiter(
                {" ", ",", ";", ":"}
            )(string),
            each List.Count(
                Splitter.SplitTextByEachDelimiter(
                    {"@", "."}
                )(_)
            ) =3 and
            Text.Length( Text.Select(_, "@")) =1 and
            not Text.Contains(_, "@.")
        ), ", "
    )
```

Verify the functionality of this custom function by applying it to the sample data and comparing the results with the output from the custom column. Simply select Invoke **Custom Function** on the **Add Column** tab of the ribbon and assign an argument to each input. *Figure 11.33* shows the outcome:

	A^B_C Contact info	A^B_C getEmail
1	Wendy Darling, UK, wendy.darling@nevergrowup.co.uk	wendy.darling@nevergrowup.co.uk
2	john.darling@nevergrowup.co.uk, UK;john.boy@abc.com	john.darling@nevergrowup.co.uk, john.boy@abc.com
3	michael; michael.darling@nevergrowup	
4	Peter Pan peter.pan@neverland.com	peter.pan@neverland.com
5	tink@pixie@fairy.org Tinker Bell	
6	Captain Hook: captain.hook@piratescove.org	captain.hook@piratescove.org

Figure 11.33: Result of invoking getEmail on the sample data

Split combined cell values into rows

Splitting combined cell values is a common task when dealing with data stored in a single cell that needs separation. This process is straightforward and can be achieved by selecting **Split Column** on the ribbon in the UI. By adjusting the necessary settings in the dialog, you can effortlessly separate combined cell values into multiple columns or rows (available under **Advanced options**).

However, if you encounter multiple columns with combined cell values that need to be separated into rows specifically, repeatedly applying this process may not produce the expected outcome.

Consider this sample data:

```
let
  Data = [
    p = Lines.ToText( {"1".."3"} ) & "4",
    c = "W01",
    s1 = Text.Combine( List.Repeat( {"24x7 #(cr,lf)"}, 3) &
      {"""8x5 (9:00 - 17:00)"""} ),
    s2 = Text.Combine( List.Repeat( {"""9x5 (9:00 - 18:00)"""} &
      {"#(lf,cr)"}, 3) & {"""9x5 (9:00 - 18:00)"""} ),
    s3 = Text.Combine( List.Repeat( {""" """} & {"#(lf)"}, 2) &
      {"""9x5 (9:00 - 18:00)"""} & {"#(cr)"} & {"""9x5 (9:00 - 18:00)"""})
  ],
  Source = Table.FromRecords(
    {
      [ID = "A", Code=Data[c], Priority = Data[p], Schedule = Data[s1]],
      [ID = "B", Code=Data[c], Priority = Data[p], Schedule = Data[s2]],
      [ID = "C", Code=Data[c], Priority = Data[p], Schedule = Data[s3]]
    },
    type table [ID = text, Code = text, Priority = text, Schedule = text]
  )
in
  Source
```

The sample data is depicted in *Figure 11.34*. It clearly shows all cells in both the Priority and Schedule columns contain multiple values that need to be separated into rows:

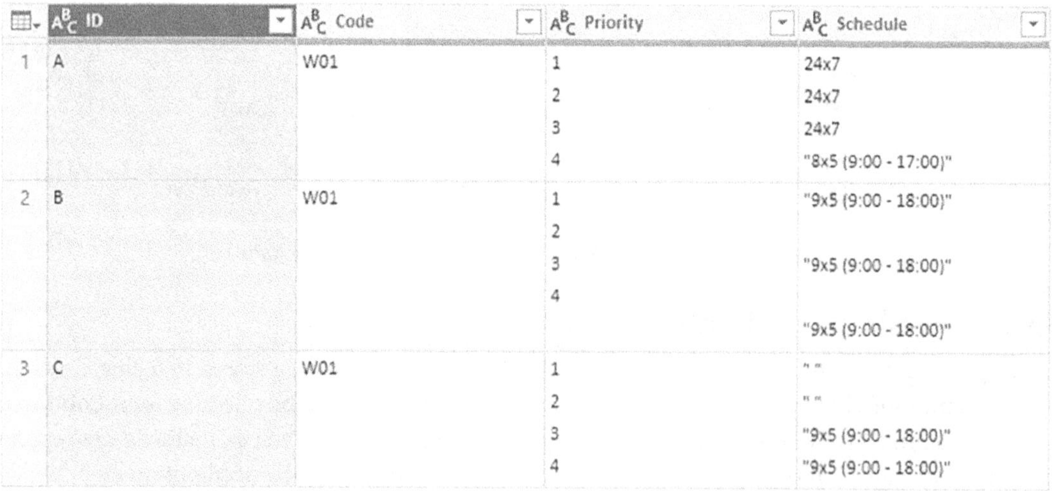

	ID	Code	Priority	Schedule
1	A	W01	1	24x7
			2	24x7
			3	24x7
			4	"8x5 (9:00 - 17:00)"
2	B	W01	1	"9x5 (9:00 - 18:00)"
			2	
			3	"9x5 (9:00 - 18:00)"
			4	
				"9x5 (9:00 - 18:00)"
3	C	W01	1	" "
			2	" "
			3	"9x5 (9:00 - 18:00)"
			4	"9x5 (9:00 - 18:00)"

Figure 11.34: Combined cell values example data

To follow along with the steps described in the next section, please transfer the provided code for this example into a new, blank query.

Goal

Preparing data for analysis by ensuring each record occupies a single row.

Transforming the table

Clearly, we are dealing with whitespace characters, which are often invisible (non-graphic). These include the space (part of the Unicode class Zs), horizontal and vertical tabs, form feeds, and newline character sequences. Newline sequences encompass carriage return, line feed, a combination of carriage return and line feed, next line, and paragraph separator characters. These could be artifacts from data extraction or user input.

In the previous section of this chapter, we explored how splitters yield a function to divide a text string into a list of text values. The `Splitter.SplitTextByWhitespace` function can be used to separate and consequently eliminate whitespace from a string. Its optional `quoteStyle` parameter specifies how quotes within text are handled. By default, `QuoteStyle.Csv` is applied, which ignores quoted strings so they are not affected by the splitting process. Accordingly, let's look at how we can transform a table:

1. On the **Add Column** tab of the ribbon, select **Custom Column**.
2. In the dialog box, enter `temp` as the new column name.
3. Remember, the invoke expression is a set of parentheses that may include an optional argument list. This initiates a function invocation. For the custom column formula, we can input `Splitter.SplitTextByWhitespace()` to initiate the splitter and receive its return value, which is a new function.
4. We can then add another invoke expression and select **Schedule** from the **Available columns** section on the right-hand side, as shown in *Figure 11.35*.

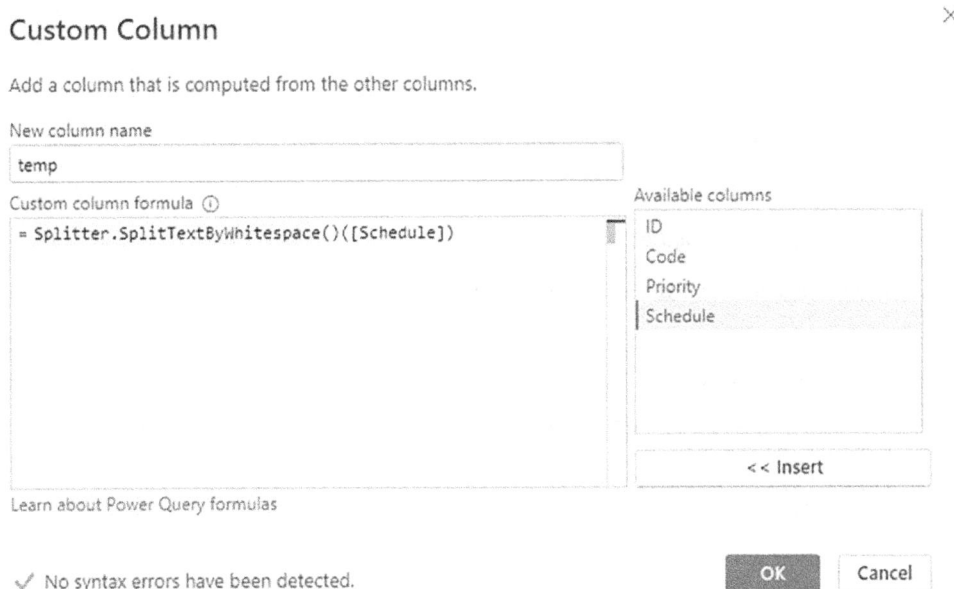

Figure 11.35: Custom Column dialog box

5. The new `temp` column contains a list of text values. By clicking on the whitespace beside a list value, a secondary preview will appear, providing a limited view of the content within the list.

   This process could be repeated for the `Priority` column as well, but managing multiple list columns can be complex, as expanding each one separately may result in unwanted duplication of rows within a table. By consolidating all lists into a single table, we can create one structure that simplifies and controls the expansion process.

6. In the **Applied Steps** section of the query settings, click on the **gear wheel** icon visible on the **Added Custom** step to reopen the **Custom Column** dialog box.

7. Here, we will modify the code to create a table that includes values from both the `Priority` and `Schedule` columns. The M code is depicted in *Figure 11.36*:

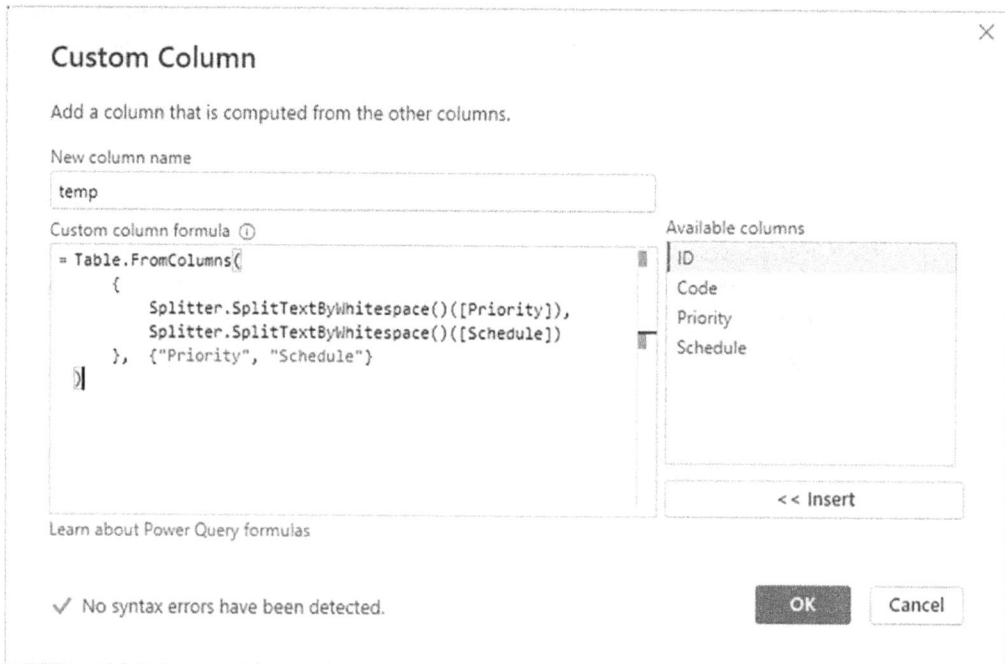

Custom Column

Add a column that is computed from the other columns.

New column name

temp

Custom column formula ⓘ

```
= Table.FromColumns(
    {
        Splitter.SplitTextByWhitespace()([Priority]),
        Splitter.SplitTextByWhitespace()([Schedule])
    }, {"Priority", "Schedule"}
)
```

Available columns

ID
Code
Priority
Schedule

<< Insert

Learn about Power Query formulas

✓ No syntax errors have been detected.

OK　　Cancel

Figure 11.36: Updating the code in the Custom Column dialog box

8. To create a table from multiple lists, use the `Table.FromColumns` function:

   a. For its first argument, specify a list of lists separated by commas that represent the column values.

   b. For the optional second argument, provide a list of column names.

9. Following these steps will create a table.

10. We can also assign column types to this nested table, eliminating the need for a Change Type step later. Inside the formula bar, between the closing parentheses of the Table.FromColumns and Table.AddColumn functions, do the following:

    a. First, insert a comma.

    b. Then add type table and a type setting record that lists each column by name and its type, like this: type table [Priority = text, Schedule = text].

11. Before expanding the nested table in the temp column, let's clean up the original Priority and Schedule columns. There are several methods to accomplish this, such as removing or selecting columns. However, since we're only interested in three columns, applying projection would be the most succinct method. This concept is thoroughly discussed in *Chapter 6, Structured Values*. In the formula bar, after the closing parenthesis of the Table.AddColumn function, insert a set of square brackets. Within these brackets, select each column you want to retain by referencing its name inside another set of square brackets, for instance, [[ID], [Code], [temp]].

12. Finally, extract the fields by expanding the nested table in the temp column, with the sideward arrows available in the header.

Here are the steps translated into M code. To incorporate this into the sample code provided, a comma should be placed directly after the closing parenthesis of the Table.FromRecords function in the Source step, which is on the first line. The subsequent in clause and the Source variable should be omitted when incorporating this code:

```
,   #"Added Custom" = Table.AddColumn( Source, "temp", each
      Table.FromColumns(
        {   Splitter.SplitTextByWhitespace()([Priority]),
            Splitter.SplitTextByWhitespace()([Schedule])
        },  {"Priority", "Schedule"}
      ),
      type table [Priority = text, Schedule = text] )[[ID], [Code], [temp]],
    #"Expanded temp" = Table.ExpandTableColumn(#"Added Custom", "temp",
        {"Priority", "Schedule"}, {"Priority", "Schedule"}
    )
  in
    #"Expanded temp"
```

The result is a transformed table that looks like this:

	ID	Code	Priority	Schedule
1	A	W01	1	24x7
2	A	W01	2	24x7
3	A	W01	3	24x7
4	A	W01	4	8x5 (9:00 - 17:00)
5	B	W01	1	9x5 (9:00 - 18:00)
6	B	W01	2	9x5 (9:00 - 18:00)
7	B	W01	3	9x5 (9:00 - 18:00)
8	B	W01	4	9x5 (9:00 - 18:00)
9	C	W01	1	
10	C	W01	2	
11	C	W01	3	9x5 (9:00 - 18:00)
12	C	W01	4	9x5 (9:00 - 18:00)

Figure 11.37: Combined cell values split into rows

Replacing multiple values

A frequently asked question in many forums goes something like this: "In my ongoing project, I'm dealing with a dataset that requires extensive value replacements across many columns. I've been using individual ReplaceValue steps, resulting in a slow and unwieldy query. Is there a more efficient method for managing bulk replacements?"

Yes, there is. Here is our sample dataset. You can transfer this code into the **Advanced Editor** and rename the query rawData:

```
let
  rawData = Table.FromColumns(
    {
      {1..3},
      {"Prdct A, 5pcs", "Product B, Qty: 10", "Prdct C; Quantity: 2"},
      {"Prdct A, 5pcs", "Product B, Qty: 10", "Prdct C; Quantity: 2"},
      {"Prdct A, 5pcs", "Product B, Qty: 10", "Prdct C; Quantity: 2"},
      {"Prdct A, 5pcs", "Product B, Qty: 10", "Prdct C; Quantity: 2"},
      {"Prdct A, 5pcs", "Product B, Qty: 10", "Prdct C; Quantity: 2"}
    }, type table
    [
      ID=Int64.Type, Description=text, Description2=text,
      Description3=text, Description4=text, Description5=text
    ]
  ),
  reSized = Table.Repeat( rawData, 100 )
in
  reSized
```

Figure 11.38 shows a small portion of the sample table:

	1²₃ ID		A⁸c Description		A⁸c Description2	
1		1	Prdct A, 5pcs		Prdct A, 5pcs	
2		2	Product B, Qty: 10		Product B, Qty: 10	
3		3	Prdct C; Quantity: 2		Prdct C; Quantity: 2	
4		1	Prdct A, 5pcs		Prdct A, 5pcs	
5		2	Product B, Qty: 10		Product B, Qty: 10	

Figure 11.38: Limited view of the sample table

The following query will generate a `Replacements` table, which aids in visualizing the replacement process. The `Old` column contains the `oldValue`, a substring we aim to replace with the `newValue` found in the adjacent `New` column:

```
let
    Source = Table.FromRows(
        {{"Prdct", "Product"}, {"pcs", " pieces"}, {"Qty", "Quantity"}},
        type table [Old=text, New=text]
    )
in
    Source
```

Figure 11.39 shows the full `Replacements` table:

	A⁸c Old		A⁸c New	
1	Prdct		Product	
2	pcs		pieces	
3	Qty		Quantity	

Figure 11.39: Replacements table

Goal

- Obtain uniformity (e.g., replacing N/A, na, and none with one consistent value).
- Correct typographical errors, misspellings, or inaccuracies.

Accumulating a result

In our solution query we won't leverage the actual `Replacements` table shared earlier; instead, we'll use two lists that represent each column of that table. This means the `oldValue` and `newValue` must align and share the same positional index within their respective lists. The following code features the more advanced `List.Accumulate` function, which will be addressed in greater detail in *Chapter 13, Iteration and Recursion*.

Let's break down this solution:

```
let
    Old = List.Buffer({"Prdct",    "pcs",    "Qty" }),
    New = List.Buffer({"Product", " pieces", "Quantity"}),
    Iterations = List.Buffer({0..List.Count(Old)-1}),
    Replacer =
        List.Accumulate(
            Iterations,
            rawData,
            (s, a) => Table.ReplaceValue(
                s,
                Old{a},
                New{a},
                Replacer.ReplaceText,
                List.Select(
                    Table.ColumnNames(rawData), each
                    Text.StartsWith(_, "Description")
                )
            )
        )
in
    Replacer
```

The goal of this query is to substitute specific substrings in columns of which the name begins with Description. We will substitute elements from an Old list with corresponding elements from a New list within the selected columns. Here's how the query operates:

- `Old = List.Buffer({"Prdct", "pcs", "Qty" })`

  The Old list comprises the substrings intended for replacement. Using List.Buffer ensures the list is evaluated once and retained in memory for improved performance. However, buffering values into memory does not guarantee a performance gain and will need to be tested.

- `New = List.Buffer({"Product", " pieces", "Quantity"})`

  The New list contains substrings set to replace the corresponding substrings in the Old list. List. Buffer is incorporated to enhance performance, although it's not guaranteed.

- `Iterations = List.Buffer({0..List.Count(Old)-1})`

  The Iterations list generates a list of indices and loads that into memory.

- `Replacer = List.Accumulate(...)`

  This function iterates over the `Iterations` list, essentially providing indices for both the `Old` and `New` lists. It applies a transformation to the `rawData` table, which refers to the query containing the sample dataset. If you've named that query with sample data differently, you'll need to update this reference accordingly.

- `(s, a) => Table.ReplaceValue(...)`

  The seed, denoted as `s`, is the initial value, which in this case is the table `rawData`. The accumulator, denoted as `a`, will assume each value in the list `{0.. List.Count(Old)-1}`, essentially representing the indices to pass all of the elements in the `Old` and `New` lists.

- `Table.ReplaceValue( s, Old{a}, New{a}, Replacer.ReplaceText, ...)`

  This function replaces all instances of the substring `Old{a}` with `New{a}` within the specified columns of the table.

- `List.Select( Table.ColumnNames(rawData), each Text.StartsWith(_, "Description"))`

  This expression selects which columns to apply the replacement to. It selects all columns whose name begins with `Description`.

Figure 11.40 shows a small portion of the transformed sample table:

🔢 ID	AᴮC Description	AᴮC Description2
1	1 Product A, 5 pieces	Product A, 5 pieces
2	2 Product B, Quantity: 10	Product B, Quantity: 10
3	3 Product C; Quantity: 2	Product C; Quantity: 2
4	1 Product A, 5 pieces	Product A, 5 pieces
5	2 Product B, Quantity: 10	Product B, Quantity: 10

Figure 11.40: Limited view of the result

This solution will prove to be more efficient and dynamic when replacing multiple text values in specific columns of a table. `List.Accumulate` allows for a performant row-by-row and column-by-column replacement of values without hardcoding, making the query more maintainable. Buffering the `Old` and `New` lists is an optimization step that ensures these lists are only evaluated once, enhancing performance, generally speaking, although this will always require testing.

Combining rows conditionally

Here's another common requirement: transforming these multi-row records, in this case from a sample bank statement (*Figure 11.41*), into a single row.

To achieve that, we have to gather and combine all details from the boxed rows and transform them into single records, to yield a six-row table, a partial view of which can be seen here:

	Date	A^B_C Details	$ Debit
1	05-02-24	CloudBliss Shopping	-30,99
2	05-02-24	Grocery Store	-15,50
3	null	Nature's Pantry	null
4	null	Card number 564	null
5	05-02-24	PowerPro Utilities	-90,00
6	null	Period: January 2024	null
7	null	Account: 123456789	null
8	null	Reference Number: PPU-7890	null
9	06-02-24	Gourmet Bistro	-75,50
10	null	Date: February 6, 2024	null
11	null	123 Main Street, Anytown	null
12	null	Card number 564	null

Figure 11.41: Sample bank statement data

Here is the sample data for you to explore and experiment with:

```
let
    Source = Table.FromRows(
        {
            {#date(2024, 2, 5), "CloudBliss Shopping", -30.99},
            {#date(2024, 2, 5), "Grocery Store",-15.5},
            {null, "Nature's Pantry", null},
            {null, "Card number 564", null},
            {#date(2024, 2, 5), "PowerPro Utilities", -90.0},
            {null, "Period: January 2024", null},
            {null, "Account: 123456789", null},
            {null, "Reference Number: PPU-7890", null},
            {#date(2024, 2, 6), "Gourmet Bistro", -75.50},
            {null, "Date: February 6, 2024", null},
            {null, "123 Main Street, Anytown", null},
            {null, "Card number 564", null},
            {#date(2024, 2, 6), "TrustWise Bank", -150},
            {null, "ATM cash withdrawl", null},
            {null, "Location: 456 Oak Street, Anytown", null},
            {null, "Card number 843", null},
            {#date(2024, 2, 6), "HappyTimes: PQE-789012", 5}
        }, type table [Date=date, Details=text, Debit=Currency.Type]
    )
in
    Source
```

Goal

Preparing data for analysis by ensuring each record occupies a single row.

Group By's comparer to the rescue

Several strategies can be employed in a scenario like this, with the versatile `Table.Group` function often proving to be the most effective, especially in cases where all related records share a common key. However, difficulties emerge when no shared keys are present and generating them is not straightforward.

In this case, for instance, the number of rows that belong together fluctuates; there's no fixed pattern to rely on. From another perspective, using the `date` column as a key is insufficient for segregating and combining these records. That is because there are likely to be multiple transactions on any given date. Without an additional marker to distinguish them, it's not a viable option. However, `Table.Group` does provide an optional comparer that we can take advantage of. Let's explore that possibility:

1. First, we use the UI to generate the majority of the M code. Select the `Date` column and go for **Group By** on either the **Home** or **Transform** tab of the ribbon.
2. Set it to **Advanced**, input a new column name, `Description`, and select an operation. The specific operation doesn't matter at this point as we'll update it later. Choose the `Details` column.
3. Since we've selected **Advanced**, we can now add another aggregation. This time, for the `Debit` amount, set either **Min** or **Max** as the operation – either is fine – and select the `Debit` column (see *Figure 11.42*). Click **OK**.

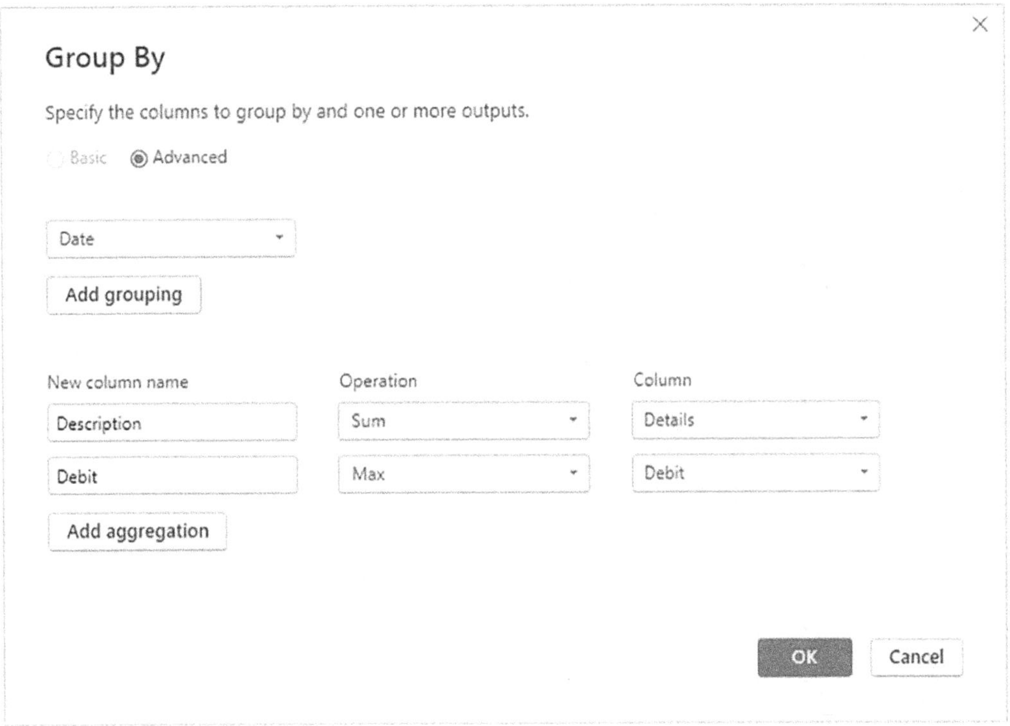

Group By

Specify the columns to group by and one or more outputs.

○ Basic ● Advanced

Date ▾

Add grouping

New column name	Operation	Column
Description	Sum ▾	Details ▾
Debit	Max ▾	Debit ▾

Add aggregation

OK Cancel

Figure 11.42: Group By dialog box

4. We can now modify the code within the formula bar. It's clear that text values cannot be summed, so we will substitute the `List.Sum` function with `Text.Combine` and provide a space as its second argument, the separator.

5. Since there is always only one debit amount per transaction, it doesn't matter whether you choose `List.Min` or `List.Max`; both will yield the same result.

6. `Table.Group` takes an optional fourth argument, `groupKind`. We can pass `GroupKind.Local` to indicate that our data is sorted by key(s) and that sequence should be respected.

Let's now concentrate on its fifth argument, the optional comparer. It's crucial to understand that when a custom comparer function is passed, it takes precedence over the specified key and assumes responsibility for creating new groups. This means a row might be placed in a group whose keys differ from its own.

Here's our custom comparer function: `(x, y)=> Number.From(y[Date] <> null)`. It is passed two values at a time, the current (x) and next row (y) value, and creates a new group if the `Date` on the next row is not `null`. In other words, if this evaluates to `false`, `Number.From` returns a 0 (zero) and it assigns the row to the current group. However, when it evaluates to `true`, `Number.From` returns the value 1 and generates a new group.

Here's the data and full solution we just created:

```
let
    Source = Table.FromRows(
      {
        {#date(2024, 2, 5), "CloudBliss Shopping", -30.99},
        {#date(2024, 2, 5), "Grocery Store",-15.5},
        {null, "Nature's Pantry", null},
        {null, "Card number 564", null},
        {#date(2024, 2, 5), "PowerPro Utilities", -90.0},
        {null, "Period: January 2024", null},
        {null, "Account: 123456789", null},
        {null, "Reference Number: PPU-7890", null},
        {#date(2024, 2, 6), "Gourmet Bistro", -75.50},
        {null, "Date: February 6, 2024", null},
        {null, "123 Main Street, Anytown", null},
        {null, "Card number 564", null},
        {#date(2024, 2, 6), "TrustWise Bank", -150},
        {null, "ATM cash withdrawl", null},
        {null, "Location: 456 Oak Street, Anytown", null},
        {null, "Card number 843", null},
        {#date(2024, 2, 6), "HappyTimes: PQE-789012", 5}
      }, type table [Date=date, Details=text, Debit=Currency.Type]
    ),
    #"Grouped Rows" = Table.Group( Source,
```

```
      {"Date"},
      {
        {"Description", each Text.Combine([Details], " "), type text},
        {"Debit", each List.Max([Debit]), type number}
      },
      GroupKind.Local,
        (x, y)=> Number.From(y[Date] <> null)
    )
 in
      #"Grouped Rows"
```

Figure 11.43 shows the outcome after applying this transformation:

🔲 ▾	🗓 Date	▾	AᴮC Description	▾	1.2 Debit	▾
1		05-02-24	CloudBliss Shopping		-30,99	
2		05-02-24	Grocery Store Nature's Pantry Card number 564		-15,5	
3		05-02-24	PowerPro Utilities Period: January 2024 Account: 123456789 Referenc...		-90	
4		06-02-24	Gourmet Bistro Date: February 6, 2024 123 Main Street, Anytown Car...		-75,5	
5		06-02-24	TrustWise Bank ATM cash withdrawl Location: 456 Oak Street, Anytow...		-150	
6		06-02-24	HappyTimes: PQE-789012		5	

Figure 11.43: Transformed sample data

Summary

This chapter began by laying the groundwork for key concepts in the M language, which is crucial for understanding some of the intricacies discussed later on. We explored techniques such as splitting, combining, comparing, and replacing values, among others, using illustrative examples for enhanced comprehension. These techniques will prove invaluable in elevating data quality. Achieving proficiency will require dedication and regular practical application in your daily routine – an investment that is well worth the effort for its reward.

In the next chapter, you will learn about what an error is and how errors can be raised, contained, and detected, as well as the tools in your error handling toolkit.

Learn more on Discord

Join our community's Discord space for discussions with the author and other readers:

`https://discord.gg/vCSG5GBbyS`

12

Handling Errors and Debugging

Error handling in Power Query's M language involves techniques for managing and resolving errors that may arise during the evaluation of an expression. By utilizing expressions and functions such as `try`, `otherwise`, and `catch`, you can gracefully handle potential errors and effectively control the execution flow. Additionally, the Power Query editor offers a convenient built-in feature called the **Applied Steps** pane, which allows you to step through the code, facilitating the identification of issues within your query.

This chapter provides you with an overview of the error-handling capabilities and debugging strategies in Power Query. It aims to equip you with the necessary knowledge to effectively address errors and ensure your queries are more future-proof. By understanding common errors that can occur in the M language and applying the techniques discussed here, you will establish a solid foundation for handling errors and creating more robust queries.

This chapter covers the following topics:

- What is an error?
- Error containment
- Error detection
- Raising errors
- Error handling
- Strategies for debugging
- Common errors
- Putting it all together

Technical requirements

To make the most of this chapter, we encourage you to open your favorite Power Query editor and try out the provided samples. By executing and exploring these scripts, you will gain a deeper understanding of how to handle errors and debug.

What is an error?

In Power Query's M language, one of the fundamental building blocks is the expression, which is responsible for producing a value upon evaluation. When an error is encountered, it indicates that the evaluation of the expression failed and could not be completed successfully. Errors can have various causes, such as invalid identifiers or operations, incompatible data types, and more. Understanding, preventing, and effectively handling errors is crucial for creating queries that are more robust and reliable.

When evaluating an M expression, there are two possible outcomes:

- **The production of a single value**

  This indicates that the evaluation process was successful, and the expression was able to generate a result.

  ```
  let
      result = 1 / 0
  in
      result
  ```

  Division by zero does not raise an error but returns infinity.

- **Raising an error**

  When an error is raised, it indicates that the evaluation of an expression failed to produce a value. The error itself is not considered to be a value in the Power Query M language. The error record contains details about the cause of the problem during evaluation. This helps to identify the operation responsible for the error and assists in troubleshooting.

  ```
  let
      result = 1 / "0"
  in
      result
  ```

  Division by a text type operand returns an `Expression.Error`.

Before delving into error handling, it is important to understand how errors can be contained, detected, and raised, which will lay the foundation for effective error handling. Combining both preventive and error-handling techniques ensures you can build more reliable and resilient queries that deliver the expected result.

Error containment

Power Query's M language integrates containment-based programming principles. Let's explore what that means for the evaluation of expressions.

Containment and propagation means that even if an error occurs while evaluating a particular value or member expression, it doesn't necessarily stop the entire evaluation process. Instead, the error can be "contained" without automatically propagating to the top-level expression.

When an error occurs, it will cause the evaluation of the current member expression to stop; it effectively unwinds, or reverses, through the previously evaluated parts of the expression. However, as long as an error can be contained, it does not propagate to the top-level expression and a value may still be produced.

Imagine you have a table that contains a cell with an error; this error can be contained within a record field. The entry will be marked as having an error, and the error record will be saved so it can be propagated as needed. This ensures that with every subsequent attempt to access that cell, the exact same error is raised. For example, consider the following code snippet that has an error:

```
let
    A = 1 / "0",
    B = [a = A]
in
    B
```

A contained error within a record field's value only propagates when accessed.

List, Record, and Table member expressions, as well as `let` expressions, are evaluated using lazy evaluation. This means that if nothing attempts to access an erroneous value, its expression may never be evaluated, and it may not even raise an error.

Power Query's key mechanisms are containment and propagation. This means that even if there's an error in some part of the data, it doesn't necessarily cause the entire evaluation process to terminate entirely. Instead, if an error can be confined, the evaluation of the expression is continued. However, the error will still propagate through expressions that access it.

Error detection

When working in Power Query, encountering errors is a natural part of the development process, regardless of whether you design queries through the **user interface** (**UI**), modify existing code, or write M code from scratch.

When you add "real-world" data into the mix, errors become a part of life that you have to deal with and manage, a process that starts with error detection.

Errors are classified into two types:

* Step-level errors
* Cell-level errors

What separates the two is their containment.

Step-level errors propagate to the top-level expression and cause the evaluation of the entire query to terminate, causing the query to fail. To address step-level errors, it's essential to determine where the error was raised. The **Applied Steps** section within the **Query Settings** pane is where you need to go for a step-by-step evaluation of your query. By selecting each step and evaluating it, starting all the way at the top and moving down, you can pinpoint the exact location (step) where the error occurred and analyze the underlying issue(s). This approach helps to identify these types of errors efficiently.

Most common step-level errors are due to the following:

- Data source errors
- Unknown or missing identifiers
- Syntax errors
- Cyclic reference (or circular reference) errors

```
Identifying cell-level errors is a different matter entirely. By default, you
can see a thin line directly underneath the column header, which is part of the
column profiling options (see Figure 12.1). When the entire line shows a green
color, it means no errors are detected. But here's the catch: the standard
column profiling scan range is limited to the top 1000 rows. However, you can
easily switch to scan the entire dataset in the status bar.
```

At this time, you do not have to worry about understanding the following piece of M code. The script is only meant to illustrate the effects of the column profiling scan range. Enter this code into a new blank query to see and try it for yourself:

```
let
    t = Table.FromColumns(
        {
            List.Transform( {1..2500},
                each if Number.Mod(_, 68) =0 then ... else _                )
        }
    )
in
    t
```

Unchanged, scanning the top 1000 rows shows 14 errors when hovering over that tiny column profile line. However, feel free to select a different **Data Preview** view on the **View** tab as seen in *Figure 12.1* such as **Column quality**, **Column distribution**, or **Column profile**.

Changing the column profiling scan range in the status bar from the top 1000 rows to scanning the entire dataset can have implications for error detection and performance. In this example, the number of errors increased from 14 to 36 when the scan range was expanded. This highlights the importance of being vigilant when validating data. Superficially, it might appear error-free until query runtime when you are confronted with unexpected failures. It is important to be aware of this as the initial impression of error-free data may be deceiving.

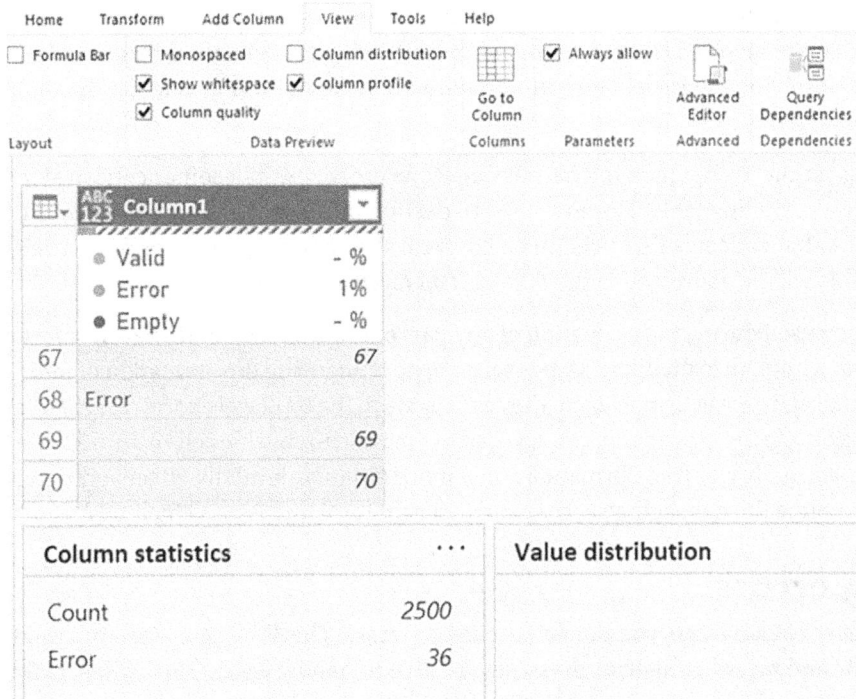

Figure 12.1: View tab with Data Preview options and enabled column quality and profile

Once the presence of cell-level errors has been confirmed, you can take necessary actions by selecting **Keep errors** in the **Reduce Rows** section under **Keep rows** on the **Home** tab. This invokes the M function called `Table.SelectRowsWithErrors` from the UI, generating a new table that includes only the rows containing at least one error in any of its cells. If you, optionally, provide it a list with column names, the function will focus on checking for errors solely within the cells of those specified columns. By utilizing this approach, you can isolate the problematic rows quickly for further investigation.

To view details about a raised error, you can simply click on the white space in a cell containing an error value. This action will display a secondary preview in the preview pane, *Figure 12.2*, that shows the information from the error record:

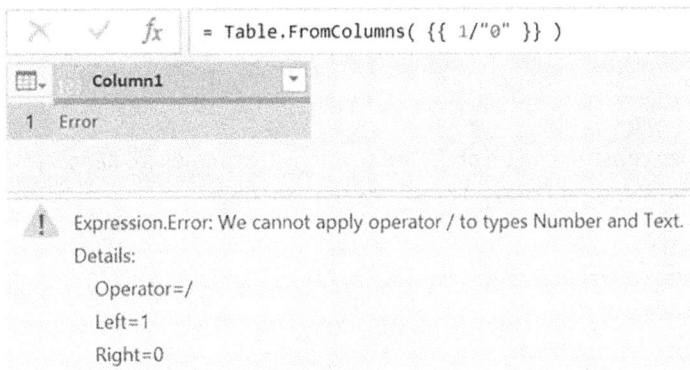

Figure 12.2: Error detail view

That information includes the cause of the problem during evaluation, the error message, operators, and values that are involved. These details aid in identifying the operation responsible for the error and assist in resolving the issue. More information on error resolution is in the upcoming sections within this chapter.

By exploring various techniques and harnessing some creativity, it becomes conceivable to design a cell-level error reporting table. However, before delving into a more advanced topic like that, there are other essential concepts that need to be covered. Rest assured, an example of a cell-level error reporting table will be addressed in the *Putting it all together* section.

Errors can be raised during the evaluation of any part of the expression. However, errors can also be handled from within an expression. Step-level errors occur during the evaluation of individual query step, and, if not appropriately managed, they propagate to the top-level expression, halting the entire query execution. On the other hand, cell-level errors pertain to specific cells within a table, indicating issues with data quality or transformations on a more granular level. By effectively detecting errors, you can streamline the debugging process and focus on resolving issues efficiently.

Raising errors

In Power Query's M language, you can define custom errors. This is helpful when you want to provide more specific and meaningful error messages, be able to handle exceptional cases, enforce custom data validation rules, or improve the overall user experience for example.

The error expression

To raise an error, simply call the error-raising expression `error` and use a text value to provide the desired error message you want to display. For example, this expression will raise the following error:

```
error "Invalid data, you did not provide a table."
```

Errors provide an error record; therefore, you can also specify a record to include more information about the error. This error record should contain fields such as `Reason`, `Message`, and `Detail`. Here's an example of how to raise an error with a custom error record:

```
error [
    Reason = "Invalid data, you did not provide a table.",
    Message = "The data provided is not valid.",
    Detail = [Operator = "&", Left = "123", Right = "321"]
]
```

However, you can also construct an error record from the text values for `Reason`, `Message`, and `Detail` as any, leveraging the standard library, `Error.Record` function:

```
error Error.Record(
    "Invalid data, you did not provide a table.",
    "The data provided is not valid.",
    [Operator = "&", Left = "123", Right = "321"]
)
```

This returns the same error record as illustrated in the previous example.

Defining custom errors in the M language has been enhanced further with the introduction of structured error messages in mid-2022. This update included the addition of two new fields to the error record: Message.Format and Message.Parameters.

Message.Format provides a structure to produce a concatenated error message to be displayed to the user. Within a string, a pair of single quotes can be used to access items from the Message.Parameters list, in this form: #{x}, where x is the zero-based index number for the parameter value to be inserted. For example, #{0} represents the first item from the Message.Parameters list.

Message.Parameters is a list containing values from which items can be requested and inserted into the error message string at specified positions. Don't worry if at this time you do not fully understand the following code. Enter this M code into a new blank query and rename that query fxDivision to try it out:

```
(dividend as number, divisor as number) as number =>
  let
      IsZero = divisor = 0,
      Division = if IsZero
        then ( error [
            Message.Format = "Encountered: '#{0}', resolution: '#{1}'",
            Message.Parameters = { "division by zero error",
                "only numbers <> 0 are allowed divisors.",
                dividend, divisor}
          ] ) [Error]
        else dividend / divisor
  in
      Division
```

Passing an argument value of 0 to the divisor of this custom function, for example, fxDivision(3, 0), will cause the following error: An error occurred in the '' query. Expression.Error: Encountered: 'division by zero error', resolution: 'only numbers <> 0 are allowed divisors.' This can be seen in the following image:

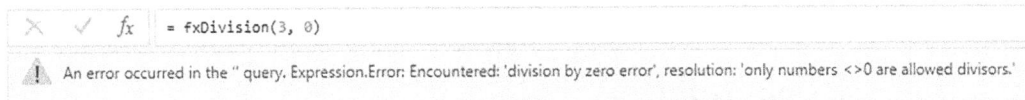

Figure 12.3: Custom error message

Furthermore, these structured error message fields also provide a means to quickly and easily obtain all information about the error without the need for custom text parsing. Input values can be obtained from the error field Detail and any of the string inputs in the error message from the Message.Parameters list, which can be valuable for error reporting and analysis.

Here is an example:

```
let
    myErr = error [
        Message.Format = "Encountered: '#{0}', resolution: '#{1}'",
        Message.Parameters = { "division by zero error",
            "only numbers <> 0 are allowed divisors" }
        ],
    CatchErr = try myErr,
    Detail = CatchErr[Error][Message.Parameters]{1}

in
    Detail
```

This returns `only numbers <> 0 are allowed divisors` but you can return any item with its zero-based index position. For example, when building more complex error-handling reports, you could extract one or multiple items. When displaying input values within error messages, all primitive values will be displayed as text. Any structured values are displayed using their literal type name (such as `Table`, `Record`, or `List`).

When both error fields `Message.Parameters` and `Message.Format` are specified, the `Message.Format` takes precedence and is used to generate a string that will overwrite the `Message.Parameters` in the error that is propagated.

Specifying a `Message.Format` without `Message.Parameters` is valid as long as no parameter inputs are expected in the provided format string.

Specifying `Message.Parameters` without a `Message.Format` will output a null value instead of a parameters list in the error that is propagated.

Finally, the `Message.Format` and `Message.Parameters` have no effect on the error fields `Reason` and `Detail`.

Overall, structured error messages in Power Query's M language significantly simplify the error logging and reporting process, as they offer a systematic and predefined way to obtain essential error details without the need for text parsing. By using this feature, you can create meaningful error messages for users and facilitate better analysis of data issues within your workflows.

The … (ellipsis) operator

Besides the error expression, the M language also includes the ellipsis operator (three dots); it's important to understand that this will not only raise an error but also provide a predefined error message. Although, depending on the version of your M (mashup) engine, that message could be something like **Expression.Error: Not Implemented** or **Expression.Error: Value was not specified**. Here is an example of how the ellipsis operator can be used:

```
let
    complexCode =
```

```
            if 1 + 1 = 2
            then ...
            else "¯\_(ツ)_/¯ That's not right."
    in
        complexCode
```

This shortcut can be particularly helpful when developing complex expressions. Assign the ellipsis to a code branch that's still in development; you can think of it as a placeholder for the part you are still working on. This will allow you to execute and test the other branch in your code, keeping the development process moving forward.

Creating custom errors offers a number of possibilities such as providing more informative error messages, handling exceptional cases, or even enforcing company data validation rules, and enhancing the overall user experience.

Error handling

Implementing error-handling strategies extends beyond addressing raised errors alone. It is as much about making choices and using techniques available in the M language to effectively mitigate errors and ensure the robustness of your data transformation workflows. When working with data, it's common to encounter errors such as missing values, incompatible data types, and unexpected or invalid calculations. To address these challenges, every technique should be considered. The aim is to implement error-handling strategies that will help avoid, manage, and resolve errors right where they occur, ensuring a predictable outcome as a result. Here's what is in your toolkit:

*   **Coalesce, dealing with nulls**

    Power Query's M language supports null propagation, which means that if a value is null in a sequence of operations, the result will be null. The a field in myRecord illustrates this. It is this behavior that helps to prevent errors that can arise from performing operations on null values. The following is an example of this:

    ```
    let
        myRecord =
            [
                a = 1 + null,
                b = List.Sum( {1, null} ),
                c = List.Count( null ),
                d = List.Count( x ?? y ?? {} ),
                x = null,
                y = null
            ]
    in
        myRecord
    ```

But when a null is passed as an argument to a function that expects another type, it can become the root cause of an error, as field c in myRecord will show. Conditional logic could be a remedy but in *Chapter 4, Understanding Values and Expressions*, you already learned that the M language also includes a coalescing operator, which is a double question mark (??).

Coalesce operates on two values, returning the left if it's not null, otherwise taking the right. More arguments can be included to form a chain of values or expressions, separating them by the coalescing operator. If all values in the chain evaluate to null, a null is returned. Implementing coalesce makes the code more succinct and readable, as shown in the following code:

```
let
    c = List.Count( x ?? y ?? {} ),
    x = null,
    y = null
in
    c
```

Here, in x ?? y ?? {}, only three values make up the chain, x, y, and an empty list. Since the empty list is the first non-null value, that value is returned as an argument to the List. Count function.

* **Optional item or field access**

  The default in the M language is required item and field access, meaning that when referencing something that isn't there, an error will be raised. However, you can quickly switch from required to optional item or field access by adding a (single) question mark at the end. The following is an example of this:

  ```
  let
      itemThree = {1..3}{3}?
  in
      itemThree
  ```

  The list we are accessing contains 3 values; therefore, the zero-based index for the last list item is 2. Since we are applying optional item access, this expression will not raise an error but return a null value instead.

  The same applies to field access, illustrated in the following code snippet:

  ```
  let
      fieldThree = [One = 1, Two = 2][Three]?
  in
      fieldThree
  ```

The record we are accessing contains 2 fields; none of those fields go by the name Three meaning required field access will raise an error. Since we are applying optional field access, this expression will not raise an error but return a null value instead.

- **MissingField.Type enumerator**

When you see optional missingField as nullable number in the parameter list of a standard library M function, it means that the function allows you to control its behavior when it encounters missing record fields or table columns. By default, all specified fields or columns are required, and any missing ones will raise an error. However, functions with a MissingField.Type parameter offer a flexible solution to handle these situations. There are three options available:

- MissingField.Error (0 or null): This is the default option and indicates that if any fields or columns are missing, an error will be raised.
- MissingField.Ignore (1): When this option is selected, missing fields or columns are simply ignored. They do not raise an error and are excluded from the output.
- MissingField.UseNull (2): Selecting this option includes missing fields or columns in the output, but their values are set to null. This allows you to retain a complete set of data while indicating the absence of specific information.

```
Various Record and Table functions provide this optional MissingField.
Type parameter, allowing you to tailor the behavior of these functions to
your specific needs, such as Record.RemoveFields, Table.RemoveColumns,
Record.RenameFields, Table.RenameColumns, Record.ReorderFields, Table.
ReorderColumns, Record.SelectFields, Table.SelectColumns, Record.
TransformFields, and Table.FromRecords.
```

Being aware of the MissingField.Type empowers you to handle potential issues effectively by overriding the default error-raising behavior and choosing to ignore missing fields or use null values instead.

- **if expression, conditional logic**

You can use the conditional statement if-then-else to check for specific conditions. For example, you can check if one or a combination of values meets certain criteria before performing any calculations on it, preventing potential errors:

```
let
    a = null ?? {},
    b = if ( a <> null and a <> {} )
        then List.Count( a )
        else 1
in
    b
```

Conditional logic lets you create a branch in your code.

- **try expression**

  A try expression tries to evaluate an expression and creates a record. Depending on whether
  the try expression handled an error or not, it produces either the output value for the expression or the error from the record that was generated:

  ```
  let
      triedExpressions =
          [
              validExpression = try 1/0,
              invalidExpression = try 1/"0"
          ]
  in
      triedExpressions
  ```

  It's important to understand that the scope for a try expression is limited to the expression
  that follows directly after it.

- **try and otherwise**

  A try-otherwise construct allows you to attempt an operation and provide a default expression
  in case an error is raised. Consider this:

  ```
  let
      a = "24-2-2024",
      b = try Date.FromText( a, [Culture="en-us"])
          otherwise "no valid date"
  in
      b
  ```

  Only when the try expression returns an error is the default expression evaluated. It helps to
  gracefully handle errors in a succinct and readable manner.

- **try and catch**

  This simplifies the implementation of adaptive error handling, the reason being that unlike
  otherwise, a one-parameter catch function has access to the error record try returns. This
  eliminates the need for a more verbose custom function approach. Let's examine this record:

  ```
  [
      myInput = error "A",
      newValue = myInput + 1,
      catchMyError = try newValue catch (e)=> if e[Message] = "A"
          then "Oh no you've caught myInput error!"
          else e[Reason] & " message: " & e[Message],
      somethingElse = 1 + 1
  ]
  ```

When the error is raised by `myInput`, it propagates to `newValue` and, subsequently, to `catchMyError`, and now, depending on the error message that is returned, a specific error handling scenario will follow within this `catch` clause.

However, a zero-parameter `catch` function does not receive error record details from `try` and is, in that sense, equivalent to the `try-otherwise` construct. It's important to realize that this approach is only suitable when all errors should be handled and dealt with in the exact same manner.

- **Try and custom function**

  This became a legacy technique with the introduction of the `catch` keyword into the M language in June 2022. Although you might still find it used in M code scripts predating the catch introduction, the one-parameter catch function is now the standard method for adaptive error handling.

- **Standard library functions**

  The M language also provides two standard library functions that can aid in error handling: `Table.ReplaceErrorValues` and `Table.RemoveRowsWithErrors` allow you to replace or remove error values from tables. Understanding the scope and limitations of these functions will help you make informed decisions when applying them in your data transformation workflows:

  - `Table.ReplaceErrorValues`: Replaces error values in the specified columns of the table with a new value from a list with `errorReplacement` lists. The format of this list containing lists is as follows: `{ {column1, value1}, ... }`.

    Only one replacement value per column is allowed, and specifying a column more than once within the list with `errorReplacement` lists will raise an error.

  - `Table.RemoveRowsWithErrors`: This function creates a table by removing the rows from the table that have at least one error value in any of its cells. If you provide this function an argument for its optional second parameter, which takes a list with column names, it will only inspect the cells in those specified columns for errors and remove corresponding rows from the table.

In summary, Power Query's M language offers various error prevention methods as well as error-handling techniques. It is important to note that the choice depends on the specific use case and requirements of the data transformation process. Usually, a combination of methods and techniques is required to ensure data integrity and reliability.

Strategies for debugging

Debugging is an integral part of the development process, and encountering situations where the code behaves unexpectedly is inevitable. Effective debugging strategies play a crucial role in identifying and rectifying errors while also enhancing code comprehension. General best practices for debugging M code include the use of comments, renaming steps for readability, breaking down complex expressions, and testing.

Let's look at them in greater detail:

- Comments are not just placeholders for thoughts or code descriptions; they serve as critical pointers that guide the debugging process. They can help you and others understand the purpose and functionality of different code sections, making it easier to locate and fix issues. Moreover, comments can be used to mark areas of code that require further review or are prone to errors.

- By default, Power Query assigns generic names to each step. These names don't provide much insight into what the step is doing. By renaming steps to something more descriptive, you make the code easier to read and understand. This can be particularly helpful when you or someone else is trying to debug the code, as it provides a better understanding of what each step is intended to do. Descriptive step names also make the code easier to maintain and update. If you need to modify your query in the future, it's much easier to find steps when steps are well-named.

- Break down complex expressions into smaller, more manageable parts. The M language, with its functional nature, allows for the creation of complex nested expressions. While these expressions can be powerful, they can also be challenging to debug when things go wrong. By breaking down complex expressions, you can isolate and examine each part individually, making it easier to identify the root cause of an issue. This approach not only simplifies debugging but also enhances code readability and maintainability when tied to well-named variables.

- Testing your M code is a proactive debugging approach that helps identify errors before they become problematic, ensuring that your code works correctly. Moreover, testing will be required each time a change is made to the code.

- Next to these generic best practices, there is a powerful debugging strategy that deserves attention. You are familiar with the concept of the `let` and the record expressions; both are used to create more complex expressions in the M language. When it comes to problem solving and debugging, however, the record expression is extremely powerful.

- Record expressions allow field names to be written without the quoted notation (in most cases), which is convenient and improves the readability of the code. But more importantly, the record expression is very flexible. That is because you can quickly change its return value, for example, you can return the entire record, which allows you to see all fields and values at a glance. If one of them shows an error, you would immediately know where to start the debugging process. Let's look at an example:

```
[
    NumE = Number.E,
    RoundUp = Number.RoundUp( NumE, 0),
    Times Two = RoundUp *2
]
```

Alternatively, you can return a selection of one or more fields with selection and projection:

```
[
    NumE = Number.E,
    RoundUp = Number.RoundUp( NumE, 0),
    Times Two = RoundUp *2
] [ [RoundUp], [Times Two] ]
```

Finally, you can return a single value by applying field access:

```
[
    NumE = Number.E,
    RoundUp = Number.RoundUp( NumE, 0),
    Times Two = RoundUp *2
] [Times Two]
```

Record expressions offer better debugging capabilities compared to the let expression. While the let expression only returns a single value—even if it's structured—the record expression allows you to view all fields and values at the same time. This feature is particularly useful when troubleshooting complex or nested expressions:

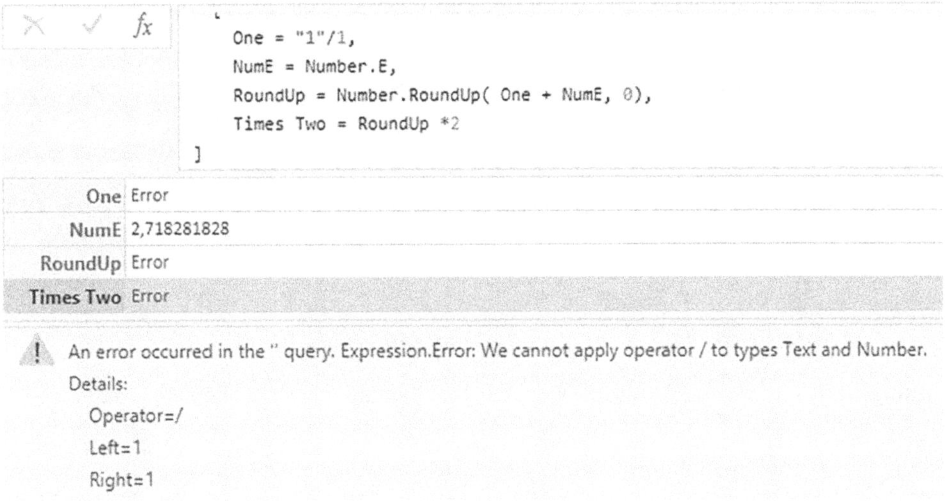

Figure 12.4: Reviewing all record fields for easy debugging

At a single glance, you can view all fields in the record. It shows three errors, and the RoundUp and Times Two fields contain the propagated error raised by One when dividing a text by a number type, making the error easy to trace and fix.

Effective debugging is achieved by thoughtful query design, implementing a mix of measures like adding comments, renaming steps, breaking down complex expressions, leveraging the record expression, and incorporating error handling; all of these combined contribute to not only more robust but also maintainable code.

Common errors

As you encounter and handle errors in your Power Query workflows, it's essential to review patterns and learn from them. Analyzing common errors and understanding their root cause can guide you in refining your error-handling approach. Therefore, this section focuses on some of the most common errors you are likely to encounter. Furthermore, it is helpful to understand that multiple errors can be encountered during debugging, and syntax errors will always be raised first as they make it impossible for the M (mashup) engine to parse the provided code.

Syntax errors

Syntax errors in an expression are typically identified during the code-writing phase. These errors indicate that there is an issue with the pattern or structure of the provided expression.

A missing comma on line 3 returns `Expression.SyntaxError: Token ',' expected:`

```
let
    A = 1,
    B = 0
    result = A / B
in
    result
```

An additional comma inside the list on line 2 returns `Expression.SyntaxError: A ',' cannot precede a '}':`

```
let
    maxValue = List.Max( {1, 4, 6, 8, } )
in
    maxValue
```

However, be aware that syntax error messages can sometimes be misleading.

A missing closing parenthesis returns `Expression.SyntaxError: Token ',' expected:`

```
let
    maxValue = List.Max( {1, 4, 6, 8 }
in
    maxValue
```

An additional closing parenthesis returns `Expression.SyntaxError: Token ',' expected:`

```
let
    maxValue = List.Max( {1, 4, 6, 8 }))
in
    maxValue
```

However, when adding a comma at the end of line *2*, the closing parenthesis remains missing:

```
let
    maxValue = List.Max( {1, 4, 6, 8 },
in
    maxValue
```

It will return Expression.SyntaxError: Token Literal expected, not the more obvious Expression.
SyntaxError: A ',' cannot precede a 'in'.

The most common causes for an Expression.SyntaxError are additional or missing commas, parentheses, and brackets, among others. Therefore, the way to resolve them is to meticulously examine the expression for any additional or missing commas, parentheses, brackets, and the like.

Dealing with errors – a top priority

Whenever a step causes errors in your query, we recommend dealing with those first before performing further action. Leaving errors unaddressed can impact your query. The way Power Query is implemented can cause errors to be ignored by functions like Table.RemoveRowsWithErrors. For example, this is the query where intentional errors are caused through type conversion of mixed-type columns.

On line *17*, blank rows are removed from the table using Table.SelectRows. However, this operation does not address any of the cell-level errors that occurred due to the incompatible type conversion. When the Table.RemoveRowsWithErrors function is applied on line *21* to remove rows with errors, errors persist, and the resulting table will include a row with errors:

```
let
  Source = Table.FromColumns(
    {
      {123, 34, 12, "txt", null},
      {123, "txt", 34, 12, null},
      {"txt", 123, 34, 12, null},
      {123, "txt", "34", 12, null}
    }
  ),
  ChType = Table.TransformColumnTypes( Source,
    {
      {"Column1", Int64.Type},
      {"Column2", Int64.Type},
      {"Column3", Int64.Type},
      {"Column4", Int64.Type}
    }),
  RemoveBlanks = Table.SelectRows( ChType, each
    not List.IsEmpty(
      List.RemoveMatchingItems( Record.FieldValues(_), {"", null})
```

```
    )),
    RemoveErrors = Table.RemoveRowsWithErrors( RemoveBlanks )
in
    RemoveErrors
```

Even though we instructed Power Query to remove all errors, errors remain.

The key to resolving this lies in the order of operations; best practice is to deal with errors right away. By right-clicking the step named `RemoveErrors` in the **Applied Steps** section of the **Query Settings** pane and selecting **Move before**, you change the order of operations. This adjustment ensures that `Table.RemoveRowsWithErrors` is executed before `Table.SelectRows` to remove blank rows. As a result, errors caused by type conversion are eliminated correctly, and the query returns a single valid row of data without any persistent errors.

DataSource.Error, could not find the source

This error occurs when the data source is inaccessible. Common causes include the user not having access to the data source or the source has been moved:

```
let
    Source = Excel.Workbook(
        File.Contents( "C:\ThereIsNoSuchFile.xlsx"), null, true
    )
in
    Source
```

```
DataSource.Error: Could not find file 'C:\ ThereIsNoSuchFile.xlsx'.
```

An unknown or missing identifier

An identifier serves as a name used to refer to a specific value, such as a query, a variable (step), or a record field name. Identifiers can be categorized into regular identifiers and quoted identifiers. Quoted identifiers allow the use of any sequence of characters, including keywords, spaces, operators, and punctuators, for example, `#"error logic"`. Regular identifiers, on the other hand, are used to name and access fields and are also known as generalized identifiers, which do not require this quoted notation.

When you encounter an error message similar to `The name 'xxxxx' wasn't recognized. Make sure it's spelled correctly.`, it indicates that you have referenced an identifier that cannot be found. To resolve this issue, you need to investigate where that unknown identifier is used and determine which value it should refer to, in order to accurately update it. Alternatively, you may need to create a variable with that name if it doesn't exist and assign that the appropriate value. When it specifically refers to the name `'_'`, the culprit is the missing `each` keyword.

An unknown function

This error raises the same message: `Expression.Error: The name 'list.Max' wasn't recognized.` Make sure it's spelled correctly, as encountered with an unknown or missing identifier. Common causes are spelling errors and incorrect casing:

```
let
    maxValue = list.Max( {1, 4, 6, 8 } )
in
    maxValue
```

M function names adhere to a consistent pattern, comprising a function category followed by a period and a name. When a name consists of compound words, the convention is to capitalize the first letter of each appended word. For example, consider a function for selecting rows in a table, which is part of the `table` functions category and has the name `SelectRows`. The qualified function, therefore, is denoted as `Table.SelectRows`. Being aware of this convention helps to spot errors in function names faster.

The introduction of Intellisense in Power Query marked a significant improvement in the development experience for users of Power BI Desktop (September 2018 release), Excel 365, and Excel 2019 versions. With Intellisense enabled, developers can begin typing a function or variable name and will be presented with a drop-down list of potential completions. Users can quickly select the desired function or variable from the suggestions without having to type it out completely, thereby reducing the likelihood of errors and typos.

> However, users needed to be aware of an issue that was present with Intellisense. That could lead to duplicated terms, for example, when typing `list.` to search for `List.Max`, Intellisense could autocomplete the user selection to `listList.Max`. If you are encountering this, here are two ways to avoid that:
>
> 1. Omit the period when typing the function, such as: `TableSelectR`
> 2. Entering, for example, only the capitalized letters from a function name. Optionally typing out more, like `tsrow` for `Table.SelectRows`
>
> Both methods would yield the desired function without duplication of terms.

An unknown column reference

When you encounter an error message like `Expression.Error: The column 'xxxxx' of the table wasn't found.`, it indicates that you have a hard coded column reference that does not match any of the column names present in the table.

There are several reasons for this error to occur:

- There may be user input errors, such as a misspelled column name when defining the reference.
- Changes may have been made to the column names in the data source after the initial query design, leading to mismatched references.

- Columns may have been omitted from the data source, and as a result, the references to those missing columns are causing the error.
- A user might have made modifications to a preceding step of the query, which caused the column reference to become incorrect, and so on.

The following code snippet is an example of an instance where such an error might occur:

```
let
    Source = #table(2, {{1, 2}}),
    RenameCols = Table.RenameColumns( Source,
        {
            {"Column 1", "ColumnA"},
            {"Column 2", "ColumnB"}
        } )
in
    RenameCols
```

To resolve this error, you should carefully review the code and cross-check column references against actual column names in the table. Verify that column names are present, spelled correctly, and have the correct casing. When making changes to either the data source or any preceding steps, make sure to update all affected column references accordingly, further downstream in the code. This error will persist until all column name issues have been resolved.

Alternatively, you can adopt a different strategy to mitigate this error. If possible, consider using M functions that allow for an optional `missingField` parameter. This parameter enables you to control the function's behavior when a missing field is encountered, providing more flexibility in handling such situations. Moreover, you can explore the option of using dynamic column references instead of hardcoding names. By utilizing dynamic column references, your queries can adapt to changes as they occur.

An unknown field reference

This is very similar to the unknown column reference error but occurs when attempting field access, selection, or lookup, and the specified field name does not match any of the actual field names within the record (or table row).

The reason and resolution for this error are similar to dealing with the unknown column reference error with the important addition that if this error is raised when performing (required) field access or lookup, the specified field name is expected to be present:

```
let
    GetName = [Initial = "M", Name="Mashup"][Name2] // required, error
in
    GetName
```

You can switch to optional field access by adding a single question mark after the field access or lookup operator, like so: [Name2]?. This will return a null instead of raising an error when the field is not found within the record:

```
let
    GetName = [Initial = "M", Name="Mashup"][Name2]? // optional, null
in
    GetName
```

To resolve this error, you should carefully review the code and cross-check field references against the actual field names in the record. Verify that field names are present, spelled correctly, and have the correct casing.

If possible, consider using M functions that allow for an optional missingField parameter. This parameter enables you to control the function's behavior when a missing field is encountered, providing more flexibility in handling such situations. Moreover, you can explore the option of using dynamic field references instead of hardcoded names. By utilizing dynamic field references, you can adapt to changes in field names.

Not enough elements in the enumeration

The M language uses a zero-based index for tables and lists. Learn all about lists and item access, which allows you to extract a list element based on its position, in *Chapter 6, Structured Values*. Like field access or lookup, item access is also performed required by default, meaning the specified position is expected to be present.

Consider this query: the function List.Numbers generates a list with 3 elements or list items { 1, 2, 3 }; applying item access and passing the value 3 as an index number will attempt to extract the fourth item from the list of values, raising Expression.Error: There weren't enough elements in the enumeration to complete the operation:

```
let
    ItemAccess = List.Numbers( 1, 3, 1 ){3} // required, error
in
    ItemAccess
```

You can switch to optional item access by adding a single question mark after the item access operator, like so: {3}?:

```
let
    ItemAccess = List.Numbers( 1, 3, 1 ){3}? // optional, null
in
    ItemAccess
```

This will return a null instead of raising an error when the requested index position is not present in the list. Alternatively, you can adopt a different strategy. Consider using a standard library function such as List.Range:

```
let
    ItemAccess = List.Range( List.Numbers( 1, 3, 1 ), 3, 1 ) // {}
in
    ItemAccess
```

This function will return an empty list instead of raising an error when the offset number exceeds the number of elements in the list.

Formula.Firewall error

These are the results of Power Query's Data Privacy Firewall. Its purpose is simple: it exists to prevent Power Query from unintentionally leaking data between sources. They raise an error like:

```
Formula.Firewall: Query 'Query1' (step 'Source') references other queries or
steps, so it may not directly access a data source. Please rebuild this data
combination.
```

Or:

```
Formula.Firewall: Query 'Query1' (step 'Source') is accessing data sources that
have privacy levels which cannot be used together. Please rebuild this data
combination.
```

Often, you'll find two methods to resolve this error without disabling the Firewall. You can combine Query1 and Query2 into a single query or turn these queries into a zero parameter function to avoid the Formula.Firewall error. While the latter works in both Power BI Desktop and Excel, it doesn't work in the Power BI service.

Learn more about the Formula.Firewall error in *Chapter 15, Optimizing Performance*.

Expression.Error: The key didn't match any rows in the table

This error occurs when Power Query is unable to find the name it's searching for. Common causes include a misspelled or changed name, insufficient privileges of the account used to access the table, or multiple credentials for a single data source, which isn't supported in the Power BI service. The Expression.Error in the following code is caused by non-matching table keys values in the lookup expression:

```
let
    Source = Table.FromRows(
        {
            {"YourTable", "Table", #table(2, {{1, 2}}) },
            {"YourTable2", "Table", #table(2, {{1, 2}}) }
        }, {"Item", "Kind", "Data"}
```

```
        ),
        Navigation = Source{[Item= "myTable", Kind="Table"]}[Data]
    in
        Navigation
```

To resolve the error in this example, you need to change myTable to YourTable on line 8 of the M code.

This error is frequently encountered when using the Folder connector to combine files. When using the Folder connector, all files are processed based on a selected example file's structure. For example, if you select an Excel file with a table named myData, all other files in the folder will be treated as Excel files with a table called myData. If there are variations in the files' structures, such as a misspelled or differently named table, the Expression.Error may occur during data combination. To avoid raising errors or losing data, it is essential to carefully review and verify the structure of the files and ensure consistency before combining them with this specific technique.

Expression.Error: The key matched more than one row in the table

When you encounter an error message like Expression.Error: The key matched more than one row in the table, it indicates that the lookup operation is returning more than a single row. This error arises when utilizing the item access operator { } to look up a row in a table, with key fields and values provided within square brackets, [ ]. The Power Query M (mashup) engine uses this syntax specifically for tables with primary keys in case of navigation or drill-down; all table's keys fields and matching field values are listed to uniquely identify the desired row. The Expression.Error here is caused by failing to specify values for all keys in the lookup expression:

```
    let
        Source = Table.FromRows(
            {
                {"YourTable", "Table", #table(2, {{1, 2}}) },
                {"YourTable2", "Table", #table(2, {{1, 2}}) }
            }, {"Item", "Kind", "Data"}
        ),
        Navigation = Source{[Kind="Table"]}[Data]
    in
        Navigation
```

To address the error from the example, you need to include the Item field and assign it a matching value on line 8 of the M code.

This error emerges when manual modifications are made to UI-generated M code. It can also occur when the lookup method is manually applied to tables lacking sufficient key-matching values or when the table may contain duplicate rows. To prevent this error, use the Table.Keys function to ascertain whether the table has primary keys. It will return a list with a record containing two fields: Columns as a list of column names that form the primary keys for the table, if any, and Primary as a Boolean value. Ensuring a matching value is supplied for each key field will avoid raising this error.

Expression.Error: Evaluation resulted in a stack overflow and cannot continue

A stack overflow error occurs when the evaluation of your M code exhausts the available memory in the call stack. This can happen due to a bug in your code, such as evaluating a recursive function without any kind of end condition. Recursive functions can lead to a stack overflow when they repeatedly call back into themselves without any proper termination condition. Common ways to resolve a stack overflow include implementing a control structure:

```
let
    NoEnd = (x) => @NoEnd (x + 1)
in
    NoEnd(0)
```

To illustrate the `if-then-else` statement on line 2, check if x is less than 100. If the condition is true, the function calls itself recursively with the operation x + 1 as new input. Otherwise, if x is equal to or greater than 100, the function returns the value of x, terminating recursive calls:

```
let
    NoEnd = (x) => if x <100 then @NoEnd(x + 1) else x
in
    NoEnd(0)
```

The key is to ensure that the termination condition will eventually be met during the execution of the function. Without a proper termination condition, the function will keep calling itself indefinitely, leading to a stack overflow error.

Furthermore, you can consider replacing recursion with iteration using functions like `List.Transform`, `List.Generate`, or `List.Accumulate`. These iterative functions can perform the same tasks as recursive functions but in a more memory-efficient manner, reducing the risk of stack overflow errors. Remember to verify termination conditions and optimize the M code for better performance and reliability.

Putting it all together

Throughout this chapter, you have gained insights into various aspects of error handling in Power Query. You have learned about the nature of errors, how to raise them intentionally, as well as how errors are contained, detected, and ultimately handled. With this foundational knowledge in hand, it is time to consolidate your learning by delving into two practical examples that showcase real-world scenarios of error handling in action. These examples will provide a deeper understanding of how to prevent errors, make deliberate choices, and address errors when they arise.

Feel free to design your own approach to these scenarios before diving into them. If you are not comfortable translating that into M code, that is absolutely fine. You can still create an outline and think of obstacles that have to be overcome. This will allow you to compare your strategy to the one suggested here. But remember, there are a multitude of solutions to any given problem, and this book only covers one possible approach.

Column selection

A very common task is selecting columns from a table. This can easily be done through the UI. However, can you think of a method to facilitate column selection with the aim of making this process more user-friendly, robust, and reliable?

Building a custom solution

We will guide you through the process and code development, explaining each part step by step. After we have covered everything, we will share the complete code sample so you can see how everything falls into place.

Let's first focus on user-friendliness. As the M language is case-sensitive, and it's easy to make a spelling error, let's explore how we can provide a list with column numbers instead of a list with column names. However, here's an important consideration: the column numbers should not be zero-based. From an intuitive standpoint, we are accustomed to start counting from one.

It would also be user-friendly to provide a toggle for selecting or deleting columns. Imagine a scenario where a user wants to keep all columns except one or a few. Requesting users to provide a list of all other column positions would be cumbersome and error-prone. To streamline the process, including an option to toggle between keeping or deleting the specified columns would greatly enhance usability and reduce potential mistakes.

With these considerations in mind, we have identified three key input parameters for our custom function. First, we need a table to perform the operation on; second, a list with column positions (in a one-based format) will indicate the specific columns that require action; and finally, a Boolean that serves as a toggle option to determine whether to keep or delete the provided columns will add a level of ease-of-use for users. Let's look at an example:

```
2    ( myTable as table, optional colPositions, optional keepOrDelete as
logical ) as table =>
```

Explicit parameters specify the input of a function and its required data type. Therefore, using explicit parameters in custom functions is a best practice that serves as a first line of defense in ensuring the function accepts only arguments of the specified type. However, for the colPositions parameter, explicit typing has intentionally been omitted. While including parameter documentation is a common approach to inform users of the expected argument types, here, custom error logic has been implemented to provide specific information to the user when an argument is passed that is not of the expected type, specifically, a list. By customizing the error message, we can offer more meaningful feedback to the user, guiding them on how to meet the argument value requirements:

```
4        // Custom error, provide more specific information to the user.
5        l = if not Value.Is( colPositions, type nullable list )
6            then error "Pass a list with column positions, starting number is 1.
7            For example: { 1, 3, 5 } will keep or delete columns 1, 3 and 5 from
the input table."
8            else colPositions ?? {},
```

Handling optional parameters in custom functions is crucial to prevent null values from becoming a root cause of errors. When an optional parameter is omitted, it defaults to null. To safeguard against potential issues, coalesce is utilized on line *8* to ensure that when the colPositions parameter is null, it will be replaced by an empty list {}. This way, the l variable is always guaranteed to have a valid value when passed to List.Transform, either the user-provided list or an empty list if no such list has been provided.

Additionally, coalesce is employed to set a default value for the optional keepOrDelete parameter. This ensures that if the user does not pass an argument for keepOrDelete, it will default to Keep. By doing so, the function is designed to be more user-friendly and predictable, as it eliminates the need for users to explicitly provide a value if they intend to keep specified columns:

```
9       // Coalesce set the default to selecting, not deleting columns.
10      inclOrExclCols = keepOrDelete ?? true,
```

To efficiently handle table column names, we will assign all column names to a variable. Power Query M uses a zero-based index, meaning we have to convert the user input because they were asked to provide a one-based index. Specifying column positions starting from one instead of zero makes it more intuitive for the user.

Before proceeding with the subtraction, we need to ensure that the data type of the list item within the colPositions list will conform to a number. To accomplish this, we will include error handling for cases where a value cannot be converted to a number type. By using a try-otherwise construct, we can attempt to convert each list item to a number. If successful, we perform the subtraction by one to adjust to the zero-based index. If any value in the list cannot be converted to a number, the otherwise clause takes effect for which we provided a null value; for the sake of simplicity, erroneous inputs are ignored:

```
11   allCols = Table.ColumnNames( myTable ),
12      // try-otherwise protects the evaluation of the second argument,
     returning a default null value for non-conforming value types.
13      baseZero = List.Transform( l, each try Number.From(_)-1 otherwise null
     ),
```

To generate a list of actual column names from the user input and at the same time ensure optional item access does not lead to errors, we will nest three functions. Building the logic from the inside out firstly, filtering the baseZero list, retaining only the values that are greater than or equal to zero. This precaution guarantees that optional item access will never raise an error caused by a negative index. Next, inside List.Transform, apply optional item access to obtain the corresponding column name from the allCols list. Finally, removing null values. By removing any nulls from the list, we can determine the number of valid column names that remain:

```
14   colNames = List.RemoveNulls( List.Transform( List.Select( baseZero, each
  _ >=0 ),    each allCols{_}? ) ),
```

With these steps in place, we can confidently generate an output value. To achieve this, we will:

- Leverage a double if-then-else statement to control the flow of the function. The outer if condition checks whether there are any valid column names remaining in the colNames list.

- If there are no valid column names, the function returns the input table as is, without any modification. Conversely, if there are valid column names, the second if-then-else statement, based on the inclOrExclCols value, determines whether the specified columns should be kept or removed from the input table.

By employing these control structures, we ensure that the function can handle various scenarios effectively. If users provide invalid column positions or do not specify any columns to include or exclude, the function still delivers consistent results, preventing unexpected errors and offering a smooth user experience:

```
16      newTbl = if List.Count( colNames ) >0
17         then Table.SelectColumns( myTable,
18            if inclOrExclCols
19            then colNames
20            else List.RemoveMatchingItems( allCols, colNames )
21         ) else myTable
```

Here's the full M code script including documentation.

```
let
    fxSelectColumns = ( myTable as table, optional colPositions, optional
keepOrDelete as logical ) as table =>
    let
        // Custom error logic to provide more specific information to the user.
        cols = if not Value.Is( colPositions, type nullable list )
            then error "Pass a list with column positions, starting number is
1.
            For example: { 1, 3, 5 } will keep or delete columns 1, 3 and 5
from the input table."
            else colPositions ?? {},
        /* Coalesce to set the default value to selecting columns, not deleting
them. */
        inclOrExclCols = keepOrDelete ?? true,
        allCols = Table.ColumnNames( myTable ),
        /* try-otherwise protects the evaluation of the second argument,
returning a null for non-conforming values. */
        baseZero = List.Transform( cols, each try Number.From(_)-1 otherwise
null ),
        colNames = List.RemoveNulls( List.Transform( List.Select( baseZero,
each _ >=0 ), each allCols{_}? )),
        /* a double if-then-else statement controls the flow for the table
```

```
output expression */
        newTbl = if List.Count( colNames ) >0
            then Table.SelectColumns( myTable,
                if inclOrExclCols
                then colNames
                else List.RemoveMatchingItems( allCols, colNames )
        ) else myTable
    in
        newTbl,
        fnDocumentation = [
            Documentation.Name = " Select Columns by position ",
            Documentation.Description = " Selects or Removes columns from the
input table.
            'colPositions' takes a list with one-based column postition
numbers.
            'keepOrDelete' takes a boolean, 'true'= keep and 'false' = remove
columns.
            Returns a table with fewer columns or as is when no valid values
have been passed. ",
            Documentation.Author = " Melissa de Korte ",
            Documentation.Version = " 1.0 "
        ]
in
    Value.ReplaceType( fxSelectColumns, Value.ReplaceMetadata(
        Value.Type( fxSelectColumns ),
        fnDocumentation
    )
)
```

This example showcases a range of error prevention and error-handling techniques, illustrating their role in data transformation tasks. By incorporating clear developer choices, custom errors, coalesce, optional item access, `try-otherwise`, and `if-then-else` statements, we have crafted a powerful and user-friendly method for selecting columns in a table. Each of these techniques serves a specific purpose, contributing to the overall robustness and reliability of the function.

Reporting cell-level errors

Ensuring data quality and validity is a crucial step in the data preparation process; addressing cell-level errors is paramount for maintaining the integrity of your datasets. While `Table.RemoveRowsWithErrors` might seem like a convenient option to remove rows with errors, it is not without consequence, especially if you are unsure which rows have been eliminated and the reasons behind their removal. To preserve data transparency, empower you to make informed decisions, and act when issues arise, let's look into creating an error reporting table for your query.

Building a custom solution

Like before, we'll walk you through the process and break down each section for you. Once we've gone through each part, we'll present the entire code so you can see how it all comes together seamlessly.

Most tables contain one or more key columns, which serve as unique identifiers for specific entries within the table. Therefore, it is important to provide users the option to identify key columns within their data and retain them as row identifiers in the output table. In addition, we can allow users to limit error detection to a specific selection of columns, ensuring a more focused and efficient approach.

With these considerations in mind, we have identified three input parameters for our custom function. These parameters include the input table on which the operation will be performed, an optional list containing the names of key columns, and an optional list that specifies the column names to be scanned for errors. By providing these parameters, users have granular control over the error detection process.

To ensure that only valid arguments are accepted, explicit parameters have been declared. Explicitly defining the expected data types for each parameter adds a layer of protection, preventing the function from accepting incompatible data types as input:

```
2    (myTable as table, optional keyCols as list, optional scanCols as list )
  as record =>
```

Allowing the keyCols argument to be optional provides users with flexibility, but also requires appropriate handling when a value is not provided because when keyCols is omitted, its value is null. To avoid a type mismatch error when passed as an argument to another function expecting a list type, the coalesce operator is leveraged to replace the null with an empty list.

Considering possible spelling errors in user-provided keyCols, we can validate them against the column names in the input table (colNames). By doing so, we can identify valid key column names and store them in a new variable called validKeys. This validation step not only helps to prevent potential errors but also enables us to provide a list with misspelled or non-existent key columns names, back to the user in the output. Finally, the hasKeys variable returns true or false depending on whether a valid key column is present:

```
4        colNames = Table.ColumnNames( myTable ),
5        validKeys = List.Intersect( { colNames, keyCols ?? {} } ),
6        hasKeys = List.Count( validKeys ) >0,
```

The same coalesce and validation method is used for the optional user-provided scanCols argument. When scanCols is omitted, it defaults to null, and coalesce replaces the null with an empty list, ensuring a list type is available for further processing.

To optimize the function's performance, we take a proactive step in data preparation. Any columns not required are immediately removed from the input table and stored in the newTable variable.

By eliminating unnecessary columns early, we reduce the computational load, resulting in a more efficient execution:

```
7        selCols = List.Intersect( { colNames, scanCols ?? {} } ),
8        newTable = Table.SelectColumns( myTable, if List.Count( selCols ) >0
then validKeys & selCols else colNames ),
```

Next, we make a development choice: we define a list with reserved column names. In other words, the names in the reservedNames list are not allowed to be present in the input table. Any violations detected will be stored in the nameViolations list. This enables us to provide feedback to the user:

```
9        reservedNames = { "Name", "Errors", "Reason", "Message", "Detail",
"rowIndex", "newCol" },
10       nameViolations = List.Intersect( { colNames, reservedNames } ),
```

Let's delve into the heart of this solution and create a pivotal component in constructing an error reporting table, by leveraging multiple if-then-else statements:

1. First, we examine whether any column name violations exist. If not, we proceed with a nested let expression to handle two different scenarios based on the presence of valid keys.
2. If valid keys exist, we retain all errors containing rows from the modified input table.
3. When no valid keys are present, we will add a zero-based row index column, called rowIndex, to the modified input table before invoking the Table.SelectRowsWithErrors function.

This looks like the following:

```
11       runLogic = if List.IsEmpty( nameViolations )
12         then let
13           t = if hasKeys = true
14             then Table.SelectRowsWithErrors( newTable )
15             else Table.SelectRowsWithErrors( Table.AddIndexColumn( newTable,
"rowIndex", 0, 1, Int64.Type)),
```

The t variable now holds a table containing rows with one or more errors in its cells. However, our focus is solely on the errors themselves. We will add a new column called newCol, using Record. ToTable(_), to generate a two-column table in each row. The first column, called Name, consists of field names, while the second column, called Value, contains the corresponding field values. Now we can invoke the Table.SelectRowsWithErrors function again, this time targeting the Value column to solely retrieve the errors.

Our ultimate goal is an error report, showing the error reason, message, and details. To accomplish this, we create an additional column in the nested table, leveraging the try-catch construct to extract relevant information from the error value, try [Value] catch (e) => e and saving that information to a new column named Errors.

Now that we have successfully extracted the necessary data, there is no need to retain the actual error value stored within the Value column of the nested table. You can use required projection to create a table with fewer columns: [[Name], [Errors]].

Finally, we can also optimize the outer table by omitting all columns except newCol, and the key column or the rowIndex column:

```
16          getErrors = Table.SelectColumns( Table.AddColumn( t, "newCol", each
17            Table.AddColumn( Table.SelectRowsWithErrors( Record.ToTable(_),
{"Value"}), "Errors",
18              each try [Value] catch (e)=> e )[[Name], [Errors]]
19            ), if hasKeys then validKeys & {"newCol"} else {"rowIndex",
"newCol"} ),
```

Having optimized the columns in our table, we now proceed to expand the nested table in newCol, which contains a Name and Errors column. This extraction operation will result in both widening and expanding the table, allowing us to expose a record value in the newly added Errors column.

Extracting the Reason, Message, and Detail fields from the record value in the Errors column widens the table even further, providing users with detailed insights into each error encountered:

```
20          errorTable = Table.ExpandRecordColumn(
21            Table.ExpandTableColumn( getErrors, "newCol", {"Name", "Errors"} ),
22              "Errors", {"Reason", "Message", "Detail"} )
23        in errorTable
```

We need to complete the final branch from the first if-then-else statement, meaning if we find that any column name violations exist, we will raise a custom error. The error message requests the user to rename the listed columns and try again:

```
24        else error
25        "Please rename these columns in your table first: " & Text.Combine(
nameViolations, ", " )
```

Finally, this function outputs a record value that contains four fields: a number for the Error count, an error reporting table Data, a list with Invalid key columns, and a list with Invalid scan columns:

```
27        [
28          Error count = Table.RowCount( runLogic ),
29          Data = runLogic,
30          Invalid key columns = List.Difference( keyCols ?? {}, validKeys),
31          Invalid scan columns = List.Difference( scanewCols ?? {}, selCols)
32        ]
```

Here's the full M code script including documentation:

```
let
  fxErrorReport = (myTable as table, optional keyCols as list, optional
scanCols as list ) as record =>
  let
    colNames = Table.ColumnNames( myTable ),
    validKeys = List.Intersect( { colNames, keyCols ?? {} } ),
    hasKeys = List.Count( validKeys ) >0,
    selCols = List.Intersect( { colNames, scanCols ?? {} } ),
    nTable = Table.SelectColumns( myTable, if List.Count( selCols ) >0 then
validKeys & selCols else colNames ),
    reservedNames = { "Name", "Errors", "Reason", "Message", "Detail",
"rowIndex", "nCol" },
    nameViolations = List.Intersect( { colNames, reservedNames } ),
    runLogic = if List.IsEmpty( nameViolations )
      then let
        t = if hasKeys = true
          then Table.SelectRowsWithErrors( nTable )
          else Table.SelectRowsWithErrors( Table.AddIndexColumn( nTable,
"rowIndex", 0, 1, Int64.Type)),
        getErrors = Table.SelectColumns( Table.AddColumn( t, "nCol", each
          Table.AddColumn( Table.SelectRowsWithErrors( Record.ToTable(_),
{"Value"}), "Errors",
            each try [Value] catch (e)=> e )[[Name], [Errors]] ),
            if hasKeys then validKeys & {"nCol"} else {"rowIndex", "nCol"} ),
        errorTable = Table.ExpandRecordColumn(
          Table.ExpandTableColumn( getErrors, "nCol", {"Name", "Errors"} ),
          "Errors", {"Reason", "Message", "Detail"} )
      in errorTable
      else error
        "Please rename these columns in your table first: " & Text.Combine(
nameViolations, ", " )
    in
      [
        Error count = Table.RowCount( runLogic ),
        Data = runLogic,
        Invalid key columns = List.Difference( keyCols ?? {}, validKeys ),
        Invalid scan columns = List.Difference( scanCols ?? {}, selCols )
      ],
    fxDocumentation = [
      Documentation.Name = " Create an Error Report ",
```

```
            Documentation.Description = " Returns a record containing 4 fields.
            'Error Count' shows the number of errors found in the input table.
            'Data' contains the error reporting table.
            'Invalid key columns' returns a list containing specified invalid key
    columns if any.
            'Invalid scan columns' returns a list containing specified invalid scan
    columns if any. ",
            Documentation.Author = " Melissa de Korte ",
            Documentation.Version = " 1.0 "
      ]
    in
      Value.ReplaceType( fxErrorReport, Value.ReplaceMetadata(
          Value.Type( fxErrorReport ),
          fxDocumentation
        )
      )
```

Error handling is a multifaceted aspect of robust query design that requires a comprehensive understanding of various error types and their containment, detection, prevention, and resolution methods. By embracing preventive measures, you can develop an error-handling skills set that not only addresses errors when they occur but also minimizes their occurrence. Making thoughtful choices or even implementing dynamic error handling will enable you to build more reliable queries. As you continue to refine your error-handling strategies, you will find that there are endless opportunities for creative and problem-solving approaches in the Power Query M language.

Summary

This chapter started out by creating a foundation: a shared understanding of what an error is, and how errors can be raised, contained, and detected. It explored various aspects of error handling, highlighting the importance of adopting a holistic approach. Beyond reacting to errors alone, it is crucial to proactively incorporate preventive measures into your query design. By employing a combination of these techniques thoughtfully, you can create queries that are more resilient, thus reducing the risk of errors and improving overall data quality.

In the next chapter, we will learn about the major functions and operators that allow iteration and recursion in Power Query M.

Learn more on Discord

Join our community's Discord space for discussions with the author and other readers:

`https://discord.gg/vCSG5GBbyS`

13

Iteration and Recursion

Iteration and recursion are fundamental concepts in programming that allow for the repetitive execution of code. In the context of Power Query M, these techniques greatly enhance your data transformation and manipulation abilities. Whether you're looking to apply a function across a list of values, accumulate results, or even refer to previous steps in a sequence, understanding iteration and recursion makes a big difference in these situations.

This chapter delves into key functions and operators that enable iteration and recursion in the Power Query M language. You'll learn how to loop through lists with `List.Transform`, perform a function on values with `List.Accumulate`, generate lists conditionally with `List.Generate`, and implement true recursion using the @ scoping operator.

The aim is to provide you with the skills needed to incorporate these techniques into your own data workflows. The main topics covered are:

- Iteration:
    - `List.Transform`
    - `List.Accumulate`
    - `List.Generate`
- Recursion:
    - The @ scoping operator

To get the most value from this chapter, it is helpful to be familiar with the basics of Power Query M, as covered in earlier chapters. Topics like understanding structured values and accessing values, both covered in *Chapter 6*, will come in handy.

Introduction to iteration

Iteration is a core concept in programming, important for performing repetitive actions on data. In Power Query, iteration often happens over rows in a table or items in a list.

Suppose you want to square a list of 1,000 numbers. Doing this without iteration would require writing 1,000 separate lines of code, which is both time-consuming and error-prone. With iteration, the same task can be completed with just a few lines of code.

Traditional languages like Python or Java use `for` and `while` loops for such tasks. However, the Power Query M language takes a different approach to iteration. It performs transformations on its underlying data structures by design.

For example, when you use `Table.AddColumn` to create a new column, Power Query automatically applies the specified operation to each row in the table, similar to how a `for` loop would iterate over each element in a list. The M language automatically does the iteration for you using its standard library functions.

However, to delve deeper into the capabilities of iteration in Power Query M, there are some functions specifically designed for this purpose: `List.Transform`, `List.Accumulate`, and `List.Generate`. These functions align closely with the concept of iteration as understood in the broader context of programming.

`List.Transform` and `List.Accumulate` allow you to perform an operation on each item in a list (like a `for` loop), whereas `List.Generate` mirrors the functionality of a `while` loop since it iterates based on a stopping condition. `List.Generate` allows for the creation of a list by repeatedly applying a function, continuing until a specified condition is no longer met.

In the coming sections, we'll explore these three functions—`List.Transform`, `List.Accumulate`, and `List.Generate`—that enable iteration in Power Query M. Each offers different levels of complexity and flexibility, paralleling the iterative capabilities of `for` and `while` loops in traditional programming. By mastering these functions, you can choose the most suitable approach for your data transformation needs, in much the same way you might select between a `for` or `while` loop in other programming languages.

List.Transform

When thinking of iteration, `List.Transform` is one of the go-to functions. The `List.Transform` function applies an operation to each item in a list. In other words, it takes a list and a function as inputs and then creates a new list where each output item is the result of applying that function to the corresponding item in the original list.

Let's delve into some practical situations where `List.Transform` proves useful. Imagine you have a list of numbers, say 2, 4, and 6, and you need to double each number. This scenario is a common example of iteration, where an operation is repeatedly applied to each item in a sequence.

In a general programming language, you might approach this with a `for` loop, like this:

```
for x in [2, 4, 6]
  {
    array[x] = array[x] * 2;
    x++;
  }
```

This code loops through each element in an array, doubling its value. However, in Power Query, you achieve the same result with a more concise approach using the List.Transform function. Here's an illustration:

```
List.Transform( { 2, 4 6 }, each _ * 2
```

In this example, List.Transform takes a list {2, 4, 6} and applies a function to each element. The function, defined as each _ * 2, multiplies each item by 2, producing a new list, {4, 8, 12}. The underscore (_) represents each element in the list during the iteration.

This comparison shows the difference in approaches between traditional for loops and the functional style of Power Query. While the for loop explicitly iterates over array indices, List.Transform abstracts the iteration process, focusing on the operation applied to each list element.

For a more detailed explanation of the each _ construct in Power Query, please see *Chapter 9*.

Extracting items from a list by position

Transitioning from the simple iteration example, let's delve into a more complex scenario. Imagine you're diving into an application's settings to analyze user preferences. These preferences are tucked away in a list, where each setting is either active (true) or inactive (false). Our list has 8 *Boolean* values, each tied to a different setting, such as *Notifications*, *Dark Mode*, *Location Sharing*, and *Automatic Updates*, to name a few.

Let's say our list is stored in a step named myList, looking like this:

```
{ true, false, true, false, true, true, false, true }
```

The goal is to extract the values at positions 2, 3, 5, 6, and 8 from this list. But here's a challenge: there isn't a direct function to pull out multiple items from a list based on their index position.

You might think of a function like List.Select to tackle this. This function takes a list as input, and allows you to select items based on a condition. For example:

```
List.Select(  { true, false, true, false, true, true, false, true },
  each _ = true )
```

This expression returns a list with only true values. However, due to duplicate values in the list and the requirement to pick different values, this function won't cut it. The reason is that it pinpoints items based solely on their value and not by their position in the list. Let's explore an alternative approach to solve this problem using List.Transform.

Extracting a single item from a list by its index position is straightforward. For instance, to obtain the second item from a list, you would use:

```
myList{1}
```

This snippet uses a zero-based index within curly brackets to specify the item position. The process is known as **field selection**. But what if you want to gather multiple items, say, the values at positions 2, 3, 5, 6, and 8?

Here's a manual approach that does the trick:

```
{ myList{1}, myList{2}, myList{4}, myList{5}, myList{7} }
```

The outcome of the above code is:

```
{ false, true, true, true, false }
```

Although correct, the code feels slightly verbose and lacks flexibility. This is a typical use case where the `List.Transform` function shines. We can perform an identical operation using less code. Performing this task using `List.Transform` requires two arguments:

- **List**: Start with a list of the index positions of the items you're after.
- **Function**: Create a function to retrieve the positions from the list.

Given the previous method, we can mimic a function to perform a similar operation but in a more succinct manner. Here's how you can rewrite the operation using `List.Transform`:

```
let
  myList =
    { true, false, true, false, true, true, false, true },
  RetrieveItems =
    List.Transform( {1, 2, 4, 5, 7}, each myList{_} )
in
  RetrieveItems
```

In this revised method, `List.Transform` iterates over the given index positions. For each value, it applies the function from the second argument, retrieving the corresponding items from `myList`. This approach is not only shorter but also adaptable for later tweaks. If you need to change to different positions later, simply change the index positions in `List.Transform`'s first argument and you're good to go.

Allocating a yearly budget to months

For another scenario, imagine you're working with a dataset containing the sales budget for 2024. The dataset is stored in a step called `Source` and looks as follows:

	^{ABC} Product	^{123} Budget	^{123} Year
1	iPhone 14	1000000	2024
2	MacBook Air	500000	2024
3	Amazon Echo Dot	250000	2024
4	Tesla Model 3	100000	2024
5	Nike Air Jordans	50000	2024

Figure 13.1: Table with Budget values for 2024

To follow along with this example, you can find the above dataset in the `Start of month dates` query from the exercise files accompanying the book.

Notice that, for this task, the above data is given on a yearly basis. Your goal is to distribute the budget figures across each month of the year.

To achieve this, here's what you can do:

1. Create a list of the starting dates for each month of 2024.
2. Expand this list into rows.
3. Divide the annual budget value by 12 to get the monthly figures.

Before adding any columns to our table, let's understand the required elements for the above approach.

First, we want to create a list of dates for each month in 2024. Since the number of values to generate for this scenario is fixed, this is a great scenario for `List.Transform`. Here's one way to do it.

To begin, you generate a list from 1 to 12:

```
{ 1 .. 12 }
```

Now we need a way to turn these into dates. The dataset already includes the year 2024, which we can use, and we have a list of 12 values for the month numbers.

To create a list of monthly dates, we want to begin with January 1, 2024. For each subsequent month, we can use the `Date.AddMonths` function alongside the number list to increment the date by one month in each step.

You still don't need to add anything to the table. Let's start by understanding an easy example and focus only on the number 6 in our generated list. We can turn 6 into `June 1, 2024`, by writing:

```
Date.AddMonths( #date( 2024, 1, 1 ), 6 - 1 )
```

Here, the number 6 is reduced by 1 and then used to increase the initial date by that many months. When you grasp the above concept, it becomes easier to manipulate our dataset.

Our objective is to add a column with a list to each row. This list will show all the first-of-the-month dates for that row's year. We accomplish this by processing a sequence of 12 values with the `List.Transform` function.

With the knowledge in hand of how we can add months to a date, here's how we implement this. Let's introduce a new column in our main table. The new column takes the existing year column and incorporates a sequence of 12 values. The code for this looks like this:

```
Table.AddColumn(
  Source,
  "Date",
  (x)=> List.Transform( {1..12},
        each Date.AddMonths( #date(x[Year], 1, 1), _ - 1 )),
  type {date} )
```

This script creates a new `Date` column to a table called `Source`, which is our primary table in the **Applied Steps** pane. It uses the `Year` information from each row of this table. The challenge here lies in the scope used within the expression. Normally, the `Table.AddColumn` function would use an each expression in its third argument to define a function. This is a shorthand way of creating a function with the underscore symbol as a variable name. `List.Transform` also by default uses the each expression to define a function expression in its second argument. But, using two functions with the same variable name (underscore) creates ambiguity.

If both the `List.Transform` function and the `Table.AddColumn` function use the each keyword, a reference to the underscore (parameter name) can only access the variable within its own context. However, for our example, we require the `List.Transform` functions (inner scope) to access the `Year` value in the table (outer scope).

To solve this, our code defines a custom function for the outer scope (the `Source` table) using the variable x. This allows us to reference the `Year` column from the `Source` table when we are inside the context of the `List.Transform` function.

As a final step, this code ascribes the data type in the fourth argument of `Table.AddColumn`. That's defined as a list type containing dates. The result of adding this step is shown in the following image:

```
= Table.AddColumn( Source, "Date",
    (x)=> List.Transform( {1..12}, each Date.AddMonths( #date( x[Year], 1, 1 ), _ - 1 ) ),
    type {date} )
```

	A^B_C Product	1²₃ Budget	1²₃ Year	Date
1	iPhone 14	1000000	2024	List
2	MacBook Air	500000	2024	List
3	Amazon Echo Dot	250000	2024	List
4	Tesla Model 3	100000	2024	List
5	Nike Air Jordans	50000	2024	List

List

01/01/2024
01/02/2024
01/03/2024
01/04/2024
01/05/2024
01/06/2024
01/07/2024
01/08/2024
01/09/2024
01/10/2024
01/11/2024
01/12/2024

Figure 13.2: Rows containing a list with all start-of-month dates of the year

After creating the column, click the arrows at the right of the Date column header, and select **Expand to New Rows**. This action will produce a table with the starting date for every month in 2024:

	ABC Product	123 Budget	123 Year	Date
1	iPhone 14	1000000	2024	01/01/2024
2	iPhone 14	1000000	2024	01/02/2024
3	iPhone 14	1000000	2024	01/03/2024
4	iPhone 14	1000000	2024	01/04/2024
5	iPhone 14	1000000	2024	01/05/2024
6	iPhone 14	1000000	2024	01/06/2024
7	iPhone 14	1000000	2024	01/07/2024
8	iPhone 14	1000000	2024	01/08/2024
9	iPhone 14	1000000	2024	01/09/2024
10	iPhone 14	1000000	2024	01/10/2024
11	iPhone 14	1000000	2024	01/11/2024
12	iPhone 14	1000000	2024	01/12/2024

Figure 13.3: Table with budget repeated for each month in the year

To finish, divide the budget column by 12. The easiest way to do that is to select the **Budget** column, navigate to **Transform**, choose **Standard**, then **Divide**, and input the value 12. After confirming, you'll have a dataset displaying your budget allocated by month.

	ABC Product	1.2 Budget	123 Year	Date
1	iPhone 14	83333.33333	2024	01/01/2024
2	iPhone 14	83333.33333	2024	01/02/2024
3	iPhone 14	83333.33333	2024	01/03/2024
4	iPhone 14	83333.33333	2024	01/04/2024
5	iPhone 14	83333.33333	2024	01/05/2024
6	iPhone 14	83333.33333	2024	01/06/2024
7	iPhone 14	83333.33333	2024	01/07/2024
8	iPhone 14	83333.33333	2024	01/08/2024
9	iPhone 14	83333.33333	2024	01/09/2024
10	iPhone 14	83333.33333	2024	01/10/2024
11	iPhone 14	83333.33333	2024	01/11/2024
12	iPhone 14	83333.33333	2024	01/12/2024

Figure 13.4: Yearly budget allocated by month

So far, we've seen how List.Transform is a useful function for iterating over lists and performing actions on each element. But what if you need more control, especially when the outcome of one iteration needs to influence the next? That's where List.Accumulate comes into play, providing a more advanced set of features.

List.Accumulate

List.Accumulate is another powerful iterator. Just like List.Transform, the function goes through items in a list one after another, performing a specified action on each item. Yet, unlike most iterators, List.Accumulate has a memory.

As it generates new values, it can access both the new item in the list and the result of the previous iteration. This trait allows it to perform an operation and use the outcome of this operation as input for the next step.

At a glance, you may see some similarities with recursion, which we will cover later in this chapter. However, the essence of List.Accumulate isn't quite recursion. It's more like a cumulative operation, where each step is built upon the outcome of the previous one, hence the name **accumulate**. This distinction allows List.Accumulate to perform tasks where outcomes of earlier steps influence the next operations. So how does that work?

Function anatomy

The syntax of the function is as follows:

```
List.Accumulate(
    list as list,
    seed as any,
    accumulator as function )
```

These terms may be a little abstract, so let's look deeper into each of them:

- list: This is the initial list to work with. The function iterates over each value in this list when applying logic.
- seed: The seed is your starting point. It's the initial value you begin with before going through the items in your list.
- accumulator: Contains a set of instructions of what List.Accumulate should do with each item in the list as it goes through them one by one. The accumulator is a function with two variables: the accumulated value (which starts as the seed) and the current item from the list. It performs a specified action, creating a new accumulated value, and then moves on to the next item in the list, carrying the accumulated value with it.

Let's see how this works with an example. Consider a scenario where you have a list containing the numbers 1 through 5, and you aim to multiply these values together. The desired result is the product of 1 * 2 * 3 * 4 * 5, which equals 120.

In a traditional programming environment, you might use a loop structure to accumulate this product, like this:

```
y = 1
for x = 1 to 5
  {
```

```
    y = y * array[x];
  }
```

This loop iteratively multiplies the accumulator variable y by each element in the array. Similarly, in Power Query, the `List.Accumulate` function achieves the same outcome in a more functional style:

```
List.Accumulate(
  { 1, 2, 3, 4, 5 },
  1,
  ( state, current ) => state * current )
```

The output of this function is 120. Here's how this works:

- `list`: This function iterates through the values 1 to 5.
- `seed`: The operation begins with the value 1, which is referred to as the state value in the first step.
- `accumulator`: It takes the state value and multiplies it by the current item in the list being iterated.

The process can be visualized as illustrated in *Figure 13.5*. Each step of the function mirrors the loop's iteration, multiplying the accumulating state with the current element.

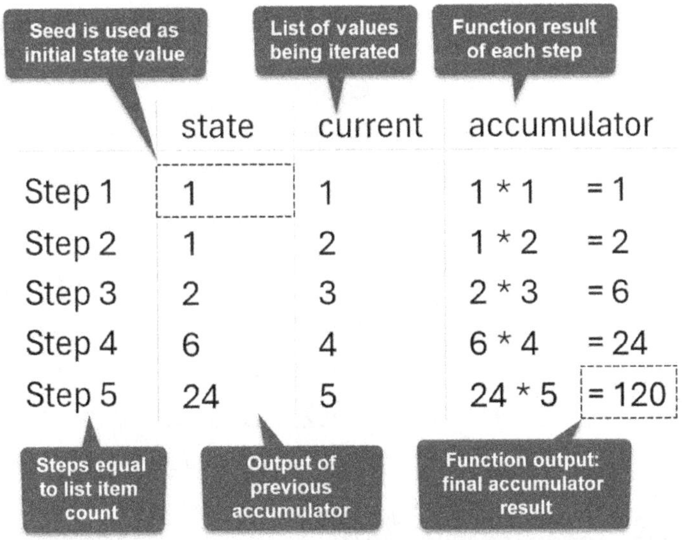

Figure 13.5: Iteration steps for List.Accumulate

Since the function iterates over the list, the number of steps is equal to the number of items in the list. It then uses the accumulator function to perform an operation for each step. Notice that the outcome is the result of the final step. The steps preceding the final steps are not returned in any way.

Let's look closer at how the accumulator function works. The accumulator function uses two input parameters. While you have the liberty to name these parameters as you wish, for clarity, they are named state and current here:

- state represents the accumulated value. In the first iteration, it is equal to the seed value. As the function iterates and applies the accumulator function, the state value evolves with each step, reflecting the output of the last accumulator result.
- current represents the values from the list being processed. In the first iteration, it equals the first value in the list; in the subsequent step, it moves to the second value, continuing in this manner until it moves through all the values in the list.

To visualize this even better, we can adjust the List.Accumulate statement to keep the running total values:

```
List.Accumulate(
  { 1, 2, 3, 4, 5 },
  {1},
  ( state, current ) =>
    state & { List.Last( state ) * current }
)
```

The output of the revised function is {1,1,2,6,24,120}. The logic of these steps is laid out in the following figure:

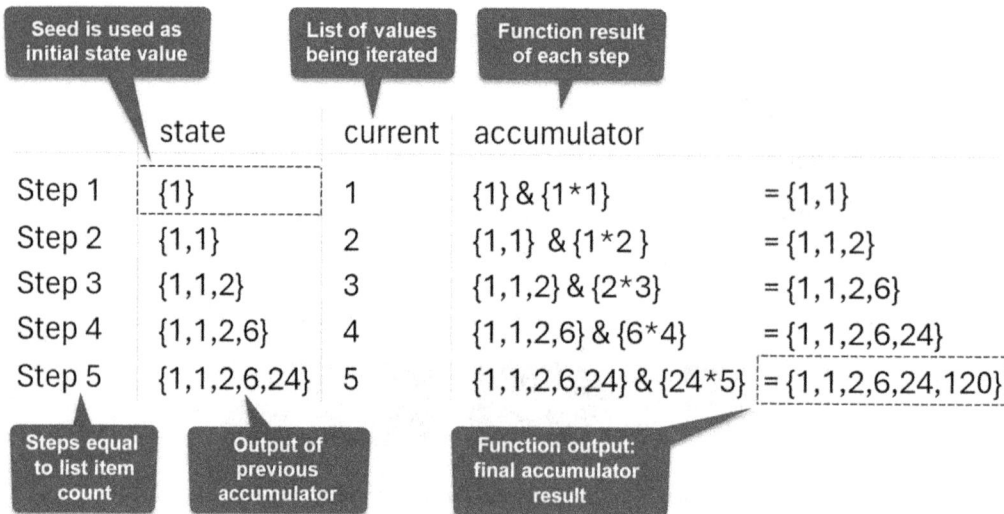

Figure 13.6: List.Accumulate logic for storing results in a list

Instead of returning only the result of the multiplication, the above logic stores the accumulator result of each step in a list. With each iteration, the accumulator grabs the last item from the list and multiplies it with the current value. It then adds the result to the last accumulator result. It does that by combining two list values. An expression like {1} & {1} combines the two lists into one, resulting in {1,1}.

The above examples illustrate the flow of the `List.Accumulate` function. However, you will typically find different scenarios where the function proves useful. Let's look at a more useful example where `List.Accumulate` shines.

Replacing multiple values

So, for which scenarios would you use `List.Accumulate` instead of other iterators? The function is an iterator, meaning it performs an operation repeatedly. More importantly, `List.Accumulate` can access the result of a previous iteration and take it to the next iteration. It's those scenarios where `List.Accumulate` has capabilities most other functions don't have. To follow along with the following example, you can find the data in the accompanying exercise file of this chapter in the query `ListAccumulate Manual Replacement`.

Imagine a scenario where you need to clean the following data:

	A^B_C Names	
1	Rick_de_Groot!	
2	Greg-Deckler!	
3	Melissa.de_Korte	
4	Brian.Julius!	
5	John.Doe!	
6	Jane_Smith!	
7	Sally.Jones!	
8	Tommy_Shelby!	

Figure 13.7: Dataset to clean

You want to return a column that contains the names, with proper spaces in between and without special characters. Removing the special characters would normally require four replacement operations with very similar logic. The only difference is a different set of values being replaced. The characters _, -, and . should be replaced by a space, and the exclamation marks should be removed.

These operations are very similar, and we should be able to replicate them in a `List.Accumulate` function. To get started, let's see what the code looks like for a regular replace values operation.

If you right-click the **Names** column, select **Replace Values**, and replace each underscore with a space, you end up with the following code:

```
Table.ReplaceValue(
    Source,
    "_",
    " ",
    Replacer.ReplaceText,
    {"Names"}
)
```

Performing this operation four times will add four steps to your query. Let's see how we can instead use List.Accumulate to store this logic in a single step.

When setting up a List.Accumulate statement, we first need to identify the values to iterate and the seed value:

- **Values to iterate:** The purpose of this function is to replace an old value with a new value. In each iteration, we therefore need access to both the old and the new value. That means we need to store the items in either a list or a record.

- **Seed value:** The seed determines the starting value of the List.Accumulate operation. Since we will be replacing values in a table, we provide the original table here.

Here's what the List.Accumulate expression looks like:

```
1   List.Accumulate(
2       { {"_"," "}, {"-", " "}, {".", " "}, {"!",""} }, // Sets of replacements
3       Source, // Initial table value (seed)
4       ( state, current ) =>
5         Table.ReplaceValue(
6           state,      // Table being updated with each replacement
7           current{0}, // Character to be replaced - first item from the current pair
8           current{1}, // Replacement character - second item from the current pair
9           Replacer.ReplaceText,{"Names"} // Column name where replacements are made
10        )
11  )
```

Figure 13.8: Using the List.Accumulate expression

In this code, line *2* contains our replacement values. It's a list where each inner list contains both the old and the new values. Line *3* refers to the original table called Source where we replace values.

When running the function, with each iteration (and therefore each replacement), the state value changes to the new table with the replaced values. To illustrate this, have a look at the following image.

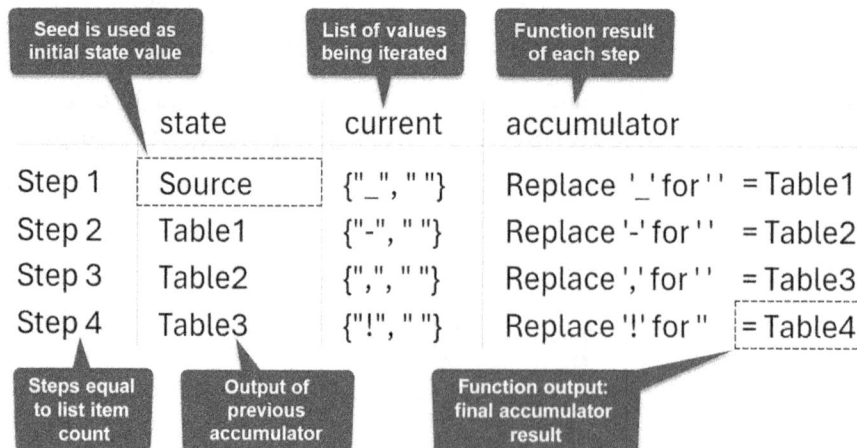

Figure 13.9: Step-by-step replacement logic for List.Accumulate

Figure 13.9 shows how we start with a table called Source. Then, with each replacement, the contents of the table change, illustrated by the versions **Table1** up to **Table3**, The results of **Table1** up to **Table3** are not separate tables that can be accessed but are computed in memory to build up to the result, **Table4**.

After completing these steps, you'll get a cleaned-up dataset, as shown in *Figure 13.10*.

	ABC Names
1	Rick de Groot
2	Greg Deckler
3	Melissa de Korte
4	Brian Julius
5	John Doe
6	Jane Smith
7	Sally Jones
8	Tommy Shelby

Figure 13.10: Cleaned dataset using the List.Transform function

You might have noticed that our code specifies exact replacements, which may not provide you with the flexibility you want. A more maintainable approach could be to store the old values and their corresponding new values in a table and use those as input. Here's how to go about it.

Our original list of replacements looks like this:

```
{ {"_"," "}, {"-", " "}, {".", " "}, {"!",""} }
```

It's a list containing nested lists with both the value to replace and the value to replace it with. Suppose you instead store these values in a table called Replacements.

The code requires a list of smaller lists as input. Each inner list has two elements: the value to be replaced and the value it should be replaced with. What if you kept these pairs in a table named Replacements instead? See *Figure 13.11* for what this Replacements table would look like.

	ABC Old	ABC New
1	_	
2	-	
3	.	
4	!	

Contains a space

Contains an empty string

Figure 13.11: Table with replacements

The goal is to convert this table into a list format similar to what List.Accumulate uses. The function Table.ToRows can help us here. It turns each row of the table into a separate list. Have a look at *Figure 13.12*, where Table.ToRows changes the above table into a list of lists, one for each row:

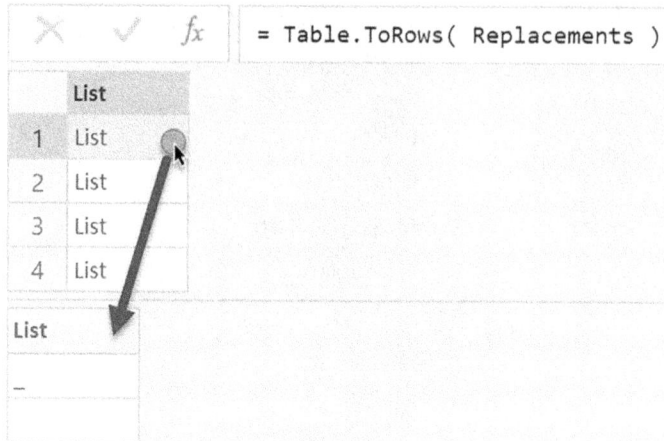

Figure 13.12: Table.ToRows converts a table into a list containing lists for each row in the table

That's the format we need as input for our function. When we replace the original replacement list with the Table.ToRows expression, we end up at our final formula:

```
List.Accumulate(
    Table.ToRows( Replacements ), // Dynamic replacement list
    Source,
    ( state, current ) =>
      Table.ReplaceValue(
        state,
        current{0},
        current{1},
        Replacer.ReplaceText,{"Names"}
      )
)
```

The formula now references the Replacements table in the second line. This design choice pays off when you need to make changes. If you want to add or adjust replacements, just update the table. The function automatically picks up these changes. You can find the solution and underlying data in the exercise files that come with this book.

As we've seen, List.Accumulate offers a level of control that simpler functions can't match. For simple iterations, List.Transform may be all you need. However, if your work requires carrying results from one iteration to the next, List.Accumulate becomes indispensable.

Up next, we'll dive into List.Generate. This function serves a similar purpose but with a twist: instead of iterating through a set number of items, it keeps going as long as a specific condition holds true.

List.Generate

The List.Generate function is one of the most powerful functions in the M language. It allows you to perform iterations repeatedly, based on specified conditions and transformations. However, it's also one of the most complex functions available.

List.Generate differs from static methods like List.Numbers and List.Accumulate(which we discussed in *Chapter 6, Structured Values*). While static methods rely on predefined inputs, List.Generate brings an element of flexibility. It allows you to input functions as arguments. These functions instruct how the list forms, from its start to its end, based on your unique logic. This concept is especially useful when you hit the limits of what static methods can achieve.

The List.Generate function has both iterative and recursive aspects:

- **Iteration aspect:** List.Generate iterates through a process, creating a list based on specified conditions. It requires a starting value, has a step function that defines how to get to the next value, and continues as long as a specified condition is true. This iterative process is similar to a while loop, executing a step, checking a condition, and proceeding or terminating based on that condition. The structure of List.Generate embodies the essence of iteration.

- **Recursion flavor:** Although not recursive in the conventional sense, the way List.Generate can create a sequence of values based on prior computations has similarities with recursion. The step function can reference the previously computed value, just like List.Accumulate does. It is similar to how recursion reuses the output of an operation, although without the function calling itself, which would be true recursion.

So why might you prefer List.Generate over other methods?

Advantages of List.Generate

The List.Generate function has benefits over other methods, especially traditional recursion, covered in the next section. The most important advantages are:

- **Performance efficiency:** List.Generate usually performs better than traditional recursion. Recursion makes multiple separate function calls and adds the intermediary results to a stack. This process is notoriously slow. In contrast, List.Generate works within one context. This means it tends to use less memory and runs faster.

- **Traceable iteration:** When using List.Generate, it's easy to track the outcome of each iteration since the result is stored as a value in the generated list. This gives a clear view of how each iteration contributes to the final list. On the other hand, in a recursive setup, as covered in the next chapter, you only see the outcome of all iterations. That can make it more difficult to follow the logical flow and to debug each step.

- **Ease of understanding:** List.Generate has a clear structure which makes the code easier to read and understand. Each part of the function is well defined, helping you quickly grasp its logic. In contrast, recursion often involves complex, interlinked calls that may require more time to understand.

So how does the function work?

Function anatomy

Clarifying how List.Generate works involves not only understanding its syntax but also understanding the sequential flow of its four key arguments: Initial, Condition, Next, and Selector. These arguments make up the instructions for the dynamic list that the function will generate.

The List.Generate function in M language uses the following syntax:

```
List.Generate(
    Initial as function,
    Condition as function,
    Next as function,
    optional Selector as nullable function
) as list
```

Each argument in List.Generate takes a function as its value. This sets it apart from many other M language functions. Here's a more detailed look at each argument:

We can describe these arguments as:

- Initial: This is your starting point. It can be a simple value like a number or a more complex structure like a record. The list starts building from here.

- Condition: The Condition argument acts as a test a value needs to pass before List.Generate considers adding it to the list. Initially, it evaluates the starting value. If this initial value doesn't meet the condition, the function returns an empty list right away. If the initial value does pass the test, the function proceeds to generate the subsequent item in the list using the Next argument. However, this new value is only added to the list if it, too, meets the condition. The function keeps generating and evaluating new items this way until it encounters a value that fails the condition, at which point, list generation stops.

- Next: This is where each new value in the list is formed. The function you place here defines the logic for generating subsequent values in the list.

- Selector: This optional argument lets you modify the final list. For instance, if you start with a list of records, you can use this to select only specific fields. Alternatively, you can use it to change each value, such as adding a prefix or converting it to a different type of value.

Let's examine how the function works using examples. All examples used throughout this section are available in the accompanying exercise files of this book.

The following code creates a list of numbers ranging from 1 to 9:

```
List.Generate(
    () => 1,        // starting value: 1
    each _ < 10,    // as long as the value is smaller than 10
    each _ + 1      // increment each value by 1 )
```

So what happened here?

- () => 1: The function starts with an initial value of 1, supplied as a zero-parameter function.
- each _ < 10: The function evaluates this condition for each value it generates, including the initial value. Once the condition fails, the function stops generating new list values. In our example, the condition ensures that the list will stop growing once a value reaches 9.
- each _ + 1: This is the rule for creating each subsequent value. We instructed the function to increment each value by *1*.

The operation of List.Generate can be compared to a traditional while loop found in many programming languages. The similarity lies in how both structures manage iteration and condition checking. Here's how a while loop might look, mirroring the logic of List.Generate:

```
y = 1
while (y < 10)
   {
     y = y + 1;
   }
```

In this while loop:

- The loop starts with y set to 1, similar to the initial value in List.Generate.
- It continues as long as y is less than 10, paralleling the condition check in List.Generate.
- The value of y increases by 1 in each iteration, like the increment step in List.Generate.

Both List.Generate and the while loop begin with an initial value, compute the next value in the sequence, check this new value against a condition, and decide whether to continue the process or stop. This comparison shows how List.Generate operates in a recursive-like manner, tracking the last generated value, using it as input for the next calculation, and determining whether to include it in the list or halt based on a specified condition.

This earlier example made use of the three mandatory arguments. They provide the input logic to create the main list. There is, however, an optional fourth argument in List.Generate: the selector, which allows you to transform the underlying list. Let's see how easily this works with another example.

Suppose you want to create a list with 12 sentences, one for each month of the year. In it, you want to return a sentence that says: January 1, 2024 is on a Monday. To achieve that, we would have to perform the following steps:

- Use List.Generate to create a list of all dates within a year that are at the start of the month.
- Use the selector to transform these dates into the right format.

To create a list containing all start-of-month values in 2024, you can use the statement in *Figure 13.13.*

	List
1	*01/01/2024*
2	*01/02/2024*
3	*01/03/2024*
4	*01/04/2024*
5	*01/05/2024*
6	*01/06/2024*
7	*01/07/2024*
8	*01/08/2024*
9	*01/09/2024*
10	*01/10/2024*
11	*01/11/2024*
12	*01/12/2024*

```
= List.Generate(
    () => #date( 2024,1,1 ),      // starting value
    each _ < #date( 2025,1,1 ), // only for 2024
    each Date.AddMonths( _, 1)  // increment by month
)
```

Explanation:

- **Generates a sequence of dates**
- **Beginning on January 1, 2024**
- **Increasing by one month at a time**
- **Up to December 1, 2024**

Figure 13.13: Create a sequence of dates using List.Generate

This logic instructs the function to start on January 1, 2024. Then, as long as the date is before January 1, 2025, it will increment each value by 1 month.

To transform the list into the desired format, you could use a function like List.Transform. However, it is even more convenient to use the selector argument of List.Generate to transform your list. The selector argument applies a function on the list generated by the first three arguments of List.Generate. That allows you to keep your logic within the same function.

Check this out:

```
List.Generate(
    () => #date( 2024,1,1 ),     // starting value
    each _ < #date( 2025,1,1 ), // only for 2024
    each Date.AddMonths( _, 1), // increment by month
    each Date.ToText( _, "MMMM d, yyyy") & " is on a "
        & Date.ToText( _, "dddd") )
```

In this example, the selector argument does three things:

- It uses Date.ToText to format the underlying dates in the format MMMM d yyyy, which, for the first value, equals January 1, 2024.
- Concatenates the string "is on a" to the first value.
- Uses the Date.ToText function to add the day of the week value to the string.

This code gives us a list with the desired text values:

	List
1	January 1, 2024 is on a Monday
2	February 1, 2024 is on a Thursday
3	March 1, 2024 is on a Friday
4	April 1, 2024 is on a Monday
5	May 1, 2024 is on a Wednesday
6	June 1, 2024 is on a Saturday
7	July 1, 2024 is on a Monday
8	August 1, 2024 is on a Thursday
9	September 1, 2024 is on a Sunday
10	October 1, 2024 is on a Tuesday
11	November 1, 2024 is on a Friday
12	December 1, 2024 is on a Sunday

Figure 13.14: Output after applying the selector function

To reach this output, we were able to work with a relatively simple `List.Generate` statement. There are, however, situations where you need to incorporate multiple values to reach the desired outcome. To do that, we need variables, which we will cover next.

Handling variables using records

In more complex scenarios, you might need to keep track of multiple variables as you generate a list. In Power Query's `List.Generate` function, you can use records to manage this complexity. As you might remember from *Chapter 6*, a record is a collection of name-value pairs, making it convenient for tracking multiple variables simultaneously.

Consider a scenario where you want to produce a list of numbers from 1 to 10 and, in addition to the numbers themselves, you want to indicate whether each number is even. To achieve this, you must maintain two key variables during the list-generation process:

- The current number in the sequence.
- Whether or not that number is even.

Since these variables will change with each iteration, we can use records to store how values change. Let's look at an example.

Previously, we saw a basic example that generated a list of numbers from 1 to 10 without any added complexity, which looked as follows:

```
List.Generate(
    () => 1,        // starting value: 1
    each _ < 10,    // as long as the value is smaller than 10
    each _ + 1      // increments each value by 1
)
```

The initial code is effective for creating a basic list, but it's not equipped to manage more than one variable. To introduce the concept of records, let's modify the example to use a record with just one field:

```
List.Generate(
    () => [ num = 1 ],
    each [num] <= 10,
    each [ num = [num] + 1 ]
)
```

- **Initial Value:** We start with a record that contains one field named num, set to 1.
- **Condition:** The condition applies field selection to [num] to retrieve its value. It then verifies whether this value is less than or equal to 10.
- **Next:** In each iteration, the num field within the record is incremented by 1.

This operation returns a list of records:

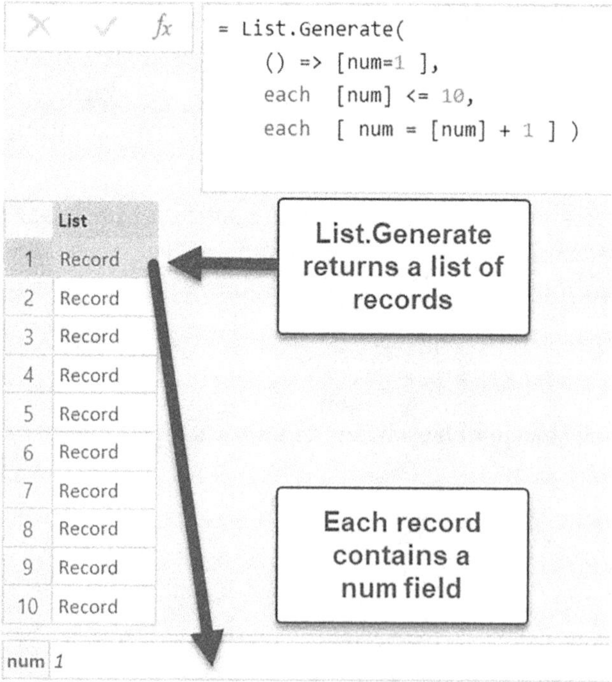

Figure 13.15: List.Generate returns a list of records

As the above figure indicates, looking into the details of individual records isn't always simple. There are two common ways to do this:

- Click the empty space next to each record to show what's inside.
- Use the selector argument to convert the record into a more easily inspected value.

However, we suggest a different, more effective approach. To make it easier to inspect the record's contents while you're working on your code, you can turn your list of records into a table. You can easily do this with the Table.FromRecords function. Simply store your List.Generate function within Table.FromRecords, and you're all set:

✕ ✓ *fx*	= Table.FromRecords(

```
= Table.FromRecords(
        List.Generate(
            () => [num=1 ],
            each  [num] <= 10,
            each  [ num = [num] + 1 ] ) )
```

▦▾	ABC 123 **num**	▾
1		1
2		2
3		3
4		4
5		5
6		6
7		7
8		8
9		9
10		10

Figure 13.16: Using Table.FromRecord to visualize the content of records

To delve deeper into using List.Generate, let's include another variable in the record to identify if the num value is even. This involves two key steps:

- Add a new field to the record defined in the initial argument.
- Specify how this field will change in each iteration by modifying the next function.

Here's what that looks like:

```
= Table.FromRecords(
    List.Generate(
        () => [num=1,                    IsEven = Number.IsEven( 1 ) ],
        each  [num] <= 10,
        each  [ num = [num] + 1, IsEven = Number.IsEven( [num] + 1 ) ] ) )
```

ABC 123 num		ABC 123 IsEven	
1	1	FALSE	
2	2	TRUE	
3	3	FALSE	
4	4	TRUE	
5	5	FALSE	
6	6	TRUE	
7	7	FALSE	
8	8	TRUE	
9	9	FALSE	
10	10	TRUE	

Figure 13.17: Using records to define multiple variables in List.Generate

In the updated example, the record now has an additional IsEven field. Notice that our condition remains the same, still focused on evaluating if the num field is less than or equal to 10. The additional field in our record doesn't impact this, as field selection can still isolate the value of the num column.

The advantage of using Table.FromRecords is its transparency; you can easily verify the outputs. After ensuring the results meet your expectations, you can remove the Table.FromRecords function from your code.

After verifying your code, you will often find yourself only needing a single field from the output record. Suppose you're interested in only extracting values from the IsEven field. You can then use the selector as follows:

```
List.Generate(
    () => [num=1, IsEven = Number.IsEven( 1 ) ],
    each [num] <= 10,
    each [ num = [num] + 1,
            IsEven = Number.IsEven( [num] + 1 ) ],
    each [IsEven]
)
```

List.Generate alternatives

While this example is valid, it's worth noting that this scenario could have been addressed more simply using List.Transform:

```
List.Transform(
    {1..10},
    each Number.IsEven( _ )
)
```

The List.Transform function takes a list as input and iterates over each item in the list by applying the function in the second argument. This approach not only simplifies the code but likely executes faster as well.

The takeaway here is to carefully consider your options before using List.Generate, which can be elaborate in its code and is relatively complex. An option like List.Transform is easier to both understand and maintain.

When deciding on which function to use and you know the number of iterations in advance, consider options such as:

- List.Transform: More suitable when each element in your list operates independently, without a need for any recursive logic.
- List.Accumulate: Useful for tasks that resemble recursive operations, as it carries the result from one iteration to the next until all iterations are completed.

What are useful List.Generate scenarios

There are a lot of use cases List.Generate can solve, yet you will often find that you can achieve the same outcomes using either List.Accumulate or List.Generate. Some scenarios where List.Generate is useful are as follows:

- **Pagination:** When dealing with APIs that return paginated results, List.Generate can iterate through each page to compile a complete dataset. Only when there are no more pages does it stop iterating.
- **Date Ranges:** When you want to create a list of dates that fall between two specific dates.
- **Custom Sequences:** When you're not limited to numbers or dates, List.Generate can churn out lists that follow complex custom logic, such as a running total, Fibonacci sequence, or prime numbers.
- **Text Manipulation:** Similar to the *multiple spaces between words* problem that we will solve with recursion later this chapter, you can use List.Generate to create a list of each modified text string until your condition is met.

Let's look at a few practical examples that use List.Generate to create the right outcome.

Looping through API data using List.Generate

The `List.Generate` function sets itself apart from `List.Accumulate` by using a condition to keep generating values. This allows the function to keep on generating new values until a condition is no longer met. This capability is invaluable when you're working with APIs, which is what we will look at right now.

So, what is an API? *API* stands for **application programming interface**. It's essentially a set of rules and protocols for fetching data from an application. For instance, let's say we're using an API from a library database to collect all the books an author has written. One challenge is that we may not know how much data will be returned. This is where the `condition` argument of `List.Generate` comes in handy. You can set it up so it keeps running until there is no more data to fetch.

Understanding the Open Library API

We'll use the Open Library API for our example. Open Library serves as a catalog of nearly every book ever published. Not only does the website have web pages you can browse but it also offers an API to pull data directly.

Before we get started, it's essential to understand how this API works. Visit Open Library's API documentation at the following link to learn more: `https://openlibrary.org/developers/api`.

This online manual provides instructions for how to interact with the API. For our exercise, we'll focus on gathering a complete list of works by the author Stephen King. To do that, we need to know how to work with the **Authors API**.

You can read more about it by navigating to this link: `https://openlibrary.org/dev/docs/api/authors`.

This page provides the exact format you need to use when sending a request to Open Library's database. If you scroll down to the *Works by an Author* section of that page, you'll find specific requests you can make to the API:

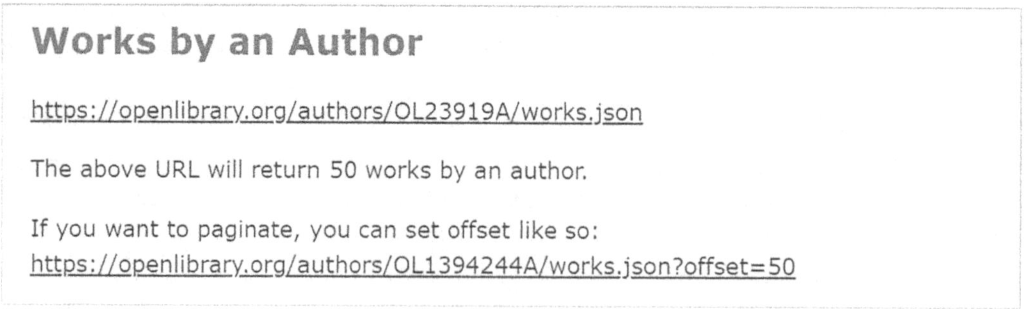

Works by an Author

https://openlibrary.org/authors/OL23919A/works.json

The above URL will return 50 works by an author.

If you want to paginate, you can set offset like so:
https://openlibrary.org/authors/OL1394244A/works.json?offset=50

Figure 13.18: Instructions for the API call

Here are some things you need to know about API calls:

- **URL Format for API Call**: An API call to fetch an author's works would look like this: `https://openlibrary.org/authors/OL23919A/works.json`.

- **Author Identifier Key:** To retrieve data for a particular author, you will need to specify their identifier key. For example, the identifier for the author in the URL above is `OL23919A`.
- **Data per API Call:** Each API call retrieves up to 50 works by the author.
- **Offsetting Records:** You can specify an offset in the URL to choose which set of 50 records you want to retrieve.

Retrieving the author identifier key

To find the correct URL for the works of Stephen King, we can navigate to `https://openlibrary.org/` and enter his name in the *search box*. In the search results, click on his *name* to navigate to the author page. You will end up at:

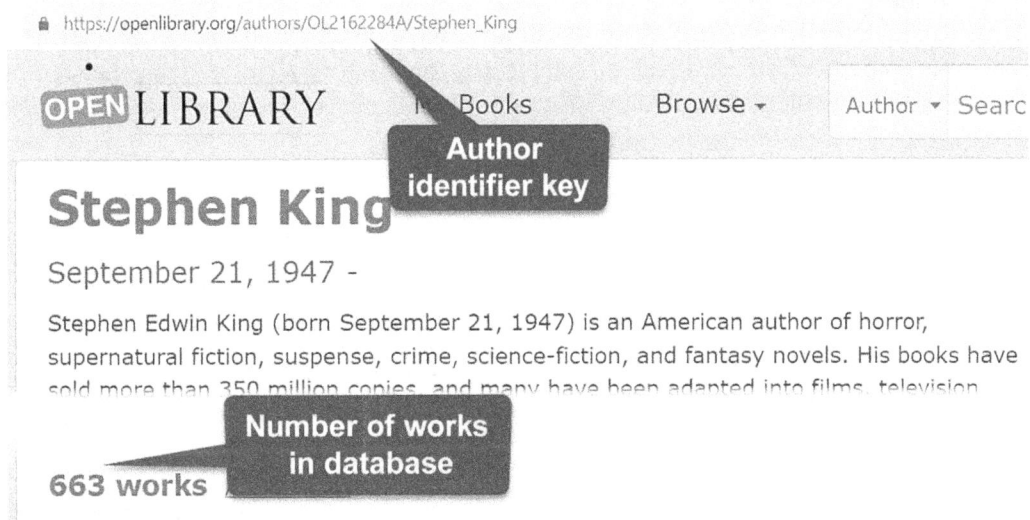

Figure 13.19: Author page for Stephen King at openlibrary.org

At the time of this writing, Open Library lists *663* works by Stephen King. The URL of his author page contains his identifier: `OL2162284A`. Armed with this information, we can now start writing our API call.

Validating the API call

Before diving into more complex logic, we should first ensure the API call is both valid and returns data. If you take the sample URL provided in the documentation and include *Stephen King's key identifier*, you get this URL: `https://openlibrary.org/authors/OL2162284A/works.json`. Although you could test it by pasting it into a web browser, we'll validate it within Power Query. To do that:

1. Open **Power Query.**
2. Click on **New Source**, and then select **Web.**
3. In the pop-up box that appears, paste the URL and click **OK:**

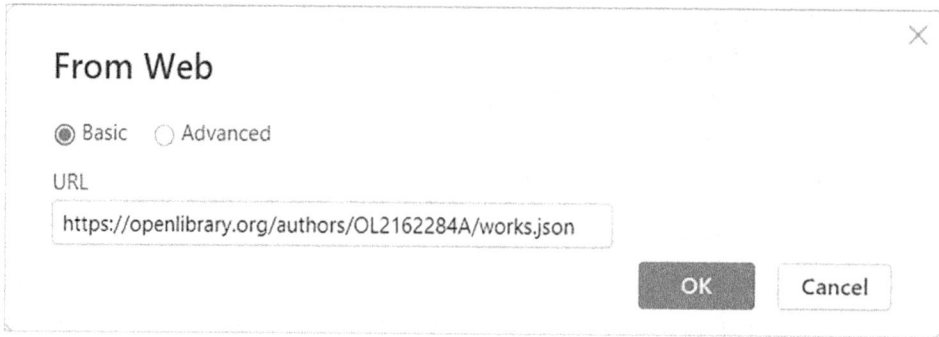

Figure 13.20: Making an API call using the web functionality

This action imports the data returned by the API. Power Query may also auto-generate additional steps, such as expanding records or listing columns. If that happens, remove all these auto-generated steps and keep only the one called Source. This returns a record containing nested values, looking as follows:

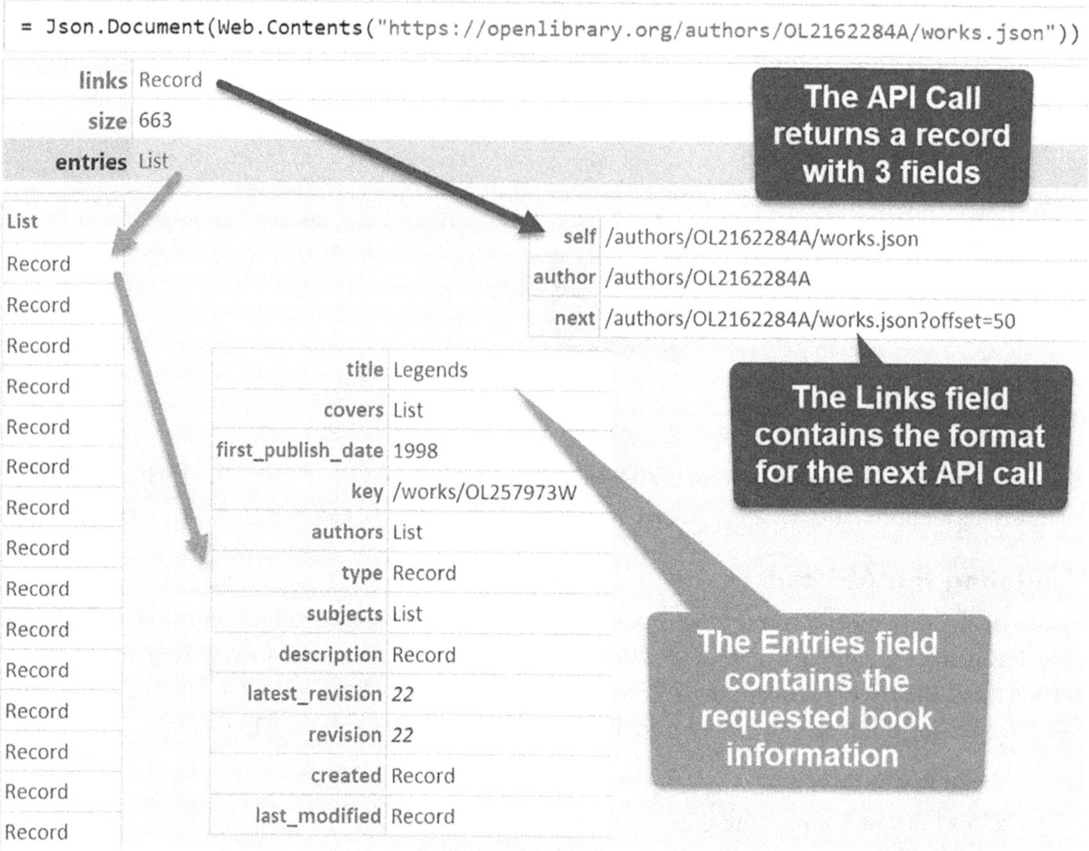

Figure 13.21: API call results for the Authors API

Examining API call results

When you select the **Source** step, you'll see that the API call returns a record with three fields:

- **links**: This contains a record with link details, including the author identifier and URLs for the current and next API calls.
- **size**: This tells you the number of records available for the author.
- **entries**: This list contains the actual information you're looking to retrieve, like book titles.

Understanding these fields helps you decide how to approach pagination.

Handling data limitations

It's important to note how the API communicates the end of the available data. When there are no more records to retrieve, the **next** URL will be missing from the `links` field. Also, if you manually execute an API call that skips to an offset without data, the `entries` field will return as empty.

We can test this by either looking for the latest API call with data or providing an arbitrary number as an offset. For example, if you attempt an API call that aims to skip 999 records and fetch the next 50, if no such records exist, the `entries` list will come back empty:

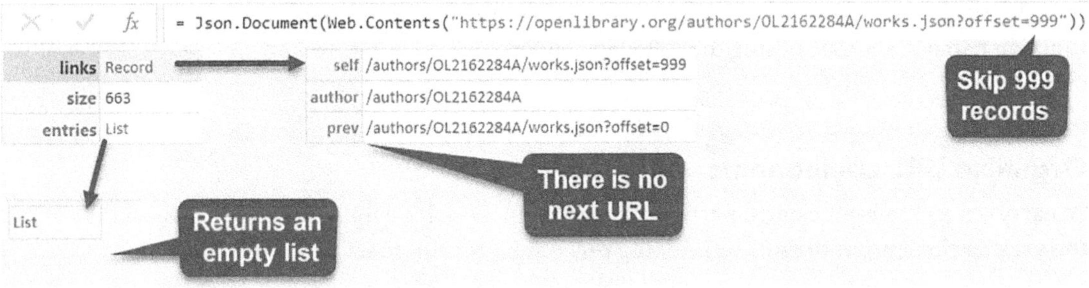

Figure 13.22: API call that returns an empty list and misses the "next" URL

Strategies for retrieving data

Based on these fields, there are different strategies for retrieving all records from the API. Here are some possible strategies based on the fields returned:

- Use `List.Generate` to build a function that uses the **next** URL in the **links** record for each subsequent API call. Stop when the API no longer returns a **next** URL.
- Use `List.Generate` to check for entries in the **entries** list. Continue making API calls as long as this list has data.
- Calculate the total number of pages required for all records, considering the limit of 50 items per API call and the number of records in the database (**size**). Then, create a function that iterates through these pages using calculated offsets.

For the purposes of this tutorial, we will focus on the first two strategies involving `List.Generate`.

Components for a List.Generate statement

To use the List.Generate function for pagination, you need to:

1. Create a function to interact with the API.
2. Organize URL components.
3. Define the logic for iterating through API responses.

Create a function to interact with the API

For cleaner code, it's helpful to first define a function that will call the API. When you initially selected **New Source**, chose **Web**, and then input the API URL in Power Query, it generated the following code:

```
Json.Document(
  Web.Contents(
    "https://openlibrary.org/authors/OL2162284A/works.json"
  )
)
```

To make our List.Generate function easier to manage, we can turn this code into a standalone function. This enables us to simply feed the API URL into the function when needed. To do so, create a function named fxGetData using the following code:

```
( myURL as text ) => Json.Document(Web.Contents( myURL) )
```

Organize URL components

To carry out API calls efficiently, particularly for pagination, it's helpful to neatly categorize and save the various elements of the API URL. Doing this prepares your query for future API calls.

You'll notice that the first API call uses the full URL:

```
"https://openlibrary.org/authors/OL2162284A/works.json"
```

Compare this with the next parameter you get for pagination:

```
"/authors/OL2162284A/works.json"
```

The next parameter is incomplete. It misses the front portion (https://openlibrary.org), which is essential to form a functional URL.

Dividing the URL into segments

To make our pagination task simpler, we'll divide the complete API URL into two segments:

- BaseURL: The constant beginning, https://openlibrary.org, which remains constant between calls.
- OffsetSuffix: The variable tail of the URL that adjusts according to the specific data being retrieved, like /authors/OL2162284A/works.json for the first call.

The benefit of a modular URL approach

Breaking the URL into these parts provides flexibility. Use BaseURL for the initial API call, and pair it with the OffsetSuffix specific to that call. For subsequent API calls, combine BaseURL with the next fragment received for pagination.

With this approach in mind, here's how you can prepare your query with the different URL components:

```
let
  fxGetData =
    ( myURL as text ) => Json.Document(Web.Contents( myURL ) ),
  BaseURL = "https://openlibrary.org/",
  OffsetSuffix = "authors/OL2162284A/works.json"
in
  OffsetSuffix
```

This approach offers a clean and organized way to manage API calls, making it easier to construct URLs for both the initial and subsequent calls.

Having broken down and organized the URL components, we're now ready to move on to preparing a structured pagination statement.

List.Generate statement using an offset URL

Now that we have organized our URL components into BaseURL and OffsetSuffix, we can use them to build a robust List.Generate statement. This statement will handle our API calls in a loop, making multiple requests until there is no more data available for the specific author. The List.Generate function we need looks like this:

```
1   List.Generate(
2       () =>
3         [
4           Request = fxGetData( BaseURL & OffsetSuffix ),          Initial
5           HasNext = true
6         ],
7       each [HasNext],                                             Condition
8       each
9         [
10          Request = fxGetData( BaseURL & [Request][links][next] ),  Next
11          HasNext = Record.HasFields( [Request][links], "next")
12        ],
13      each [Request]                                             Selector
14  )
```

Figure 13.23: Statement for looping through an API using an offset URL

The function consists of four main arguments: Initial value, Condition, Next argument, and Selector.

Initial value

The initial value is a record that consists of two fields:

- Request Field: The Request field makes the first API call. It combines BaseURL and AuthorSuffix to form the initial API URL. For example, the URL might look like this: https://openlibrary. org/authors/OL2162284A/works.json

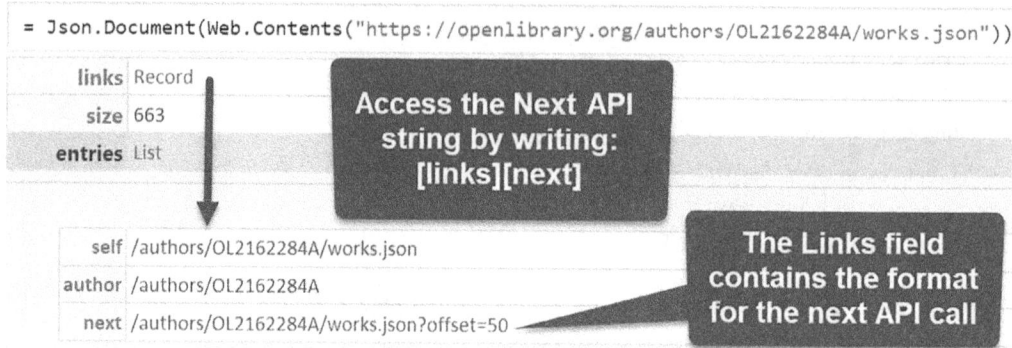

```
= Json.Document(Web.Contents("https://openlibrary.org/authors/OL2162284A/works.json"))
```

links	Record
size	663
entries	List

Access the Next API string by writing: [links][next]

self	/authors/OL2162284A/works.json
author	/authors/OL2162284A
next	/authors/OL2162284A/works.json?offset=50

The Links field contains the format for the next API call

Figure 13.24: The API URL

- HasNext Field: The HasNext field sets the initial condition for pagination to true. This is because a valid API URL will always return some records. If no records are returned, it usually means the author doesn't exist in the database.

Condition

Here, we simply check the HasNext field to decide if we need to make another API call. If HasNext is true, the function will make another request.

Next argument

The next argument prepares the function for the next API call. It consists of two fields:

- Updating Request: This field forms the URL for the next API call. It takes BaseURL and appends the next link from the last API call.
- Updating HasNext: This checks if the last API call had a next link. This is captured in

```
[ Request = fxGetData( BaseURL & [Request][links][next] ) ]
```

If it has a next url, this returns true. If not, it returns false, ending the loop. The preceding code drills down into multiple records by using the field selection operation three times. To recap how this works, refer to *Chapter 6, Structured Values*.

Selector

The last part of the function is the Selector. This specifies what the function should return. In this case, it will return only the Request field because that's where the relevant API data is stored. If we omit this argument, we will get a list of records as a result.

List.Generate statement testing for empty API

The approach we took above made use of the next component for the URL that specifies an offset. That, however, isn't the only approach we could take. Alternatively, we can test whether the API call contains data.

We can incorporate that logic in the following way:

```
1   List.Generate(
2     () =>
3       [
4         Counter = 0,                                              Initial
5         Request = fxGetData( 0 )
6       ],
7     each not List.IsEmpty( [Request][entries] ),     Condition
8     each
9       [
10        Counter = [Counter] + 50,                            Next
11        Request = fxGetData( [Counter] + 50 ) ],
12    each [Request]                                              Selector
13  )
```

Figure 13.25: Statement for looping through an API using a manual offset

Initial value

The function starts with an initial record that has two fields:

- Counter: This field starts at zero and will be incremented by 50 for each subsequent API call. This serves as the offset for the API request URL.
- Request: This field contains the data returned by the API call. It uses the fxGetData function to fetch data starting at the zero offset.

Condition

The condition argument decides when to stop further API calls. It focuses on the Request field, which holds a list of retrieved API values. The function continues if this list isn't empty, which we check using:

```
each not List.IsEmpty( [Request][entries] )
```

If the list is empty, the loop stops, indicating that all data has been collected.

Next argument

This part updates the record for the next iteration:

- Counter: Increments the counter by 50, which will serve as the offset for the next API call.
- Request: Retrieves the next set of data based on the new offset.

Selector

The selector each [Request] specifies what the function will return. We are only interested in the Request field because it contains the API data we need.

Compared to the approach where we used the next URL component, the offset approach simplifies things. There's no need to track whether a next link exists or not. All we have to worry about is whether there are more entries to retrieve, which we easily check with List.IsEmpty.

Turning records into desired output

The output of both List.Generate functions is a list of records:

	List
1	Record
2	Record
3	Record
	Record
13	Record
14	Record

Figure 13.26: List of records as output of List.Generate

Suppose we want to return a list of book titles and their release date. We will have to delve deeper into the record values to retrieve that information. When you drill into the different lists and records from the API call, you can find the following information:

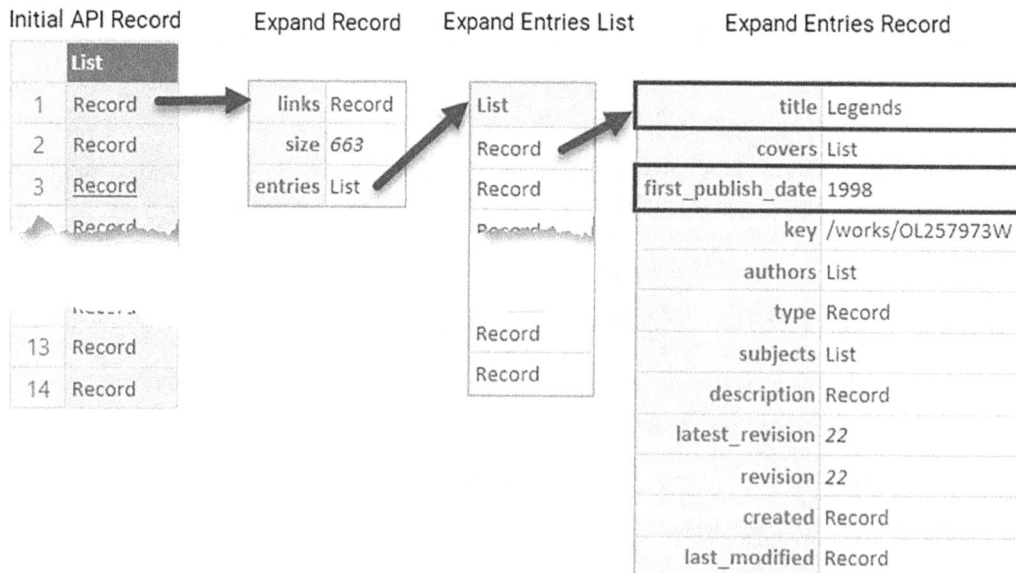

Figure 13.27: Objects returned by API call

Having a list of records is not the desired output format we'd like. Instead, it would make more sense to see the actual information within the records. That means we should transform the list of records. From the current setup, the easiest way to return the desired information in a readable format is:

1. Go to the **Transform** tab and select **To Table**.
2. Click on the two opposite arrows in Column1's column header and expand the **entries** field.
3. Click the two opposite arrows in the header of the entries column and select **Expand to New Rows**
4. Repeat the previous action and, this time, select the fields **title** and **first_publish_date**.

You will end up with the following table:

	ABC 123 title		ABC 123 first_publish_date	
1	Legends		1998	
	The World's Best Fantasy Horror Ninth Ann Collection		null	
20	The Several hall of Fam		null	
21	The Living Dead		2008	
22	The Science Fiction Weight-Loss Book		null	
23	Treasury of Great Short Stories		null	
24	The Dark Descent		November 8, 1990	
25	Scary!		August 27, 1998	

2 COLUMNS, 663 ROWS   Column profiling based on top 1000 rows

Figure 13.28: A table from the API with all works from Stephen King

The output of this operation is a table with the columns `title` and `first_publish_date`. This table is easy to read, and you can incorporate it into your dataset in an easy way. That rounds up the first illustrations of `List.Generate`. As you've seen, setting up an API connection can feel complex. It requires you to understand how to access different objects in M and learn how to loop through them. However, once you get comfortable with this, it's a very powerful technique for your toolkit.

Up next, we have another common use case that makes use of `List.Generate`; we'll look at creating a running total.

Creating an efficient running total

A common scenario for data analysts is creating a running total. While it's easier and often makes more sense to create it in DAX, there are scenarios where having your running total in Power Query makes sense.

A running total is the cumulative sum of a series of values. An example where you see a running total used is in financial reporting. Actual sales are often compared to budget sales using year-to-date calculations.

Power Query lacks a dedicated function for running totals. Instead, people often resort to using functions like `List.Range` or `List.FirstN`. However, these methods can be inefficient. They calculate the total by summing an ever-expanding range of numbers, meaning the same number is included in a sum operation again and again. This can slow down the calculation.

A more efficient approach is to use functions with recursive-like capabilities, such as `List.Generate` or `List.Accumulate`. These functions perform a calculation, save the result in a list, and then proceed to the next number. Each new number is added to the previously stored total. This way, the function doesn't have to recalculate the entire range each time, with significant performance gains as a result.

Suppose you have a table with sales throughout the year, as shown in the following image:

	ABC Period	123 Sales
1	Jan 2024	900
2	Feb 2024	850
3	Mar 2024	925
4	Apr 2024	875
5	May 2024	910
6	Jun 2024	725
7	Jul 2024	750
8	Aug 2024	740
9	Sep 2024	900
10	Oct 2024	925

Figure 13.29: Sales data

To follow along, start by opening the accompanying exercise file of this chapter.

If you're looking to add a column that displays year-to-date sales, using `List.Generate` can be a solution. However, generating a list of running total values is just part of the job. You also need to integrate these values into your existing table. Here's how to break down the task:

1. Obtain the list of values that will be used to calculate the running total.
2. Compute running total values using `List.Generate`.
3. Split the existing table into separate lists, each representing a column.
4. Restore the table by combining all lists.

Let's see how this works in practice.

Obtain the list of values

To get started, we have the data from the above figure stored in a step named `Source`. We'll store the values we want to use for the `List.Generate` formula in a separate step. To do that, create a new step by clicking the **fx** symbol next to the formula bar. This creates a new step that references `Source`. Rename this step `RTValues`.

Next, we reference the Sales column using field selection. The formula to do that is:

```
Source[Sales]
```

For our running total, we will reference this list repeatedly. To ensure good performance, it's a good idea to buffer the list of values into memory using List.Buffer. That gives us:

```
List.Buffer( Source[Sales] )
```

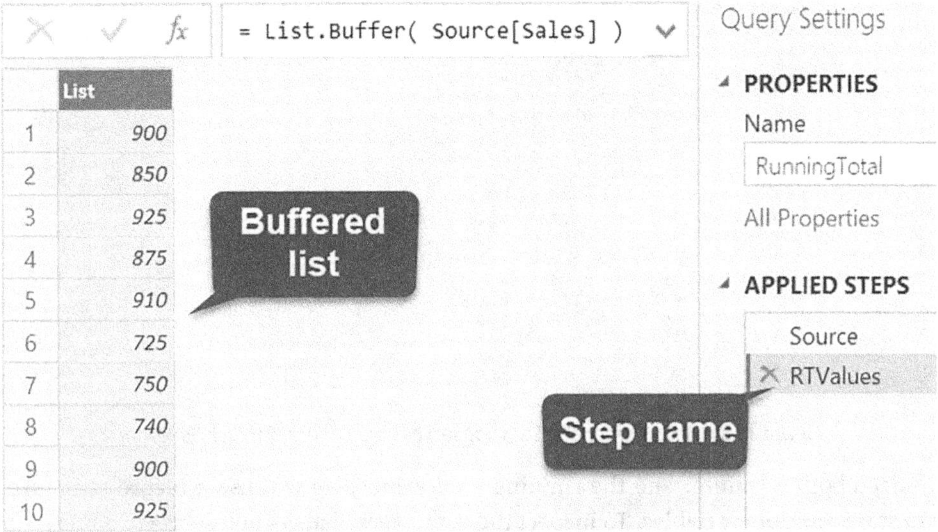

Figure 13.30: List of values for running total

That gives us a list of values that are the base for our running total.

Compute running total values with List.Generate

Now it's time to create a List.Generate expression that returns the running total of these values. Earlier in this chapter, you learned that List.Generate uses a condition to evaluate when to stop computing values. After we end up in the situation illustrated in the above image, here's what you can do:

- Create a new step in the **Applied Steps** pane that references the RTValues step.
- Build the List.Generate formula that uses RTValues for the running total.

Now, let's construct the List.Generate function. It uses the RTValues list to count the items in the running total. We'll incorporate a counter in List.Generate. This counter increases with each step. Computing the running total values stops when the counter equals the list's total number of values.

To set up this counter, you can write:

```
List.Generate(
    () => 0,
    each _ < List.Count ( RTValues ),
    each _ + 1
)
```

This results in a list with the numbers 0 to 9:

```
= List.Generate(
      () => 0,
      each _ < List.Count ( RTValues ),
      each _ + 1 )
```

List	
1	0
2	1
3	2
4	3
5	4
6	5
7	6
8	7
9	8
10	9

Figure 13.31: An incrementing list that serves as a counter for List.Generate

Since we need both a counter and the running total values, we will use a record structure that allows us to store multiple variables. To inspect the data, we will also enclose the formula with Table. FromRecords. Equivalent code that uses records looks as follows:

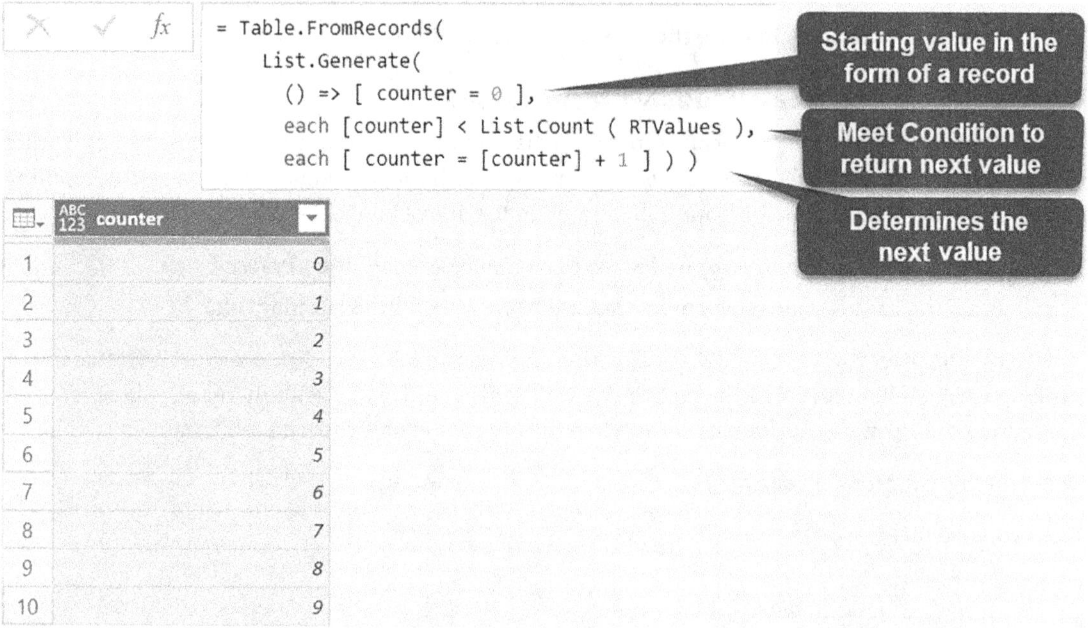

```
= Table.FromRecords(
      List.Generate(
            () => [ counter = 0 ],
            each [counter] < List.Count ( RTValues ),
            each [ counter = [counter] + 1 ] ) )
```

Starting value in the form of a record

Meet Condition to return next value

Determines the next value

ABC 123 counter	
1	0
2	1
3	2
4	3
5	4
6	5
7	6
8	7
9	8
10	9

Figure 13.32: List.Generate function using a record for variables

Notice that this new expression would not work with only referencing the value by providing the underscore. This was only possible in the initial version because there was a single value for each iteration. Since we now want to pick a value from a record, we should also specify which field we are referring to.

To calculate the running total, you need to introduce an additional variable. This variable will exist both in the initial record and in the function responsible for updating values. Here's the modified code:

```
Table.FromRecords(
  List.Generate(
    () => [ counter = 0,
            RT      = RTValues{0} ],
    each [counter] < List.Count ( RTValues ),
    each [ counter = [counter] + 1,
           RT      = [RT] + RTValues{[counter] + 1} ]

  )
)
```

In this code:

- A new field called RT has been added to the initial record. The value RTValues{0} sets the initial running total using the first element from the RTValues list.
- In the third argument, an extra field for the running total (RT) is also included. This calculates the running total by adding the next value to the existing sum.

To break down the logic:

- counter is a variable that increments by one each time the function iterates.
- RT represents the running total.

By using the counter, you can retrieve the corresponding element from the RTValues list to update the running total. For instance, when counter is 0, the code fetches RTValues{0}; when it's 1, it fetches RTValues{1}, and so on. This way, you can compute the running total efficiently. This is the result of the preceding code:

	counter	RT
1	0	900
2	1	1750
3	2	2675
4	3	3550
5	4	4460
6	5	5185
7	6	5935
8	7	6675
9	8	7575
10	9	8500

Figure 13.33: Create a running total using List.Generate

The output of *Figure 13.33* is exactly what we are looking for. There are two remaining changes to make:

1. The code we used still uses `Table.FromRecords` to visualize the contents of each record. We can now remove it since our output is correct.

2. After performing *step 1*, we are left with a list of records. We only need the running total field from the record instead of returning the records themselves. We can use the selector to select the field.

The following code gives us a list with only the running total:

```
List.Generate(
        () => [ counter = 0, RT = RTValues{0} ],
        each [counter] < List.Count ( RTValues ),
        each [ counter = [counter] + 1,
               RT      = [RT] + RTValues{[counter] + 1} ],
        each [RT]
)
```

Next, we need to find a way to attach the running total values to our list. An effective way to do that is to split the original table into lists, where each list represents a column. We then combine these lists with the running total lists and restore the table.

Split the existing table into separate lists

The first step is to transform the table shown in *Figure 13.34* into individual lists, with each list representing a column. To accomplish this, create a new step called `TableColumns` and apply the `Table.ToColumns` function on the `Source` step:

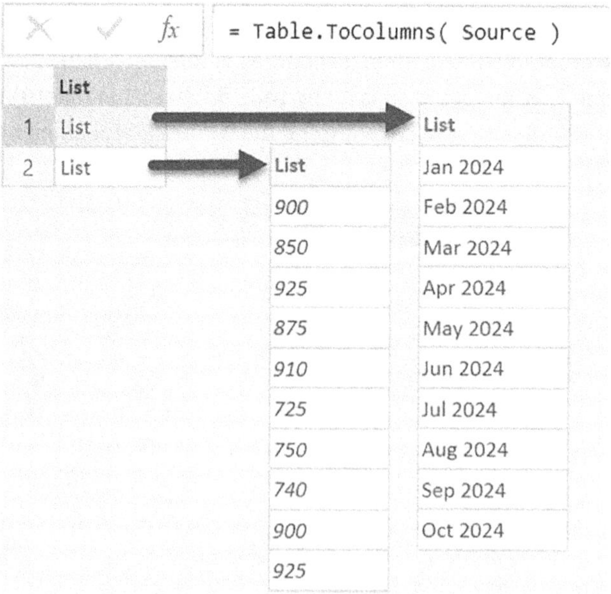

Figure 13.34: Sales table transformed into a list with two column value lists

Restore the table by combining all lists

The next step is to reassemble the table by merging all the separate lists back together. A good candidate for this operation is the `Table.FromColumns` function.

The `Table.FromColumns` function accepts two arguments to create a table:

- `Lists`: A list that includes other lists, each containing the values for a specific column.
- `Columns`: A list that includes the names of the columns.

To combine the column values into a single nested list, you can use the following expression:

```
TableColumns & { RunningTotal }
```

This merges our separate lists of column values into one unified list:

	List
1	List
2	List
3	List

Figure 13.35: Lists of column values

To create a table using this combined list, you can use the `Table.FromColumns` function like this:

```
Table.FromColumns( TableColumns & { RunningTotal } )
```

	ABC Column1	123 Column2	ABC 123 Column3
1	Jan 2024	900	900
2	Feb 2024	850	1750
3	Mar 2024	925	2675
4	Apr 2024	875	3550
5	May 2024	910	4460
6	Jun 2024	725	5185
7	Jul 2024	750	5935
8	Aug 2024	740	6675
9	Sep 2024	900	7575
10	Oct 2024	925	8500

Figure 13.36: Table with missing column names and types

This expression will return a table that includes all the original columns, along with the new `RunningTotal` column.

The table is almost complete, but it lacks two crucial elements:

- A data type for the `RunningTotal` column.
- Proper column names.

You have two options to set the data type for the `RunningTotal` column. The first is to add a separate step that specifies the column types. The second option is to directly assign a data type to the `RunningTotal` column using the `Value.ReplaceType` function. Here's how to do it:

```
Value.ReplaceType( RunningTotal, type {Int64.Type} )
```

The above data type is only valid for whole numbers. If your values have decimals, you can replace `{Int64.Type}` with `{number}`.

To specify the column names when using the `Table.FromColumns` function, you can include them as a list in the second argument. To retrieve the column names from the original table, you can use `Table.ColumnNames`. Additionally, you need to add `RunningTotal` as a new column name. The expression below creates our list of column names:

```
Table.ColumnNames( Source ) & {"Running Total"}
```

You can combine these steps into one expression and what you get is:

```
Table.FromColumns(
   TableColumns &
     {Value.ReplaceType( RunningTotal, type { Int64.Type } )},
   Table.ColumnNames( Source ) & {"Running Total"} )
```

This single statement will create a table with the `Running Total` column, properly typed and named, along with the original columns:

	ABC Period	123 Sales	123 Running Total
1	Jan 2024	900	900
2	Feb 2024	850	1750
3	Mar 2024	925	2675
4	Apr 2024	875	3550
5	May 2024	910	4460
6	Jun 2024	725	5185
7	Jul 2024	750	5935
8	Aug 2024	740	6675
9	Sep 2024	900	7575
10	Oct 2024	925	8500

Figure 13.37: Output table including the Running Total column

The running total example is a great illustration of how you can iteratively apply logic until a condition fails. However, it's good to remember that we could have solved this same scenario using List.Accumulate. Both approaches work effectively. It's up to you to decide which function you prefer.

So far, we have looked at iterators like List.Transform and List.Accumulate. Both are powerful iterators that work for a fixed number of iterations. This chapter also introduced List.Generate, which allows you to perform an operation until a specified condition is no longer met. The remaining topic for this chapter is recursion. You'll learn what it is and how you can best use it.

Recursion

Recursion is a programming term that sounds more complex than it really is. Simply put, recursion happens when a function calls itself within its own definition. Think of it as a loop, but instead of using a typical for or while loop, the function uses itself to perform an operation multiple times.

Recursion is helpful for addressing problems where you need to repeat a task but the number of repetitions isn't known beforehand. This operation requires an ending condition so that the iterations stop when they reach a specific condition, preventing infinite repetitions.

The concept of recursion has also been compared to the concept of Russian dolls. Imagine opening a Russian doll to find another one inside, and another inside that, and so on. This process continues until you reach the smallest doll that can't be opened further. Each step is like a function calling itself, eventually reaching a point where it can no longer do so.

Why is recursion important?

While the M language already offers a rich set of built-in functions, some operations need extra flexibility and a recursive element. For example, you might have hierarchical data—like an organizational chart—that you need to unpack. Or, you may have nested objects that you want to flatten.

Admittedly, for most situations that require a recursive element, we recommend making use of List.Generate. It performs better than traditional recursion and is easier to troubleshoot. However, the book wouldn't be complete without delving into traditional recursion.

So, when do we find recursion acceptable? You may encounter a situation where a recursive function is easier to write and the number of iterations is relatively low. Since performance won't be an issue here, using recursion is perfectly fine. In all other situations, we stick to our recommendation of, using List.Generate instead.

Recursion versus iteration: a brief comparison

Before diving deeper, it's worth distinguishing recursion from its closely related counterpart: iteration. Both recursion and iteration perform repetitive tasks, but they do so in fundamentally different ways.

In iteration, a set of instructions (the loop) is executed repeatedly until it reaches the end of the input. Suppose you have a list of values to transform. The List.Transform function can apply an operation on each item in the list, which is considered iteration. The length of the list is known beforehand, and the number of iterations is predictable.

Recursion, on the other hand, captures the repetitive task within the function itself. It repeatedly performs an expression that includes a condition until that condition is no longer met. This often results in cleaner, more elegant code, but at the expense of greater memory usage and usually slower performance.

So how does recursion work in practice?

Recursive functions

When writing recursive functions, the concept of scope is important. The concept of scope refers to the environment where a variable or function is accessible. Generally, scope helps you reference a variable defined in another step or another query. Yet, for a recursive function, we want to create a reference to the function itself.

With that in mind, let's introduce the @ symbol, known as the scoping operator or the inclusive-identifier-reference.

What is the @ scoping operator?

In the M language, the @ symbol is designed to resolve challenges when accessing variables. The @ allows a function to refer to itself or another variable within its own definition.

Variables in M are usually not part of the environment of the expression they are defined in. That means self-referencing is generally not possible. This is where the @ symbol comes in. It allows a variable to be part of its environment, thereby supporting recursive function calls.

Inclusive-identifier-reference

The @ is formally known as the inclusive-identifier-reference, a term that lends itself to the concept of scope in programming. The term consists of three words:

- **Inclusive:** The symbol @ includes the identifier (i.e., variable or function) within its own scope.
- **Identifier:** This is the variable or function you're trying to access.
- **Reference:** You're pointing to a particular identifier within the code.

The @ is the opposite of what is known as an exclusive identifier reference. Exclusive identifiers cannot be part of their own environment, causing errors if you attempt to self-reference.

Using recursive functions

Some challenges require you to repeatedly check a condition and perform an operation. In these situations, recursive functions show their value.

A typical subject that lends itself to recursion is the calculation of factorial numbers. A factorial number is the product of all positive integers less than or equal to a given positive integer.

To calculate the factorial of 5, represented as 5!, you multiply 5 x 4 x 3 x 2 x 1, resulting in 120. To write this in Power Query, you could write:

```
let
  Factorial =
    ( n ) =>
    if n <= 1
      then 1
      else n * @Factorial ( n - 1 ) // '@' is used here
  in
    Factorial ( 5 )
```

In this code, the @ symbol enables the Factorial function to call itself, making the function recursive. This self-calling is evident in the part that says @Factorial. When the if statement evaluates to false, the code multiplies the current number n by the number n minus 1. Then, the function starts over, this time using n-1 as its starting value.

The process continues until the if statement is true. At that point, the function stops running because there's no self-reference. If you omit the @ symbol and just use Factorial, Power Query will generate an error. This happens because the function can't recognize itself without the @.

We will now delve more deeply into how you can incorporate the @ operator in your code.

How to use the @ operator

Having seen the @ operator used in an example, you're probably wondering how to incorporate it into your Power Query M code. Here are four steps to incorporate the scope operator in your custom functions:

Step 1: Write your initial code

Start by writing your function in the usual manner, without the @ symbol. For example, if you're creating a Factorial function, your initial code might look like this:

```
Factorial =
  (n) => if n <= 1 then 1 else n * (n - 1)
```

This first step creates the function by taking an input value n and performing the operation once. The function checks whether n is one or less. If it's greater, it multiplies n by n - 1.

Before thinking of including recursion, it's always important to include an if condition. This condition serves as a safety measure to prevent the function from entering an infinite loop. Also, make sure to give your function a name, as you'll need it later for the recursive call.

Step 2: Identify the recursive call

Next, identify where your function should call itself. In our Factorial example, the recursive call involves n * (n - 1). In each iteration, the function multiplies the current value by itself -1.

Step 3: Add the @ operator

Now it's time to incorporate the @ symbol into your code. Recall that we named our function earlier. You'll use that name here.

Modify your function to include both the @ symbol and the function's name in the part where it calls itself. Your revised Factorial function should look like this:

```
Factorial =
    (n) => if n <= 1 then 1 else n * @Factorial(n - 1)
```

The function will keep calling itself as long as the if condition is false. When this happens, the code reaches the @Factorial part and then starts from the beginning using n-1 as input.

Step 4: Test your function

Execute your function to confirm it works as intended. Run it through various scenarios to ensure the @ operator performs the recursion as expected.

By following these four steps, you're prepared to use the @ operator in your custom functions. You'll not only know how to implement recursion but also safeguard it from endless loops. Ready for another example?

Removing consecutive spaces

Let's explore a real-world example to understand recursion better. Suppose you have a dataset with a column filled with sentences, but the spacing between words is inconsistent. Your goal is to tidy it up so that you never have more than one space between words.

For example, you might have a sentence like Hard " work   beats   luck", where the spaces between words vary. You can solve this by using a formula like Text.Replace:

```
Text.Replace( MyString, "  ", " " )
```

This replaces double spaces with a single space. Doing this once gives you "Hard   work   beats luck". Although improved, the first three words still have extra spaces—three and two, to be precise. You'll need to run this operation twice more to clean up the spacing fully.

However, since each sentence in your dataset may have varying numbers of spaces between words, you'll want to repeat this action as needed. To avoid excessive calculations, it's important to include a test condition that checks for remaining consecutive spaces in the string. Here's how you can do that:

```
let
  MyString = "Hard    work   beats   luck",
  Replace =  if Text.Contains( MyString, "  " )
             then Text.Replace( MyString, "  ", " " )
             else MyString
in
  Replace
```

This way, you only apply the Text.Replace function if the condition is met, saving computational resources.

Now we have both a replacement operation and a condition to identify consecutive spaces. The next step is to create a way to repeat this operation, and that's where recursion is useful. To implement recursion, we need to store our logic within a function. This is important because the @ symbol operates by repeatedly calling a function.

Here's how you turn the code into a function:

```
( MyString as text ) as text =>
  let
    Replace =
      if Text.Contains ( MyString, "  " )
        then Text.Replace ( MyString, "  ", " " )
        else MyString
  in
    Replace
```

In this function, we define a parameter named MyString that takes a text string as input. We then use this parameter within our function's logic.

The current version of our function can only replace a single double space in one go. To enable ongoing checks and replacements, we can incorporate recursion using the @ operator. Here's the improved function code:

```
let
  fxDeSpace = ( MyString as text ) as text =>
    let
      Replace =
        if Text.Contains ( MyString, "  " ) then
          @fxDeSpace ( Text.Replace ( MyString, "  ", " " ) )
        else
          MyString
    in
      Replace
in
  fxDeSpace
```

To arrive at this code, we performed the following steps:

- Assigned the name fxDeSpace to our function.
- Inside the function, we added a reference to its own name, prefixed by the @ operator (@ fxDeSpace).

The important detail here is wrapping `Text.Replace` with `@fxDeSpace`. What happens is, if the `Text.Contains` function confirms the presence of consecutive spaces, the function will replace the double with a single space and then call itself again from the beginning. This cycle continues until no more double spaces are found. At this point, the function stops calling itself.

Performance considerations using recursion

Recursion can be an elegant way to solve problems that have recursive structures, like generating factorials or reaching into hierarchical data. However, recursion isn't without downsides, especially when it comes to performance.

When you use recursion, each recursive call creates a new layer in the call stack—a temporary memory storage where your program keeps track of its tasks. If your function calls itself too many times, the stack can overflow, causing your query to fail.

When a stack overflow occurs, you'll encounter an error message that indicates the stack size has exceeded its limit. This happens when your recursive function doesn't have a proper exit condition, or the recursion depth is too high.

```
To prevent this, make sure to include logic in your recursive function to
ensure it will eventually terminate. Also, keep an eye on the recursion depth.
If you're getting the stack limit error, it's a sign you should consider
alternative approaches.
```

Recursion is often not our first choice to compute our calculations. There are more efficient methods often relating to `List.Generate` or `List.Accumulate`, which we covered earlier in this chapter.

Summary

In this chapter, we explored two important concepts: iteration and recursion. Beginning with iteration, we examined the role of the `List.Transform` and `List.Accumulate` functions. Both perform their tasks on a list with a fixed number of items, like a `for` loop. While `List.Transform` serves its purpose for straightforward operations, `List.Accumulate` is also helpful for scenarios requiring access to the result of earlier iterations.

We then delved into the `List.Generate` function, which allows you to dynamically create lists based on custom conditions and logic, similar to a `while` loop. The function has good performance, provides an easy way to debug its results, and is the preferred choice over traditional recursion in most use cases.

Lastly, we tackled the concept of `true` recursion, facilitated in M through the @ scoping operator. Although recursion comes with a cost in terms of memory and speed, you can consider using it for tasks involving a limited number of iterations and where writing a recursive function simplifies the code.

Throughout the chapter, we emphasized the importance of choosing the appropriate method—iteration or recursion—based on the specific requirements of your data transformation tasks. Keep your expression as simple as possible, but when required, don't be afraid to reach out to the complex techniques described in this chapter. They can significantly enhance your data manipulation capabilities in Power Query M.

Learn more on Discord

Join our community's Discord space for discussions with the author and other readers:

`https://discord.gg/vCSG5GBbyS`

14

Troublesome Data Patterns

Reshaping and preparing data for analysis is often a combination of art and science, blending theory and skills with creative problem-solving. There are a wide range of troublesome data patterns, from dealing with stacked data to multiline headers and beyond. Challenges are not limited to the structure of the data alone but often also include inconsistencies and other complexities that can arise from the unique nature of the data itself or specific business rules and requirements.

When we think about problem-solving, it's important to remember that there are many different approaches and techniques. In this book, we're not claiming to have all the answers or that these methods are best. Rather, we aim to offer a collection of ideas and spark your imagination to help you kick-start your problem-solving journey, making you confident in facing any troublesome data pattern that crosses your path.

The examples provided throughout this chapter are a starting point. As you progress and read through it, our hope is not only to combine theory with practical knowledge but also to inspire you to view problem-solving as a creative process because, ultimately, the best solution is the one you develop for your own unique data challenge.

There are countless scenarios that would fit well in this chapter; however, there are not enough pages to do them all justice. Therefore, we have opted to explore two examples in depth, and these topics are:

- Extracting fixed patterns
- Extracting and combining data

Given the recurring discussions on online forums, it's clear they reflect common challenges users face in the real-world.

We will turn our attention to pattern matching first, kicking things off by exploring aspects that could play a role in identifying and extracting meaningful patterns from data.

Pattern matching

Pattern matching is an essential skill often associated with regular expressions (or regex), which is important for identifying and manipulating specific patterns in textual data. Although the Power Query M language lacks direct support for regex, it provides a wealth of functions that can help address these types of requirements. In this section, we explore pattern matching within the constraints of Power Query, highlighting some key techniques and strategies for addressing these challenges.

Basics of pattern matching

Pattern matching is incredibly useful for finding and extracting specific character sequences from data. That process relies heavily on the use of text functions. The M language is equipped with various functions that operate on text values. These functions can facilitate certain aspects relevant to pattern matching. They offer a range of capabilities, from basic to more advanced string operations.

Here, we'll delve into various considerations and functions relevant to pattern matching. While this is by no means a complete or extensive list, it should give you a sense of the potential and versatility of M functions in handling pattern-matching scenarios.

Case sensitivity

In Power Query's M language, case sensitivity refers to the ability to distinguish between uppercase and lowercase letters as separate characters. Recognizing this aspect of M is crucial when handling textual data, as functions that involve comparing or replacing text are all impacted by that sensitivity when matching characters. However, there are text functions that can perform case-insensitive operations; meaning that when you compare two strings, the comparison will not consider the case of the letters. For example, Text would then be equal to text in a case-sensitive comparison. These functions are equipped with an optional comparer.

In situations where a function lacks a comparer, modifying the case of a text to achieve uniformity can be a good strategy. Using Text.Lower, Text.Upper, or Text.Proper to standardize the letter casing can circumvent that. To illustrate:

Text.Lower("Power Query") will return power query.

Text.Upper("Power Query") will return POWER QUERY.

Text.Proper("power query") will return Power Query.

These are simple methods to standardize text before further processing.

Contains versus exact match

When looking for Power Query in the string Power Query is awesome!, we can determine the second string contains the first but there is no exact match. Requirements for pattern matching can vary – sometimes you may need to confirm the presence of a substring, a contains-type scenario, while other times an exact match is essential. Functions such as Text.Start, Text.End, Text.Middle, and Text.Range can return a substring to match. They are also helpful in identifying a specific pattern.

While `Text.Contains` offers a straightforward method to check if a substring exists within a string, `Text.PositionOf` can be used to find the position of a substring within a string. If it returns a number greater than or equal to 0, the substring exists. If it returns -1, the substring is not present.

Allowed characters

Determining which characters are relevant to your pattern is crucial, like uppercase or lowercase letters, numerals, a selection of special characters, or a combination of all of them. The M language includes functions that can selectively keep or remove characters, such as `Text.Select` or `Text.Remove`, for example. To illustrate:

`Text.Select("Power Query", {"o", "e"})` will return oee.

`Text.Remove("Power Query", {"o", "e"})` will return Pwr Qury.

Handling one or more elements

Are you handling one thing, like a single word, or several things, like a string or sentence? If several, does that need to be split into smaller units? When dealing with more than one item, you will resort to list operations, like `List.Select`, `List.Transform`, and others. Returning a single value often involves `Text.Combine`. That function takes a list of text values and joins or concatenates them into a single string; optionally, including a separator between each list item.

Wildcards

Wildcards are symbols used to represent one or more characters in a text string. They are often used in search and pattern-matching operations. Although Power Query doesn't natively support wildcards, it does not mean wildcards cannot be mimicked in M. Standard library functions like `Text.StartsWith` or `Text.EndsWith`, for example, make it straightforward to find strings that start or end with certain text. However, other wildcard behaviors are often more intricate and require custom logic to replicate.

Now that we've introduced aspects of pattern matching, let's dive into examining some specific examples. We will demonstrate how pattern matching can be used in various contexts. Through these examples, including practical applications and nuances of pattern matching, we hope to enhance your ability to recognize and implement solid approaches to pattern matching in your own workflows.

Extracting fixed patterns

Extracting fixed patterns from a text string is a task that many users find challenging. This often involves extracting types of ID codes – like system IDs, SKUs, document numbers, tracking numbers, or billing codes – from larger strings of text. The challenge lies in the fact that no two scenarios are exactly alike. To help you navigate this topic we will explore several examples to tackle these types of requirements, ensuring you have the know-how to handle a wide range of fixed patterns successfully, such as prefixed codes or codes that follow a pattern, like four letters followed by five numbers and so on. Every example comes with its own dataset that you can use to follow along.

Example 1, prefixed

Let's take a look at a practical example. Our task is to extract specific codes. The codes we are interested in have a distinct pattern: each one begins with the letters DGPQ, followed by a sequence of five numerals. This means our codes will always start with DGPQ and that is followed by a string of numbers, such as DGPQ12345. It's important to note that all codes consistently follow this pattern and there will only ever be one code contained within a string.

Our approach involves identifying and extracting these codes from within a larger text string. We need to scan each text, recognize the DGPQ prefix, and extract that code:

```
let
    Source = Table.FromColumns(
        {{"The code DGPQ33446 is important for this task.",
        "Unique document identifier: DGPQ13295.",
        "Please use the code DGPQ36006 to access the system.",
        "For verification, enter DGPQ30881 on the website.",
        "The transaction ID DGPQ78388 must be noted.",
        "DGPQ10273 is the code for your appointment.",
        "Reference code DGPQ36144 is included in the report.",
        "To complete registration, use DGPQ90158 as your code.",
        "Package with tracking number DGPQ52287 has been shipped."}},
        type table [String=text]
    )
in
    Source
```

Let's break down the code for this sample dataset, focusing on each individual part:

1. `let`

   The `let` clause is the first part of a `let` expression, where the `in` clause is the last part. A `let` expression allows the creation of one or more variables that each have an expression assigned to it and are separated by commas.

2. `Source`

   This is a step or variable name in your query. It is followed by an equal sign and assigned an expression to store a value.

3. `Table.FromColumns`

   This function is used to create a table from a list.

   a. `{{"String1", "String2", "String3"}}`

      The first argument is a list that contains a column values list for each column to create. This example shows one list within the list.

b. `type table [String=text]`

An optional second argument, which has been assigned a *table type* that specifies a *column name* and ascribes a *column type* for each column in the table.

4. `in`

The final part of a `let` expression is the `in` clause. Whatever is specified after it will produce the outcome for that `let` expression – in this case, the value stored within the `Source` variable.

Follow along with these steps to add a **Code** column to the sample table. This process requires multiple functions. It is a common practice to nest these functions, working from the inside out. However, nesting a record expression allows you to easily review the results of all the intermediate steps, which is great for optimizing and troubleshooting code:

1. Navigate to **Add Column** and choose **Custom Column**.
2. Enter `Code` as the new column name.
3. `[ ]`

Initialize a record expression by entering `[ ]`, a set of square brackets. Inside a record, a comma-delimited list of field names and field values can be created.

4. `n = Text.PositionOf([String], "DGPQ", Occurrence.First)`

To pinpoint the position of the `DGPQ` prefix, the function `Text.PositionOf` can be used. If that returns a positional index number greater than or equal to `0`, the substring exists; else, if the substring is not found, it returns `-1`.

5. `result = Text.Range([String], n, 9)`

Enter a comma to create a new field within the record. With that position, the full code can be obtained by taking the range of characters starting from that positional index, n, and extracting 4+5 =9 characters from the text.

6. `[result]`

Finally, to return the value of `result`, apply field access by placing your cursor after the closing square bracket of the record initializer, and in a new set of square brackets, enter the **field name** from which to obtain the value and click **OK**.

While formatted here for clarity, in the formula bar, the M code should look like this:

```
Table.AddColumn(Source, "Code", each
    [
        n = Text.PositionOf([String], "DGPQ", Occurrence.First),
        result = Text.Range( [String], n, 9 )
    ][result]
)
```

Or, when you prefer nesting expressions, like this:

```
Table.AddColumn(Source, "Code", each
    Text.Range( [String],
        Text.PositionOf([String], "DGPQ", Occurrence.First
        ), 9
    )
)
```

Figure 14.1 shows the output of this approach.

▦	A^B_C String		$^{ABC}_{123}$ Code	
1	The code DGPQ33446 is important for this task.		DGPQ33446	
2	Unique document identifier: DGPQ13295.		DGPQ13295	
3	Please use the code DGPQ36006 to access the system.		DGPQ36006	
4	For verification, enter DGPQ30881 on the website.		DGPQ30881	
5	The transaction ID DGPQ78388 must be noted.		DGPQ78388	
6	DGPQ10273 is the code for your appointment.		DGPQ10273	
7	Reference code DGPQ36144 is included in the report.		DGPQ36144	
8	To complete registration, use DGPQ90158 as your code.		DGPQ90158	
9	Package with tracking number DGPQ52287 has been shipped.		DGPQ52287	

Figure 14.1: Result of example 1

Perfect. Now, it's good practice to review your approach and identify limitations and areas for improvement. For this exercise, let's proceed under the assumption that the likelihood of changes to our pattern or requirement is nonexistent. With that in mind, the primary concern that emerges is the lack of error handling. Error handling is crucial for scenarios where the substring DGPQ, isn't found within the text. In such instances, the Text.PositionOf function returns -1. If not managed, this will raise the error The 'offset' argument is out of range. in the Text.Range function.

As a matter of fact, incorporating a conditional statement would be a very effective method to manage this type of scenario. The improved M code could look like this:

```
Table.AddColumn(Source, "Code", each
    let n = Text.PositionOf([String], "DGPQ", Occurrence.First) in
    if n > -1 then Text.Range( [String], n, 9 ) else ""
)
```

1. `let n = Text.PositionOf([String], "DGPQ", Occurrence.First) in`

    Nesting a let expression enables us to assign the result of an expression to a variable. In this instance, we created a variable named n, which holds the result of the Text.PositionOf expression. Now we can refer to the outcome of that expression multiple times by referring to n, without the need to repeat this formula within the code.

2. `if n > -1 then Text.Range( [String], n, 9 ) else ""`

A let expression is always concluded by an in clause. Following the in clause, you can return a variable or write another expression. Here, we have chosen a conditional statement that performs a logical test. When this yields true, the result expression is executed, but when it yields false, the else clause takes effect, and an empty text string is returned. This acts as a safeguard, verifying the presence of the substring before executing the Text.Range function. This is crucial in preventing errors and ensuring the code performs as intended in scenarios where the substring may be missing in the input string.

To achieve the same result using a record expression, you will assign the conditional statement to a new field within the record, like so, before returning its field value:

```
Table.AddColumn(Source, "Code", each
    [
        n = Text.PositionOf([String], "DGPQ", Occurrence.First),
        r = if n > -1 then Text.Range( [String], n, 9 ) else ""
    ][r]
)
```

In this example alone, we have illustrated nesting functions, using a record and a let expression. We discussed these methods' pros, cons, and considerations in *Chapter 8, Working with Nested Structures*, but ultimately everyone develops their own coding style. When it comes to driving adoption, trouble-shooting, and clarity, we promote the use of the record expression.

Example 2, pattern

Unlike the previous scenario, where all codes had a fixed prefix, codes in this example start with four capital letters, followed by a sequence of five digits. This means our target codes may begin with any four-letter uppercase combination, such as ABCD12345 or EFGH67890. Note that this pattern of four letters followed by five numbers is consistent throughout the dataset.

Our strategy in this case would be to split the string into character sequences, aka words, and scan through those, identifying and extracting each code that meets these criteria. Here is the sample dataset; it contains 6 valid codes:

```
let
    Source = Table.FromColumns(
        {{"The code CHLO33446 is important for this task.",
        "Unique document identifier: JXKE13295.",
        "Please use the code SBT36006 to access the system.",
        "For verification, enter ERKZ30881 on the website.",
        "The transaction ID YNZ78388 must be noted.",
        "IHCY10273 is the code for your appointment.",
        "Reference code SSK36144 is included in the report.",
        "To complete registration, use PRLL90158 as your code.",
```

```
            "Package with tracking number MGAK52287 has been shipped."}},
            type table [String=text]

    )

in

    Source
```

Follow along with these steps to add a **Code** column to this sample table. That process requires multiple functions. We will leverage a record expression:

1. Navigate to **Add Column** and choose **Custom Column.**

2. Enter Code as the new column name.

3. [ ]

    Initialize a record expression by entering [ ], a set of square brackets.

4. w = Text.Select([String], {"A".."Z", "0".."9", " "})

    Valid characters are capitalized letters and numerals. Let's include a space. That space can be used to split each string into smaller units or words. Using the Text.Select function, we can keep only those characters from the input string. Add a comma at the end to create a new field in this record.

5. s = Text.Split(w, " ")

    Split each string on the space character, to return a list with text values, and add a comma at the end to create a new field in this record.

6. r = List.Select(s, each Text.Length(_) =9)

    For our initial attempt, we will select any list element with a total length of nine characters, as that seems like a good starting point. Add a comma at the end to create a new field in this record.

7. a = List.First(r)

    Upon examination of the intermediate results, this does provide the expected outcome. We can extract the answer with a function like List.First.

8. [a]

    Access field a to return its value, after the closing bracket of the record expression.

While formatted here for clarity, in the formula bar the M code should look like this:

```
Table.AddColumn(Source, "Code", each
    [
        w = Text.Select([String], {"A".."Z", "0".."9", " "}),
        s = Text.Split( w, " "),
        r = List.Select( s, each Text.Length(_) =9),
        a = List.First( r )
    ][a]
)
```

Figure 14.2 Shows the output of this approach.

	A^BC String	ABC 123 Code
1	The code CHLO33446 is important for this task.	CHLO33446
2	Unique document identifier: JXKE13295.	JXKE13295
3	Please use the code SBT36006 to access the system.	*null*
4	For verification, enter ERKZ30881 on the website.	ERKZ30881
5	The transaction ID YNZ78388 must be noted.	*null*
6	IHCY10273 is the code for your appointment.	IHCY10273
7	Reference code SSK36144 is included in the report.	*null*
8	To complete registration, use PRLL90158 as your code.	PRLL90158
9	Package with tracking number MGAK52287 has been shipped.	MGAK52287

Figure 14.2: Result of example 2

The task has been completed successfully. Let's take a brief moment to review this approach for potential oversights and areas for enhancement. Think about how the process could be fine-tuned and consider the likelihood that the pattern or requirement may change over time. Here are some points to consider for improvement:

- **Letter casing:** The current method only considers capitalized letters. This automatically excludes other nine-letter words containing lowercase letters, including any wrongly cased codes – those will not be identified.

- **Pattern validation:** The pattern itself, four letters followed by five digits, has not been validated. This omission may lead to invalid results.

- **Risk of data loss:** There is a risk of data loss in cases where more than a single code is contained within a string. The current process will not capture all instances; it will only capture the first value that survives the `List.Select` criteria.

To develop a more robust solution that tackles all of these potential issues, enhancing the accuracy and effectiveness, we will leverage this modified sample dataset in the next example:

```
let
    Source = Table.FromColumns(
        {{"The code CHLO33446 is IMPORTANT.",
        "Unique document identifier: JXKE13295.",
        "Please use the code SBT36006 to access the system.",
        "For verification, enter ERKZ30881 and MdKZ85426.",
        "The transaction ID YNZ78388 must be noted.",
        "IHCY10273 is the code for your appointment.",
        "Reference code SSK36144 is included in the report.",
        "To complete registration, use PRLL90158 as your code.",
        "Package with tracking number MGA5K2287 has been shipped."}},
        type table [String=text]
```

```
    )
in
    Source
```

Again, you can follow along with the steps to add a **Code** column to the table:

1. Navigate to **Add Column** and choose **Custom Column.**
2. Enter Code as the new column name.
3. `[ ]`

   Initialize a record expression by entering [ ], a set of square brackets. Inside a record, a comma-delimited list of field names and field values can be created.

4. `w = Text.SplitAny( [String], "., :")`

   Split the input string. Include the space and punctuation characters, to split each string into smaller parts. The splitting occurs on any character specified in the second argument of Text.SplitAny, returning a list of text values. Enter a comma at the end to create a new field in the record.

5. `r = List.Select( w, each Text.Length(_) =9 and Text.Start(_, 4)=Text.Select( _,` `{"A".."Z", "a".."z"}) and Text.Range(_, 4, 5)=Text.Select(_,{"0".."9"}))`

   Select any element from that list, r = List.Select(w, each, that conforms to the desired pattern. This means a total length of nine characters, Text.Length(_) =9 and, where the first four are letters, Text.Start(_, 4)=Text.Select(_,{"A".."Z", "a".."z"}), and the final five are digits, Text.Range(_, 4, 5)=Text.Select(_,{"0".."9"})). Include a closing parenthesis in the List.Select function and a comma to add a new field.

6. `a = Text.Combine( r, ", ")`

   Extract and combine all of the results into a single string.

7. `[a]`

   Apply field access to obtain the value for a.

While formatted here for clarity, in the formula bar, the M code should look like this:

```
Table.AddColumn(Source, "Code", each
    [
        w = Text.SplitAny( [String], "., :"),
        r = List.Select( w, each
                Text.Length(_) =9 and
                Text.Start(_, 4)=Text.Select(_,{"A".."Z", "a".."z"}) and
                Text.Range(_, 4, 5)=Text.Select(_,{"0".."9"})
            ),
        a = Text.Combine( r, ", ")
    ][a]
)
```

Figure 14.3 shows the output of the revised method.

	A^B_C String	ABC 123 Code
1	The code CHLO33446 is IMPORTANT.	CHLO33446
2	Unique document identifier: JXKE13295.	JXKE13295
3	Please use the code SBT36006 to access the system.	
4	For verification, enter ERKZ30881 and MdKZ85426.	ERKZ30881, MdKZ85426
5	The transaction ID YNZ78388 must be noted.	
6	IHCY10273 is the code for your appointment.	IHCY10273
7	Reference code SSK36144 is included in the report.	
8	To complete registration, use PRLL90158 as your code.	PRLL90158
9	Package with tracking number MGA5K2287 has been shipped.	

Figure 14.3: Result of the revised example 2

Example 3, splitters

Splitter functions in the M language are particularly valuable for specific pattern extraction scenarios. There is a collection of these functions, all of which have been thoroughly discussed and exemplified in *Chapter 11, Comparers, Replacers, Combiners, and Splitters*. However, since fixed-width data formats are very common in numerous legacy systems, it's only fitting that we address that specific scenario here as well. Unlike delimited formats, where fields are separated by characters like commas or tabs, fixed-width formats solely rely on the position of data within a string. This distinction often presents challenges: fields are embedded within a large block of text without clear separators. Understanding how to parse such data effectively is essential. Here's a sample dataset:

```
let
    Source = Table.FromRows({
        {"Hardware ZEQNNZE        Nails - 2 inch      4SPYBBU8    WRPBOSGEHTFD300
            2024-01-10"},
        {"Software CGUL2L         Antivirus SW        ZH1R987S2   SADBT0        150
            2024-01-11"},
        {"Hardware OY6IL4VFH21 Hammer - 5kg           O08AUF8JG   80LC6OMO      75
            2024-01-12"},
        {"Software DLTQ80V7X      Operating System    NZ8DD797    AB9MTEI09L    200
            2024-01-13"},
        {"FurnitureWCPKVSZJX      Office Chair        FTHJK       QQMR1QZMR71 50
            2024-01-14"},
        {"FurnitureZRE4CCR1       Office Desk         OYOWTO7IOQMFSNGRQ5        40
            2024-01-15"},
        {"Hardware WJAA7DHJ       Screwdriver Set     EO65VPCJ    IGC2FHI8G     120
            2024-01-16"},
        {"Software JX6URB9HI      Database Software   1430D1ADFC4 3YD7QU07T8OF300
            2024-01-17"},
```

```
        {"Hardware 1ADXHN       Electric Drill      AK3M3MJMY6M XUBQZP7R      60
           2024-01-18"},
        {"FurnitureD20R63MNM6  Bookshelf            4G6GD3G     373NWC1I9JT55
           2024-01-19"}
     }, type table [Column1=text])
  in
     Source
```

The most effective splitter for handling fixed-width data is `Splitter.SplitTextByPositions`. This splitter takes a list of positional index numbers. Each index listed needs to be greater than or equal to 0, and each subsequent value equal to or larger than the one before it. These indices specify the zero-based location in the text where splitting occurs, aligning perfectly with the inherent structure of fixed-width data formats. The following table shows how to determine these positions based on known field lengths of a legacy system and, very importantly, also includes the field order:

Field	Length	Position	Method	Order
Item type	10	0	Zero-based starting position = 0	0
Item code	12	9	Previous field length -1	1
Description	20	21	Prev field len + Prev position	2
Supplier code	12	41	Prev field len + Prev position	3
Manufacturer code	12	53	Prev field len + Prev position	4
Quantity	6	65	Prev field len + Prev position	5
Date	10	71	Prev field len + Prev position	6

Table 14.1: Determining positions and field order

There are three codes within each line of data that we need to extract: an **Item Code**, **Supplier Code**, and **Manufacturer Code.** We will demonstrate two methods, the first leveraging `Splitter.SplitTextByPositions`. This knowledge of how to determine each position, coupled with the known field order – depicted in the table – ensures we can easily solve this. Let's add a custom **Code** column. Here we go:

1. Navigate to **Add Column** and choose **Custom Column.**
2. Enter Code as the new column name.
3. [ ]

   Initialize a record expression by entering [ ], a set of square brackets.

4. `s = Splitter.SplitTextByPositions({0, 9, 21, 41, 53, 65, 71})([Column1])`

   The `Splitter.SplitTextByPositions` takes one argument, a list with positions, and returns a function. To invoke this function, simply add another set of parentheses, which is the function invocation operator, and pass the column name. Enter a comma at the end to create a new field.

5. `r = List.Transform( {1, 3, 4}, (x)=> Text.Trim( s{x} ))`

In the table, we can look up the field order, a zero-based index of each field to extract. The **Item Code** (*1*), **Supplier Code** (*3*), and **Manufacturer Code** (*4*) correspond to a list item in s. We can create a list with these indices to iterate, extracting those elements and removing any excess spaces all in one operation. Add a comma at the end to create another field.

Remember: (x)=> is equal to (_)=> and equal to the each expression, which also takes the underscore as its only variable, as explained in *Chapter 9, Parameters and Custom Functions*.

6. `a = Text.Combine( r, ", ")`

Combine all results into a single string.

7. `[a]`

Return the value for field a by applying field access to the record expression.

While formatted here, in the formula bar, the M code should look like this:

```
Table.AddColumn( Source, "Code", each
    [
        s = Splitter.SplitTextByPositions({0, 9, 21, 41, 53, 65, 71})
([Column1]),
        r = List.Transform( {1, 3, 4}, (x)=> Text.Trim( s{x} )),
        a = Text.Combine( r, ", ")
    ][a]
)
```

Figure 14.4 displays the output of this method when the **Monospaced** option, located in the **View** tab, is enabled. Using the monospaced view temporarily allows users to effortlessly and visually verify that they are handling fixed-width data.

	A^B_C Column1		ABC 123 Code
1	Hardware ZEQNNZE	Nails - 2 i...	ZEQNNZE, 4SPYBBU8, WRPBOSGEHTFD
2	Software CGUL2L	Antivirus S...	CGUL2L, ZH1R987S2, SADBT0
3	Hardware OY6IL4VFH21	Hammer - 5k...	OY6IL4VFH21, OO8AUF8JG, 80LC6OMO
4	Software DLTQ80V7X	Operating S...	DLTQ80V7X, NZ8DD797, AB9MTEI09L
5	FurnitureWCPKVSZJZ	Office Chai...	WCPKVSZJX, FTHJK, QQMR1QZNR71
6	FurnitureZRE4CCR1	Office Desk...	ZRE4CCR1, OYOWTO7IOQMF, SNGRQ5
7	Hardware WJAA7DHJ	Screwdriver...	WJAA7DHJ, EO65VPCJ, IGC2FHI8G
8	Software JX6URB9HI	Database So...	JX6URB9HI, 143OD1ADFC4, 3YD7QU07T8OF
9	Hardware 1ADXHN	Electric Dr...	1ADXHN, AK3M3MJMY6M, XUBQZP7R
10	FurnitureD20R63MNM6	Bookshelf ...	D20R63MNM6, 4G6GD3G, 373NWC1I9JT5

Figure 14.4: Result of example 3

Unless modifications are made to the underlying report of the legacy system, a method such as this requires virtually no maintenance and there is no need to incorporate error handling. Therefore, to explore these types of scenarios further, we will explore an alternative, one that doesn't rely on a splitter function but can equally take advantage of these fixed positions. We will use the exact same sample dataset.

> It is important to understand that the M engine generates M code while you interact with the **User Interface (UI)**. This process includes updating references to variables, also known as step names, within expressions. However, if you insert custom code that depends on specific variables, further UI interactions may disrupt this or other related steps.
>
> To prevent such problems, remember that the M engine is indifferent to step order because it follows the dependency chain of the let expression. By placing your custom variables above the Source step, you minimize the risk of UI interactions affecting manually written steps unintentionally.

A critical part of this next method involves manually writing a custom variable, which holds crucial information for our operation. In *Chapter 8, Working with Nested Structures*, we showcased how the List. Zip function forms a new list of lists by pairing elements from all of its input lists with corresponding index positions, where each nested list contains an element from List 1 (positions) followed by an element from List 2 (field length). To enhance efficiency, especially since we will reference this list repeatedly, we will store it in memory. Although this particular code does not directly reference a variable from the let expression, as a general best practice, we recommend placing it above the Source step:

```
s = List.Buffer( List.Zip(
    {
        {0, 9, 21, 41, 53, 65, 71},
        {10, 12, 20, 12, 12, 6, 10}
    }
)),
```

By now, you should be familiar with the initial steps of that process; therefore, we will primarily focus on the logic for the custom column formula itself:

1. Initialize a record expression and name its first field r.
2. We know the field order from the legacy system, the zero-based index of each field, and aim to extract the **Item Code** (*1*), **Supplier Code** (*3*), and **Manufacturer Code** (*4*) from a text string. This can be done by placing their positions in a list for iteration: List.Transform({1, 3, 4}, (x)=> …).
3. We will extract each field's full length, including trailing spaces, to remove them: Text.Trim(…).
4. Within Text.Trim, use the Text.Range function to extract the three fields, passing the string from Column1 as the first argument value: Text.Range([Column1], …).

5. For the second argument, we will dive deeper. The variable s is a list of lists, corresponding to each field within the string. We can retrieve the relevant corresponding list with s{x}, where x is the current value from the list we are iterating inside List.Transform.

    Since the result of s{x} is a list with two elements, the first being the position and the second being the field length, we can apply item access once more to extract the position value by adding {0}. The argument to the second parameter of Text.Range should now look like this: s{x}{0}.

6. As the third parameter, it expects a count that corresponds to the field length, which is the second item in each of the nested lists, requiring a small modification: s{x}{1}.

7. Check if you have a closing parenthesis for the Text.Range function. If not, include it and add a comma at the end so that we can create a new field in our record.

8. Define a field named a and assign this expression to concatenate all results: Text.Combine(r, ", ").

9. Finally, apply field access to the record expression to retrieve the value for a:

```
[
    r = List.Transform( {1, 3, 4}, (x)=>
            Text.Trim(
                Text.Range( [Column1], s{x}{0}, s{x}{1} )
            )
        ),
    a = Text.Combine( r, ", ")
][a]
```

Here's how the full expression should look inside the formula bar:

```
Table.AddColumn( Source, "Code", each
    [
        r = List.Transform( {1, 3, 4}, (x)=>
                Text.Trim(
                    Text.Range( [Column1], s{x}{0}, s{x}{1} )
                )
            ),
        a = Text.Combine( r, ", ")
    ][a]
)
```

Example 4, substitution

Another approach for extracting fixed patterns is substitution. This technique, potentially the most elaborate of them all, requires transforming each valid character into a symbol that represents a type. For instance, every letter is converted into a caret (^), each number into a hashtag (#), and every separator into an underscore (_). This process results in one uniform pattern, simplifying identification and extraction.

While defining such an elaborate approach can be effective, it's often unnecessary given the number of more straightforward alternatives. However, in specific niche cases, substitution may be justified. Here's our sample dataset for this example:

```
let
    Source = Table.FromColumns(
        {{"The code CHLO-33-446 is IMPORTANT.",
        "Unique document identifier: JXKE-13-295.",
        "Please use the code SBT3-6006 to access the system.",
        "For verification, enter ERKZ-30-881 and MdKZ-85.426.",
        "The transaction ID YNZ-78-388 must be noted.",
        "IHC-Y10-273 is the code for your appointment.",
        "Reference code SSK-36-144 is included in the report.",
        "To complete registration, use PRLL-90-158 as your code.",
        "Package with tracking number MGA5-K22.87 has been shipped."}},
        type table [String=text]
    )
in
    Source
```

In this scenario, valid codes are defined as follows: They start with four letters – uppercase, lowercase, or a combination – followed by a separator, which is either a hyphen (-) or a period (.), two digits, another separator, and finally, a set of three digits. The overall length of this pattern is consistently 11 characters. Accordingly, target codes may appear as `ABCD-12-345`, `efgh-67.890`, or `IjkL.01.321`, for example.

Aside from the fundamental replacement of values, the remaining steps have a high degree of similarity to *Example 3*, the *Splitters* alternative approach:

1. First, assemble a replacements list. This list includes a substitution value for every valid character and is loaded into memory. Although this does not directly reference a variable from the let expression, as a general best practice, we will place it above the `Source` step. The code is as follows:

    ```
    replacements = List.Buffer(
        List.Zip({{"A".."Z"}, List.Repeat({"^"}, 26)}) &
        List.Zip({{"0".."9"}, List.Repeat({"#"}, 10)}) &
        List.Zip({{"-", "."}, List.Repeat({"_"}, 2)})
    ),
    ```

2. Add a custom `Code` column to the table and initialize a record expression [ ], to extract all valid codes.

3. Leverage `List.ReplaceMatchingItems` to replace all characters in each string. This requires a list of replacements in the format {oldValue, newValue}, and the function also comes equipped with an optional comparer. After completing all replacements, concatenate all list items to form a single text string:

```
replVal = Text.Combine(
    List.ReplaceMatchingItems(
        Text.ToList([String]),
        replacements,
        Comparer.OrdinalIgnoreCase
    )
)
```

4. In the `replVal` string we can now identify each instance of the generic pattern that looks like this: ^^^^_##_### and collect their positions within a list:

```
lookUp = Text.PositionOf( replVal, "^^^^_##_###", Occurrence.All)
```

5. Use the lookup list to iterate and extract results from the input string, like so:

```
getMatches = Text.Combine(
    List.Transform(
        lookUp,
        (x)=> Text.Range([String], x, 11 )
    ), ", "
)
```

6. Since we used a record expression to generate all values, what's left is to return the final result stored in the getMatches field (by applying field access):

```
[
    replVal = Text.Combine(
        List.ReplaceMatchingItems(
            Text.ToList([String]),
            replacements,
            Comparer.OrdinalIgnoreCase
        )
    ),
    lookUp = Text.PositionOf( replVal,
        "^^^^_##_###",
        Occurrence.All
    ),
    getMatches = Text.Combine(
        List.Transform(
            lookUp,
```

```
                (x)=> Text.Range([String], x, 11 )
            ), ", "
        )
    ][getMatches]
```

Here's how that looks inside the formula bar:

```
Table.AddColumn( Source, "Code", each
    [
        replacements = List.Buffer(
            List.Zip({{"A".."Z"}, List.Repeat({"^"}, 26)}) &
            List.Zip({{"0".."9"}, List.Repeat({"#"}, 10)}) &
            List.Zip({{"-", "."}, List.Repeat({"_"}, 2)})
        ),
        replVal = Text.Combine(
            List.ReplaceMatchingItems(
                Text.ToList([String]),
                replacements,
                Comparer.OrdinalIgnoreCase
            )
        ),
        lookUp = Text.PositionOf( replVal, "^^^^_##_###", Occurrence.All),
        getMatches = Text.Combine(
            List.Transform(
                lookUp,
                (x)=> Text.Range([String], x, 11 )
            ), ", "
        )
    ][getMatches]
)
```

Figure 14.5 displays the expected outcome for this method.

🔲▾ A^B_C String	▾	ABC 123 Code	▾
1	The code CHLO-33-446 is IMPORTANT.	CHLO-33-446	
2	Unique document identifier: JXKE-13-295.	JXKE-13-295	
3	Please use the code SBT3-6006 to access the system.		
4	For verification, enter ERKZ-30-881 and MdKZ-85.426.	ERKZ-30-881, MdKZ-85.426	
5	The transaction ID YNZ-78-388 must be noted.		
6	IHC-Y10-273 is the code for your appointment.		
7	Reference code SSK-36-144 is included in the report.		
8	To complete registration, use PRLL-90-158 as your code.	PRLL-90-158	
9	Package with tracking number MGA5-K22.87 has been shipped.		

Figure 14.5: Result of example 4

We've noted that there are likely more straightforward alternatives, even in cases when you rely on inspecting each individual character. To demonstrate, let's use the same sample dataset as the previous example.

1. Add a custom Code column and initialize a record expression: [ ].

2. Split each string into words. Add a comma to create a new field.

    ```
    w = Text.Split( [String], " ")
    ```

3. Select list items that match the pattern. Start disregarding words that do not meet the minimum character requirement (less than 11 characters). In all other cases, test the value by removing all valid characters from each segment and checking if the remaining text length is equal to zero. Add a comma at the end.

    ```
    r = List.Select(w, (x)=> if Text.Length(x) < 11 then false
        else Text.Length(
            Text.Remove(Text.Start(x, 4), {"A".."Z", "a".."z"}) &
            Text.Remove(Text.Range(x, 4, 1) & Text.Range(x, 7, 1), {"-",
    "."}) &
            Text.Remove(Text.Range(x, 5, 2) & Text.Range(x, 8, 3),
    {"0".."9"})
        ) = 0
    )
    ```

4. `a = Text.Combine( List.Transform(r, (x)=> Text.Start(x, 11)), ", ")`

    From the list items that remain, extract the first 11 characters.

5. `[a]`

    Extract the value from field a by applying field access.

Inside the formula bar, the M code should look like this:

```
Table.AddColumn( Source, "Code", each
  [
    w = Text.Split( [String], " "),
    r = List.Select( w, (x)=> if Text.Length(x) <11 then false else
    Text.Length(
    Text.Remove(Text.Start( x, 4),{"A".."Z", "a".."z"}) &
    Text.Remove(Text.Range( x, 4, 1) & Text.Range( x, 7, 1),{"-", "."}) &
    Text.Remove(Text.Range( x, 5, 2) & Text.Range( x, 8, 3),{"0".."9"})
    )=0 ),
    a = Text.Combine( List.Transform(r, (x)=> Text.Start(x, 11)), ", ")
  ][a]
)
```

Example 5, regex

Power Query does not natively support regex, but it can be implemented by using the `Web.Page` function to execute **JavaScript** (**JS**) code. Generally, the performance of this method is a major concern, especially when applied to larger datasets. Therefore, it's crucial to balance the want with the need for regex to ensure the benefits outweigh the drawbacks in terms of performance and user experience.

Our task is to extract postal codes from this sample dataset. These postal codes each have a length of 5 digits and can be found in different places within the address strings:

```
let
  Source = Table.FromColumns({
    {
      "Boulevard des Écoles 73, 31000 Lyon",
      "6 Boulevard du Château, 69001 La Ville Rose Toulouse",
      "Rue Saint-Martin 65, 31000 Lyon",
      "Chemin Victor Hugo 143, 69001 Bordeaux",
      "Avenue des Vignes 7, 67000 Toulouse",
      "74 Quai de la République 69001 Latin Quarter Paris",
      "55 Boulevard de la Liberté, 67000 La Petite France Strasbourg",
      "82 Chemin des Jardins, 59000 Paris"
    }}, type table [Address = text]
  )
```

```
 in
    Source
```

A common method is to create a custom function that uses the Web.Page function to run JavaScript. This process requires a text value with a `<script>` tag to insert JavaScript code into an HTML document. Anything between `<script>` and `</script>` is executed as JavaScript. Our task is to create JS code that performs a regex operation. It needs to identify and extract sequences of five digits from the input text string passed to the custom function. Afterward, the Web.Page function will output a table showing the HTML document's contents, organized in basic elements. This table can then be accessed to retrieve the results. Although we are not experts in JS code, here's how that can look. Adhering to best practices, we will implement this custom function above the `Source` step:

```
fxRegex = (input as text) as text =>
    Web.Page(
        "<script>
            var a ='" & input & "';
            var b = a.match(/\d{5}/g);
            document.write(b);
        </script>"
    ){0}[Data]{0}[Children]{1}[Children]{0}[Text],
```

Figure 14.6 shows how this should look from inside the **Advanced Editor:**

```
1   let
2       fxRegex = (input as text) as text =>
3           Web.Page(
4               "<script>
5                   var a = '" & input & "';
6                   var b = a.match(/\d{5}/g);
7                   document.write(b);
8               </script>"
9           ){0}[Data]{0}[Children]{1}[Children]{0}[Text],
10      Source = Table.FromColumns({
11          {
```

Figure 14.6: Incorporating the fxRegex function above the Source step

Here's a detailed breakdown of components within this code and their function:

1. `fxRegex = (input as text) as text =>`

   This declares a function named `fxRegex` that takes one parameter, `input`, of type text. The function will return a text-type value.

2. `Web.Page(...)`

   This function allows us to create a web page in memory, a workaround to running JavaScript, which does support regular expressions, in Power Query. Anything between the `<script>` and `</script>` tags is treated and executed as JavaScript code.

3. `var a ='" & input & "';`

   This line declares a JavaScript variable named a. The single quote (') following the equal sign (=) initiates a string in JavaScript. Subsequently, the double quote (") signals the end of a text string in M, temporarily escaping JS notation. This enables the concatenation of the input parameter value (& input) in M code. After injecting the input value, M concatenates a new string (& ") and resumes in JavaScript, closing the string with a single quote (').

4. `var b = a.match(/\d{5}/g);`

   This line initializes a JavaScript variable, b, and uses JavaScript's match method with a regex pattern, where \d matches any digit, {5} specifies exactly five digits in a row, and g is a global search flag to find all matches. Regular expressions can be quite specific. You may need to adjust this pattern when applying it to different scenarios.

5. `document.write(b);`

   This line writes the result of the regex match to the HTML document.

6. `){0}[Data]{0}[Children]{1}[Children]{0}[Text]`

   This part accesses the output generated by Web.Page and navigates through the **document object model (DOM)** to obtain the text written by document.write(b). It sequentially applies item access and field access, multiple times, to retrieve the content.

   With the custom fxRegex function in place, we can apply its logic to each row within the table, storing the results in the Postal Code column. Since a custom function is just like any other function in M, we will choose **Custom Column** and enter: fxRegex([Address]).

In the formula bar, the M code should look like this:

```
Table.AddColumn(Source, "Postal Code", each fxRegex( [Address] ))
```

Figure 14.7 shows the output of this method.

	A^BC Address		ABC 123 Postal Code	
1	Boulevard des Écoles 73, 31000 Lyon		31000	
2	6 Boulevard du Château, 69001 La Ville Rose Toulouse		69001	
3	Rue Saint-Martin 65, 31000 Lyon		31000	
4	Chemin Victor Hugo 143, 69001 Bordeaux		69001	
5	Avenue des Vignes 7, 67000 Toulouse		67000	
6	74 Quai de la République 69001 Latin Quarter Paris		69001	
7	55 Boulevard de la Liberté, 67000 La Petite France Strasbourg		67000	
8	82 Chemin des Jardins, 59000 Paris		59000	

Figure 14.7: Result after invoking the fxRegex function on our sample

> Important note: While this JavaScript method is supported in Power BI Desktop and Excel, for example, it is not available in the Power BI service. In the Power BI service, regular expressions can be implemented through scripting in Python or R. However, enabling scheduled refresh will also require a personal gateway to be installed on the computer where the workbook and the R or Python installations are located.

The task was completed with success. Let's evaluate this approach. We already called out that the performance of this specific technique can quickly become an issue because it creates a web page in memory for each row in the table to run the JavaScript code and execute the regex. The main problem, however, from our perspective is that we did not think about or try using standard library M functions at all. This brings up an important question: Is it possible to solve this challenge with nothing other than standard M functions? Let's reuse our sample dataset and find out.

You can follow along with these steps to add a `Postal Code` column to the table:

1. Navigate to **Add Column** and choose **Custom Column**.
2. Enter `Postal Code` as the new column name.
3. `[ ]`

   Initialize a record expression by entering [ ], a set of square brackets.

4. `w = Text.SplitAny([Address], Text.Remove([Address], {"0".."9"}))`

   Split the input string. As a separator, we will use the `Text.Remove` function to include all characters from the input string, with the exception of any numerals. Add a comma at the end to create a new field within the record.

5. `r = List.Select( w, each Text.Length(_) =5)`

   Select all elements from the list that have a total length of 5 characters. Enter a comma at the end of the line to add another field.

6. `a = Text.Combine(…, ", ")`

   Combine all of the results into a single string.

7. `[a]`

   Extract the field value by applying field access to the record.

While formatted here for clarity, the M code in the formula bar should look like this:

```
Table.AddColumn(Source, "Postal Code", each
    [
        w = Text.SplitAny([Address],
            Text.Remove([Address], {"0".."9"})),
        r = List.Select( w, each Text.Length(_)=5),
        a = Text.Combine(r, ", ")
    ][a]
)
```

This relatively concise code achieves the expected outcome and is guaranteed to perform better than the initial regex operation. But does that mean there's no hope if you're in a tough spot and the only solution seems to be using regex? Not necessarily. There's one option left: optimizing the initial regex approach.

Optimization can often feel like a mystery. It involves extensive testing and is a blend of both art and science. However, sometimes simply rethinking an approach can make all the difference. We're not sure who first introduced this concept, but the principle is astonishingly simple and effective. Create a web page to run the JavaScript code only once.

We will leverage the same sample dataset. Now, with the intention to execute the JS code only once, all values will have to be passed into that single function call. In JavaScript terms, it needs to receive an array of values, perform the regex operation on that array, and structure the output in such a way that Power Query can understand it. Here's the most crucial piece of that puzzle, creating an array:

1. Get the `Address` column values as a list: `Source[Address]`.
2. Wrap `Json.FromValue(...)` around it to convert the list into JSON format, preparing it to be processed in a JavaScript environment.
3. Wrap `Text.FromBinary(...)` around it as the `Json.FromValue` function returns a binary data type. However, the Web.Page function requires a text string input. The `Text.FromBinary` function converts the binary data (the JSON-formatted list of addresses) into a text string:

```
Text.FromBinary( Json.FromValue( Source[Address] ))
```

This allows us to pass the entire `Address` column as an array of values, which can be injected into the JavaScript code. Consequently, the JavaScript code that executes the regex operation must be modified to iterate this array. Again, we are by no means experts in JS code, but consider the following code:

```
OutputList = Web.Page(
    Text.Combine({
        "<script>",
        "var arr = ",
        Text.FromBinary( Json.FromValue( Source[Address] )),
        ";",
        "var output = []; ",
        "for (var i in arr){",
        "   var matches = arr[i].match(/\d{5}/g);",
        "   output[i] = matches ? '\""' + matches.join('|') + '\""' :
'\""\"";",
        "}; ",
        "document.write('{' + output.join(',') + '}');",
        "</script>"
    })
){0}[Data]{0}[Children]{1}[Children]{0}[Text]
```

Here's a detailed breakdown of elements within the provided code and their function:

1. `Web.Page(...)`

   This function takes a text value and creates an in-memory web page that executes the JavaScript code present between the `<script>` and `</script>` tags.

2. `Text.Combine({...})`

   This function takes a list of comma-delimited text values and combines them into a single text. That list contains different text strings separated by commas. All of them except for one M expression are segments of JS code.

3. `var arr =`

   Initializes a JavaScript array with the name `arr`.

4. `Text.FromBinary( Json.FromValue( Source[Address] ))`

   Converts the `Address` column from the `Source` table into a JSON string and then into a text value, which will be the content of the JavaScript array named `arr`.

5. `; (semicolon)`

   This marks the end of a statement in JavaScript, an instruction to be executed.

6. `var output = [];`

   Declares an empty JavaScript array named `output`.

7. `for (var i in arr){`

   The `for` loop in JavaScript iterates over each address in the `arr` array.

8. `var matches = arr[i].match(/\d{5}/g);`

   Uses a regular expression to find sequences of five digits in each address and stores them in a variable named `matches`. If there are multiple matches within a single address, they are all included in this matches array.

9. `output[i] = matches ? '\""' + matches.join('|') + '\""' : '\""\""';`

   The *ternary operator* shorthand for an `if-else` statement. It is used here as `condition ? IfTrue : IfFalse` and checks if the matches variable is non-null and non-empty. If true, it joins all elements into a single string, separated by a `|` character. If `false`, it assigns an empty text string as a placeholder. This ensures the output array has an equal length when compared to the `arr` input array, meaning one value per table row.

10. `document.write('{' + output.join(',') + '}');`

    Writes the output array as a string to the HTML document and concatenates a `{` (curly bracket) at the start and one `}` to the end of the comma-delimited string, creating a textual representation of the list syntax in M code.

11.){0}[Data]{0}[Children]{1}[Children]{0}[Text]

This part navigates through the document of the generated HTML page to access the text written by the JavaScript code.

Figure 14.8 shows the return value for the OutputList expression, a string.

{"31000","69001","31000","69001","67000","69001","67000","59000"}

Figure 14.8: The return value for OutputList, a text value

The final step – converting this text value, OutputList, into an actual list with text values – is surprisingly easy: Expression.Evaluate(OutputList). This list contains one value for each row, which we'll add as a new Postal Code column to the Source table. You can follow along with these instructions:

1. To insert a manual step, click on the **fx** button.
2. Replace the returned variable name with Table.ToColumns(Source). This transforms the Source table into a list of its columns.
3. To add another list of column values that contains the transformed OutputList values, we can leverage the combination operator – the ampersand, &.
4. Add {Expression.Evaluate(OutputList)} after the ampersand. The expression is enclosed in a set of curly brackets, {}, turning it into a list within a list.
5. Place your cursor in front of the expression and enter Table.FromColumns(to start converting the combined lists back into a table.
6. Place your cursor at the end of the expression, add a comma, and then provide a list of column names. Since we added a new column, include its name, Table.ColumnNames(Source) & {"Postal Code"}, in a similar manner.
7. Add the closing parenthesis,), to finish the expression.

Although formatted here, inside the formula bar the M code should look like this:

```
Table.FromColumns(
    Table.ToColumns(Source) & {Expression.Evaluate(OutputList)},
    Table.ColumnNames(Source) & {"Postal Code"}
)
```

This concludes the extracting fixed patterns section. Each method, whether straightforward or more elaborate or complex, provides unique possibilities and demonstrates Power Query's flexibility in handling text data. Surely, if we put our minds to it, we can easily come up with another dozen ways to tackle these types of challenges. However, remember that the choice of method ultimately depends on the specific requirements, data, and complexity of the pattern that needs to be extracted. Your growing expertise and imagination are key to unlocking so much more potential.

Transitioning to the second part of this chapter, we shift our focus to combining data. This crucial process allows users to append information from various tables, sheets, or workbooks, for example.

Combining data

Although the process of extracting and combining data may seem straightforward at a glance, it can quickly turn into a complex and demanding task. The level of complexity largely depends on the characteristics of the data and its organization. From the perspective of this section, it's important to understand that by combining data we mean an append operation, typically seen when consolidating files.

In the real world, data often originates from various sources and is managed by multiple users, which complicates maintaining consistency across all files. Excel workbooks, in particular, is a very common format, as Excel is used extensively across many industries for numerous data-related tasks.

In this section, we'll delve into techniques and strategies to overcome challenges commonly faced when working with multiple Excel files. While some are specific to the nature of Excel, others are more generic and applicable across different scenarios.

Basics for combining data

An **ETL** process (**Extract, Transform,** and **Load**) begins by connecting to a data source. Before you begin, it is essential to have a good understanding of the task and clarify requirements as much as possible. Although this is by no means an extensive list, here are some points to keep in mind, especially when dealing with multiple files:

1. **Data location:** This refers to the unique address that identifies where the data is stored. This can be a path to a local directory or file, a URL leading to a cloud storage service, or a path to a network drive, for example. It is important to understand that locations and file names are not static; they can change over time due to numerous reasons, like system migrations, data reorganization, and so on.

   That's where parameters come in. They act like variables and allow you to store and manage a value that can be used inside your queries. This is not only efficient but also simplifies maintenance. Parameters enable you to easily update and change a value without having to modify each query where that value is used. When files, folders, or even entire databases are moved, you can quickly restore all dependent queries by updating the parameter that stores the value. Parameters are covered in *Chapter 9, Parameters and Custom Functions.*

2. **Data source:** To be able to read data, a connector is used. Therefore, you need to identify where data is coming from and if a connector is available for that source. For example, is it a locally stored file, a folder on a network drive, a SharePoint Online folder, or something else altogether? When there is no default connector available for the source, you can develop your own. That process is covered in *Chapter 16, Enabling Extensions*, of this book.

   Most accessing data functions leverage a connector and a location to extract data from the source. These functions typically return a **Navigation** table, primarily used by the Power Query user interface to provide a navigation experience over the exposed data. This helps a user visually identify and select specific data for further processing.

3. **Data selection:** Data can be dumped into a folder and spread across multiple files. It's important to know which files should be considered, and if selection is required, what criteria to apply. For example, a date range, specific file extension, or another relevant attribute.

4. **Data Organization:** Understanding how data is organized within files is essential. Are you dealing with one or multiple sheets and tables in a workbook? Could you encounter files with no data? Is the absence of data of interest and how should you deal with that circumstance?

5. **Data structure:** Since our focus is on Excel files, you need to examine how data within each file is structured. Is it presented on sheets or in Excel tables? In the latter case, are all Excel tables named properly for easy identification? In the former case, a method has to be developed to identify where relevant data is located that can be applied to all files involved.

6. **Data consistency:** Check for uniformity across different files, like matching column names, consistent value types in like-named columns, and so on.

    You may encounter naming conventions. As column headers can be used as labels on a report, ask yourself if those names are suitable and clearly describe the data. Or, you may encounter prefixed column names, something like `1-1-2024 Stock On Hand`, for example. That in itself will make all `Stock On Hand` columns unique. However, by extracting the date, a pattern like that can easily be remedied.

7. **Data collections:** Is all data within the selected files *the same*? If it is homogeneous, it can be consolidated into a single table. If not, there are most likely multiple distinct datasets present. Identify each one: what do they represent, and what, if any, outputs are required from them? Remember that a separate query has to be developed for each table to generate from the data.

    Imagine files from a financial department, that each have balance sheets, budgets, income statements, expenses, and so on. Obviously, they are not and do not describe "the same" thing. What data should be collected for the analysis?

8. **Data transformation:** Lastly, does the data have to be transformed before it can be combined? Did you spot patterns or problems in the data to address? Are applied transformations dynamic? Do you need to incorporate error reporting?

    The most simple and effective data model optimization strategy is to only bring what you need, nothing else. Selecting columns and rows early may have additional benefits like query folding. Query folding is discussed in *Chapter 15, Optimizing Performance*.

Hopefully, it's becoming clear that what's often brushed off as a simple task can actually have a number of layers that add more and more complexity. Nonetheless, the key to success lies in thoughtful query design. It is worth thinking about how query preparation and development impact the ETL process, even at its core, by considering basic things such as step order and avoiding redundancy, for example. In essence, the time and effort spent designing well-structured queries pays off in maintainability, reliability, and ultimately the quality of insights you can derive from the analysis that follows.

Now that we've introduced aspects of combining data, let's dive into a practical example. Our goal is to illustrate various key elements that were described here. While each dataset and its requirements possess a distinct character, the aim is to lay a foundational framework that can help develop more robust strategies for these types of challenges, enabling you to incorporate those elements into your own workflows.

Keeping this in mind, let's start our exploration by diving into a practical example.

Extract, transform, and combine

In this section, we're focusing on working with multiple Excel files stored in a folder. To get the most out of it, we recommend actively following along with the steps provided. It's important to note that there are numerous methods to achieve the desired outcome. In this part of the chapter, our goal is to walk you through one specific solution, illustrating various techniques that have been discussed throughout this book. A final note: the screenshots are from Power BI Desktop (*version: 2.124.1805.0*); there may be some differences if you're using a different version.

Before we proceed, it's crucial to understand the task at hand and examine how the raw data is organized within the files.

Get and inspect data

The data used in this example is available for download here: https://github.com/PacktPublishing/The-Definitive-Guide-to-Power-Query-M-/. It is a folder containing nine files. The first three files, illustrated in *Figure 14.9*, should be combined to reflect the expected outcome shown in the final file shown here:

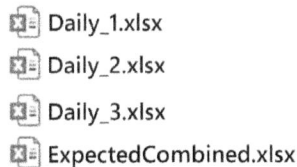

Daily_1.xlsx

Daily_2.xlsx

Daily_3.xlsx

ExpectedCombined.xlsx

Figure 14.9: Files to combine and expected result file

Take a moment to review the three source files. A snapshot is shown in *Figure 14.10*.

Figure 14.10: Limited view of a source file

Compare the inputs with the intended result from `ExpectedCombined.xlsx`, partially shown in *Figure 14.11*.

	A	B	C	D	E	F	G	H	I
1	Name	Date	DOW	Occupancy | This Year | My Prop	Occupancy | This Year | Comp Set	Occupancy | % Chg | My Prop	Occupancy | % Chg | Comp Set	Occupancy | Index (MPI)	Occupancy | Rank
2	Daily_1.xlsx	5/22/2023	Mon	89.393939393939391	93.126385809312623	69.540229885057471	73.553719008264466	95.992063492063494	5 of 6
3	Daily_1.xlsx	5/23/2023	Tue	100	98.59571322985957	87.5	77.158034528552463	101.42428785607196	1 of 6
4	Daily_1.xlsx	5/24/2023	Wed	70.707070707070713	84.405025868440504	28.205128205128204	48.119325551232166	83.771161704611785	6 of 6
5	Daily_1.xlsx	5/25/2023	Thu	61.616161616161612	77.605321507760536	9.3189964157706093	12.419700214132762	79.396825396825392	5 of 6
6	Daily_1.xlsx	5/26/2023	Fri	71.717171717171733	46489230745	10.59190031152648	797743	285583 48513	5 of 6
...									
19	Daily_3.xlsx	2023	Thu	72.0315.894 08425	79.171741778 9117	-21. 10 5062	-3 0354 2804749558	9 3271255	5 of
20	Daily_3.xlsx	5/26/2023	Fri	73.684210526315795	77.611940298507463	-19.185059422750424	-18.16082983773941	94.939271255060731	4 of 5
21	Daily_3.xlsx	5/27/2023	Sat	88.421052631578945	96.865671641791039	-6.052631578947369	3.723418306696606	91.282134457870399	5 of 5
22	Daily_3.xlsx	5/28/2023	Sun	84.210526315789465	93.283582089552226	-10.526315789473683	-0.22264368763915232	90.273684210526312	5 of 5

Figure 14.11: Limited view of the expected result

The method we're about to explore demonstrates how to build a manageable solution, mirroring what the UI provides when **Combine & Transform Data** is chosen. It's a highly effective, customizable, and modular approach, allowing for easy collaboration and handoff to others, even when it contains advanced M code or sophisticated concepts.

Given that file locations are likely to change over time, we will initiate our modular approach by creating a parameter.

Location parameter

We have stored all downloaded files in a folder called `Sample files`, in the root directory of the system. Instead of hardcoding that path in any data-accessing query, create a parameter to store its value. That parameter value can easily be updated without the need to alter any M code and, in most cases, without ever opening the Power Query Editor.

Right-click on a blank area within the **Queries** pane and select **New Parameter,** from the quick access menu, depicted in *Figure 14.12*, or select it from the **Manage Parameters** button menu located on the **Home** tab:

Queries [0]

Paste

New Query   ▶

New Parameter...

New Group...

Expand All

Collapse All

Figure 14.12: Quickly create a new parameter from the Queries pane

This action opens the **Manage Parameters** dialog box, shown in *Figure 14.13*, displaying all parameters in the current file and providing a central place to create, manage, and delete them. Each parameter is stored and visible as a separate query in the **Queries** pane.

In M, a query name is considered an identifier, and the quoted notation is applicable under certain conditions, such as when a query name includes spaces. To avoid that, opt for a space-free name such as FolderLocation. Make sure to keep the **Required** option checked. For **Type**, choose **Text**, and specify the **Current Value**. In our case, that is C:\Sample files (note that your file path may differ):

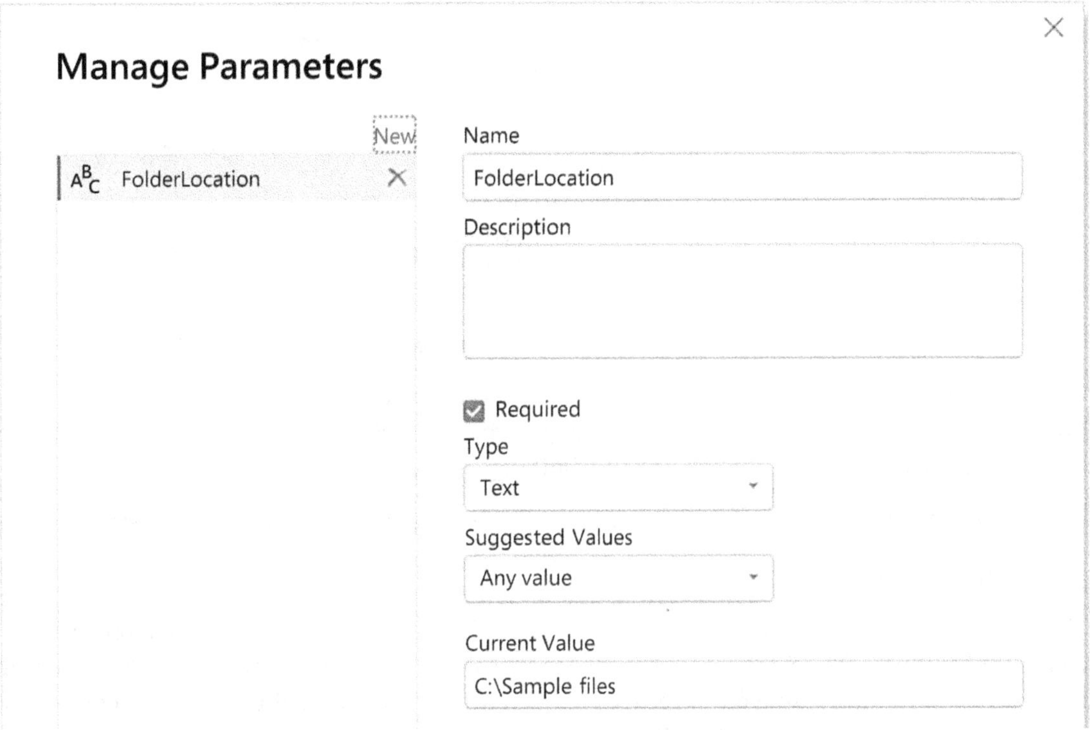

Figure 14.13: Manage Parameters dialog

With this building block in place, we can now move forward by establishing a connection to the data.

Connect to data

Use the **New Source** button located on the **Home** tab. Choose the **Folder connector** and switch the **input type** from **Text** (indicated by the **ABC** icon) to **Parameter**, setting the **FolderLocation** parameter as its **value**. Completing this action will display the folder contents, illustrated in *Figure 14.14*. Along with it, you'll find command buttons, each offering different functionality. Here is a brief description:

1. **Combine & Transform Data:** This option should only be selected when all folder contents, including subfolders, are to be processed in exactly the same manner. This does not offer a means to select files and combining data will fail when the file format, structure, or consistency varies. For example, if the "example file" is an Excel file and a table named myData was selected from the navigation experience, all files would be treated as Excel files that contain a myData table.

2. **Transform Data:** This option should be selected to manually control file selection and transformations in the Power Query Editor before combining data.

3. **Cancel:** This will abortthe connecting to data operation.

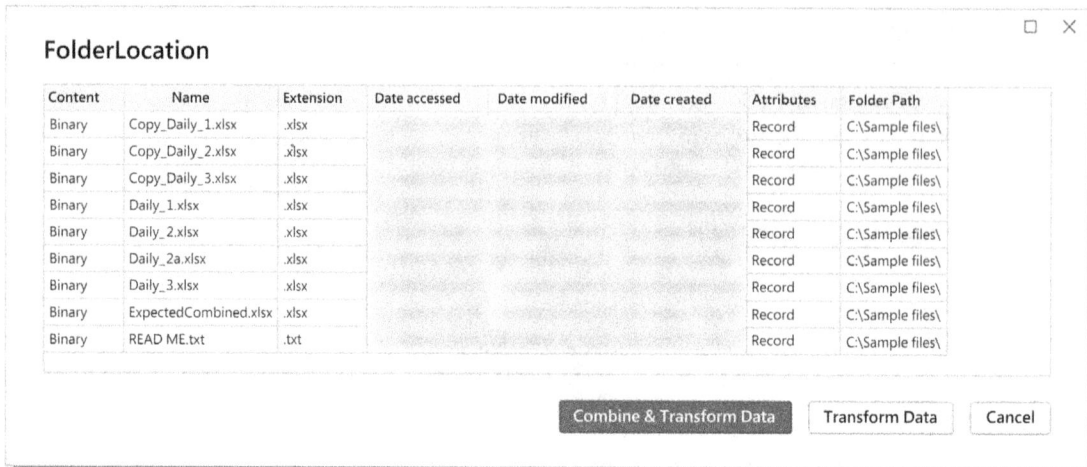

Content	Name	Extension	Date accessed	Date modified	Date created	Attributes	Folder Path
Binary	Copy_Daily_1.xlsx	.xlsx				Record	C:\Sample files\
Binary	Copy_Daily_2.xlsx	.xlsx				Record	C:\Sample files\
Binary	Copy_Daily_3.xlsx	.xlsx				Record	C:\Sample files\
Binary	Daily_1.xlsx	.xlsx				Record	C:\Sample files\
Binary	Daily_2.xlsx	.xlsx				Record	C:\Sample files\
Binary	Daily_2a.xlsx	.xlsx				Record	C:\Sample files\
Binary	Daily_3.xlsx	.xlsx				Record	C:\Sample files\
Binary	ExpectedCombined.xlsx	.xlsx				Record	C:\Sample files\
Binary	READ ME.txt	.txt				Record	C:\Sample files\

Figure 14.14: Folder contents and available command buttons

The objective is to craft a solution that enables selecting specific files, therefore choose **Transform Data**. This action creates a new query, called Query1 if that name doesn't already exist. It contains the data shown in *Figure 14.14* and serves as a new building block.

After setting up this connection, it's time to select the files that are needed for our analysis.

Filter files

The only transformation we need to apply to Query1 is a filter to select files that are of interest to the combine operation – the top three files depicted in *Figure 14.9*. To set that process in motion, we will use the drop-down menu from the Extension column header, go to **Text filters**, choose **Begins with**, and enter .xls, which generates the following code, visible in the formula bar:

```
Table.SelectRows(Source, each Text.StartsWith([Extension], ".xls"))
```

To make sure the comparison is performed in a case-insensitive manner, pass Comparer.OrdinalIgnoreCase as the third argument value to the Text.StartsWith function. Furthermore, files should only be considered if their name starts with Daily_ To do this, follow these steps:

1. From the formula bar, copy the full Text.StartsWith function.
2. Place your cursor before the final closing parenthesis.
3. Enter the **and** operator.
4. Paste the copied logic.
5. Update the code and enter the field [Name] as text and Daily_ as a substring.
6. Rename this step SelectFiles.

Although formatted here, the code should now look like this:

```
Table.SelectRows(Source,
    each Text.StartsWith([Extension], ".xls") and
```

```
        Text.StartsWith([Name], "Daily_", Comparer.OrdinalIgnoreCase)
    )
```

Overall strategy

Power Query's **folder** connector includes a **Combine & Transform Data** option. This uses a user-selected sample file to develop transformation logic that will uniformly be applied to all files within the folder. However, that design process understandably lacks the flexibility to select specific files or extract particular data collections, like tables or worksheets, from these files. For those proficient in the M language, tweaking all relevant queries is feasible, while many others struggle.

Therefore, we are going to take a different approach: building a custom solution resembling that of **Combine & Transform Data** but introducing the necessary flexibility during its step-by-step development, tailoring the process precisely to our requirements, all the while gaining a better understanding of how these solutions are organized – modular, easy to maintain, and well suited to a wide range of scenarios.

To achieve the desired result, several transformations have to be performed:

1. Remove empty rows and columns.
2. Extract part of the business name from the document header.
3. Extract the body of data from the worksheet.
4. Deal with multiple header rows.

To start this development process, we'll need to select an appropriate sample. Which file is the most suitable for that purpose? And let's anticipate that we may want to switch to a different sample file in the future. As it is another input, we can store that in a parameter.

Choose a sample file

The `Binary` value in the `Content` column (*Figure 14.14*) contains the Excel file data. You should think of that as the value to transform. In other words, it is an input value and to build a transformation pattern for all files, a sample is required. Upon examination of the files, we found `Daily_2.xlsx` suitable. It appears to be the most challenging and complete. You can follow these steps:

1. Right-click on the whitespace beside the `Binary` value for `Daily_2.xlsx`.
2. Choose **Add as new Query**.
3. Rename that new query `BinarySample`.

	Content	A^B_C Name	A^B_C Extension
1	Binary	Daily_1.xlsx	.xlsx
2	Binary	Daily_2.xlsx	.xlsx
3	Binary	Daily_2a.xlsx	.xlsx
4	Binary	Daily_3.xlsx	.xlsx

Figure 14.15: First three columns from Query1 query

File parameter

The binary content is an input value. When developing a structured and modular approach, create a parameter for that. Here's how to do it:

1. Choose **Manage Parameters** and select **New parameter** from the options.
2. Assign the name BinaryFile, which reflects its purpose, making it easy to identify.
3. Choose **Binary** for **Type** and **Suggested Values**.
4. Enter BinarySample for **Default Value** and also set it for **Current Value**.

Transformation pattern

We will keep the modular approach going, setting up a transformation development query that takes the BinaryFile parameter as its input value:

1. Right-click on the BinaryFile parameter query.
2. Choose **Reference** from the available options.

   This adds a new query and shows the file in the **Preview** pane.

3. Double-click the file to invoke the **Excel.Workbook** function.
4. Rename this query TransformData.

Now the content of the selected Excel file is visible, as depicted in *Figure 14.16*.

A^B_C Name	Data	A^B_C Item	A^B_C Kind
1 Daily	Table	Daily	Sheet

Figure 14.16: Contents from the sample file

This marks another pivotal moment in the development process. It's possible that the file contents, unlike *Figure 14.16*, yield a table containing more than one row. In scenarios where data is uniform and should be consolidated into a single table, the process of selecting relevant rows, choosing a sample, and creating a parameter as previously illustrated repeats.

On the other hand, if file contents here show multiple distinct sets of data are present, a new query will have to be created for each separate table to develop. Then, duplicate this query, provide an appropriate name, and repeat the forthcoming process for each of them.

Alright, now, taking potential inconsistencies across files into account that may hamper accurate data identification, proactive measures can be implemented. Instead of immediately drilling down into the Data column, a safeguard can be put in place that is able to address some level of inconsistency between files, such as letter casing. To illustrate, we will apply a filter on rows where Kind is equal to Sheet and Name is equal to Daily, and make sure this comparison is performed in a case-insensitive manner:

```
Table.SelectRows( Source,
    each Text.Lower([Name]) = "daily" and [Kind] = "Sheet"
)
```

Understand that a `filter` expression like this will never return more than a single row as sheet names have to be unique within a workbook and letter casing is not considered. This makes it safe to drill down into the `Data` column by applying a combination of optional item and field access:

1. Inside the formula bar, after the closing parenthesis, apply optional item access, `{0}?`, to get the first record from the table.

2. This should be directly followed by optional field access, `[Data]?`, to return the value from the requested field.

3. In the **Applied Steps** pane, rename this step `RAW`.

Now the content of the selected sheet is visible, in part, as depicted in *Figure 14.17*.

A^B_C Column3	A^B_C Column4	ABC 123 Column5	ABC 123 Column6	
null Daily by Date Performance Data - Preliminary		*null*	*null*	*null*
null My Property: Business Name2		*null*	*null*	*null*
null Comp Set: Location4 #444444, Location5 #555555, Location 6 #66666...		*null*	*null*	*null*
null	*null*	*null*	*null*	*null*
null	*null*	*null*	*null*	*null*
null Job Number: 37165322 Staff: User1 Created: May 15, 2023 Curr...		*null*	*null*	*null*
null	*null*	*null*	*null*	*null*
null	*null*	*null*	*null* Occupancy	
null Date	DOW		*null* This Year	
null	*null*	*null*	*null* My Prop	
null 05/22/2023	Mon		*null*	96,84210526
null 05/23/2023	Tue		*null*	97,89473684

Figure 14.17: Partial view of the data on the Daily sheet

Remove blank rows

Looking at the data, there are quite a number of completely blank columns and rows. It seems a good strategy to remove them first, and the UI offers this feature for rows:

1. On the **Home** tab, choose **Remove Rows** then **Remove Blank Rows**.

2. In the **Applied Steps** pane, rename that step `NoEmptyRows`.

That action produced the following M code, visible in the formula bar:

```
Table.SelectRows(RAW,
    each not List.IsEmpty(
        List.RemoveMatchingItems( Record.FieldValues(_), {"", null})
    )
)
```

Remove blank columns

There is no equivalent feature to remove blank columns. Instead, we will have to develop that logic. But let's take inspiration from the `NoEmptyRows` step:

1. We can reuse part of it. Go ahead and copy the M code from the each keyword until the second-to-last closing parenthesis from the formula bar.

2. Click the **fx** in front of the formula bar to insert a manual step.

3. Inside the formula bar, you can see the previous step name, place the cursor before it, and enter the function `Table.SelectColumns(`

4. Move your cursor to the end and place a comma. The second parameter expects a list with column names to keep. That logic will be provided by another expression, producing a list with all column names based on a condition, like so:

   a. Enter the `List.Select` function.

   b. Pass it the current column names: `Table.ColumnNames(NoEmptyRows)`

   c. Follow this with a comma and paste the copied logic as the condition `each not List. IsEmpty(List.RemoveMatchingItems(Record.FieldValues(_), {"", null}))`

   d. This operation won't be performed row by row but column by column; therefore, `Record.FieldValues(_)` will have to be replaced by `Table.Column( NoEmptyRows, _)`, producing a list with column values.

   e. Lastly, insert the closing parenthesis in the `Table.SelectColumns` function.

5. Rename this step `NoEmptyCols`.

Following the provided steps closely, the expression should now look like this:

```
Table.SelectColumns( NoEmptyRows,
    List.Select( Table.ColumnNames(NoEmptyRows),
        each not List.IsEmpty(
            List.RemoveMatchingItems(
                Table.Column( NoEmptyRows, _),
                {"", null}
            )
        )
    )
)
```

As a result, all columns containing only blanks and/or nulls have been removed.

Given the high probability of needing to remove empty columns when working with Excel files in the future, transforming this task into a custom function appears to be a logical step. This approach comes with additional benefits – let's discover them.

Custom functions

The significant amount of logic involved in performing this operation references the table from the `NoEmptyRows` step three times. It would be great to offload that to a function parameter. Let's create a custom function above the `Source` step in the **Advanced Editor**. This will also enhance the readability and reusability of the code in the future.

1. Copy the expression assigned to the `NoEmptyCols` step.

2. Insert a new step above `Source` and call it: `fxNoEmptyCols =`

3. Before we paste the logic, we aim to turn this into a custom function:

    a. Enter the function initializer – parentheses with a goes to sign: `() =>`

    b. This function requires one parameter – a table-type input value. Let's call it `tbl` and specify its type: `tbl as table`

    c. The function's return value is `table` as well. We can specify that between the closing parenthesis and the goes to sign: `as table`

    d. After the goes to sign, paste the copied code, and replace all table references with the `tbl` input parameter.

When done, the variable and its expression will look like this:

```
fxNoEmptyCols = (tbl as table) as table => Table.SelectColumns( tbl,
    List.Select( Table.ColumnNames( tbl ),
            each not List.IsEmpty (
                List.RemoveMatchingItems(
                    Table.Column( tbl, _),
                    {null, ""}
                )
            )
        )
    ),
```

Now we have that custom function in place, it's time to update the logic assigned to the `NoEmptyCols` step. Inside the formula bar, change the expression into:

```
fxNoEmptyCols( NoEmptyRows )
```

Extract header data

Before removing all document header rows (see *Figure 14.18*), a key piece of information needs to be extracted from the header. The last word on the second line, `Name2`, is a `Property ID`, which has to be included in a new column, in the final output:

A^BC Column3	A^BC Column4
1 Daily by Date Performance Data - Preliminary	*null*
2 My Property: Business Name2	*null*
3 Comp Set: Location4 #444444, Location5 #555555, Location 6 #66666...	*null*
4 Job Number: 37165322 Staff: User1 Created: May 15, 2023 Curr...	*null*

Figure 14.18: Showing document header rows

When devising a strategy to extract that `Property ID`, it's crucial to avoid hard-coding field references, since consistency across files is not guaranteed. Relying on a hard-coded reference may cause errors or return incorrect values.

There are two steps to retrieving this Property ID: first, extract the entire string from the header. Second, extract the last word from that string. A record expression is useful here as it allows you to look inside and review intermediate results during development or at a later stage when troubleshooting. Open the **Advanced Editor**, create a new variable at the top, and call it GetPropertyID:

1. Initialize the record expression: [ ].
2. Call the first field PropertyString and assign an expression to obtain the second row from the table as a record: NoEmptyCols{1}.
3. Transform the record into a list by wrapping Record.ToList(…) around it.
4. Extract the first list item by subsequently wrapping List.First(…) around it.
5. Include a comma at the end, to create a new field for this GetPropertyID record.
6. Call that second field PropertyID and assign it an expression to split the string:

   Text.Split(PropertyString, " ") This returns a list.

7. Extract the last list item by wrapping List.Last(…) around it.
8. Return the PropertyID value through field access.

Here's how that record expression should look. It returns the text value Name2:

```
GetPropertyID = [
    PropertyString = List.First( Record.ToList(NoEmptyCols{1})),
    PropertyID = List.Last( Text.Split( PropertyString, " "))
][PropertyID],
```

With the PropertyID successfully extracted, we can include this value in the final output at a later stage in the data transformation process.

Remove rows

The header and footer information is positioned in the first column of the table, and all adjacent cells extending to the far right are empty. We can leverage a familiar pattern to eliminate these rows as the process is similar to that of NoEmptyRows, but we'll keep that step as is and in place for the purpose of extracting the PropertyID:

1. Copy the entire second argument value from the NoEmptyRows step: each   not List.IsEmpty(List.RemoveMatchingItems(Record.FieldValues(_), {"", null})).
2. Then, go to the last step in the **Applied Steps** pane, NoEmptyCols, and place a filter on any field. That will generate a new step and some code. Replace the second argument within this step with the code copied earlier from NoEmptyRows.
3. The inner Record.FieldValues(_) returns a list of field values in the same order as the column order in the table. To omit values from the first column, wrap List.Skip(…) around this expression.
4. Rename the step RemoveRows.
5. At the bottom, two rows remain in total. Simply select **Remove Rows**, then **Remove Bottom Rows** from the **Home** tab to exclude them, and rename this step GetDataRange.

Although formatted here, the combined syntax for RemoveRows should look like this:

```
Table.SelectRows(NoEmptyCols,
    each not List.IsEmpty(
        List.RemoveMatchingItems(
            List.Skip( Record.FieldValues(_)), {"", null}
        )
    )
)
```

The development process is progressing nicely, yet guaranteeing data from each file is accurately placed into corresponding columns during an append operation requires them to have matching names.

New headers

The first three rows of this intermediate table contain headers (see *Figure 14.19*). In an Excel workbook, headers are often placed within merge cells. As a result, one cell will contain this value and others will be blank. There is a common five-step pattern to resolve this: **Transpose** the table, **Fill Down**, **Merge Columns**, **Transpose** back, and **Promote Headers**. These steps can all be performed through the UI, with no coding required.

	A^B_C Column3	A^B_C Column4	123 Column6	
1		*null*	*null* Occupancy	
2	Date	DOW	This Year	
3		*null*	*null* My Prop	
4	05/22/2023	Mon	96,84210526	
5	05/22/2023	Tue	97,89473684	

Figure 14.19: Partial view of the intermediate table

However, there are alternatives. We will provide one here. This requires splitting the table and transforming header rows separately from the data rows, in combination with a trick to fill columns to the right by transforming each individual table row, a record, into a table and invoking **fill down**. That process was demonstrated in *Chapter 8, Working with Nested Structures*.

1. On the **Home** tab, choose **Keep Rows**, then **Keep Top Rows**, and enter 3. Inside the formula bar, the code reads `Table.FirstN(GetDataRange,3)`.

2. Place your cursor directly after the equal sign in the formula bar and enter `Table.TransformRows(`.

3. Place your cursor at the end, enter a comma, the each expression followed by `Record.ToTable(_)`, and add a closing parenthesis to `Table.TransformRows` to review intermediate results.

4. To fill down values within the `Value` column, wrap `Table.FillDown( …, {"Value"})` around it.

5. Extract the `Value` column as a list by adding `[Value]` directly after the closing parenthesis of the `Table.FillDown` function. This returns a list, with a nested list for each row, as shown in *Figure 14.20*.

6. Rename the step GetHeaderRows:

```
Table.TransformRows(
    Table.FirstN(GetDataRange,3),
    each Table.FillDown( Record.ToTable(_), {"Value"})[Value]
)
```

	List
1	List
2	List
3	List

Figure 14.20: GetHeaderRows produces a list of lists.

Keeping a modular approach, now is a good time to break the logic out into a new step. Insert a manual step by clicking **fx** in front of the formula bar:

1. Values need to be combined by their position: List.Zip(GetHeaderRows).
2. Now all list items can be transformed: List.Transform(…, each Text.Combine(_, " | ")) to return a single text value for each column, depicted in *Figure 14.21*.
3. Rename this step Headers:

```
List.Transform(
    List.Zip( GetHeaderRows ),
    each Text.Combine( _, " | ")
)
```

	List
1	Date
2	DOW
3	Occupancy | This Year | My Prop
4	Occupancy | This Year | Comp Set
5	Occupancy | % Chg | My Prop

Figure 14.21: Headers list, showing the first five items

Finally, it's time to get the data section and assign these headers to the columns:

1. Click **fx** to create a manual step and replace Headers with GetDataRange inside the formula bar. This will return the value associated with that variable/step.
2. Skip the top three rows: Table.Skip(GetDataRange, 3).
3. Rename columns, using List.Zip to create rename lists: Table.RenameColumns(…, List.Zip({Table.ColumnNames(GetDataRange), Headers})).

4.   Rename the step GetTable.

```
Table.RenameColumns(
    Table.Skip( GetDataRange, 3),
    List.Zip({Table.ColumnNames(GetDataRange), Headers} )
)
```

Reverting to a previous step midway in a query is no issue at all. However, it's important to be cautious as query interactions afterward like inserting or modifying steps through the UI may disrupt variable references within expressions. A practical solution to minimize that risk is positioning these steps in a safer location, like above the Source step, where query interaction is unlikely, similar to the placement of the custom function and field-accessing record expression.

To reposition both the GetHeaderRows and Headers steps, open the **Advanced Editor** window. From there, select **Cut**, and then **Paste** these steps on a new line inserted between the let clause and the initial expression. This rearrangement ensures the steps are less likely to be affected by changes made from the UI at a later stage. After repositioning these steps in the Advanced Editor, the step order will resemble that shown in *Figure 14.22*.

```
1   let
2       GetHeaderRows = Table.TransformRows( Table.FirstN(GetDataRange,3), each
3           Table.FillDown( Record.ToTable(_), {"Value"})[Value]
4       ),
5       Headers = List.Transform( List.Zip( GetHeaderRows ), each Text.Combine( _, " | ")),
6       GetPropertyID = [
7               PropertyString = List.First( Record.ToList(NoEmptyCols{1})),
8               PropertyID = List.Last( Text.Split( PropertyString, " "))
9           ][PropertyID],
10      fxNoEmptyCols = (tbl as table) as table => Table.SelectColumns( tbl,
11          List.Select( Table.ColumnNames(tbl),
12              each not List.IsEmpty ( List.RemoveMatchingItems( Table.Column( tbl, _), {null, ""})) )
13          ),
14      Source = Excel.Workbook( BinaryFile ),
```

Figure 14.22: Repositioned steps in the Advanced Editor

A Changed Type step will top all polls on *steps that raise errors*. Maybe unjustly so, as defining data types is intended to help avoid errors and ensure accurate results.

Data types

It is advisable to set column types as late as possible, toward the end of the query development process. When defining data types, you can also specify locale. This enables a more accurate interpretation of dates and numbers. Data types are defined at the field/column level. Setting a column's data type through the UI triggers a type conversion to a nullable type, and invokes the Table.TransformColumnTypes function.

Let's set the type for the Date column. Click the **ABC123** to the left of the column name and set it to **date**. That generates the following syntax:

```
Table.TransformColumnTypes(ExpandContent,{{"Date", type date}})
```

A culture can be specified as the third parameter. Pass en-US for the *United States*:

```
Table.TransformColumnTypes(ExpandContent,{{"Date", type date}}, "en-US")
```

According to the specification of the expected outcome file, we are close to completion of this initial data preparation phase. All columns should be converted to text. While there might be discussions about the appropriateness of that data type, it's worth noting text values can be converted to any primitive data type – a safe choice.

Examine the expression inside the formula bar closely. It's important to recognize that we're dealing with a nested structure: a list within a list for which the format is { columnName, typeName }. And there should be one list for every column whose type to set. This pattern can be made dynamic and more succinct.

1.   Inside the formula bar, delete the nested structure {{"Date", type date}}.
2.   Enter the List.Transform(function.
3.   Pass it the Headers list as the first argument. This contains all column names.
4.   Transform each column name to the format { columnName, typeName }, like so: each {_, type text}. Include a closing parenthesis to the function.

Although formatted here, this is what the expression looks like:

```
Table.TransformColumnTypes( GetTable,
    List.Transform( Headers, each {_, type text}), "en-US"
)
```

Every column has now been assigned the text data type, showing an ABC icon in front of its name.

Adding a field

The final step in this transformation process is inserting the Property ID, which assigns the GetPropertyID value to every row in the table. Simply follow these steps:

1.   Navigate to **Add Column** and choose **Custom Column**.
2.   Provide a column name: Property ID.
3.   Enter the GetPropertyID reference in the formula section.
4.   Rename the step InsertPropertyID.

Inside the formula bar, ascribe the type to this column by entering a comma before the closing parenthesis, followed by type text:

```
Table.AddColumn(SetColTypes, "Poperty ID", each GetPropertyID, type text)
```

The data from this sample file has now been shaped exactly like the ExpectedCombined file. It's time to consider if and how to deal with empty files and errors.

Empty file condition

Determine whether acting on empty files is necessary for the purpose of query optimization or reporting. This is not hard to implement. Keep in mind that when no intervention is made, an error will be raised, but more about that in a moment.

For our requirement, active reporting on empty files isn't necessary. Yet, monitoring and assessing whether any modifications need to be made to optimize the query can be beneficial. When the data identification criteria of the RAW step fail, an empty table is returned, providing an opportunity to modify the query's output. Here's how:

1. Click **fx** in front of the formula bar to insert a manual step.
2. Enter this expression: = if Table.IsEmpty(RAW) then "File is empty." else InsertPropertyID
3. Rename that step Result:

```
if Table.IsEmpty( RAW ) then "File is empty." else InsertPropertyID
```

This conditional statement acts like a switch, determining whether to output a text string or table value. Keeping this as the final step in the query ensures that the entire sequence of transformation operations remains visible and accessible from the **Applied Steps** pane.

When placed out of order, **Applied Steps** will show all operations collapsed into one single step. There's no technical requirement to keep the Result variable as the final query step, because there is no impact on how it operates or the structure of the M code. Nonetheless, the placement does significantly influence the UI experience, impacting future query development and hand-off. Consequently, it's advisable to document this strategic choice and its function in a comment. *Right-click* the **Result** step name, choose **Properties**, and enter a **Description**, as illustrated in *Figure 14.23*. An information icon will be displayed in the **Applied Steps** section afterward.

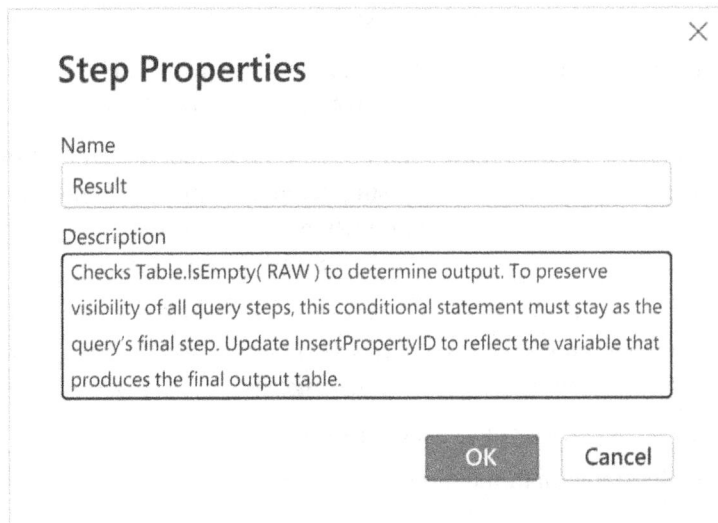

Figure 14.23: Insert comments for documentation

The TransformData query contains the entire data transformation process. It has been developed and applied to a single sample file. But in order to process all files in the exact same manner, it has to be converted into a function query that can be invoked on all selected files within the folder.

Query, create function

You can convert a query into a function query with help from the UI. It's essential to have a modular setup in place because the query **Create Function** option will ask to provide a parameter for each argument passed to the function. In this case, there is only one input, the **BinaryFile** already set up as a parameter.

Right-click **TransformData** and select **Create Function**. A dialog box will appear, prompting you to enter a name for the new function. As illustrated in *Figure 14.24*, enter fxCollectData. This action generates a function query called fxCollectData, and places both the **BinaryFile** parameter and **TransformData** in a folder called fxCollectData.

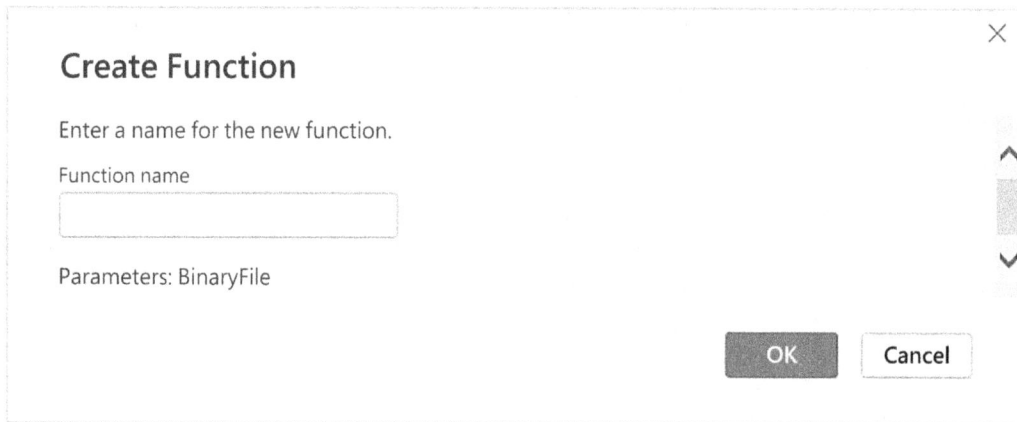

Figure 14.24: The Create Function dialog

Organize your queries by moving FolderLocation, and BinarySample into the fxCollectData folder. This can be achieved by *dragging* and *dropping* them or by *right-clicking* and selecting **Move to group**.

Return to Query1, rename it CombinedData, and keep the Name and Content columns. This can be done through the UI by selecting them and choosing **Remove Columns | Remove Other Columns**, or, for more succinct and clean code, by applying projection, adding [[Name], [Content]] at the end of the SelectFiles expression inside the formula bar. For the following step, we will assume projection was used.

There are several methods to transform structured values within a table. These were covered in *Chapter 8, Working with Nested Structures*. Here, we will leverage the Table.TransformColumns function:

1. Click **fx** in front of the formula bar to insert a manual step.
2. Enter the function between the equal sign and the variable name: Table.TransformColumns(.

3. As the second argument, it expects a transformation operations list: {"Content", each fxCollectData(_)}.

4. Add the closing parenthesis to the Table.TransformColumns function and rename this step InvokedFunction:

```
Table.TransformColumns( SelectFiles, {"Content", each fxCollectData(_)})
```

	A^B_C Name	ABC 123 Content
1	Daily_1.xlsx	Table
2	Daily_2.xlsx	Table
3	Daily_2a.xlsx	**File is empty.**
4	Daily_3.xlsx	Table

Figure 14.25: Contents in the Content column after invoking fxCollectData

After transforming the values inside the **Content** column shown in *Figure 14.25*, an empty file is present. Regardless, a monitoring workflow has to be implemented for as long as the empty file switch is applied to the TransformData query.

Set up monitoring

Setting up a monitoring workflow to receive notifications about empty files is straightforward in the Power BI service. Start by duplicating the CombinedData query and rename this duplicate EmptyFiles. Then, isolate all relevant rows by applying a filter. Go ahead and also rename this filter step to EmptyFiles:

```
Table.SelectRows(InvokedFunction, each [Content] = "File is empty.")
```

As this query is intended to facilitate monitoring, its helpful to include the file location in the output. Select the Source step. This shows a column is present that contains this value. It's called Folder Path but had been omitted earlier. Now select the SelectFiles step. Here, we have applied projection to limit the columns. Therefore, to include this column and place it in front as the first column in the table, insert [Folder Path], as shown here:

```
[[Folder Path], [Name], [Content]]
```

This EmptyFiles query can be loaded into the data model, as a standalone, hidden table. To enable notification, create a simple DAX measure, like so:

```
EmptyFileCount_ModelName = COUNTROWS( EmptyFiles )
```

This measure can be placed in a visual providing the ability to set up a threshold trigger within the Power BI service, such as a card. Once that is all done and the threshold value is crossed, you or your team can be alerted automatically to investigate.

Finetuning

Next, return to the `CombinedData` query. Here, for as long as the empty file switch is applied to the `TransformData` query, rows meeting that criterion will have to be excluded. Regardless of whether any rows currently satisfy that condition, call it `NoEmptyFiles`:

```
Table.SelectRows(InvokedFunction, each [Content] <> "File is empty.")
```

When this `NoEmptyFiles` step is omitted, encountering an empty file will raise an error. Moreover, processing files in bulk could reveal other issues over time, which may potentially cause an error to be raised. Proactively incorporating a strategy to address this scenario can be warranted. *Chapter 12, Handling Errors and Debugging,* provides a method to capture errors for reporting, providing the means to implement a similar but separate workflow to that of managing empty files.

When files causing failures are identified, additional transformation logic will likely be required to fix the underlying issue. Here's how the process of modifying or updating the M code applied through the `fxCollectData` custom function will look:

1. Start by pinpointing a file that raises an error during processing.
2. Navigate to the `BinarySample` query and select the `SelectFiles` step.
3. Drill down into the `Content` column for the identified file.
4. Remove the `Imported Excel workbook` step when that was generated automatically, to show the selected file as a file in the **Preview** pane.
5. Move to the `CollectData` query and identify the step where errors occur.
6. Incorporate additional logic or update code accordingly, to resolve that.
7. Select the `CombinedData` query, and confirm no issues remain. When errors persist, repeat these steps until all issues have been cleared.

Under no circumstance should you modify the `fxCollectData` query directly; this query is linked to reflect any changes made to `CollectData`. However, that link will be severed once `fxCollectData` has been opened in the Advanced Editor. Luckily, the user will be prompted beforehand with a warning message, as shown in *Figure*. Press **Cancel** to abort. Equally, when not prompted with this warning, which indicates the connection is already lost, any modifications to `CollectData` will not sync to `fxCollectData`. In such cases, to reestablish a linked function query, a new function will have to be generated from the `CollectData` query and the `InvokedFunction` step needs to be updated.

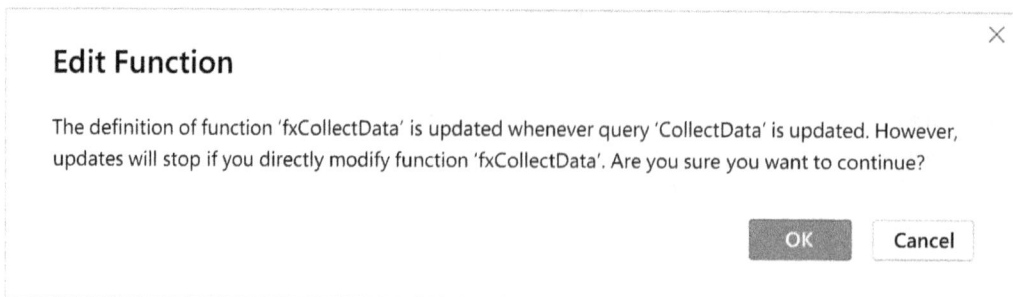

Figure 14.26: Warning message when trying to open the Advanced Editor for the fxCollectData query

Without incorporating error reporting, you might want errors to persist and cause failures to signal there is an issue that needs to be addressed. For now, we will assume error reporting has been implemented, and it is safe to exclude all rows with errors. Choose **Remove Rows**, then **Remove Errors** on the **Home** tab, and rename the step RemoveErrors.

The content from all files can now be combined.

Combine files

Click the expand column option, in the header of the Content column. This allows you to select and expand columns from the nested tables. *Click* on the sideward arrow icon. By default, all fields will be selected and, when enabled, disable the **Use original column name as prefix** option at the bottom before clicking **OK**.

This will add a new step to the query. Inside the formula bar, you can see it passed two hard-coded lists to the Table.ExpandTableColumn function. That first list contains columnNames to expand from each nested table and the second list, newColumnNames, to assign to the parent table. This helps avoid conflicts between names in the existing and new columns. However, the risk a file will suddenly include fields called Name or Content is extremely low, therefore that final list can be deleted. As for the first list, that can be replaced by a function providing all column names from the CollectData query dynamically. After these modifications, the expression within the formula bar will look like this – rename that step ExpandAllColumns:

```
Table.ExpandTableColumn(RemoveErrors, "Content",
    Table.ColumnNames(CollectData)
)
```

Having successfully combined data from all three files, each corresponds to a week's worth of data, producing one comprehensive table consisting of 21 rows and 22 columns. All values are formatted as text, mirroring the ExpectedCombined.xlsx file. With all the necessary data compiled and structured according to the predefined specifications, we are well positioned to move forward and begin transformations for the analytics phase.

Summary

In this chapter, we have highlighted practical aspects of data manipulation and preparation by focusing on two very different topics: extracting fixed patterns and combining data from multiple Excel files. Although they feel worlds apart, these skills, among many others, are both essential for transforming raw data into insightful, actionable information.

By breaking down processes into manageable pieces, underscoring the importance of a methodical approach as well as creative problem-solving, we aimed to offer a collection of ideas, fuelling your imagination to tackle any challenge. The next chapter focuses on another critical area: optimizing performance. You will learn about factors that influence, and methods to improve, query performance.

Learn more on Discord

Join our community's Discord space for discussions with the author and other readers:

https://discord.gg/vCSG5GBbyS

15

Optimizing Performance

While returning accurate data is important, the speed of your queries greatly affects the user experience. Long refresh times for your datasets may result in timeouts, and waiting for the results of your transformations in the Power Query editor can be frustrating. In this chapter, we will delve into strategies to optimize the performance of your queries. We will first look at memory usage when evaluating queries and how using too much memory slows down your queries. We will then look at different strategies to prevent this from happening.

We'll look at the importance of query folding and how you can ensure that the data source processes as many transformations as possible. Then, we'll cover the formula firewall, a tool designed to protect your queries from exposing sensitive information. We'll explain what triggers errors related to this and discuss its effect on your queries. Additionally, we'll examine how storing data in memory (buffering) can make your queries run faster. Finally, we'll offer tips for selecting a data source, keeping these considerations in mind.

We will cover the following topics:

- Understanding memory usage when evaluating queries
- Query folding
- The formula firewall
- Optimizing query performance
- Performance tips

Understanding memory usage when evaluating queries

Retrieving data and performing transformations does not come for free. To run queries, Power Query requires memory. Some approaches require more memory than others. Understanding how to improve memory usage therefore helps when optimizing queries. *So how does that work?*

Queries are executed within a **mashup container,** a dedicated process responsible for query evaluation. You can see the number of mashup containers used by going to the **Task Manager** and opening the processes for Power BI Desktop:

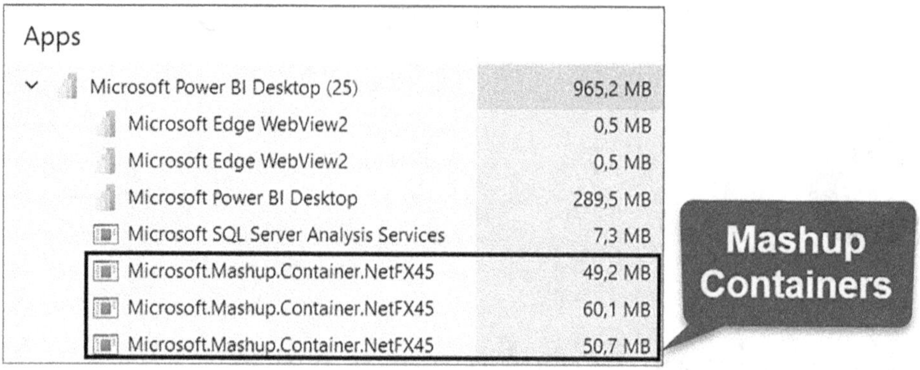

Figure 15.1: Mashup containers show up in the Task Manager

The memory given to each container depends on where you're running Power Query. Common environments include Power BI Desktop, the Power BI service, and the on-premises data gateway. So what happens when container memory runs low?

When a mashup container's memory needs exceed its allocated limit during query evaluation, Power Query begins paging (transferring) query data to disk storage. This paging process leads to a notable decrease in query performance, as disk access is significantly slower than memory access. Therefore, being aware of the memory limitations and managing your queries accordingly is important for optimizing performance in Power Query.

Memory limit variations and adjustments

The memory limit for each mashup container depends on the execution environment, and in some cases, you can adjust it. These are the environments that are typically used:

- **Gateway machine:** The memory per container is calculated automatically for machines running the on-premises gateway. While you can't set any limits yourself, increasing the memory and speed of the machine can improve query refresh times.

- **Power BI service:** You can't change the memory limit here. However, if you're using a premium version of Power BI, you get more resources, which may improve performance.

- **Power BI Desktop:** You can adjust how much memory is used here. You'll find this option under **File > Options and Settings > Options**, in the **Data Load** tab.

For Power BI Desktop, as of the time of writing, the standard maximum memory allocation for each query evaluation is 432 MB. You can adjust this in Power BI Desktop by going to **File**, choosing **Options and Settings**, and then selecting **Options**. You can alter the query memory settings in the **Data Load** tab:

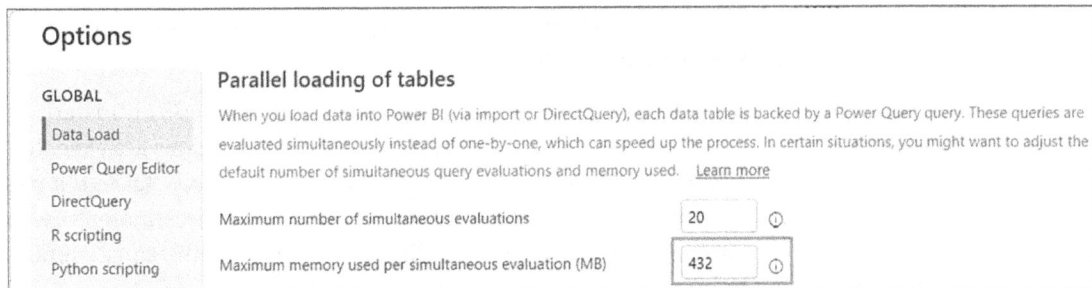

Figure 15.2: You can set a maximum amount of memory for query evaluation in Power BI Desktop

Remember, the maximum memory that can be assigned to a query depends on the total memory available on your machine.

To achieve faster query execution in Power Query, the primary strategies involve managing memory usage. This includes:

- Minimizing memory consumption at import.
- When using memory, ensuring the data volume is as small as possible.

Next, we'll explore some strategies to help you do this.

Query folding

Query folding is one of the most important aspects for optimizing your queries' performance and is useful for any developer who connects to external data sources. It's a process where the evaluation of a query is offloaded to the data source itself.

> During query folding, Power Query's mashup engine converts a query's transformations into the data source's native language. This approach combines multiple transformation steps into one efficient query that the data source can execute.

Doing so transfers the computational load of these transformations from the local environment, where Power Query operates, directly to the data source, like an SQL database. Any remaining transformations that can't be folded are performed locally.

The primary goal of query folding is to reduce memory usage in Power Query by using the computational power of the data source to process queries and transformations. For instance, suppose you connect to a table in an SQL database and want to retrieve data for only the last week.

Instead of importing all data first and then filtering, query folding instead sends a precise query to retrieve only the relevant rows. That has two benefits:

1. **Optimizing resource usage:** Query folding uses the strengths of data sources by transferring the workload of query transformations directly to them. When transformations are executed on your local machine, it requires extracting all the data from a data source through a network, which is then processed in the Power Query engine. This can be resource-intensive and time-consuming. In contrast, your data source, typically a server or database, can generally handle these tasks more quickly and efficiently than your local system.

2. **Minimizing network data transfer:** An essential byproduct of this approach is the reduction in data transfer across the network. Instead of pulling large volumes of unprocessed data onto your local environment for transformation, query folding ensures that only the necessary, processed data is retrieved. This means only the necessary data (after selecting specific rows/columns) is sent over the network, which saves the bandwidth and time required for data transfer.

In addition to these key benefits, understanding query folding is crucial for two more reasons. Firstly, query folding is essential for using Direct Query and Dual storage mode tables in Power BI. These modes depend on query folding to send data requests directly to the database.

Secondly, query folding plays an important role in incremental refresh scenarios. Incremental refresh is a feature that allows loading data from a specific point in time. For example, in a table with millions of rows spanning 20 years, you can update only a recent portion of the data using incremental refresh. However, this is only feasible when the data source supports query folding, allowing your query to fetch just the necessary subset of data. Without query folding, the entire dataset must be retrieved and filtered locally, which is far less efficient.

So, how does query folding work in practice?

Query folding in action

To understand query folding, let's reflect on the M script. The M script creates a detailed plan for handling the data. It instructs Power Query on what steps to take, in what order, and how to combine these steps effectively.

Whenever we want to access a data source, we use data-accessing functions to the data source. Let's say we connect to an SQL database. The below image illustrates a query that connects to a table called Track:

```
1  let
2      Source = Sql.Database( Server, Database ),
3      dbo_Track = Source{[Schema="dbo",Item="Track"]}[Data]
4  in
5      dbo_Track
```

	1²₃ ⌕ TrackId ▼	AᵇC Name ▼	1²₃ AlbumId ▼	AᵇC Composer
1	1	For Those About To Rock (We Salute You)	1	Angus Young, f
2	2	Balls to the Wall	2	
3	3	Fast As a Shark	3	F. Baltes, S. Kau
4	4	Restless and Wild	3	F. Baltes, R.A. S
5	5	Princess of the Dawn	3	Deaffy & R.A. S

Query settings ＞

∨ Properties

Name

Track

∨ Applied steps

　🖫 Source ⚙ 📝

✕ ▦ dbo_Track

The query up to this step will be evaluated by the data source.

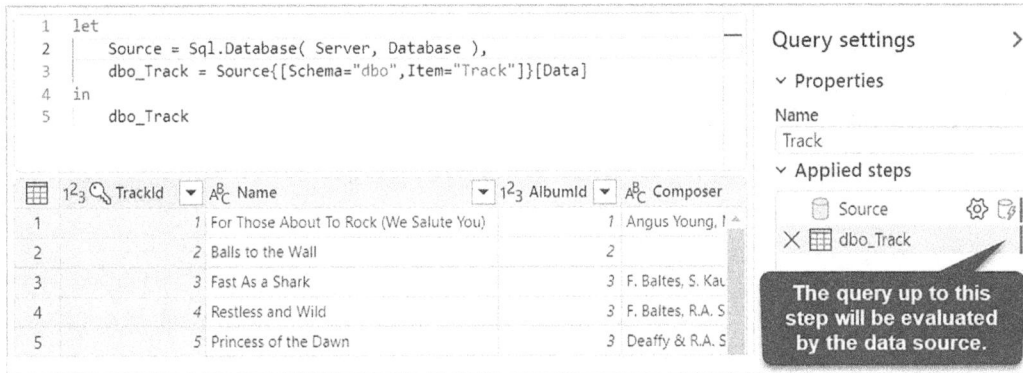

Figure 15.3: A query that connects to an SQL database

In the new Power Query experience, you can find indicators beside each step. When the step has a green **database icon with a lightning sign,** this indicates a step will fold (more about this later). To inspect what Power Query does under the hood, select any foldable step, right-click, and press **View data source query:**

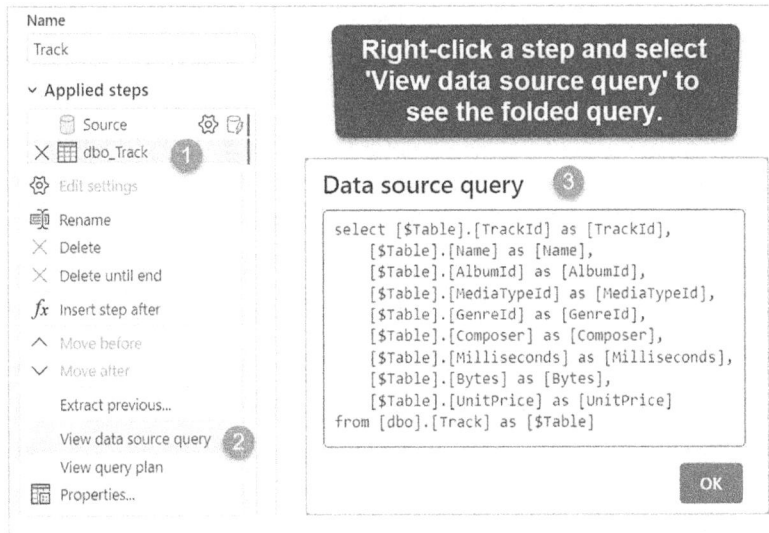

Name

Track

∨ Applied steps

　🖫 Source ⚙ 📝

✕ ▦ dbo_Track ①

⚙ Edit settings

🖹 Rename

✕ Delete

✕ Delete until end

ƒx Insert step after

∧ Move before

∨ Move after

　Extract previous...

　View data source query ②

　View query plan

🖽 Properties...

Right-click a step and select 'View data source query' to see the folded query.

Data source query ③

```
select [$Table].[TrackId] as [TrackId],
       [$Table].[Name] as [Name],
       [$Table].[AlbumId] as [AlbumId],
       [$Table].[MediaTypeId] as [MediaTypeId],
       [$Table].[GenreId] as [GenreId],
       [$Table].[Composer] as [Composer],
       [$Table].[Milliseconds] as [Milliseconds],
       [$Table].[Bytes] as [Bytes],
       [$Table].[UnitPrice] as [UnitPrice]
from [dbo].[Track] as [$Table]
```

OK

Figure 15.4: When View data source query is enabled for a step, you can view the folded query

You end up at a screen showing a popup with the folded query, a native SQL query. What that means is that the database server executes this query.

Now, let's make some changes to the query. Instead of showing all columns, I have selected five columns only. By checking the data source query of this new **RemoveColumns** step, we now get a different query that selects only the relevant columns, as shown in the following screenshot:

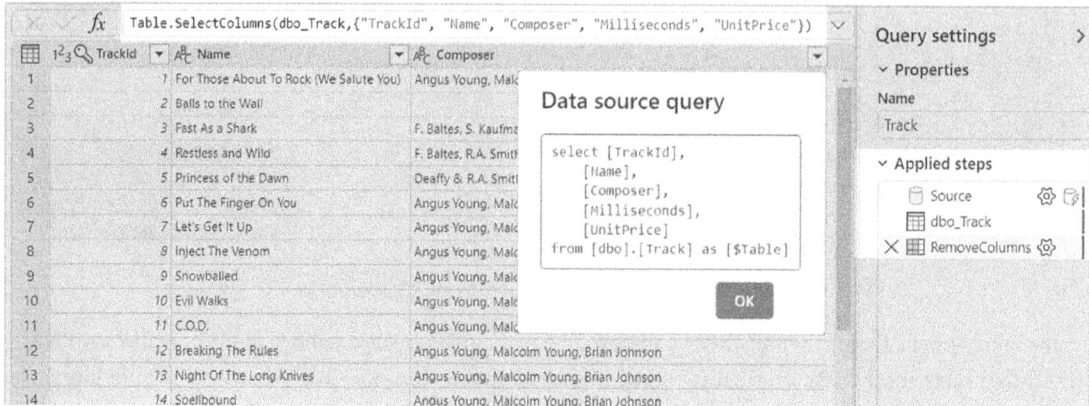

Figure 15.5: This data source query represents the selection of some columns

Think about this for a minute. Without query folding, Power Query would have to import all data (including unnecessary columns). After importing this, it would then discard the irrelevant columns. In other words, it would use unnecessary resources to import and then remove data.

However, thanks to query folding, Power Query sends a query that retrieves only the necessary fields. This approach has two fundamental benefits. Firstly, it significantly improves performance as only relevant data is transferred to the engine. Secondly, it enables users who may not be well versed in the query language of the data source (such as SQL) to still benefit from an automatically generated data source query.

It's important to note that there aren't explicit indicators in the old Power Query interface to show whether a step is being folded. To check if a step folds in this environment, right-click on it and look for the **Native Query** option. If this option is unavailable (grayed out), it indicates that it is unclear whether that step folds. This could mean folding has stopped, or the connector is unsure whether this step folds. We will delve more into this later in this chapter.

Now you've been introduced to query folding, you might wonder how Power Query decides which operations can be folded. In other words, what is the process behind query evaluation in this context?

Query evaluation

Most queries consist of several applied steps. To evaluate a query, the following steps take place:

1. **Initial retrieval:** The Power Query engine gathers the query's M code. It also collects data source credentials and data source privacy levels.

2. **Read data source metadata:** The engine queries the data source for metadata. This step determines the data source's capabilities and whether certain operations can be folded.

3. **Generate data source query:** Based on the information received, the engine determines (using the query folding mechanism) what information it can extract from the data source, and which transformation should happen inside the Power Query engine. Based on this, it generates a data source query and sends information to the transformations engine.

4. **Retrieve data:** The Power Query engine then receives the data as requested from the data, based on the earlier query.

5. **Execute remaining:** Any transformations that couldn't be folded are now carried out by the M engine on the retrieved data.

6. **Load data:** This processed data is loaded into the designated destination, such as Power BI or Excel.

As we said, the primary function of query folding in Power Query is to convert transformations into a data source query that the data source can execute. The connection to the data source is initially established using a function from the accessing data functions family. Query folding primarily targets the transformation steps that immediatelyfollow the step that connects to the data. The effectiveness of query folding in translating these transformations into a data source query depends on the capabilities of the connector being used with the data source.

Folding, not folding, and partial folding

Unfortunately, Power Query connectors are not smart enough to translate all M code to a data source query. Some operations cause query folding to break. Later in this chapter, we'll look into strategies to maintain query folding.

With that in mind, the following outcomes are possible:

- **Full query folding:** All transformations occur at the data source, and the Power Query engine receives the output.
- **Partial query folding:** A subset of transformations are folded and sent to the data source. The remaining steps that are not translated are processed in the Power Query engine.
- **No query folding:** When none of the applied steps can be transformed to the language of the data source, all transformations are done in the Power Query engine. It may be that the connector does not support query folding or that the particular transformation is not supported.

If your data source works with a query language, it likely supports query folding. You can think of sources like databases, OData feeds, and Active Directory. However, data sources like Excel files, CSV, or web sources don't support query folding.

As you've just learned, understanding how query folding works in your Power BI queries is important for reducing memory usage. But that would be hard if you didn't know which steps fold and which don't. To help in this area, Power Query provides a range of tools that can tell you whether a transformation folds.

Tools to determine foldability

Power Query has three main tools that allow you to determine whether a step folds. These tools are:

- View data source query
- Step folding indicators
- Query plan

In the following section, we'll delve into each one of them and show you how you can use them.

View data source query

As we saw earlier, the **View data source query** option is the first tool to determine whether a step folds. When you right-click on a step, you can find an option that says **View data source query**:

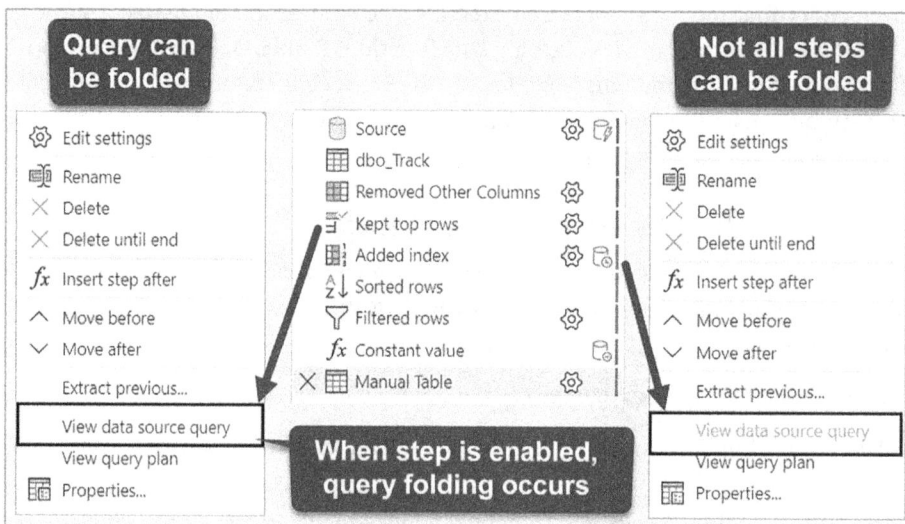

Figure 15.6: View data source query

When the feature is active, you can see the data source query that has been generated. If the feature appears grayed out, it indicates that some steps in your query are not foldable. However, this doesn't necessarily mean that your entire query is non-foldable; it could be partially foldable, or the connector might not support this feature. The **View native query** option is specific to certain database connectors that generate SQL queries. It is not applicable for connectors based on OData.

The advantage of this approach is that it works in both the old and new Power Query experiences. In the old Power Query experience, this option appears with the text **View native query**. The downside of this method is that you would have to go through each step to see whether it folds. Luckily there are other options available, which we will cover next.

Query folding indicators

Another option to determine foldability is by using the query folding indicators. These are available in the new Power Query experience and provide visual cues within the Power BI Query Editor. They provide information on whether each step in your query is being folded or whether a particular step is breaking the fold. This is useful because it signals which subsequent operations will be processed outside the data source.

Each step in your query will display one of the following indicators:

Indicator	Icon	Description
Folding		Indicates that this part of the query will be processed by the data source.
Not Folding		Indicates that this step will be processed outside the data source.
Might Fold		Whether or not a query step will be processed by the data source is uncertain and will be determined during query execution. Likely happens for ODBC or Odata connections.
Uncertain		Indicates an uncertain query plan, often due to providing a manual table or using transformations/connectors unsupported by the query plan tool and indicators.
Unknown		Indicates that there is no query plan available, which could be due to an error or because the query involves data formats other than tables.

* When an applied step in a query displays a specific folding indicator, any subsequent steps that have a vertical line with the same color as this indicator share the same query folding status.

Figure 15.7: An overview of the available query folding indicators

These indicators provide information about how Power Query interacts with your data source and whether it leverages the data source's processing capabilities. Let's look at an example.

Suppose we use the Sql.Database function to connect to an SQL database. This connector supports query folding and tries to transform any transformation on the underlying data to a data source query. We can use the expression:

```
Sql.Database( ServerAddress, DatabaseName )
```

The following image is the result of performing a range of transformations:

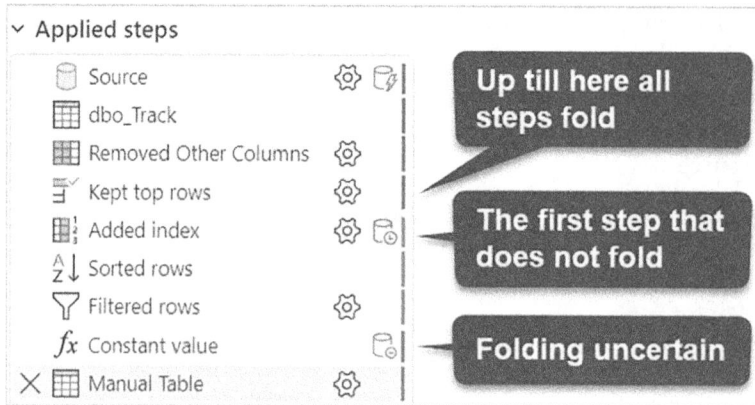

Figure 15.8: The query folding indicators signal the folding status of each applied step

The first four steps in this query are successfully folded, meaning Power Query can transform them into a query the data source understands. The first step displays the folding indicator, and the following three steps are marked with a vertical line of the same color, indicating their folded status.

However, a shift occurs at the **Added index** step, where we encounter the *Not Folding* indicator for the first time. This is a turning point for optimizing your query, as it indicates that further steps building onto this one will not fold and will be handled by the Power Query engine instead.

It's important to note that the presence of the *Not Folding* indicator does not mean the entire query fails to fold; it simply highlights that a portion of the query, starting from this point, does not fold, although other parts may still do so.

Another aspect to remember is that the current query plan (required for query folding) exclusively supports tables. Therefore, when a step involves adding a constant value that does not have a corresponding query plan, it is assigned the *Uncertain* folding indicator, reflecting this limitation.

The query folding indicators provide an easy way to determine query foldability. Yet with the new Power Query experience, there's another method you can use, the query plan.

Query plan

The query plan offers a third method to assess query folding. So what is the query plan? A query plan contains the mashup engine's instructions on how it executes a query on your data. It's a helpful tool to analyze the order in which the engine performs its operations. The new Power Query interface allows you to explore the M engine's generated query plan. To access it, right-click on any step in your query and select **View query plan**:

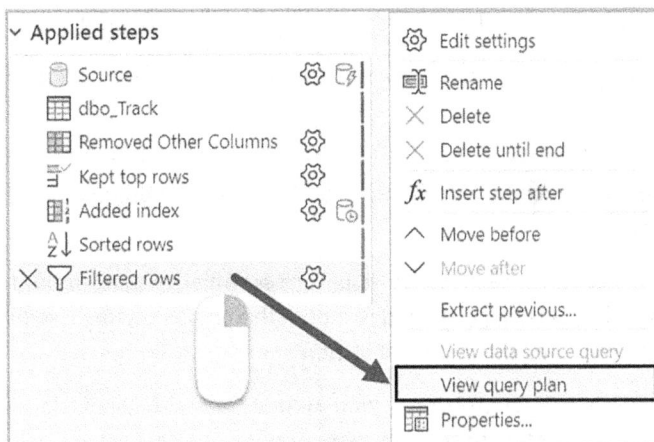

Figure 15.9: Viewing the query plan

Upon doing this, a window pops up, displaying the various steps of the query plan:

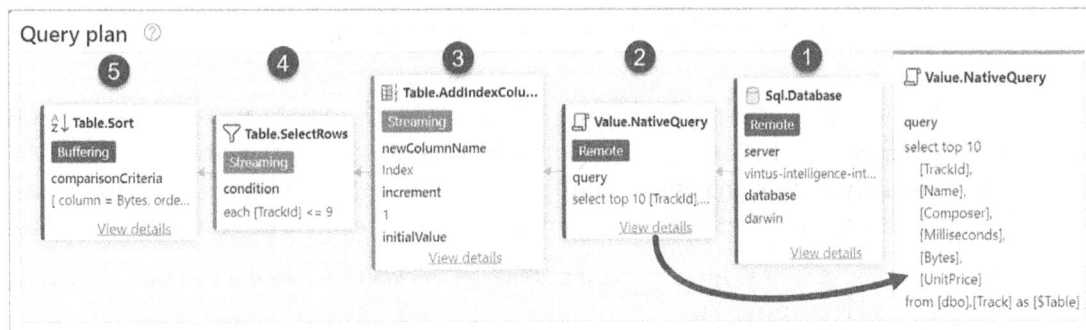

Figure 15.10: The query plan generated by the Power Query engine

The query plan represents all steps leading up to the selected one. It's read from right to left, and you can probably see how it relates to the applied steps in *Figure 15.9*. The following happens:

1. Connection to an SQL database, using *query folding*.

2. Retrieval of the top 10 rows using a *native query*, also via *query folding*.

3. Addition of an index column, which breaks *query folding*. This change is indicated by a shift from a *Remote* label to *Streaming*.

4. The query then filters the relevant rows.

5. Finally, the remaining rows are sorted.

However, the sequence in the query plan might not always align with the order of the applied steps. This may be confusing at first since you may be wondering why your first applied step is not the first transformation in the query plan.

The Power Query engine optimizes the query by potentially doing the following:

- **Combining steps:** The engine may choose to combine steps, like performing multiple filtering steps at once.
- **Removing steps:** If a future step makes an earlier one irrelevant, the query plan may remove it.
- **Reordering steps:** When the output remains the same, the engine may reorder steps to maximize query folding.

In the above query plan, the engine filters rows before sorting them, even though the applied steps order does the reverse. The revised query plan is more efficient, as sorting a reduced dataset requires fewer resources while producing the same outcome.

Operations that fold successfully in the query plan are marked with Remote labels in their boxes. For instance, clicking on the **Details** text in *step 2* lets you preview the data source query. You can use these visual cues to see whether important steps of your query successfully fold.

When you notice critical steps don't fold, consider restructuring your query or rewriting your transformations to improve foldability, thereby potentially improving performance. This can involve breaking down complex operations into simpler ones that fold or rearranging steps to allow more **Remote** executions.

You have now learned about three tools to verify whether a query (step) folds. We would like to point out that you can also verify whether a query step folds by using the **Query Diagnostics** feature. However, we don't generally recommend using it, as the information it provides is hard to interpret. Also, compared to the three tools outlined above, it requires unnecessary effort to determine query folding.

With an understanding of how to identify folding steps, let's now delve into the types of operations that typically fold and those that do not.

Operations and their impact on folding

In this section, we will delve into which operations fold and which won't. While the query folding mechanism does not support the same operations for each data source, you can apply some general principles. Sources like relational databases (SQL Server, Oracle, etc.), cubes (SSAS, SAP Hana/BW, and Google Analytics), Azure Data Explorer, OData, and premium dataflows support query folding. Since SQL databases belong to the most common data sources, the following examples revolve around SQL.

Foldable operations

The only operations that are capable of folding are transformations. Typically, if a transformation fits within a SELECT statement, it's likely to be foldable. Such statements can include clauses like WHERE, GROUP BY, and JOIN. You can also create columns with simple expressions compatible with SQL databases.

The following types of operations typically fold nicely:

- **Modifying columns:** Involves selecting, removing, renaming, or reordering columns that align with the SELECT clause in SQL

- **Custom calculations:** Only supports basic logic like text transformations, math, and even specific data type changes fitting within the SELECT clause
- **Sorting columns:** Corresponds to the ORDER BY clause in SQL
- **Filtering rows:** Aligns with the WHERE clause in SQL
- **Grouping data:** Is associated with the GROUP BY clause
- **Joining tables:** Non-fuzzy joins fall under the JOIN clause.
- **Appending queries:** Use the UNION ALL operator for appending queries.
- **Pivoting and unpivoting data:** These operations, aligning with the PIVOT/UNPIVOT operators in SQL, allow for data reorganization, changing its structure for better analysis.

It's important to be aware that certain transformations in Power Query may return different outcomes depending on whether they are executed by the Power Query engine or by the data source. This difference arises from the varying ways in which Power Query and many databases handle specific operations. Let's consider two examples to illustrate this:

- **Handling of null values in joins:** In Power Query, when you perform a left outer join, it treats two null values as equivalent, and a join may return values. However, in many database systems, null values are not considered equal. This difference in handling null values can lead to differences in the outcome of a join operation between Power Query and the database.
- **Case sensitivity in filters:** Suppose you filter a column for the city name Mexico in Power Query. By default, the operation is case-sensitive. However, when this query is folded and executed at the data source, it might ignore capitalization, as some databases do not consider the case when filtering text. That means the same operation could return different results depending on where it's executed.

Therefore, when translating Power Query code to native data source code, consider these potential differences. They could result in variations in the returned data for the same dataset based on where and how the query is processed. An alternative for those who want more control over their queries is to create a custom query and use it with the Value.NativeQuery function. We will explore this function in greater detail later in this chapter when delving into strategies for maintaining query folding.

Non-foldable operations

Query folding is a powerful feature in Power Query, but it has limitations due to certain non-foldable operations. We will now cover the limitations, which are operations that don't fold.

Transformations

When thinking of operations that don't fold, one of the most important categories is those of transformations. Despite many connectors effectively translating M code into data source queries, numerous transformations can still stop folding. This typically occurs when the connector lacks support for a specific transformation or the data source has no equivalent. Common non-foldable transformations include:

- Adding index or ranking columns.
- Combining or appending different data sources.

- Combining queries with different privacy levels.
- Operations without an equivalent in the data source. Some examples are Transpose, Keep Bottom N Rows, and Capitalizing the first letter of each word in a string.

There's no guarantee a type of operation folds. For example, converting a value to the text type might be foldable, but changing it to the time type might not. Connectors also receive updates so that some operations may be supported in the future. While most users who want to optimize query folding focus on transformations, other areas also impact folding, for instance, privacy levels.

Data source privacy levels

Another aspect impacting query folding is data source privacy levels. Working with data sources with incompatible privacy levels can trigger the formula firewall, which prevents query folding. The details of privacy levels and their effects on query folding and the formula firewall will be explored later in this chapter. Let's look at another area that can prevent query folding, that of providing native database queries.

Native database queries

Using native database queries typically breaks query folding. This occurs when employing the `Value.NativeQuery` function or custom statements in data access functions. However, there are instances where custom queries can still allow folding, which we'll examine in the upcoming section on maintaining query folding.

Functions designed to prevent query folding

Some functions are designed to prevent query folding from happening. The `Table.StopFolding` function is an example. It ensures that subsequent operations are executed within the Power Query engine. You might use these in scenarios where the data source, despite supporting folding, is extremely slow.

Similarly, the functions `List.Buffer`, `Table.Buffer`, and `Binary.Buffer` also stop folding by loading data into memory. Buffer functions and their role in optimization will be covered later in this chapter.

Considering these factors, what strategies can you use to preserve query folding for as long as possible?

Strategies for maintaining query folding

In this section, we'll explore various scenarios that can break query folding and look at methods to counteract these. To perform query folding examples yourself, you would need access to a data source that supports query folding, like a database. Since this book focuses on M code, the following examples, which show ways to maintain query folding, are meant to be read along.

Rearranging steps

The order in which you perform your operations can impact whether queries fold. To ensure your query runs as quickly as possible, rearranging steps is an excellent strategy so that the data source performs as many operations as possible.

For example, suppose we have a dataset with music tracks, and we want to perform the following transformations:

- **RemoveColumns:** Select the columns TrackId, Name, Composer, and Milliseconds from the original table.
- **KeepTopRows:** Keep only the first 10 rows from the table.
- **Filter_TrackID:** Filter the TrackIds with a value of 5 or higher.

The following image shows the query folding indicators for each step:

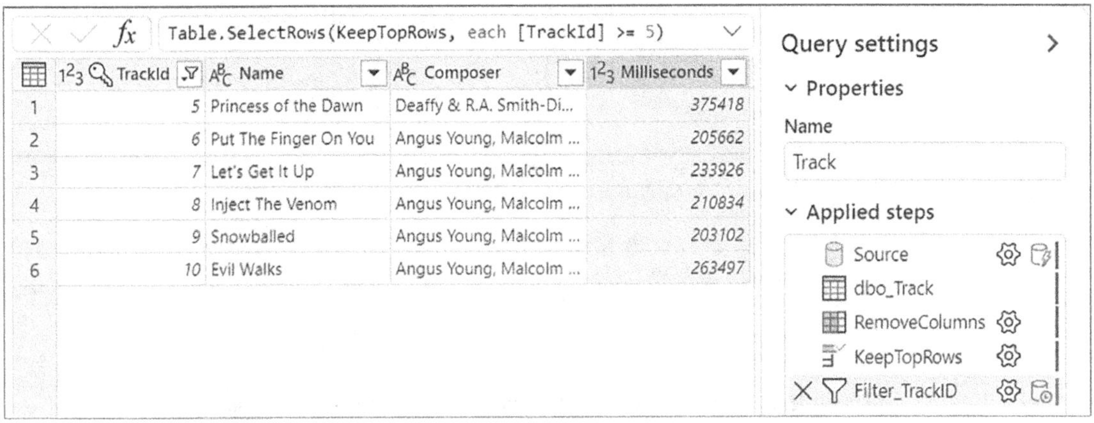

Figure 15.11: Query folding indicators show whether or not a step will fold

The first four steps fold, meaning the data source executes them. However, the last step, **Filter_TrackID**, does not fold; Power Query executes it after loading the previous data. This is surprising because filtering values is usually a supported query folding operation.

In such situations, it's worth experimenting with the sequence of your query steps. Changing the order may improve the connector's ability to maintain query folding through more of the query's steps. For example, consider moving the **Filter_TrackID** step to an earlier point in the sequence. Here's what the restructured query looks like:

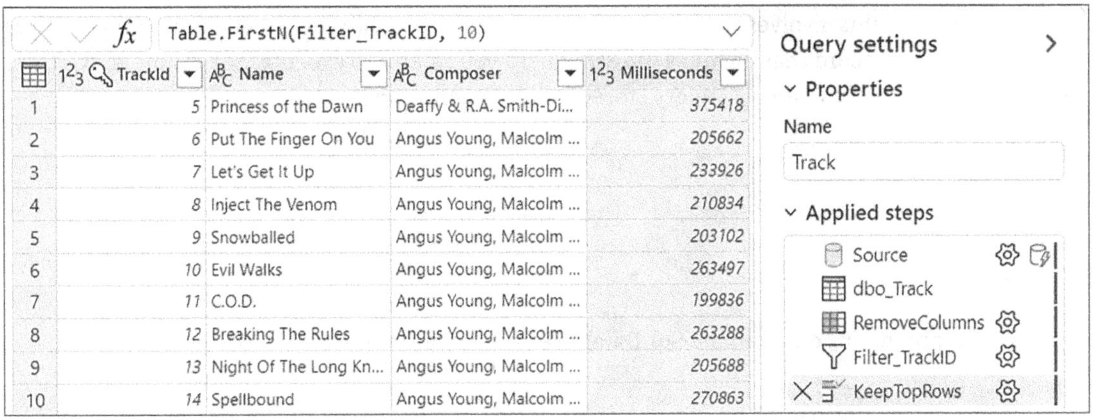

Figure 15.12: All steps in the query fold

Notice how query folding now works for all the applied steps? In the above scenario, moving around steps also results in a different outcome so that it may be undesired. But it does show that the order in which you perform steps can change whether a transformation will fold.

You can also inspect the query that Power Query generates for the data source by right-clicking the **KeepTopRows** step and selecting **View data source query**. The output query is as follows:

```
Data source query

select top 10
    [_].[TrackId],
    [_].[Name],
    [_].[Composer],
    [_].[Milliseconds]
from
(
    select [TrackId],
        [Name],
        [Composer],
        [Milliseconds]
    from [dbo].[Track] as [$Table]
) as [_]
where [_].[TrackId] >= 5
```

Figure 15.13: A data source query is generated through query folding

This query may not be as optimal as a manually written SQL query, but it is much better than loading all the data and then applying the transformations in Power Query. However, nothing is stopping you from passing your own SQL queries, which we will discuss next.

Working with native queries

When using Power Query, those with SQL expertise can pass a more optimized query. However, it's important to keep a few considerations in mind to ensure successful query folding with custom SQL queries.

The primary method for connecting to an SQL database in Power Query is through the Sql.Database function. Typically, this involves specifying a server address and database name. Additionally, you can specify an options record that includes the SQL query you intend to execute. For example, consider a scenario where you have an SQL query stored in a step named myQuery:

```
myQuery =
  "SELECT TOP (10)
    [TrackId],[Name], [Composer], [Milliseconds]
  FROM [dbo].[Track]
  WHERE [TrackId] >= 5"
```

You can incorporate this query in the **Sql.Database** function as follows:

```
Sql.Database( ServerAddress,
              DatabaseName,
              [ Query= myQuery ] )
```

Executing the custom SQL query provides us with the following output:

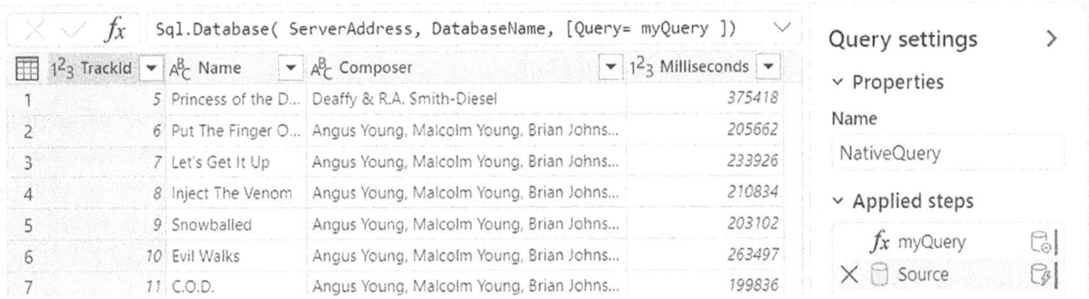

Figure 15.14: Query folding occurs for the custom SQL query

The indicators confirm that this query is processed at the data source level, which you might have expected. However, let's examine what happens when we apply a simple operation, like filtering a row in this table – an operation typically picked up by the query folding mechanism. Surprisingly, the *Not Folding* indicator reveals that query folding does not occur for the **Filter_Name** step:

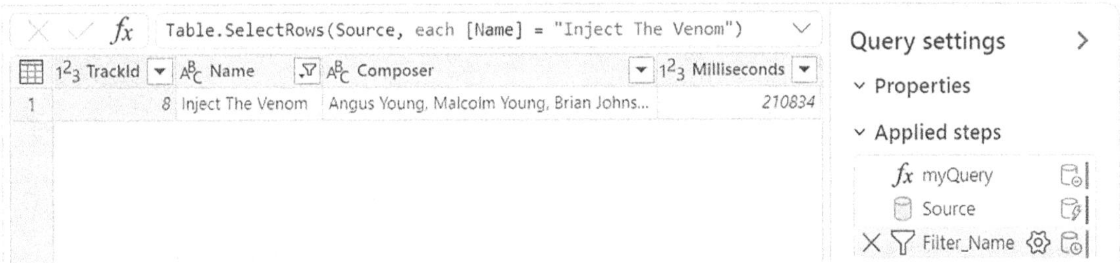

Figure 15.15: Query folding does not happen for the steps following a custom SQL query

While we can pass a custom SQL query to the Sql.Database function, any subsequent steps do not benefit from query folding, which is not ideal.

The good news is that there's a solution when working with native SQL queries. We can use the Value.NativeQuery function to incorporate query folding with custom SQL queries. *How does this work?* Instead of inputting the SQL statement directly into the Sql.Database function, we should provide it to the Value.NativeQuery function:

```
1   let
2       myQuery =
3       "SELECT TOP (10)
4           [TrackId], [Name], [Composer] ,[Milliseconds]
5        FROM [dbo].[Track]
6        WHERE [TrackId] >= 5",
7       Source = Sql.Database( ServerAddress, DatabaseName ),
8       NativeQuery = Value.NativeQuery( Source, myQuery, null, [EnableFolding = true] )
9   in
10      NativeQuery
```

Figure 15.16: A custom SQL query passed to the Value.NativeQuery function

Here's what the process looks like:

1. First, establish a connection to the database using the `Sql.Database` function.
2. Next, set up the `Value.NativeQuery` function:

    a. Pass the database connection as the first argument to the `Value.NativeQuery` function.
    b. Include the custom SQL query as a string in the second argument.
    c. Specify `null` to indicate that no optional parameters are required.
    d. To ensure query folding occurs, include an options record with `EnableFolding` set to true.

With this setup, if we attempt to filter the `Name` column for the value `Inject the Venom`, we now observe that query folding is effectively applied to all steps in the query:

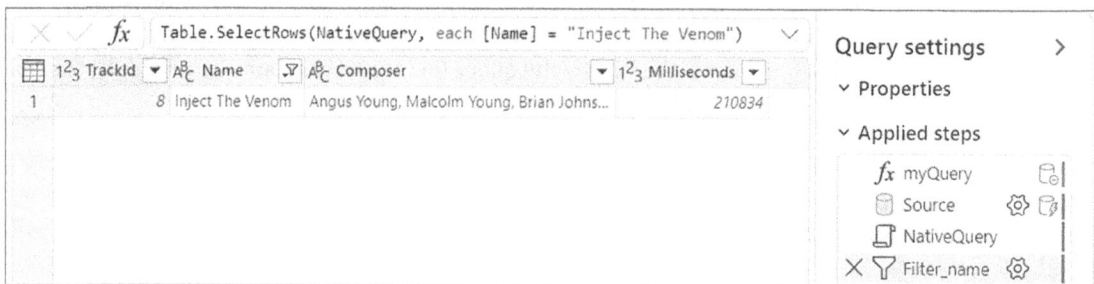

Figure 15.17: Value.NativeQuery allows for query folding while providing a custom SQL query

Looking at the data source query, we can now see both the custom SQL query we provided and the additional folded code using the query folding mechanism:

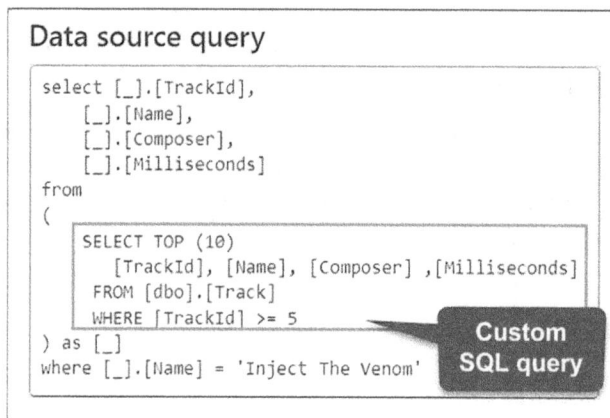

Figure 15.18 The data source query generated by the query folding mechanism

Remember to set the `EnableFolding` option to `TRUE` for this to work.

Rewriting code

Sometimes, you might encounter a scenario where a specific operation doesn't support query folding, even though you'd expect it to. As discussed earlier in this chapter, you can determine the foldability of a step by looking at the query folding indicator, inspecting the query plan, or determining if the step has **Data source query** enabled when you right-click it.

If a step does not fold, rewriting the expression could lead to a version that supports query folding. Let's take an example. In the following table, the TrackID column has a null value in row 5:

1²₃ TrackId	A⁸_C Name	A⁸_C Composer	1²₃ Milliseconds
1	1	For Those About ...	Angus Young, Malc...	343719
2	2	Balls to the Wall	null	342562
3	3	Fast As a Shark	F. Baltes, S. Kaufma...	230619
4	4	Restless and Wild	F. Baltes, R.A. Smit...	252051
5	null	Princess of the D...	Deaffy & R.A. Smit...	375418
6	6	Put The Finger O...	Angus Young, Malc...	205662
7	7	Let's Get It Up	Angus Young, Malc...	233926
8	8	Inject The Venom	Angus Young, Malc...	210834

Figure 15.19: A snapshot of the data used for query folding

Suppose you want to select IDs 3, 6, and 8. You could achieve this using the List.Contains function, which translates into the IN operator in SQL and supports query folding. That looks like the following:

```
Table.SelectRows( Source,
    each List.Contains( {3, 6, 8 }, [TrackId] ) )
```

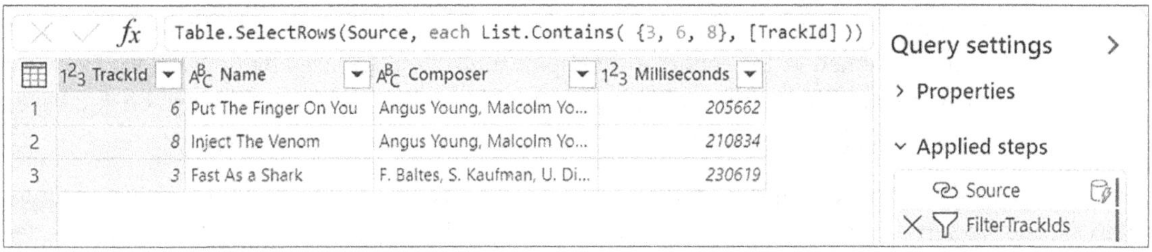

Figure 15.20: List.Contains is a transformation that can fold

However, a challenge arises when you need to include null values in your selection. In SQL, null values aren't allowed within an IN clause, leading to a situation where the original expression doesn't fold:

```
Table.SelectRows( Source,
    each List.Contains( {3, 6, 8, null}, [TrackId] ) )
```

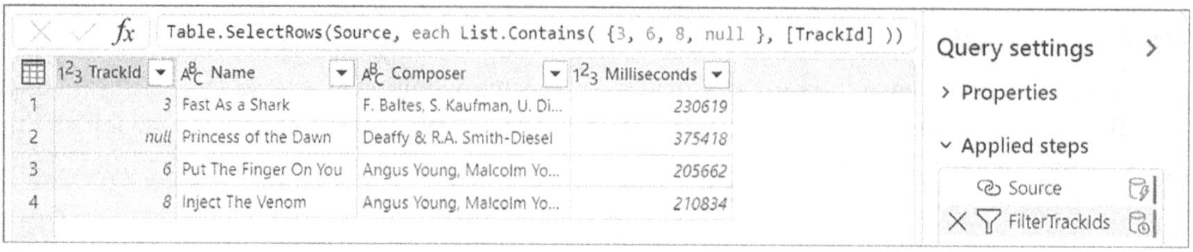

Figure 15.21 Folding does not occur when including null values in List.Contains

To overcome this, you can experiment by incorporating the null condition separately from the List.Contains function:

```
Table.SelectRows( Source,
    each List.Contains( {3, 6, 8 }, [TrackId] )
        or [TrackId] = null )
```

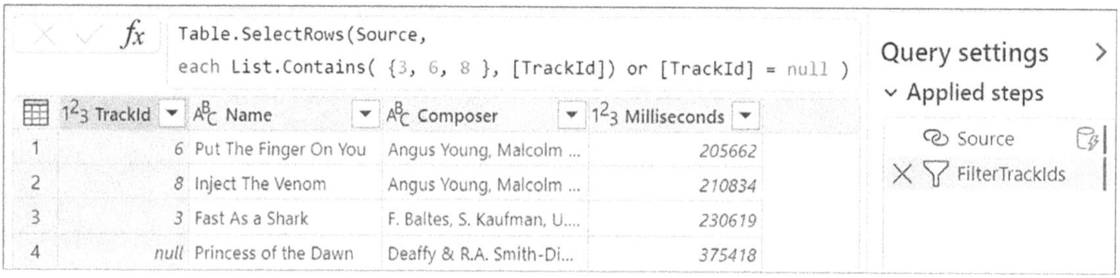

Figure 15.22: Query folding works when executing the test for null values separately

As you can see, query folding now works for the entire query and provides the same output.

Using cross-database folding

A common challenge with query folding arises when working with data across different databases. Power Query is not designed to fold queries that span multiple databases by default. An example where you may run into this limitation is when performing operations like merges between databases. However, when these databases are hosted on the same server, there's a workaround.

Let's illustrate this with an example. Consider a scenario where we want to compare customer email addresses between two databases to identify similarities. For this example, we'll refer to these databases as AW (AdventureWorks) and CT (Contoso), each containing a table with a similar structure:

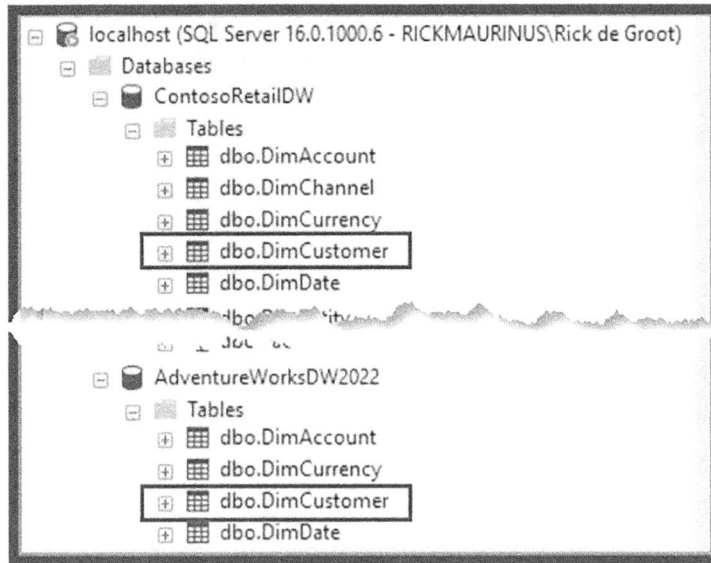

Figure 15.23: Two identical table names in different databases on the same server

We approach the task with two distinct queries and use data from both the AW (AdventureWorks) and CT (Contoso) databases. Each query connects to its respective database and retrieves information from the customer table. Specifically, we focus on the BirthDate and EmailAddress fields from both databases:

```
let
    Source = Sql.Database("localhost", "ContosoRetailDW"),
    Navigation = Source{[Schema = "dbo", Item = "DimCustomer"]}[Data],
    #"Removed other columns" = Table.SelectColumns(Navigation, {"EmailAddress", "BirthDate"})
in
    #"Removed other columns"
```

```
let
    Source = Sql.Database("localhost", "AdventureWorksDW2022"),
    Navigation = Source{[Item = "DimCustomer", Schema = "dbo"]}[Data],
    #"Removed other columns" = Table.SelectColumns(Navigation, {"EmailAddress", "BirthDate"})
in
    #"Removed other columns"
```

Figure 15.24: The queries that retrieve columns from the customer tables in two different databases

The query folding indicators for both queries show that all steps in these individual queries have been successfully folded. Here's a look at the data source query for the CT database:

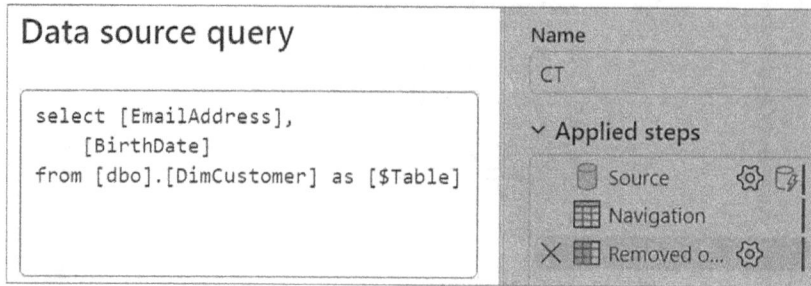

Figure 15.25: The data source query generated by the query folding mechanism

The next step involves merging the data from these two queries. To accomplish this:

1. Navigate to the **Home** tab and select **Merge Queries**.
2. Then choose **Merge queries as New**.
3. In the dialog box that appears, we choose **EmailAddress** as the field to merge on and select a **Left Outer** join.

That provides us with the following setup:

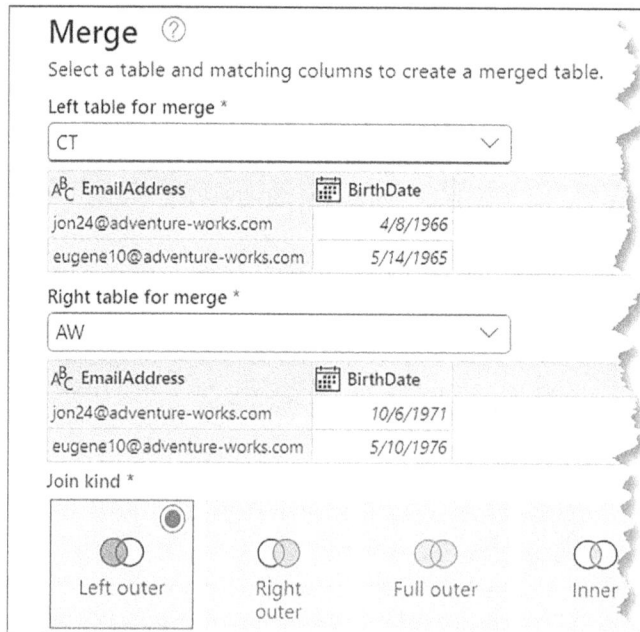

Figure 15.26: Performing a left outer join using EmailAddress as the join column

Following the merge, we expand the BirthDate column to allow a direct comparison within the query. The result is as follows:

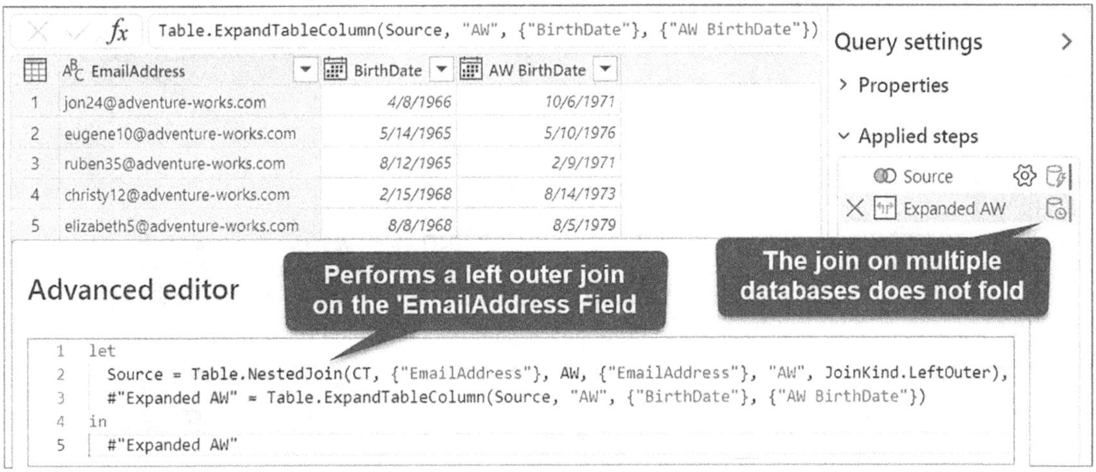

Figure 15.27: Joining queries and expanding a field does not fold when using multiple databases

While our initial attempt at merging data from the AW (AdventureWorks) and CT (Contoso) databases successfully combined the email addresses with the relevant birthdates, this merge operation broke query folding. Instead, the processing takes place within the Power Query engine. Although the separate queries are foldable, the subsequent merge is not. So, is there anything we can do to fix this?

This is where the EnableCrossDatabaseFolding option within the Sql.Database function proves useful. The Sql.Database function typically requires inputs such as a server and database names. However, it also allows for additional parameters, one of which is the EnableCrossDatabaseFolding option. This setting is designed to facilitate query folding across multiple databases, as long as they are located on the same server.

Initially, we connected to the CT database using the expression:

```
Sql.Database("localhost", "ContosoRetailDW")
```

To make use of query folding across databases, this expression can be modified to:

```
Sql.Database(
  "localhost",
  "ContosoRetailDW",
  [EnableCrossDatabaseFolding = true])
```

For query folding to work, we should apply the same modification to the AW database connection. The revised approach results in a scenario where the join operation between the two databases is efficiently processed through query folding:

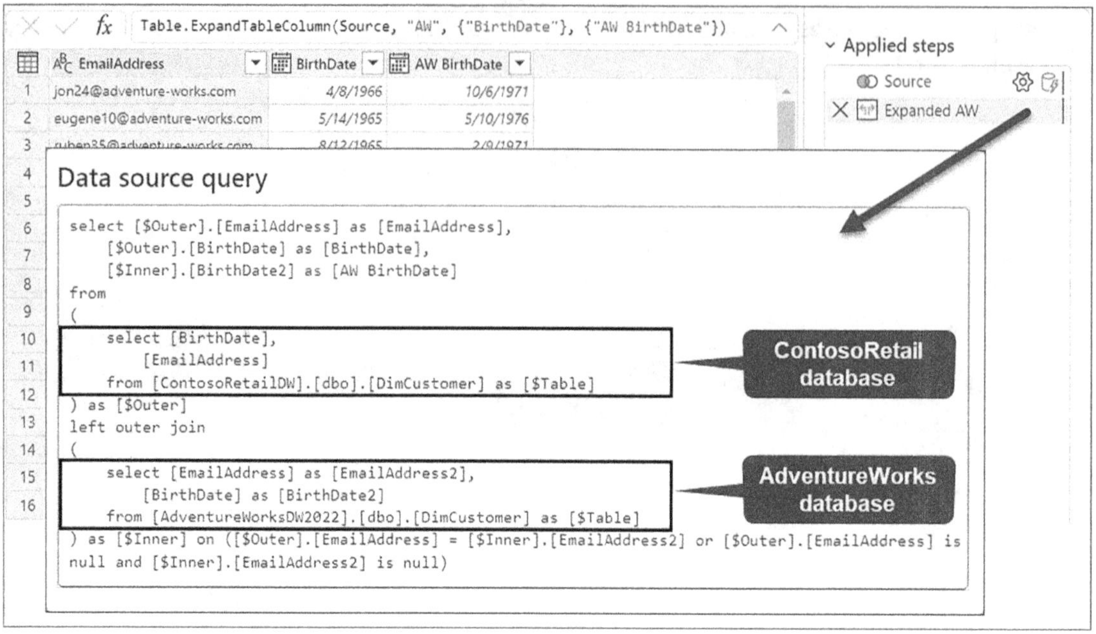

Figure 15.28: A data source query that joins tables from multiple databases on the same server

As the image shows, cross-database query folding allows the data source itself to handle the transformation workload, rather than relying on the Power Query engine. That even works when operations reference multiple databases on the same server.

To conclude, this section has introduced query folding as an important aspect of optimizing your queries. It is best practice to have your data source do the heavy lifting for your transformations. With the strategies provided, you now know multiple ways to maintain query folding for as long as possible. With this knowledge in hand, we encourage you to apply these strategies to your daily work and see for yourself how it impacts performance.

Up next is another important topic, the formula firewall. It is a feature that can impact query folding, but also a common source of frustration when it blocks your queries from running.

The formula firewall

When working with queries, combining different data sources is common. It's likely that after some fiddling you run into an error that prevents you from combining your data. This error is the result of the formula firewall that Power Query has, also known as the data privacy firewall. So, what exactly is the formula firewall, and *how can you work with it?*

What is the formula firewall?

The **formula firewall** is a Power Query feature that prevents accidental data transfer between sources. This feature is particularly important when dealing with sensitive information. It was designed because of query folding. Query folding allows Power Query to convert data transformations into a data source query that a data source can execute directly.

Imagine a situation where you're working with two queries in Power Query. Query1 holds sensitive information, like social security numbers. Using an inner join, you aim to use this data to extract relevant details from Query2. However, for efficiency, you want to avoid importing the entire SQL table associated with Query2 into Power Query. Importing the whole table only to filter out the unnecessary rows later is not optimal. After all, using query folding is a more efficient approach, as it only imports the required data.

However, while query folding is effective, it also introduces a potential risk. In the process of query folding, sensitive information from Query1, such as social security numbers, could unintentionally be embedded into the data source query for Query2. If someone with database expertise—or anyone monitoring your network—were to intercept this query, they could potentially access the confidential information embedded within it.

This is where the formula firewall comes into play. Its purpose is to prevent such situations where sensitive data might be unintentionally embedded in queries sent to external sources. To recognize where a potential risk lies, the formula firewall uses partitions.

Understanding partitions

When evaluating a query with the formula firewall active, Power Query splits the query and its dependencies into partitions. These partitions are essentially groups of one or more steps. Whenever a partition references another, the formula firewall intervenes by substituting the reference with a call to a specific function, named `Value.Firewall`. This function ensures that partitions do not access each other directly. Instead, all references must first be evaluated by the firewall. Data is allowed into the current partition only after the firewall authorizes the interaction between partitions.

As you can imagine, the way partitions are created is incredibly important. Including fewer or more steps within a single partition could determine whether the firewall becomes involved. However, the process of partitioning queries is complex and beyond the scope of this book. For those interested in a deeper understanding of this process, further reading is available at `https://learn.microsoft.com/en-us/power-query/data-privacy-firewall`. We will refer to this page throughout the rest of this chapter.

The fundamental principle of the formula firewall

The formula firewall operates on a fundamental principle concerning partitions. This principle is split into two key points:

- **Referring to other partitions**: A partition can use data or results from another partition. That partition can be another query or a partition within the same query.
- **Accessing compatible data sources**: A partition can obtain data from external sources, provided they have a compatible privacy level.

Either of the two is possible, but not both at the same time. Violating this rule will result in one of two formula firewall messages:

- **Error from referencing**:

  ```
  Formula.Firewall: Query 'X' (step 'Y') references other queries or steps,
  so it may not directly access a data source. Please rebuild this data
  combination.
  ```

- **Error from accessing incompatible data sources**:

  ```
  Formula.Firewall: Query 'X' (step 'Y') is accessing data sources with
  incompatible privacy levels. Please rebuild this data combination.
  ```

From just reading the above statements, it's hard to understand what's happening for a Formula Firewall error, but hold on. We're about to make this a lot clearer. In the next section, we will explore the reasons behind these errors and discuss strategies to resolve them.

Firewall error: Referencing other partitions

The first firewall error we'll discuss is the error triggered when referencing other partitions. The error message for this error is:

```
Formula.Firewall: Query 'X' (step 'Y') references other queries or steps, so it
may not directly access a data source. Please rebuild this data combination.
```

It's important to grasp why this error pops up because it blocks your queries from producing any results. This means you won't be able to update your data or view the outcomes of your transformations. Unfortunately, solving the Formula Firewall error without knowing its underlying mechanics can be difficult.

Consider the example shown in the following image:

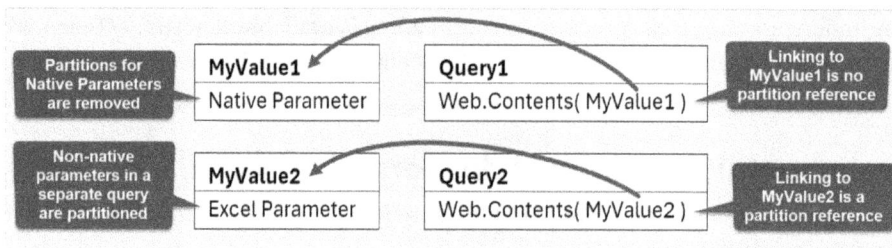

Figure 15.29: Two similar queries where one runs into the Formula Firewall error

Here, you see two similar queries, but only one encounters the Formula Firewall error. In **Query1**, there's a reference to a parameter named **MyValue1**, created through the user interface. The partitioning process automatically removes partitions from such native parameters, allowing **Query1** to run smoothly.

However, if you manually set up a parameter that pulls a value from an Excel file, as seen with **MyValue2**, the partitioning process treats this differently. It doesn't remove the partition, so any reference to **MyValue2** is seen as referencing a partition.

Consequently, when **Query2** tries to use **MyValue2** with the **Web.Contents** function to reach another data source while at the same time referencing another partition, it triggers the formula firewall.

Let's work through an example to see this error in action. To follow along with the below examples, you can download the exercise files from the GitHub repository of this book.

Connecting to a URL using native parameters

A common operation to retrieve data is to connect to a URL. Examples of this could be to retrieve movie scores from IMDb, get data from a table on Wikipedia, or return the latest weather forecast information. Regardless of what information you need, you can connect to a website using Power Query's web connector. Doing so makes for an easy use case to illustrate the formula firewall. Here's how.

Suppose you want to connect to the PowerQuery.How website and retrieve the HTML code. First, you'll create a parameter in Power Query:

1. Go to the **Home** tab and select **Manage Parameters**.
2. Then choose **New** and name this parameter myURLParameter.
3. Set it to **type text**, and assign the value https://powerquery.how/.

Performing these steps gives you:

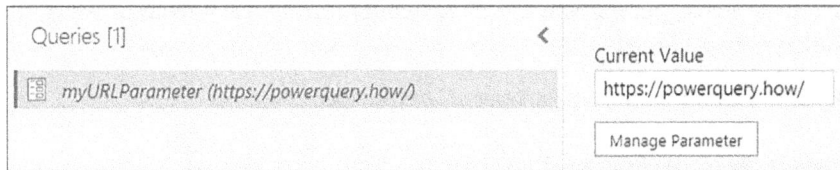

Figure 15.30: A parameter containing a URL to connect to

This newly created parameter, including a static URL, does not directly access data sources.

Next, let's set up a query to connect to the website and fetch the HTML code. In the Queries area, right-click, select **New Query**, then click **Web**. In the dialog box, choose the URL type, select **Parameter** from the dropdown, and refer to **myURLParameter**:

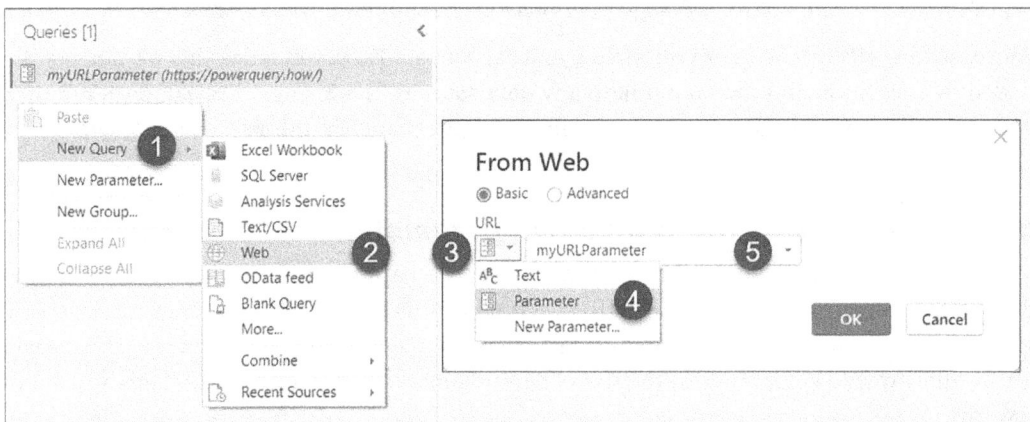

Figure 15.31: Creating a web query that uses a parameter as a URL

You'll be prompted to choose a connection method when connecting to a web source for the first time. Select **Anonymous** and then **Connect**. In the following screen, tick the box in front of **HTML Code** to return the HTML content. Confirm by clicking **OK**:

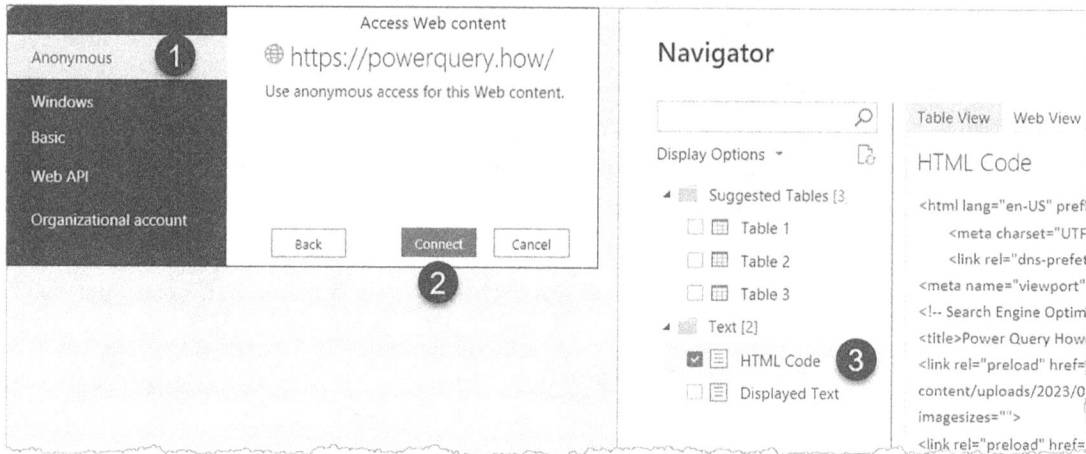

Figure 15.32: Selecting web content access and data retrieval options

By completing these steps, you retrieve the HTML content from the website using a hardcoded parameter, resulting in two queries.

The first query is the parameter myURLParameter, defined as:

```
"https://powerquery.how/" meta [IsParameterQuery=true, Type="Text",
IsParameterQueryRequired=true]
```

The second query is called HTML Code and is defined as:

```
Web.BrowserContents(myURLParameter)
```

Up to this stage, the formula firewall has not flagged any problems and has successfully returned the HTML code. This smooth operation is due to the partitioning process, as detailed on Microsoft's website. This process removes partitions from native parameters established via the Power Query user interface.

In our case, the HTML Code query refers to myURLParameter. However, since this parameter is not included in a partition and does not link to any data sources, the formula firewall does not trigger any alerts. Let's now move on to a situation where a slight change in the setup leads to the Formula Firewall error.

Connecting to a URL using an Excel parameter

Now, let's modify our approach slightly. Instead of a native parameter, we'll retrieve the URL to connect to from a table value from an Excel file. A setup like this allows for end users to make changes to a URL in an easy-to-access Excel file, without the need to fiddle with Power Query. This provides a user-friendly way to enter input, at the risk of running into the formula firewall. Let's find out how this works.

To follow along, make sure you have downloaded the `ExcelParameterFile` file from the book's GitHub repository. It contains a table titled `ParameterTable`, which has a single column called URL, holding the text value `https://powerquery.how/`. This looks as follows:

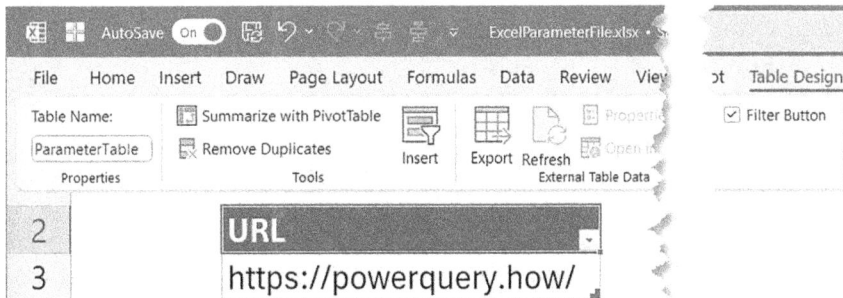

Figure 15.33: An Excel file containing the URL for our query

First, save this file in your preferred location. To connect to it, go to **New Query**, choose **Excel Workbook**, and find the file. When you open it, a window will pop up. Here, select `ParameterTable` and click **OK**:

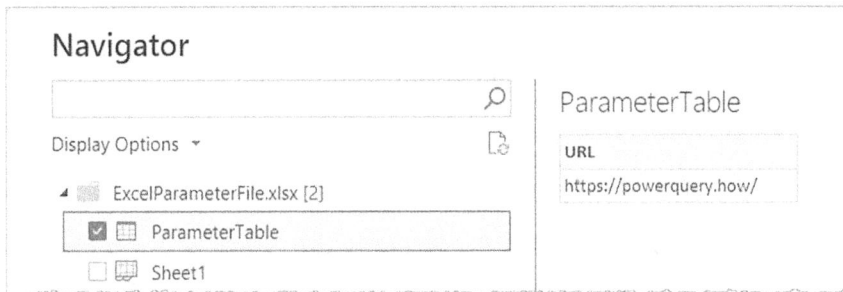

Figure 15.34: Selecting data from the Excel Workbook Navigator

After importing the data, you will find a table with a single cell that holds the URL. To use this URL in your queries, you should extract the value from this cell. To do this, right-click on the cell and choose the **Drill Down** option. This step will return the cell value for you:

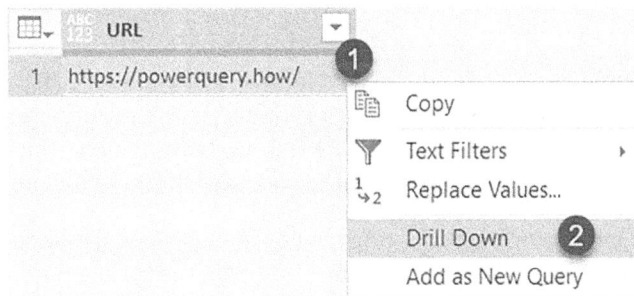

Figure 15.35: Drill down on a table value to return its value

The query generated to extract the value from the Excel file looks like this:

```
let
  Source = Excel.Workbook(File.Contents(
    "C:\Data\ExcelParameterFile.xlsx"), null, true),
  ParameterTable_Table =
    Source{[Item="ParameterTable",Kind="Table"]}[Data],
  URL = ParameterTable_Table{0}[URL]
in
  URL
```

Rename this query myExcelURL. Do you recall the earlier situation where we used myURLParameter? What if we replace that with myExcelURL, the parameter from our Excel file? Try using this in a query:

```
Web.BrowserContents( myExcelURL )
```

After making this change, you'll encounter an error that looks like the following:

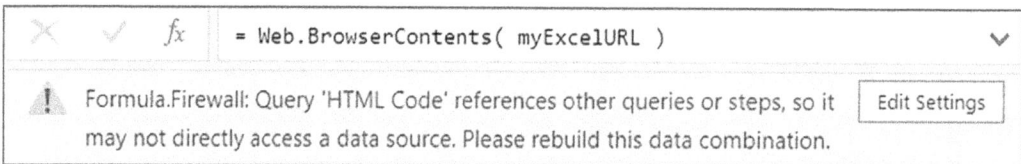

Figure 15.36: The Formula Firewall error when referencing queries connecting to a data source

Why does this error arise, especially when we successfully used a parameter in the previous example? To understand this, let's focus on the fundamental principle of the formula firewall: *"A partition can either reference other partitions or access data from sources that have a compatible privacy level. It cannot do both at the same time."*

In our initial example, there were two reasons for the absence of an error. Firstly, the myURLParameter was a native, hardcoded parameter that did not access any external data sources. Secondly, the partitioning process excluded the native parameter from its scope, meaning its reference was not considered as a reference to another partition.

The situation changes with a parameter derived from an Excel file. Such a parameter accesses data from another source (the Excel file), and thus, it's included in the partitioning process. When the Web.BrowserContents function attempts to access a website (PowerQuery.How) and simultaneously references a partition (the Excel parameter), it breaches the firewall's fundamental rule.

Partitioning in Power Query can be pretty complicated. Even reading the Microsoft documentation on it will leave you with a lot of remaining questions. However, the main point to remember is this: if you reference one query to get data from a source, like our Excel file, and then try to use that data in another query to access a source, it breaks the rules of the formula firewall. So, what's the best way to fix this issue?

Resolving the firewall error

When we attempt to reference the Excel parameter from this different partition, we breach a key firewall rule. We cannot access a data source (in this case, the web request) and simultaneously reference another partition (the Excel parameter). Yet, there are plenty of scenarios where you want to be able to use a data point that is stored elsewhere, in this case, the Excel URL. Our objective is to enable the query to retrieve the URL from the external source while finding a way to keep the logic within the same partition. To achieve this, we will explore two possible methods.

Method 1: Using a function

The first method involves storing the myExcelURL parameter logic within a function. A function stores logic into reusable code but does not execute it. When we then call this function in a query, the accessing of data happens within the partition where the function is called. This is different from referencing a query because, in that situation, the accessing of the data occurs in the other query, which will be seen as a separate partition and potentially triggers the firewall.

To create this function, you can add a simple function definition that refers to the previous step at the end of your query:

```
let
   Source = Excel.Workbook(File.Contents(
       "C:\Data\ExcelParameterFile.xlsx"), null, true),
   ParameterTable_Table =
     Source{[Item="ParameterTable",Kind="Table"]}[Data],
   URL = ParameterTable_Table{0}[URL],
   myFunction = () => URL
in
   myFunction
```

This script creates a function. Make sure to name it fxMyExcelURL. Use this function in another query to make a web request, like this:

```
   Web.BrowserContents( fxMyExcelURL() )
```

Doing this allows you to make your request successfully without running into the formula firewall. You can find this solution in the exercise files of this chapter.

Method 2: Integrating the logic into one query

A second approach is integrating all the logic of accessing the Excel file into the same query. Doing so ensures that all related steps fall within a single partition, which allows using the parameter to access an external data source under the formula firewall's rules.

To consolidate the steps, you can take the logic of the Excel Workbook query and add a new step at the end of the query. In that step, you can reference the URL from the Excel workbook as follows:

```
let
  Source = Excel.Workbook(File.Contents(
    "C:\Data\ExcelParameterFile.xlsx"), null, true),
  ParameterTable_Table =
    Source{[Item="ParameterTable",Kind="Table"]}[Data],
  myContainedExcelURL = ParameterTable_Table{0}[URL],
  HTMLCode = Web.BrowserContents( myContainedExcelURL )
in
    HTMLCode
```

Combining these steps into a single query allows the partitioning process to keep the steps that access data within the same partition. This approach successfully resolves the first Formula Firewall error. To see this for yourself, you can find the complete query in this chapter's exercise files.

By applying the above steps, you end up in the following situation:

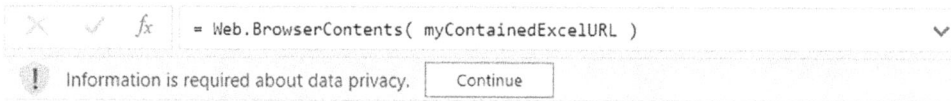

Figure 15.37: Prompt for setting privacy levels

The error informs you that it requires additional information about data privacy. If you press **Continue** and select **Public**, your query will return its results. However, by choosing **Private** or **Organizational**, your query may lead to the second type of Formula Firewall error, which we will discuss next.

Firewall error: Accessing compatible data sources

The second firewall error can happen when you combine data sources with incompatible privacy levels. Remember how the firewall is meant to prevent unintended data leakage? That's what this error is about. The message for this error is:

```
Formula.Firewall: Query 'X' (step 'Y') is accessing data sources with incompatible
privacy levels. Please rebuild this data combination.
```

Consider the scenarios depicted in the following image:

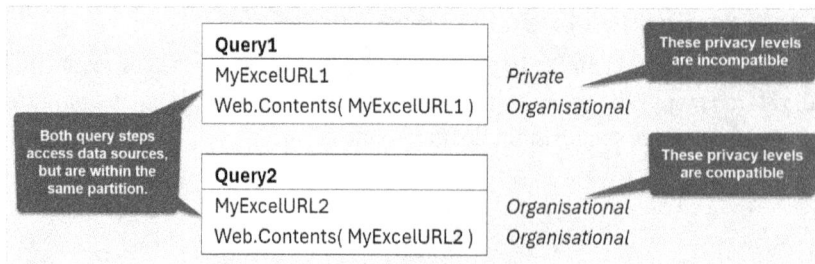

Figure 15.38: Two queries where one contains data sources that are incompatible

The image shows two queries. Focusing on **Query1**, it accesses data from two external sources. If the **Web.Contents** step tried to reference another partition, it would normally trigger a "referencing other partitions" error due to simultaneously accessing a data source and referencing another partition. However, that's not the issue here as the data is within the same query. That allows the partitioning process to put both steps within the same partition. The real problem for **Query1** is a mismatch in privacy levels: the data source **MyExcelURL1** is marked as '**Private**, while the **Web.Contents** step is set to the **Organizational** privacy level. Because these levels don't match, Power Query reports the second firewall error for accessing incompatible data sources.

Query2 doesn't encounter this error because both steps in the query involve data sources with matching privacy levels. Therefore, the formula firewall allows both data sources to combine.

Understanding this might seem complex, but don't worry. We'll break down this example further with a practical case. To grasp the error message fully, it's essential to first learn about privacy levels.

Understanding privacy levels

In Power Query, each data source can be assigned a privacy level. These levels are important for determining how data from different sources can be combined.

Here's an overview of the privacy levels and their effects on query folding:

- **Public:** Data from a **Public** source can be freely combined with other data sources.
- **Organizational:** This setting allows data to be combined only with other **Organizational** sources.
- **Private:** The most restrictive setting. **Private** data does not combine with other sources, maintaining strict isolation.

Think of privacy levels like this: if you label a data source as **Private**, it won't mix with other data in queries. This keeps sensitive information safe and separate. Data marked as **Organizational** can only be mixed with other **Organizational** data. **Public** data offers the most flexibility as it can easily be combined with any other data source that permits it. This typically includes data sources with their privacy levels set to **Public** or **None**.

Setting privacy levels

When you attempt to combine a data source without a set privacy level, Power Query prompts you to choose one. To set privacy levels manually:

1. In Power BI Desktop:

   - Navigate to the **Home** tab on the Power Query ribbon and select **Data Source Settings**.
   - Choose the data source to modify and click **Edit Permissions** to set its privacy level.

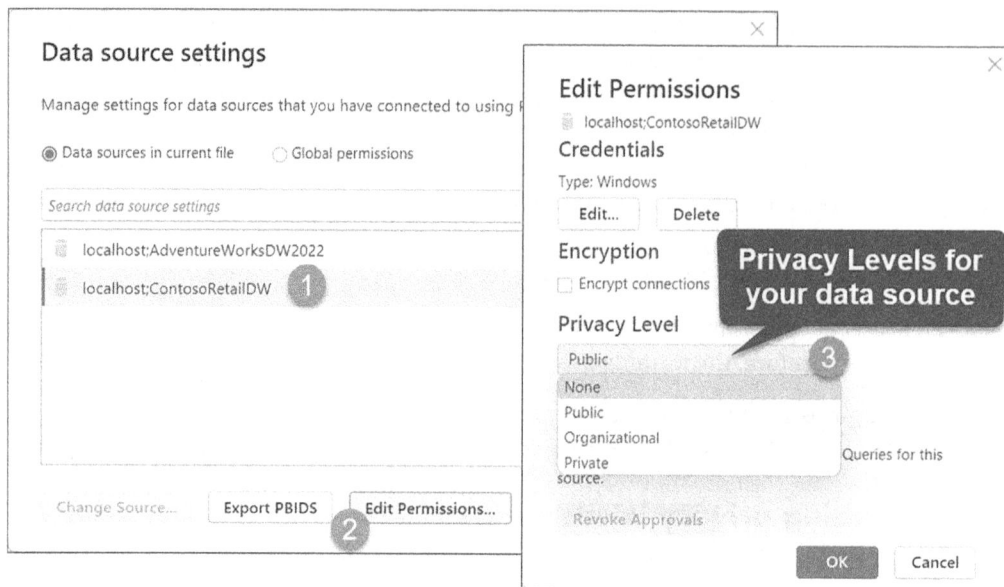

Figure 15.39: Setting privacy levels in Data source settings

2. In the Power BI service:

    •   Access settings via the top-right gear icon, then select **Manage Connections and Gateways.**

    •   Find your data source and set the **Privacy Level** at the bottom of the screen.

So, what does this have to do with the formula firewall?

Resolving the firewall error

Let's revisit our previous example where we retrieved a URL from an Excel file. This action prompted an error message requesting privacy-level information for the data sources:

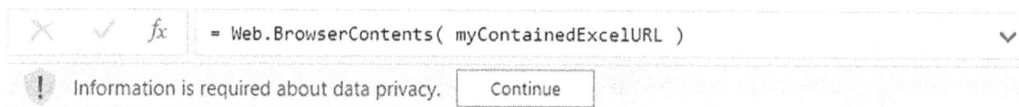

Figure 15.40: Error message requesting information on privacy levels

The above message requires information about the data privacy level of the web request. To resolve this error, we perform one of two methods.

Method 1: Setting compatible privacy levels

Whether or not we receive the Formula Firewall error depends on the privacy level settings:

•   **Public:** Your query will execute immediately unless the Excel file we connect to has its privacy level set to **Private** or **Organizational**, which causes a firewall error. The privacy levels **None** and **Public** are both compatible.

- **Organizational:** Setting the query to **Organizational** prompts a check of the Excel file's privacy level. The query runs smoothly if the file we combine with is set to **Organizational**. Any other privacy level will trigger the Formula Firewall error.
- **Private:** Selecting **Private** invariably leads to a firewall error.

Let's say we want to set the privacy level to **Organizational**. We encounter a firewall error when selecting **Continue** and assigning **Organizational** to our data source. This happens because, while we set the web request to **Organizational**, the privacy level for the Excel file connection is still undefined.

To resolve this:

1. Navigate to **Data Source Settings**.
2. Locate the Excel file under **Data sources in current file**.
3. Use **Edit Permissions** to set the Excel file's privacy level to **Organizational**.
4. Confirm your choice, then return to your query.
5. Click **Refresh Preview** to update your queries.

After these steps, your queries should function without privacy-level-related errors.

Method 2: Ignoring privacy levels

Another method to prevent the Formula Firewall error is to ignore the privacy level settings. The formula firewall's role as a gatekeeper between your data sources can slow down query performance. This feature is important for preventing data leaks, especially in query folding scenarios. However, you have an alternative if you're dealing with non-sensitive data.

In Power BI Desktop, you can choose to ignore privacy levels. This may also help to improve the performance of your queries as any compatibility checks can be skipped.

In situations like our previous example, where you're asked to set privacy levels, continuing without setting them triggers a specific pop-up message:

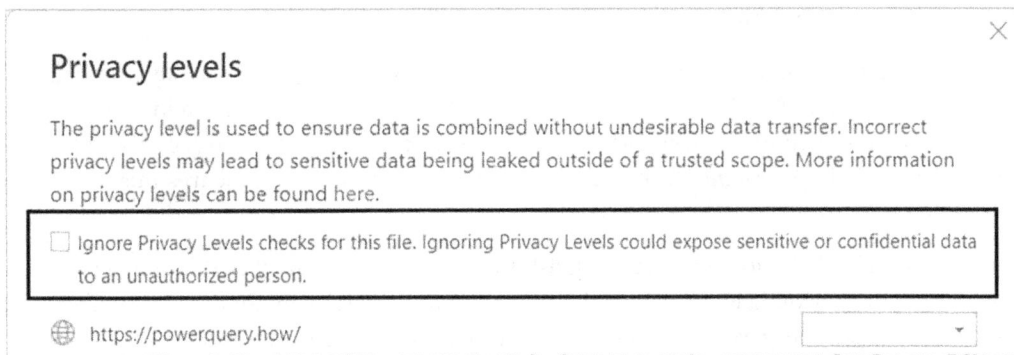

Figure 15.41: Privacy levels notification – option to ignore privacy levels

You have the choice to select **Ignore Privacy Levels**. Opting for this allows your query to execute without running into privacy-related Formula Firewall errors.

To find this setting:

- Navigate to **File**, then **Options and Settings,** and click **Options.**
- Select **Always ignore Privacy Level settings** in the **Privacy** section.

That looks as follows:

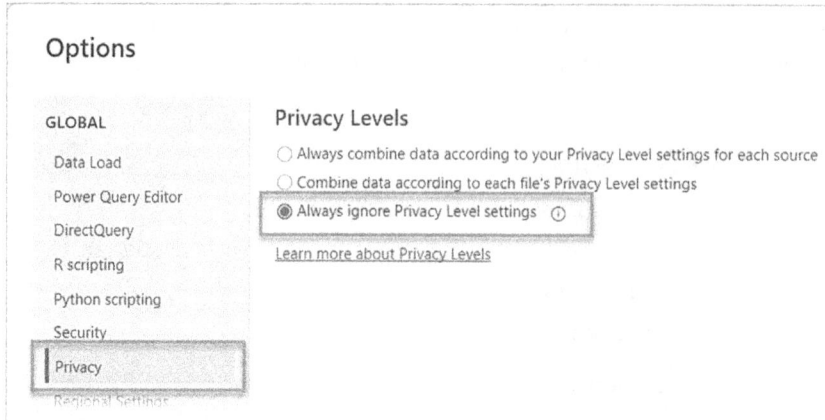

Figure 15.42: The Options menu to configure Privacy Levels

> **Important:** Using this setting might expose sensitive or confidential data. Additionally, this setting is only applicable in Power BI Desktop. The Power BI service does not respect this setting, and you'll need to configure the appropriate privacy levels.

To conclude, this chapter has demonstrated how to address various Formula Firewall errors using specific strategies. We solved the partition referencing error by consolidating logic within a single query and creating a custom function. For the data privacy error, we either aligned data privacy levels or ignored privacy settings entirely.

However, it's important to note that the examples provided in this chapter do not support refreshing in the Power BI service. This limitation arises because the example involves fetching a URL in one query and using it in another. Power Query's engine requires that the base URL of a web request is explicitly visible to the M engine. Our dynamic referencing of the URL obscures this, leading to a dynamic queries error.

Despite this specific limitation for a web request, the techniques outlined in this chapter remain effective for resolving Formula Firewall situations. For instance, if these methods were applied to filter a database query, the query would successfully refresh in the Power BI service.

So far, you've learned how to deal with the formula firewall and what you can do to ensure query folding takes place for your queries. In the next section, we'll look at other strategies to improve the performance of our queries.

Optimizing query performance

Power Query operates within a constrained environment. Specifically, each mashup container has a limited amount of resources. This limitation is an important factor to consider when creating queries. It is important to reduce the data volume right at the beginning of your query for fast queries. By doing so, you not only speed up the query process but also prevent exceeding resource limits that cause paging and can lead to slow performance or failures.

As previously discussed, using the query folding mechanism is one of the most effective strategies for optimizing performance. However, there are scenarios where your data source does not support query folding, or a required transformation breaks the folding process. In such cases, the strategy shifts toward minimizing the memory footprint of your query. So, what are some effective methods to achieve this?

Prioritize filtering rows and removing columns

It's worth emphasizing here that one of the first steps you should focus on is reducing your dataset to keep only what is necessary. You can do that by:

- **Filtering rows**: As early as possible in your query, prioritize filtering your rows to include only the necessary ones. By reducing the number of rows, you decrease the amount of data that Power Query needs to keep in memory, leading to faster processing and less memory usage.
- **Removing unnecessary columns**: Like filtering rows, removing unnecessary columns is equally important. This practice trims the data volume and simplifies your data model, making it easier to work with and understand.

Both operations make sense from a computing perspective. But besides these, there's another distinction to make for the type of operations to perform first.

Buffering versus streaming operations

Performing operations at the data source is often faster than doing them locally. However, when performing operations locally, you can find two types of operations: buffering and streaming. So, what are these operations, and what is their relationship to performance?

Buffering operations

Buffering operations are those that require reading the entire dataset to produce a result. These operations are resource-intensive and demand a complete scan of the data up to the previous step. This also means that the amount of memory used is proportional to the size of the input.

Consider an example where we sort a dataset and then retrieve the top 1000 rows. In this case, the whole dataset is needed to determine the top 1000 rows accurately, even if you only want to return a small part of the data. On the other hand, if you first select the top 1000 rows and then sort them, the sorting process only needs to keep these 1000 rows in memory. It can do that by simply retrieving the top 1000 rows, never requiring the full dataset. In this scenario, the sorting is considered a buffering operation.

Buffering operations are not limited to sorting data. They also include certain types of joins, grouping data, and altering the structure of your table, such as through pivot or transpose operations. Likewise, operations that return unique values or add a ranking column require scanning the entire table. These are the types of operations that use a lot of resources and should be limited when optimizing performance.

Streaming operations

In contrast to buffering operations, streaming operations do not require scanning the entire dataset to return a result. A good example of this is the filtering operation. Filtering a list or table processes data in a streaming manner. As data flows through, Power Query evaluates and returns results progressively. This means that for a preview screen in the Power Query Editor, only a portion of the data is needed to fill the top 1000 rows. This also directly leads to a more responsive Power Query Editor as it can show your data previews quicker. Typical streaming operations include adding columns, filtering rows, and selecting columns. Objects that support streaming include those of the table, list, and binary type.

Maximizing streaming transformations helps reduce memory consumption and avoid performance issues when running a query. Knowing this, you may wonder how to identify whether you're working with a streaming or buffering operation. The answer is that you can determine this in the new Power Query interface by using the query plan.

Using the query plan

The query plan is a feature in the new Power Query experience that is meant to provide more information about the evaluation of your query. Whenever you want to know more details on the evaluation of a particular step, right-click on the step and select **Query Plan**.

For instance, let's look at a simple query:

```
1   let
2       Source = Sql.Database("localhost", "ContosoRetailDW"),
3       Navigation = Source{[Schema = "dbo", Item = "DimCustomer"]}[Data],
4       RemoveOtherColumns = Table.SelectColumns(Navigation, {"EmailAddress", "BirthDate"}),
5       AddIndex = Table.AddIndexColumn(RemoveOtherColumns, "Index", 0, 1, Int64.Type),
6       FilterTop20 = Table.SelectRows(AddIndex, each [Index] <= 20),
7       SortRows = Table.Sort(FilterTop20, {{"BirthDate", Order.Ascending}})
8   in
9       SortRows
```

Figure 15.43: A database query with a range of transformations

This query connects to an SQL database, selects some columns, adds an index column, filters the top 20 rows, and sorts the table.

To analyze the query plan for the **SortRows** step, right-click on the step and select **View query plan**:

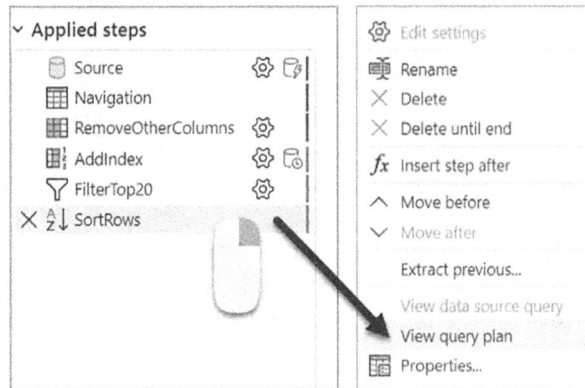

Figure 15.44: Right-click on a step to select View query plan

This action will open a window displaying the query plan:

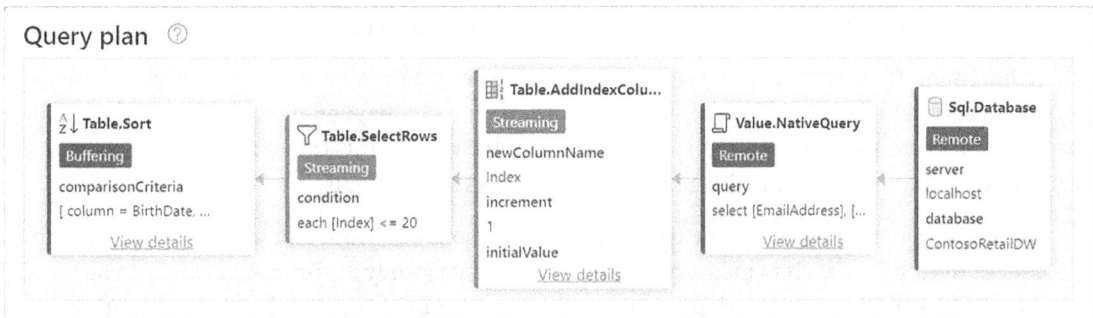

Figure 15.45: Query plan indicates how a step is evaluated

The query plan visualizes the evaluation path of your query. It begins on the right, showing the connection to the SQL database, and progresses to the left, leading to the final step of sorting the table.

Within the plan, you can encounter three types of indicators for each step:

- **Remote**: Steps marked as *Remote* indicate operations performed at the data source. When a step folds, you can view the native query by selecting **View details**.
- **Streaming**: These steps do not require scanning all the data to return a result. They process the data as it streams through, retrieving only the rows needed to populate the preview.
- **Buffering**: Steps with this indicator require a full scan of the data from the previous step.

The query plan not only reveals whether an operation is buffering or streaming but also shows which steps are folded and the underlying queries at the data source. What's good to remember about memory is that when (part of) your query does not fold, operations from that point are performed in memory of the Power Query engine.

Optimization Tip: Prioritize query folding where possible. After folding is no longer feasible, use streaming operations before buffering. This approach ensures your data quickly populates the preview data, reducing wait times while developing. Only use buffering operations when necessary to complete your queries. Strategically sequencing these operations can significantly reduce the time it takes for a preview to load when modifying your query.

You just learned about the types of operations that require either a partial or full scan of your dataset. Another strategy to improve your query performance is by storing parts of your query in memory before applying an expensive operation. This can be done by using buffer functions, which we will discuss next.

Using buffer functions

Buffer functions in the M language, identified by the suffix .Buffer, play an important role in improving the performance of Power Query operations. They temporarily save data in your computer's memory. This process, called **buffering**, can speed up your queries but also has some limitations.

Buffer functions are most useful in scenarios where Power Query may execute multiple requests to fetch the same data from an external source. This situation can happen during complex operations that require accessing data repeatedly, such as in detailed row-by-row transformations. You also see this when using a replacement table to perform multiple replacements.

Since repeatedly requesting the same data can be slow, especially from an external source, you may consider buffering the data into memory. In that way, the data is only retrieved once and can be reused from memory. Another scenario where you benefit from the buffer function is when computing a running total. The performance improves considerably when you buffer the values for the running total.

On the other hand, if you buffer a large amount of data in memory and surpass the memory limit of your mashup container, the system starts moving data between RAM and storage (paging). This slows down your queries due to the slower access speed compared to RAM. To ensure your queries are fast, it's therefore important to consider your query's memory footprint. In the next section, we'll look at different approaches to creating a running total and how buffer functions help improve the query performance.

The impact of buffering and running totals

In this section, we will use an example to measure the performance and memory consumption of different approaches. Unfortunately, Power Query has no easy built-in way to measure its performance. Whereas query diagnostics are available in Power BI Desktop, the feature makes it hard to interpret its metrics.

For a more accurate measurement of query speed, we have used a tool called **SQL-profiler** and connected it to our Power BI dataset. We have computed our refresh times by refreshing each query separately three times and taking the average refresh time. Let's see what our setup looks like.

The setup

Consider a dataset containing parking transactions, each with an associated payment amount:

	ABᶜ Transaction ID	ABᶜ Meter Code	Transaction DateTime	1²₃ Amount Paid
1	1250162207	12028002	11/7/2023 7:30:00 AM	26
2	1250162278	19232002	11/7/2023 7:31:00 AM	152
3	1250131414	19127010	11/7/2023 4:20:00 AM	967
4	1250134465	5073002	11/7/2023 4:48:00 AM	4
5	1250134860	19161010	11/7/2023 4:52:00 AM	673

Figure 15.46: Sample parking transactions dataset

You can follow along with this example by using the exercise files provided on the GitHub page of this book.

Our goal is to calculate a cumulative total of these payments. To calculate the running total, we use two functions: List.Sum and List.FirstN. List.FirstN selects values up to a particular row, and List.Sum adds these values to give a cumulative total. We begin by adding an index column starting at 1, increasing by 1 for each row. This forms the basis of our query:

```
let
    Source = myCSV,
    AddedIndex =
        Table.AddIndexColumn(Source, "Index", 1, 1, Int64.Type)
in
    AddedIndex
```

Next, we'll explore four methods to compute a running total:

1. From regular table
2. From buffered table
3. From buffered column
4. From buffered column and using List.Generate

Each method offers an alternative approach to calculating the running total, potentially affecting the efficiency and performance of the process.

Method 1: Running total from regular table

For the first method, we will add a new column with the following expression:

```
List.Sum( List.FirstN( AddedIndex[Amount Paid], [Index] ))
```

This formula calculates the running total for each transaction:

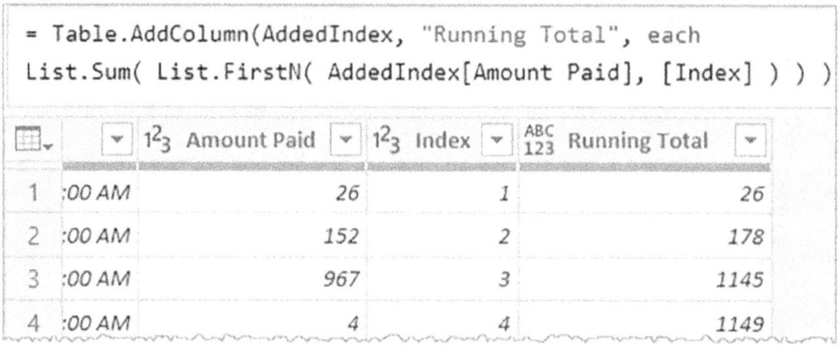

```
= Table.AddColumn(AddedIndex, "Running Total", each
List.Sum( List.FirstN( AddedIndex[Amount Paid], [Index] ) ) )
```

	1²₃ Amount Paid	1²₃ Index	ᴬᴮᶜ₁₂₃ Running Total
1	:00 AM	26	1	26
2	:00 AM	152	2	178
3	:00 AM	967	3	1145
4	:00 AM	4	4	1149

Figure 15.47: Adding a running total without buffering values

When evaluating the performance of this method in Power BI, we observe:

- **Processing time:** It takes an average of 128 seconds.
- **Data retrieved:** The method retrieves 1.88 GB of data.

Given that the original data file is only 393 KB, the substantial amount of data processed suggests that Power Query reads the file multiple times. This inefficiency is a significant downside of using a regular table for running total calculations.

Method 2: Running total from buffered table

Method 2 introduces a variation in calculating the running total. Instead of using a regular table, this method involves buffering the table in memory. This is achieved with the `Table.Buffer` function, as demonstrated in the following query:

```
let
  Source = myCSV,
  AddedIndex =
    Table.AddIndexColumn(Source, "Index", 1, 1, Int64.Type),
  BufferTable = Table.Buffer( AddedIndex ),
  AddRunningTotal = Table.AddColumn(BufferTable, "Running Total",
    each List.Sum( List.FirstN( BufferTable[Amount Paid], [Index] )))
in
  AddRunningTotal
```

In this step, `Table.Buffer` loads the data into memory. The advantage here is that instead of making multiple requests to the source file, the data is now stored in memory. Subsequent operations on this table instead can use the in-memory data.

The performance metrics for this method in Power BI Desktop show a notable improvement:

- **Processing time:** Reduced to an average of 61 seconds.
- **Data retrieved:** Only 394 KB of data is retrieved.

This approach increases query speed by 52.3% and reduces its data consumption. The total data retrieved is now in line with the size of the original CSV file. This also shows how effective the `Table.Buffer` function is for optimizing performance.

Method 3: Running total from buffered column

Earlier in this chapter, we stressed the importance of minimizing memory usage for the mashup engine. Following this principle, method 3 buffers only the specific column used in the running total calculation. This approach reduces the memory footprint and hopefully reduces the query's refresh time.

The query structure for this method is as follows:

```
let
  Source = myCSV,
  AddedIndex =
    Table.AddIndexColumn(Source, "Index", 1, 1, Int64.Type),
  BufferColumn = List.Buffer( AddedIndex[Amount Paid] ),
  AddRunningTotal = Table.AddColumn(AddedIndex, "Running Total",
    each List.Sum( List.FirstN( BufferColumn, [Index] )))
in
  AddRunningTotal
```

In this query, the `BufferColumn` step specifically targets the **Amount Paid** column for buffering.

The performance results for this method show another significant improvement:

- **Processing time**: Remarkably reduced to an average of 1.2 seconds.
- **Data retrieved**: Amounts to 786 KB.

This method achieves a staggering 99.1% reduction in refresh time compared to the original query. An interesting observation is that the method accesses the CSV file twice—most likely once for the original table and once to buffer the column used in the running total calculation. This shows that the amount of data retrieved is not always an indicator of the speed of the query. Instead, this scenario indicates a strategic balance between memory efficiency and processing speed.

Does this mean there's nothing left to improve? Well, not exactly. The `List.FirstN` method for creating a running total is not the most efficient one. To improve things even further, we can make use of the `List.Generate` function.

Method 4: Running total from buffered column using List.Generate

The `List.FirstN` method, while functional, is not the most efficient for summing values in a running total calculation. It requires retrieving and adding a range of values for each row. An alternative and more efficient technique is the use of the `List.Generate` function. This method computes the running total by adding each new value to the previously calculated total rather than recalculating the sum over an ever-increasing range of values each time. For an in-depth discussion about this `List.Generate` method, see *Chapter 14*, but for now, let's explore this method in the current context.

The query using `List.Generate` is as follows:

```
let
    Source = myCSV,
    BufferedColumn = List.Buffer( Source[Amount Paid] ),
    RunningTotal =
      List.Generate (
        () => [ RT = BufferedColumn{0}, RowIndex = 0 ],
        each [RowIndex] < List.Count( BufferedColumn ),
        each [ RT = List.Sum( { [RT], BufferedColumn{[RowIndex] + 1} }),
              RowIndex = [RowIndex] + 1 ],
        each [RT] ),
    CombineTables = Table.FromColumns(
      Table.ToColumns( Source )   & { RunningTotal },
      Table.ColumnNames( Source ) & { "Running Total" }   )
in
    CombineTables
```

This method still buffers only a single column. The `List.Generate` function then efficiently computes the running total. Lastly, the original table columns are combined with the newly created running total column.

The performance of this revised method in Power BI Desktop is as follows:

- **Processing time**: Remarkably reduced to an average of 201 milliseconds.
- **Data retrieved**: Amounts to 786 KB.

This method shows a remarkable 99.8% improvement in processing time compared to the original approach.

The following table summarizes the performance of these four different methods:

Method	Description	Processing Time	Data Retrieved	Improvement
1	`List.FirstN` + Regular Table	128 seconds	1.88 GB	0.0%
2	`List.FirstN` + Buffered Table	61 seconds	394 KB	52.3%
3	`List.FirstN` + Buffered Column	1.2 seconds	786 KB	99.1%
4	`List.Generate` + Buffered Column	201 milliseconds	786 KB	99.8%

Table 15.1: Comparing the performance of different methods

As this section showed, buffer functions like `List.Buffer` and `Table.Buffer` can significantly impact the memory used to perform calculations in M, especially when your query accesses your data source multiple times. You can try one of these functions whenever you notice your query using much more memory than required. While this is an excellent optimization, don't forget to look for alternative approaches that make more efficient use of memory, just like `List.Generate` in this example.

The performance of your queries not only depends on how you structure your query. An important consideration is the speed of your data sources, which we will cover next.

Data source considerations

When dealing with slow queries, a good question is where your queries spend their time. Even if you manage to keep the memory footprint of your queries small, if your data source is slow, you will wait for your data to come in. In other words, choosing the right data source can greatly impact your query performance.

Data sources and speed

While it's not always feasible to swap to a different data source, it's good to be aware of some general rules of data sources and their performance. Here are a few pointers on what to think of:

- **Relational databases:** These databases tend to perform better than files. A bonus is that many database connectors support query folding and allow you to load your data incrementally.
- **Files:** Store data in CSV or text files when working with files. They perform much better than JSON, XML, and Excel files.
- **Network location:** Retrieving files from a network location like OneDrive or SharePoint tends to be slower than local files. While developing, it is a good idea to consider storing your files locally.
- **Web/internet:** Connecting to web services or APIs may be slow. Similarly, importing large quantities of data over the internet can be slow.

When working with the above data sources, they likely contain your source data. You may find yourself in a situation where the nature of these sources is slowing down your queries, especially when you're working with legacy data sources or data from network locations. If you find yourself in that situation, you can consider making use of a feature called dataflows, which we will cover next.

Using dataflows

Some data sources can be challenging to optimize. They may not support query folding, are naturally slow, or lack the resources to handle large data requests. You may be unable to do much to speed them up in these cases. However, if you're working with data from a slow source, consider using a dataflow, also known as an analytical dataflow.

A dataflow connects to a data source using Power Query. You can set it up to collect data from your slow source regularly. Once it gathers the data, the dataflow stores it in Power BI's Azure Data Lake Storage. Here, the data is kept in a format known as **CDM** (**Common Data Model**) folders. This folder includes CSV files for each part of your data and a JSON metadata file that describes the data's content and structure.

Now, remember that data source that used to be slow? You can use the dataflow to store its data. Instead of connecting directly to the slow source, your queries can connect to the dataflow in Power Query, which can significantly speed up your query processing.

For companies with Power Premium, the enhanced compute engine is a great feature to improve dataflows. This engine speeds up how fast dataflows respond to your requests. The best part is its ability to use query folding. Queries sent to retrieve data from the dataflow are executed against the cache in SQL rather than the CDM folder for dataflows without this feature turned on.

We've discussed how dataflows can be a great platform to store the data from your slow data sources. Another advantage is their ability to store your queries' output. When you have many queries in the query editor, it tends to become slow, most likely due to the overhead of loading queries in the background. To make the user interface faster, it's useful to reduce the number of queries. A good way to do this is by saving some of your queries' logic in a dataflow. Then, you can create a single query that connects to this dataflow to get the results of your original queries. This approach not only speeds up the user interface but also makes your queries refresh faster as the dataflow simply returns the output of your queries instead of calculating it during refresh time.

To learn more about dataflows, you can read this article: `https://learn.microsoft.com/en-us/power-bi/transform-model/dataflows/dataflows-create`.

Performance tips

Optimizing performance is a complicated topic, even after learning about all the different perspectives in this chapter. As with all optimization topics, you'll have to test different approaches for your situation. However, we have several general performance tips:

- Connect your query to a fast data source. If your source system is slow, consider moving the data to a faster source or storing your data in a dataflow.

- Maximize the number of steps that your query folding mechanisms can fold. If you're adept at SQL, consider crafting an efficient SQL query and apply the `EnableFolding` parameter. If SQL is not your strength, prioritize placing foldable steps early in your query. This approach helps ensure that your data source handles most of the transformations.

- When your query steps no longer fold, the next focus should be reducing your query's memory usage. That means filtering rows and removing columns as soon as possible. Also reduce your query size as much as possible before performing expensive buffering operations such as a group by, pivoting, or joins. Subsequent steps then only need to apply their logic on a smaller dataset.

- Use buffer functions for steps that repeatedly request data. When doing that, make sure to buffer only the data that is required. This means that if you need to buffer the column values only, only buffer that column; don't buffer the entire table.

While the above are general recommendations to make your queries performant, we also have some recommendations that improve query speed while developing in the query editor:

- Consider working with a subset of your data to speed up your development. Filter rows as early as possible so the remaining query has fewer processing needs.

- Attempt to use streaming operations as much as possible at the start of your query. This ensures the preview screen populates quickly and provides a better developing experience. Once buffering operations come in, your query will need to evaluate all the rows in your dataset.

- Once the number of transformations and queries increases, Power Query tends to get sluggish. Consider storing (part of) your logic in a dataflow to reduce the amount of resources used while developing.

Summary

In this chapter, we have learned the multi-faceted approach required to optimize performance in Power Query. We have delved into areas such as the effective use of query folding and strategies for navigating the formula firewall. The difference between buffering and streaming operations, along with the careful use of buffer functions and the importance of reducing memory usage in your queries, were important areas of focus.

Key to this chapter is the understanding that the careful management of memory aspects helps improve query performance. By integrating these concepts and approaches, you are now equipped with a comprehensive understanding of the various elements that contribute to the performance optimization of your Power Query operations.

In the following chapter, we will focus on working with extensions. You'll learn the fundamental concepts required to create a custom connector and what tools are involved in the process.

Learn more on Discord

Join our community's Discord space for discussions with the author and other readers:

`https://discord.gg/vCSG5GBbyS`

16

Enabling Extensions

Power Query supports a wide array of different data source connectors for accessing and retrieving data from a variety of different data sources. In fact, Power BI Desktop natively supports almost 200 different data source connectors, most of which have been covered in *Chapter 3, Accessing and Combining Data*. In addition, many of these data source connectors are generic for various data format standards and protocols such as the **Open Data Protocol (OData)**, **Open Database Connectivity (ODBC)**, **JavaScript Object Notation (JSON)**, **Extensible Markup Language (XML)**, and Parquet. Support for these common standards and protocols significantly expands the potential data sources for Power Query to thousands, if not tens of thousands of potential sources.

Even with all the data sources already supported by Power Query, there is still a need to support additional data sources. In particular, various web services often provide an **application programming interface (API)** that must be used to access their data. This chapter demonstrates how to create custom extensions for Power Query to handle these kinds of scenarios, including the following topics:

- What are Power Query extensions?
- Preparing your environment
- Creating a custom connector
- Installing and using a custom connector

Technical requirements

You will require the following to complete the tasks in this chapter:

- Visual Studio Code
- Power Query SDK

What are Power Query extensions?

In short, Power Query extensions are primarily pieces of M code that add to the global environment. Refer to *Chapter 7, Conceptualizing M*, to understand more about the global environment. Extensions are primarily used to create custom data connectors but can also be used to create a library of reusable custom functions.

These extensions come in four different file types (file extensions):

- m: This is a simple text file containing M code.
- Pq: This is a simple text file containing M code.
- mez: This is a standard ZIP file containing custom connector files. Can use a standard ZIP file and rename it from `file.zip` to `file.mez`.
- pqx: This is an **Open Packaging Conventions** (**OPC**) ZIP file containing custom connector files. Typically packaged using the `System.IO.Packaging` .NET library, this packaging format allows the digital signing of the file and is the format for Microsoft-certified connectors.

As noted, `.mez` and `.pqx` files are collections of files used to build custom data source connectors. We will explore creating a custom connector later in this chapter. These file collections always include a single `.m` or `.pq` file, which is the primary file that holds the custom connector code.

It's important to note that Power Query extensions are implemented using the `section` keyword and functions within the section are exposed to the global environment using the `shared` keyword. Sections are implemented as standard M code with some special syntax rules.

Consider the following code. Note the special use of semicolons (;) within the `section` syntax. Just as multiple expressions within a `let` statement are separated with a comma (,), multiple expressions within a `section` are separated by semicolons:

```
section MyAwesomeExtension;

shared MyAwesomeExtension.DoSomething = (firstNumber as number, secondNumber as
number) as number =>
    MyAwesomeExtension.SquareNumber(firstNumber) + MyAwesomeExtension.
SquareNumber(secondNumber);

MyAwesomeExtension.SquareNumber = (paramNumber as number) as number =>
paramNumber * paramNumber;
```

This section has one shared function, `MyAwesomeExtension.DoSomething`, and one internal function only accessible within the section, `MyAwesomeExtension.SquareNumber`. The `MyAwesomeExtension.DoSomething` function calls `MyAwesomeExtension.SquareNumber` to square the two numbers and add them together.

Paste this code into a text editor and save the file with a file name of `MyAwesomeExtension.pq`. Place this file into the `[Documents]\Microsoft Power BI Desktop\Custom Connectors` folder. You may have to create this folder.

Open Power BI Desktop and navigate to **File | Options and settings | Options**. Under the **GLOBAL** heading, choose **Security**, and then under **Data Extensions**, select the radio button for **(Not Recommended) Allow any extension to load without validation or warning**:

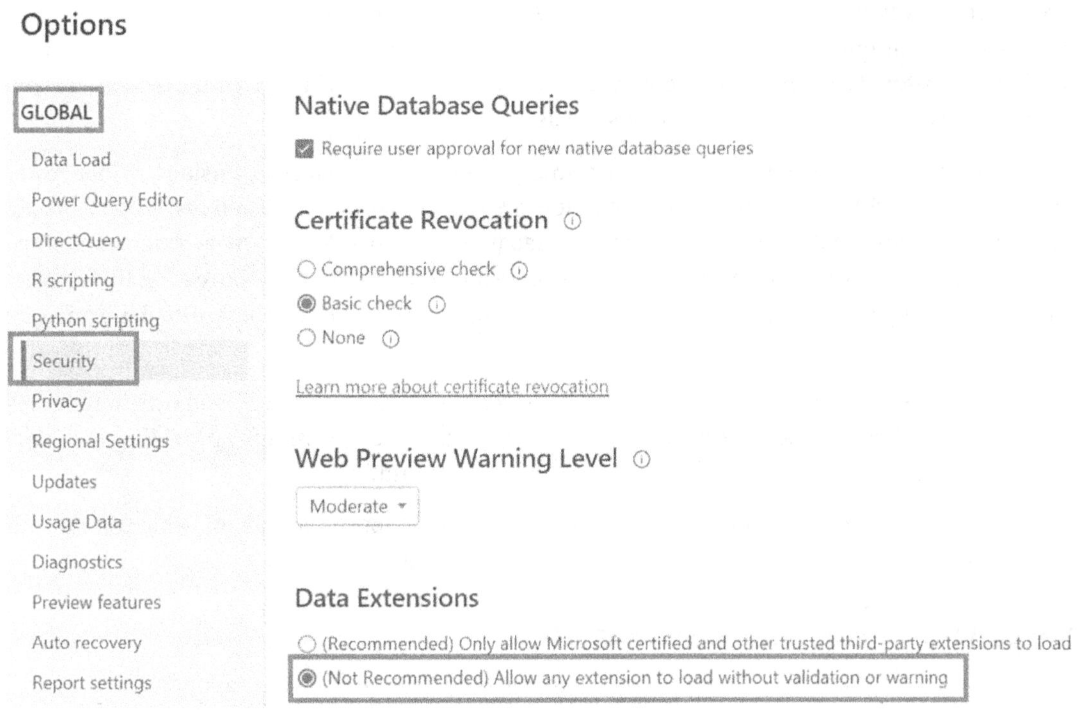

Options

Figure 16.1: Enable uncertified extensions

Close Power BI Desktop and then relaunch Power BI Desktop. Open the Power Query editor in Power BI Desktop and create the following query:

```
let
    Source = MyAwesomeExtension.DoSomething(10, 5)
in
    Source
```

This query returns 125, the result of squaring 10 and 5 and adding them together. Note that only the MyAwesomeExtension.DoSomething function is exposed to and can be used in the query. The MyAwesomeExtension.SquareNumber function cannot be referenced as it is not prefaced with the shared keyword.

At this point, you should be able to understand the basic structure and nature of Power Query extensions but may be asking yourself how you might use them.

What can you do with extensions?

There are two primary uses for extensions within Power Query:

- Custom function library
- Custom data source connectors

As you have already seen, you can use extensions to provide a library of custom, reusable functions for use within your queries. Instead of copying and pasting code between projects, you can instead include your custom functions in a section with the shared keyword. While this ability exists, it is not the primary use for extensions and is not widely used.

Custom data source connectors are the other primary use for Power Query extensions. While Power BI Desktop comes with almost 200 connectors, there are still many other data sources, especially data sources that use custom APIs, which are not included in the product. Power Query extensions allow developers to create custom connectors that connect to these additional data sources. In this chapter, we use Discord, a popular instant messaging and **Voice over Internet Protocol** (**VoIP**) platform as an example.

Custom connectors can be used to create new data sources or customize and extend existing sources. When installed, these connectors extend Power Query's global environment, providing new data access functions are not present within the M language by default.

The rest of this chapter focuses on the creation of a custom data source connector, which starts with the processing of preparing your environment for development.

Preparing your environment

To prepare your environment, you must download and install two software components:

- Visual Studio Code
- Power Query **software development kit (SDK)**

In addition, the custom connector example covered in this chapter connects to Discord, a popular voice and instant messaging social platform. We will use the Discord API to connect to a Discord server and retrieve information. To use Discord, we will also want to install and configure two additional components, namely:

- Internet Information Services
- Discord

Let's look at how to get these software components installed and configured.

Getting Visual Studio Code

There are currently two versions of Power Query: a version released in 2017 that works as an extension for Visual Studio 2017 and 2019 and a new version (currently in preview on the publication date for this book) that works with Visual Studio Code.

For this book, we will be working with the new version of the Power BI SDK for **Visual Studio Code**. To get started, download and install the latest version of Visual Studio Code here: https://code. visualstudio.com/download.

If you are only familiar with Visual Studio 2017, 2019, or 2022, you will likely find Visual Studio Code somewhat unfamiliar and perhaps a bit vexing to work with. In fact, you would not be ostracized if you feel that the acronym GUI stands for Gratuitously Unintuitive Interface when it comes to Visual Studio Code. There are many differences and odd quirks in the Visual Studio Code product that can cause confusion. While a full treatment of the experience within Visual Studio Code is beyond the scope of this book, significant effort has been made to point out where and how to navigate Visual Studio Code for the purposes of creating a custom connector. In addition, the steps within the *Creating a custom connector* section have been specifically designed to minimize the number of odd errors or messages. Therefore, follow the steps in that section closely.

> **Pro tip:** Sometimes, simply saving your work, closing the folder, and then reopening the folder works wonders.

Once you have Visual Studio Code installed, the next step is to install the Power Query SDK.

Getting the Power Query SDK

The Power Query SDK can be downloaded from the Visual Studio Marketplace: `https://marketplace.visualstudio.com/items?itemName=PowerQuery.vscode-powerquery-sdk`. If you instead have Visual Studio 2017 or 2019, then you can download and install the older version of the SDK here: `https://marketplace.visualstudio.com/items?itemName=Dakahn.PowerQuerySDK`. The instructions found in this book assume that you are using the new SDK for Visual Studio Code.

Clicking the **Install** button on the web page for the new Power Query SDK for Visual Studio Code launches Visual Studio Code and brings up the installation page for the Power Query SDK. Simply click the **Install** button here to download and install the SDK.

Once the Power Query SDK is installed, the next step is to configure a local web server.

Setting up Internet Information Services

Internet Information Services is a web server that can be configured on any Windows PC. To configure Internet Information Services on your local computer, follow these steps:

1. Type `Turn Windows features on and off` into the Windows search bar and launch the **Windows Features** dialog.

2. Select the check box next to **Internet Information Services:**

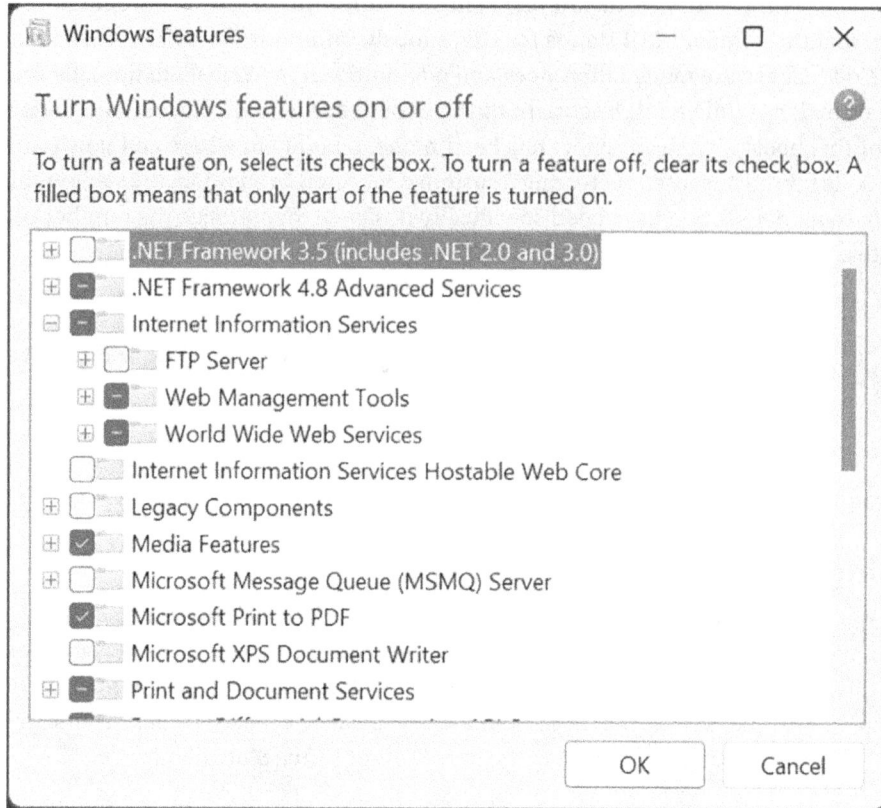

Figure 16.2: Turn on Internet Information Services

3. Click the **OK** button to configure **Internet Information Services**. By default, this automatically selects **Web Management Tools** and **World Wide Web Services** but not **FTP Server.** This is fine for our purposes.

In our example custom connector, we will be using OAuth for authentication. **OAuth** stands for **Open Authentication** and is an open standard that allows users to grant limited access to a website or service to third-party applications. We will use the local Internet Information Services as an endpoint for a redirect **uniform resource identifier (URI)** required by the OAuth protocol.

Note that it is not overly important what redirect URI is provided and the actual URI involved doesn't necessarily even have to actually exist in some cases, including in the case of this example. All that is required is that some web server is available to serve as the redirect URI endpoint.

As an alternative to using a local web server as our endpoint, we could, in theory, use nearly any OAuth redirect URI, such as `https://oauth.powerbi.com/views/oauthredirect.html`. However, this can be risky if the domain name and thus web service are not within the control of the developer as that endpoint may, at some point, no longer be valid and would thus potentially cause an error in the authentication process.

Note that this kind of "**not valid**" error is different from a page simply not existing for a web server. For example, `jazzysneakers123.com` is not a valid domain name and thus will generate an error in the authentication process if someone attempts to use `jazzysneakers.com` as a redirect URI. This is different from using an invalid page for a domain name that exists and responds to requests as a web server. In the latter case, a **404 page not found** message is generated and this will not automatically cause the authentication process to fail.

For our development purposes, we will use the local Internet Information Services and we can refer to this web server as localhost. Obviously, this would not be sufficient for a production custom connector since not everyone has a local web server installed and configured by default. Production scenarios would require the developer to set up a generally available web server and corresponding redirect URI. This kind of production scenario is beyond the scope of this book but this could be as easy as setting up a WordPress blog site with or without a custom domain.

The next step is to install and configure Discord, so let's get started with it!

Setting up Discord

To set up Discord for use with the Discord API, we require the following:

- Discord client
- Discord server
- Discord application (app)
- OAuth configuration

Let's review how to get and configure each of these items.

Discord client

To download and install the Discord client, use a web browser to navigate to `https://discord.com`. Click the **Download for Windows** button on the home page and then run the installation to install Discord. Alternatively, you can use the **Open Discord in your browser** button instead.

Discord server

To create a Discord server, simply click the + icon in the left navigation of the Discord client, as shown in the following figure:

Figure 16.3: Add a Discord server

Choose what kind of server to create and provide a name for your server. Click the **Create** button to create the server. Once created, the server will appear in the left navigation pane of the Discord client.

The next step is to create a Discord application.

Discord app

To use the Discord API, we need to create a Discord app. To create a Discord app, follow these steps:

1. Use a web browser and navigate to the following web page: https://discord.com/developers/
   applications.

2. Click the **New Application** button.

3. Provide a name for the application and then click the **Create** button:

CREATE AN APPLICATION

Are you a game dev? We may already have your app in our database. Reach out to our **Dev Support** for more info and to claim your game!

NAME *

Power Query

✔ By clicking Create, you agree to the Discord Developer Terms of Service and Developer Policy.

Cancel   Create

Figure 16.4: Create a Discord app

4. Click the **Create** button to create the application.

After clicking the **Create** button, you are transported to the application's settings page. This is where we can perform the next step, configuring OAuth, so let's do that next. This application can be added to a Discord server although for our purposes that will not be necessary.

Discord OAuth configuration

To use the API to send requests to the Discord API on behalf of a user, the user must first authorize the app. The configuration for this is done on the application's settings page and requires the following steps:

1. Click the **OAuth2** link in the left navigation pane of the application settings page.

2. Note the **CLIENT ID** under **Client information**. Copy and save this client ID as we will need it later when creating our custom connector.

3. Next, click the **Reset Secret** button shown in the following screenshot:

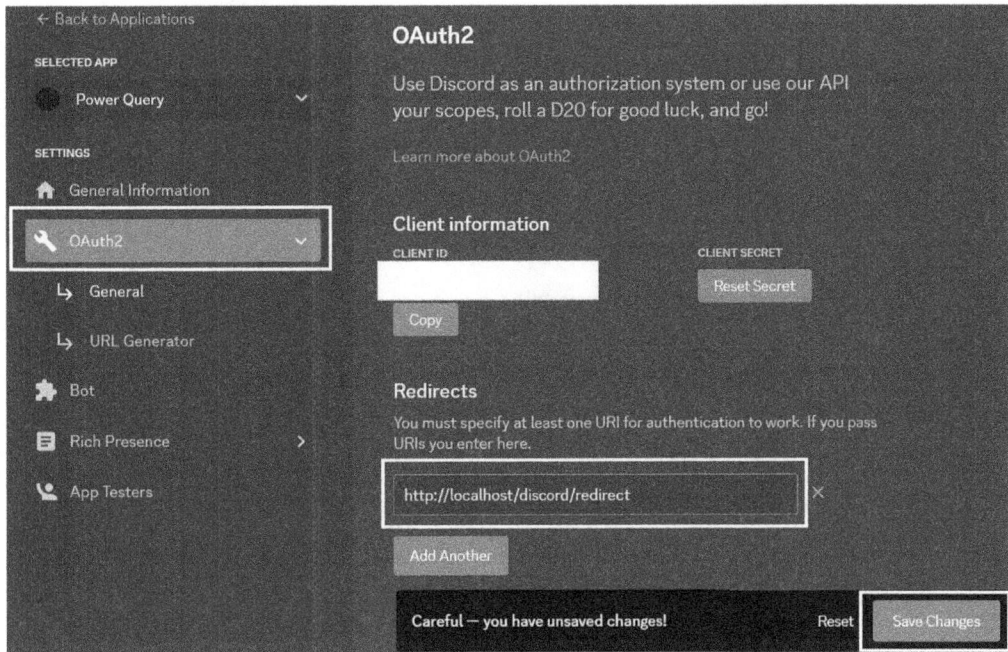

Figure 16.5: Add an OAuth2 application redirect

4. Make sure to use the **Copy** button to copy your client secret key and save this key. You will need it when creating the custom connector.

5. Now click the **Add Redirect** button and add the redirect http://localhost/discord/redirect, as shown in *Figure 16.5*.

6. Finally, click the **Save Changes** button to save the redirect.

The http://localhost/discord/redirect web page does not actually exist. In fact, any URI that used localhost could be used for this step. What is important is that localhost refers to our local PC where a local web server is running as configured in the *Setting up Internet Information Services* section.

We have now finished preparing the environment. Let's now move on to creating a custom connector or extension.

Creating a custom connector

With Visual Studio Code, the Power Query SDK installed, our local environment configured with IIS, and Discord elements created and configured, we can now create a custom connector for Power Query.

The full code for the custom connector for this book is available in the GitHub repository found here: https://github.com/PacktPublishing/The-Definitive-Guide-to-Power-Query-M-/tree/main/ Chapter%2016. You can either download the TDGTPQM_Discord.zip file from *Chapter 14* in the repository, extract the files, copy and paste the connector folder somewhere on your PC, and then open the folder in Visual Studio Code (**File | Open Folder...**), or you can follow along with the rest of this section where we build the connector from scratch.

In either case, you will be well served by reading the code explanations throughout the rest of this section. The rest of this section assumes that you are creating the custom connector from scratch.

The steps to create the connector are as follows:

1. Create the extension project.
2. Configure authentication.
3. Configure navigation and content.

Let's look at the first step: creating an extension project.

Creating an extension project

As noted earlier, we will be creating our custom connector in Visual Studio Code, Microsoft's current preferred approach as of this book's publication. To create the extension project, do the following:

1. Launch Visual Studio Code if it is not running already.
2. Access the **EXPLORER,** expand the **POWER QUERY SDK** section, and then create a new extension project by clicking the **Create an extension project** button:

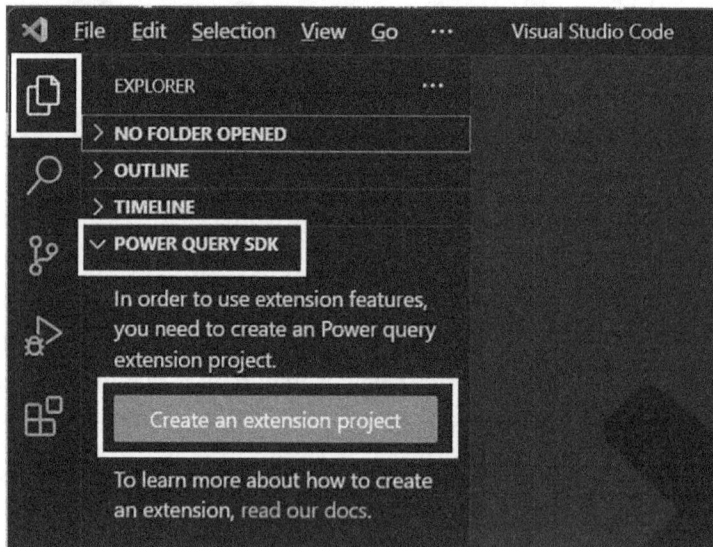

Figure 16.6: Create an extension project

3. When prompted, enter TDGTPQM_Discord as the **New project name** and press the *Enter* key.
4. When prompted for a folder for the workspace, create a new folder named TDGTPQM_Discord, select that folder, and press the **Select workspace** button.

The following file and folder structure is created:

- TDGTPQM_Discord

  - .vscode

    - settings.json

- bin
    - AnyCPU
    - Debug
    - TDGTPQM_Discord.mez
- resources.resx
- TDGTPQM_Discord.pq
- TDGTPQM_Discord.proj
- TDGTPQM_Discord.query.pq
- TDGTPQM_Discord.png
- TDGTPQM_Discord.png
- TDGTPQM_Discord.png
- TDGTPQM_Discord.png
- TDGTPQM_Discord.png
- TDGTPQM_Discord.png
- TDGTPQM_Discord.png
- TDGTPQM_Discord.png

Let's take a closer look at the files created:

- settings.json: A **JavaScript Open Notation (JSON)** file that holds workspace settings.
- TDGTPQM_Discord.mez: This file is contained in the directory bin\AnyCPU\Debug and is the actual extension built by the Power Query SDK that you deploy and use as your custom connector.
- resources.resx: An XML file that mainly stores strings used within the extension.
- TDGTPQM_Discord.pq: This is the main code file for the custom connector. Only a single .pq file is allowed and its format is that of an M section.
- TDGTPQM_Discord.proj: An XML file that contains project settings.
- TDGTPQM_Discord.query.pq: Mainly used as a method of creating test queries. This file simply contains the following code:

```
let
    result = TDGTPQM_Discord.Contents()
in
    result
```

This file simply references a function (TDGTPQM_Discord.Contents) defined within the TDGTPQM_Discord.pq, as we will see later. This code is sufficient for our purposes and will remain unchanged.

- .png files: Icons used by the connector.

To write our custom connector, we will be working with the TDGTPQM_Discord.pq file, so let's explore this file in greater detail.

TDGTPQM_Discord.pq

This file contains the main code logic for the custom connector and is the file we will be modifying to create our custom connector. The entire custom connector is implemented as a section as per this code at the top of the file:

```
// This file contains your Data Connector logic
[Version = "1.0.0"]
section TDGTPQM_Discord;
```

As explained previously, `section` documents show how extensions are implemented in M.

Below this section definition, we find the following code:

```
[DataSource.Kind="TDGTPQM_Discord", Publish="TDGTPQM_Discord.Publish"]
shared TDGTPQM_Discord.Contents = (optional message as text) =>
    let
        _message = if (message <> null) then message else "Hello World",
        a = "Hello from HelloWorld: " & _message
    in
        a;
```

`TDGTPQM_Discord.Contents` is the main function we will use to return the contents of our connector. Note the shared keyword preceding the function definition. This means that this function can be referenced outside of the section.

Also, note the definition for `DataSource.Kind` and `Publish.DataSource.Kind` is defined as `TDGTPQM_Discord`. Using the `shared` keyword along with a `DataSource.Kind` literal attribute definition for the function associates the function with a specific data source, the `TDGTPQM_Discord` data source.

The next block of code is the definition record for the associated data source, `TDGTPQM_Discord`:

```
// Data Source Kind description
TDGTPQM_Discord = [
    Authentication = [
        // Key = [],
        // UsernamePassword = [],
        // Windows = [],
        Anonymous = []
    ]
];
```

The data source definition record defines the data source's supported authentication types. In this case, only anonymous or implicit authentication is supported as currently defined.

In addition to the `DataSource.Kind` literal attribute, there is also a `Publish` literal attribute associated with the `TDGTPQM_Discord.Contents` function. The block of code below the data source definition record is the `Publish` record definition:

```
// Data Source UI publishing description
TDGTPQM_Discord.Publish = [
    Beta = true,
    Category = "Other",
    ButtonText = { Extension.LoadString("ButtonTitle"), Extension.
LoadString("ButtonHelp") },
    LearnMoreUrl = "https://powerbi.microsoft.com/",
    SourceImage = TDGTPQM_Discord.Icons,
    SourceTypeImage = TDGTPQM_Discord.Icons
];
```

The `Publish` record is used by the Power Query **user interface** (UI) (Power Query editor, for example) to display the data source extension via the **Get Data** dialog. These settings can be adjusted to change the behavior of certain UI elements such as the category in which the data source connector is displayed, whether the connector is in Beta or not, and the **Learn More** link for the connector.

This `Publish` record references an additional record, `TDGTPQM_Discord.Icons`, which holds references to the `.png` image files:

```
TDGTPQM_Discord.Icons = [
    Icon16 = { Extension.Contents("TDGTPQM_Discord16.png"), Extension.
Contents("TDGTPQM_Discord20.png"), Extension.Contents("TDGTPQM_Discord24.png"),
Extension.Contents("TDGTPQM_Discord32.png") },
    Icon32 = { Extension.Contents("TDGTPQM_Discord32.png"), Extension.
Contents("TDGTPQM_Discord40.png"), Extension.Contents("TDGTPQM_Discord48.png"),
Extension.Contents("TDGTPQM_Discord64.png") }
];
```

These are the icons displayed within the Power Query UI for the connector.

This completes our detailed exploration of the `TDGTPQM_Discord.pq` file. You might be surprised about the small amount of code required to create a custom connector; make no mistake, the default extension project created by the Power Query SDK is already a functioning custom connector. That said, this connector right now does not really do anything other than essentially return the equivalent of `Hello World`.

With our extension project created, we can now move on to writing our custom code for authentication.

Configuring authentication

With our base extension project created and explained, it is now time to turn our attention to customizing the extension to meet our needs of connecting to Discord. Our first task in this regard is to code and configure the authentication for the connector.

Discord uses the OAuth security protocol for authentication. There are other authentication types available:

- Anonymous
- AAD
- Username and password
- Windows
- Key

Each of these authentication mechanisms is unique. More information about these additional authentication types can be found here: `https://learn.microsoft.com/en-us/power-query/handling-authentication`.

OAuth authentication is by far the most complex authentication method for Power Query extensions and thus why it was chosen for this book as an example. As mentioned previously, OAuth stands for Open Authentication and is an open standard that allows users to grant limited access to a website or service to third-party applications. In our case, the user is granting our third-party custom connector limited access to their Discord information.

The OAuth protocol allows access without the user having to share their credentials (usernames and passwords).

> OAuth provides a secure and standardized way for users to authorize external applications to access their data or perform actions on their behalf.

Instead of credentials like usernames and passwords, OAuth uses the exchange of client secrets and access tokens between the user, the application requesting access, and the service providing the resources.

By implementing OAuth, service providers can ensure that user credentials remain protected and are not exposed to external applications. OAuth enables users to control and revoke access to their resources at any time, providing them with increased security and control over their data.

Overall, OAuth plays a crucial role in enabling secure and controlled access to resources, promoting interoperability, and enhancing user privacy in various web and mobile applications. You have very likely seen OAuth authorization prompts in the past, though you may not have recognized what they were.

To implement our OAuth authentication, we need to perform the following steps:

1. Add client ID and client secret files.
2. Add configuration settings.
3. Create OAuth functions.
4. Modify the data source definition.

5. Add a credential.

6. Test the connection.

Adding client ID and client secret files

The first step in configuring the authentication for our custom connector is to add files to store our application's client ID and client secret. To do this, perform the following steps:

1. With the extension project open, select **File** | **New File** from the Visual Studio Code menu.

2. When prompted, enter client_id as the file name, press the **Enter** key, and then press the **Create File** button.

3. The client_id file is automatically opened in Visual Studio Code. On line *1*, simply paste in the client ID that you saved as part of the *Discord OAuth configuration* section.

4. Repeat these steps but, this time, use client_secret for your file name and paste in your client secret saved as part of the *Discord OAuth configuration* section.

The files you just created will be used as part of the OAuth configuration settings for our custom connector, so let's add those configuration settings now.

Adding Configuration Settings

Configuration settings are simply variables defined within our custom connector. These variables can be thought of as global variables in the sense that any expression or function defined within our custom connector can access and use these variables.

To add the configuration settings, do the following:

- At the top of your file, you will see the following line:

```
Section TDGTPQM_Discord;
```

- Paste the following code immediately under the preceding line:

```
// OAuth Configuration Settings
client_id = Text.FromBinary(Extension.Contents("client_id"));
client_secret = Text.FromBinary(Extension.Contents("client_secret"));
redirect_uri = "http://localhost/discord/redirect";
authorize_uri = "https://discord.com/api/oauth2/authorize?";
token_uri = "https://discord.com/api/oauth2/token";

// Static variables
api_uri = "https://discord.com/api";

// Connector window
windowWidth = 1200;
windowHeight = 1000;
```

To better explain the variables created, consider the following:

- client_id: This reads the client_id file created in the *Adding client ID and client secret files* section and stores its value.

- client_secret: This reads the client_id file created in the *Adding client ID and client secret files* section and stores its value.

- redirect_uri: This stores the redirect URI used when configuring the Discord OAuth in the *Discord OAuth configuration* section. This must be the same redirect URI used in that configuration.

- authorize_uri: This holds the value for Discord's OAuth authorization URI.

- token_uri: This holds the value for Discord's token-granting URI.

- api_uri: This stores the base Discord API URI.

- WindowWidth: This defines the window width for the authentication dialog.

- WindowHeight: This defines the window height for the authentication dialog.

With these configuration variables/settings in place, we can now move on to implementing the required functions defined by Power Query's OAuth authentication type, so let's do that now.

Creating OAuth functions

Power Query's OAuth authentication type requires the implementation of two fields, StartLogin and FinishLogin. There are also two optional fields that can be implemented, Refresh and Logout. Each of these fields must specify a function defined within our custom connector. We will implement the required fields/functions but not the optional fields/functions as part of this custom connector.

Between the data source record definition, TDGTPQM_Discord, and the TDGTPQM_Discord.Publish record definition, insert the following code:

```
//
// OAuth2 flow definition
//
StartLogin = (resourceUrl, state, display) =>
    let
        AuthorizeUrl = authorize_uri
            & Uri.BuildQueryString(
                [
                    client_id = client_id,
                    redirect_uri = redirect_uri,
                    response_type = "code",
                    scope = "identify email connections guilds guilds.members.
read"
                ]
            )
    in
        [
```

```
                LoginUri = AuthorizeUrl,
                CallbackUri = redirect_uri,
                WindowHeight = windowHeight,
                WindowWidth = windowWidth,
                Context = null
        ];

FinishLogin = (context, callbackUri, state) =>
    let
        Parts = Uri.Parts(callbackUri)[Query]
    in
        TokenMethod(Parts[code]);

TokenMethod = (code) =>
    let
        Response = Web.Contents(
            token_uri,
            [
                Content = Text.ToBinary(
                    Uri.BuildQueryString(
                        [
                            client_id = client_id,
                            client_secret = client_secret,
                            grant_type = "authorization_code",
                            code = code,
                            redirect_uri = redirect_uri
                        ]
                    )
                ),
                Headers = [#"Content-type" = "application/x-www-form-
urlencoded", #"Accept" = "application/json"]
            ]
        ),
        Parts = Json.Document(Response)
    in
        Parts;
```

It should be noted that the internal workings of Power Query's OAuth authentication type are somewhat murky. Scant explanation or documentation is provided by Microsoft outside of implementation code samples. The code here is based on Microsoft's sample GitHub connector, which can be found here: https://github.com/microsoft/DataConnectors/tree/master/samples/Github.

The `StartLogin` and `FinishLogin` function definitions will vary depending on the specifications of each API. These functions implement the information and structures required by the Discord API. Let's start by taking a closer look at the `StartLogin` function.

The `StartLogin` function begins the OAuth authentication process by building out the authorization URI expected by the Discord API. This value is stored by the `AuthorizationUrl` expression. In effect, this expression is simply building a URI with specific query string parameters. The actual URI that is built is the following: `https://discord.com/api/oauth2/authorize?client_id=1128020929558098050&redirect_uri=http%3A%2F%2Flocalhost%2Fdiscord%2Fredirect&response_type=code&scope=identify%20guilds%20guilds.members.read%20email%20connections`.

Notice that the base authorization URI comes from our `authorize_uri` variable defined in the *Adding configuration settings* section. The query string contains our `client_id` (yours will be different) along with our `redirect_uri`, a `response_type` of `code`, and a `scope` parameter. The code response type tells the Discord API what kind of authorization response we are looking to receive, and the `scope` defines the permissions we are seeking to grant our third-party custom connector.

The `StartLogin` function returns a record containing the following fields:

- `LoginUri`: This is the `AuthorizeUrl` expression, which ultimately is the URI provided earlier: `https://discord.com/api/oauth2/authorize?client_id=1128020929558098050&redirect_uri=http%3A%2F%2Flocalhost%2Fdiscord%2Fredirect&response_type=code&scope=identify%20guilds%20guilds.members.read%20email%20connections`
- `CallbackUri`: Our `redirect_uri` configuration variable/setting
- `WindowHeight`: Our `WindowHeight` configuration variable/setting
- `WindowWidth`: Our `WindowWidth` configuration variable/setting
- `Context`: `null`

To gain a better understanding of how this works, simply paste the URI provided earlier (`AuthorizeUrl`) into a web browser. A Discord authorization prompt appears indicating that a third-party application is seeking the following permissions:

- Access your username, avatar, and banner.
- Access your email address.
- Access your third-party connections.
- Know what servers you're in.
- Read your member info (nickname, avatar, roles, etc.) for servers you belong to.

This list of permissions comes from the `scope` query string parameter of the URI. Click the **Authorize** button. You are now redirected to the `redirect_uri` specified, `http://localhost/discord/redirect`. This page does not actually exist, so your local web server returns a `404 Not Found` page. However, look closer at the URI in the browser; the URI will be something like this: `http://localhost/discord/redirect?code=WV9s0kMY3Rg6AsPvCzj6CgbgnUvwz0`.

Note the code parameter in the query string. Since we requested a `response_type` of code, this is the code returned by the Discord server. We then use this code in the `FinishLogin` function to generate an access token and complete our authorization process. This is done by feeding the code (`Parts[code]`) into the `TokenMethod` function.

In effect, the `FinishLogin` method retrieves the response from our `redirect_uri` and feeds the code query string parameter value to the `TokenMethod` function. The `TokenMethod` function completes the process of retrieving our OAuth access token.

To better understand this process, we can use Postman (`postman.com`) to emulate the behavior, as shown in the following screenshot. Postman is an API platform that includes tools that are commonly used to emulate complex API interactions such as authentication. Here in this Postman request, we have chosen a `POST` operation (as opposed to `GET`):

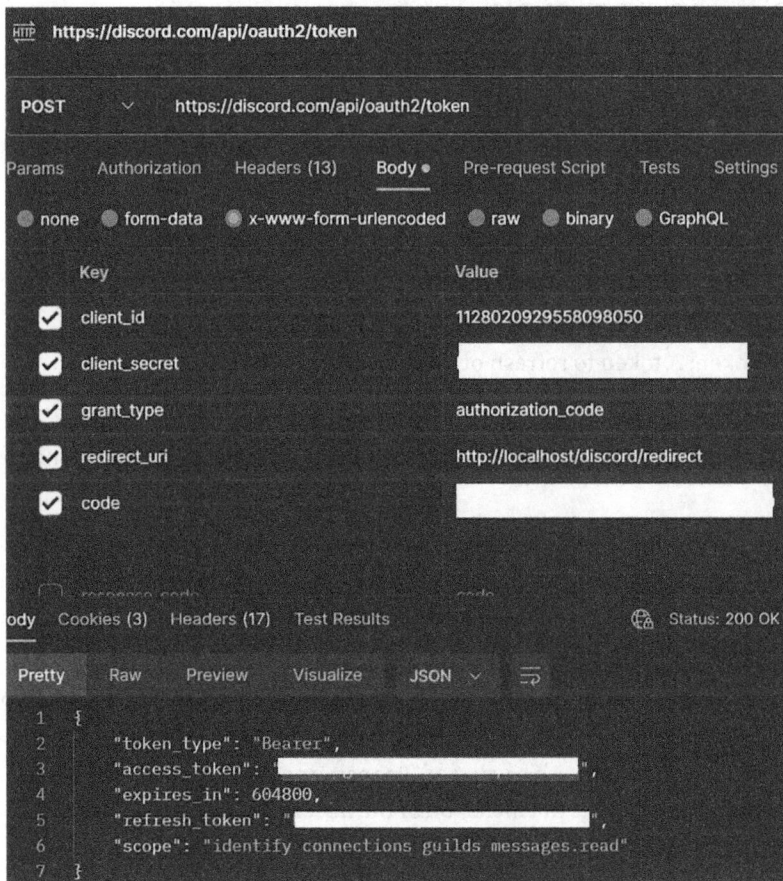

Figure 16.7: Retrieving the OAuth access token via Postman

Our custom connector behaves the same because we have included a **Headers** element within our `Web.Contents` function call within the `TokenMethod` function. Within *Figure 16.7*, we have specified a post to the URI `https://discord.com/api/oauth/token`, which is the same as the `token_uri` we are using in our custom connector.

Within the **Body** of our Postman request, we have specified the body is x-www-form-urlencoded, the same as implemented in our **Headers** for the Content-type within the TokenMethod function. Within that body, we are encoding the following information:

- client_id: This is our client ID generated in the *Discord OAuth configuration* section.
- client_secret: The client secret generated in the *Discord OAuth configuration* section.
- grant_type: This is set to authorization_code as required by the Discord OAuth API.
- redirect_uri: Our redirect URI defined in the *Discord OAuth configuration* section, http://localhost/discord/redirect.
- code: This is the code returned from the initial Discord API authorization call. In our custom connector, this is the code generated and put into the query string of our redirect_uri. If you pasted the example URI (AuthorizationUrl), it is this code: http://localhost/discord/redirect?code=WV9s0kMY3Rg6AsPvCzj6CgbgnUvwz0.

Each of these pieces of information is also encoded into our request made within the TokenMethod function.

In *Figure 16.7*, you can also see the response provided by Discord. The Discord token URI responds with the following information in JSON format:

- token_type: The type of token being returned, in this case, Bearer
- access_token: The Bearer access token
- expires_in: When the token expires
- refresh_token: A token to refresh our token
- scope: The scope of the access token

Note in our TokenMethod function that we expect a Json.Document to be returned as a response (Response).

While the specifics of the exact parameters passed within these requests vary between API OAuth implementations, overall, the provided M code should work with minimal modifications for most OAuth authentication scenarios. Luckily for us, Power Query's OAuth authentication type handles much of the heavy lifting from here on out.

For example, if we were to continue our example in Postman, for each subsequent API request (for example, getting a list of the servers for the user), we would need to include the access token in a parameter called Authorization with a value of "Bearer <access_token>". However, Power Query's OAuth authentication type handles the inclusion of the necessary headers automatically for us during these subsequent API requests.

Now that we have implemented the required OAuth authentication type functions, we can modify our data source record definition to change the authentication type from **Anonymous** to **OAuth**.

Modifying the data source record definition

With our required OAuth functions implemented, we can now modify our Data Source definition record to change from **Anonymous** authentication to **OAuth** authentication. To do this, follow these steps:

1. Find the Data Source definition record, `TDGTPQM_Discord`.

2. Replace the record definition with the following code. Notice that we now specify the `OAuth` authentication type provided as a record that specifies our `StartLogin` and `FinishLogin` functions for the corresponding `OAuth` authentication type fields:

```
// Data Source Kind description
TDGTPQM_Discord = [
    TestConnection = (dataSourcePath) => {"TDGTPQM_Discord.Contents"},
    Authentication = [
        OAuth = [
            StartLogin = StartLogin,
            FinishLogin = FinishLogin
        ]
    ]
];
```

With our OAuth authentication type now defined, it is time to test `OAuth` authentication for our custom connector. To do this, we must first add a credential.

Adding a credential

Adding a credential within Visual Studio Code emulates the behavior of the Power Query UI (such as Power Query editor) when you sign in or authenticate in order to connect to a data source.

To add a credential, follow these steps:

1. If you have not already, choose **File | Save All** from the Visual Studio Code menu.

2. Expand **POWER QUERY SDK** in the **Explorer** pane.

3. Click **Run TestConnection function**. Note that you receive an error:

   ```
   Failed to run the query due to Error: Failed to run the query due to Error:
   Unable to find credential for 'TDGTPQM_Discord/TDGTPQM_Discord'
   ```

4. Click **Evaluate current file**. Note that you again receive an error message:

   ```
   Credentials are required to connect to the TDGTPQM_Discord source. (Source
   at TDGTPQM_Discord.)
   ```

5. Click **Set credential**.

6. When prompted with **Choose the data source kind**, choose `TDGTPQM_Discord` from the list.

7. When prompted with **Choose a query/test file**, choose `TDGTPQM_Discord.query.pq` from the list.

8. When prompted with **Choose an authentication method**, choose **OAuth** from the list.

> Note that if you instead only see **Anonymous** listed, this is one of the many "quirks" of Visual Studio Code. Try saving your work and executing *Steps 3* and *4* again. If that does not work, choose **File | Close Folder** from the menu, save your work if prompted, and then reopen the folder using **File | Open Folder…**.

9. Once the folder is reopened, expand the **POWER QUERY SDK** section of the **Explorer** pane and pick back up from *Step 5*.

10. A dialog like the following should be displayed:

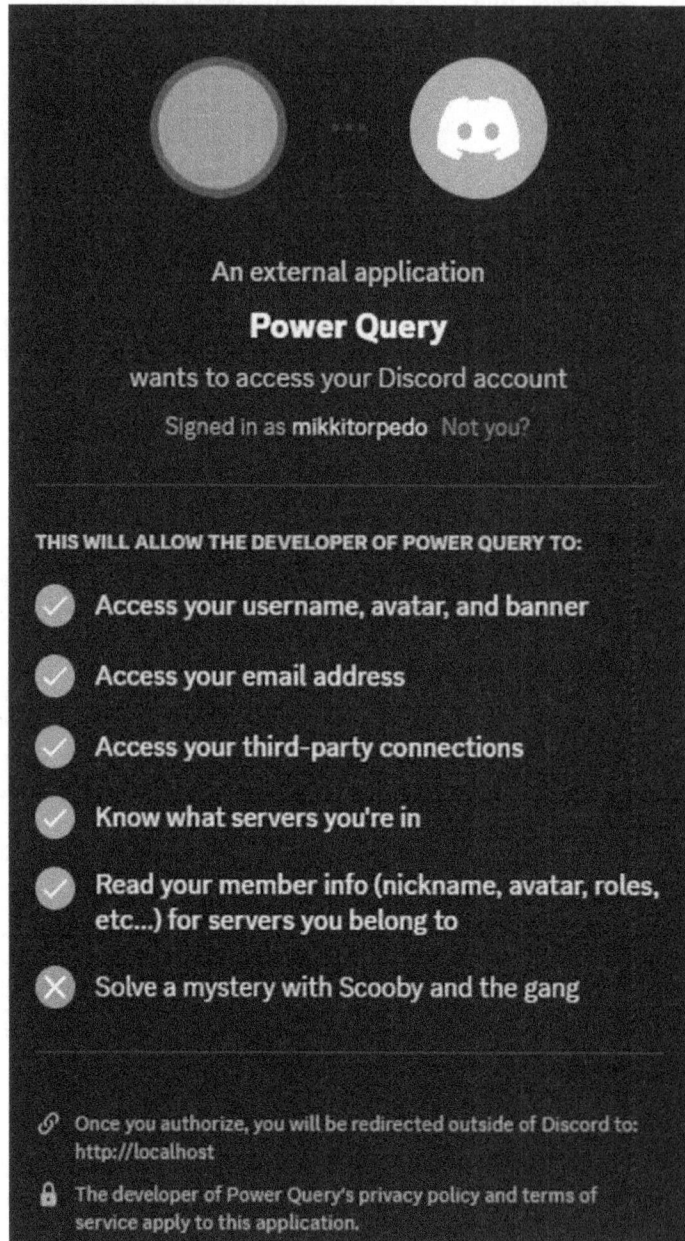

Figure 16.8: Discord authorization dialog

11. Click the **Authorize** button.

You should receive the message **New OAuth credential has been generated successfully.**

With our credential in place, we can now test our connection.

Testing the connection

While our custom connector still does not do very much other than essentially respond with the ubiquitous "Hello World" text, testing the connection at this stage does validate that our OAuth credential is present.

To test the connection, follow these steps:

1. Expand the **POWER QUERY SDK** section in the **Explorer** pane.
2. Click **Run TestConnection function**. This time, no error is displayed.
3. Make sure that the TDGTPQM.pq file is selected in the **EXPLORER** pane and then click **Evaluate current file**. This time, a PQTest result tab appears with a Value starting with Hello from TDGTPQM_Discord:.

Once our custom connection is successfully tested, confirming that our OAuth credential is created and present within Visual Studio Code, we can now move on to making our custom connector retrieve data from the Discord API.

Configuring navigation and content

It is now time to start making our custom connector actually retrieve and present data from Discord. If you consider the user experience in the Power Query editor when connecting to a data source, you follow this experience:

1. Choose **Get Data** and then pick a data source connector.
2. Sign in or authenticate according to the authentication options presented.
3. Often, a **Navigator** dialog is displayed where you can navigate folders and tables to retrieve preview data.
4. You choose tables of data within the **Navigator** dialog and press the **OK** button to retrieve the data.

We have already implemented our authentication type, OAuth. With respect to implementing the rest of the steps in M code, we essentially need to implement this process in reverse order by doing the following:

1. **Add API call data retrieval functions**: These functions will implement the actual data retrieval from the Discord API. This is how the data will be retrieved and displayed within the **Preview** panel of the **Navigator** dialog as well as how the data will be retrieved and loaded into the Power Query editor and eventually the data model.
2. **Add navigation functions**: These functions will present the **Navigator** dialog (the left-hand navigation panel) and link this navigation to the appropriate data retrieval operations (API call functions) implemented in *Step 1*.
3. **Modify the TDGTPQM.Contents function**: Finish the implementation of the **Navigator** dialog by modifying the TDGTPQM.Contents function to initialize the navigation.

Let's look at implementing the first step in this process: creating the M code to perform API calls.

Adding API call functions for data retrieval

For our custom Discord connector, we wish to implement three different data retrieval operations related to the following:

- Information associated with the identity of the user
- Information related to the servers or guilds to which the user belongs
- Information associated with the identity of the user within each server/guild

The information retrieved here is fairly basic and may not have much analytical value. However, this basic connector could be expanded upon to retrieve the number of messages posted to each server/guild, and so on.

To implement these data retrieval operations, do the following. Immediately above the data source kind definition, TDGTPQM_Discord, insert the following three functions:

```
// ** Identity
TDGTPQM_Discord.GetIdentity = () as table =>
    let
        apiCall = Json.Document(
            Web.Contents(
                api_uri,
                [
                    RelativePath = "users/@me"
                ]
            )
        ),
        output = Table.FromRecords({apiCall})
    in
        output;


// ** Servers (Guilds)
TDGTPQM_Discord.GetGuilds = () as table =>
    let
        apiCall = Json.Document(
            Web.Contents(
                api_uri,
                [
                    RelativePath = "users/@me/guilds"
                ]
            )
        ),
        output = Table.FromList(apiCall, Splitter.SplitByNothing(), null, null,
ExtraValues.Error)
```

```
        in
            output;


    // ** Member User
    TDGTPQM_Discord.GetGuildMember = (guildid as text) as table =>
        let
            apiCall = Json.Document(
                Web.Contents(
                    api_uri,
                    [
                        RelativePath = "users/@me/guilds/" & guildid & "/member"
                    ]
                )
            ),
            output = Table.FromRecords({apiCall})
        in
            output;
```

These functions are extremely similar. Let's first take a look at the `TDGTPQM_Discord.GetIdentity` function. This is the function that retrieves the information associated with the identity of the user. As we can see in the function definition, this function returns a table type (as `table`) and has no parameters. Reading the `apiCall` expression backward, we construct a URI consisting of our base `api_uri` as created in *Adding configuration settings* and the relative path of `users/@me`. This URI then becomes `https://discord.com/api/users/@me`.

We use `Web.Contents` to retrieve the response from this URI call and specify that these contents are a `Json.Document`. The output expression then retrieves the information within this JSON document using the `Table.FromRecords` function.

The next function, `TDGTPQM.GetGuilds`, retrieves information related to the servers, or guilds in Discord API parlance, to which the user belongs. This function also takes no parameters and returns a table. The API call is made to the following URI: `https://discord.com/api/users/@me/guilds`.

The output expression is slightly different. Instead of processing records, we are processing a list using the `Table.FromList` function.

You might naturally wonder how we can possibly know how to process the response from the API call, and whether to use the `Table.FromRecords` function or the `Table.FromList` function. The answer is by carefully reading the documentation provided by the API we are calling. However, a good trick is to use Postman to generate and view the response. You can do that by following these steps:

1. Paste the `AuthorizationUrl` into a web browser and press the *Enter* key. For reference, this URI is `https://discord.com/api/oauth2/authorize?client_id=1128020929558098050&redirect_uri=http%3A%2F%2Flocalhost%2Fdiscord%2Fredirect&response_type=code&scope=identify%20guilds%20guilds.members.read%20email%20connections`

2. Copy the code query string parameter value returned as part of the redirect_uri.

3. As shown in *Figure 16.7*, use Postman to request an access token using the code as one of the encoded parameters.

4. Use this access token in another Postman request to the API call:

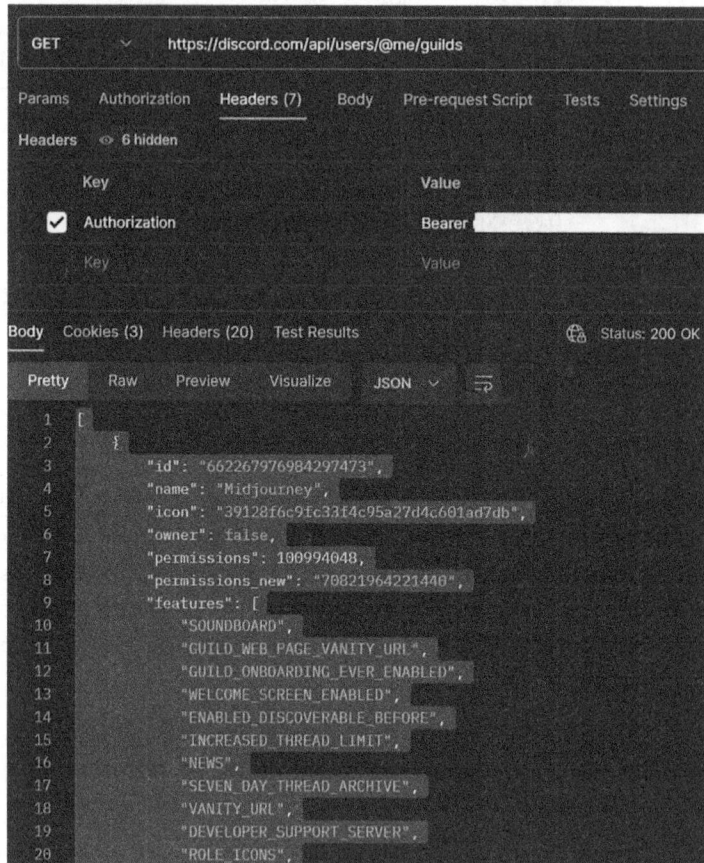

Figure 16.9: Discord API call using Postman

As you can see in *Figure 16.9*, we have initiated a GET request to the Discord API endpoint of https://discord.com/api/users/@me/guilds. We have included an Authorization parameter in our **Headers** with a value of "Bearer <access token>". In the bottom panel, we can view the response returned from the API call.

5. Copy the response returned and paste this data into a file.

6. Use the Power Query editor UI to retrieve and expand/process the information in the file.

7. View the M code generated in the **Advanced Editor**.

8. Copy the relevant M code from the **Advanced Editor** and paste this code as the output expression for our function.

Hopefully, this helps you understand how to create the M code for your data retrieval functions. Let's finish this section by taking a quick look at the final data retrieval function, TDGTPQM_Discord.GetGuildMember.

The `TDGTPQM_Discord.GetGuildMember` function retrieves the information associated with the identity of the user within each server/guild. This function also returns a table as output but also takes a single parameter, `guildid`. This parameter is used within the API call to specify the server/guild from which to retrieve the user information. The API call is in the following format: `https://discord.com/api/users/@me/guilds/<guildid>/member`.

The output expression uses `Table.FromRecords` to transform the response into a table.

This completes our explanation of the API call data retrieval functions. We can now move on to the functions that will provide our navigation experience within the **Navigatior** dialog in the Power Query editor UI.

Adding navigation functions

With our API call data retrieval functions coded, we can now implement the functions that present the user experience within the **Navigatior** dialog of the Power Query editor UI.

To implement the navigation functions, we first need to code a helper function: `Table.ToNavigationTable`. The code for this function is taken directly from Microsoft's example code found here: `https://github.com/microsoft/DataConnectors/tree/master/samples/NavigationTable`.

Add the following function to the end of the custom connector code:

```
// Navigation Tables Functions
Table.ToNavigationTable = (
    table as table,
    keyColumns as list,
    nameColumn as text,
    dataColumn as text,
    itemKindColumn as text,
    itemNameColumn as text,
    isLeafColumn as text
) as table =>
    let
        tableType = Value.Type(table),
        newTableType = Type.AddTableKey(tableType, keyColumns, true) meta [
            NavigationTable.NameColumn = nameColumn,
            NavigationTable.DataColumn = dataColumn,
            NavigationTable.ItemKindColumn = itemKindColumn,
            Preview.DelayColumn = itemNameColumn,
            NavigationTable.IsLeafColumn = isLeafColumn
        ],
        navigationTable = Value.ReplaceType(table, newTableType)
    in
        navigationTable;
```

In short, this function transforms a table by adding the metadata expected by the **Navigator** dialog UI within the Power Query experience. The metadata added includes the following list:

- `NavigationTable.NameColumn`
- `NavigationTable.DataColumn`
- `NavigationTable.ItemKindColumn`
- `Preview.DelayColumn`
- `NavigationTable.IsLeafColumn`

Currently, you must manually add this function to your code. However, Microsoft has indicated that this function may eventually become part of the M standard library.

This function takes the following arguments:

- `table`: The table you wish to convert to a navigation table.
- `keyColumns`: The primary key (unique values) columns for your table.
- `nameColumn`: The column used for the display name in the **Navigator** dialog.
- `dataColumn`: The column containing a table or a function that returns a table. This is the actual data that will be retrieved if selected in the **Navigator** dialog.
- `itemKindColumn`: The column that specifies the type of icon to display in the **Navigator** dialog. The values in this column can be one of the following:

    - `Cube`
    - `CubeDatabase`
    - `CubeView`
    - `CubeViewFolder`
    - `Database`
    - `DatabaseServer`
    - `DefinedName`
    - `Dimension`
    - `Feed`
    - `Folder`
    - `Function`
    - `Record`
    - `Sheet`
    - `Subcube`
    - `Table`
    - `View`

- `itemNameColumn`: The column that specifies how data preview is handled in the **Navigator** dialog. Most often, the value in the `itemKindColumn` is the same as the value in the `itemNameColumn`.

- isLeafColumn: The column that specifies whether the item can be expanded or not. This column should contain a logical or Boolean value.

Additional information about this function can be found here: `https://learn.microsoft.com/en-us/power-query/handling-navigation-tables`.

Next, immediately above the `TDGTPQM_Discord.GetIdentity` function, add the following three functions:

```
TDGTPQM_Discord.UsersNavigation = () as table =>
    // Navigation
    //** Users Navigation
    let
        objects = #table(
            {"Name", "Key", "Data", "ItemKind", "ItemName", "IsLeaf"},
            {
                {"Me", "me", TDGTPQM_Discord.GetIdentity(), "Record", "Record",
true}
            }
        ),
        Navigation = Table.ToNavigationTable(objects, {"Key"}, "Name", "Data",
"ItemKind", "ItemName", "IsLeaf")
    in
        Navigation;

TDGTPQM_Discord.GuildsNavigation = () as table =>
    // Navigation
    //** Guilds (Server) Navigation
    let
        objects = #table(
            {"Name", "Key", "Data", "ItemKind", "ItemName", "IsLeaf"},
            {
                {"Servers", "guilds", TDGTPQM_Discord.GetGuilds(), "Table",
"Table", true}
            }
        ),

        Navigation = Table.ToNavigationTable(objects, {"Key"}, "Name", "Data",
"ItemKind", "ItemName", "IsLeaf")
    in
        Navigation;

TDGTPQM_Discord.MemberNavigation = () as table =>
    // Navigation
    //** Membership Navigation
```

```
    let
        servers = Table.ExpandRecordColumn(TDGTPQM_Discord.GetGuilds(),
"Column1", {"name", "id"}, {"Name", "Key"}),
        addDataColumn = Table.AddColumn(servers, "Data", each TDGTPQM_Discord.
GetGuildMember([Key])),
        addItemKindColumn = Table.AddColumn(addDataColumn, "ItemKind", each
"Record"),
        addItemNameColumn = Table.AddColumn(addItemKindColumn, "ItemName", each
"Function"),
        addIsLeafColumn = Table.AddColumn(addItemNameColumn, "IsLeaf", each
true),

        Navigation = Table.ToNavigationTable(addIsLeafColumn, {"Key"}, "Name",
"Data", "ItemKind", "ItemName", "IsLeaf")

    in
        Navigation;
```

The first two functions, TDGTPQM_Discord.UsersNavigation and TDGTPQM_Discord.GuildsNavigation, are nearly identical. In both cases, there is an objects expression that defines a table with the following columns:

- Name
- Key
- Data
- ItemKind
- ItemName
- IsLeaf

For each, a single navigation leaf node is defined. The TDGTPQM_Discord.UsersNavigation function defines the following values for the single row in this table:

- Me
- me
- TDGTPQM_Discord.GetIdentity()
- Record
- Record
- true

According to this definition, the word Me will appear in the **Navigator** dialog for this node. The unique name or key for the node is me. The data retrieved by selecting this node is the data retrieved by our API call data retrieval function, TDGTPQM_Discord.GetIdentity. The icon and preview displays are specified as being a Record and, finally, the final value of true specifies that this is a leaf (endpoint) node and not an expandable folder.

The TDGTPQM_Discord.GuildsNavigation function is nearly identical but specifies a Data column value of our API call data retrieval function, TDGTPQM_Discord.GetGuilds. Also, we specify that the icon and data preview should be handled as a Table instead of a Record.

In both cases, this table is then fed to the Table.ToNavigationTable function with the additional parameters referencing the appropriate columns within our objects table.

The TDGTPQM_Discord.MemberNavigation function presents a more complex dynamic navigation. This function uses our TDGTPQM_Discord.GetGuilds API call data retrieval function to retrieve a list of servers to which the user belongs. The records returned are expanded for the name and id columns returned by the API call and renamed as Name and Key, respectively. We then add the additional columns required by the Table.ToNavigationTable function including a Data column where we call our TDGTPQM_Discord.GetGuildMember function, passing in the Key (id of server/guild) as its sole parameter. We also specify an ItemKind column where we specify a value of Record and an IsLeaf column that holds the logical value true.

For the ItemName column, instead of specifying the same value used for the ItemKind column (Record), we specify a value of Function. This is necessary because this is a dynamically generated navigation table.

This completes our explanation of the navigation table functions. We are now ready to finish our custom connector by modifying the TDGTPQM_Discord.Contents function, so let's do that next.

Modifying the contents function

It's time to finish our custom connector code. The final modification required is to modify the TDGTPQM_Discord.Contents function in order to present the top level of our navigation that will appear in the **Navigator** dialog of the Power Query UI. Instead of returning a single text string, we can instead present the **Navigator** dialog that allows the user to select the data they wish to retrieve from Discord. To do that, follow these steps:

1. Locate the TDGTPQM_Discord.Contents function within your custom connector code.

2. Replace the TDGTPQM_Discord.Contents function with the following:

```
[DataSource.Kind="TDGTPQM_Discord", Publish="TDGTPQM_Discord.Publish"]
shared TDGTPQM_Discord.Contents = () =>

    let
        objects = #table(
            {"Name", "Key", "Data", "ItemKind", "ItemName", "IsLeaf"},
            {
                {"Users", "usersFolder", TDGTPQM_Discord.
UsersNavigation(), "Folder", "usersFolder", false},
                {"Servers", "guildsFolder", TDGTPQM_Discord.
GuildsNavigation(), "Folder", "guildsFolder", false},
                {"Membership", "membershipFolder", TDGTPQM_Discord.
MemberNavigation(), "Folder", "membershipFolder", false}
```

```
                }
            ),
            Navigation = Table.ToNavigationTable(objects, {"Key"}, "Name",
    "Data", "ItemKind", "ItemName", "IsLeaf")
        in
            Navigation;
```

As you can see, the code for this is very similar to our first two navigation functions, TDGTPQM_Discord.UserNavigation and TDGTPQM_Discord.GuildsNavigation. We again define an objects expression that returns a table with the columns expected by the Table.ToNavigationTable function.

Each of the rows in this table contains a name (Name) and unique key (Key) as well as a specification of an ItemKind of Folder, ItemName of Folder, and IsLeaf of false. For the Data column, we specify values of our corresponding navigation table functions as appropriate, namely:

- TDGTPQM_Discord.UserNavigation
- TDGTPQM_Discord.GuildsNavigation
- TDGTPQM_Discord.MemberNavigation

Similar to the navigation functions, we feed this objects table to our Table.ToNavigationTable function as output from the TDGTPQM_Discord.Contents function.

Now that we have completed the coding of our custom connector, we are finally ready to install and start using this connector within Power BI Desktop.

Installing and using a custom connector

To do this, please follow these steps:

1. With your project open in Visual Studio Code, save your work by clicking **File | Save All** in the menu.
2. Expand the **POWER QUERY SDK** section in the **EXPLORER** pane.
3. Click **Run TestConnection function** and ensure no errors are displayed.
4. Make sure that the TDGTPQM.pq file is selected in the Explorer pane and then click the **Evaluate current file**. This time, the **PQTest result** tab should display the following information:

Name	Key	Data	ItemKind
Users	usersFolder	[Table]	Folder
Servers	guildsFolder	[Table]	Folder
Membership	membershipFolder	[Table]	Folder

Figure 16.10: TDGTPQM.pq evaluation output

As you can see, this is the top level of how our navigation will be displayed in the **Navigator** dialog of the Power Query UI and directly corresponds to the specifications of our objects expression from our TDGTPQM_Discord.Contents function.

5. Click the bin\AnyCPU\Debug folder link in the **EXPLORER** pane to expand this folder.

6. Right-click the TDGTPQM_Discord.mez file and choose **Reveal in File Explorer**.

7. Copy the TDGTPQM_Discord.mez file.

8. While in File Explorer, navigate to your **Documents** directory.

9. Create a folder called Microsoft Power BI Desktop.

10. Navigate into the Microsoft Power BI Desktop folder.

11. Create a folder called Custom Connectors.

12. Navigate into the Custom Connectors folder.

13. Paste the TDGTPQM_Discord.mez file.

14. Open Power BI Desktop.

15. In the ribbon, navigate to **File | Options and settings | Options**.

16. In the **Options** dialog, choose **Security** in the left navigation.

17. Under **Data Extensions**, select the radio button for **(Not Recommended) Allow any extension to load without validation or warning**".

18. Click the **OK** button.

19. Restart Power BI Desktop.

20. From the **Home** tab in the ribbon, choose **Transform Data** to open the Power Query editor.

21. From the **Home** tab in the ribbon of the Power Query editor, choose **New Source | More**.

22. In the search bar, enter tdgtpqm.

23. Choose the **TDGTPQM_Discord (Beta)** connector and then press the **Connect** button. The following dialog is displayed:

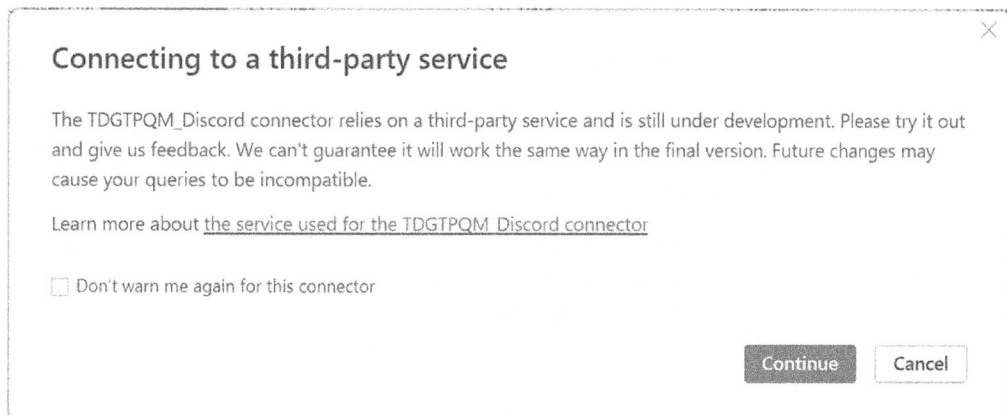

Connecting to a third-party service

The TDGTPQM_Discord connector relies on a third-party service and is still under development. Please try it out and give us feedback. We can't guarantee it will work the same way in the final version. Future changes may cause your queries to be incompatible.

Learn more about the service used for the TDGTPQM_Discord connector

☐ Don't warn me again for this connector

Continue   Cancel

Figure 16.11: Third-party service connection notification

24. Press the **Continue** button.

25. Click the **Sign-in** button.

26. Authorize the application by clicking the **Authorize** button in the dialog box.

27. Click the **Connect** button.

28. The **Navigator** dialog is displayed:

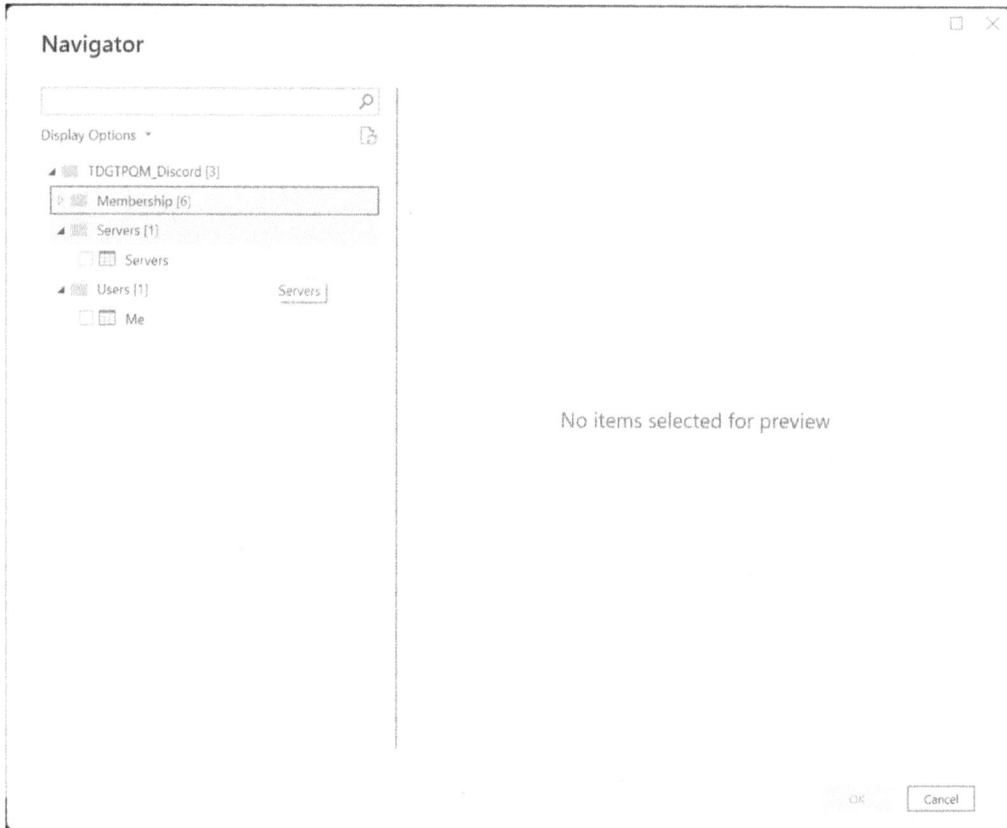

Figure 16.12: TDGTPQM._Discord custom connector Navigator dialog in Power Query editor

Congratulations! You have successfully created a custom connector for Power Query that connects to and retrieves data from the Discord API. You can use this connector in a similar manner to the default connectors included with Power BI Desktop.

Bear in mind that this is just one example of creating a custom connector to retrieve data from an API. There are hundreds, if not thousands, of custom APIs from which you can retrieve data. By learning how to code custom connectors for Power Query, the sky is the limit regarding how many and the types of data sources you can connect to.

Summary

In this chapter, we dove into the world of extending Power Query's capabilities by adding a custom function library and creating a custom connector. Power Query is a powerful data transformation and integration tool, but its true potential can be unleashed by developing your own connectors to access specialized data sources or APIs. This allows you to bring in data from unique systems or services that are not natively supported by Power Query.

We began by preparing a development environment, including configuring Visual Studio Code, the Power Query SDK, and elements of Discord, our target data source. Next, we created and explained the base template for custom Power Query extensions. We then coded and configured OAuth authentication for our custom connector. Additionally, we wrote the custom M code for retrieving data from the Discord API and presenting a navigation experience for the **Navigator** dialog found in Power Query UI. Finally, we demonstrated how to install and use the custom connector in Power BI Desktop.

Throughout the chapter, we have thoroughly explained the development process and anatomy of a custom connector, breaking down its components and code to explain its purpose. We examined how to define the connector's metadata, establish connections, handle authentication, and implement data retrieval and transformation logic.

You have reached the end of this book, which is what we feel to be the most definitive single resource for the M language that exists anywhere. If you have read this entire book, you have learned a wealth of information about the M language, from the basic elements of the M language to the abstract concepts that underpin M and everything in between. Along the way, we have provided many practical examples of how to use M to solve challenging data transformation problems, as well as best practices for coding M. It is our sincere hope that you have enjoyed this journey and feel empowered to leverage all the capabilities of the M language.

Learn more on Discord

Join our community's Discord space for discussions with the author and other readers:

```
https://discord.gg/vCSG5GBbyS
```

‹packt›

Other Books You May Enjoy

If you enjoyed this book, you may be interested in these other books by Packt:

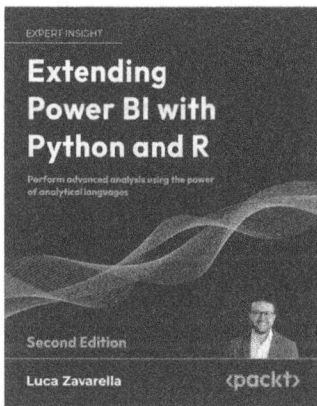

Extending Power BI with Python and R - Second Edition

Luca Zavarella

ISBN: 9781837639533

- Configure optimal integration of Python and R with Power BI
- Perform complex data manipulations not possible by default in Power BI
- Boost Power BI logging and loading large datasets
- Extract insights from your data using algorithms like linear optimization
- Calculate string distances and learn how to use them for probabilistic fuzzy matching
- Handle outliers and missing values for multivariate and time-series data
- Apply Exploratory Data Analysis in Power BI with R
- Learn to use Grammar of Graphics in Python

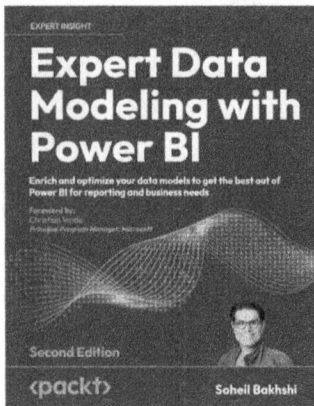

Expert Data Modeling with Power BI - Second Edition

Soheil Bakhshi

ISBN: 9781803246246

- Implement virtual tables and time intelligence functionalities in DAX to build a powerful model
- Identify Dimension and Fact tables and implement them in Power Query Editor
- Deal with advanced data preparation scenarios while building Star Schema
- Discover different hierarchies and their common pitfalls
- Understand complex data models and how to decrease the level of model complexity with different approaches
- Learn advanced data modeling techniques such as calculation groups, aggregations, incremental refresh, RLS/OLS, and more
- Get well-versed with datamarts and dataflows in PowerBI

Packt is searching for authors like you

If you're interested in becoming an author for Packt, please visit authors.packtpub.com and apply today. We have worked with thousands of developers and tech professionals, just like you, to help them share their insight with the global tech community. You can make a general application, apply for a specific hot topic that we are recruiting an author for, or submit your own idea.

Share your thoughts

Now you've finished *The Definitive Guide to Power Query (M)*, we'd love to hear your thoughts! Scan the QR code below to go straight to the Amazon review page for this book and share your feedback or leave a review on the site that you purchased it from.

https://packt.link/r/1835089720

Your review is important to us and the tech community and will help us make sure we're delivering excellent quality content.

Index

M

Download a free PDF copy of this book

Thanks for purchasing this book!

Do you like to read on the go but are unable to carry your print books everywhere?

Is your eBook purchase not compatible with the device of your choice?

Don't worry, now with every Packt book you get a DRM-free PDF version of that book at no cost.

Read anywhere, any place, on any device. Search, copy, and paste code from your favorite technical books directly into your application.

The perks don't stop there, you can get exclusive access to discounts, newsletters, and great free content in your inbox daily

Follow these simple steps to get the benefits:

1. Scan the QR code or visit the link below

https://packt.link/free-ebook/9781835089729

2. Submit your proof of purchase
3. That's it! We'll send your free PDF and other benefits to your email directly

www.ingramcontent.com/pod-product-compliance
Lightning Source LLC
Chambersburg PA
CBHW081457190326
41458CB00015B/5267